INTRODUCTION TO
AMERICAN HIGHER EDUCATION

Written primarily for students in higher education and student affairs graduate programs, *Introduction to American Higher Education* is a groundbreaking textbook that combines classic scholarship pertaining to colleges and universities with the most cutting-edge perspectives in the field.

The book is divided into five sections and contains 25 essential readings on the following topics:

- Faculty
- Teaching, Learning and Curriculum
- College Students
- Organizations, Leadership and Governance
- Higher Education Policy

Each section includes chapters on community colleges and four-year institutions, as well as a substantive overview written by Ann E. Austin, Clifton F. Conrad, Laura I. Rendón, Adrianna J. Kezar, and Edward P. St. John. This impressive volume ensures that faculty members will no longer have to compile their own collections of articles and chapters for use in introductory courses—*Introduction to American Higher Education* brings together the best scholarship in one comprehensive text.

Shaun R. Harper is on the faculty in Higher Education, Africana Studies, and Gender Studies at the University of Pennsylvania.

Jerlando F. L. Jackson is on the faculty in the Higher, Postsecondary, and Continuing Education program at the University of Wisconsin-Madison, where he also serves as Director of Wisconsin's Equity and Inclusion Laboratory (Wei Lab).

INTRODUCTION TO AMERICAN HIGHER EDUCATION

Shaun R. Harper and Jerlando F. L. Jackson

Editors

with Ann E. Austin, Clifton F. Conrad,
Adrianna J. Kezar, Laura I. Rendón, and
Edward P. St. John

Routledge
Taylor & Francis Group

NEW YORK AND LONDON

First published 2011
by Routledge
270 Madison Avenue, New York, NY 10016

Simultaneously published in the UK
by Routledge
2 Park Square, Milton Park, Abingdon, Oxon OX14 4RN

Routledge is an imprint of the Taylor & Francis Group, an informa business

Typeset in Times New Roman by Swales & Willis Ltd, Exeter, Devon
Printed and bound in the United States of America on acid-free paper by Sheridan Books, Inc.

Library of Congress Cataloging in Publication Data
   Introduction to American higher education / Shaun Harper and Jerlando Jackson,
   editors ; with Ann E. Austin . . . [et al.].
   p. cm.
   Includes index.
   1. Education, Higher—United States. 2. Universities and colleges—United States.
   I. Harper, Shaun R., 1975– II. Jackson, Jerlando F. L., 1973– III. Austin, Ann E.
   LA227.4.I58 2010
   378.73—dc22
   2010014665

ISBN 13: 978–0–415–80325–0 (hbk)
ISBN 13: 978–0–415–80326–7 (pbk)

Contents

III. STUDENTS
LAURA I. RENDÓN, SECTION EDITOR

IV. ORGANIZATIONS, LEADERSHIP AND GOVERNANCE
ADRIANNA J. KEZAR, SECTION EDITOR

V. POLICY
EDWARD P. ST. JOHN, SECTION EDITOR

Preface

Almost every higher education or student affairs graduate program offers a required course titled "Introduction to Higher Education" or some variation thereof—for example, Colleges and Universities in the United States, Foundations of Higher Education, or Higher Education in American Society—yet, no prevailing textbook previously existed for primary use in such courses. Although there are several well-respected scholars in each focal area of study in the field, little effort had been previously devoted to pursuing consensus among them about what graduate students and other newcomers to the field ought to read and know. In the absence of a major text for assignment in the foundational course, many professors, for years, have compiled their own collections of journal articles and book chapters for pairing with books that are only partially relevant to those who do not yet possess an advanced understanding of higher education as a multidimensional field of study. In our view, a textbook was necessary to unify baseline knowledge about the functions, purposes, and intricacies of postsecondary education in the United States.

Introduction to American Higher Education is intended primarily for adoption in relevant courses taken by graduate students in their first year of study. We also envision it being useful to others who may enter into higher education work via nontraditional pathways—for example, someone who accepts an entry-level position in student affairs without a master's degree, or a more senior-level administrator who comes to higher education after having spent the majority of her or his career in an entirely different industry. This book contains 25 essential readings (five chapters per section that are woven together by thoughtful prefaces written by expert scholars), along with insightful statements on the past and future of the field. Respected professors at a variety of colleges and universities have determined that the five chapters in each section represent *some* themes and topics that would be appropriate for colleagues who seek to evolve from novice to expert. This book on its own will not confer expertise upon those who read it. However, exposure to the selected content will provide access to terms, concepts, philosophical positions and tensions, and the organizational and structural norms that are characteristic of this complex enterprise called higher education. Furthermore, this text simultaneously honors classic contributions to the literature and represents the freshest, most cutting-edge thinking in the field.

AN INCLUSIVE CROSS-SECTOR OVERVIEW

The book is organized around five focal areas of study in higher education: (1) Faculty; (2) Curriculum, Teaching and Learning; (3) Students; (4) Organizations, Leadership and Governance; and (5) Policy. These are areas the Association for the Study of Higher Education (ASHE), the premier professional organization for those who conduct research on higher education, uses to organize sessions for its annual meeting. Prolific and highly-respected resident experts in each area (three of whom are ASHE past presidents) were invited to serve as section editors. Their presence in this volume represents the breadth and multidimensionality of the field. Each reacted responsibly to the task of selecting a quintet of readings that best capture important concepts and complexities in her or his area of expertise.

Although one of us primarily studies higher education leadership issues and the other conducts research mostly pertaining to college students, we felt it was important to produce a volume that offers a balanced overview of the field. Hence, each section includes the exact same number of readings that have been deemed essential by groups of faculty who conduct research in the area. Also included are some chapters that focus on how various aspects of colleges and universities are uniquely experienced by women and racial/ethnic minority faculty, as well as diverse student populations.

Some foundational texts introduce student affairs as an important aspect of higher education (for example, *Student Services: A Handbook for the Profession*). But to be an effective student affairs administrator, one must understand how colleges and universities work beyond the boundaries of student affairs. This book is inclusive of research on students, student outcomes, and student development, but also introduces much-needed perspectives on what occurs inside classrooms, at governance and decision-making tables, and at state and federal policy levels. Regardless of their interests or career aspirations, readers of this text will discover intersecting problems and possibilities across the five areas of study, as opposed to being narrowly exposed to just one facet of the field.

WHAT ABOUT COMMUNITY COLLEGES?

Less than a decade ago, one of us completed coursework for a Ph.D. without having been assigned a single publication to read that pertained to community colleges—they were rendered insignificant and were never even mentioned in class discussions. Unlike other important books in the field that somehow manage to contain little to nothing about community and technical colleges, we decided to be deliberately inclusive of them here. Each section includes at least one essential related reading that is situated in the community college context. Why? In Fall 2007, 42.4% of undergraduate students were enrolled at community colleges. Thus, it is an important context to consider as one endeavors to learn about the landscape of postsecondary education in the United States.

We suspect that some may ask, "Since I only intend to work at four-year institutions, why is it necessary for me to learn about community colleges?" We have three responses to this question. First, one cannot legitimately claim to be committed to developing expertise on American higher education without being exposed to the institutions that enroll nearly half its students. To know nothing about community colleges makes one an insufficiently prepared student of higher education. Second, as Tatiana Melguizo notes in the Epilogue of this book, articulation agreements between community colleges and four-year institutions are expected to be strengthened over the next few years. Those who work at universities, say in undergraduate admissions or degree progress offices, are required to know much about community college curricula, student characteristics, and transfer policies. This is true even at highly-selective private universities. Moreover, we can reasonably posit that faculty and student affairs professionals who understand the context from which community college transfer students come might do a better job of facilitating seamless transitions and meeting those students' needs. Our final reaction is this: people do not know for sure where they will be working 3, 13, or even 30 years into the future—there are 2,265 community and technical colleges from which to choose.

HISTORICAL BEGINNINGS: A NOTE ON HOW TO USE THIS BOOK

Readers may notice that higher education history is not one of the sections in this book. We opted instead for a prologue from eminent historian John R. Thelin, who is also an ASHE past president. In the Prologue, Thelin lists several books and articles that have been deemed exemplary by seven fellow historians. We believe *Introduction to American Higher Education* works best when it is paired with one of the history books that Thelin names. Those who teach the course that introduces graduate students to higher education as a field of study might consider starting the semester, for example, with Frederick Rudolph's *The American College and University: A History* to establish historical context for many of the topics, tensions, organizational norms, and structural nuances that students will later encounter in our book. Without proper historical framing, we are afraid that readers may find some dimensions of colleges and universities utterly contradictory and confusing. A good history text will help explain much about contemporary cultures and conflicts described in the 25 chapters published in this volume.

ACKNOWLEDGMENTS

We remain indebted to those who taught us the fundamentals of higher education as a field of study at Indiana University and Iowa State University, especially George Kuh, Ed St. John, Don Hossler, Andrea Walton, Guadalupe Anaya, Deborah Faye Carter, John Bean, Nancy Chism, Mary F. Howard-Hamilton, Daniel Robinson, Walter Gmelch, John Schuh, Larry Ebbers, Nancy Evans, and Florence Hamrick. Our appreciation is also extended to colleagues and students at Penn and UW-Madison with whom we learn, critically analyze, and research important problems pertaining to American higher education. We especially thank Keon M. McGuire and Byron K. Sharer Robertson, our graduate research assistants who aided in retrieving sources and documents for this project. A portion of any praise we receive for this book rightfully belongs to Sarah Burrows, our former editor at Routledge, who posed to us an intriguing pair of questions: "Why doesn't your field have an introductory textbook, and will you guys please consider proposing one?" Quite honestly, without Sarah's prompting we likely would have never undertaken this project—the field will benefit from her wisdom and faith in us to responsibly produce such an important volume.

We also salute a dozen of our most significant faculty colleagues with whom we routinely conspire and occasionally collaborate to advance the field: anthony lising antonio, Estela Mara Bensimon, Elton J. Crim, Brandon D. Daniels, Lamont A. Flowers, Linda Serra Hagedorn, Frank Harris III, Sylvia Hurtado, James T. Minor, Lori D. Patton, L. Allen Phelps, and Damon A. Williams. These scholars inspire us, we admire and appreciate their work, and our scholarship is enhanced by their feedback and collaborative input. Last, but not least, our sincerest gratitude belongs to the five section editors, the 26 members of their advisory groups, Professor John R. Thelin, and the five early/mid-career colleagues who composed the future-focused Epilogue for our book. Working with each of these celebrity scholars was most rewarding.

Shaun R. Harper
Philadelphia, Pennsylvania

Jerlando F. L. Jackson
Madison, Wisconsin

Prologue on Studying the History of American Higher Education

One characteristic of a scholarly field or learned profession is its declaration of a common body of knowledge. Herein one finds agreement among expert colleagues about the essential works that define the topic and provide an initiation into the field for new scholars. Over the past half century, the study of higher education in the United States has evolved as a topic of disciplined inquiry and cumulative knowledge that now joins with law, medicine, sociology, and economics in the ranks of established fields. Less clear, however, is the foundation of historical works that ought to provide an introductory grounding. To explore and attempt to clarify this question, I have relied on a survey and correspondence with several leading historians of higher education at universities in the United States. My roster of consultants includes the following professors who study and teach courses on the history of American higher education: Roger Geiger (The Pennsylvania State University), Andrea Walton (Indiana University), James Axtell (The College of William & Mary), Amy E. Wells (University of Mississippi), Christian Anderson (University of South Carolina), Luther Spoehr (Brown University), and Timothy Caine (University of Illinois at Urbana-Champaign).

Each colleague was asked to provide me an annotated list of key works upon which they relied, respectively, as core readings in introducing students to a historical perspective on the study of higher education. The results were fascinating in that these short lists of works displayed the extremes of consensus and diversity. In sum, these historians of higher education confirmed the adage invoked by statisticians: "Never the center without a spread." How true this turned out to be in identifying the historical base for a serious, systematic introduction to higher education as a field.

The cumulative bibliography included, to one extreme, the hearty perennials of classic works by established historians who happened also to write well on topics with enduring significance. Beyond this relatively small common ground, the remaining recommendations represented remarkable imagination and variety. It was the mixed message that suggests a new generation of higher education graduate students are in store for exciting and sometimes unexpected readings which, I think, will reaffirm to an older generation of colleagues why the history of higher education has emerged and will endure as a substantive, fascinating topic that has attracted some of our best writers and readers.

CONSENSUS ON MAJOR BOOKS

A staple of historical study of higher education, both for writers and readers, are the substantial books on significant topics. This observation may be obvious, but it is important because in some fields of the social and behavioral sciences, it is the journal article, not the published book, that is the premiere coin of the scholarly realm. Nine titles surfaced time and time again in the independent rosters filed by the established scholars. These core books are as follow:

Frederick Rudolph, *The American College and University: A History* (University of Georgia Press, 1990).

Clark Kerr, *Uses of the University* (Harvard University Press, 1963).

Charles Homer Haskins, *The Rise of the Universities* (Cornell University Press, 1925).

Barbara Miller Solomon, *In the Company of Educated Women: A History of Women and Higher Education in America* (Yale University Press, 1985).

John R. Thelin, *A History of American Higher Education* (Johns Hopkins University Press, 2004).

Laurence R. Veysey, *The Emergence of the American University* (University of Chicago Press, 1965).

Roger Geiger, Editor, *The American College in the Nineteenth Century* (Vanderbilt University Press, 2000).

James D. Anderson, *The Education of Blacks in the South, 1860–1935* (The University of North Carolina Press, 1988).

Christopher Jencks and David Riesman, *The Academic Revolution* (Double Day Anchor, 1968).

ENDURING BOOKS WORTH SPECIAL NOTE

In addition to the nine "major" texts listed above, there were a handful of books on special topics that were highly praised by several correspondents. Although these did not fall into the small group of consensus works, they are sufficiently memorable as to warrant special note:

W. Bruce Leslie, *Gentlemen and Scholars: College and Community in the "Age of the University," 1865–1917* (The Pennsylvania State University Press, 1992).

David O. Levine, *The American College and The Culture of Aspiration, 1915–1940* (Cornell University Press, 1986).

Jerome Karabel, *The Chosen: The Hidden History of Admissions and Exclusion at Harvard, Yale, and Princeton* (Houghton Mifflin, 2005).

One aim of many introductory courses dealing with higher education is to provide new students with a sampling of and appreciation for the raw materials of historical research. Namely, the documents, letters, reports, newspaper articles, and memoirs that constitute the primary sources left as part of the historical record by participants and observers of significant events. These are distinguished from the more familiar and obvious secondary sources of articles and books later written by scholars. Two excellent works for primary sources and historical documents are the following anthologies—one published almost a half century ago and dealing with over two centuries of events and issues; and the second, published recently and focused on academic debates about higher education since 1940:

Richard Hofstadter and Wilson Smith, Editors, *American Higher Education: A Documentary History* (University of Chicago Press, 1961).

Thomas Bender and Wilson Smith, Editors, *American Higher Education Transformed, 1940–2005: Documenting the National Discourse* (Johns Hopkins University Press, 2008).

Also, there was strong agreement that the *ASHE Reader on the History of Higher Education*, edited by Harold Wechsler and Lester Goodchild, provided graduate students with an invaluable, voluminous reference work on key books and articles about the development of higher education.

JOURNAL ARTICLES

One healthy characteristic of the historical scholarship on higher education is that there has been a lively, fertile writing and publication of journal articles that provide original research and fresh interpretation on both familiar and unexpected topics. The price of such originality and productivity is that the titles and topics are so sufficiently diverse and numerous that professors are less likely to agree on a small number of essential articles than was the case in recommendations about the most significant books. What follows is a sampling of provocative journal articles which, at the time of their publication, prompted scholars and graduate students to rethink the boundaries and innards of higher education as a field:

John S. Whitehead and Jurgen Herbst (1986). How to think about the Dartmouth case. *History of Education Quarterly, 26*(3), 333–349.
James Axtell (1971). The death of the liberal arts college? *History of Education Quarterly, 11*(4), 339–352.
Roger L. Geiger (1992). The historical matrix of American higher education. *History of Higher Education Annual, 12,* 7–34.
Linda Eisenmann (1997). Reconsidering a classic: Assessing the history of women's higher education a dozen years after Barbara Solomon. *Harvard Educational Review, 67*(4), 689–717.
Peter Wallenstein (1999). Black southerners and non-black universities: Desegregating higher education, 1935–1967. *History of Higher Education Annual, 19,* 121–148.

CONCLUSION

I was invited to provide a historical context appropriate for an introduction to higher education textbook, and identify a list of essential books and articles on the history of colleges and universities in the United States. Noted above are writings that simultaneously satisfy several criteria. Each selection brings justifiable acknowledgement to an accomplished author in the field, while demonstrating interesting research methodologies and a compelling writing style that will be useful to graduate students and other readers of this book. No single selection will cover the entire history of higher education landscape—nor will they please all scholars or exhaust all good possibilities. This Prologue, however, does illustrate that historical writing about higher education in the United States has both an abundant, lively past and an intriguing future.

John R. Thelin
University Research Professor
University of Kentucky

About the Editors and Section Editors

Shaun R. Harper is on the faculty in the Graduate School of Education, Africana Studies, and Gender Studies at the University of Pennsylvania. His research focuses on race and gender in American higher education, Black male college access and achievement, the effects of college environments on student behaviors and outcomes, and gains associated with educationally purposeful student engagement. He has published nine books and more than 60 peer-reviewed journal articles, book chapters, and other academic publications. His books include *Student Engagement in Higher Education: Theoretical Perspectives and Practical Approaches for Diverse Populations* (Routledge, 2009); *College Men and Masculinities* (Jossey-Bass, 2010); and the fifth edition of *Student Services: A Handbook for the Profession* (Jossey-Bass, 2011). *The Journal of Higher Education, Journal of College Student Development, Teachers College Record, American Behavioral Scientist*, and several other well-regarded journals have published his research. Additionally, Harper has delivered over 30 keynote addresses and presented more than 125 research papers, workshops, and symposia at national education conferences. His professional honors include the 2010 Outstanding Contribution to Research Award from the National Association of Student Personnel Administrators, the 2010 Early Career Award from the American Educational Research Association (Division G), and the 2008 Early Career Award from the Association for the Study of Higher Education. Harper has prior administrative experience in student activities, sorority and fraternity affairs, graduate admissions, and academic program administration. His Ph.D. in higher education is from Indiana University.

Jerlando F. L. Jackson is on the faculty in the Educational Leadership and Policy Analysis Department at the University of Wisconsin-Madison. He also serves as the Coordinator of the Higher, Postsecondary, and Continuing Education graduate program and as a Faculty Affiliate for the Wisconsin Center for the Advancement of Postsecondary Education. In addition, he is Director of Wisconsin's Equity and Inclusion Laboratory (Wei Lab). Jackson's research primarily explores workforce diversity and workplace discrimination in higher education. He is credited with over 90 publications, 125 presentations, and has published the following books: *Ethnic and Racial Administrative Diversity: Understanding Work Life Realities and Experiences in Higher Education* (Jossey Bass, 2009); *Strengthening the African American Educational Pipeline: Informing Research, Policy, and Practice* (SUNY Press, 2007); and *Toward Administrative Reawakening: Creating and Maintaining Safe College Campuses* (Stylus, 2007). His articles have appeared in a range of journals, including: *The Review of Higher Education, Research in Higher Education, Teachers College Record, American Behavioral Scientist*, and *Peabody Journal of Education*. Jackson has served as editor-in-chief of the ASHE Reader Series, senior associate editor for the *Journal of the Professoriate*, chair of the affirmative action committee for the American Educational Research Association (Division J), and on the editorial boards of the *Review of Higher Education* and the *Journal of College Student Development*. His Ph.D. in higher education is from Iowa State University.

Ann E. Austin is Professor of Higher, Adult and Lifelong Education at Michigan State University, where she held the inaugural Mildred B. Erickson Distinguished Chair from 2005 to 2008. Her research focuses on faculty careers, roles, and development; organizational change and transformation in universities and colleges; reform in doctoral education; and the improvement of teaching and learning in postsecondary contexts. Austin is Co-Principal Investigator of the Center for the Integration of Research, Teaching and Learning (CIRTL) and Director of the Global Institute for Higher Education at Michigan State. Her books include *Rethinking Faculty Work: Higher Education's Strategic Imperative* (Jossey-Bass, 2007) and *Paths to the Professoriate: Strategies for Enriching the Preparation of Future Faculty* (Jossey-Bass, 2004). Austin is a past president of the Association for the Study of Higher Education. Her Ph.D. in higher education is from the University of Michigan.

Clifton F. Conrad is Professor of Higher Education at the University of Wisconsin-Madison. For the past three decades, Conrad's research has focused primarily on advancing knowledge and understanding of college and university curriculum at the undergraduate and graduate levels, in the liberal arts and sciences as well as across professional fields. His books include *College & University Curriculum: Placing Learning at the Epicenter of Courses, Programs and Institutions* (Pearson, 2007); *The SAGE Handbook for Research in Education: Engaging Ideas and Enriching Inquiry* (SAGE, 2006); *Emblems of Quality: Developing and Sustaining High-Quality Programs* (Allyn & Bacon, 1997); and *A Silent Success: Master's Education in the United States* (Johns Hopkins University Press, 1993). Conrad is a past president of the Association for the Study of Higher Education. His Ph.D. in higher education is from the University of Michigan.

Adrianna J. Kezar is Associate Professor of Higher Education and Associate Director of the Center for Higher Education Policy Analysis at the University of Southern California. She has published extensively on the topics of higher education leadership, change, governance, diversity issues, and philosophical questions. Kezar's books include *Organizing Higher Education for Collaboration* (Jossey-Bass, 2009); *Rethinking Leadership in a Complex, Multicultural, and Global Environment: New Concepts and Models for Higher Education* (Stylus, 2009); *Higher Education for the Public Good: Emerging Voices from a National Movement* (Jossey-Bass, 2005); and *Taking the Reins: Institutional Transformation in Higher Education* (Praeger, 2003). She formerly served on the Board of Directors for the Association for the Study of Higher Education and as editor-in-chief of the *ASHE Higher Education Report* series. Her Ph.D. in higher education is from the University of Michigan.

Laura I. Rendón is Professor of Higher Education at Iowa State University. She has been inducted into the Iowa Academy of Education and is a former fellow of the Fetzer Institute. Rendón's current research focuses on access, retention, and graduation of low-income, first-generation college students and the transformation of teaching and learning to emphasize wholeness and social justice. Her books include *Sentipensante (Sensing/Thinking) Pedagogy: Educating for Wholeness, Social Justice and Liberation* (Stylus, 2008) and *Educating a New Majority: Transforming America's Educational System for Diversity* (Jossey-Bass, 1996). Her scholarly work on diversity and student success has been featured in *The Chronicle of Higher Education* and the PBS documentary, *The College Track*. Rendón is a past president of the Association for the Study of Higher Education. Her Ph.D. in higher education is from the University of Michigan.

Edward P. St. John is the Algo D. Henderson Collegiate Professor of Higher Education at the University of Michigan. His scholarship is primarily concerned with education for a just society. St. John's interest in equity in higher education stems from three decades of research on education policy. He presently serves as series editor for *Readings on Equal Education* and directs the Promoting Equity in Higher Education project through the National Center for Institutional Diversity. His books include *Education and the Public Interest: School Reform, Public Finance, and Access to Higher Education* (Springer, 2009); *Public Funding of Higher Education: Changing Contexts and New Rationales* (Johns Hopkins University Press, 2005); and *Refinancing the College Dream: Access, Equal Opportunity, and Justice for Taxpayers* (Johns Hopkins University Press, 2003). His Ed.D. in Administration, Planning and Social Policy is from the Harvard University Graduate School of Education.

Advisory Groups

The five section editors consulted 26 experts in their respective content areas for advice and recommendations on the publications that were ultimately selected for inclusion in this book. Listed below are colleagues who generously contributed to the advisory groups.

Faculty
Roger G. Baldwin, Michigan State University
John M. Braxton, Vanderbilt University
KerryAnn O'Meara, University of Maryland
Jack H. Schuster, Claremont Graduate
    University
Mary Deane Sorcinelli, University of
    Massachusetts Amherst
Christine A. Stanley, Texas A&M University

Curriculum, Teaching and Learning
Jennifer Grant Haworth, Loyola University
    Chicago
Jason Johnson, West Virginia University
Lisa R. Lattuca, The Pennsylvania State
    University
Michael B. Paulsen, University of Iowa
Frank Tuitt, University of Denver

Students
Alberto F. Cabrera, University of Maryland
Sylvia Hurtado, UCLA
George D. Kuh, Indiana University
Amaury Nora, University of Texas at San
    Antonio
Frances K. Stage, New York University

Organizations, Leadership and Governance
Jay Dee, University of Massachusetts Boston
Jeni Hart, University of Missouri
James T. Minor, Southern Education
    Foundation
Robert A. Rhoads, UCLA
William G. Tierney, University of Southern
    California

Policy
Michael B. Paulsen, University of Iowa
Laura W. Perna, University of Pennsylvania
Patricia Somers, University of Texas at Austin
Scott L. Thomas, Claremont Graduate
    University
Caroline Sotello Viernes Turner, Arizona
    State University

I

FACULTY

Ann E. Austin, Section Editor

Faculty members are central to the work of higher education institutions, and not surprisingly, have been an important focus of research by scholars over the past several decades. The literature on the faculty, while not as extensive as the research and writing on college students, has been growing steadily. Literature in this area tends to focus on several themes and questions. Who are the faculty? What does it mean to be an academic professional? What are the roles and responsibilities of faculty members? How do discipline and institutional type play a role in defining faculty identity, faculty work, and faculty careers? To what extent and in what ways do broader contextual factors—issues and pressures in the broader societal context—relate to the experiences, careers, and work of faculty members? The chapters included in this section reflect these recurring issues in the literature on the faculty in American universities and colleges. Taken as a whole, they provide some historical background about the development of the academic profession over approximately 300 years, describe core elements that define academic work, highlight key factors that create variability in faculty members' experiences, and analyze pressures in the societal context that affect faculty work today, bringing both opportunity and challenge.

In Chapter 1, Jack H. Schuster and Martin J. Finkelstein examine the history of American higher education, arguing that the social, economic, and political forces influencing colleges and universities over time contributed to developments in the definition, qualifications, and roles of faculty members. These defining developments occurred in two phases. First, in the nineteenth century, the number and size of higher education institutions increased and a process of professionalization occurred, leading to the emergence of a permanent, specialized professoriate. The process of professionalization involved formal preparation provided in graduate education, growing specialization in teaching areas, the emergence of the academic as a disciplinary expert, and the idea of academic work as constituting a lifelong career. The second phase occurred in the twentieth century, during which the academic career, defined by disciplinary specialization, expanded and diversified.

The three roles of teaching, research, and service, each connected to disciplinary expertise, came to define academic work. In the two and a half decades after the Second World War, a period of massive expansion in American higher education, the faculty became more diverse. Reinforced by the socializing processes of the graduate schools and the role of the disciplinary societies, the importance of disciplinary identification and specialization continued to define the meaning of academic work. Since 1970, significant changes have occurred in the context and nature of faculty work, including a major increase in the number of part-time faculty and evidence of declining faculty commitment to their institutions. Schuster and Finkelstein raise the question of whether, in response to changes in the societal context, another major shift is occurring in the academic profession and whether universities and colleges will find the faculty members they need in this new century.

Burton R. Clark provides a sociological analysis of academic work in the United States in Chapter 2. He argues that "the academic profession is a multitude of academic tribes and territories," due to two major factors that define the nature of an academic's work: disciplinary specialization and institutional differentiation. Disciplinary cultures are characterized by different values, approaches, and practices regarding teaching and research, work assignments and habits, career paths, forms of authority, and professional and scholarly associations. As the chapter highlights, faculty work in medicine, as an example, is very different from faculty work in any of the humanities. Institutional differences are also quite powerful in determining the nature of academic work, affecting teaching loads, the proportion of academics employed in part-time as compared to full-time positions, the nature of students taught (the extent of their need for remediation, for example), the ways in which faculty interact with their peers, the relative strength of the institutional culture versus the disciplinary culture, and the extent of faculty influence and authority in institutional issues.

The interactions between disciplinary differentiation and institutional differentiation create, according to Clark, many different faculty experiences and careers. Additionally, he argues, the differentiations related to discipline and institution relate to five systemic problems: (1) deprofessionalization due to increasing faculty involvement in remediation; (2) burnout and erosion of scholarly life due to excessive teaching; (3) weakening of professional control and professionalism from increasing administrative management of faculty; (4) fragmentation of academic culture; and (5) decreasing intrinsic rewards in academic work. Clark's overall conclusion is that academic professionalism in the United States is weakening in the face of the many different forms of academic life. He urges resistance to the increase in part-time faculty, greater commitment to intellectual work as central to the profession, greater involvement of faculty members in institutional management, more connection among the different cultures of the academy, and greater emphasis on the intrinsic rewards of the academic profession.

Other chapters in this section echo the theme of differentiation and difference that affect the lives and work of academics. In Chapter 3, Barbara K. Townsend and Vicki J. Rosser illuminate aspects of faculty work and life in one sector of American higher education, the community college. This sector is markedly different in mission focus than the research university, which is often used as the dominant context in which to study or discuss the academic profession. Townsend and Rosser summarize the debates and perspectives concerning whether community college faculty should be engaged in some form of scholarly activity, typically conceived more broadly in that context to include, for example, interpretative work, presentations, performances, exhibits, and curriculum development, as well as traditional academic articles, chapters, and books. They explain that while more research is needed concerning the relationship of teaching and scholarship at community colleges, some researchers, as well as some community college leaders and faculty, believe that with faculty involvement in scholarly activities, teaching is enhanced, learning opportunities for students are increased, and institutional prestige increases. Townsend and Rosser used a major database, the National Study of Postsecondary Faculty, to analyze faculty workloads, engagement in scholarly activities, and time spent in instruction in 2004 as compared to 1993. They present their findings, which showed more hours spent on work, more time spent on scholarly activities, and a greater percentage of time spent on instruction in the latter year. Chapter 3 illustrates the importance of recognizing and studying how faculty professional experiences and the expectations they face relate to specific institutional types. It also serves as a reminder of the particular need to expand knowledge about faculty work in the community college, a sector where a large proportion of students are educated and faculty are employed.

One major concern in higher education today is the need for attracting and retaining a diverse faculty. Increasing the diversity of the faculty—particularly recruiting and retaining women and faculty of color—is especially important to ensure that higher education institutions are tapping into the wide and diverse array of talent in society. Equally important is the goal of having instructors and professors who reflect the growing diversity of the student population. In Chapter 4, Caroline Sotello Viernes Turner, Juan Carlos González, and J. Luke Wood offer an extensive literature review, analysis, and synthesis of more than 250 articles, books, chapters, reports, and dissertations published between 1998 and 2007 on the topic of faculty of color in higher education. The authors first examine what the literature reveals about support and challenges for faculty of color at the department, institution, and national levels. Building on this analysis, they then present recommendations found in the literature that can be implemented within and across the three contexts of department, institution, and nation. Among the many recommendations highlighted, they emphasize the need to provide for faculty of color, at each context level, greater research support, more mentoring, and opportunities to participate in collaborative communities. The chapter is part of a growing body of work that examines the characteristics, experiences, and professional interests and needs of various groups among the increasingly diverse faculty. A central theme among much of that literature is a call for designing and studying strategies that support the success of the full array of faculty members now participating in the academy.

Finally, Judith M. Gappa, Ann E. Austin, and Andrea G. Trice assert in Chapter 5 that faculty are the intellectual capital of a college or university, and therefore constitute the greatest asset of the institution. However, like Schuster and Finkelstein, they see several major changes affecting higher education overall, and faculty work specifically. Fiscal constraints and increased competition, calls for higher education institutions to be more accountable, increasing enrollments and greater diversity among students, and the availability of new technologies are creating a changing environment for faculty work. One effect of these factors is the shifting pattern of faculty appointments. A tripartite system of appointments is emerging (e.g., tenure-track appointments, renewable contracts, and fixed-term appointments), which may create a bifurcated faculty characterized by inequities between permanent faculty and those in less-permanent appointments. A second outcome of the contextual factors affecting higher education institutions is decline in the autonomy of the faculty, as greater control over faculty work and institutional decisions moves toward administrators.

Third, the many demands on faculty members (e.g., supporting the learning needs of diverse students and engaging in entrepreneurial work) mean an expanding workload and an escalation in the pace of academic work. Fourth, a sense of academic community and collegiality may diminish as faculty members have less time for interpersonal interactions and as aspects of faculty roles are "unbundled" and assigned to specialists (such as, for example, the technical design of online courses). Fifth, new expectations that faculty members face (e.g., to use new technologies in their research and teaching) will require continuous professional development. These themes concerning how societal pressures and changes are affecting colleges and universities are addressed in much of the recent literature on faculty work. The impact of these factors on the academic profession deserve the attention of institutional leaders committed to supporting academic workplaces in which faculty can excel and institutional missions can be achieved with excellence; faculty members themselves seek to understand the contexts and choices relevant to their work; prospective faculty members consider embarking on academic careers; and faculty advisors seek to prepare future faculty for the challenges and opportunities they will encounter.

CONCLUSION

In addition to the themes they highlight, the five chapters in this section also provide examples of the kind of scholarly work that has been done concerning the faculty. We see historical analysis in Schuster and Finkelstein's chapter; sociological perspectives demonstrated in Clark's work; the benefits of literature analysis, synthesis, and review in the Turner, González, and Wood chapter; quantitative analysis in Townsend and Rosser's work; and a qualitative, analytical, synthetic approach in Gappa, Austin, and Trice's chapter. Other approaches can also be found in the literature, including, for example, interview studies, case studies, longitudinal research, and narratives and life histories of faculty lives. The work on faculty issues addresses important questions about identity and meaning in faculty work, roles and responsibilities, disciplinary and institutional contexts, and societal expectations and pressures that impact academic workplaces and faculty lives. However, important questions remain, especially as the faculty becomes more diverse and as higher education institutions develop new responses to external expectations. The study of the academic profession offers inviting questions to researchers and thoughtful findings for the consideration of institutional leaders, current and aspiring faculty members, and higher education policymakers.

1

The American Faculty in Perspective

Jack H. Schuster and Martin J. Finkelstein

The turbulent environmental forces challenging the higher education enterprise in the closing decade of the twentieth century include, most tangibly, changes in the composition of the faculty and the nature of their appointments, in the makeup and preparation of student bodies, and in the resources available to higher education; less tangible (but no less momentous) changes have occurred in public expectations for higher education and in the technologies that influence how we go about organizing and implementing the teaching and learning enterprise.

What might these shifts mean for the American faculty? What kind of faculty will the nation require to meet these challenges? As we address this question, it is instructive to begin with a look at the historical record. That record suggests at least one striking conclusion: when the number and intensity of external social/economic/political pressures impinging on the higher education system reach a "critical mass," the system is forced to reequilibrate itself to accommodate the pressures, not only responding quantitatively, but adapting qualitatively as well. As American higher education expanded in response to the nation's transition to a secular, industrial, urban society with an emergent middle class (Veysey, 1965), it adopted new purposes, functions, and modes of operation (Trow, 1973). Shifts occurred in faculty roles, work activities, and careers, and indeed, there was a reformulation of the very definition of a college or university faculty member and of qualifications to serve in that role.

For nearly four centuries, since the founding of Harvard College, academic staff of one sort or another have stood (or sat) in front of a group, large or small, of physically present students of one sort or another. For more than half that period, college teaching changed little and could best be described as an odd job taken on by fresh graduates of baccalaureate programs as a way station on the path to some other career, for example, the ministry, business, law, medicine, government, or farming. During the past 150 to 175 years, however, an extraordinary change has occurred in the role of academic staffs—their responsibilities, backgrounds, and career paths—both reflecting and making possible in the United States the transformation to a mass system of higher education and, beyond that, practically universal access (Trow, 1973).

These historical shifts in the roles and responsibilities of academic staffs proceeded in two basic phases: professionalization in the nineteenth century, and expansion and diversification in the twentieth century (Metzger, 1987). Professionalization began in the first quarter of the nineteenth century and gained momentum after the Civil War, roughly paralleling the emergence of the American university (Veysey, 1965; Finkelstein, 1983). Expansion and diversification marked the post–World War II period; and it remains ongoing and impressive, although the rate of growth in numbers of institutions, students, and academic staff has slowed since the 1970s (Jencks and Riesman, 1968; Metzger 1987; Kerr, 1991). Current environmental turbulence suggests that we are on the cusp, as it were, of a third tectonic shift.

Reviewing such historical transitions provides an important perspective on the historical development of faculty work and careers, allowing us to unfreeze some of our assumptions about the "essentialness" and "invariability" of who faculty are and what they do and providing us with the necessary floating frame within which to contemplate the future. It is our belief that this overview of how the academic profession evolved on these shores will both allow us to perceive more clearly the current condition of academic life—poised, we argue, at the threshold of momentous change—and enable us to discern more reliably the key issues that will shape academic work and careers in the new century.

THE COLLEGE TEACHING CAREER CIRCA 1800

During the seventeenth century and the first half of the eighteenth, the teaching staffs of American colleges were composed entirely of tutors, typically young men, often no more than twenty years of age, who had just received their baccalaureate degree and were preparing for careers in the ministry (Morison, 1936). Their responsibilities were pastoral-custodial as well as pedagogical in nature. Ideally, a single tutor was assigned to shepherd a single class through the prescribed four-year curriculum. As Morison (1936, p. 127) observed, "Tutors were with their pupils almost every hour of the day [in the classroom recitations, in study halls, and at meals], and slept in the same chamber with some of them at night. They were responsible not only for the intellectual, but also for the moral and spiritual development of their charges." In reality, however, the tutorship during this era functioned more as a "revolving door," whether at Harvard or at Yale, Brown, Dartmouth, or Bowdoin. For prior to 1685, very seldom did a tutor see a class through all four years, and only six of the forty-one tutors during this period remained at Harvard for more than three years (Finkelstein, 1984, pp. 8–9).

During the second half of the eighteenth century, these staffs of tutors began to be supplemented by a small cadre of "permanent" faculty: the first professors. Carrell (1968) could identify only ten professors in all of American higher education in 1750. By 1800, while the number of colleges had doubled, professorial ranks had multiplied tenfold to more than one hundred. All in all, by the onset of the nineteenth century, some two hundred individuals had served as professors in nineteen American colleges.

The pattern that had been in place at Harvard for more than a century and at Yale for more than a half century was adopted almost immediately by those colleges founded during the second half of the eighteenth century. At Brown, for example, within five years of its founding, a core permanent faculty had already emerged with Howell's promotion from tutor to professor to join President and Professor James Manning. By 1800 Brown's five tutors had been supplemented by three permanent professors (*Historical Catalogue*, 1905). At Princeton, by 1767, two decades after its founding, three permanent professors had joined the three tutors (Wertenbaker, 1946). At Dartmouth, during the administration of John Wheelock (1779–1817), several professors were appointed to supplement the single professor who, together with two or three tutors, had constituted the entire faculty during the preceding administration of Eleazar Wheelock (Richardson, 1932, p. 820).

Although these professors discharged responsibilities very similar to those of the tutors in terms of supervising recitations, study halls, chapel, and discipline, they were distinguishable from the tutors in at least three crucial respects. First, professors did not take general charge of a whole class of students; rather, they were appointed in a particular subject area such as natural philosophy, divinity, or ancient languages and, for the most part, provided instruction in that area of specialization. Second, they were generally older than the tutors (by at least five to ten years) and more experienced (the majority had some postbaccalaureate professional preparation in theology, law, or medicine).[1] Third, they stayed on—that is, they were relatively permanent.

Carrell's analysis (1968) of 124 biographical sketches of professors during the second half of the eighteenth century illuminates the particular meaning of a "permanent" appointment prior to 1800. First, a professorship implied a career at a single institution, most frequently one's alma mater. Nearly 40% of Carrell's sample taught at their own alma mater; proportions ranged from just over one-third at the College of Philadelphia (later the University of Pennsylvania) to five-sixths (83%) at Harvard. Indeed, seven out of eight taught at only one institution during their careers, and a practically invisible one in forty taught at three or more institutions. Second, although often enduring, a professorial position was typically a "non-exclusive" career. In analyzing the lifetime occupational commitment of his sample, Carrell reported that about 15% identified themselves exclusively as professional teachers, and roughly 20% described themselves *primarily* as professional teachers but with a secondary occupation in the ministry, medicine, or law, whereas over half ($n = 68$) identified themselves primarily as practitioners of one of the traditional professions and only secondarily as professional college teachers (often having taken up professoring after a lengthy stint as a minister or a practicing physician).

Although college teaching typically was not an exclusive career, or even the first choice, of a majority of eighteenth-century professors, it became a long-term commitment for many—once the move had been made. In analyzing indicators of the extent of professors' occupational commitment *during their teaching tenure*, Carrell found strikingly varied results: 45% identified themselves as college teachers exclusively, while about one-quarter identified themselves as college teachers only primarily or secondarily. In the latter two categories, clergy were heavily represented in the first, and physicians and lawyers made up the greater portion of the second, suggesting that clergy were more likely than the other learned professions to develop a primary commitment to the professorial role, once assumed.

An important question remains: to what extent did appointments as tutors lead to professorial appointments? Alternatively, were these types of appointments typically compartmentalized from each other? In fact, the tutorship remained a separate, temporary career track for young people moving on. It rarely led to entering the professorial ranks: no tutors at Harvard became Harvard professors; one in ten tutors at Yale during this period moved on to a professorship; and one in five at Brown. The professors were typically drawn from outside the ranks of the tutors, although at a few places, such as Yale, the majority of the professors had at one time or another served as tutors (Finkelstein, 1983).

By 1800, then, college teaching was becoming a *bifurcated* occupation. The majority of college teachers were still young, inexperienced tutors, providing general custodial supervision as well as instruction to students for what would be a brief postbaccalaureate engagement before they, the tutors, moved on with their lives and into other careers. An emerging minority were more experienced professionals drawn from other fields (the ministry, medicine, law) who moved into professorships in a teaching field following a career in their profession, often at their alma mater, and who typically continued in the faculty role as a second and/or secondary career.

NINETEENTH-CENTURY PROFESSIONALIZATION

Faculty professionalization during the nineteenth century meant at least four things. First, it marked the beginnings of *specialization* in teaching; that is, faculty usually were hired to teach in a particular field rather than to lead a cohort of freshman through the entire prescribed baccalaureate course (this had begun to occur during the second half of the eighteenth century [Carrell, 1968]). Second, associated with specialization in teaching was the notion that academic staffs should have *formal preparation*, through *graduate* education, for the specializations they taught (not merely general preparation in one of the learned professions); and until the last quarter of the nineteenth century, such training was available only in European universities (McCaughey, 1974; Tobias, 1982). Third, the time dedicated to preparation meant that college teaching no longer made sense as a transitory position but ordinarily required and sustained a *lifelong career commitment* (Carrell, 1968; McCaughey, 1974). Finally, specialization, coupled with the requisite advanced subject-matter preparation, spawned the conception of the academic as *expert*. This in turn provided the basis for subsequently advancing claims to academic freedom and faculty professional autonomy (Scott, 1966; Baldridge et al., 1978; Tobias, 1982).

The professionalization phase proceeded in two relatively distinct stages—two minirevolutions separated by a half century. The first quarter of the nineteenth century witnessed the ascent of a core of permanent, specialized professors as the centerpiece of academic staffing, quickly supplanting the tutorship as the modal appointment type at the leading institutions. This new breed of older academic staff, appointed to teach a particular subject, had some "professional training" in theology, law, or medicine (if not in their teaching field) and tended to stay on in their teaching role (whatever their original career choice might have been). They remained largely independent of the more temporary tutorship, thereby perpetuating a bifurcated staffing system. However, the professors replaced the tutors as the center of academic gravity.

How can we account for this first big step in the evolving professionalization of the academic career—the rise of the permanent faculty and their displacement, in only two decades, of the class of temporary, "revolving door" tutors as the instructional heart of the academy? Several "environmental" pressures appear to provide necessary, if not sufficient, conditions for driving the shift. The first is sheer growth in opportunity: increase in size of some of the leading institutions (Yale, for example, doubled its enrollment in twenty years) and increase in the number of institutions as a result of the "College Movement," however modest that growth may seem in light of later, accelerated expansion (Rudolph, 1962; Burke, 1982). A second set of factors can be seen in changing church-related careers—the most important occupational sector competing with colleges for would-be faculty members. Calhoun (1965), examining the New Hampshire clergy in the late eighteenth and early nineteenth centuries, reports a radical shift in clerical career patterns, which he attributes to the increasing secularization and urbanization of the populace. The average terms of service in local parishes, which throughout the eighteenth century had as often as not been measured in whole adult lifetimes, began to resemble the tenures of modern college and university presidents. This new hazard of job insecurity meant that the challenge of obtaining even so tenuous a position, coupled with the low salaries of clergy hired by rural and small-town congregations, led many ministers to seek to enhance their careers by developing options—such as launching colleges and becoming professors themselves (Tobias, 1982). The correlation of these developments in clerical careers with the ascent of the permanent professorship is lent further credence by the fact that by the beginning of the nineteenth century, clergymen were demonstrably more likely than their fellow professionals in law and medicine to identify themselves primarily as college teachers.

Although the "professor movement" had created by 1825 a relatively large cohort of career college teachers, their preparation, the nature of their work, and the structure of their careers were not yet fully "professionalized" in our contemporary sense. The postgraduate preparation of faculty in their teaching specialty (as distinguished from the ministry, law, or medicine) remained a rarity, except at Harvard. The majority of faculty members continued to be drawn to their initial appointments as professor from nonacademic jobs, primarily in school teaching or the ministry, secondarily in law or medicine. Any semblance of a career grounded in their academic discipline typically ended with their *institutional* career. That is, the modal pattern at some institutions was for the majority of faculty to move into nonacademic careers following their stints, however lengthy, as college teachers (50% of the full professors at Brown did so, and 60% at Bowdoin, although this pattern did not hold at Harvard and Yale).[2] And irrespective of their length of institutional service, most faculty in the first half of the nineteenth century still evidenced relatively low engagement with a field of study in terms of their scholarly publication patterns and associational involvements. Only a single faculty member at Brown, Bowdoin, Harvard, and Yale was involved to any significant extent in the activities of the learned societies of the day. And, excluding the medical faculty, it was only these same solo faculty members who were publishing in their areas of academic appointment.[3] While many professors in the first quarter of the nineteenth century were actively pursuing concurrent "public" careers, virtually none was rooted in their academic specialization. Beyond the budding multifaceted careers of a few men such as Benjamin Silliman at Yale and Parker Cleaveland at Bowdoin, visible on the academic public lecture circuit, the vast majority of professors expended their extra-institutional time in less scholarly pursuits, devoted to church related or civic activities. Fully three-quarters of the professors at Dartmouth, two-thirds of those at Bowdoin, and half of those at Brown were engaged in itinerant preaching and work with missionary societies. Somewhat lower proportions were actively involved in community life, principally by holding political office at the local or even national level, assuming leadership roles in civic associations unrelated to education or intellectual culture (e.g., tree-planting societies), or, in fewer cases, holding membership in state historical societies (Packard, 1882; *Historical Catalogue*, 1905; Tobias, 1982).

By mid-nineteenth century, the confluence of a number of social and intellectual forces gained sufficient momentum to propel (catapult, really) the professionalization process to the next level, and this was a critical step in the shaping of modern academic life. The progressive secularization of American society was penetrating the classical college, subjugating the demands of piety to the secular religion of progress and materialism and reflecting the needs of a growing industrial economy (Hofstadter and Metzger, 1955; Brubacher and Rudy, 1968). At the same time, the rise of science and the tremendous growth of scientific knowledge was breaking apart the classical curriculum and giving rise to the development of the academic disciplines (distinguishing, thereby, the professional from the amateur) and spawning systematic research and graduate education (Berelson, 1960; Veysey, 1965; Wolfle, 1972; Oleson and Voss, 1979). Larger numbers of Americans were studying abroad in Germany and, on their return, importing their versions of the German university and the German idea of research into the United States (Hofstadter and Metzger, 1955). Once graduate education and disciplinary specialization took hold in earnest in the last quarter of the nineteenth century, it was but a short step to the establishment of the major (now familiar) learned societies and their sponsorship of specialized, disciplinary journals: for example, the American Chemical Society began in 1876, the Modern Language Association in 1883, the American Historical Association in 1884, the American Psychological Association in 1892, and on and on (Berelson, 1960).

These developments together provided American higher education with the capability of producing graduate-trained specialists and created clear career opportunities for the specialists thereby produced. Thus the impetus was provided for furthering—completing, in some respects—a second-order restructuring of faculty roles and careers.

This second-order shift was marked by the emergence of the faculty role as specialist in a discipline. Advanced graduate training in a discipline (in contrast to professional training in theology, law, and medicine), together with scholarly publication and participation in the activities of learned societies, was already evident well before 1850 at a few institutions, most notably

Harvard. By 1845, for example, some 70% of the Bowdoin faculty were publishing in their field of specialization (about half authoring primarily textbooks); nearly one-third of them were active in professional associations (Packard, 1882). About half the Brown faculty were publishing in their field of specialization at this time, and by the Civil War, fully one-half were affiliated with the major disciplinary and scientific associations of the day. It was not until the second half of the century (the 1860s and 1870s for the most part), however, that institutions such as Dartmouth and Williams began basing appointments on discipline related credentials and began hiring individuals directly out of the European and nascent American graduate schools (Finkelstein, 1983). And it was then, too, that one discerns the emergence of interinstitutional mobility: faculty, trained in a discipline, moving to more attractive positions at other institutions as emergent disciplinary loyalties supplanted local institutional commitments.

The professorial role as expert, as it began to take form in the immediate pre–Civil War period, gave rise to two significant, interrelated shifts in the professors' institutional careers during the last quarter of the nineteenth century. First was the emergence of new academic ranks (assistant and associate professor) and the forging of these new roles into a career sequence that at once gave shape to the career course and regulated movement through the junior ranks to a full professorship. Concomitantly, there was an expansion and professionalization of the junior faculty. Together, these developments served to integrate into a seamless structure the dual career track system (temporary tutors and a small core of permanent professors) that had characterized the early part of the nineteenth century.

The ranks of instructor and assistant professor made their appearance quite early in the annals of some institutions, but they did not become standard practice anywhere until the last quarter of the nineteenth century; nor did they serve as feeders to the senior ranks initially. These junior faculty roles, however, came to represent not merely changes in nomenclature, but rather significant departures from the tutorship, leading at some institutions to the disappearance of the tutorship and at others to its transformation into an instructorship. Most critically, by the 1870s and 1880s at most institutions the junior roles came to function as feeders to the full professorial ranks. By 1880 the junior faculty grew to equal or surpass in size the senior faculty at many institutions; and they were increasingly entering their academic careers directly from graduate training in their specialties or from junior appointments at other institutions. The essential features of the twentieth-century faculty role were becoming the norm—a far cry from the composition of faculties in the first quarter of the nineteenth century.

All of these structural changes in the academic career follow from the emergence of the discipline as the central organizing principle of academic life and the university as the dominant organizational form. Beginning in the 1850s the bare outline of a concurrent "public" career rooted in a faculty member's disciplinary expertise, as an educator and/or as a proponent of culture (rather than of religion), was becoming discernible at many institutions. At Brown, for example, the immediate pre–Civil War period saw the first instance of a faculty member using his expertise in the service of state government: the appointment of a chemistry professor to head the Rhode Island board of weights and measures. By the end of the Civil War, the proportion of the Brown faculty involved in itinerant preaching and other clerical activities had dropped from more than one-third at midcentury to one-eighth. Although a large majority of the faculty remained involved in civic and community affairs (about 75%), a change in the nature of that involvement had taken place: only a single faculty member was directly involved in elective politics, while the majority were involved in distinctively cultural, academic, or education-related activities such as membership on boards of education; holding office in national honor, art, or historical societies; and service on state and federal government commissions (*Historical Catalogue*, 1905). At Bowdoin, by the eve of the Civil War, four of seven faculty members were engaged in extra-institutional roles as specialists, educators, and public men of letters. Parker Cleaveland was holding public lectures on mineralogy, and Alpheus Packard on education; President James Woods and Professor Packard were engaging in commissioned writing for the Maine Historical Society; and Thomas Upham was producing pamphlets for the American Peace Association (Packard, 1882).[4]

The growing centrality of the discipline was intruding into new professional claims for a role in areas of college governance, especially faculty appointments and curricular decisions, that had been the province of college presidents; these areas had traditionally been driven by religious as distinguished from scholarly considerations. Such claims on the part of professors were evident during the pre–Civil War period in the struggles, albeit amicable ones, between the old- and new-guard faculty concerning the relative emphasis on moral development and student discipline versus purely academic concerns (Dwight, 1903). The assertions of faculty prerogatives were reflected both more dramatically and less amicably in the post–Civil War period; they took the form of veritable faculty revolts at some of the more traditional institutions. At Williams, for example, the faculty, concerned about student performance and academic standards, confronted Mark Hopkins, the prototypical old-time college president, over their determination to enforce regular class attendance via a marking system. Two years earlier the faculty had succeeded in instituting annual written examinations; and in 1869, at the faculty's insistence, admissions standards were tightened and the practice of sending lists of class standings (the equivalent of the modern registrar's grade report) to all parents was initiated, despite enrollment shortfalls. By 1872 these conflicts had precipitated Hopkins's resignation and the inauguration of Paul Ansel Chadbourne, who had come to Williams eight years earlier as only the second European-trained specialist on the faculty (Rudolph, 1956, pp. 223–24).

At Dartmouth a decade later, fifteen of the twenty-two resident faculty petitioned the Board of Trustees for the dismissal of President Samuel Colcord Bartlett. At issue was the president's attempt to secure the appointment of a new professor of Greek whose religious qualifications appeared to the faculty to exceed the candidate's scholarly qualifications. Although Bartlett survived the challenge and lingered on for another decade, his successor, William Jewett Tucker, recognized in his 1893 inaugural address the emergence of a "New Dartmouth," a new kind of college staffed by a new kind of faculty (Tobias, 1982).

The faculty, it could be said, by century's end had scaled one plateau. Consolidation and deeper professionalization lay ahead.

CONSOLIDATION AND ELABORATION IN THE EARLY TWENTIETH CENTURY

By 1915 one indicator that the "new" academic profession had turned a collective corner was the founding of the American Association of University Professors (AAUP). The coming together of eighteen academic luminaries from seven of the leading universities to charter the first national organization of professors suggests a newfound sense of collective professorial self-consciousness and a sense of colleagueship or fraternity in the service of scientific progress. As Edwin R. A. Seligman of Columbia, one of the founders, proclaimed: "Loyalty to our institution is admirable, but if our institution for some unfortunate reason stands athwart the progress of science, or even haltingly follows that path, we must use our best efforts to convince our colleagues and the authorities of the error of their ways. . . . In prosecuting this end, we need both individual and collective efforts. The leisure of the laboratory and of the study accounts for much; but almost equally important is the stimulus derived from contact with our colleagues" (cited by Hofstadter and Metzger, 1955, p. 471). Yet this sense of collective consciousness was, in one important sense, highly restricted: in terms of who was to be included in the collectivity. In the AAUP's initial constitution, membership was limited to "recognized" scholars with at least ten years' experience in the professoriate. Although the base was broadened in 1920 to include professors with three or more years of experience, nonetheless the cadre that was conscious of itself collectively constituted a small, exclusive contingent of professionalized scholars within the professoriate.

Initial membership included 867 research-oriented full professors; seven years later, about four thousand faculty members, constituting some 6% of the professoriate, could be counted among the AAUP's members. But among even this select group, strictly professional concerns were secondary to institutional ones. John Dewey had sought to direct the energies of the new organization toward developing professional standards for the university-based scholar and away from intervention into faculty-administrative disputes at the institutional level. But the membership clearly saw the association's primary function as that of a grievance committee assisting individual faculty in internal campus disputes, and during the early years, the organization was overwhelmed by the grievances brought to its attention (Hofstadter and Metzger, 1955).

The focus on such faculty-administrative concerns heralded the persistent, if imperfect, arrival of the modern university scholar. Indeed, the two-decade period between the world wars was largely one of consolidating the gains of the preceding quarter century. Discipline-based graduate study and research grew at an unprecedented rate. The annual production of doctorates increased fivefold: from 620 in 1920 to nearly 3,300 in 1940. More discourses and pronouncements on graduate education were published than in any previous or subsequent twenty-year period, excepting the present era. A cycle of intense, second-order specialization was evident in the differentiation of yet more specialized subareas within the disciplines. To illustrate, the social sciences spawned in quick succession the Econometric Society (1930), the American Association of Physical Anthropologists (1930), the Society for the Psychological Study of Social Issues (1936), the American Society of Criminology (1936), the Rural Sociological Society (1937), the Society for Applied Anthropology (1941), and the Economic History Association (1941), among others. And these societies, in turn, sponsored more specialized scholarly journals, for example, the *Journal of Personality* (1932), *Econometria* (1933), *Sociometry* (1937), and the *Public Administration Review* (1940). By the mid-1940s, the dominance of the graduate research model as we know it was clearly established, as was the professoriate's claim to that crucial desideratum of professionalization, namely, specialized expertise (Berelson, 1960).

On campus, the recognition of disciplinary expertise as the sine qua non of faculty work translated into gradually relieving the faculty of responsibilities for overseeing student discipline; this had been, after all, the major noninstructional function of the faculty during the eighteenth and nineteenth centuries. Although the first deans of students emerged with the advent of the university in the last quarter of the nineteenth century (Brubacher and Rudy, 1968, p. 322), what became known as the student personnel movement began in the 1920s and gained momentum throughout the 1930s and 1940s. The movement established on campuses across the nation an infrastructure designed to address the nonintellectual, nonacademic needs of college students. This infrastructure, featuring deans of students, counseling, student health services, career development, and so on, was, to be sure, a response to a broad array of convergent forces, including the tremendous growth and diversification of student bodies; a reaction against the more narrow German influence on higher education; and an expression of John Dewey's educational philosophy. Nonetheless, these various forces also served to provide the occasion (and organizational means) for the faculty collectively to shed nonacademic responsibilities that had grown anachronistic by the interwar period.

The faculty's disciplinary expertise expressed itself on campus not only in casting off old responsibilities, but also in adding new ones. Organizationally, the increasing recognition of the faculty's claim to professional expertise brought an enhanced role in campus decision making. Faculty governance structures had existed statutorily at several leading institutions, including Harvard, Princeton, and Pennsylvania, as early as the mid-eighteenth century, closely paralleling the emergence of the professorship. And by the second half of the nineteenth century, faculty bodies had developed considerable authority at Yale, Cornell, and Wisconsin. However, although precedent may have placed student discipline and admission and graduation requirements within their purview, faculty prerogatives in key areas, such as curriculum, educational policy, and especially faculty personnel decisions (appointments and promotions) and the selection of academic administrators, were not clearly established at most institutions; not infrequently, faculty input in these areas was ignored (Cowley, 1980).

But the 1930s saw the blossoming of faculty committee structures on most leading campuses. By 1939 Haggerty and Works found that two-fifths of the faculty employed by institutions served by the North Central Association were on average sitting on two committees each. Although two-thirds of such committees concentrated on administrative functions, a significant minority focused on issues of educational policy. These developments culminated in the report of the AAUP Committee on College and University Government (Committee T) that set forth five overarching principles for faculty participation in institutional governance.[5] Taken together, these principles mandated a role for faculty in the selection of administrators, in the formulation and control of educational policy, and in the appointment and promotion process. The role promulgated was largely *consultative*, but the AAUP document has at its foundation the premise that "faculty were not hired employees to be manipulated by president and trustees, but were academic professionals whose role involved teaching and contributing to the direction and major decisions of an institution" (Orr, 1978, pp. 347–48).

Perhaps fundamentally, the expertise of professors translated on their own campuses into leverage that enabled them to win tenure rights. Throughout the nineteenth century, the professoriate had labored without provisions for job security, as mere employees of their campuses who were subject to the will of presidents and trustees. Although many full professors were on *indefinite* appointments, that simply meant that no length of term had been specified in their contract. Indefinite appointments were never the equivalent of *permanent* appointments, either in intent or in law; and individuals on such appointments could be dismissed at any time (Metzger, 1973). Moreover, for junior faculty neither a recognized set of procedures nor a timetable was yet established for attaining even these indefinite appointments that were the reward of a full professorship. An individual faculty member might serve his institution for fifteen or twenty years and be dismissed at any time—without reason and without a hearing. Such dismissals occurred again and again, even at institutions with a tradition of faculty power, such as Yale and Wisconsin. In its historic 1940 Statement of Principles on Academic Freedom and Tenure, culminating fourteen years of negotiation, the AAUP articulated the concept of *permanent* faculty tenure, designed a means for regularizing the flow of tenure decision making (that is, by stipulating a six-year probationary period), and endorsed procedures to ensure due process on nonreappointment. By that time, the AAUP had sufficient stature to gain widespread institutional acceptance of its pronouncement. And by that time, too, most institutions had already formalized the system of academic ranks to provide the infrastructure of career progression (Orr, 1978).

Off-campus, that recognition of the faculty's specialized expertise brought them into public service on a scale heretofore unknown. Although the discipline-based "public service" role of the professional scholar had germinated during the Progressive era and World War I, the number of faculty involved had been relatively small and their national exposure highly circumscribed.

Thus, during the heyday of the Wisconsin Idea (1910–11), some thirty-three faculty members held official positions both with the state and within the university, mostly as agricultural experts or with the state railroad or tax commissions; thirteen others, including economists, lawyers, and political scientists, were "on call" at the capital as needed. Even so, less than 10% of the university faculty participated directly, and this group was drawn from only a handful of disciplines (Veysey, 1965).

During World War I, the faculty's public service to the nation was offered primarily through two vehicles: the National Board for Historical Service and the Committee on Public Information. The former, linked to the leadership of the American Historical Association, directed the efforts of several dozen historians for the revision of secondary-school social studies curricula. Under the Committee on Public Information, about one hundred social scientists were commissioned to prepare wartime propaganda pamphlets, while others were employed to monitor foreign-language newspaper editorials to detect disloyalty (Gruber, 1976).

The national "Brain Trust" assembled by President Franklin D. Roosevelt to address the social and economic dislocation wrought by the depression provided on an unprecedented scale a highly visible public showcase for faculty talent. Between 1930 and 1935, forty-one independent and state-supported universities granted nearly three hundred leaves to full-time faculty for the express purpose of serving the federal government (Orr, 1978). A much larger number of faculty served state and local governments "on overload." In the early 1940s, it was to academics that the federal government turned once again in support of the national defense effort associated with World War II. The Manhattan Project, which gave birth to the atomic bomb, is only the most dramatic and famous of innumerable faculty-assisted wartime projects. After the war this newfound visibility contributed to the legitimation of the professional role of the college teacher. The esteem in which members of the academic profession were held by the public increased, as did the prestige attached to an academic career.[6]

The growing recognition of faculty as professionals served not only to elevate the profession but also to broaden entry into it. Professionalization permitted (although it by no means assured) the introduction of achievement-related criteria of success and a concomitant reduction in the salience of the ascriptive characteristics of social class and religious preference. Thus, by 1940, Catholics and Jews surged to constitute nearly one-quarter of what had been an exclusively Protestant profession; the sons of farmers and manual laborers were increasingly joining the sons of businessmen and professionals; and *daughters* were now joining the sons, making up fully 13% of a sample of faculty affiliated with institutions accredited by the North Central Association (Kunkel, 1938; Lipset and Ladd, 1979).

By World War II, the various components of the contemporary academic role had thus crystallized into the highly differentiated model of today—teaching, research, and institutional and public service, all rooted in the faculty member's disciplinary expertise. The "modern era" of faculty roles and academic work had begun.

GROWTH AND DIVERSIFICATION, 1940–1969

The twenty-five-year period between the end of World War II and the close of the 1960s (when the analyses in this volume begin) was one characterized by unprecedented growth for American higher education and its academic staffs. The rate of expansion, peaking in the late 1960s with the establishment by most states of large and diverse public systems of higher education designed to achieve goals of very broad—even universal—access, nearly doubled the ranks of college faculty between 1940 and 1960, from about 120,000 to 236,000 (Harris, 1972, p. 484) and almost doubled again in a single decade, 1960–70, from 236,000 to 450,000 (NCES, 1980).[7] The number of new positions created between 1965 and 1970 alone exceeded the total number of positions extant in 1940 (Lipset and Ladd, 1979).

This explosive growth was closely associated with diversification. Most critically, faculty were pursuing careers in institutions with a much wider range of missions. By 1969 seven of ten faculty members were employed in the public sector (home to less than half of them in 1940), and fully one in six faculty were employed at two-year institutions (Harris, 1972). Although the majority of faculty were teaching in the liberal arts fields throughout this period, by 1960 the professions were beginning to rival the liberal arts in doctoral degree production (Berelson, 1960)—a harbinger of developments to come. Demographically, the gradual opening up of faculty ranks to women and to individuals from more diverse religious (non-Protestant) and racial or ethnic (nonwhite, non-European) backgrounds continued to proceed—if, initially, at glacial speed (Steinberg, 1974).

In the midst of such modest, though expanding diversification of faculty characteristics, we nevertheless find a growing normative homogenization of the profession in at least one crucial aspect: the hold of the academic disciplines on faculty loyalties and commitments. Thus while student enrollments were burgeoning and diversifying, a critical component of what Jencks and Riesman (1968) referred to as the "academic revolution," the influence of one's field, exercised primarily through the socialization experience of graduate school and later through the disciplinary associations, had been *narrowing* the definition of the proper scope and standards of academic work. This model of the university scholar and her or his scholarship suffused the early professional socialization experience of that large, dominant cohort of faculty hired to staff the great expansion of higher education during the 1960s; and the broad acceptance of this outlook and orientation, through the influence of this robust, energetic generation of faculty, had largely penetrated the whole American system by the late 1960s.

THE LAST QUARTER CENTURY: THE SEEDS OF A THIRD REVOLUTION?

Since the consummation of the "academic revolution" described by Jencks and Riesman and the concomitant crystallization of the model of modern academic man (only more recently "woman" in any significant numbers), American higher education has been pushed, forcefully, in new directions by the economic, demographic, and technological changes to which we alluded earlier. Many believe that the face of American higher education will have changed, perhaps much of it beyond recognition, over the next generation (indeed, perhaps over the next decade). How are these competing forces of change and stasis being resolved? How are the changes that are already manifest reshaping the nature of faculty work and careers? And how will they do so in the future?

Emerging evidence, reported in subsequent chapters, suggests that the "academic revolution" of the 1960s is fraying at the edges, that changes are well under way in the nature of faculty life and work. Faculty careers, for example, appear to be becoming (1) less *exclusive*, that is, there is increasing traffic between college teaching and other employment, especially in the career and professional fields; and (2) less *preemptive*, that is, less of a career preoccupation that demands and consumes all available time. For part-time faculty, this is true by definition (except for the many part-timers holding down two or more such jobs). But increasingly, for regular, full-time faculty, there are competing claims: economic pressures have led some to redirect some of their energies to extramural pecuniary pursuits (other concurrent employment); a lack of congruence between individual faculty orientations and changing institutional missions has led others to disengage from institutional life and to pursue other life interests. Many observers have for some time decried the decline of "academic citizenship" (Cross, 1994). We note that this putative retreat comes anomalously at a time when commitments to enhancing the quality of campus life *should* be increasing (given the burgeoning contingent of senior faculty, who by virtue of their loyalty and know-how have traditionally been the most valuable academic citizens) and when that interest needs to be intensified (as proportionately fewer full-time faculty positions exist, a fact that devolves more institutional responsibility on the shrinking proportion of regular, full-time faculty). Increasing attention has been paid in recent years to the teaching role; and indeed a significant and rapidly growing segment of the faculty—part-timers and others not eligible for tenure—have their responsibilities by *definition* limited to teaching.

Questions such as these are relevant not only to the American faculty as an aggregate body, but especially to the cohorts of new entrants that colleges and universities have begun hiring in recent years (Finkelstein, Seal, and Schuster, 1998a, 1998b). How will the more general shifts play out with respect to this critical group who will, after all, serve as the American faculty of the first quarter of the twenty-first century? And to the new demographic mix of students they will encounter? Will these changes inevitably constitute a new "revolution" in American academic life? Or will they merely amount to a minor turbulence on the order of the one the system fostered after World War II, something that can readily be accommodated? And whatever the disruption, will we have the faculty that the nation requires to staff its colleges of the new century?

NOTES

1. Seven of the eight professors at Brown during the eighteenth century had such training (*Historical Catalogue*, 1905), as did all ten professors at Harvard (Eliot, 1848).
2. It should be noted, however, that those full professors who left teaching averaged nearly two decades in their institutional positions (21.2 years at Brown; 18.5 years at Bowdoin), so that college teaching still constituted a significant span in their careers.
3. The four "active" faculty were Caswell at Brown, Cleaveland at Bowdoin, Peck at Havard, and at Yale, Silliman, who had in 1824 founded the *American Journal of Science*. Although many of their colleagues were publishing *something*, their work consisted chiefly of collections of sermons and addresses made at commencements and other public occasions (Finkelstein, 1984, p. 16).
4. Other institutions lagged a decade or more behind these developments. At Dartmouth, as late as 1851, three-quarters of the faculty continued to participate actively in the community as preachers, licentiates, or ordained ministers, and as civic boosters. By the late 1870s, however, the proportion of faculty engaged in clerical activities had plummeted to 15%, while over half of the faculty were then significantly engaged in scientific associations in their fields of specialization (Tobias, 1982). At Wisconsin, by the early 1870s university professors were called upon to head the state geological survey (Curti and Carstensen, 1949).
5. That Committee T was the second committee organized by the AAUP (in 1916, one year after the association's founding) indicates the importance the professoriate attached to what came to be called "shared governance." The committee's name, *College and University Government*, reflects that the more contemporary *governance* is latter-day terminology; it was not customarily employed for these purposes until after World War II.
6. Bowen (1978) has documented the close association of public attitudes toward academe and levels of faculty salaries. He pinpointed World War II as marking a major upturn in both the level and the rate of real growth in faculty salaries.
7. The numbers are for faculty at the rank of instructor or above offering resident, degree-credit instruction. Both full-time and part-time faculty are included, but not those offering nondegree instruction or instruction off-campus. The figure for 1940 is estimated from the total instructional staff figure.

REFERENCES

Baldridge, J. Victor, David Curtis, George Ecker, and Gary Riley. 1978. *Policy Making and Effective Leadership: A National Study of Academic Management*. San Francisco: Jossey-Bass.
Berelson, Bernard. 1960. *Graduate Education in the United States*. New York: McGraw-Hill.

Bowen, Howard R. 1978. *Investment in Learning: The Individual and Social Value of American Higher Education*. San Francisco: Jossey-Bass.

Brubacher, John, and Willis Rudy. 1968. *Higher Education in Transition*. Rev. ed. New York: Harper and Row.

Burke, Colin. 1982. *American Collegiate Populations*. New York: New York University Press.

Calhoun, Daniel. 1965. *Professional Lives in America*. Cambridge, MA.: Harvard University Press.

Carrell, William. 1968. "American College Professors: 1750–1800." *History of Education Quarterly* 8:289–305.

Cowley, William H. 1980. *Professors, Presidents, and Trustees*. Ed. Donald Williams. San Francisco: Jossey-Bass.

Cross, K. Patricia. 1994. "Academic Citizenship." *American Association for Higher Education Bulletin 1994–1995* 47, nos. 1–10: 3–5.

Curti, Merle E., and Vernon Carstensen, 1949. *The University of Wisconsin: A History*. Vol. 2, 1848–1925. Madison: University of Wisconsin Press.

Dwight, Timothy. 1903. *Memories of Yale Life and Men*, 2845–1899. New York: Dodd, Mead.

Eliot, Samuel. 1848. *A Sketch of the History of Harvard College*. Boston: Little and Brown.

Finkelstein, Martin J. 1983. "From Tutor to Professor: The Development of the Modern Academic Role at Six Institutions during the Nineteenth Century." *History of Higher Education Annual* 399–121.

———. 1984. *The American Academic Profession: A Synthesis of Social Scientific Inquiry since World War II*. Columbus: Ohio State University Press.

Finkelstein, Martin J., Robert K. Seal, and Jack H. Schuster. 1998a. *The New Academic Generation: A Profession in Transformation*. Baltimore: Johns Hopkins University Press.

———. 1998b. *New Entrants to the Full-Time Faculty of Institutions of Higher Education*. Statistical Analysis Report NCES no. 92–252. Washington, DC: National Center for Education Statistics.

Gruber, Marilyn. 1976. *Mars and Minerva*. Baton Rouge: Louisiana State University Press.

Haggerty, William, and George Works. 1939. *Faculties of Colleges and Universities Accredited by the North Central Association of Colleges and Secondary Schools, 1930–1937*. Publication no. 12. Chicago: Commission on Institutions of Higher Education, North Central Association.

Harris, Seymour E. 1972. *A Statistical Portrait of Higher Education*. New York: McGraw-Hill.

Historical Catalogue of Brown University, 1764–1904. 1905. Providence, RI: Brown University.

Hofstadter, Richard, and Walter Metzger. 1955. *The Development of Academic Freedom in the United States*. New York: Columbia University Press.

Jencks, Christopher, and David Riesman. 1968. *The Academic Revolution*. Garden City, NY: Doubleday.

Kerr, Clark. 1991. *The Great Transformation in Higher Education, 1960–1980*. Albany: State University of New York Press.

Kunkel, B. W. 1938. "A Survey of College Faculties." *American Association of University Professors Bulletin* 24 (March): 249–62.

Lipset, Seymour, and Everett C. Ladd Jr. 1979. "The Changing Social Origins of American Academics." In *Qualitative and Quantitative Social Research*, eds. Robert Merton, James S. Coleman, and Peter H. Rossi. Glencoe, IL: Free Press.

McCaughey, Robert M. 1974. "The Transformation of American Academic Life: Harvard University, 1821–1892." *Perspectives in American History* 8:239–334.

Metzger, Walter P. 1973. "Academic Tenure in America: An Historical Essay." In *Faculty Tenure*, by Commission on Academic Tenure in Higher Education. San Francisco: Jossey-Bass.

———. 1987. "The Academic Profession in the United States." In *The Academic Profession: National, Disciplinary, and Institutional Settings*, ed. Burton R. Clark. Berkeley: University of California Press.

Morison, Samuel E. 1936. *Harvard College in the Seventeenth Century.* Cambridge: Harvard University Press.

National Center for Education Statistics (NCES). 1980. *The Condition of Education 1980, Statistical Report*. Washington, DC: U.S. Government Printing Office.

Oleson, Alexandra, and John Voss, eds. 1979. *The Organization of Knowledge in Modern America, 1860–1880*. Baltimore: Johns Hopkins University Press.

Orr, Kenneth B. 1978. "The Impact of the Depression Years, 1929–39, on Faculty in American Colleges and Universities." PhD diss., University of Michigan, Ann Arbor.

Packard, Alpheus, ed. 1882. *History of Bowdoin College*. Boston: James Ripley Osgood and Co.

Richardson, Leon D. 1932. *History of Dartmouth College*. Vol. 2. Hanover, NH: Dartmouth College Publications.

Rudolph, Frederick. 1956. *Mark Hopkins and the Log*. New Haven, CT: Yale University Press.

——. 1962. *The American College and University: A History*. New York: Random House.

Scott, W. Richard. 1966. "Professionals in Bureaucracies—Areas of Conflict." In *Professionalization*, eds. Howard M. Vollmer and D. L. Mills. Englewood Cliffs, NJ: Prentice Hall.

Steinberg, Stephen. 1974. *The Academic Melting Pot: Catholics and Jews in American Higher Education*. New York: McGraw-Hill.

Tobias, Marilyn. 1982. *Old Dartmouth on Trial*. New York: New York University Press.

Trow, Martin. 1973. "Problems in the Transition from Elite to Mass Higher Education." In *Policies for Higher Education, from the General Report on the Conference on Future Structures of Post-Secondary Education*. Paris: Organization for Economic Cooperation and Development.

Veysey, Laurence R. 1965. *The Emergence of the American University*. Chicago: University of Chicago Press.

Wertenbaker, Thomas J. 1946. *Princeton, 1746–1896*. Princeton, NJ: Princeton University Press.

Wolfle, Dale. 1972. *The Home of Science*. New York: McGraw-Hill.

2

Small Worlds, Different Worlds

The Uniquenesses and Troubles of American Academic Professions

Burton R. Clark

The academic profession is a multitude of academic tribes and territories.[1] As in days of old, it is law, medicine, and theology. It is now also high-energy physics, molecular biology, Renaissance literature, childhood learning, and computer science. Built upon a widening array of disciplines and specialties, it hosts subcultures that speak in the strange tongues of econometrics, biochemistry, ethnomethodology, and deconstructionism. Driven by a research imperative that rewards specialization, its fragmentation is slowed, though not fully arrested, by limited resources to fund all the new and old lines of effort in which academics would like to engage. Already very great, knowledge growth builds in a self-amplifying fashion. Subject differentiation follows in train, not least in a national system of universities and colleges, such as the American, that is both hugely based on research and generously inclusive in adding subjects to the now-endless list of what legitimately can be taught. As subjects fragment, so does the academic profession, turning it ever-more into a profession of professions.

No less important in the differentiation of the academic profession in America is the dispersion of faculty among institutions in a system that, when viewed internationally, must be seen as inordinately large, radically decentralized, extremely diversified, uniquely competitive, and uncommonly entrepreneurial. A high degree of institutional dispersion positions American faculty in many varied sectors of a national "system" that totaled 3,600 institutions in the mid-1990s: a hundred-plus "research universities" of high research intensity; another hundred "doctoral-granting" universities that grant only a few doctorates and operate off of a small research base; five hundred and more "master's colleges and universities," a catch-all category of private and public institutions that have graduate as well as undergraduate programs, offering master's degrees but not doctorates; still another six hundred "baccalaureate colleges," heavily private and varying greatly in quality and in degree of concentration on the liberal arts; a huge array of over 1,400 two-year colleges, 95 percent public in enrollment, whose individual comprehensiveness includes college-transfer programs, short-term vocational offerings, and adult education; and finally a leftover miscellany of some seven hundred "specialized institutions" that do not fit into the above basic categories.[2]

These major categories in turn contain much institutional diversity. Buried within them are historically black colleges, Catholic universities, women's colleges, fundamentalist religious universities and colleges, and such distinctive institutions as the Julliard School (of Music), the Bank Street College of Education, and Rockefeller University. The American faculty is distributed institutionally all over the map, located in the educational equivalents of the farm and the big city, the ghetto and the suburbs, the darkened ravine located next to a coal mine and the sunny hill overlooking a lovely valley.

Disciplinary and institutional locations together compose the primary matrix of induced and enforced differences among American academics. These two internal features of the system itself are more important than such background characteristics of academics as class, race, religion, and gender in determining work-centered thought and behavior. These primary dimensions convert simple statements about "the professor" in "the college" or "the university" into stereotypes. We deceive ourselves every time we speak of *the* college professor, a common habit among popular critics of the professoriate who fail to talk to academics in their varied locations and to listen to what they say. Simple summary figures and averages extracted from surveys, e.g., "68 percent of American professors like their mothers" or "On the average, American professors teach eight and a half hours a week," also should be avoided. Understanding begins with a willingness to pursue diversity.

DIFFERENT WORLDS, SMALL WORLDS

The disciplinary creation of different academic worlds becomes more striking with each passing year. In the leading universities, the clinical professor of medicine is as much a part of the basic work force as the professor of English. The medical academic might be found in a cancer ward, interacting intensively with other doctors, nurses, orderlies, laboratory assistants, a few students perhaps, and many patients in a round of tightly scheduled activities that can begin at six in the morning and extend into the evenings and weekends. Such academics are often under considerable pressure to generate income from patient-care revenues; their faculty groups negotiate with third-party medical plans and need a sizeable administrative staff to handle patient billing. Salaries may well depend on group income, which fluctuates from year to year and is directly affected by changes in the health-care industry and the competitive position of a particular medical school-hospital complex. Even in a tenured post, salary may not be guaranteed. Sizeable research grants must be actively and repetitively pursued; those who do not raise funds from research grants will find themselves encumbered with more clinical duties.

The humanities professor in the leading universities operates in a totally different environment. To begin with, teaching "loads" are in the range of four to six hours a week, office hours are at one's discretion, and administrative assignments vary considerably with one's willingness to cooperate. The humanities academic typically interacts with large numbers of beginning students in introductory classes in lecture halls; with small numbers of juniors and seniors in specialized upper-division courses; and with a few graduate students in seminars and dissertation supervision around such highly specialized topics as Elizabethan lyric and Icelandic legend. Much valuable work time can be spent at home, away from the "distractions" of the university office.

About what is the humanities academic thinking and writing? Attention may center on a biography of Eugene O'Neill, an interpretation of what Jane Austen really meant, an effort to trace Lillian Hellman's political passions, or a critique of Derrida and deconstructionism. Professors seek to master a highly specialized segment of literature and maximize individual interpretation. The interests of humanities professors are reflected not only in the many sections and byways of such omnibus associations as the Modern Language Association but also in the specificities of the Shakespeare Association of America, the Dickens Society, the D. H. Lawrence Society of North America, the Speech Association of America, the Thomas Hardy Society of America, and the Vladimir Nabokov Society. Tocqueville's famous comment on the propensity of Americans to form voluntary associations is nowhere more true than in the academic world.

Disciplinary differences are of course not limited to the sharp contrast between life in a medical school and in a department of English. The work of Tony Becher and others on the cultures of individual disciplines has shown that bodies of knowledge variously determine the behavior of individuals and departments.[3] Disciplines exhibit discernible differences in individual behavior and group action, notably between "hard" and "soft" subjects and "pure" and "applied" fields: in a simple fourfold classification, between hard-pure (physics), hard-applied (engineering), soft-pure (history), and soft-applied (social work). Across the many fields of the physical sciences, the biological sciences, the social sciences, the humanities, and the arts, face-to-face research reveals varied work assignments, symbols of identity, modes of authority, career lines, and associational linkages. Great differences in the academic life often appear between letters and science departments and the many professional-school domains in which a concern for the ways and needs of an outside profession must necessarily be combined with the pursuit of science and truth for its own sake. The popular images of Mr. Chips chatting up undergraduates and Einsteinian, white-haired, remote scholars dreaming up esoteric mathematical equations are a far cry from the realities of academic work that helps prepare schoolteachers, librarians, social workers, engineers, computer experts, architects, nurses, pharmacists, business managers, lawyers, and doctors—and, in some academic locales, also morticians, military personnel, auto mechanics, airport technicians, secretaries, lathe operators, and cosmetologists. For over a century, American higher education has been generous to a fault in admitting former outside fields, and new occupations, into the academy—a point made by historians of higher education and of the professions.[4]

Because research is the first priority of leading universities, the disciplinary differentiation of every modern system of higher education is self-amplifying. The American system is currently the extreme case of this phenomenon. Historic decentralization and competitiveness prompted Charles William Eliot at Harvard and others at the old colleges of the last half of the nineteenth century to speed up the nascent evolution from the age of the college to the age of the university. This evolution turned professors loose to pursue specialized research and to teach specialized subjects at the newly created graduate level, even as students were turned loose to pick and choose from an array of undergraduate courses that was to become ever more bewildering. Throughout the twentieth century and especially in the last fifty years, the reward system of promoting academics on the grounds of research and published scholarship has become more deeply rooted in the universities (and would-be universities and leading four-year colleges) with almost every passing decade. The many proliferating specialties of the knowledge-producing disciplines are like tributaries flowing into a mammoth river of the research imperative.

The most serious operational obstacles to this research-driven amplification are the limitations of funding and the institutional need to teach undergraduates and beginning graduate students the codified introductory knowledge of the various fields. There also remains in American higher education the long-standing belief in the importance of liberal or general education—a task, we may note, that Europeans largely assign to secondary schools. The saving remnant of academics who uphold the banner of liberal and general education are able to sally forth in full cry periodically—the 1920s, the late 1940s, the 1990s—to group some specialties into more general courses, narrow the options in distribution requirements from, say, four hundred to one hundred courses, insist that teaching take priority over research, and in general raise a ruckus about the dangers of the specialized mind. Meanwhile, promotion committees on campus continue their steady scrutiny of individual records of research-based scholarship. Central administrators work to build an institutional culture of first-rateness, as it is defined competitively across the nation and the world according to the reputations of noted scholars and departments. Sophisticated general educators and liberal-arts proponents in the universities recognize the primacy of the substantive impulse and learn how to work incrementally within its limits.

Institutional Differentiation

As powerful as self-amplifying disciplinary differences have become in dividing the American professoriate, institutional diversity now plays an even more important role. This axis of differentiation places approximately two-thirds of American academics in settings other than that of doctoral-granting universities. We find about a fourth of the total faculty in the colleges and universities that offer degree work as far as the master's; a small share, about 7 percent, in the liberal-arts colleges; and a major bloc of a third or so (over 250,000) in the nearly 1,500 community colleges.[5] In student numbers in 1994, the universities had just 26 percent of the total enrollment; the master's level institutions, 21 percent; the baccalaureate colleges, 7 percent; the specialized institutions, 4 percent; and the community colleges, 43 percent—by far the largest share.[6] The two-year colleges admit over 50 percent of entering students. There is no secret that academics in this latter section do an enormous amount of the work of the system at large.

These major locales exhibit vast differences in the very basis of academic life, namely, the balance of effort between undergraduate teaching and advanced research and research training. Teaching loads in the leading universities come in at around four to six hours a week, occasionally tapering down to two to three hours—a class a week, a seminar a week—while sometimes, especially in the humanities, rising above six. The flip side is that faculty commonly expect to spend at least half their time in research, alone or in the company of graduate students, other faculty, and research staff. We need not stray very far among the institutional types, however, before we encounter teaching loads that are 50, 100, and 200 percent higher. The "doctoral-granting universities" that are not well supported to do research often exact teaching loads of nine to twelve hours, as do the liberal-arts colleges, especially those outside the top fifty. In master's colleges, loads of twelve hours a week in the classroom are common. In the community colleges, the standard climbs to fifteen hours and loads of eighteen and twenty-one hours are not unknown. Notably, as we move from the research universities through the middle types to the two-year institutions, faculty involvement shifts from advanced students to beginning students; from highly selected students to an open-door clientele; from young students in the traditional college age-group to a mix of students of all ages in short-term vocational programs as well as in course work leading toward a bachelor's degree. In the community colleges, students in the college-transfer track are numerically overshadowed by students in terminal vocational programs, and both are frequently outnumbered by nonmatriculated adults who turn the "college" into a "community center."

The burdens of remedial education are also much heavier as we move from the most to the least prestigious institutions. The open-door approach, standard in two-year colleges and also operational in tuition-dependent four-year colleges that take virtually all comers, means that college teachers are confronted with many underprepared students. Those who work in the less-selective settings also more frequently work part-time. During the last two decades, the ranks of the part-timers have swollen to over 40 percent of the total academic work force,[7] with heavy concentrations in the less prestigious colleges and especially in the community colleges, where over half the faculty operate on a part-time schedule. At the extreme opposite end of the institutional prestige hierarchy from those who serve primarily in graduate schools and graduate-level professional schools in the major universities we find the full-time and, especially, part-time teachers of English and mathematics in downtown community colleges, who teach introductory and subintroductory courses over and over again—the rudiments of English composition, the basic courses in mathematics—to high-school graduates who need remediation and to adults struggling with basic literacy.

With the nature of work varying enormously across the many types of institutions that make up American postsecondary education, other aspects of the academic life run on a parallel course. If we examine the cultures of institutions by discussing with faculty members their basic academic beliefs, we find different worlds. Among the leading research universities, the discipline is front and center, the institution is prized for its reputation of scholarship and research, and peers are the primary reference group. A professor of physics says, "What I value the most is the presence of the large number and diverse collection of scientists who are constantly doing things that I find stimulating." A professor of biology tells us that his university "has a lot of extremely good departments . . . there are a lot of fascinating, interesting people here." A political scientist adds that what he values most "is the intellectual level of the faculty and the graduate students. . . . Good graduate students are very important to me personally and always have been, and having colleagues that are smart is important." And a professor of English states that his institution "is a first-rate university . . . we have a fine library, and we have excellent teachers here, and we have first-rate scholars." Academics in this favored site have much with which to identify. They are proud of the quality they believe surrounds them, experiencing it directly in their own and neighboring departments and inferring it indirectly from institutional reputation. The strong symbolic thrust of the institution incorporates the combined strengths of the departments that in turn represent the disciplines. Thus, for faculty, disciplinary and institutional cultures converge, creating a happy state indeed.

The leading private liberal-arts colleges provide a second favored site. Here, professors often waxed lyrical in interviews about the small-college environment tailored to undergraduate teaching: "It is a very enjoyable setting. The students—the students we get in physics—are a delight to work with," "I can't put it in a word, but I think that it is one of the least constraining environments I know of," "It is a better form of life," or "My colleagues are fantastic. The people in this department are sane, which in an English department is not always the case." These institutions retain the capacity to appear as academic communities, not bureaucracies, in their overall integration and symbolic unity.

But soon we encounter sites where faculty members are troubled by inchoate institutional character and worried about the quality of their environment. In the lesser universities, and especially in the comprehensive colleges that have evolved out of a teachers-college background, at the second, third, and fourth levels of the institutional prestige hierarchy, the setting may be summed up in the words of one professor:

> I think the most difficult thing about being at an institution like [this one] is that it has a difficult time coming to terms with itself. I think the more established institutions with strong academic backgrounds don't have the problem that an institution that pretty much is in the middle range of higher educational institutions around the country does. I'm not saying that [this place] is a bad institution, but it certainly doesn't have the quality students, the quality faculty, the quality programs of the University of Chicago, Harvard, Yale. . . . When it talks about standards, what sort of standards? When it talks about practicality, how practical does it have to be? . . . It doesn't have a strong sense of tradition.

Compared to the research universities, the overall institutional culture is weaker and less satisfying for many faculty members at the same time that disciplinary identifications are weakened as heavy teaching loads suppress research and its rewards.

In these middle-level institutions, professors often spoke of their relationship with students as the thing they value most. Students begin to replace peers as the audience of first resort. That shift is completed in the community colleges, with the identifications of faculty reaching a high point of student-centeredness. In a setting that is distinctly opposed to disciplinary definitions of quality and excellence, pleasures and rewards have to lie in the task of working with poorly pre-pared students who pour in through the open door. For example: "We are a practical teaching college. We serve our community and we serve . . . the students in our community and give them a good, basic, strong education. . . . We are not sitting here on our high horses looking to publish" and "I really do like to teach, and this place allows me to teach. It doesn't bog me down with having to turn out papers." In the community colleges, the equity values of open door and open access have some payoff as anchoring points in the faculty culture. But in the overall institutional hierarchy, where the dominant values emphasize quality, selection, and advanced work, the community-college ideology can play only a subsidiary role. The limitations cannot be missed: "It would be nice to be able to teach upper-division classes."

As go work and culture, so go authority, careers, and associational life. To sum up the story on authority: in the leading universities faculty influence is relatively strong. Many individuals have personal bargaining power; departments and professional schools are semiautonomous units; and all-campus faculty bodies such as senates have primacy in personnel and curricular decisions. University presidents speak lovingly of the faculty as the core of the institution and walk gently around entrenched faculty prerogatives. But as we move to other types of institutions, faculty authority weakens and managerialism increases. Top-down command is noticeably stronger in public master's colleges, especially when they have evolved out of a teachers-college background. The two-year colleges, operating under local trustees much like K-12 schools, are quite manage-rial. Faculty in these places often feel powerless, even severely put upon. Their answer (where possible under state law) has been to band together by means of unionization. The further down the general hierarchy of institutional prestige, the more widespread the unions become, especially among public sector institutions.

To sum up the associational life of faculty: in the leading universities, faculty interact with one another across institutional boundaries in an extensive network of disciplinary linkages—formal and informal; large and small; visible and invisible; local, regional, national, and international. When university specialists find national "monster meetings" not to their liking, they go anyway to participate in a smaller division or section that best represents their specific interests, or they find kindred souls in small, autonomous meetings of several dozen people. In the other sectors, however, involvement in the mainline disciplinary associations declines; there is less to learn that is relevant to one's everyday life, and travel money is scarce in the institutional budget. Academics then go to national meetings when they are held in their part of the country. They look for special sessions on teaching; they break away to form associations (and journals) appropriate to their sec-tor. Community-college teachers have developed associations in such broad areas as the social sciences and the humanities, e.g., the Community College Humanities Association, and in such special fields as mathematics and biology, e.g., the American Mathematics Association for Two-Year Colleges.[8]

Different worlds, small worlds. Institutional differentiation interacts with disciplinary differ-entiation in a bewildering fashion that steadily widens and deepens the matrix of differences that separate American academics from each other.

SYSTEMIC PROBLEMS

When we pursue the different worlds of American professors by emphasizing disciplinary and institutional conditions, deep-rooted problems that are otherwise relegated to the background or only dimly perceived come to the fore. Five systemic concerns may be briefly stated as problems of secondarization, excessive teaching, attenuated professional control, fragmented academic cul-ture, and diminished intrinsic reward and motivation.

Secondarization and Remediation

The long evolution from elite to mass to universal access in American postsecondary education has not been without its costs. One major undesirable effect is a change in the conditions of the academic life that occurs when academics confront poorly educated students who come out of a defective secondary-school system and flow into higher education by means of open access. Academic work then revolves considerably around remedial education. Faced with entering students whose academic achievement is, for example, at the level of ninth-grade English, faculty first have to help the student progress to the twelfth-grade or traditional college-entry level, thereby engaging in the work of the high school. Mathematics instructors may find themselves facing students whose achievements measure at the sixth-grade level and hence need to complete some elementary schoolwork as well as their secondary education. Well known by those who teach in nonselective four-year colleges and especially in community colleges, this situation may seem surprising, even shocking, to others. But like the night and the day, it follows from the structure and orientation of American secondary and postsecondary education. If secondary schools graduate students whose achievement is below the twelfth-grade level, as they commonly do, and if some colleges admit all or virtually all who approach their doors, then college faculties will engage in K-12 work. Remedial education is spread throughout American higher education, from leading universities to community colleges, but it is relatively light when selectivity is high and quite heavy when selection is low or even nonexistent.

The problem of teaching poorly prepared students is compounded in the two-year college by its concentration on the first two years of the four-year undergraduate curriculum and on short-term vocational and semiprofessional programs. This curricular context calls for repetitive teaching of introductory courses. Since community colleges experience much student attrition during and after the first year of study, due to a variety of personal, occupational, and academic reasons, teaching is concentrated in first-year courses. In each department it is usually the general introductory course or two that must be taught over and over again, with little or no surcease. Upper-division courses, let alone graduate courses, are rarely available. While some course diversity can be found at the second-year level, the departmental task is to cover the introductory materials semester by semester, year in and year out. The teaching task is then closer to secondary-school teaching than what is found in selective universities. The task of remedial education adds to the downward thrust, requiring subcollege work on a plane below the regular first-year instruction.

Inherent and widespread in current American education, this teaching context receives relatively little attention in academic and public discussions. It is virtually an institutional secret that academic life is so often reduced to the teaching of secondary-school subjects. With due respect to the difficulties of the work, and the often deep devotion of involved staff to the welfare of under-prepared students and immigrant populations, this widely found situation amounts to a dumbing down of the intellectual life of academic staff. Subject content is limited to codified introductory material. Educational euphemisms allow us to blink at this undesired effect of American-style comprehensive secondary schooling and universal higher education, but they do not allow us to escape it. The situation marginalizes faculty. Eroding "the essential intellectual core of faculty work," it deprofessionalizes them.[9]

Excessive Teaching

The complaint that professors do too much research and too little teaching has been prevalent for almost a hundred years. When William James wrote about "the Ph.D. octopus" shortly after the turn of the century, he pointed to the increasing preoccupation of professors in the emerging universities with specialized research, graduate students, and doctoral programs. Since then the protest of too much research has been a perennial battle cry of the American reformer seeking more emphasis on undergraduate programs and on their general or liberal education components in particular. The 1980s and early 1990s have seen a strong resurgence of this point of view inside and outside the academy. Careful critics beamed their messages at research universities, would-be universities, and even four-year private and public colleges that have opened their faculty reward systems to the research imperative. They understand that professors teach when they supervise students in the preparation of master's and doctoral theses. They are sometimes aware that in the best private liberal-arts colleges professors involve their undergraduate students in research as an effective way to teach and to learn.[10] But the critical comment overall has turned into a generalized charge that "professors" should do less research and more teaching, meaning undergraduate teaching. In the popular press, and even in the academic press, careful targeting is forgone. In the extreme, a minimization of teaching by professors is portrayed as part of a "scam."

But across the dispersed American professoriate, the reality is the reverse: more academics teach too much than teach too little. Fifteen hours of classroom teaching each week is far too much for the maintenance of a scholarly life; even twelve hours is excessive. But as noted earlier, most institutional sectors present such loads, specifying assignments that are two to three times greater than that of professors in research-based institutions. Twelve and fifteen hours a week in the classroom at the college level tend to push professors out of their disciplines. A sense of being a scholar is reduced as the "physicist" becomes entirely a "teacher of physics," the "political scientist" a "teacher of political science"—and then mainly as teachers of introductory courses only. Interest flags in what is going on in the revision of advanced topics; command of the literature weakens. Excessive teaching loads apparently are now becoming a source of academic burnout, importing into higher education the teacher burnout long noted as a problem in the K-12 system. A 1989 Carnegie Foundation faculty survey found that the share of the full-time faculty "intending to retire early" was 25 percent in research universities, 26 percent in liberal-arts colleges, and a huge 49 percent in two-year colleges.[11] A setting characterized by heavy introductory teaching propels academics toward early retirement twice as much—one-half of the total staff!—as settings where professors have light teaching loads, involvement in research, and a more scholarly life as traditionally defined.

Weakened Professional Control

As indicated earlier, command structures are not unheard of in American colleges and universities. Professors in research universities and leading private four-year colleges certainly encounter trustee and administrator influence. Their professional position is also increasingly challenged by the professionalization of administrative occupations clustered around central management; in the words of Gary Rhoades, "faculty are increasingly 'managed' professionals in organizations increasingly run by 'managerial professionals.'"[12] But academics in these favored sites generally have strong countervailing power of a professional kind that is rooted in their personal and collective expertise. Department by department, professional school by professional school, they exercise much internal control. They expect to dominate in choosing who to add to the faculty and what courses should be taught. They expect to be consulted in many matters rather than to receive orders from those in nominally superior positions. But in public and private comprehensive colleges and especially in community colleges, the foundations of authority change. Subject expertise becomes more diffuse, occasionally amounting only to sufficient knowledge in the discipline to teach the introductory course to poorly prepared students, while at the same time the role of trustees and administrators is strengthened, sometimes approaching the top-down supervision found in local school districts. Such managerialism is particularly evident in public-sector institutions, especially when they are exposed to state assertions of accountability.

Adding greatly to the vulnerability of academic professionals to political and administrative dictate is the marginal position of part-time faculty. In all institutional sectors, part-timers have long been with us: witness the traditional use and abuse of faculty spouses in part-time work in foreign language departments of research universities. But the use of part-timers grew greatly during the last two decades as a form of mobile and inexpensive labor. It unfortunately turns out that floating student "clienteles" require dispensable academic staff, hence the deteriorating situation for staff in community colleges where a majority of faculty now serve part-time. The part-timers themselves have only marginal influence, and their large numbers weaken the influence of full-time faculty vis-à-vis trustees and administrative staff. A relatively powerless proletariat exists in American academic life, centered in employment that is part-time and poorly paid.

Experiments are underway in the two-year colleges, we should note, to create new forms of academic professionalism that are centered on "the disciplines of instruction" rather than on disciplinary affiliation.[13] This approach emphasizes the importance of translating knowledge into more understandable forms by such means as course revision and media preparation. Certain attitudes about teaching, as well as forms of teaching, become the possible basis for professional identity. But while community-college instruction has become a career in its own right, it remains highly unlikely that a strong sense of professionalism can be constructed when disciplinary foundations are weak, part-time work is the main form of employment, and top-down bureaucratic control remains widespread.

Fragmented Academic Culture

All-encompassing academic values are increasingly hard to find in American academic life. The claims frequently made by reformers that academics must somehow find their way back to agreement on core values and assume an overarching common framework become less realistic with each passing year. Different contexts, especially institutional ones, promote different values. Even common terms assume different meanings. "Academic freedom" in one context means mainly the right to do as one pleases in pursuing new ideas; in another, not to have an administrator dictate the teaching syllabus one uses; in another, the right to teach evolution in a college where the local board of trustees is dominated by creationists; in yet another, the right to join an extremist political group. Promotion criteria vary from an all-out emphasis on research productivity to weight put solely on undergraduate instruction, from complicated mixtures of teaching and research and several forms of "service" to heavy weighting of years on the job and seniority rights. As mentioned earlier, professional schools must value their connection to outside professions as well as to other parts of their universities, thereby balancing themselves between two sets of values in a way not required in the letters and science departments. The grounds for advancement then become particularly contentious. All such differences in outlook among academics widen as differentiation of academic work continues.

Diminished Intrinsic Reward and Motivation

Under all the strengths and weaknesses of American academic life, we find the persistent problem of the professional calling. When academic work becomes just a job and a routine career, then such material rewards as salary are placed front and center. Academics stay at their work or leave for other pursuits according to how much they are paid. They come to work "on time" because they must (it is nailed down in the union contract); they leave on time because satisfaction is found after work is concluded. But when academic work is still a calling, it "constitutes a practical ideal of activity and character that makes a person's work morally inseparable from his or her life. It subsumes the self into a community of disciplined practice and sound judgment whose activity has meaning and value in itself, not just in the output or profit that results from it."[14] A calling transmutes narrow self-interest into other-regarding and ideal-regarding interests: one is linked to peers and to a version of a larger common good. The calling has moral content; it contributes to civic virtue.

Professionalization projects seek to provide vehicles by which multitudes of workers are transported to a calling, where they find intrinsic motivation as well as the glories of high status and the trappings of power. The academic profession is lucky in that it has abundant sources of intrinsic motivation in the fascinations of research and the enchantments of teaching. Many academic contexts offer a workaday existence rich in content and consequence. As a confederative gathering, the academic profession's continuing promise lies considerably in the provision of a variety of contexts that generate "absorbing errands."[15] In that promise lies the best hope in the long term for the recruitment and retention of talent. But when such contexts fade away or become severely weakened, the errands run down and talented people search for other fascinations and enchantments. The systemic problems I have identified—secondarization, excessive teaching, weakened professional control, fragmented academic culture—point to structural and cultural conditions that run down the academic calling.

WHAT, IF ANYTHING, CAN BE DONE?

In a large, decentralized, and competitive system of higher education, apace with great differentiation of institutions and disciplines, student growth and knowledge growth have badly fractured the American academic profession. From a cross-national perspective, the resulting system has had major advantages. More than elsewhere, the system at large has been able to combine academic excellence and scientific preeminence with universal access and weak standards. It has been flexible, even to a fault, with various sectors adjusting to different demands and numerous colleges and universities fashioning individual niches. But a heavy price has been paid, not least in the systemic problems I have identified that seriously weaken the American academic work force. The ever-extending differentiation that is integral to the success of the system produces a host of academic subworlds that downgrade the academic profession overall. They establish conditions hostile to the best features of professionalism.

Can these conditions be reduced, reversing the drift toward secondarization, the weight of excessive teaching, the weakening of professional control, the fragmentation of academic culture, and the diminishing of intrinsic motivation and reward? These weaknesses do not just hurt the professoriate; they also injure universities and colleges. They undermine the hopes of the nation that a well-trained and highly motivated professoriate will continue to staff an academic system second to none.

Four broad ideas can frame future directions of reform. First, *the intellectual core of academic work throughout the system should be protected and strengthened.* It may be helpful to students in the short run to offer them remedial instruction; it may be helpful to high-turnover clienteles and tight institutional budgets to invest heavily in part-time academics. But such major developments are injurious to the state of the academic profession and hence in the long term to the institutions that depend upon its capability. Higher education has enough to do without including the work of the secondary school. Success in secondary-school reform that instilled serious standards for the high-school diploma would be a major step for those who teach in postsecondary education. Part-timeness needs to be taken seriously, since nothing runs down a profession faster than to shift its work from full-time labor requiring credentialed experts to an operation that can be staffed by casual laborers who must live by their wits as they flit among jobs. Limits on the use of part-timers can be set in institutions: 20 or 25 percent of the total staff is enough; 50 percent is highly excessive and should be seen as institutionally injurious.

Second, *constant attention must be paid to the integration of academic personnel with managerial personnel.* As the gap grows between "faculty" and "administration" inside universities and colleges, faculty seek to promote their special interests more and administrators increasingly see themselves as the only ones who uphold overall institutional concerns. "Shared governance" only works when it is shared to the point where some academics sit in central councils and the rest of the academic staff feel they are appropriately represented, or where decision-making is extensively decentralized to deans and department heads and faculty sit close to these newly strengthened "line managers," or in various other complicated combinations of centralized and decentralized decision-making.

Personal leadership has its place in academe, but the window of opportunity for arbitrary top-down policy generally does not last very long. Anything worth doing in a university or college requires a number of people who want it to happen and will work at it for a number of years. Academic values, as defined by the academic staff, need to be constantly mixed throughout the organizational structure with the influence of the new managerial values that will be even more necessary in academic institutions in the future than they are now. The linking of academics with overall, long-term institutional interests is central in academic management; with it comes extended professional authority.

Third, *indirect forms of linkage among divergent academic cultures need to be better understood and promoted.* The search for clarified common goals comes up empty-handed. Rhetoric that embraces complex universities and colleges falls back on eternal clichés about research, teaching, and service. Meanwhile, the separate departments and professional schools go on generating their separate cultures. How do these cultures then connect, if at all? Both as modes of reasoning and as knowledge domains, they often have some overlap with neighboring fields. With interdisciplinary fields also helping to bridge the gaps, the many specialties of academics may be seen (in the words of three acute observers) as connected in "chains of overlapping neighborhoods." The connections produce "a continuous texture of narrow specialties," a "collective communication," and "a collective competence and breadth." Academics are partially integrated through "interlocking cultural communities."[16] Then, too, the socialization of graduate students into academic ways still counts for something—an integrating force among university graduates spread out among different types of institutions. Models of behavior also radiate from one type of institution to another. For example, the image of liberal education most strongly embodied in small private liberal-arts colleges clearly serves as a model of what undergraduate education in large public four-year colleges could be if appropriately funded and properly carried out. The many different types of institutions comprising the American system do not operate as value-tight compartments.

Fourth, *the intrinsic rewards of the academic life need to be highlighted and respected.* As earlier reported, academics in diverse settings point to the special joys of teaching, or of doing research, or of combining the two. They speak of the pleasure of shaping the minds of the young, of making discoveries, of carrying forward the intellectual heritage of the nation and the world. They sense that at the end of the day they may have done something worthwhile. They point to such psychic rewards as reasons to be in academic work and as reasons to resist the lure of greater material rewards elsewhere. There is still some devotion to a calling.

Academic fanatics who are fully caught up in this now oddly shaped calling can even feel, as Max Weber put it in a famous essay, that they are in the grip of "a demon who holds the fibers of their very lives."[17] We find the academic demon everywhere: in the professor so intensely interested in her writing that she never checks the clock; in the college teacher who acts way beyond the call of duty as personal mentor and substitute parent for marginal students; in the academic scientist who is in the laboratory instead of at home at two o'clock in the morning; in the lecturer who will not stop talking long after the bell has rung and has to be forced out of the lecture hall or classroom; in the dying academic who works up to the last week, even the last day. George Steiner wrote of the world of "the absolute scholar" as "a haunting and haunted business," a place where "sleep is a puzzle of wasted time, and flesh a piece of torn luggage that the spirit must drag after it. . . ."[18]

Even in modest dosages, academic professionalism centered on intrinsic features of the work at hand leads to committed productivity that political and bureaucratic controls cannot generate—nor can "market forces" guarantee. Those who seek to replace professional commitment with the nuts and bolts of bureaucratic regulation run down the calling; they take intellectual absorption out of the absorbing errand. Wise academic leaders and sophisticated critics sense that only professional norms and practices are ingrained, person by person, in everyday activity to constructively shape motivation and steer behavior. They then attend to the conditions of professional inspiration and self-regulation. Positioned between state and market, academic professionalism, however fragmented, remains a necessary foundation for performance and progress in higher education.

NOTES

1. This chapter is based largely on two books and two prior articles that report the results of research on academic life in Europe and America: Burton R. Clark, ed., *The Academic Profession: National, Disciplinary and Institutional Settings* (Berkeley and Los Angeles, Calif.: University of California Press, 1987); Burton R. Clark, *The Academic Life: Small Worlds, Different Worlds* (Princeton, N.J.: Carnegie Foundation for the Advancement of Teaching and Princeton University Press, 1987); Burton R. Clark, "The Academic Life: Small Worlds, Different Worlds," *Educational Researcher* 18 (5) (1989): 4–8; and Burton R. Clark, "Faculty: Differentiation and Dispersion," in Arthur Levine, ed., *Higher Learning in America: 1980–2000* (Baltimore, Md.: Johns Hopkins University Press, 1993), 163–178. For other research-based studies of American academics reported in the 1980s and 1990s, see Martin J. Finkelstein, *The American Academic Profession: A Synthesis of Social Scientific Inquiry Since World War II* (Columbus, Ohio: Ohio State University Press, 1984); Howard R. Bowen and Jack H. Schuster, *American Professors: A National Resource Imperiled* (New York: Oxford University Press, 1986); and Robert T. Blackburn and Janet H. Lawrence, *Faculty at Work: Motivation, Expectation, Satisfaction* (Baltimore, Md.: Johns Hopkins University Press, 1995).
2. Carnegie Foundation for the Advancement of Teaching, *A Classification of Institutions of Higher Education,* 1994 ed. (Princeton, N.J.: Carnegie Foundation for the Advancement of Teaching, 1994), xiv.
3. Tony Becher, *Academic Tribes and Territories: Intellectual Enquiry and the Cultures of Disciplines* (Milton Keynes, England: The Open University Press, 1989).
4. See Walter Metzger, "The Academic Profession in the United States," in Clark, ed., *The Academic Profession: National, Disciplinary, and Institutional Settings,* 123–208; and R. H. Wiebe, *The Search for Order, 1877–1920* (New York: Hill and Wang, 1967).
5. Arthur M. Cohen and Florence B. Brawer, *The American Community College,* 3d ed. (San Francisco, Calif.: Jossey-Bass, 1996), 86.
6. Carnegie Foundation for the Advancement of Teaching, *A Classification of Institutions of Higher Education,* xiv.
7. For tracking the growth of part-time faculty, see David W. Leslie, Samuel E. Kellams, and G. M. Gunne, *Part-Time Faculty in American Higher Education* (New York: Praeger, 1982); Judith M. Gappa, *Part-Time Faculty: Higher Education at a Crossroads,* ASHE-ERIC Higher Education Research Report No. 3 (Washington, D.C.: Association for the Study of Higher Education, 1984); and Judith M. Gappa and David W. Leslie, *The Invisible Faculty: Improving the Status of Part-Timers in Higher Education* (San Francisco, Calif.: Jossey-Bass, 1993).
8. Cohen and Brawer, *The American Community College,* 98.

9. Earl Seidman, *In the Words of the Faculty: Perspectives on Improving Teaching and Educational Quality in Community Colleges* (San Francisco, Calif.: Jossey-Bass, 1985), 275.

10. See Robert A. McCaughey, *Scholars and Teachers: The Faculties of Select Liberal Arts Colleges and Their Place in American Higher Learning* (New York: Barnard College, Columbia University, 1994).

11. Carnegie Foundation for the Advancement of Teaching, "Early Faculty Retirees: Who, Why, and with What Impact?," *Change* (July/August 1990): 31–34. On burnout in community colleges, see Cohen and Brawer, *The American Community College,* 90–93.

12. Gary Rhoades, "Reorganizing the Faculty Work Force for Flexibility," *Journal of Higher Education* 67 (6) (November/December 1996): 656.

13. Cohen and Brawer, *The American Community College,* 96–100.

14. Robert N. Bellah, Richard Madsen, William M. Sullivan, Ann Swidler, and Steven M. Tipton, *Habits of the Heart: Individualism and Commitment in American Life* (Berkeley and Los Angeles, Calif.: University of California Press, 1985), 66.

15. A metaphor attributed to Henry James. Exact reference unknown.

16. For a fuller account of these metaphors and perspectives offered respectively by Michael Polanyi, Donald T. Campbell, and Diana Crane, see Clark, *The Academic Life,* 140–142.

17. Max Weber, "Science as a Vocation," in H. H. Gerth and C. Wright Mills, eds., *From Max Weber: Essays in Sociology* (New York: Oxford University Press, 1946), 156.

18. George Steiner, "The Cleric of Treason," in *George Steiner: A Reader* (New York: Penguin Books, 1984), 197–198.

3

The Extent and Nature of Scholarly Activities among Community College Faculty

Barbara K. Townsend and Vicki J. Rosser

Community college has long been known as a teaching institution whose faculty members concentrate on teaching to the exclusion of scholarly activities. But particularly in the 1980s and 1990s, it has been exhorted to encourage its faculty to conduct scholarship. A major advocate of this position has been George Vaughan (1986, 1988, 1991, 1992), a former community college president and well-known scholar about the community college. Although, perhaps, the most vociferous, Vaughan is not alone in his calls for community college faculty to participate in scholarly endeavors. Other researchers who have supported the engagement of community college faculty members in some form of scholarship include Cohen and Brawer (1977), Outcalt (2002), and Palmer (1991).

These calls for scholarly activity are best understood in the context of distinctions among different kinds of scholarship, distinctions clearly set forth by Boyer (1990) in his *Scholarship Reconsidered*. Boyer argued for reconsidering scholarship in terms of four kinds of faculty work: the scholarship of discovery or what is commonly understood as basic research, the scholarship of synthesis, the scholarship of application or applied research, and the scholarship of teaching. According to Boyer, each of these kinds of scholarly work is valuable and "dynamically interact, forming an interdependent whole" (p. 25).

Vaughan (1991) reflected this differentiation among kinds of scholarship in his call for scholarship among community college faculty members. Noting that "research is but one form of scholarship" (p. 5), Vaughan argued that the majority of community college faculty and administrators "should concern themselves with scholarship rather than research" (1988, p. 28). Similarly, Parilla (1987), when president of Montgomery Community College, asserted that community college faculty members, rather than conducting basic research, should conduct "interpretive, rationalistic scholarship" (p. 111) that would help faculty members in their teaching, partly through their "maintaining currency in one's teaching field" (p. 11). Additionally, in 1988 the American Association of Community Colleges Commission on the Future of Community Colleges advocated "a broad definition of scholarship that goes beyond traditional research to include 'integrating knowledge, through curriculum development, . . . applying knowledge, through service, and . . . presenting knowledge, through effective teaching'" (as cited in Vaughan & Palmer, 1991, p. 1).

The primary reason the individuals cited above advocate engagement in scholarly activities is their belief that the community college's claim to be an excellent teaching institution is suspect if at least some of its faculty members do not conduct scholarship (e.g., Vaughan, 1988). In other words, they believe that productive scholars are better teachers than those who do not practice some form of scholarship.

The relationship between teaching and scholarship has been hotly contested for many decades. Braxton (1996) conducted a thorough review of the literature on this topic and concluded that there are three positions about the possible relationship. Some contend that there is no relationship (e.g., Finkelstein, 1984). Others claim that conducting research or scholarly activities negatively affects one's teaching partly because the time involved in doing the research takes away time from teaching (e.g., Boyer, 1990). And still others assert that scholarship positively affects or benefits one's teaching (e.g., Parilla, 1987; Vaughan, 1988). As example of this position, Vaughan (1988) argues that "outstanding teaching requires constant learning and intellectual renewal and cannot exist without these essential elements of scholarship" (p. 28). Furthermore, "[t]eaching without scholarship is the brokering of information, not the providing of intellectual leadership" (p. 29).

There is limited evidence about the relationship between scholarship and teaching in any sector, but particularly in the community college. The one existing study was conducted by Mahaffey and Welsh (1993) in 1990. The researchers surveyed 127 faculty members at Midlands Technical College and interviewed eight full-time faculty identified as "scholar-teachers" (p. 33), so titled because they had been honored by their institution for one or more presentations or publications within the previous three years. Demographically, the scholar-teachers in the study were more likely to have a doctorate and to teach transfer-level courses than were other faculty. Faculty who participated in scholarly activities "self-reported positive benefits to their teaching" (p. 34) and received more teaching awards than did faculty who were not conducting scholarship.

Whether or not supported empirically, the idea that conducting some form of scholarship enhances teaching has support among some who work in the community college. In a national survey of community college faculty members' attitudes and trends, Huber (1998) asked about the extent to which these faculty agreed with the statement, "Generally speaking, to be a good teacher, one must be engaged in research" (p. 85). As might be expected of faculty working at an institution devoted to teaching, 50% of the respondents either somewhat or strongly disagreed with the statement. However, 7% strongly agreed and 20% somewhat agreed.

A community college faculty member, Douglas Heath (1996) suggested a move away from the "tired, old teaching-versus-research debate" (p. 112) toward asking "what constitutes appropriate professional growth" (p. 112) for community college faculty. More specifically, he asked "What do we believe to be the kinds of professional growth that qualify someone to *continue* [italics added] to teach freshmen and sophomores?" (p. 112). His answer is that faculty members need to participate in some kind of scholarly activity, but not necessarily that of basic research.

EXTENT OF AND INTEREST IN SCHOLARLY ACTIVITIES

Whether or not scholarly activities benefit one's teaching in the community college, at least some community college faculty members are expected to participate in scholarly activities. Five percent of the respondents to Huber's (1998) national survey of community college faculty indicated that "regular research activity is expected" (p. 80) of them. Additionally, independent of whether it is expected of them, "research and/or comparable scholarly activities" (p. 79) require, on average, over six hours a week of all the respondents' time.

Even if not required of community college faculty, research, at least in some form, appears to be an option for many. A search of the National Education Association (NEA) community college collective bargaining contracts (via Higher Education Contract Analysis System) revealed that 520 of the 624 collective bargaining contracts mentioned research (NEA, 2008). The primary areas in which the word research is noted relate to publication and scholarship, professional development, creative achievement, grant writing, sabbaticals, and reassigned time. For example, the Community College of Spokane provides an opportunity whereby faculty members can earn Professional Improvement Units (PIUs) that allow "independent research and development activities which are in excess of the normal contractual obligations and beyond the professional responsibilities of the academic employee" (NEA, 2008). Similarly, at the University of Hawai'i Community Colleges, "faculty workload is not limited to instruction. It may include disciplinary research, scholarly activities, or creative endeavors. . . ." (NEA, 2008).

Additional evidence that some community faculty members seek greater participation in scholarly activities exists. There are occasional calls by community college faculty who teach in the hard sciences for greater "scholarly opportunities for two-year college geosciences faculty and their students" (Semken, 2002) and for more "participation and leadership of two-year college faculty in the geosciences education community" (Macdonald, 2002). Also, a new journal has recently been created by Ocean County [Community] College in New Jersey. The journal, named *apropos*, is described as "a national journal of scholarship" that seeks "scholarly articles published by two-year college professors" (Ocean County College, n.d.). The articles may be "research, pedagogical, or creative" in nature (Ocean County College, n.d.).

ADDITIONAL REASONS FOR PARTICIPATION IN SCHOLARLY ACTIVITIES

Aside from the general belief that scholarly activities benefit one's teaching, there are other reasons why some community college leaders, as well as some community college faculty members, want more scholarly engagement. These reasons include the desire to prepare students to conduct research and the increased professional and institutional prestige that may result if at least some community college faculty members are practicing scholars.

Since at least the 1970s, undergraduate research has been encouraged at four-year colleges and universities (Council on Undergraduate Research, n.d.) and since the mid-1990s it has really been stressed at these institutions (Thomas & Gillespie, 2008). This interest in undergraduate research is not unique to baccalaureate degree-granting institutions: community colleges also support faculty conducting research with their students. Perez (2003) conducted a national study of undergraduate research in community colleges and found that 7 (15%) of the 47 institutions responding to his survey indicated some involvement of undergraduate students with research "under the mentorship of faculty members" (p. 70). Four of the institutions used their own funds while the other three used grant funding to support this work. More recently, Cejda and Hensel (2008) conducted a study examining undergraduate research at community colleges and found that both basic and applied research is being conducted. They also learned that this research "is currently more of an effort by individual faculty members than an institutional program" (p. 2). Certainly some individual community college faculty members are interested in working with their students to conduct research, as evidenced by conference program presentations of such activity (e.g., Longtine, 2008). Also, Montgomery [Community] College has been host since 1993 of the Beacon Conference for Student Scholars at Two-Year Colleges, an annual conference in which the top three papers representing scholarship accomplished by the students and their mentors are presented (Montgomery College, n.d.).

There are several motivating factors behind some community college faculty members' desire to work with undergraduate students on research projects. According to Cejda and Hensel (2008), the most common one is that this research is seen as improving the preparation of students. This is so whether those be future transfer students or students in applied programs who could benefit from understanding "research activities that meet the needs of the various constituencies that will employ the students" (p. 4). In other words, students will gain greater critical thinking skills and have more opportunity to develop research skills. Other reasons why faculty participate in undergraduate research include benefits to the faculty members working with the students, such as "travel funds, special assistance in grant writing, release time, and merit pay for service" (Perez, 2003, p. 72). An increase in institutional as well as one's own professional prestige is also cited as a factor (Perez, p. 72).

Interest in increasing institutional prestige through faculty scholarship may be particularly salient currently. At the same time that enrollments in doctoral programs are increasing, there is a decrease in the availability of tenure-track positions (Curtis & Jacobe, 2006). Also, the limited number of faculty positions at research-extensive and intensive institutions cannot accommodate all those who seek faculty positions (Austin, 2002). Additionally, some individuals who have earned a doctorate may be place-bound after graduation with a nearby community college as the only available postsecondary institution at which to teach. It may be that institutional support of faculty scholarship could make the community college a more attractive work site for those who want to conduct scholarship as well as teach (Laabs, 1987).

Another factor is the development of what has been termed "the community college baccalaureate" (Floyd, Skolnik, & Walker, 2005), a baccalaureate degree awarded by the community college. Currently, at least one community college in each of 16 states has been authorized to award the baccalaureate degree, although some of these institutions have subsequently become four-year schools (Townsend, Bragg, & Ruud, 2008). Community colleges offering a baccalaureate degree need to hire faculty qualified to teach upper-division students. According to regional accrediting associations, these qualifications typically include possessing a doctorate. Such faculty may want to do scholarship in addition to teaching and, indeed, may be expected to do some to meet programmatic accreditation requirements for the new baccalaureate degrees.

As discussed above, there are various reasons why some community colleges and some community college faculty members may desire greater participation in scholarly activities; there is also evidence that some faculty members are doing such activities. Thus, it seems germane to examine available national, self-reported data about faculty work roles of community college faculty members for evidence of scholarly activities and to see if these activities have increased since the 1990s. Since some critics maintain that increased scholarly activities may negatively impact time spent on teaching, this study also seeks to determine if possible increased participation in scholarly activities occurred at the expense of time spent on instructional activities.

METHODS AND DATA SOURCE

Are community college faculty in the twenty-first century participating in more scholarly activities and spending less time in teaching than in the previous decade? This study sought to compare the extent and nature of full-time community college faculty's workload in 1993 with that of community college faculty in 2004, with a particular focus on scholarly output. The research questions were the following:

1. Did full-time community college faculty in the early twenty-first century conduct more scholarship than did full-time community college faculty in the early 1990s?
2. Was more time spent on community college instruction in the early 1990s than in the early twenty-first century?

To answer the study's two questions, we used data from two iterations of the National Study of Postsecondary Faculty (NSOPF) 1993 and 2004 restricted datasets. Both NSOPF databases are considered nationally representative samples of faculty members in higher education institutions. We chose to use only the 1993 and 2004 NSOPF databases because analysis of the 1999 data indicated it was an aberrant year in terms of faculty members' workload. Another reason for using 1993 and 2004 datasets was the change in the questions asked in the different iterations of the NSOPF survey. The 1993 and 2004 questions are more similar than are those in the 1999 survey and, thus, could be combined more effectively across the databases.

Because faculty roles are largely shaped by their employing institution's dominant mission, we focused on full-time instructional faculty at public two-year colleges. This focus allowed us to examine possible differences in the faculty's teaching and research activities. For the purpose of this individual-level study, 6,700 faculty members were selected as a subset from the two national samples: 4,300 faculty members from the 1993 NSOPF data set, and 2,400 from the 2004 NSOPF data set (sample size numbers have been rounded).

Faculty members' workload was measured in terms of the following: (a) overall workload defined as hours worked per week (including paid and unpaid activities at institution, and paid and unpaid activities not at institution); (b) teaching workload defined as number of credit courses taught, number of student contact hours, and total classroom credit hours generated; and (c) research or scholarly output within the last two years defined as number of creative works juried and nonjuried media; book reviews; books, texts, and reports; presentations and exhibits; patents and software.

Tests of statistical significance (t tests) were conducted using SPSS (version 15.0) to examine the mean differences between the 1993 and 2004 workload measures. Proper weighting procedures were applied; see Thomas and Heck (2001) for further explanation of the weighting approach used in this study. Descriptive statistics provide an appropriate way to examine faculty members' workload within each surveyed year. While these databases are nationally representative, we present these statistical differences with a note of caution; the respondents from the two subsets are different individuals from 1993 to 2004. However, examining these data as distinct snapshots in time may provide initial indicators regarding the scholarly output that may be occurring within the community colleges.

RESULTS

Table 3.1 provides a recap of community college faculty members' workload activities. The reported extent and nature of full-time community college faculty members' workload was significantly different in 2004 from that reported in 1993. Full-time faculty in the 2004 study reported a significantly longer ($p = .00$) average work week (49.17 hours) than did faculty in the 1993 study (46.66 hours). The increase occurred in the number of hours per week on paid tasks at the institution (40.48 in 2004 vs. 36.52 in 1993, $p = .00$) and the number of hours per week on unpaid tasks outside the institution (4.5 in 2004 vs. 3.79 in 1993, $p = .00$). While there was a significant decline in the reported number of hours per week on unpaid institutional tasks in 2004 (4.43 vs. 5.86 in 1993, $p = .00$), the decline in the reported number of hours on paid tasks outside the institution was nonsignificant (2.55 in 2004 vs. 2.68 in 1993, $p = .26$).

TABLE 3.1
Faculty Members' Workload Activities

Workload activity	1993 (n = 4,300)*	2004 (n = 2,400)*
Average work hours/week	46.66	49.17*
Hours per week on paid tasks at the institution	36.52	40.48*
Hours per week on paid tasks outside the institution	2.68	2.55
Hours per week on unpaid tasks at the institution	5.86	4.43*
Hours per week on unpaid tasks outside the institution	3.79	4.50*
Average office hours / week	9.15	7.15*
Credit courses taught per semester	3.79	4.50*
Total credit and non-credit courses / semester	4.06	4.94*
Total hours per week teaching credit courses	16.33	18.27*
Percent of time spent on instruction	70%	84%*
Juried articles	0.15	0.25*
Nonjuried articles	0.12	0.41*
Book reviews, chapters, creative works	0.18	0.27*
Presentations	1.26	1.73*
Exhibitions and performances	1.78	2.58*
Books, textbooks, reports	0.44	0.24*
Patents, computer software	0.08	0.03*

(Significance =.05 or less) *Sample size numbers have been rounded.

However, the decline in office hours per week was significant (7.15 in 2004 vs. 9.15 in 1993, $p = .00$).

Not only did faculty in the 2004 study report a significantly longer work week, they also reported a significantly higher number of credit courses taught per semester (4.50 vs. 3.79 in 1993, $p = .00$) and a significantly higher total number of both credit and noncredit courses taught per semester/quarter (4.94 vs. 4.06 in 1993, $p = .00$). Similarly, in 2004, faculty reported more time spent in total hours per week teaching credit courses: 18.27 vs. 16.33 hours in 1993 ($p = .00$). Perhaps for these reasons, faculty in the 2004 study spent almost 84% of their time on instruction as compared to almost 70% for faculty reporting in 1993 ($p = .00$).

Even though faculty members in the 2004 study spent so much of their time on instruction, in the aggregate these faculty members generated significantly more scholarly output, as measured in this study, than did faculty in the 1993 study. In 2004 community college faculty reported .25 juried and .41 nonjuried articles ($p = .00$) as compared to .15 juried and .12 nonjuried journal articles in 1993 ($p = .00$). Similarly, in 2004 the community college faculty in the aggregate reported .27 book reviews, chapters, and creative works as compared to .18 book reviews, chapters, and creative works for faculty in the 1993 study. The amount of presentations was also significantly larger (1.73 for 2004 respondents vs. 1.26 for 1993 respondents, $p = .00$) as were the number of recent exhibitions and performances (2.58 in 2004 vs. 1.78 in 1993, $p = .00$).

However, faculty in the 2004 study reported significantly fewer recent books, textbooks, and reports than did 1993 faculty: .24 in 2004 vs. .44 in 1993 ($p = .00$). The 2004 cohort also reported significantly fewer recent patents and computer software: .03 in 2004 vs. .08 in 1993 ($p =.00$).

DISCUSSION

The results of this study provide two snapshots of full-time community college members' work during different decades. In most areas, these snapshots indicate a significant difference in the work of faculty members in the 2004 NSOPF study as compared to those in the 1993 survey.

Faculty in the 2004 study reported a longer work week and spent a greater percentage of their work week on instruction. This finding may indicate that the faculty's work week has been extended by their allocating more time to service, research, and teaching. While faculty members in 2004 show an increase in the number of paid tasks within the institution, a decrease is reflected in their paid tasks outside. At the same time, there was an increase in their unpaid tasks outside and a decrease in unpaid internal tasks. It may be that in 2004 their institutions were in need of more in-depth task work that warranted paid time, possibly at the cost of conducting unpaid work. Similarly, time spent on unpaid tasks conducted outside of the institution increased while time spent on paid tasks remained fairly equal. This finding may suggest that community college faculty continue to have a strong affinity to their external service commitments within their local communities.

At the same time, faculty members in the 2004 study had a significantly greater scholarly output of juried and nonjuried articles and presentations; book reviews, chapters, and creative works; presentations; and exhibitions and performances. Whether this increase in scholarly output occurred because community colleges during the 1990s began to stress scholarship for their faculty is unknown. However, the current NEA collective bargaining contracts indicate that there may be institutional incentives for participating in some kind of scholarly activity.

If the number of refereed publications is considered a measure of participation in the "external discourse community" (Prager, 2003), it would appear that full-time community college faculty in the 21st century are participating in this community to a greater extent than did faculty in 1993 and with no decline in their teaching responsibilities. Just as the scholarly output increased from 1993 to 2004, so too did the teaching output. From this perspective, it appears that community college faculty in 2004 were doing more than were community college faculty in 1993.

However, the finding that full-time community college faculty members in 2004 reported more scholarly productivity than did those in 1993 needs to be interpreted with caution. While scholarly output in the form of articles was higher for the faculty in 2004, this increase may be partially a result of "the increasing number and diversity of publication outlets (particularly in an age of online publishing)" so that more articles are accepted for publication (Sax, Hagedorn, Arrendondo, & DiCrisi, 2002, p. 428). Also, an increase in the number of articles and presentations may also reflect the trend toward multiple-authored rather than single-authored work in certain disciplines (Roberts, Davis, Zanger, Gerrard-Morris, & Robinson, 2006). A more positive interpretation is that some of the increased scholarly input may stem from a growing interest and participation in undergraduate research activities at the community college.

IMPLICATIONS FOR RESEARCH AND PRACTICE

Whether an increase in scholarly activity by community college faculty members is a positive development is unclear. Certainly, people like Vaughan (1986, 1988, 1991, 1992) see a positive link between faculty scholarship and effective teaching. Yet, the research on this link is mixed (see Braxton, 1996), and little of it has been conducted in the community college setting.

Future research on this topic could include national surveys asking full-time community college faculty about their perceptions of the relationship between scholarship and teaching, both in general and in their own teaching. Asking community college students, particularly those participating in undergraduate research projects, about their perceptions of the value of their faculty conducting scholarship would provide a missing element in the discussion about the relationship of teaching and scholarship.

Additionally, faculty should be asked not only about the extent of their scholarly activities, if any, but also about the extent to which their institution encourages and supports them conducting scholarship. Long-term faculty could be interviewed about their perceptions of any institutional changes regarding expectations for scholarship and the possible effect of changing expectations upon institutional culture and the classroom.

It may be that faculty participation in scholarly activities is important for some faculty and not for others. If more research indicates, as did that of Mahaffey and Welsh (1993) that those faculty who conduct scholarship "self-report positive benefits to their teaching" (p. 33), it behooves community college senior administrators to consider providing some incentives for scholarly activity, whether they be release time, conference travel money, or small grants for equipment or other resources needed for the activity. In so doing, the administration may also make the community college a more attractive job site for prospective faculty, an important consideration given the massive impending faculty retirements that have been predicted (Shults, 2001).

REFERENCES

Austin, A. E. (2002). Preparing the next generation of faculty: Graduate school as socialization to the academic career. *Journal of Higher Education, 73*(1), 94–122.

Boyer, E. L. (1990). *Scholarship reconsidered: Priorities of the professoriate*. Lawrenceville, NJ: Princeton University Press.

Braxton, J. M. (1996). Contrasting perspectives on the relationship between teaching and research. *New Directions for Institutional Research, 90*, 5–14.

Cejda, B. D., & Hensel, N. (2008, Fall). CUR focus: Undergraduate research in community colleges: A summary of the CUR/NCIA conversations. *CUR Quarterly, 29*(1), 1–5.

Cohen, A. M., & Brawer, F. B. (1977). *The two-year college instructor today*. New York: Praeger Special Studies.

Council on Undergraduate Research. (n.d.). CUR timeline. Retrieved on October 6, 2008, from http://www.cur.org/timeline.html

Curtis, J. W., & Jacobe, M. F. (2006). Consequences: An increasingly contingent faculty. In *AAUP contingent faculty index 2006* (pp. 5–16). Washington, DC: AAUP.

Finkelstein, M. J. (1984). *The American academic profession: A synthesis of social scientific inquiry since World War II*. Columbus, OH: Ohio State University Press.

Floyd, D. L., Skolnik, M., & Walker, K. (Eds.). (2005). *Community college baccalaureate: Emerging trends and policy issues*. Sterling, VA: Stylus.

Heath, D. E. (1996). On the professional growth of community college geographers. *Journal of Geography, 95*(May/June), 112–116.

Huber, M. T. (1998). *Community college faculty attitudes and trends, 1997* (no. R309A60001; NCPI-4-03). Stanford, CA: National Center for Postsecondary Improvement.

Laabs, T. R. (1987). Community college tenure: Teach or research? *Community/Junior College Quarterly of Research and Practice, 11*, 267–273.

Longtine, C. A. (2008, August). *Undergraduate research and the two-year college: A population-level and interclonal study of stem-galling fly Eurosta solidaginis*. Presentation at 93rd ESA Annual Meeting, Milwaukee, WI.

Macdonald, R. H. (2002, October). *Increasing the participation and leadership of two-year college faculty in the geosciences education community: Results of a NAGT planning workshop*. Paper presented at annual meeting of the Geological Society of America, Denver, CO.

Mahaffey, J., & Welsh, M. F. (1993). Scholarship and the vitality of a community college faculty. *Community College Review, 21*(1), 31–41.

Montgomery College. (n.d.). *Beacon: A conference for student scholars at two-year colleges*. Retrieved on October 6, 2008, from http://www.beaconconference.org/

National Education Association. (2008). *Higher Education Contract Analysis System (HECAS) Collective bargaining issues*. Washington, DC: NEA. Retrieved on October 12, 2008, from http://www.nea.org/hecas/HECAS

Ocean County College. (n.d.). *Apropos, a national journal of scholarship submission requirements.* Retrieved on October 6, 2008, from http://www.ocean.edu/ campus/PAR/apropos.html

Outcalt, C. (Ed.). (2002). Community college faculty: Characteristics, practices, and challenges. *New Directions for Community Colleges, 118,* 1–6.

Palmer, J. C. (1991). Nurturing scholarship at community colleges. *New Directions for Community Colleges, 19*(4), 69–77.

Parilla, R. E. (1987). Scholarship in community colleges. *College Teaching, 35*(3), 111–112.

Perez, J. A. (2003). Undergraduate research at two-year colleges. *New Directions for Teaching and Learning, 93,* 69–77.

Prager, C. (2003). Scholarship matters. *Community College Journal of Research and Practice, 27,* 579–592.

Roberts, G. A., Davis, K. S., Zanger, D., Gerrard-Morris, A., & Robinson, D. H. (2006). Top contributors to the school psychology literature: 1996–2005. *Psychology in the Schools, 43*(6), 737–743.

Sax, L. J., Hagedorn, L. S., Arrendondo, M., & DiCrisi, F. A. (2002). Faculty research productivity: Exploring the role of gender and family-related factors. *Research in Higher Education, 43*(4), 423–446.

Semken, S. C. (2002). What are the scholarly opportunities for two-year college geosciences faculty and their students? Paper presented at annual meeting of the Geological Society of America, Denver, CO.

Shults, C. (2001). *The critical impact of impending retirements on community college leadership.* AACC Research Brief AACC-RB-01-05. Washington, DC: AACC.

Thomas, E., & Gillespie, D. (2008). Weaving together undergraduate research, mentoring of junior faculty, and assessment: The case of an interdisciplinary program. *Innovative Higher Education, 33,* 29–38.

Thomas, S. L., & Heck, R. H. (2001). Analysis of large-scale secondary data in higher education research: Potential perils associated with complex sampling designs. *Research in Higher Education, 42,* 517–540.

Townsend, B. K., Bragg, D., & Ruud, R. (2008). *The adult learner and the applied baccalaureate: National and state-by-state inventory.* Retrieved November 22, 2008, from http://education.missouri.edu/orgs/ cccr/projects.php

Vaughan, G. B. (1986). In pursuit of scholarship. *AACJC Journal, 56*(4), 12–16.

Vaughan, G. B. (1988). Scholarship in community colleges: The path to respect. *Educational Record, 69*(2), 26–31.

Vaughan, G. B. (1991). Scholarship and the community college professional: Focusing the debate. *New Directions for the Community College, 19*(4), 3–15.

Vaughan, G. B. (1992). The community college unbound. *New Directions for Community Colleges, 20*(2), 23–34.

Vaughan, G. B., & Palmer, J. C. (1991). Editors' notes. *New Directions for Community Colleges, 76,* 1–2.

4

Faculty of Color in Academe

What 20 Years of Literature Tells Us

Caroline Sotello Viernes Turner, Juan Carlos González,
and J. Luke Wood

The increasing demographic diversity in the U.S. population begun in the past century continues into this century. The new millennium also brings a heightened awareness of the importance of global and national understanding of cross-cultural perspectives. Such trends and transitions contribute to the shaping of American higher education. Efforts toward faculty racial and ethnic diversity are fueled by the increasing diversity of the student body (Cook & Córdova, 2006; Cora-Bramble, 2006), compelling arguments about the need to prepare all students for a diverse society (antonio, 2002; C. A. Stanley, 2006; Umbach, 2006), continuing evidence that a diverse faculty is important to the success of a diverse student body (Hagedorn, Chi, Cepeda, & McLain (2007), evidence that a diverse faculty assists in the recruitment of students of color to higher education (Alger & Carrasco, 1997; antonio, 2000), and the contributions of diverse faculties to the engagement of new scholarship (Alger, 1999; Christian-Smith & Kellor, 1999; A. M. Padilla, 1994; Turner, 2000; Urrieta & Méndez Benavídez, 2007) and approaches to teaching (antonio, 2000; M. Garcia, 2000; Pineda, 1998; Turner, 2000; Umbach, 2006; Vargas, 2002).

To better prepare students for an increasingly diverse society, campuses across the country are engaged in efforts to diversify the racial and ethnic makeup of their faculties. These efforts are perhaps the least successful of campus diversity initiatives as faculty of color remain underrepresented and their achievements in the academy almost invisible. According to *The Chronicle of Higher Education Almanac* ("Number of Full-Time Faculty Members," 2007–2008), in 2005 faculty of color made up only 17% of total full-time faculty, with 7.5% Asian, 5.5% Black, 3.5% Hispanic, and 0.5% American Indian. When figures reported for the full professor rank are examined, we see that fewer than 12% of full professors in the United States were people of color: 6.5% Asian, 3% Black, 2% Hispanic, and 0.3% American Indian. For female faculty of color, the numbers are even more dismal: In 2005, only 1% of full professors were Black, 1% Asian, 0.6% Hispanic, and 0.1% American Indian.

According to Bland, Meurer, and Maldonado (1995) and Patterson, Thorne, Canam, and Jillings (2001), literature analyses and syntheses are important as a means of periodically bringing coherence to a research area, contributing new knowledge revealed by integrating single studies, and informing scholars and practitioners of the state of the field. From 1988 to 2007, more than 300 scholars published 211 studies and produced 41 doctoral dissertations related to the underrepresentation of faculty of color. We found it inspirational that so many scholars have written about issues pertaining to faculty of color in the past 2 decades. This chapter reviews and synthesizes these studies with the goal of informing scholars and practitioners of the current state of the field. During this process, we developed an interpretive framework to present common elements across publications.

We hope that this analysis will highlight critical information for practitioners and researchers as they attempt to further understand the departmental, institutional, and national processes to create, attract, and sustain a diverse professoriate.

METHOD

Our search for and collection of academic resources related to faculty of color began in 2005. We began collecting, annotating, and synthesizing resources from various academic databases for the years spanning 1988 to 2005. This produced more than 160 resources, including books, journal articles, book chapters, conference papers, Web sites, and videotapes. In 2007, searches for new material that had been written about faculty of color from 2004 to 2007 produced about 117 new references.

As a result of the plethora of publication and resource types included in both the 2005 and the 2007 searches and because of space constraints, we decided to focus our analysis on journal articles, books, dissertations, reports, and book chapters, eliminating conference papers, video resources, and Web sites. Even then, we had 252 pieces of literature to include in our analysis. Table 4.1 shows our search results in 5-year increments.

Google Scholar (accessible at http://www.scholar.google.com), a comprehensive academic search engine, was our major source for identifying, collecting, and checking references. This search engine is able to perform exhaustive searches of all academic work—from the easy-to-find academic articles to the hard-to-locate book chapters. According to Google Scholar (2007), articles in the academic search engine are sorted "the way researchers do, weighing the full text of each article, the author, the publication in which the article appears, and how often the piece has been cited in other scholarly literature." Supplementary article and report searches were conducted through (a) Education Resources Information Center (ERIC), (b) Blackwell Synergy, (c) Journal Storage (JSTOR), (d) Informaworld, (e) the Wilson Index, (f) Ebscohost Electronic Journal Service, (g) Wiley Interscience, (h) Project Muse, (i) the Springer Collection, (j) Questia Online Libraries, (k) Galegroup, (l) PsycINFO, and (m) the Sage Publications Collection. Dissertation searches were performed through Proquest Digital Dissertations. Additional book resources were identified through the Missouri Education and Research Libraries Information Network (MERLIN) and through the Arizona State University, Tempe, Campus Library Catalog. Our search keywords encompassed the following terms: *African American faculty, Black faculty, Native American faculty, Indian faculty, Indigenous faculty, Asian faculty, Asian American faculty, Hispanic faculty, Latino faculty, Latina faculty, Chicano faculty, Chicana faculty, women of color faculty, underrepresented minority faculty,* and *minority faculty.*

TABLE 4.1
Review of Literature Related to Faculty of Color, by Type of Publication, in 5-Year Increments

5-year increment	Journal articles	Dissertations	Books	Reports	Book chapters	Total
2003–2007	86	15	9	9	5	124
1998–2002	25	11	15	6	7	64
1993–1997	12	14	8	9	4	47
1988–1992	7	1	2	3	4	17
Total	130	41	34	27	20	252

After all references were collected and annotated, we began our analysis. All resources were reviewed with attention to their (a) research purpose, (b) research questions, (c) methodology, (d) theoretical framework, (e) findings, (f) recommendations, and (g) conclusions. We then identified emerging themes from the literature individually and cross-checked them in a team discussion. Then, themes were distilled and pictorially depicted using Inspiration (Inspiration, 2007), a software program used to develop, map, and organize themes in a visual treelike format. This analytical process produced about 230 tree branches, with each branch representing a different idea found in the literature about the experience of faculty of color. Inside each tree branch, each author and year of publication were included, so as to thicken the branches of the issues most addressed in the literature. The complete analysis is too complex to show here. A conceptualization of it is shown in Figures 4.1 and 4.2.

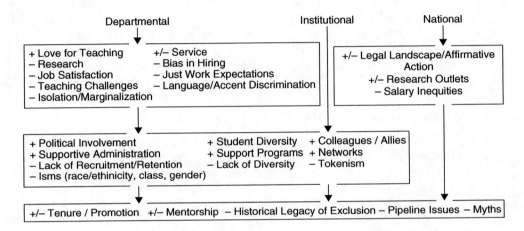

FIGURE 4.1   Supports (+) and challenges (–) within and across departmental, institutional, and national contexts

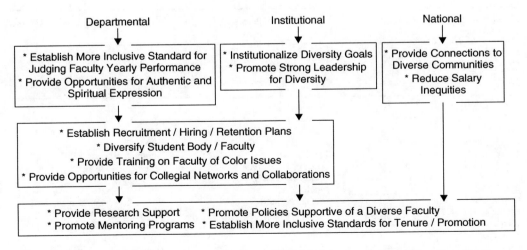

FIGURE 4.2   Recommendations for departmental, institutional, and national contexts

FRAMEWORK FOR ANALYSIS

Publications by more than 300 scholars, including 252 journal articles, dissertations, reports, books, and book chapters, are analyzed here. Figure 4.1 captures the richness of the themes emerging from this extant literature. Factors that positively (represented with a plus sign) or negatively (represented with a minus sign) affected the workplace experience of faculty of color are pictured here from three contexts: (a) the departmental, (b) the institutional, and (c) the national. In Figure 4.1, when boxes cut across various contexts, this means that faculty of color were affected positively or negatively across contexts. Although elements in the departmental context, where working relationships among peers are most intense, are critical to the work life experience of faculty of color, as explicated in the literature included in this study, the importance of a positive and welcoming institutional and national context cannot be denied. The national context is made up of professional organizations and journals that are receptive to the research of the individual faculty member, the off-campus climate, and the legal landscape, including the impact of challenges to affirmative action on the experience of faculty of color. According to the literature, elements such as lack of diversity cut across the departmental and institutional contexts, and mentorship crosses all contexts: national, institutional, and departmental.

EMERGING THEMES: SUPPORTS AND CHALLENGES

In this section, themes identified across publications are listed below within departmental, institutional, and national contexts. Paragraphs briefly describing the various themes introduce each subsection. Words italicized within a paragraph denote themes that are listed within each introductory paragraph along with the relevant references where elaboration on the theme can be found. At least three references had to cite the factor listed to be included in Figure 4.1. Tables 4.2–4.10 relate to the framework presented in Figure 4.1. References for publications documenting each theme are presented alphabetically in three columns, starting from the top left and ending on the bottom right.

TABLE 4.2
+ Love for Teaching

Hill-Brisbane & Dingus (2007) Turner (2003)	C. A. Stanley (2007a)	Turner & Myers (2000)

TABLE 4.3
+ / – Service

Aguirre (2005)	Gregory (2001)	Skachkova (2007)
Aguirre & Martinez (1993)	Hamlet (1999)	E. Smith (1992)
Alemán & Renn (2002)	Hill-Brisbane & Dingus (2007)	C. A. Stanley (2007a)
Alexander-Snow & Johnson (1999)	W. J. Johnson (1996)	Takara (2006)
Arnold (2006)	Jones (2002)	Tierney & Rhoads (1993)
Baez (2002)	Loder et al. (2007)	Tomlinson (2006)
Bensimon et al. (2000)	McKenzie (2002)	Turner et al. (1996)
Bradley (2005)	Moule (2005)	Turner & Myers (2000)
Brayboy (2003)	Niemann (1999)	Urrieta & Méndez Benavidez (2007)
Brown et al. (2007)	Niemann (2003)	Valladares (2007)
Chesler et al. (2005)	A. M. Padilla (1994)	Vasquez et al. (2006)
Cowan (2006)	Rains (1995)	Whetsel-Ribeau (2007)
	Sámano (2007)	Wong & Bainer (1991)

TABLE 4.4
– Research

Aguirre (2005)	M. García (2000)	D. G. Smith et al. (2004)
Aguirre et al. (1993)	Gregory (2001)	C. A. Stanley (2007a, 2007b)
Benjamin (1997)	Hamlet (1999)	Takara (2006)
Bradley (2005)	Louis (2007)	Thompson & Dey (1998)
De la luz Reyes & Halcón (1988)	Niemann (2003)	Turner (2002a)
Delgado Bernal & Villalpando (2002)	Pepion (1993)	Turner & Myers (2000)
Fenelon (2003)	Rendón (2000)	B. N. Williams & Williams (2006)

TABLE 4.5
– Job Satisfaction

Aguirre (2000)	Kauper (1991)	E. Smith (1992)
Astin et al. (1997)	Laden & Hagedorn (2000)	D. G. Smith et al. (2004)
Blackburn & Lawrence (1995)	Morell-Thon (1998)	Tack & Patitu (1992)
Chused (1988)	Niemann (2003)	Thompson & Dey (1998)
Flowers (2005)	Niemann & Dovidio (2005)	Turner & Myers (2000)
Holcomb-McCoy & Addison-Bradley (2005)	Olivas (1988)	Van Ummersen (2005)
Isaac & Boyer (2007)	Peterson-Hickey (1998)	Whetsel-Ribeau (2007)
Jones (2002)	Ponjuan (2005)	Witt (1990)
	Rains (1995)	

TABLE 4.6
– Teaching Challenges

Aguirre (2000, 2005)	Johnsrud & Sadao (1998)	Sampaio (2006)
Bradley (2005)	Kauper (1991)	Skachkova (2007)
Brayboy (2003)	Marbley (2007)	G. Smith & Anderson (2005)
Hassouneh (2006)	Saavedra & Saavedra (2007)	C. A. Stanley (2006)
Hendrix (2007)		

TABLE 4.7
– Isolation and Marginalization

Aguirre (2000, 2005)	Ginorio (1995)	Rendón (1996)
Aguirre & Martinez (1993)	C. M. Gonzalez (2002)	Reyes (2005)
Alemán & Renn (2002)	M. C. González (1995)	Sadao (2003)
Alexander-Snow & Johnson (1999)	Hamlet (1999)	J. W. Smith & Calasanti (2005)
Awe (2001)	Hune (1998)	C. A. Stanley (2006, 2007a)
Baez (2003)	Hune & Chan (1997)	Takara (2006)
Benjamin (1997)	K. W. Jackson (1991)	Thompson & Dey (1998)
Brayboy (2003)	Jacobs et al. (2002)	Tomlinson (2006)
Burden et al. (2005)	B. J. Johnson & Pichon (2007)	Townsend-Johnson (2006)
Carmen (1999)	Maher & Tetreault (2007)	Turner (2002b, 2003)
Chused (1988)	McKenzie (2002)	Turner et al. (1996)
Clark (2006)	Moses (1989)	Turner & Myers (1997, 2000)
Cowan (2006)	Niemann (1999)	TuSmith & Reddy (2002)
Cuádraz (1992)	R. V. Padilla & Chávez Chavez (1995)	Valladares (2007)
De la luz Reyes & Halcón (1988)	Pollard (2006)	Van Ummersen (2005)
Essien (2003)	Rains (1995)	Whetsel-Ribeau (2007)
		Wong & Bainer (1991)

TABLE 4.8
– Bias in Hiring

Alemán & Renn (2002)	Delgado-Romero et al. (2007)	Owino (2000)
Brayboy (2003)	W. J. Johnson (1996, D. R. Johnson, 2006)	Reyes & Ríos (2005)
Brown et al. (2007)	Johnston (1997)	Slater (1999)
Chapman (2001)	Kayes (2006)	D. G. Smith (2000)
Chesler et al. (2005)	Maturana (2005)	D. G. Smith et al. (2004)
Chused (1988)	Mickelson & Oliver (1991)	C. A. Stanley (2006)
Clark (2006)	Niemann (1999)	Tuitt et al. (2007)
De la luz Reyes & Halcón (1988)	Olivas (1988)	Turner & Myers (2000)

TABLE 4.9
– Unjust Work Expectations

Aguirre & Martinez (1993)	Johnsrud & Sadao (1998)	A. M. Padilla (1994)
Baez (2000, 2002)	Jones (2002)	Porter (2007)
Bensimon et al. (2000)	Loder et al. (2007)	Rains (1995)
Bradley (2005)	McLean (2007)	Sámano (2007)
Brayboy (2003)	R. Mitchell & Rosiek (2006)	Sampaio (2006)

TABLE 4.10
– Language/Accent Discrimination

Alemán & Renn (2002)	McLean (2007)	Saavedra & Saavedra (2007)
Guang-Lea & Louis (2006)	Nevarez & Borunda (2004)	Turner & Myers (2000)

Departmental Context

Within the departmental context, faculty of color *love of teaching* was noted as a primary reason for their persistence in academe. However, undervaluation of their *research* interests, approaches, and theoretical frameworks and challenges to their credentials and intellect in the *classroom* contribute to their *dissatisfaction with their professorial roles.* In addition, *isolation,* perceived biases in the *hiring process, unrealistic expectations* of doing their work and being *representatives of their racial/ethnic group,* and *accent discrimination* are noted negatives described in the literature. Although *service* can be detrimental to faculty of color as they progress toward tenure and promotion, it can also be what provides inspiration and passion as they fulfill their desire to serve in response to the needs of their communities. In fact, according to Baez (2000), service "may set the stage for a critical agency that resists and redefines academic structures that hinder faculty success" (p. 363).

Bridging Departmental and Institutional Contexts

Several themes described within the departmental context were also noted within an institutional context. Although we know that professional *networks, colleagues, and allies* can exist in all three contexts pictured here, the literature reviewed spoke about these factors primarily within the departmental and institutional context. These factors, coupled with the presence of *student diversity, faculty research/teaching/professional development support programs, a political* understanding of the importance of sharing accomplishments with those who might provide departmental and institutional opportunities for advancement, and a *supportive administration* contribute to the creation of a positive departmental and institutional work environment. However, *lack of campus student/faculty diversity* and being the *token* person of color coupled with a perceived *lack of departmental/institutional effort to recruit*, hire, and *retain* faculty of color contribute negatively to the experience of faculty of color. In addition, the literature widely documents the negative, interlocking workplace effects *of racism, classism and sexism.* (See Tables 4.11–4.20.)

TABLE 4.11
+ Networks

Baez (1997)	J. C. González (2007a, 2007b)	A. M. Padilla (1994)
Essien (2003)	Hill-Brisbane & Dingus (2007)	Turner & Myers (2000)
Frierson (1990)	Lasalle (1995)	

TABLE 4.12
+ Student Diversity

antonio (2003)	Frierson (1990)	Guiffrida (2005)

TABLE 4.13
+ Colleagues/Allies

Baez (1997)	Hill-Brisbane & Dingus (2007)	C. A. Stanley (2006)
Buttner et al. (2007)	Marbley (2007)	Turner & Myers (2000)
Frierson (1990)	A. M. Padilla (1994)	

TABLE 4.14
+ Support Programs

Daley et al. (2006)	Moradi & Neimeyer (2005)	Segura (2003)
Gooden et al. (1994)	R. V. Padilla & Chávez Chavez (1995)	D. G. Smith et al. (2004)
Kosoko-Lasaki et al. (2006)	Piercy et al. (2005)	Soto-Greene et al. (2005)
Medina & Luna (2000)	Segovia (1994)	Waitzkin et al. (2006)
		Yager et al. (2007)

TABLE 4.15
+ Political Involvement

De la luz Reyes & Halcón (1988)	McKenzie (2002)	R. V. Padilla & Chávez Chavez (1995)
C. González (2007)		

TABLE 4.16
+ Supportive Administrative Leadership

Buttner et al. (2007)	Marbley (2007)	C. A. Stanley (2006)
C. González (2007)	Morris (2000)	C. A. Stanley & Lincoln (2005)
MacLachlan (2006)	Sámano (2007)	

TABLE 4.17
– Lack of Diversity

Aguirre (2000)	Hune (1998)	Olivas (1988)
Alemán & Renn (2002)	Hune & Chan (1997)	Opp & Gosetti (2002)
Alger et al. (2000)	Hurtado et al. (1999)	Owino (2000)
antonio (2003)	J. F. L. Jackson & Phelps (2004)	Peoples (2004)
Arnold (2006)	Jacobs et al. (2002)	Perna (2003)
Benjamin (1997)	Kirkpatrick (2001)	Perna et al. (2007)
Beutel & Nelson (2006)	Knowles & Harleston (1997)	Ponjuan (2005)
Bradley (2005)	Lindsay (1991)	Rai & Critzer (2000)
Chesler et al. (2005)	Maher & Tetreault (2007)	Reyes & Ríos (2005)
Cole & Barber (2003)	MacLachlan (2006)	E. Smith (1992)
Cook & Córdova (2006)	Maturana (2005)	P. W. Smith et al. (2002)
Carnes et al. (2005)	Milem & Astin (1993)	C. A. Stanley (2007a)
Cora-Bramble (2006)	Millett & Nettles (2006)	Takara (2006)
Cowan (2006)	Mitchell & Lassiter (2006)	Thompson & Dey (1998)
Essien (2003)	Moody (1988)	Tierney & Rhoads (1993)
Fenelon (2003)	Myers & Turner (2001, 2004)	Turner et al. (2002)
Frierson (1990)	Nelson et al. (2007)	Turner & Myers (1997)
J. C. González (2007b)	Nevarez & Borunda (2004)	TuSmith & Reddy (2002)
Gregory (2001)	Niemann (2003)	Vasquez et al. (2006)
Greiner & Girardi (2007)	Nieves-Squires (1991)	Witt (1990)
Holland (1995)		Wong & Bainer (1991)

TABLE 4.18
– Lack of Recruitment/Retention

Adams & Bargerhuff (2005)	K. Johnson (2003)	
Aguirre (2000)	Kayes (2006)	C. A. Stanley (2006, 2007a)
Alemán & Renn (2002)	Maher & Tetreault (2007)	J. M. Stanley et al. (2007)
Alex-Assenoh et al. (2005)	Marbley (2007)	Subervi & Cantrell (2007)
Carmen (1999)	Mickelson & Oliver (1991)	Tierney & Rhoads (1993)
Clark (2006)	Morris (2000)	Townsend-Johnson (2006)
Cora-Bramble (2006)	Moss (2000)	Turner (2003)
Cowan (2006)	Nelson et al. (2007)	Turner et al. (1996)
Cross (1994)	Niemann (1999)	Turner & Taylor (2002)
Daley et al. (2006)	Opp & Smith (1994)	TuSmith & Reddy (2002)
Delgado-Romero et al. (2007)	Price et al. (2005)	Vasquez et al. (2006)
Hall (2006)	Pura (1993)	Whetsel-Ribeau (2007)

TABLE 4.19
– Isms (Race/Ethnicity, Class, Gender, Sexual Orientation)

Aguirre (2000)	Ginorio (1995)	Olivas (1988)
Aguirre et al. (1993)	C. M. Gonzalez (2002)	R. V. Padilla & Chávez Chavez (1995)
Akins (1997)	J. C. González (2007b)	Rai & Critzer (2000)
Alemán & Renn (2002)	Gregory (1995, 2001)	Saavedra & Saavedra (2007)
Alexander-Snow & Johnson (1999)	Gumataotao-Lowe (1995)	Slater (1999)
Arnold (2006)	Hall (2006)	P. W. Smith et al. (2002)
Baez (1997)	Hamlet (1999)	Stanley (2006, 2007a)
Benjamin (1997)	Harris (2007)	Stein (1994)
Bower (2002)	Holcomb-McCoy &	Takara (2006)
Bradley (2005)	Addison-Bradley (2005)	Tomlinson (2006)
Brayboy (2003)	Horton (2000)	Turner (2002b, 2003)
Brown et al. (2007)	Hune (1998)	Turner & Myers (1997, 2000)
Carmen (1999)	Hurtado et al. (1999)	TuSmith & Reddy (2002)
Carr et al. (2007)	K. W. Jackson (1991)	Valladares (2007)

Chesler et al. (2005)
Cuádraz (1993)
Delgado-Romero et al. (2007)
De la luz Reyes & Halcón (1988)
Essien (2003)
Fenelon (2003)
A. García (2005)

Jacobs et al. (2002)
W. J. Johnson (1996)
K. Johnson (2003)
Johnsrud & Sadao (1998)
Mickelson & Oliver (1991)
Niemann (1999, 2003)

Vasquez et al. (2006)
Wheeler (1996)
Witt (1990)
Whetsel-Ribeau (2007)
Wong & Bainer (1991)

TABLE 4.20
– Tokenism

Aguirre (2000)	De la luz Reyes & Halcón (1988)	Niemann (2003)
Aguirre et al. (1993)	Fairbanks (2005)	Rains (1995)
Alemán & Renn (2002)	C. M. Gonzalez (2002)	Sámano (2007)
Alexander-Snow & Johnson (1999)	Guang-Lea & Louis (2006)	Segura (2003)
Bradley (2005)	Marbley (2007)	Skachkova (2007)
Brayboy (2003)	Medina & Luna (2000)	Takara (2006)
Chused (1988)	Niemann (1999)	Turner & Myers (2000)

National Context

In a national context, the processes of hiring and retaining faculty of color are influenced by the legal landscape, notably national debates on affirmative action and its application. Often, failure to systematically implement *affirmative action* policies is described as a contributing factor to the underrepresentation of minority faculty. The Supreme Court ruling in *Grutter v. Bollinger* (2003) provides the most recent judicial addition to the affirmative action debate. In this case, the court ruled that maintaining diversity in postsecondary institutions among students was a compelling interest for using race as a factor in university admissions. The court cited the need to prepare students for an increasingly diverse global society as a cause (in part) of this decision. Although this case was specific to the usage of diversity in student admissions processes, "many elements of the decisions lend support to the faculty diversity legal debate" (Springer, 2002, pp. 5). Thus, this case has begun to shift the sentiment of some scholars who see this decision as an important step toward enacting policies that aid faculty diversification efforts. However, others have expressed fear that the programs and policies they currently have in place to support faculty diversity will cause their institution to be vulnerable to lawsuits. On the basis of marked increases in the number of publications regarding faculty of color since the *Grutter* decision, the ruling may have contributed to an increase of articles regarding faculty of color in academe (see Table 4.1). Another national theme that emerged from the literature was *research as an outlet* for faculty of color. Scholars described the challenges faculty of color face because of the illegitimization of their research and methodologies in academic culture, scholarly journals, disciplinary associations, professional networks, and funding entities. For example, Stanley (2007b), in her article "When Counter Narratives Meet Master Narratives in the Journal Editorial-Review Process," described her experiences with the editorial review process and called on "journal editors and reviewers to examine their roles as disciplinary gatekeepers and to break the cycle of master narratives in educational research in the editorial review process" (p. 14). Additionally, national studies of *salary inequities* focus on the effect of pay on the representation of diverse faculty and variance in salary by race, ethnicity, and institutional type. (See Tables 4.21–4.23.)

TABLE 4.21
± Legal Landscape/Affirmative Action

Alemán & Renn (2002)	Hamlet (1999)	Slater (1999)
Alexander-Snow & Johnson (1999)	Jacobs et al. (2002)	E. Smith (1992)
Alger (1999, 2000)	Maher & Tetreault (2007)	P. W. Smith et al. (2002)
Ashraf & Shabbir (2006)	Maturana (2005)	Springer (2004)
Baez (2002)	Myers & Turner (2001)	Takara (2006)
Basri et al. (2007)	Nevarez & Borunda (2004)	Tomlinson (2006)
Blackshire-Belay (1998)	Niemann (1999, 2003)	Turner et al. (1996)
Brown et al. (2007)	Niemann & Dovidio (2005)	Turner (2003)
Chesler et al. (2005)	Peoples (2004)	Turner & Myers (1997)
Cowan (2006)	Rai & Critzer (2000)	Turner & Taylor (2002)
Delgado-Romero et al. (2007)	Sánchez (2007)	Vasquez et al. (2006)
Guang-Lea & Louis (2006)	Skachkova (2007)	Witt (1990)

TABLE 4.22
± Research Outlets

Alemán & Renn (2002)	Moule (2005)	Stanley (2007b)
Alexander-Snow & Johnson (1999)	A. M. Padilla (1994)	Turner (2000)
Louis (2007)	Reyes & Ríos (2005)	Turner & Myers (2000)

TABLE 4.23
– Salary Inequities

Alemán & Renn (2002)	Renzulli et al. (2006)	Witt (1990)
Myers & Turner (2001)	Toutkoushian et al. (2007)	

Bridging Departmental, Institutional, and National Contexts

Across departmental, institutional, and national settings, the literature identifies major barriers to the tenure and promotion of faculty of color, such as negative student evaluations, undervaluation of research, and unwritten rules and policies regarding the tenure process. Conversely, the integration of policies that recognize contributions to diversity is an important step toward rethinking standards for hiring and *tenure and promotion* processes. For example, in 2004, the University of California system adopted Academic Personnel Policy No. 210 ("Section II: Appointment and Promotion," 2002), which states that "teaching, research, professional and public service contributions that promote diversity and equal opportunity are to be encouraged and given recognition in the evaluation of the candidate's qualifications" (p. 4) for appointment and promotion. This policy, which was revised and placed into effect in 2005, can serve as a model for other institutions seeking to place value on faculty contributions to diversity efforts when determining hiring, tenure, and promotion decisions. On one hand, faculty who were not successful in the tenure process often lacked *mentorship* to aid their incorporation into academia. On the other hand, scholarship on successful faculty revealed that mentorship was a critical support to their professional success. The *historical literature* on faculty of color indicates that underrepresentation, segregation, and exclusion are still prevalent in the educational system. These concerns, coupled with *pipeline* issues and pervasive *myths* in the recruitment and hiring process, maintain a lack of diversity in the professoriate. (See Tables 4.24–4.28.)

Although campus climate is a major factor noted in the literature on faculty of color (Alemán & Renn, 2002; Bradley, 2005; Ginorio, 1995; Guang-Lea & Louis, 2006; Holcomb-McCoy & Addison-Bradley, 2005; Horton, 2000; Hurtado, Milem, Clayton-Pedersen, & Allen, 1999; Jacobs, Cintrón, & Canton, 2002; Niemann, 2003; Niemann & Dovidio, 2005; Piercy et al.,

TABLE 4.24
± Tenure/Promotion

Alemán & Renn (2002)	Hune & Chan (1997)	Sampaio (2006)
Akins (1997)	Jacobs et al. (2002)	Slater (1999)
Baez (1997, 2002)	C. Johnson (2001)	P. A. Smith & Shoho (2007)
Basri et al. (2007)	B. J. Johnson & Harvey (2002)	Stanley (2006, 2007a)
Bensimon & Tierney (1996)	Jones (2001, 2002)	Thompson & Dey (1998)
Blackshire-Belay (1998)	Laden & Hagedorn (2000)	Tierney & Rhoads (1993)
Brown et al. (2007)	Maher & Tetreault (2007)	Townsend-Johnson (2006)
Chesler et al. (2005)	Marbley (2007)	Turner et al. (1996)
Cowan (2006)	Morell-Thon (1998)	Turner & Myers (2000)
Fenelon (2003)	Niemann (1999, 2003)	Turner & Taylor (2002)
Gregory (2001)	Pepion (1993)	TuSmith & Reddy (2002)
Guang-Lea & Louis (2006)	Perez (2001)	Valladares (2007)
Harris (2007)	Perna (2003)	Whetsel-Ribeau (2007)
Hassouneh (2006)	Perna et al. (2007)	Witt (1990)
Hendricks (1996)	Ponjuan (2005)	B. N. Williams & Williams (2006)
Hendrix (2007)	Rai & Critzer (2000)	Wong & Bainer (1991)

TABLE 4.25
± Mentorship

Alex-Assenoh et al. (2005)	Gregory (2001)	C. A. Stanley (2006, 2007a)
Arnold (2006)	Hendricks (1996)	J. M. Stanley et al. (2007)
Barnett et al. (2003)	Holland (1995)	Tierney & Rhoads (1993)
Blackshire-Belay (1998)	Johnsrud (1994)	Turner et al. (1996)
Burden et al. (2005)	Kosoko-Lasaki et al. (2006)	Turner & Thompson (1993)
Chesler et al. (2005)	Lewellen-Williams et al. (2006)	Turner & Myers (1997)
Daley et al. (2006)	Millett & Nettles (2006)	Turner & Myers (2000)
Dixon-Reeves (2003)	Moss (2000)	Vasquez et al. (2006)
Frierson (1990)	Nelson et al. (2007)	Waitzkin et al. (2006)
A. García (2000)	Nevarez & Borunda (2004)	D. A. Williams & Williams (2006)
C. M. Gonzalez (2002)	A. M. Padilla (1994)	Yager et al. (2007)
	Peterson-Hickey (1998)	

TABLE 4.26
– Pipeline Issues

Alemán & Renn (2002)	B. J. Johnson & Pichon (2007)	Nelson et al. (2007)
Chesler et al. (2005)	Jordan (2006)	P. W. Smith et al. (2002)
Cross (1994)	Lindsay (1991)	J. M. Stanley et al. (2007)
Hernández & Davis (2001)	Moody (1988)	Turner & Myers (1997, 2000)
Jacobs et al. (2002)	Myers & Turner (2001, 2004)	Turner & Taylor (2002)
K. Johnson (2003)		

TABLE 4.27
– Historical Legacy of Exclusion

Aguirre et al. (1993)	W. J. Johnson (1996)	Slater (1999)
Castellanos & Jones (2003)	Lindsay (1991)	E. Smith (1992)
Chesler et al. (2005)	Maher & Tetreault (2007)	Turner & Taylor (2002)
Gregory (2001)	Moody (2004)	Weems (2003)
Hurtado et al. (1999)	Rai & Critzer (2000)	

TABLE 4.28
– Myths

Assensoh (2003)	Kayes (2006)	D. G. Smith et al. (1996)
Chapman (2001)	Maturana (2005)	C. A. Stanley (2007a)
Cho (2002)	Morris (2000)	Townsend-Johnson (2006)
Hune (1998)	Peoples (2004)	Turner et al. (1996)
K. Johnson (2003)	Pura (1993)	Turner & Myers (2000)
D. R. Johnson (2006)	D. G. Smith (2000)	Wong & Bainer (1991)

2005; Price et al., 2005; Ponjuan, 2005; Stanley, 2006; Whetsel-Ribeau, 2007), it is not included as a separate category in Figure 4.1. Our reasoning is that campus climate is an all-encompassing term that includes many of the supports and challenges already addressed in our model.

EMERGING THEMES: RECOMMENDATIONS

Figure 4.2 represents the major recommendations derived from the literature that address challenges presented in Figure 4.1. Similar to Figure 4.1, Figure 4.2 differentiates among three contexts—departmental, institutional, and national. Some recommendations are pictured as cutting across multiple contexts because they are applicable in each of them. For example, as in Figure 4.1, in Figure 4.2, a recommendation that cuts across all three contexts is *promote mentoring programs.*

Themes identified across publications are listed below within departmental, institutional, and national contexts. Listed after each theme are the references in which elaboration on the theme can be found. At least three references had to cite the factor listed for it to be included here.

Departmental Context Recommendations

Although most recommendations noted in the literature cited here applied to the departmental context, they were not exclusive to this context. According to the literature, departments need to *diversify their processes for how they judged faculty* pre- and post-tenure. The literature described new and/or alternative ways of thinking, teaching, writing, and just being an academic brought to higher education by current faculty of color. Their new approaches to research, teaching, and service are, in many cases, in conflict with traditional approaches leading to poor evaluations and lack of publications. This means that in a *publish or perish* environment based on traditional ways of knowing, many faculty of color may be at a disadvantage (see Table 4.29). Second, as the faculty diversifies and brings to the academy different ways of knowing, it is important that they are given the opportunity for individual expression—*authentic and spiritual.* The literature in this area is growing and indicates the need for departments to recognize the underlying messages conveyed to faculty of color that devalue their research and writing in an oppressive fashion (see Table 4.30). For example, Louis (2007) urged scholars to accept, as legitimate ways of knowing, "knowledge systems that do not necessarily conform to Western academic standards."

TABLE 4.29
Establish More Inclusive Standards for Judging Faculty Yearly Performance

Bensimon & Tierney (1996)	Louis (2007)	Rains (1995)
Bensimon et al. (2000)	Moule (2005)	C. A. Stanley (2006, 2007a, 2007b)
Cooper & Stevens (2002)	Pepion (1993)	Turner & Taylor (2002)
Hayden (1997)	Perez (2001)	Urrieta & Méndez Benavídez (2007)
Jones (2002)		

TABLE 4.30
Provide Opportunities for Authentic and Spiritual Expression

Astin & Astin (1999)	Jones (2000)	Rendón (2000)
Guang-Lea & Louis (2006)	Louis (2007)	C. A. Stanley (2007b)
Hall (2006)		

Additionally, departments should recognize that some scholars may believe that "the spiritual aspect of life is as important to the search for knowledge as is the physical" (p. 134).

Institutional Context Recommendations

D. A. Williams and Wade-Golden (2006) defined chief diversity officers (CDOs) as "the 'face' of diversity efforts [that] carry formal administrative titles like vice provost, vice chancellor, associate provost, vice president, assistant provost, dean, or special assistant to the president for multicultural, international, equity, diversity, and inclusion" (p. 1). Furthermore, D. A. Williams and Wade-Golden (2007) stated that "today's CDOs are often seen as change agents who are appointed to create an environment that is inclusive and supportive of all members of the institution in order to maximize both human and institutional capital" (p. iii). As institutions begin to recognize the importance of the role of the CDO to diversifying the faculty, it is critical to understand that although they may be centrally responsible, they should not be solely responsible for this important work. As the roles of CDOs increase and become more defined, it is important that that they continue their work to *institutionalize diversity goals* and to *promote strong campus leadership* that advocates for faculty diversification (see Tables 4.31 and 4.32). The following citations present work in support of the types of institutional factors important to the goal of increasing the racial and ethnic representation of faculty of color.

Departmental and Institutional Contexts Recommendations

The literature reviewed in this study underscores the importance of having *departmental and institutional plans* that systematically promote progress toward the *goal of diversifying the faculty*. Part of the plan should also include training to increase knowledge and sensitivity of all campus staff, faculty, and higher level administrators on issues facing faculty of color in the

TABLE 4.31
Institutionalize Diversity Goals

Alicea-Lugo (1998)	Guang-Lea & Louis (2006)	Sánchez (2007)
Brayboy (2003)	Harvey & Valadez (1994)	Sámano (2007)
Chapman (2001)	W. J. Johnson (1996)	C. A. Stanley (2007b)
Colby & Foote (1995)	Johnston (1997)	Tack & Patitu (1992)
Cowan (2006)	Maturana (2005)	

TABLE 4.32
Promote Strong Leadership for Diversity

Alexander-Snow & Johnson (1999)	Maturana (2005)	C. A. Stanley & Lincoln (2005)
Arnold (2006)	Opp & Gosetti (2002)	Toutkoushian et al. (2007)
Buttner et al. (2007)	Price et al. (2005)	Whetsel-Ribeau (2007)
Fox (2005)	Sámano (2007)	Wong & Bainer (1991)
MacLachlan (2006)	C. A. Stanley (2006, 2007a)	

workplace. The alignment of diversity efforts at both levels of the organization is critical for progress to take place. In addition, the literature suggests that *increasing the campus presence of students and faculty of color* may lead to a synergy that supports the retention and development of both groups as well as attracting others. A more diverse environment has the potential to alleviate isolation for people of color on campus. As colleges and universities become diverse, it will also be important for students, staff, faculty, and administrators to be provided with *training on the issues faced by faculty of color.* Another recommendation emerging from this study, which can build scholarly community at the departmental and institutional levels, is deliberate efforts to provide opportunities for *collegial networking and cross-disciplinary collaborations* (see Tables 4.33–4.36).

TABLE 4.33
Establish Recruitment/Hiring/Retention Plans

Alger (1999)	Hayden (1997)	Opp & Smith (1994)
Bowser et al. (1993)	Johnston (1997)	Peoples (2004)
Chapman (2001)	Jones (2001)	Peterson-Hickey (1998)
Colby & Foote (1995)	Kauper (1991)	Plata (1996)
Chused (1988)	Kayes (2006)	Pura (1993)
Clark-Louque (1996)	Kirkpatrick (2001)	Sámano (2007)
Cooper & Stevens (2002)	Light (1994)	C. A. Stanley (2007a)
Cross & Slater (2002)	Mickelson & Oliver (1991)	J. M. Stanley et al. (2007)
Delgado-Romero et al. (2007)	Moody (1988)	Stein (1994)
C. González (2007)	Moreno et al. (2006)	Tippeconnic & McKinney (2003)
J. C. González (2007a)	Morris (2000)	Turner (2002a)
Granger (1993)	Moss (2000)	Wong & Bainer (1991)
Harvey & Valadez (1994)	Opp & Gosetti (2002)	

TABLE 4.34
Diversify Student Body/Faculty

Adams & Bargerhuff (2005)	Frierson (1990)	Morris (2000)
Alex-Assensoh (2003)	C. González (2007)	Myers & Turner (2001)
antonio (2002, 2003)	J. C. González (2007a)	Price et al. (2005)
Barnett et al. (2003)	Guang-Lea & Louis (2006)	Pura (1993)
Fox (2005)	Kauper (1991)	Sánchez (2007)
	Kirkpatrick (2001)	

TABLE 4.35
Provide Training on Faculty-of-Color Issues

Adams & Bargerhuff (2005)	Plata (1996)	Whetsel-Ribeau (2007)
Peoples (2004)	Sámano (2007)	Wong & Bainer (1991)
Pineda (1998)	C. A. Stanley (2006, 2007a)	

TABLE 4.36
Provide Opportunities for Collegial Networks and Collaborations

Alexander-Snow & Johnson (1999)	Gregory (2001)	Plata (1996)
Baez (1997)	W. J. Johnson (1996)	Stein (1994)
Bowser et al. (1993)	B. J. Johnson & Harvey (2002)	Thomas & Hollenshead (2001)
Butner et al. (2000)	MacLachlan (2006)	Turner & Myers (1997)
Essien (2003)	Moses (1989)	Valladares (2007)
	A. M. Padilla (1994)	Wong & Bainer (1991)

National Context Recommendations

To achieve success in the recruitment and retention of faculty of color, communities of color and institutions of higher education must create relationships with one another, recognizing the importance of increased faculty racial and ethnic diversity and working in collaboration to achieve this goal. With regard to the hiring of Latino faculty, C. González (2007) stated that "the Hispanic community must establish a strong working relationship with institutions of higher learning and use power in a measured and sustained way" (p. 159) to encourage faculty diversification. Likewise, institutions must establish and maintain *connections to diverse communities* in support of the service and incorporation needs of faculty of color. Additionally, institutions must begin to address and reduce *salary inequities* between majority and minority faculties. (See Tables 4.37 and 4.38.) Pay inequities invalidate and devalue the contributions of diverse faculties and increase the likelihood that they will reject position offers or leave institutions early. Furthermore, disparities in the allocation of research space, graduate student research support, and funding for conference participation must be viewed as an extension of salary inequity issues. These funding inequities should be addressed for incoming and current faculty of color through policies that promote equity.

Departmental, Institutional, and National Contexts Recommendations

Recommendations cutting across all three contexts include the critical need for *research support* for faculty of color, particularly for nontenured faculty (see Table 4.39). Support can come from departmental, institutional, or national sources, including federal, state, professional organization, and foundation funding. However, although research support can be in the form of funding, it may also include opportunities to participate in nationwide workshops and seminars designed to assist junior faculty of color in the grant-getting and publication processes. The best of these programs would emphasize collaborative and not hierarchical professional socialization. Having

TABLE 4.37
Provide Connections to Diverse Community

C. González (2007)	Sámano (2007)	Urrieta & Méndez Benavídez (2007)
J. C. González (2007a, 2007b)	J. M. Stanley et al. (2007)	
K. P. Gonzalez & Padilla (2007)	Turner & Thompson (1993)	
Gregory (2001)		

TABLE 4.38
Reduce Salary Inequities

Myers & Turner (2001)	Renzulli et al. (2006)	Toutkoushian et al. (2007)

TABLE 4.39
Provide Research Support

Alex-Assenoh et al. (2005)	J. C. González (2007a, 2007b)	Turner (2003)
Bradley (2005)	Louis (2007)	Turner & Myers (1997, 2000)
Dixon-Reeves (2003)	C. A. Stanley (2006)	Wong & Bainer (1991)
Fox (2005)	J. M. Stanley et al. (2007)	

mentors along their career path is a leading factor contributing to the growth and development of faculty of color. Because mentorship is so critical, programs providing *opportunities for mentorship* should be made available at the departmental, institutional, and national levels. Such connections within all contexts, including internationally, play an important role in the development of faculty and in the promotion and tenure process. In addition, having different rubrics for evaluating tenure and promotion worthiness are mentioned in the literature. For example, value should be placed, during tenure and promotion evaluations, on contributions to diversity efforts and for faculty outreach to diverse on-campus communities, off-campus local communities, and diverse national communities. Also, emerging from the literature are recommendations to promote policies supportive of a diverse faculty (see Table 4.40). Included among these factors are the need to level the field with regard to inequitable pay for faculty of color and women employed in minority-serving institutions when compared with salaries paid in predominantly White institutions. Renzulli, Grant, and Kathuria (2006) referred to this phenomenon as "economic subordination" (p. 507). Overarching policies that create multilevel pathways to the professoriate and continue to support careers are also reported as important for implementation across contexts. Finally, practices that promote the building of scholarly and collaborative communities as opposed to individualism and competitiveness are recommended. (See Tables 4.41 and 4.42.)

TABLE 4.40
Promote Policies Supportive of a Diverse Faculty

Adams & Bargerhuff (2005)	J. C. González (2007a)	Renzulli et al. (2006)
Arnold (2006)	Granger (1993)	Sámano (2007)
Astin (1992)	Guang-Lea & Louis (2006)	Stanley (2007a)
Bowser et al. (1993)	W. J. Johnson (1996)	J. M. Stanley et al. (2007)
Bradley (2005)	Moody (1988)	Vasquez et al. (2006)
Chapman (2001)	Niemann (1999)	Wong & Bainer (1991)
Fox (2005)		

TABLE 4.41
Promote Mentoring Programs

Alexander-Snow & Johnson (1999)	Kosoko-Lasaki et al. (2006)	J. M. Stanley et al. (2007)
Alex-Assenoh et al. (2005)	Lewellen-Williams et al. (2006)	C. A. Stanley & Lincoln (2005)
Arnold (2006)	Moss (2000)	Stein (1994)
Barnett et al. (2003)	A. M. Padilla (1994)	Tippeconnic & McKinney (2003)
Bradley (2005)	Piercy et al. (2005)	Turner & Myers (1997)
Dixon-Reeves (2003)	Sámano (2007)	Waitzkin et al. (2006)
W. J. Johnson (1996)	Soto-Greene et al. (2005)	Wong & Bainer (1991)
Johnsrud (1994)	C. A. Stanley (2006, 2007a)	Yager et al. (2007)
Kirkpatrick (2001)		

TABLE 4.42
Establish More Inclusive Standards for Tenure and Promotion

Alexander-Snow & Johnson (1999)	Jones (2002)	C. A. Stanley (2006, 2007a, 2007b)
Bensimon & Tierney (1996)	Moule (2005)	Turner & Taylor (2002)
Bensimon et al. (2000)	Pepion (1993)	Louis (2007)
Cooper & Stevens (2002)	Perez (2001)	Urrieta & Méndez Benavídez (2007)
Fenelon (2003)	Rains (1995)	Wong & Bainer (1991)
Hayden (1997)		

SPANNING 2 DECADES: METHODOLOGICAL APPROACHES AND THE STUDY OF FACULTY OF COLOR

Between 1988 and 2007, a number of publications on faculty of color were conceptual in nature. In addition, a cursory analysis of empirical research conducted during this time frame revealed the preferred usage of the following research methodologies: (a) interviews, (b) surveys and questionnaires, (c) large data sets, and (d) a combination of multiple qualitative methods (document analysis, interviews, and observations). An examination of the preferred research methodologies used during this period (divided into 5-year periods) is provided, as well as some citations relevant to these approaches.

Between 1988 and 1992, the preferred data collection approaches to the study of faculty of color in academe appeared to be surveys and questionnaires (Chused, 1988; Nieves-Squires, 1991; E. Smith, 1992) and (to a lesser extent) interviews—sometimes used in conjunction with other methods (Kauper, 1991; Nieves-Squires, 1991). Various forms of data collection were used by other researchers, such as auto-ethnographic narratives (Cuádraz, 1992), historical analysis (Lindsay, 1991), and the usage of large data sets (Mickelson & Oliver, 1991).

From 1993 to 1997, the primary data collection methods used were surveys (Aguirre, Martinez, & Hernández, 1993; Clark-Louque, 1996; Hendricks, 1996; Holland, 1995; Johnston, 1997), interviews (Baez, 1997; Cuádraz, 1993; D. R. Johnson, 1996; Knowles & Harleston, 1997; Lasalle, 1995; Turner & Thompson, 1993), and some combination of qualitative methods (i.e., archival and document analysis in conjunction with interviews and/or observations; Hayden, 1997; Pepion, 1993; Pura, 1993; Rains, 1995). Also used to a lesser degree were historical analysis (Gregory, 1995) and the analysis of large data sets (Akins, 1997; Milem & Astin, 1993).

From 1988 to 2002, the use of interviews as the primary form of data collection appeared to be preferred (Astin & Astin, 1999; Baez, 2000; Carmen, 1999; Morell-Thon, 1998; Peterson-Hickey, 1998; Pérez, 2001; Turner, 2002b). However, interviews were often combined with observations (Gonzalez, 2002; C. Johnson, 2001; Morris, 2000; Thomas & Hollenshead, 2001) and large data set analyses (Myers & Turner, 2001; Turner & Myers, 2000). Also, the use of large data sets seemed to increase during this period (antonio, 2002; Opp & Gosetti, 2002; Owino, 2000; Thompson & Dey, 1998). Additional publications indicate the continued use of surveys and questionnaires (Awe, 2001; Chapman, 2001; Hernández & Davis, 2001), narratives (Jacobs, Cintrón, & Canton, 2002; Medina & Luna, 2000), and historical analysis (Gregory, 2001).

Publications from 2003 to 2007 illustrate that researchers used interviews (Burden, Harrison, & Hodge, 2005; Carr, Palepu, Szalacha, Caswell, & Inui, 2007; J. C. González, 2007a, 2007b; McLean, 2007; Skachkova, 2007; Urrieta & Méndez Benavídez, 2007; B. N. Williams & Williams, 2006), analysis of large data sets (Ashraf & Shabbir, 2006; Isaac & Boyer, 2007; Perna, 2003; Perna, Gerald, Baum, & Milem, 2007; Porter, 2007; Toutkoushian, Bellas, & Moore, 2007), and surveys and questionnaires (Hagedorn, Chi, Cepeda, & McLain, 2007; Holcomb-McCoy & Addison-Bradley, 2005; Stanley, 2007a, 2007b; Subervi & Cantrell, 2007; Umbach, 2006). Also, historical research approaches (Weems, 2003) and narrative data analysis (Sámano, 2007; Stanley, 2006) were used during this period (although to a lesser degree). Authors also published studies that used a combination of qualitative research methods (interviews, observations, and document analysis; Hill-Brisbane & Dingus, 2007).

Table 4.43 shows a fairly consistent use by researchers of similar methodological approaches to examine the status of faculty of color throughout the 20-year time period.

TABLE 4.43
Methodological Approaches and the Study of Faculty of Color

5-year increment	Methodological approach
1988–1992	Interviews, surveys/questionnaires
1993–1997	Interviews, multiple qualitative methods,[a] surveys/questionnaires
1998–2002	Interviews, surveys/questionnaires, large data set(s), observations/interviews
2003–2007	Interviews, surveys/questionnaires, large data set(s)

a Multiple qualitative methods: archival/document analysis combined with the usage of interviews and/or observations.

SPANNING 2 DECADES: ISSUES EXAMINED IN THE STUDY OF FACULTY OF COLOR

Findings from our examination of publications included in this study (i.e., journal articles, dissertations, books, reports, and book chapters) document that the total number of publications on faculty of color has visibly increased over each 5-year period examined (1988–1992, 1993–1997, 1998–2002, and 2003–2007). The largest total publication increase occurred during the 2003–2007 period (see Table 4.1). This increase may be linked to the 2003 *Grutter v. Bollinger* Supreme Court decision, although there is no evidence to prove this link. In general, most of the publications during the time periods examined were journal articles, except from 1993 to 1997 when more dissertations were produced.

Several publications on faculty of color from 1988 to 1992 focused on the intersection of race and ethnicity and gender (Chused, 1988; Cuádraz, 1992; Lindsay, 1991; Moses, 1989; Nieves-Squires, 1991; Tack & Patitu, 1992; Witt, 1990). Also heavily researched was the lack of diversity in the academy (Frierson, 1990; Lindsay, 1991; C. D. Moody, 1988; Olivas, 1988; E. Smith, 1992) and job satisfaction (Chused, 1988; Tack & Patitu, 1992; Turner & Myers, 2000; Witt, 1990). During this time span, some publications focused on faculty of color career decisions (Kauper, 1991) and occupational stress (E. Smith, 1992).

Scholarly publications from 1993 to 1997 focused on (a) the socialization process for faculty of color (Bensimon & Tierney, 1996; Lasalle, 1995; Tierney & Rhoads, 1993; Turner & Thompson, 1993); (b) lack of faculty diversity (Benjamin, 1997; Holland, 1995; Milem & Astin, 1993; Tierney & Rhoads, 1993); (c) strategies for faculty racial/ethnic diversification (Colby & Foote, 1995; Knowles & Harleston, 1997; Light, 1994; Opp & Smith, 1994; Plata, 1996; Pura, 1993; D. G. Smith, Wolf, & Busenberg, 1996); (d) isms (with regard to race/ethnicity, class, gender, and sexual orientation; Aguirre et al., 1993; Akins, 1997; Ginorio, 1995; W. J. Johnson, 1996); (e) tenure and promotion issues (Akins, 1997; Pepion, 1993; Tierney & Rhoads, 1993); and (f) isolation and marginalization in the academy (Aguirre & Martinez, 1993; Benjamin, 1997; Hune & Chan, 1997; Padilla & Chávez Chavez, 1995; Rendón, 1996). Additionally, literature demonstrating the importance of faculty and academic administrator mentorship in support of the retention of faculty of color and the attraction of students to faculty careers was addressed (Holland, 1995; Johnsrud, 1994; Padilla, 1994; Segovia, 1994; Wheeler, 1996).

From 1998 to 2002, there was a continuation of literature documenting the intersection of race/ethnicity and gender among faculty (Aguire, 2000; Alemán & Renn, 2002; Moss, 2000; Opp & Gosetti, 2002; Owino, 2000; Perna, 2003; Rai & Critzer, 2000; Turner, 2000, 2002b). This literature was accompanied by publications on specific female faculty of color groups such as African American women (Hamlet, 1999; McKenzie, 2002; Thomas & Hollenshead, 2001), Latinas (Alicea-Lugo, 1998; Medina & Luna, 2000), and Asian women (Hune, 1998). Some publications on African American male faculty were also evident during this period (Jones, 2000, 2002).

During this time frame, research on faculty of color also focused on (a) stress and coping (Butner, Burley, & Marbley, 2000; Thomas & Hollenshead, 2001; Thompson & Dey, 1998), (b) job satisfaction (Laden & Hagedorn, 2000; Morell-Thon, 1998), (c) myths (Cho, 2002; D. G. Smith, 2000), (d) different ways of knowing (A. W. Astin & Astin, 1999; Rendón, 2000), (e) service (Baez, 2000; Hamlet, 1999; McKenzie, 2002; Turner & Myers, 2000), (f) lack of diversity in the academy (Aguirre, 2000; Hune, 1998; Owino, 2000; Thompson & Dey, 1998), (g) recruitment and retention concerns (Carmen, 1999; Morris, 2000; Moss, 2000; Niemann, 1999), (h) isms (with regard to race/ethnicity, class, gender, and sexual orientation; Gonzalez, 2002; Horton, 2000; Rai & Critzer, 2000; Slater, 1999), (i) tokenism (Aguirre, 2000; Medina & Luna, 2000; Niemann, 1999), (j) bias in hiring (Chapman, 2001; Slater, 1999; D. G. Smith, 2000), (k) tenure and promotion issues (Blackshire-Belay 1998; Niemann, 1999; TuSmith & Reddy, 2002), (l) isolation and marginalization (Alemán & Renn, 2002; Awe, 2001; Hamlet, 1999), and (m) affirmative action and legal issues (Alexander-Snow & Johnson, 1999; Alger, 1999; Turner & Taylor, 2002). Additionally, two guidebooks specific to the recruitment and retention of faculty of color emerged, one that focused on the search committee process (Turner, 2002a) and the other designed to aid faculty of color to succeed in the academy (M. García, 2000).

From 2003 to 2007, emergent issues from the published literature reflected an interest in faculty of color and (a) their unique scholarly contributions (Fenelon, 2003; Louis, 2007; Tippeconnic & McKinney, 2003; Urrieta & Méndez Benavídez, 2007), (b) their perceptions of teaching and use of critical and alternative pedagogy (Hassouneh, 2006; McLean, 2007; Saavedra & Saavedra, 2007; Sampaio, 2006; G. Smith & Anderson, 2005), (c) job satisfaction (Flowers, 2005; Holcomb-McCoy & Addison-Bradley, 2005; Isaac & Boyer, 2007; Niemann & Dovidio, 2005; Ponjuan, 2005), (d) resiliency (Cora-Bramble, 2006; J. C. González, 2007a, 2007b), (e) lack of diverse faculty representation (Essien, 2003; Fenelon, 2003; Myers & Turner, 2004; Ponjuan, 2005), (f) service (Bradley, 2005; Brayboy, 2003; Skachkova, 2007; Urrieta & Méndez Benavídez, 2007), (g) recruitment and retention concerns (Clark, 2006; K. Johnson, 2003; Kayes, 2006; Turner, 2003), (h) isms (with regard to race/ethnicity, class, gender, and sexual orientation; Holcomb & Addison-Bradley, 2005; Stanley, 2007a; Valladares, 2007), (i) tokenism (Bradley, 2005; Fairbanks, 2005; Sámano, 2007; Segura, 2003), (j) bias in hiring (Maturana, 2005; Reyes & Ríos, 2005; Stanley, 2006), (k) tenure and promotion issues (Cowan, 2006; Perna, 2003; Sampaio, 2006), (l) isolation and marginalization (B. J. Johnson & Pichon, 2007; Reyes, 2005; Tomlinson, 2006; Townsend-Johnson, 2006), and (m) affirmative action and legal issues (Ashraf & Shabbir, 2006; Springer, 2004; Takara, 2006).

The predominant research emphasis during this time frame was scholarship on mentoring (Alex-Assenoh et al., 2005; Barnett, Gibson, & Black, 2003; Dixon-Reeves, 2003; Kosoko-Lasaki, Sonnino, & Voytko, 2006; Lewellen-Williams et al., 2006; C. A. Stanley & Lincoln, 2005; J. M. Stanley, Capers, & Berlin, 2007; Waitzkin, Yager, Parker, & Duran, 2006; Yager, Waitzkin, Parker, & Duran, 2007). Additionally, two interrelated fields experienced a growth in scholarly attention: (a) research on faculty and graduates of color in the science, technology, engineering, and mathematics fields (MacLachlan, 2006; Millett & Nettles, 2006; Nelson, Brammer, & Rhoads, 2007) and (b) literature on faculty of color in the health fields (Burden et al., 2005; Carnes, Handelsman, & Sheridan, 2005; Carr et al., 2007; Daley, Wingard, & Reznik, 2006; D. A. Mitchell & Lassiter, 2006; Soto-Greene, Sanchez, Churrango, & Salas-Lopez, 2005; Yager, Waitzkin, Parker, & Duran, 2007).

Table 4.44 indicates that some issues emerging from the published literature examined in this study appeared to remain somewhat constant, whereas others were added over different time periods. Scholarly interest in the intersection of gender with racial/ethnic diversity among the faculty, mentorship, job satisfaction, isms (with regard to race/ethnicity, class, gender, and sexual

TABLE 4.44
Emerging Issues

5-year increment	Emerging issues
1988–1992	Intersection of gender, lack of diversity, job satisfaction
1993–1997	Socialization process, strategies for diversification, mentorship, lack of diversity, isms, tenure & promotion, isolation/marginalization
1998–2002	Intersection of gender, different ways of knowing, stress & coping, job satisfaction, myths, service Lack of diversity, recruitment & retention, isms, tokenism, bias in hiring, tenure & promotion, isolation/marginalization, affirmative action/legal issues
2003–2007	Scholarly contributions, teaching & pedagogy, job satisfaction, resiliency, mentorship, STEM fields Health fields, service, lack of diversity, recruitment & retention, isms, tokenism Bias in hiring, isolation/marginalization, tenure & promotion Affirmative action/legal issues

orientation), tenure and promotion, isolation and marginalization, and lack of diversity in the academy appear to hold researchers' attention over the 20-year span. Additions that stood out during 1998–2002 are respect for different ways of knowing and myths surrounding concerns related to the recruitment and retention of faculty of color. Additional issues receiving attention from 2003 to 2007 are scholarly contributions made by a diverse professoriate, resiliency, and experiences of faculty of color in science, technology, engineering, mathematics, and health fields.

FURTHER RESEARCH

Further work is needed to capture insights from other sources. Even though we compiled and analyzed a comprehensive list of publications for this chapter, as stated earlier conference papers, videotapes, and Web sites, although identified, were excluded in the analysis provided here. It is also likely that we have not captured all existing publications on this subject. However, the works presented here likely represent the major themes on faculty diversity to be captured in journal articles, books, dissertations, reports, and book chapters written over the past 20 years.

However, our analysis has identified major gaps in the literature. First, most publications located and examined here focus on faculty of color within public 4-year university settings. As a result, more work examining faculty of color within community college, technical college, private college, for-profit college, minority-serving institutions, and faith-based campus environments needs to be conducted. Second, there is almost nothing written on issues related to faculty of color and the intersection of race/ethnicity and sexual orientation. Delgado-Romero, Manlove, Manlove, and Hernandez (2007) stated that "one aspect of Latino/a faculty experience that is virtually absent from the research literature is the experience of Latino/a lesbian, gay, bisexual, and transgendered (LLGBT) faculty" (p. 43). Third, most of the literature analyzed here underscores the value of mentoring within departmental, institutional, and national contexts. Further work on the importance of such connections within an international context can be undertaken as these colleagues are critical to faculty development as well as in the promotion and tenure process. In fact, more comparative studies on faculty of color within a global context would be a welcome addition to the extant literature. Fourth, although our study showed that the literature, in general, reflected emerging themes across institutional types and racial/ethnic affiliation, more work needs to be done to examine sets of issues that are unique or specific to various racial/ethnic groups and to faculty women of color. For example, Turner and Myers (2000) began to identify themes that are specific to faculty by racial/ethnic affiliation and gender. Fifth, although several themes, such as mentorship, have been shown to support the recruitment and retention of faculty of color, more work needs to be done on how such factors can be implemented nationwide to contribute to the resolution of the critical problem examined in this chapter. Finally, empirical research needs to be conducted on the critical, emerging institutional role of the executive-level campus diversity officer, the CDO, and his or her impact on diversifying the faculty.

IMPLICATIONS

This review and synthesis of extant literature on faculty of color has implications for policy-makers, administrators, faculty, and graduate students. In essence, this analysis highlights the complexity of the faculty of color experience in higher education by providing an integration of single studies conducted over an extensive time period and by presenting themes derived from these studies. In addition, the literature collected for this study addresses supports, challenges, and recommendations that cut across departmental, institutional, and national contexts. Those involved in making policies and decisions may find this analysis useful in understanding the interrelated factors affecting faculty of color hiring and persistence. For example, transcending context and time frame, mentoring is a factor described in the literature as critical to the persistence of faculty of color.

In conclusion, challenges afford opportunities. All involved in higher education have an opportunity to support others as they encounter the challenges presented in this chapter. According to our analysis, these challenges remain over time and appear to be pervasive in the social fabric of the academy. We must dissipate these barriers by helping faculty, staff, and students understand the nature of the barriers across contexts, as discussed in the literature, that impede the progress of potential and current faculty of color. By understanding challenges, supports, and recommendations described across single studies, there is an opportunity to develop strategies applicable in the contexts described here (departmental, institutional, and national) that can contribute to the creation of a more welcoming and affirming academic environment for faculty of color.

REFERENCES

Asterisks denote references included in the literature review/synthesis.

*Adams, K., & Bargerhuff, M. E. (2005). Dialogue and action: Addressing recruitment of diverse faculty in one Midwestern university's college of education and human services. *Education, 125,* 539–545.

*Aguirre, A. (2000). Women and minority faculty in the academic workplace: Recruitment, retention, and academic culture. *ASHE-ERIC Higher Education Report, 27*(6).

*Aguirre, A. (2005). The personal narrative as academic storytelling: A Chicano's search for presence and voice in academe. *International Journal of Qualitative Studies in Education, 18,* 147–163.

*Aguirre, A., & Martinez, R. O. (1993). *Chicanos in higher education: Issues and dilemmas for the 21st century* (ASHE-ERIC Higher Education Report No. 3). Washington, DC: ERIC Clearinghouse on Higher Education, George Washington University, in cooperation with the Association for the Study of Higher Education.

*Aguirre, A., Martinez, R., & Hernández, A. (1993). Majority and minority faculty perceptions in academe. *Research in Higher Education, 34,* 371–385.

*Akins, D. (1997). *The economics of tenure: Understanding the effects of ethnicity, status and discipline on faculty attitude, workload and productivity.* Unpublished doctoral dissertation, University of Southern California.

*Alemán, A. M. M., & Renn, K. A. (Eds.). (2002). *Women in higher education: An encyclopedia.* Santa Barbara, CA: ABC-CLIO.

*Alexander-Snow, M., &Johnson, B. J. (1999). Perspectives from faculty of color. In R. J. Menges (Ed.), *Faculty in new jobs: A guide to settling in, becoming established, and building institutional support* (pp. 88–117). San Francisco: Jossey-Bass.

*Alex-Assensoh, Y. (2003). Race in the academy: Moving beyond diversity and toward the incorporation of faculty of color in predominately white colleges and universities. *Journal of Black Studies, 34,* 12–27.

*Alex-Assenoh. Y. M., Givens., T., Golden., K., Hutchings, V. L., Wallace, S. L., & Whitby, K. J. (2005). Mentoring and African-American political scientists. *Political Science and Politics, 38,* 283–285.

*Alger, J. R. (1999). When color-blind is color-bland: Ensuring faculty diversity in higher education. *Stanford Law & Policy Review, 10,* 191–204.

*Alger, J. R. (2000). How to recruit and promote minority faculty: Start by playing fair. *Black Issues in Higher Education, 17,* 160–163.

Alger, J. R., & Canasco, G. P. (1997, August). *The role of faculty in achieving and retaining a diverse student population.* Paper presented at the AACRAO Policy Summit, Denver, CO.

*Alger, J. R., Chapa, J., Gudeman, R. H., Marin, P., Maruyama, G., Milem, J. F., et al. (2000). *Does diversity make a difference? Three research studies on diversity in college classrooms.* Washington, DC: American Council on Education & the American Association of University Professors.

*Alicea-Lugo, B. (1998). Salsa y adobo: Latino/Latina contributions to theological education. *Union Seminary Quarterly Review, 52,* 129–144.

antonio, A. L. (2000). Faculty of color and scholarship transformed: New arguments for diversifying faculty. *Diverse Digest, 3*(2), 6–7.

*antonio, A. L. (2002). Faculty of color reconsidered: Reassessing contributions to scholarship. *Journal of Higher Education, 73,* 582–602.

*antonio, A. L. (2003). Diverse student bodies, diverse faculties: The success or failure of ambitions to diversify faculty can depend on the diversity of student bodies. *Academe, 89*(6). Retrieved January 6, 2008, from http://www.aaup.org/AAUP/ pubsres/academe/2003/ND/Featanto.htm?PF=l

*Arnold, J. (2006). *Moving beyond access: Institutionalizing best practices for the inclusion of underrepresented faculty and administrators.* Unpublished doctoral dissertation, University of Pennsylvania, Philadelphia.

*Ashraf, J., & Shabbir, T. (2006). Are there racial differences in faculty salaries? *Journal of Economics and Finance, 30,* 306–316.

*Assensoh, A. B. (2003). Trouble in the promised land: African American studies program and the challenges of incorporation. *Journal of Black Studies, 34,* 52–62.

*Astin, A. W. (1992). The unrealized potential of American higher education. *Innovative Higher Education, 17,* 95–114

*Astin. A. W. & Astin. H. S. (1999). *Meaning and spirituality in the lives of college faculty: A study of values, authenticity, and stress.* Los Angeles: University of California, Higher Education Research Institute.

*Astin, H. S., antonio, a. i., Cress, C. M., & Astin, A. W. (1997). *Race and ethnicity in the American professoriate, 1995–1996.* Los Angeles: University of California, Higher Education Research Institute.

*Awe, C. (2001). *The socialization of junior tenure-track faculty members in research universities.* Unpublished doctoral dissertation, University of Illinois, Urbana-Champaign.

*Baez, B. (1997). *How faculty of color construct the promotion and tenure process.* Unpublished doctoral dissertation, Syracuse University.

*Baez, B. (2000). Race-related service and faculty of color: Conceptualizing critical agency in academe. *Higher Education, 39,* 363–391

*Baez, B. (2002). *Affirmative action, hate speech, and tenure: Narratives about race, law, and the academy.* Independence, KY: Routledge Falmer.

*Baez, B. (2003). Outsiders within? *Academe, 89*(4). Retrieved January 6, 2008, from http://www.aaup. org/AAUP/pubsres/academe/2003/JA/Feat/beaz.htm

*Barnett, E., Gibson, M., & Black, P. (2003). Proactive steps to successfully recruit, retain, and mentor minority educators: Issues in education. *Journal of Early Education and Family Review, 10*(3), 18–28.

*Basri, G., Boechat, M. I., Island, E., Ledesma, M., Oakley, J., Pitts, L., et al. (2007). *Study group on university diversity: Overview report to the regents.* Oakland: Office of the President, University of California. Retrieved January 8, 2008, from http://www.universityofcalifornia.edu/news/2007/ diversityreport0907.pdf

*Benjamin, L. (Ed.). (1997). *Black women in the academy: Promises and perils.* Gainesville: University Press of Florida.

*Bensimon, E. M., & Tierney, W. G. (1996). *Promotion and tenure: Community and socialization in academe.* Albany: State University of New York Press.

*Bensimon, E. M., Ward, K., & Sanders, K. (2000). *The department chair's role in developing new faculty into teachers and scholars.* Boston: Anker.

*Beutel, A. M., & Nelson, D. J. (2006). The gender and race-ethnicity of faculty in top social science research departments. *Social Science Journal, 43,* 111–125.

*Blackburn, R. T., & Lawrence, J. H. (1995). *Faculty at work: Motivation, expectation, satisfaction.* Baltimore: Johns Hopkins University Press.

*Blackshire-Belay, C. (1998). Under attack: The status of minority faculty members in the academy. *Academe, 84*(4), 30–36.

Bland, C. J., Meurer, L., & Maldonado, G. (1995). A systematic approach to conducting a non-statistical meta-analysis of research literature. *Academic Medicine, 70,* 642–653.

*Bower, B. L. (2002). Campus life for faculty of color: Still strangers after all these years? *New Directions for Community Colleges, 118,* 79–88.

*Bowser, B. P., Auletta, G. S., & Jones, T. (1993). *Confronting diversity issues on campus.* Newbury Park, CA: Sage.

*Bradley, C. (2005). The career experiences of African American women faculty: Implications for counselor education programs. *College Student Journal, 39,* 518–527.

*Brayboy, B. M. J. (2003). The implementation of diversity in predominantly White colleges and universities. *Journal of Black Studies, 34,* 72–86.

*Brown, O. G., Hinton, K. G., & Howard-Hamilton, M. (Eds.). (2007). *Unleashing suppressed voices on college campuses: Diversity issues in higher education.* New York: Peter Lang.

*Burden, J. W., Harrison, L., & Hodge, S. R. (2005). Perceptions of African American faculty in kinesiology-based programs at predominantly White American institutions of higher education. *Research Quarterly for Exercise and Sport, 76,* 224–237.

*Butner, B. K., Burley, H., & Marbley, A. F. (2000). Coping with the unexpected: Black faculty at predominantly White institutions. *Journal of Black Studies, 30,* 453–462.

*Buttner, E., Holly, L., Kevin, B., & Billings-Harris, L. (2007). Impact of leader racial attitude on ratings of causes and solutions for an employee of color shortage. *Journal of Business Ethics, 73,* 129–144.

*Carmen, F. (1999). *In their own voice: The experiences of counselor educators of color in academe.* Unpublished doctoral dissertation, University of New Mexico.

*Carnes. M., Handelsman, J., & Sheridan, J. (2005). Diversity in academic medicine: The stages of change model. *Journal of Women's Health, 14,* 471–475.

*Carr, P. L., Palepu, A., Szalacha, L., Caswell, C., & Inui, T. (2007). "Flying below the radar": A qualitative study of minority experience and management of discrimination in academic medicine. *Medical Education, 41,* 601–609.

*Castellanos, J., & Jones, L. (Eds.). (2003). *The majority in the minority: Expanding the representation of Latina/o faculty, administrators and students in higher education.* Herndon, VA: Stylus.

*Chapman, B. G. (2001). *Minority faculty recruitment in community colleges: Commitment, attitudes, beliefs, and perceptions of chief academic officers.* Unpublished doctoral dissertation, University of Texas at Austin.

*Chesler, M. A., Lewis, A., & Crowfoot, J. (2005). *Challenging racism in higher education: Promoting justice.* Lanham, MD: Rowman & Littlefield.

*Cho, S. (2002). Confronting the myths: Asian Pacific American faculty in higher education. In C. S. V. Turner, a. l. antonio, M. Garcia, B. Laden, A. Nora, & C. Presley (Eds.), *Racial & ethnic diversity in higher education* (2nd ed.; pp. 169–184). Boston: Pearson Custom.

Christian-Smith, L. K., & Kellor, K. S. (Eds.). (1999). *Everyday knowledge and uncommon truths: Women of the academy.* Boulder, CO: Westview Press.

*Chused, R. H. (1988). The hiring and retention of minorities and women on American law school faculties. *University of Pennsylvania Law Review, 137,* 537–569.

*Clark, R. L. (2006). *Recruitment and retention of faculty of color in Oklahoma.* Unpublished doctoral dissertation, Oklahoma State University.

*Clark-Louque, A. R. (1996). *The participation of minorities in higher education.* Unpublished doctoral dissertation, Pepperdine University.

*Colby, A., & Foote, E. (1995). *Creating and maintaining a diverse faculty* (ERIC Document Reproduction Service No. Ed. 386 261). Los Angeles: ERIC Clearinghouse for Community Colleges. Retrieved January 6, 2008, from http://www.ericdigests.org/l996–2/diverse.html

*Cole, S., & Barber, E. G. (2003). *Increasing faculty diversity: The occupational choices of high achieving minority students.* Cambridge, MA: Harvard University Press.

*Cook, B. J., & Córdova, D. I. (2006). *Minorities in higher education 2006: Twenty-second annual status report.* Washington, DC: American Council on Education.

*Cooper, J. E., & Stevens, D. D. (Eds.). (2002). *Tenure in the sacred grove: Issues and strategies for women and minority faculty.* Albany: State University of New York Press.

*Cora-Bramble, D, (2006), Minority faculty recruitment, retention and advancement: Applications of a resilience-based theoretical framework. *Journal of Health Care for the Poor and Underserved, 17,* 251–255.

*Cowan, L, Y, (2006), *An examination of policies and programs used to increase ethnic and racial diversity among faculty at research universities.* Unpublished doctoral dissertation, University of Illinois at Urbana-Champaign.

*Cross, T. (1994), Black faculty at Harvard: Does the pipeline defense hold water? *Journal of Blacks in Higher Education, 4,* 42–46.

*Cross, T., & Slater, R. (2002). A short list of colleges and universities that are taking measures to increase their number of Black faculty. *Journal of Blacks in Higher Education, 36,* 99–103.

*Cuádraz, G. H. (1992). Experiences of multiple marginality: A case of Chicana scholarship women. *Journal of the Association of Mexican American Educators, Inc, 12,* 31–43.

*Cuádraz, G. H. (1993). *Meritocracy (un)challenged: The making of a Chicano and Chicana professoriate and professional class.* Unpublished doctoral dissertation, University of California, Berkeley.

*Daley, S., Wingard, D. L., & Reznik, V. (2006). Improving the retention of underrepresented minority faculty in academic medicine. *Journal of the National Medical Association, 98,* 1435–1440.

*De la luz Reyes, M., & Halcón, J. J. (1988). Racism in academia: The old wolf revisited. *Harvard Education Review, 58,* 299–314.

*Delgado Bernal, D., & Villalpando, O. (2002). The apartheid of knowledge in the academy: The struggle over "legitimate" knowledge for faculty of color. *Equity & Excellence in Education, 35,* 169–180.

*Delgado-Romero, E. A., Manlove, A. N., Manlove, J. D., & Hernandez C. A. (2007). Controversial issues in the recruitment and retention of Latino/a faculty. *Journal of Hispanic Higher Education, 6,* 34–51.

*Dixon-Reeves, R. (2003). Mentoring as a precursor to incorporation: An assessment of the mentoring experience of recently minted Ph.D.s. *Journal of Black Studies, 34,* 12–27.

*Essien, V. (2003). Visible and invisible barriers to the incorporation of faculty of color in predominantly White law schools. *Journal of Black Studies, 34,* 63–71.

*Fairbanks, A. R. (2005). *Walking in two worlds: Making professional transitions between native and non-native worlds.* Unpublished doctoral dissertation, University of Minnesota, Minneapolis.

*Fenelon, J. (2003). Race, research, and tenure: Institutional credibility and the incorporation of African, Latino, and American Indian faculty. *Journal of Black Studies, 34,* 87–100.

*Flowers, L. A. (2005). Job satisfaction differentials among African American faculty at 2-year and 4-year institutions. *Community College Journal of Research and Practice, 29,* 317–328.

*Fox, M. J. T. (2005). Voices from within: Native American faculty and staff on campus. *New Directions for Student Services, 109*(1), 49–59.

*Frierson, Jr., H. T. (1990). The situation of Black educational researchers: Continuation of a crisis. *Educational Researcher, 19*(2), 12–17.

*García, A. (2005). Counter stories of race and gender: Situating experiences of Latinas in the academy. *Latino Studies, 3,* 261–273.

*García, M. (Ed.). (2000). *Succeeding in an academic career: A guide for faculty of color.* Westport, CT: Greenwood Press.

*Ginorio, A. B. (1995). *Warming the climate for women in academic science.* Washington, DC: Association of American Colleges & Universities.

*Gonzalez, C. M. (2002). *The Latina/o faculty: A perilous journey to the ivory tower in higher education.* Unpublished doctoral dissertation, Arizona State University, Tempe.

*González, C. M. (2007). Building sustainable power: Latino scholars and academic leadership positions at U.S. institutions of higher learning. *Journal of Hispanic Higher Education, 6,* 157–162.

*González, J. C. (2007a). Expanding our thinking of resiliency from K-12 to higher education: Resolute experiences of academic Latinas. In D. M. Davis (Ed.), *Resiliency reconsidered: Policy implications of the resiliency movement* (pp. 103–122). Charlotte, NC: Information Age.

*González, J. C. (2007b). Surviving the doctorate and thriving as faculty: Latina junior faculty reflecting on their doctoral studies experiences. *Equity & Excellence in Education, 40,* 291–300.

*Gonzalez, K. P., & Padilla, R. V. (2007). *Doing the public good: Latina/o scholars engage civic participation.* Sterling, VA: Stylus.

*González, M. C. (1995). In search of the voice I always had. In R. V. Padilla & R. Chávez Chavez (Eds.), *The leaning ivory tower: Latino professors in American universities* (pp. 77–90). Albany: State University of New York Press.

Gooden, J. S., Leary, P. A, & Childress, R. B. (1994). Initiating minorities into the professoriate: One school's model. *Innovative Higher Education, 18,* 243–253.

Google Scholar. (2007). *About Google Scholar.* Accessed on January 7, 2008, from http://scholar.google.com/intl/en/scholar/about.html

*Granger, M. W. (1993). A review of the literature on the status of women and minorities in higher education. *Journal of School Leadership, 3,* 121–135.

*Gregory, S. (1995). *Black women in the academy: The secrets to success and achievement.* New York: University Press of America.

*Gregory, S. T. (2001). Black faculty women in the academy: History, status, and future. *Journal of Negro Education, 70,* 124–138.

*Greiner, K., & Girardi, A. G. (2007). *Student and faculty ethnic diversity report* (Eric Reproduction Document Number 495714). Des Moines, IA: Iowa College Student Aid Commission. Retrieved December 23, 2007, from http://www.eric.ed.gov/ERICDocs/data/ericdocs2sql/content_storage0l/0000019b/80/28/03/f9.pdf

Grutter v. Bollinger. (2003). 539 U.S. 306.

*Guang-Lea, L., & Louis, J. (2006). Successful multicultural campus: Free from prejudice toward minority professors. *Multicultural Education, 14*(1), 27–30.

*Guiffrida, D. (2005). Othermothering as a framework for understanding African American students' definitions of student-centered faculty. *Journal of Higher Education, 76,* 701–723. Retrieved January 6, 2008, from https://dspace.lib.rochester.edu/retrieve/7328/bs0.pdf

*Gumataotao-Lowe, C. S. N. (1995). *Institutional racism in higher education: Perceptions of people of color.* Unpublished doctoral dissertation, University of Washington.

*Hagedorn, L. S., Chi, W. Y., Cepeda, R. M., & McLain, M. (2007). An investigation of critical mass: The role of Latino representation in the success of urban community college students. *Research in Higher Education, 4,* 73–91

*Hall, D. M. (2006). *Keeping hope alive: Retention of faculty of color at traditionally White four-year colleges and universities.* Unpublished doctoral dissertation, Illinois State University.

*Hamlet, J. D. (1999). Giving the sistuhs their due: The lived experiences of African American women in academia. In T. McDonald & T. Ford-Ahmed (Eds.), *Nature of a sistuh: Black women's lived experiences in contemporary culture* (pp. 11–26). Durham, NC: Carolina Academic Press.

*Harris, T. M. (2007). Black feminist thought and cultural contracts: Understanding the intersection and negotiation of racial, gendered, and professional identities in the academy. *New Directions for Teaching and Learning, 110,* 55–64.

*Harvey, W. B., & Valadez, J. (Eds.). (1994). Creating and maintaining a diverse faculty [Special issue].

New Directions for Community Colleges, 22(3). Retrieved January 6, 2008, from http://www.eric. ed.gov/ERICDocs/data/ericdocs2sql/content_storage_0l/0000019b/80/13/72/82.pdf

*Hassouneh, D. (2006). Anti-racist pedagogy: Challenges faced by faculty of color in predominantly White schools of nursing. *Journal of Nursing Education, 45*, 255–262.

*Hayden, R. E. (1997). *Faculty affirmative action: A case study of underrepresented faculty at the University of California, Irvine.* Unpublished doctoral dissertation, University of California, Irvine.

*Hendricks, F. M. (1996). *Career experiences of Black women faculty at research I universities.* Unpublished doctoral dissertation, University of Missouri—Columbia.

*Hendrix. K. G. (2007). "She must be trippin": The secret of disrespect from students of color toward faculty of color. *New Directions for Teaching and Learning, 110*, 85–96.

*Hernández, E. I., & Davis, K. G. (2001). The national survey of Hispanic theological education. *Journal of Hispanic/Latino Theology, 8,* 37–58.

*Hill-Brisbane, D. A., & Dingus, J. E. (2007). Black women teacher educators: Creating enduring afriographies as leaders and change makers. *Advancing Women in Leadership, 22*(1). Retrieved December 30, 2007, from http://www.advancing-women.com/awl/winter2007/Hill.htm

*Holcomb-McCoy, C., & Addison-Bradley, C. (2005). African American counselor educators' job satisfaction and perceptions of departmental racial climate. *Counselor Education and Supervision, 45*(1), 2–15.

*Holland, G. (1995). *The effects of mentoring experiences on the retention of African-American faculty at four-year colleges and universities.* Unpublished doctoral dissertation, Illinois State University.

*Horton, H. W. (2000). Perspectives on the current status of the racial climate relative to students, staff, and faculty of color at predominantly White colleges/universities in America. *Equity & Excellence in Education, 33*(3), 35–37.

*Hune, S. (1998). *Asian Pacific American women in higher education: Claiming visibility and voice.* Washington, DC: Association of American Colleges & Universities.

*Hune, S., & Chan, K. S. (1997). *Special focus: Asian Pacific American demographic and educational trends: Fifteenth annual status report.* Washington, DC: American Council on Education.

*Hurtado, S., Milem, J., Clayton-Pedersen, A., & Allen, W. (1999). *Enacting diverse learning environments: Improving the climate for racial/ethnic diversity in higher education* (ASHE-ERIC Higher Education Report No. 26–8). Washington, DC: George Washington University, School of Education & Human Development.

Inspiration Software. (2007). Available at http://ww.inspiration.com/

*Isaac, E. P., & Boyer, P. G. (2007). Voices of urban and rural community college minority faculty: Satisfaction and opinions. *Community College Journal of Research and Practice, 31*, 359–369.

Jackson, J. F. L., & Phelps, L. A. (2004). Diversity in the two-year college academic workforce. *New Directions for Community Colleges, 127*, 79–88.

*Jackson, K. W. (1991). Black faculty in academia. In P. G. Altbach & K. Lomotey (Eds.), *The racial crisis in American higher education* (pp. 135–148). Albany: State University of New York Press.

*Jacobs, L., Cintrón, J., & Canton, C. E. (2002). *The politics of survival in academia: Narratives of inequality, resilience, and success.* Lanham, MD: Rowman & Littlefield.

*Johnson. B. J., & Harvey, W. (2002) . The socialization of Black college faculty: Implications for policy and practice. *Review of Higher Education, 25*, 297–314.

*Johnson. B. J. & Pichon. H. 12007). The status of African American faculty in the academy: Where do we go from here? In J. F. L. Jackson (Ed.) *Strengthening the African American educational pipeline: Informing research, policy, and practice* (pp. 97–114). Albany: State University of New York Press.

*Johnson, C. (2001). *The tenure process and five minority faculty members.* Unpublished doctoral dissertation, University of Nebraska Lincoln.

*Johnson, D. R. (2006). *The hiring process: The Black experience in a community college search committee.* Unpublished doctoral dissertation, University of Texas at Austin.

*Johnson, K. (2003). *Encouraging the heart: How three University of California institutions responded to minority faculty recruitment after the implementation of Proposition 209.* Unpublished doctoral dissertation, Pepperdine University.

*Johnson, W. J. (1996). *A qualitative study of the factors affecting the recruitment and retention of African*

American faculty in Minnesota community colleges. Unpublished doctoral dissertation, University of Minnesota, Twin Cities Campus.

*Johnsrud, L. K. (1994). Enabling the success of junior faculty women through mentoring. In M. A. Wunsch (Ed.), *Mentoring revisited: Making an impact on individuals and institutions* (pp. 53–64). San Francisco: Jossey-Bass.

*Johnsrud, L. K., & Sadao, K. C. (1998). The common experience of "otherness": Ethnic and racial minority faculty. *Review of Higher Education, 21,* 315–342.

*Johnston, G. H. (1997). *Piecing together the "mosaic called diversity": One community college's ongoing experience with hiring a more diverse faculty.* Unpublished doctoral dissertation, University of Illinois at Urbana Champaign.

*Jones, L. (Ed.). (2000). *Brothers of the academy: Up and coming Black scholars earning our way in higher education.* Sterling, VA: Stylus.

*Jones, L. (Ed.). (2001). *Retaining African Americans in higher education: Challenging paradigms for retaining students, faculty and administrators.* Herndon, VA: Stylus.

*Jones, L. (Ed.). (2002). *Making it on broken promises: African American male scholars confront the culture of higher education.* Herndon, VA: Stylus.

*Jordan, D. (2006). *Sisters in science: Conversations with Black women scientists about race, gender, and their passion for science.* West Lafayette, IN: Purdue University Press.

*Kauper, M. W. (1991). *Factors which influence the career decisions of minority faculty at a predominately White liberal arts institution: A case study.* Unpublished doctoral dissertation, Indiana University Bloomington.

*Kayes, P. E. (2006). New paradigms for diversifying faculty and staff in higher education: Uncovering cultural biases in the search and hiring process. *Multicultural Education, 14,* 65–69.

*Kirkpatrick, L. (2001). *Multicultural strategies for community colleges: Expanding faculty diversity.* Washington, DC: ERIC Clearinghouse for Community Colleges.

*Knowles, M. F., & Harleston, B. W. (1997). *Achieving diversity in the professoriate: Challenges and opportunities.* Washington, DC: American Council on Education.

*Kosoko-Lasaki, O., Sonnino, R. E., & Voytko, M. L. (2006). Mentoring for women and underrepresented minority faculty and students: Experience at two institutions of higher education. *Journal of the National Medical Association, 98,* 1449–1459,

*Laden, B. V., & Hagedorn, L. S. (2000). Job satisfaction among faculty of color in academe: Individual survivors or institutional transformers? *New Directions for Institutional Research, 27*(1), 57–66.

*Lasalle, L. A. (1995). *Racing the professoriate: The socialization of faculty of color.* Unpublished doctoral dissertation, Pennsylvania State University, State College.

*Lewellen-Williams, C., Johnson, V. A., Deloney, L. A., Thomas, B. R., Goyol, A., & Henry-Tillman, R. (2006). The pod: A new model for mentoring underrepresented minority faculty. *Academic Medicine, 81,* 275–279.

*Light, P. (1994). "Not like us": Removing the barriers to recruiting minority faculty. *Journal of Policy Analysis and Management, 13,* 164–180.

*Lindsay, B. (1991). Public and higher education policies influencing African-American women. In G. P. Kelly, & S. Slaughter (Eds.), *Women's higher education in comparative perspective* (pp. 85–102). Boston: Kluwer Academic.

*Loder, T. L., Sims, M. J., Collins, L., Brooks, M., Volk, D., Calhoun, C., & Coker, A. D. (2007). On becoming and being faculty-leaders in urban education and also being African-American . . . Seems promising. *Advancing Women in Leadership Online Journal, 22*(1). Retrieved January 8, 2008, from http://www.advancingwomen.com/awl/winter2007/Loder.htm

*Louis, R. (2007). Can you hear us now? Voices from the margin: Using indigenous methodologies in geographic research. *Geographic Research, 45,* 130–139.

*MacLachlan, A. J. (2006). *Developing graduate students of color for the professoriate in science, technology, engineering and mathematics (STEM).* Berkeley, CA: Center for Studies in Higher Education. Retrieved December 24, 2007, from http://eric.ed.gov/ERICDocs/data/ericdocs2sql/content_storage_01/0000019b/80/29/de/c7.pdf

*Maher, F. A., & Tetreault, M. K. T. (2007). *Privilege and diversity in the academy.* New York: Routledge.

*Marbley, A. F. (2007). Finding my voice: An African-American female professor at a predominantly White university. *Advancing Women in Leadership Online Journal, 22.* Retrieved January 11, 2008, from http://www.advancingwomen.com/awl/winter2007/finding_my_voice.htm

*Maturana, I. M. (2005). *Factors in the search process that contribute to the recruitment and hiring of faculty of color.* Unpublished doctoral dissertation, University of Massachusetts at Boston.

*McKenzie, M. M. (2002). Labor above and beyond the call: A Black woman scholar in the academy. In S. Harley & The Black Women and Work Collective (Eds.), *Sister circle: Black women and work* (pp. 231–253). New Brunswick, NJ: Rutgers University Press.

*McLean, C. A. (2007). Establishing credibility in the multicultural classroom: When the instructor speaks with an accent. *New Directions for Teaching and Learning, 110,* 15–24.

*Medina, C., & Luna, G. (2000). Narratives from Latina professors in higher education. *Anthropology & Education Quarterly, 31,* 47–66.

*Mickelson, R. A., & Oliver, M. L. (1991). Making the short list: Black candidates and the faculty recruitment process. In P. A. Altbach & K. Lomotey (Eds.), *The racial crisis in American higher education* (pp. 149–166). Albany: State University of New York Press.

*Milem, J. F., & Astin, H. S. (1993). The changing composition of the faculty: What does it really mean for diversity? *Change, 25*(2), 21–27.

*Millett, C. M., & Nettles, M. T. (2006). Expanding and cultivating the Hispanic STEM doctoral workforce: Research on doctoral student experiences. *Journal of Hispanic Higher Education, 5,* 258–287.

*Mitchell, D. A., & Lassiter, S. (2006). Addressing health care disparities and increasing workforce diversity: The next step for the dental, medical, and public health professions. *American Journal of Public Health, 96,* 2093–2097.

*Mitchell, R., & Rosiek, J. (2006). Professor as embodied racial signifier: A case study of the significance of race in a university classroom. *Review of Education, Pedagogy and Cultural Studies, 28,* 395–409.

*Moody, C. D. (1988). Strategies for improving the representation of minority faculty in research universities. *Peabody Journal of Education, 66*(1), 77–90.

*Moody, J. (2004). *Faculty diversity: Problems and solutions.* New York: Routledge.

*Moradi, B., & Neimeyer, G. J. (2005). Diversity in the ivory White tower: A longitudinal look at faculty race/ethnicity in counseling psychology academic training programs. *Counseling Psychologist, 33,* 655–675.

*Morell-Thon, C. (1998). *Job satisfaction of Hispanic faculty in higher education.* Unpublished doctoral dissertation, University of Virginia.

*Moreno, J. F., Smith, D. G., Clayton-Pedersen, A. R., Parker, S., & Teraguchi, D. H. (2006). *The revolving door for underrepresented minority faculty in higher education: An analysis from the campus diversity initiative.* Washington, DC: Association of American Colleges & Universities.

*Morris, C. A. (2000). *Strategies for recruitment and retention of faculty of color in community colleges.* Unpublished doctoral dissertation, University of Texas at Austin.

*Moses, Y. T. (1989). *Black women in academe: Issues and strategies.* Washington, DC: Association of American Colleges & Universities.

*Moss, L. E. T. (2000). *Recruitment, retention, and mentoring of female and minority faculty in higher education.* Unpublished doctoral dissertation, Arkansas State University.

*Moule, J. (2005). Implementing a social justice perspective in teacher education: Invisible burden for faculty of color. *Teacher Education Quarterly, 32*(4), 23–42.

*Myers, S. L., Jr., & Turner, C. S. V. (2001). Affirmative action retrenchment and labor market outcomes for African-American faculty. In B. Lindsay & M. J. Justiz (Eds.), *The quest for equity in higher education: Toward new paradigms in an evolving affirmative action era* (pp. 63–98). Albany: State University of New York Press.

*Myers, S. L., Jr., & Turner, C. S. V. (2004). The effects of Ph.D. supply on minority faculty representation. *American Economic Review, 94,* 296–301.

*Nelson, D. J., Brammer, C. N., & Rhoads, H. (2007). *A national analysis of minorities in science and*

engineering faculties at research universities. Arlington, VA: National Science Foundation. Retrieved January 10, 2008, from http://cheminfo.chem.ou.edu/~djn/diversity/Faculty_Tables_FY07/07Report. pdf

*Nevarez, C., & Borunda, R. (2004). *Faculty of color: Contesting the last frontier.* Sacramento, CA: Serna Center. Retrieved December 3, 2007, from http://www.csus.edu/sernacenter/assets/scholar_reports/ nevarez_borunda.pdf

*Niemann, Y. F. (1999). The making of a token: A case study of stereotype threat, stigma, racism, and tokenism in academe. *Frontiers: A Journal of Women Studies, 20,* 111–134.

*Niemann, Y. F. (2003). The psychology of tokenism: Psychosocial realities of faculty of color. In G. Bernal, J. E. Trimble, A. K. Burlew, & F. T. L. Leong (Eds.), *Handbook of racial and ethnic minority psychology* (pp. 100–118). Thousand Oaks, CA: Sage.

*Niemann, Y. F., & Dovidio, J. F. (2005). Affirmative action and job satisfaction: Understanding underlying processes. *Journal of Social Issues, 61,* 507–523.

*Nieves-Squires, S. (1991). *Hispanic women: Making their presence on campus less tenuous.* Washington, DC: Association of American Colleges and Universities.

Number of full-time faculty members by sex, rank, and racial and ethnic group, fall 2005. (2007–2008). In *Chronicle of higher education: The 2007–08 almanac* (Vol. 54, p. 24). Retrieved January 9, 2007, from http://chronicle.com/weekly/almanac/2007/nation/0102402.htm

*Olivas, M. A. (1988). Latino faculty at the border: Increasing numbers key to more Hispanic access. *Change, 20*(3), 6–9.

*Opp, R. D., & Gosetti, P. P. (2002). Women full-time faculty of color in 2-year colleges: A trend and predictive analysis. *Community College Journal of Research and Practice, 26,* 609–627.

*Opp, R., & Smith, A. (1994). Effective strategies for enhancing minority faculty recruitment. *Community College Journal of Research and Practice, 18,* 147–163.

*Owino, A. Z. (2000). *An investigation of the hiring trends of women and minority faculty in institutions of higher learning.* Unpublished doctoral dissertation, Pennsylvania State University, State College.

*Padilla, A. M. (1994). Ethnic minority scholars, research, and mentoring: Current and future issues. *Educational Researcher, 23*(4), 24–27.

*Padilla, R. V., & Chávez Chavez, R. (1995). *The leaning ivory tower: Latino professors in American universities.* Albany: State University of New York Press.

Patterson, B. L., Thorne, S. E., Canam, C., & Jillings, C. (2001). *Meta-study of qualitative health research: A practical guide to meta-analysis and meta-synthesis.* Thousand Oaks, CA: Sage.

*Peoples, III, R. (2004). *Recruitment of minority faculty: A comparison of attitudes, beliefs, perceptions, commitments, and strategies of Texas administrators in selected community colleges.* Unpublished doctoral dissertation, Baylor University.

*Pepion, K. (1993). *Ideologies of excellence: Issues in the evaluation, promotion, and tenure of minority faculty.* Unpublished doctoral dissertation, University of Arizona.

*Pérez, E. T. (2001). *Negotiation tenure and promotion: An examination of legitimate scholarship productions, academic ambassadors and institutional dislocation of Latina/o professors in the midwest.* Unpublished doctoral dissertation. University of Nebraska.

*Perna, L. W. (2003). The status of women and minorities among community college faculty. *Research in Higher Education, 44,* 205–240.

*Perna, L., Gerald, D., Baum, E ., & Milem, J. (2007). The status of equity for Black faculty and administrators in public higher education in the south. *Research in Higher Education, 48,* 193–228.

*Peterson-Hickey, M. M. (1998). *American Indian faculty experiences: Culture as a challenge and source of strength.* Unpublished doctoral dissertation, University of Minnesota, Twin Cities Campus.

*Piercy, F., Giddings, V., Allen, K., Dixon, B., Meszaros, P., & Joest, K. (2005). Improving campus climate to support faculty diversity and retention: A pilot program for new faculty. *Innovative Higher Education, 30*(1), 53–66.

*Pineda, A. M. (1998). The place of Hispanic theology in a theological curriculum. In P. Casarella & R. Gómez (Eds.), *El cuerpo de Cristo: The Hispanic presence in the U.S. Catholic Church* (pp. 134–154). New York: Crossroads.

*Plata, M. (1996). Retaining ethnic minority faculty at institutions of higher education. *Journal of Instructional Psychology, 23,* 221–227

*Pollard, D. S. (2006). Women of color and research. In D. S. Pollard & O. M. Welch (Eds.), *From center to margins: The importance of self-definition in research* (pp. 7–20). Albany: State University of New York Press.

*Ponjuan, L. (2005). *Understanding the work lives of faculty of color: Job satisfaction, perception of climate, and intention to leave.* Unpublished doctoral dissertation, University of Michigan.

*Porter, S. R. (2007). A closer look at faculty service: What affects participation on committees? *Journal of Higher Education, 78,* 523–541.

*Price, E. G., Gozu, A., Kern, D. E., Power, N. R., Wand, G. S., Golden, S., & Cooper, L. A. (2005). The role of cultural diversity climate in recruitment, promotion, and retention of faculty in academic medicine. *Journal of General Internal Medicine, 20,* 565–571.

*Pura, R. L. (1993). *An analysis of the minority faculty recruitment strategies at a community college in an urban environment: A case study.* Unpublished doctoral dissertation, University of Texas at Austin.

*Rai, K. B., & Critzer, J. W. (2000). *Affirmative action and the university: Race, ethnicity, and gender in higher education employment.* Lincoln: University of Nebraska Press.

*Rains, F. V. (1995). *Views from within: Women faculty of color in a research university.* Unpublished doctoral dissertation, Indiana University Bloomington.

*Rendón, L. (1996). From the barrio to the academy: Revelations of a Mexican American "scholarship girl." In C. S. V. Turner, M. Garcia, A. Nora, & L. I. Rendón (Eds.), *Racial & ethnic diversity in higher education* (pp. 281–287). Boston: Pearson.

*Rendón, L. I. (2000). Academics of the heart: Maintaining body, soul, and spirit. In M. Garcia (Ed.), *Succeeding in an academic career: A guide for faculty of color* (pp. 141–154). Westport, CT: Greenwood Press.

*Renzulli, L. A., Grant, L., & Kathuria, S. (2006). Race, gender, and the wage gap: Comparing faculty salaries in predominantly White and historically Black colleges and universities. *Gender and Society, 20,* 491–510.

*Reyes, X. A. (2005). Dissonance in the academy: Reflections of a Latina professor. *Latino Studies, 3,* 274–279.

*Reyes, X. A., & Ríos, D. I. (2005). Dialoguing the Latina experiences in higher education. *Journal of Hispanic Higher Education, 4,* 377–391

*Saavedra, D. E., & Saavedra, M. L. (2007). Women of color teaching students of color: Creating an effective classroom climate through caring, challenging, and consulting. *New Directions for Teaching and Learning, 110,* 73–83.

*Sadao, K. C. (2003). Living in two worlds: Success and the bicultural faculty of color. *Review of Higher Education, 26,* 397–418.

*Sámano, M. L. (2007). *Respecting one's abilities, or (post) colonial tokenism?: Narrative testimonios of faculty of color working in predominantly White community colleges.* Unpublished doctoral dissertation, Oregon State University. Retrieved January 6, 2008, from http://ir.library.oregonstate.edu/dspace/bitstream/l957/5011/1/Samano_Dissertation.pdf

*Sampaio, A. (2006). Women of color teaching political science: Examining the intersections of race, gender, and course material in the classroom. *Political Science and Politics, 39,* 917–922.

*Sánchez, R. M. (2007). *Best practices for recruiting and hiring a diverse workforce: Appendix d-diversity and position descriptions.* Pullman, WA: Washington State University, Center for Human Rights. Retrieved January 8, 2008, from http://www.chr.wsu.edu/Content/Documents/chr/best%20practices%20booklet%209–07%20(2)pdf

Section II: Appointment and promotion. (2002). In University of California academic personnel manual (pp. APM 200–APM 420). Oakland: University of California, Human Resources. Retrieved January 8, 2008, from http://www.ucop.edu/acadadv/acadpers/apm/apm-210.pdf

*Segovia, F. F. (1994). Theological education and scholarship as struggle: The life of racial/ethnic minorities in the profession. *Journal of Hispanic/Latino Theology, 2*(2), 5–25.

*Segura, D. A. (2003). Navigating between two worlds: The labyrinth of Chicana intellectual production in the academy. *Journal of Black Studies, 34*, 28–51.

*Skachkova, P. (2007). Academic careers of immigrant women professors in the U.S. *Higher Education, 53*, 697–738.

*Slater, R. B. (1999). The first Black faculty members at the nation's highest-ranked universities. *Journal of Blacks in Higher Education, 22*, 97–106.

*Smith, D. G. (2000). How to diversify the faculty. *Academe, 86*(5), 48–52. Retrieved January 6, 2008, from http://www.aaup.org/AAUP/pubsres/ academe/2000/SO/Feat/smit.htm?PF=l

*Smith, D. G., Turner, C. S. V., Osefi-Kofi, N., & Richards, S. (2004). Interrupting the usual: Successful strategies for hiring diverse faculty. *Journal of Higher Education, 75*, 133–160.

*Smith, D. G., Wolf, L. E., & Busenberg, B. E. (1996). *Achieving faculty diversity: Debunking the myths.* Washington, DC: Association of American Colleges & Universities.

*Smith, E. (1992). *A comparative study of occupation stress in African American and White university faculty.* Lewiston, NY: Edwin Mellen Press.

*Smith, G., & Anderson, K. J. (2005). Students' ratings of professors: The teaching style contingency for Latino/a professors. *Journal of Latinos and Education, 4*, 115–136.

*Smith, J. W., & Calasanti, T. (2005). The influences of gender, race and ethnicity on workplace experiences of institutional and social isolation: An exploratory study of university faculty. *Sociological Spectrum, 25*, 307–334.

*Smith, P. A., & Shoho, A. R. (2007). Higher education trust, rank and race: A conceptual and empirical analysis. *Innovative Higher Education, 32*, 125–138.

*Smith, P. W., Altbach, P. G., & Lomotey, K. (Eds.). (2002). *The racial crisis in American higher education: Continuing challenges for the twenty-first century.* Albany: State University of New York Press.

*Soto-Greene, M. L., Sanchez, J., Churrango, J., & Salas-Lopez, D. (2005). Latino faculty development in U.S. medical schools: A Hispanic center of excellence perspective. *Journal of Hispanic Higher Education, 4*, 366–376.

*Springer, A. (2002). *How to diversify faculty: The current legal landscape.* Washington, DC: American Association of University Professors.

*Springer, A. D. (2004). Legal watch: Faculty diversity in a brave new world. *Academe, 90*(4). Retrieved January 6, 2008, from http://www.aaup.org/AAUP/pubsres/academe/2004/JA/Col/lw.htm?PF=l

*Stanley, C. A. (2006). Coloring the academic landscape: Faculty of color breaking the silence in predominantly White colleges and universities. *American Educational Research Journal, 43*, 701–736.

*Stanley, C. A. (Ed.). (2007a). *Faculty of color: Teaching in predominantly White colleges and universities.* Bolton, MA: Anker.

*Stanley, C. A. (2007b). When counter narratives meet master narratives in the journal editorial review process. *Educational Researcher, 36*(1), 14–24.

*Stanley, C. A., & Lincoln, Y. S. (2005). Cross-race faculty mentoring. *Change, 37*(2), 44–50.

*Stanley, J. M., Capers, C. F., & Berlin, L. E. (2007). Changing the face of nursing faculty: Minority faculty recruitment and retention. *Journal of Professional Nursing, 23*, 253–261

*Stein, W. (1994). The survival of American Indian faculty: Thought and action. *National Education Association Higher Education Journal, 10*, 101–114.

*Subervi, F., & Cantrell, T. H. (2007). Assessing efforts and policies related to the recruitment and retention of minority faculty at accredited and non-accredited journalism and mass communication programs. *Journalism and Mass Communication Educator, 62*(1), 27–46.

*Tack, M., & Patitu, C. L. (1992). *Faculty job satisfaction: Women and minorities in peril* (ASHE-ERIC Higher Education Report No. 4). Washington, DC: George Washington University, School of Education & Human Development.

*Takara, K. W. (2006). A view from the academic edge: One Black woman who is dancing as fast as she can. *Du Bois Review, 3*, 463–470.

*Thomas, G. D., & Hollenshead, C. (2001). Resisting from the margins: The coping strategies of Black women and other women of color faculty members at a research university. *Journal of Negro Education, 70*, 166–175.

*Thompson, C. J., & Dey, E. L. (1998). Pushed to the margins: Sources of stress for African American college and university faculty. *Journal of Higher Education, 69*, 324–345.

*Tierney, W. G., & Rhoads, R. A. (1993). *Faculty socialization as cultural process: A mirror of institutional commitment* (ASHE-ERIC Higher Education Report No. 93–6). Washington, DC: George Washington University, School of Education & Human Development.

*Tippeconnic, III, J. W., & McKinney, S. (2003). Native faculty: Scholarship and development. In M. K. P. Ah Nee-Benham & W. J. Stein (Eds.), *The renaissance of American Indian higher education: Capturing the dream* (pp. 241–256). Mahwah, NJ: Erlbaum.

*Tomlinson, L. L. (2006). *Listening to faculty of color: Diverse experiences on a predominately White campus.* Unpublished doctoral dissertation, Illinois State University.

*Toutkoushian, R. K., Bellas, M. L., & Moore, J. V. (2007). The interaction effects of gender, race, and marital status on faculty salaries. *Journal of Higher Education, 78*, 572–601.

*Townsend-Johnson, L. (2006). *African-American women faculty teaching at institutions of higher learning in the Pacific Northwest: Challenges, dilemmas, and sustainability.* Unpublished doctoral dissertation, Oregon State University.

*Tuitt, F. A., Sagaria, M. D., & Turner, C. S. V. (2007). Signals and strategies in hiring faculty of color. *Higher Education Handbook of Theory and Research, 22*, 497–535.

*Turner, C. S. V. (2000). New faces, new knowledge: As women and minorities join the faculty, they bring intellectual diversity in pedagogy and in scholarship. *Academe, 86*(5), 34–37.

*Turner, C. S. V. (2002a). *Diversifying the faculty: A guidebook for search committees* (2nd ed.). Washington, DC: Association of American Colleges & Universities.

*Turner, C. S. V. (2002b). Women of color in academe: Living with multiple marginality. *Journal of Higher Education, 73*, 74–93.

*Turner, C. S. V. (2003). Incorporation and marginalization in the academy: From border toward center for faculty of color? *Journal of Black Studies, 34*, 112–125.

Turner, C. S. V. (2006, September 29). Before starting a faculty search, take a good look at the search committee. *Chronicle of Higher Education*, pp. B32, B34.

*Turner, C. S. V., antonio, a. l., García, M., Laden, B. V., Nora, A., & Presley, C. L. (Eds.). (2002). *Racial & ethnic diversity in higher education* (2nd ed.). Boston: Pearson Custom.

*Turner, C. S. V., García, M., Nora, A., & Rendón, L. I. (Eds.). (1996). *Racial & ethnic diversity in higher education.* Needham Heights, MA: Simon & Schuster Custom.

*Turner, C. S. V., & Myers, S. L., Jr. (1997). Faculty diversity and affirmative action. In M. García (Ed.), *Affirmative action's testament of hope: Strategies for a new era in higher education* (pp. 131–148). Albany: State University of New York Press.

*Turner, C. S. V., & Myers, S. L., Jr. (2000). *Faculty of color in academe: Bittersweet success.* Boston: Allyn & Bacon.

*Turner, C. S. V., & Taylor, D. V. (2002). *Keeping our faculties: Addressing the recruitment and retention of faculty of color* (Position paper). Minneapolis: University of Minnesota, Office of the Associate Vice President for Multicultural & Academic Affairs. Retrieved January 6, 2008, from http://www.oma.umn.edu/kof/pdf/kofposition.pdf

*Turner, C. S. V., & Thompson, J. R. (1993). Socialization experiences of minority and majority women doctoral students: Implications for faculty recruitment and retention. *Review of Higher Education, 16*, 355–370.

*TuSmith, B., & Reddy, M. T. (Eds.). (2002). *Race in the college classroom: Pedagogy and politics.* Piscataway, NJ: Rutgers University Press.

Umbach, P. D. (2006). The contribution of faculty of color to undergraduate education. *Research in Higher Education, 47*, 317–345.

*Urrieta, L. Jr., & Méndez Benavídez, L. (2007). Community commitment and activist scholarship: Chicana/o professors and the practice of consciousness. *Journal of Hispanic Higher Education, 6*, 222–236.

*Valladares, S. E. (2007). *Challenges in the tenure process: The experiences of faculty of color who conduct*

social science, race-based academic work. Unpublished doctoral dissertation, University of California, Los Angeles.

*Van Ummersen, C. A. (2005). No talent left behind. *Change, 37*(6), 26–31

Vargas, L. (Ed.). (2002). *Women faculty of color in the White classroom: Narratives on the pedagogical implications of teacher diversity.* New York: Peter Lang.

*Vasquez, M. J. T., Lott, B., García-Vásquez, E., Grant, S. K., Iwamasa, G. Y., Molina, L., et al. (2006). Personal reflections: Barriers and strategies in increasing diversity in psychology. *American psychologist, 61*, 157–172.

*Waitzkin, H., Yager, J., Parker, T., & Duran, B. (2006). Mentoring partnerships for minority faculty and graduate students in mental health services research. *Academic Psychiatry, 30*, 205–217.

*Weems, R. E., Jr. (2003). The incorporation of Black faculty at predominantly White institutions: A historical and contemporary perspective. *Journal of Black Studies, 34*, 101–111.

*Wheeler, B. G. (1996). True and false: The first in a series of reports from a study of theological school faculty. *Auburn Studies.* Retrieved January 6, 2008, from http://www.auburnsem.org/study/publications_details.asp?nsectionid=2&pageid= 3&pubid=4

*Whetsel-Ribeau, P. (2007). *Retention of faculty of color as it relates to their perceptions of the academic climate at four-year predominately White public universities in Ohio.* Unpublished doctoral dissertation, Bowling Green State University.

*Williams, B. N., & Williams, S. M. (2006). Perceptions of African American male junior faculty on promotion and tenure: Implications for community building and social capital. *Teachers College Record, 108*, 287–315.

Williams. D. A,. & Wade-Golden. K. C. (2006, April 18). What is a chief diversity officer? *Inside Higher Ed.* Retrieved January 10, 2008, from http://www.insidehighered.com/workplace/2006/ 04/18/william

Williams, D. A., & Wade-Golden, K. C. (2007). *The chief diversity officer: A primer for college and university presidents.* Washington, DC: American Council on Education.

*Witt, S. L. (1990). *The pursuit of race and gender equity in American academe.* New York: Praeger.

*Wong, T. M., & Bainer, D. (1991). Ethnic-minority faculty in evangelical Christian colleges: Models in search of an identity. In D. J. Lee., A. L. Nieves., & H. L. Allen (Eds.), *Ethnic-minorities and evangelical Christian colleges* (pp. 239–258). Lanham, MD: University Press of America.

*Yager, J., Waitzkin, H., Parker, T., & Duran, B. (2007). Educating, training, and mentoring minority faculty and other trainees in mental health services research. *Academic Psychiatry, 31*, 146–151.

5

The Changing Context for Faculty Work and Workplaces

Judith M. Gappa, Ann E. Austin, and Andrea G. Trice

For almost four hundred years, higher education institutions have played a critically important role in American society. Colleges and universities prepare educated citizens, advance knowledge, and engage in service in ways that benefit individuals, communities, states, the nation, and the broader world. Ideas incubated within academe enrich our culture and help solve societal problems.

Today's institutional leaders, however, are faced with myriad challenges that only seem to grow more difficult with each passing year: for example, maintaining technological infrastructures that address both user needs and budgetary constraints; recruiting and retaining students well-matched to their institutional missions; creating environments that value student diversity; finding new sources of revenue as traditional sources of support decline; responding effectively to increasing accountability requirements; and continually enhancing the prestige and prominence of the institution. In recent years, these and other forces have been affecting American higher education institutions, challenging their traditional missions, and shifting the contours of organizational structures. The pace and extent of changes currently affecting higher education far surpass "business as usual." James Duderstadt, former president of the University of Michigan, observed that "we are entering a period in which the capacity to nourish and manage change will be one of the most important abilities of all" (2000, p. 35).

To a significant extent, it is the faculty that enables higher education institutions to meet these numerous demands and fulfill their missions. The teaching, research, creative endeavors, community involvement, professional service, and academic decision making—the work of the university or college—is carried out each day by committed faculty members. Certainly administrators provide much of the vision, leadership, and support essential to institutional success. Their work should never be undervalued. Nevertheless, it is the work of the faculty that is essential to achieving the excellence that colleges and universities envision.

Indeed, the faculty's intellectual capital, taken collectively, is the institution's foremost asset. It is also the institution's only appreciable asset (Ulrich, 1998). Other institutional assets—buildings, laboratories, classrooms, residence halls, power plants, and technology infrastructures—begin to depreciate the day they are acquired. But colleges and universities depend on their faculty members' competence and commitment to increase steadily over time to meet the institution's ever changing circumstances and goals.

Although faculty members are the primary resource for meeting today's escalating demands upon colleges and universities, these same demands are simultaneously altering the context within which they work. Today's challenges place new expectations and require new skills and abilities of faculty members. Nevertheless, many institutions have not seriously considered how support for faculty must evolve to better enable them to accomplish their work. Adding to the complexity of today's changing educational landscape, faculty members are also more diverse than ever before, as are the appointments they hold. Further, many early career faculty members seek to make their personal lives a higher priority than their senior colleagues have often done.

Taken together, these changes mean that traditional academic appointments, employment policies and practices, and supports for faculty work are no longer fully appropriate for today's faculty members and the work they undertake. For example, if faculty members working in non-tenure track appointments are to be in a position to do their best work, leaders must provide equitable working conditions and ensure these faculty members' inclusion in the campus community. If today's diverse faculty members are to satisfactorily balance their personal and professional lives, current expectations for academic careers will have to become more flexible. Likewise, as faculty members are challenged to increase their use of technology in the classroom, help generate more resources for the university, and create an academic environment that values students' diversity, many will need easy and continuous access to professional development opportunities that help them obtain the appropriate skills.

In this changing environment, developing and supporting the intellectual capital that each faculty member represents is fundamental to the ability of higher education institutions to manage change and move with strength and effectiveness into the future. For administrative leaders facing constant challenges, an energetic, diverse, and engaged faculty is their most important resource. Investment in the faculty and in the quality of the academic workplace becomes a college's or university's most critical strategic choice.

The stakes are high for institutions that choose not to make this investment. As this and later chapters point out, faculty work and workplaces have not always changed for the better, and some faculty, like their counterparts in other occupations, will leave for better circumstances. People today are not as wedded to their employers or their careers as in previous decades (Downey, March, Berkman, and Steinauer, 2001; Judy and D'Amico, 1997; Cintrón, 1999). For example, in a study focused on corporate management, Ulrich (1998) found that 50 percent of high potential managers at a global company did not think they would stay with that company long enough to retire and 90 percent personally knew someone who had voluntarily left in the past six months.

Similarly, successful faculty members make choices about where and for whom they will work. One third of respondents to the Higher Education Research Institute (HERI) survey indicated that they had considered leaving academe for another job and 28 percent had received at least one firm offer (Lindholm, Szelenyi, Hurtado, and Korn, 2005). Data regarding potential faculty members at the beginning of the academic pipeline also warrant institutional leaders' attention. Sixty-two percent of faculty in a national survey observed that their graduate students pursue academic research careers less often than in the past (Wimsatt and Trice, 2006).

How then can higher education institutions most effectively support faculty in their work and encourage commitment to the college or university? They must rethink the nature of today's academic workplace in recognition of the many and complex demands facing faculty, the shifts in faculty appointment patterns, the diversity of faculty characteristics, and the changes in societal perspectives on work. Moreover, they must also reassess and modify their current policies and practices regarding faculty work in light of the changes that have occurred. The following questions should be considered:

- What changes in faculty work, faculty characteristics, and faculty appointments, as well as in the broader societal context, require fresh perspectives on the academic workplace?
- What are the essential elements of academic work and workplaces that should be part of all faculty work, regardless of the type of appointment?
- What specific institutional policies and practices contribute to academic workplaces that support all faculty members in carrying out excellent work in service to institutional missions?

Attention to the well-being of the faculty and to the quality of the academic workplace strengthens the institution's capacity to achieve its mission and maintain its excellence, effectiveness, and health. This kind of attention enhances the quality of key outcomes, such as recruitment and retention of a diverse and highly talented faculty, increased faculty satisfaction with their work, and a higher level of faculty commitment to the organization. In sum, this kind of attention is a strategic investment in the intellectual capital of the institution.

MAJOR CHANGES AFFECTING HIGHER EDUCATION INSTITUTIONS

Contextual changes affecting higher education institutions today require the best from faculty members even as they simultaneously change the playing field, necessitating new skills and abilities in addition to the traditional talents and competencies expected of professors. Certainly, the specific impact of these forces on a particular institution is mediated by the institution's history, mission, geographical location, size, resources, and a host of other factors. Yet overall, they are having major impacts across the higher education sector and will be familiar to all institutional leaders. Of particular importance is how these forces are affecting faculty and creating an environment within which focused attention on the nature of the academic workplace becomes strategically essential.

This chapter highlights four of the most significant forces creating challenges for higher education institutions:

1. Fiscal constraints and increased competition
2. Calls for accountability and shifts in control
3. Growing enrollments and the increasing diversity of students
4. The rise of the Information Age along with expanded use of new technologies to facilitate learning

The chapter then examines the specific impacts of these four forces on faculty work and workplaces.

Fiscal Constraints and Increased Competition

Fiscal constraints and shifts in financial support for higher education form one of the most powerful pressures affecting universities and colleges today. In addition to meeting the ever-increasing costs of operating expenses and compensation packages, universities and colleges are also pressed to increase their instructional technology and overall technology infrastructure, to provide additional student services to meet the needs of more diverse student bodies, to address deferred maintenance, and to handle rising energy costs. Many higher education institutions have enriched their physical plants in recent years, as one strategy to stay competitive in response to growing student expectations for a range of amenities or expanded research endeavors. Some colleges and universities are using tuition discounting as a way to enhance their attractiveness; this strategy, however, is another pull on institutional budgets.

Although rising costs and fiscal pressures are a major challenge for private as well as public institutions, the latter are also dealing with considerable volatility in state budgets. Not only are budget allocations for higher education constrained, allocations are also unpredictable and unstable. In general, there is little expectation that state support for higher education will improve significantly if at all over the coming years, in view of the constantly rising costs of such mandated state programs as Medicare and elementary and secondary education. In a recent article, Don Boyd of the Nelson A. Rockefeller Institute of Government noted that "even if state and local governments close their current budget gaps with regular sources of revenue, instead of relying on gimmicks that provide only temporary relief, the sad conclusion is that most states will face continuing problems in financing current services and will not have sufficient resources to support real increases in spending" (Boyd, 2005, p. 1).

Federal funding, which primarily takes the form of student financial aid as well as research grants and contracts in areas deemed national priorities, also has been stagnant since the late 1970s (Breneman, Finney, and Roherty, 1997). Moreover, as public perception has shifted toward viewing individuals rather than the general society as the primary beneficiaries of higher education, financial aid has shifted from grants to loans.

These factors together contribute to a general scramble for resources by colleges and universities. As Newman, Couturier, and Scurry assert (2004, p. 4), "the search for truth" in higher education institutions "is rivaled by a search for revenues." The need for resources is fueling greater orientation toward entrepreneurialism in colleges and universities as well as increased competition and market orientation among higher education institutions. These circumstances have led some observers to assert that higher education is increasingly functioning as a commodity in a marketplace that values the knowledge and expertise that institutions compete to provide (Eckel, Couturier, and Luu, 2005; Newman, Couturier, and Scurry, 2004; Slaughter and Leslie, 1999; Slaughter and Rhoades, 2004).

Colleges and universities are responding to these fiscal pressures by using budget reductions and cost-containment strategies, striving to build their endowments, seeking to attract foundation support and private gifts, and privatizing some institutional functions, such as food services, bookstores, and remedial support for students. Under these circumstances, some institutions are urging academic departments to develop revenue-producing continuing education programs, or to seek collaborations with industry for technology development and transfer. Faculty members especially are under pressure to engage more aggressively in grant seeking.

As many institutions become more corporate in their outlook by their increasing dependence on the bottom line, the culture is changing on many campuses. Entrepreneurialism, quantifiable productivity, and efficiency are high on the list of expectations that faculty must meet. Leaders need to consider these and other potential outcomes of these shifts:

- How might a culture of increasing entrepreneurialism affect faculty members' commitment to their institutions and thus retention?
- To what extent are financial pressures creating a competitive environment that challenges a spirit of collegiality on the campus?
- Are pressures for faculty to produce revenue creating environments where those who bring in less revenue feel less respected and less equitably treated by their institutions?

CALLS FOR ACCOUNTABILITY AND SHIFTS IN CONTROL

At the same time that higher education institutions are struggling with financial constraints and increased competition for scarce resources, they also face heightened calls for accountability and responsiveness to societal needs and expectations. The public wants to see wider access; high-quality research; engagement with their surrounding communities and social and national problems; and contributions to economic development (Duderstadt, 2000; Newman, Couturier, and Scurry, 2004). Overall, however, the public appears to have less confidence and trust in higher education institutions as pillars of society than was the case a few decades ago. Criticisms are not hard to find. Employers have expressed reservations about higher education, worrying about the quality of new college graduates' preparation for the workplace. Newspaper articles and television coverage publicize high tuition, scientific misconduct, and student misbehavior. In some states, legislators have felt enough uncertainty about what is happening in public colleges and universities to deliberate over regulating faculty workloads, to institute faculty post-tenure review, to link funding directly to measurable outcomes, and to mandate periodic program reviews. As one recent example of legislative interest in regulating higher education, lawmakers in Virginia, in a broadly supported move, unanimously passed a bill requiring faculty to consider costs when selecting books for their courses (Schmidt, 2006).

The federal government is also seeking to influence the financial decisions of higher education institutions through regulatory policies pertaining to federal student financial aid and research funding. Institutions are being encouraged to refrain from tuition increases, and there are some hints that eligibility for participation in federal student aid programs could be linked to institutional decisions about tuition levels (Zusman, 2005).

Thus institutions need to pay more attention to external pressures for greater accountability and tighter control, and this need has impacted colleges and universities in several ways. At some institutions, presidential authority has increased in response to accountability and budget pressures. Simultaneously, however, decentralization has been the institutional response as some colleges and universities have chosen to push accountability down to the unit level. Strategies such as responsibility-centered budgeting provide departments and units with more autonomy, coupled with greater responsibility to engage in entrepreneurial plans to increase revenue (Zusman, 2005).

Demands for increased accountability are also changing the context in which faculty work. The following questions are worth consideration by institutional leaders:

- Do faculty members feel diminished respect for their work as tighter controls and an increased number of checks and balances become part of their daily reality?
- To what extent have faculty members experienced a loss of autonomy as, for example, requirements for quantifiable outcomes from teaching and institutional review board demands and controls have increased dramatically?

GROWING ENROLLMENTS AND INCREASING DIVERSITY OF STUDENTS

Over the past twenty-five years, total student enrollments have increased almost 50 percent, to around 17 million. Demand is expected to expand even more: the National Center for Education Statistics predicts that, by 2014, enrollments will increase another 15 percent from 2003 levels (Hussar, 2005).

In addition to general growth in the numbers of students on campus, the student body is increasingly diverse in terms of age, background, race and ethnicity, and educational expectations (Keller, 2001; Syverson, 1996). Of particular interest is the considerable growth in the number of students over the age of twenty-five; students in this cohort expect their educational experiences to be characterized by quality, convenience, low cost, relevance, and institutional responsiveness to their needs (Levine, 2000). According to the most current statistics, students twenty-five and older account for about 40 percent of undergraduate enrollments. Further, since 1980 the percentage of the student body that is composed of ethnic and racial minorities has increased, from 16 percent to more than 25 percent (Snyder and Tan, 2005).

Students and their families often view a college education as the ticket to economic success and a middle-class lifestyle. Students are looking for educational experiences that are relevant to their employment prospects, convenient to their personal commitments and life circumstances, and reasonable in cost. Nondegree programs are in demand, as are certificate programs that respond to shifts in the labor environment. Older learners with multiple responsibilities benefit from educational providers who offer extended office hours for educational services, or who provide options (for example, child care) that make pursuing education more possible. The increase in first-generation college and university students makes the availability of academic support services especially important.

Higher education institutions must have the necessary infrastructure to provide a welcoming and supportive environment and to meet the needs of this diverse student body. They must be able to create multicultural environments in which each member is valued and respected. Colleges and universities are also striving to help students enhance their international awareness and knowledge and gain facility in speaking and understanding other languages. These skills help learners prepare for work in a global economy and for participation as responsible and tolerant citizens.

As faculty members are faced with the significant challenges this diverse student body poses, institutions should consider questions such as these:

- Do faculty members across appointment types have the necessary skills to address the learning needs of first-generation students and students from diverse backgrounds?
- As students become increasingly consumer-oriented, is this adversely affecting the nature of student-faculty relationships?

THE RISE OF THE INFORMATION AGE AND THE AVAILABILITY OF NEW TECHNOLOGIES

The rapid expansion of knowledge and the pervasiveness of new technologies are two additional challenges confronting colleges and universities and their leaders. This expansion of knowledge is leading to the emergence of new areas of specialization that challenge the structure of the traditional disciplines. Simultaneously, however, the boundaries between disciplines are blurring, and new interdisciplinary fields of study are emerging. Some institutions have established cross-disciplinary units to support new developments in knowledge and the application of knowledge to societal problems. Faculty members are increasingly working in interdisciplinary contexts and participating in collaborative teams to teach or conduct research. Duderstadt (2000, p. 3) has captured the challenge and the promise confronting faculty members engaging in interdisciplinary ventures for the first time:

It has become increasingly clear that those within the academy will need to learn to tolerate more ambiguity, to take more risks. This may mean we will be less comfortable in our scholarly neighborhoods; we may have to relax the relatively stable professional selves that we have preserved for so long. Yet most will find working together much more fulfilling than working apart. Ultimately this will release incredible creativity.

Closely connected to the emergence of the Information Age is the explosion of new technologies that facilitate teaching and learning. Gumport and Chun (2005, p. 402) have suggested that advancements in technology are affecting higher education in three ways: "(1) the nature of knowledge, (2) the process of teaching and learning, and (3) the social organization of teaching and learning in higher education."

Technological developments contribute to the knowledge industry, in which faculty members become, in the words of Gumport and Chun (2005, p. 403), "knowledge consumers and knowledge producers functioning within market forces." One result is the emergence of people and policies to manage intellectual property issues that arise for faculty and for the institutions in which they work. In short, in a society that values knowledge, issues of "ownership and management of academic knowledge" (Gumport and Chun, 2005, p. 403) can affect faculty autonomy as well as academic freedom. Technological developments have also produced new research strategies that expand disciplinary inquiries while contributing to the blurring of boundaries between fields, and offer scholars new ways to interact, unbounded by time and distance.

Technological advances also affect the processes of teaching and learning. At one level, the use of technology in class and in facilitating communication simply builds on typical teacher-learner roles and relationships to make the learning process more efficient. At another level, technological innovation has had a much greater impact, bringing major changes to how learning and teaching occur. Thus, for many years, the typical learning environment involved teachers and students engaging in face-to-face classroom interactions, using books and blackboards to aid the processes of teaching and learning. But the explosion of available technologies over the past two decades has led to new ways of finding information, communicating, learning, and applying knowledge (Twigg, 2002), and even to the formation of new types of higher education institutions that specialize in online learning at any time and in any place.

These technological advances have caused faculty members to find themselves in new roles as they interact with learners and assess students' learning. Students are engaging in more individualized learning experiences, and the issues of time and location for learning are becoming more flexible (Gumport and Chun, 2005), thus requiring faculty to adjust their roles as teachers. They must learn to design and organize learning materials that can be provided via the Web. They must cultivate meaningful relationships with a diverse array of students even in virtual, computer-mediated environments, and they must be able to manage their time now that students can seek faculty interactions via computer any time of the day or night, seven days a week.

The possibilities offered by the Information Age, with its array of new technologies, seem unlimited and exciting—but the challenges, especially for faculty who use these technologies, can also be significant. The following questions are therefore worth consideration:

- To what extent does technology isolate faculty from each other even as it aids communication?
- How is technology affecting faculty members' ability to establish boundaries between their professional and personal lives?
- How can faculty members most effectively and efficiently stay current with technologies that enhance their work?

EFFECTS OF THESE MAJOR CHANGES ON FACULTY

The various factors that cause challenges for higher education institutions are also leading to significant changes in faculty careers and academic workplaces. Specific effects on faculty include:

- Changing patterns in faculty appointments
- Declines in faculty autonomy and control
- An escalating pace of work and expanding workloads
- Increasingly entrepreneurial and high-pressure environments that hinder community and institutional commitment
- A need for continuous, career-long professional development

CHANGING PATTERNS IN FACULTY APPOINTMENTS

Major changes in the nature of faculty appointments constitute one of the most significant responses by universities and colleges to the challenges posed by fiscal constraints, and by the need to stay competitive in a rapidly changing environment where flexibility, responsiveness, accountability, and cost-efficiency are key.

Changes in faculty work are situated within a general restructuring of work throughout the global economy. Handy (1994), an astute observer of societal change, has compared the emerging workplace in the global economy to the three leaves of a shamrock. One leaf contains the professional core, which is becoming a smaller proportion of the workforce. The second leaf includes freelance professionals and technicians who are self-employed and hired by organizations on an ad hoc, per-project basis. The third leaf is made up of the ever-increasing group of contingent workers who are available by the hour. In many employment sectors, the core workforce is becoming smaller as the number of contingent employees increases.

In the United States, changes in higher education have brought about a noteworthy resemblance between Handy's shamrock and the academic workplace, as Rice (2004) and Finkelstein and Schuster (2003) have highlighted. The major structural changes in faculty appointments have resulted in a tripartite system of appointments: tenure track, renewable contracts, and fixed-term or temporary. In this restructuring of academic appointments, full-time tenure-track faculty members typically follow the traditional path of the "prototypical American scholar" (Boyer, 1990) or "complete scholar" (Rice, 1996b) engaged in research, teaching, and service. Faculty with contract-renewable appointments often specialize in either teaching or research and provide flexibility to the employing institution. More and more faculty members, those who constitute the third leaf in terms of Handy's metaphor, are hired temporarily to teach specific courses.

By changing the types of faculty appointments into which talented individuals are hired, colleges and universities usually hope to gain some immediate flexibility or cost savings. But some institutions have shifted the pattern of appointment types without carefully considering the long-term impact on faculty members and the academic workplace. The shifts in faculty appointment types have created a bifurcated faculty, where those with full-time tenure-track appointments enjoy the traditional benefits of professorial work—respect, autonomy, collegiality, and opportunities for professional growth—while those who are not on the tenure track do not necessarily receive those benefits, at least not to the same extent. Furthermore, these different types of appointments cause inequities, which can undermine the sense of commitment that faculty should bring to their work. Institutions need to look carefully at the support and benefits that are in place across the various appointment types now in use. Otherwise, the intellectual capital of many faculty members may be underutilized, if they do not feel supported, respected, and thus committed to the work of the institution.

DECLINING AUTONOMY AND CONTROL FOR FACULTY

Fiscal constraints, calls for accountability, and the availability of new technologies have important implications for the nature and extent of the autonomy and control that faculty traditionally have experienced in their work. In regard to fiscal pressures, Slaughter (1993, p. 276) concludes that retrenchment in the face of budget constraints has "generally undermined faculty participation in governance and faculty authority over the direction of the curriculum." Moreover, as colleges and universities take on more entrepreneurial activities, often to attract more revenue, faculty members' autonomy and control over their work may diminish and shift toward the administrators who manage these revenue-producing activities and make important decisions about them. Furthermore, the efforts of state legislatures to hold public higher education institutions to higher levels of accountability have implications for faculty autonomy. In the context of these trends, Rhoades (1998) has suggested that faculty are losing autonomy and becoming "managed professionals" who are increasingly accountable to administrators, state legislators, governing boards, and funding agencies.

The new technologies are another major factor in faculty autonomy and control. Market forces demanding that higher education institutions be more efficient and cost-effective have caused "unbundling," or differentiation, in faculty work. The development of technology-mediated learning experiences requires an array of different skills. Traditionally, a faculty member envisions, prepares, delivers, and evaluates a course that he or she teaches. In this age of technology, however, these processes of production, distribution, and evaluation are being separated. Curriculum designers may prepare a course; technology specialists may develop the appropriate software to facilitate teaching the course online or in another technology-mediated environment; public relations specialists may market the course; a teacher may work with the students; and an evaluator may determine the effectiveness of the course, of the related technology, and of the instructor. The faculty member is still involved in helping students learn, but the course itself has become a commodity. Faculty members have traditionally believed that they "owned" their courses, but the differentiation of these aspects of teaching has diminished faculty control and ownership.

Academic freedom and autonomy have long been cherished aspects of academic work, yet the current pressures affecting higher education institutions are chipping away at faculty autonomy in subtle ways. Faculty members, regardless of their appointment types, need a sense of control and autonomy over their work, whether they have the traditional full array of teaching, research, and service responsibilities or more focused responsibility for particular parts of the academic enterprise. The creativity and energy of faculty members are enhanced when the autonomy to do their work as they think best is integral to their assignments.

ESCALATING PACE AND EXPANDING WORKLOAD

What is often called "ratcheting" is another outcome of the major factors affecting higher education institutions. External calls for greater accountability and demonstrable outcomes, institutional pressure for faculty to generate revenue, and the necessity of keeping up with the never-ending expansion of new knowledge all conspire to create seemingly endless demands and expectations of faculty members. In fact, ironically, even as the public sometimes expresses skepticism about the amount and quality of work that faculty members are perceived as doing, many faculty members themselves report that they face constant pressure to turn their attention in too many different directions, and that they find the pace of work hectic and relentless (Rice, Sorcinelli, and Austin, 2000). There does not seem to be any limit to or boundary on the amount of work for faculty to do.

Fiscal constraints lead to greater faculty workloads when support staff are reduced or course loads are increased. The prevalence of computer use adds to a sense of "information overload" and to a growing expectation among students, and often among colleagues as well, that faculty members should be available every day, around the clock. With the wide use of e-mail by both students and faculty, asking questions and sending messages at any hour is easy to do and often seems to imply an expectation for rapid response (Young, 2005). These changes in faculty workload are evident in the frequent stories published by the *Chronicle of Higher Education* about faculty members who are grappling with the pressures of work and family responsibilities, or who report that the work involved in gaining or awarding tenure in their departments continues to escalate, or who express doubt about whether the long hours of work are sufficiently balanced by intrinsic rewards to make an academic career desirable.

Many new faculty members, and graduate students aspiring to be faculty members, are expressing concern about what they perceive to be increasing expectations for higher levels of productivity. They often report feeling pulled in many directions simultaneously and wonder whether they can find workable ways to manage their personal and professional responsibilities. Finding enough time to do their work was one of the most frequently mentioned sources of stress among early-career faculty in a range of institutional types (Rice, Sorcinelli, and Austin, 2000). Some graduate students and new faculty, as they observe the stress and long hours that characterize the work lives of their senior colleagues, express uncertainty about wanting to continue pursuing their academic careers. One faculty member echoed the comments of many other respondents: "The main issue on everyone's mind is maintaining equilibrium" (Rice, Sorcinelli, and Austin, 2000, p. 17).

Finally, public calls for accountability and state oversight have led to numerous reporting requirements that involve faculty as well as administrators. Faculty members must account for how they spend their time and must justify their teaching, research, and community engagements with documented evidence of outcomes. They must prepare annual public reports enumerating the products of their work, often for distribution to a public audience. They must be able to document students' achievement and learning outcomes or explain their research in language that is accessible and interesting to the general public. Such accountability requirements take valuable faculty time.

As colleges and universities seek to recruit and retain excellent and diverse faculty members, provisions for flexibility in how faculty construct academic career paths and organize their personal and professional commitments are likely to be key ingredients of an attractive workplace. In the face of demanding workloads, faculty members—men and women alike—can work most effectively when they have the flexibility to organize their work in ways that enable them also to manage the responsibilities of their personal lives.

POTENTIAL LOSS OF THE SENSE OF AN ACADEMIC COMMUNITY

Taken together, the array of factors affecting higher education institutions—fiscal constraints, calls for greater accountability, the increasing prevalence of new technologies to facilitate teaching and research, and a diverse student body and faculty—seem, to many, to be changing the nature of the academic community. More specifically, the ratcheting of the workload experienced by many faculty members diminishes time available for casual and serendipitous collegial interaction. The commitment of many faculty members, both male and female, to handle significant personal as well as professional responsibilities means that time is at a premium for virtually everyone. The unbundling of aspects of faculty work separates faculty into specific groups by function so that fewer people see the whole picture in regard to the institution's overall mission. Some faculty members are segregated from others by institutions' failure to fully welcome and integrate non-tenure-track faculty into the intellectual life of their departments or their academic institutions. Today's faculty members' diverse backgrounds can also make the formation of strong relationships more challenging. A vibrant sense of academic community requires opportunities and occasions for faculty members to interact—and time to do so. All these trends undermine those necessary conditions.

Early-career faculty, like doctoral students planning to pursue academic careers (Austin, 2002), are especially concerned about the nature of the academic community. When early-career faculty discuss what they value and look forward to experiencing in their careers, they often mention the hope of participating in a "culture of collegiality" (Austin, 2003; Boice, 1992; Finkelstein, 1984; Rice, Sorcinelli, and Austin, 2000; Sorcinelli, 1988; Tierney and Bensimon, 1996; Whitt, 1991). Yet early-career faculty, as they begin to experience their careers, often express surprise and disappointment that their experiences do not match their hopes and expectations (Rice, Sorcinelli, and Austin, 2000).

A strong academic community that values and includes all faculty members contributes to the intellectual vibrancy of a college or university, supports the bonds of commitment that link faculty members to the institution, and creates a climate that enhances students' learning. When institutional leaders recognize the value of nurturing a community that includes all faculty members, regardless of their appointments, they enhance institutional health and success.

THE NEED FOR CONTINUOUS PROFESSIONAL DEVELOPMENT

In order to work creatively and effectively in a rapidly changing context, faculty must engage in continuous learning so as to constantly expand their repertoires of talents and skills. Support for faculty to engage in professional development directly strengthens the quality of their teaching, research, and outreach.

Understanding Students

A faculty member must understand the characteristics of diverse learners and have command of a repertoire of teaching skills in order to address different learning needs. A major challenge facing higher education is how to teach a greater number of people, who are diverse in their needs and goals, in a more efficient and less costly way. Faculty members must be able not only to meet the needs of many different students but to do so in ways that are efficient—for example, knowing a variety of strategies for teaching large classes effectively or interacting with students via the Internet.

Using Technology

New technologies present exciting opportunities for responding to students' needs, enhancing learning environments, and enriching research activities. But new technologies also require faculty to learn to think and work in new ways and to stay current with new technological developments. The World Wide Web has transformed the ways in which people interact with information, requiring adeptness at navigating myriad paths to pursue information, at developing judgments about the relative value of information, and at formulating syntheses of meaning even while knowledge changes and expands (Brown, 2002). Online teaching also involves skills additional to and different from those used in face-to-face teaching. In distance learning, for example, faculty members may teach groups of students whom they never meet in person. Through the use of computers, they have the option to incorporate real-time conversations with experts on relevant topics into their class sessions. Many faculty find it useful to know how to use instructional platforms such as Blackboard or WebCT to facilitate student-faculty interaction, ensure that students have ready access to learning materials, and monitor students' progress.

Engaging in Entrepreneurial Activity

Many universities and colleges are urging their faculty to pursue entrepreneurial opportunities—for example, expanded extension services, continuing education, patents, new programs and certificates, or new options for distance learning—that attract new revenues and constituents. But raising funds and engaging the public in new ways are activities that require skills and knowledge that not all faculty members possess. Faculty need to learn how to write successful grant proposals to obtain support for new programs, how to interact with funding agencies, and how to present their ideas in ways that convince a public outside higher education.

Increased Collaboration and Interdisciplinarity

The rapid expansion of knowledge is resulting in greater knowledge specialization and, simultaneously, in an increase in interdisciplinary work. New units are appearing on many campuses to facilitate cross-disciplinary work addressing complex problems. Such cross-disciplinary work often involves new collaborations among scholars as well as new theoretical developments and research strategies.

Although the expansion of knowledge has created greater specialization and more fragmentation of knowledge (Rice, 2004), it also, somewhat paradoxically, requires faculty members to join interdisciplinary conversations, teams, or units, to learn to think in new ways, to make new connections, and to develop new skills.

Faculty members accustomed to individual autonomy and disciplinary specialization find that they must engage in decision making with others who often, at least metaphorically, speak a different language. Such collaborations raise many questions for faculty members. For example, what are the rules of ownership of intellectual work? How does decision making occur when a number of people are involved? These questions require faculty members to sort through the values and practices that most appropriately guide academic work under new collaborative conditions.

CONCLUDING THOUGHTS

This chapter has highlighted four major external factors that create opportunities and challenges for higher education institutions: fiscal constraints and increased competition, calls for accountability, the increasing diversity of students, and the rise of the Information Age along with its new technologies. These external factors challenge today's faculty members and the traditions of academic work and life. They have led to

- Proliferation of faculty appointments off the tenure track
- Shifts in faculty members' control over and autonomy in their work
- Continuously expanding workloads
- Increasing fragmentation of faculty work, which undermines a sense of academic community
- Continuous need for faculty to engage in professional growth

Because faculty represent the institution's greatest asset, institutional leaders must pay attention to faculty work and to the quality of academic workplaces, placing these concerns among the highest institutional priorities. As we pointed out at the beginning of this chapter, the intellectual capital and commitment that faculty bring to their colleges and universities are essential to the excellence and health of their institutions. Finding ways to maximize the intellectual capital represented by the faculty—in other words, investing in the faculty—enhances the health and success of a college or university. To thrive, colleges and universities must face this strategic imperative and realign their institutional support of faculty members in ways that more fully address today's institutional missions as well as faculty members' goals and priorities.

REFERENCES

Austin, A. E. (2002). Preparing the next generation of faculty: Graduate education as socialization to the academic career. *The Journal of Higher Education, 73*(2), 94–122.

Austin, A. E. (2003). Creating a bridge to the future: Preparing new faculty to face changing expectations in a shifting content. *Review of Higher Education, 26*(2), 119–144.

Boice, R. (1992). *The new faculty member: Supporting and fostering professional development.* San Francisco: Jossey-Bass.

Boyd, D. (2005, June). *State fiscal outlook from 2005 to 2013: Implications for higher education.* Boulder, CO: National Center for Higher Education Management Systems, 2005. Retrieved March 6, 2005, from www.higheredinfo.org/analyses/

Boyer, E. (1990). *Scholarship reconsidered: Priorities of the professoriate.* Princeton, NJ: The Carnegie Foundation for the Advancement of Teaching.

Breneman, D. W., Finney, J. E., & Roberty, B. M. (1997, April). *Shaping the future: Higher education finance in the 1990s.* San Jose, CA: California Higher Education Policy Center.

Brown, J. S. (2002, March/April). Growing up digital: How the web changes work, education, and the way we learn. *Change*, pp. 11–20.

Cintrón, L. (1999). *Professional pathways: Examining work, family and community in the biotechnology industry: An executive summary.* Retrieved July 5, 2006, from http://m.radcliffe.edu/research/pubpol/ProfessionalPathways.pdf

Downey, D., March, T., Berkman, A., & Steinauer, J. M. (2001). The keys to retention [Electronic version]. *Incentive, 175*(10), 117–118.

Duderstadt, J. J. (2000). *A university for the 21st century.* Ann Arbor: University of Michigan Press.

Eckel, P. D., Couturier, L., & Luu, D. T. (2005). *Peering around the bend: The leadership challenges of privatization, accountability, and market-based state policy.* Washington, DC: American Council on Education.

Finkelstein, M. J. (1984). *The American academic profession.* Columbus: The Ohio State University Press.

Finkelstein, M. J., Liu, M., & Schuster, J. H. (2003, November). *The career trajectories of current part-time faculty: Mobility across employment and appointment statuses.* Paper presented at the annual meeting of the Association for the Study of Higher Education, Portland, OR.

Finkelstein, M. J., & Schuster, J. H. (2001). Assessing the silent revolution: How changing demographics are reshaping the academic profession. *AAHE Bulletin, 54*(2), 3–7.

Gumport, P. J., & Chun, M. (2005). Technology and higher education: Opportunities and challenges for the new era. In P. G. Altbach, R. O. Berdahl, & P. J. Gumport (Eds.), *American higher education in the twenty-first century: Social, political, and economic challenge* (2nd ed., pp. 393–424). Baltimore: Johns Hopkins University Press.

Handy, C. (1994). *The age of unreason.* Boston: Harvard Business School Press.

Hussar, W. J. (2005). *Projections of education statistics to 2014* (NCES 2005–074). U.S. Department of Education, National Center for Education Statistics. Washington, DC: U.S. Government Printing Office.

Judy, R. W., & D'Amico, C. (1997). *Workforce 2020: Work and workers in the 21st century.* Indianapolis, IN: Hudson Institute.

Keller, G. (2001, Spring). The new demographics of higher education. *Review of Higher Education, 24*(3), 219–235.

Levine, A. (2000). *Higher education at a crossroads.* Earl Pullias Lecture in Higher Education. Los Angeles: Center for Higher Education Policy Analysis, Rossier School of Education, University of Southern California.

Lindholm, J. A., Szelenyi, K., Hurtado, S., & Korn, W. S. (2005). *The American college teacher: National norms for the 2004–2005 HERI faculty survey.* Los Angeles: Higher Education Research Institute, UCLA.

Newman, F., Couturier, L., & Scurry, J. (2004). *The future of higher education: Rhetoric, reality, and the risks of the market.* San Francisco: Jossey-Bass.

Rhoades, G. (1998). *Managed professionals: Unionized faculty and restructuring academic labor.* Albany: State University of New York Press.

Rice, R. E. (1996). Making a place for the new American scholar. *New Pathways Working Paper Series, no. 1.* Washington, DC: American Association for Higher Education.

Rice, R E. (2004). The future of the American faculty: An interview with Martin J. Finkelstein and Jack H. Schuster. *Change, 36*(2), 26–35.

Rice, R. E., Sorcinelli, M. D., & Austin, A. E. (2000). Heeding new voices: Academic careers for a new generation. *New Pathways Working Paper Series, no. 7.* Washington, DC: American Association for Higher Education.

Schmidt, P. (2006, March 17). In the states. *Chronicle of Higher Education*, p. A34.

Slaughter, S. (1993). Retrenchment in the 1980s: The politics of prestige and gender. *Journal of Higher Education, 64,* 250–282.

Slaughter, S., & Leslie, L. L. (1999). *Academic capitalism: Politics, policies, and the entrepreneurial university.* Baltimore, MD: Johns Hopkins University Press.

Slaughter, S., & Rhoades, G. (2004). *Academic capitalism and the new economy: Markets, state, and higher education.* Baltimore: Johns Hopkins University Press.

Snyder, T. D., & Tan, A G. (2005). *Digest of education statistics, 2004* (NCES 2006005). U.S. Department of Education, National Center for Education Statistics. Washington, DC: U.S. Government Printing Office.

Syverson, P. (October, 1996). The new American graduate student: Challenge or opportunity? *CGS Communicator, 29*(8), 7–11.

Tierney, W. G., & Bensimon, E. M. (1996). *Promotion and tenure: Community and socialization in academe.* Albany: State University of New York Press.

Twigg, C. (2002). The impact of the changing economy on four-year institutions of higher education: The importance of the Internet. In C. Twigg (Ed.), *The knowledge economy and postsecondary education: Report of a workshop.* Washington, DC: National Academy Press.

Ulrich, D. (1998, Winter). Intellectual capital = competence X commitment. *Sloan Management Review, 39*(2), 15–26.

Whitt, E. (1991). Hit the ground running: Experiences of new faculty in a school of education. *The Review of Higher Education, 14*(2), 177–197.

Wimsatt, L. A., & Trice, A. G. (2006). *A profile of grant administration burden among faculty within the federal demonstration partnership: A report of the faculty advisory committee of the Federal Demonstration Partnership.* Washington, DC: The National Academy of Sciences.

Young, J. (2005, April 12). Knowing when to log off: Wired campuses may be causing "information overload." *Chronicle of Higher Education.*

Zusman, A. (2005). Challenges facing higher education in the twenty-first century. In P. G. Altbach, R. O. Berdahl, & P. J. Gumport (Eds.), *American higher education in the twenty-first century: Social, political, and economic challenge* (2nd ed., pp. 115–160). Baltimore: Johns Hopkins University Press.

II

CURRICULUM, TEACHING
AND LEARNING

Clifton F. Conrad, Section Editor

Since the founding of Harvard College in 1636 through the first decade of this century, there has been vigorous debate over the purposes of higher education, and in turn, myriad ideas for giving expression to alternative visions. Reflection on college and university curricula, teaching, and learning has long been linked to that ongoing debate. The five chapters in this section highlight these issues across a variety of time periods and postsecondary institutional contexts. Over the last few decades, there have emerged a number of domains of inquiry into curriculum, teaching, and learning. Three are addressed in this introduction: curriculum design, curriculum content, and teaching and learning.

CURRICULUM DESIGN

With respect to the first domain, Lisa R. Lattuca and Joan S. Stark present their academic plan in Chapter 6, which is arguably the most compelling curriculum design model in the contemporary literature. In a nutshell, it incorporates the complex and interactive external and internal forces shaping curricula, while simultaneously conceptualizing key considerations in developing and assessing programs of study. It is worth noting that curriculum design and planning has received intermittent attention in the higher education literature over the past few decades. Among the models advanced for purposes of helping facilitate the design of programs of study are Dressel's (1971) conceptualization of curriculum, Mayhew and Ford's (1971) curriculum model, Conrad's (1978) framework for curriculum planning, Conrad and Pratt's (1983) model of curricular decision making, and Haworth and Conrad's (1997) engagement theory of academic program quality.

Lattuca and Stark also illuminate longstanding debates regarding the curriculum and elaborate on forces that have shaped these discussions. They trace the multiple educational purposes of higher learning institutions over the last several centuries—from utilitarian and liberal arts missions to research missions, and most recently, a more or less bewildering diversity of institutional missions. In so doing, they describe the external and internal influences on postsecondary education, as well as key issues that have long been at the epicenter of discourse on curriculum. Such issues include: general education versus specialized education; increasing access to higher learning along with a heightened sense of responsibility to increasingly diverse student bodies;

prescribed curriculum versus curricular choice; the content of curriculum; curriculum assessment and accountability; and student preparedness. Echoing historian Frederick Rudolph's claim that the college curriculum has long been a battleground for society, Lattuca and Stark argue that college and university curricula simultaneously reflect societal pressures and shape them.

CURRICULUM CONTENT

A second domain of inquiry has been the content of curriculum, from the undergraduate through the graduate level, but especially with respect to undergraduate education. In Chapter 7, Steven Brint traces the rise of the "practical arts" (occupational and professional programs) at the expense of the classical liberal arts and sciences core over the past four decades. Brint ultimately raises the question of whether the practical arts have wholly replaced the liberal arts and sciences at most institutions of higher learning. He suggests that the arts and sciences (especially the natural sciences) have thus far been largely able to maintain their position at leading research universities.

Brint makes a compelling case that occupational and professional fields have moved closer to the core not least by modeling themselves after the arts and sciences. To that end, they have developed their own vocabularies as well as conceptual and theoretical scaffolding that often mirrors the liberal arts and sciences. And what Brint calls the "ethos of utilitarianism" among students has also contributed to the rise of the practical arts. In light of this trend away from the arts and sciences, Brint explores some initiatives taken from disciplines and fields of study normally housed in the liberal arts and sciences. Among them, he discusses the "migration" of faculty (and sometimes entire fields) in the direction of professional preparation and the rapid growth of interdisciplinary fields in the liberal arts and sciences.

In part anchored in the putative decline of the liberal arts and sciences, the "canon wars" in higher education over the past two decades have focused on the content of the liberal arts and sciences. On the one hand have been the Western traditionalists—from Allen Bloom to Lynn Cheney to Denish D'Souza—who have passionately defended the importance of placing Western Civilization at the core of undergraduate education. On the other hand have been the multiculturalists who have pushed for reform of the arts and sciences—reforms aimed at incorporating the diverse perspectives of a wide range of racial and ethnic groups and women who have seldom been incorporated into the curriculum. Nested in this continuing debate, James A. Banks provides a comprehensive portrait in Chapter 8 of the tension between the traditional canon versus multiculturalism. In a nutshell, he argues that the debate between the Western traditionalists and the multiculturalists is centered around their contrasting perspectives regarding the nature of knowledge as well as their divergent political and social interests.

Arguing that the debate has been far too polarizing, Banks conjoins the canon debate by advancing and supporting the claims of both sides and, in turn, suggests that each kind of knowledge should be taught in K-16 education. To that end, he identifies five types of knowledge: personal/cultural knowledge, popular knowledge, mainstream academic knowledge, transformative academic knowledge, and school knowledge. He argues that transformative academic knowledge is curriculum content that challenges mainstream academic knowledge and, in so doing, significantly expands the historical and literary canon. With respect to multicultural education, Banks goes on to explore major implications of such education for teaching and learning. He emphasizes that a multicultural curriculum must ultimately find expression not only in curriculum content but in our teaching as well. In particular, multicultural teaching should be aimed at helping students understand how knowledge is to be constructed. For purposes of illustration, he draws on a unit on the Westward Movement in the United States to show how teachers can draw on their own experiences as well as students' personal and cultural knowledge.

TEACHING AND LEARNING

Especially since the early 1990s, a third major domain of inquiry has evolved in the higher education literature. For reasons that continue to baffle many of us who study colleges and universities, teaching has long received attention in the literature but *learning* has remained on the periphery. Within the last two decades, however, "student learning" has been placed at the forefront of inquiry for many scholars in the field of higher education. In no small measure, this emphasis has been fueled by Ernest Boyer's (1990) foundational piece for the movement termed the Scholarship of Teaching and Learning (SoTL) and an article by Barr and Tagg (1995) that argued for a new paradigm for undergraduate education: from teaching to learning.

Anchored in this domain of scholarship, Terry O'Banion argues on behalf of a "Learning Revolution" that is spreading throughout education. In Chapter 9, this author argues for a new architecture for the learning college that overhauls the traditional architecture of community colleges. Drawing on the 12 Vanguard Learning Colleges in the League for Innovation's Learning College Project, O'Banion suggests five dimensions of a new architecture that include changes with respect to departmental structure, workload formulas, grading, late registration, and several time-bound artifacts that often undermine student learning in the community college context. In the end, he suggests that these examples are but the "tip of the iceberg" with respect to the challenges that community colleges face in crafting a new architecture that places learning (along with teaching) at the center of institutional priorities.

The final chapter in this section is anchored in a straightforward premise: the scholarship on teaching and the scholarship on learning are often represented in two overlapping but nonetheless separate domains. To illustrate, in their widely-cited article, Barr and Tagg (1995) advance a dualism ("from teaching to learning") that arguably fails to connect the two; and the phrase "teaching and learning" does not link teaching *with* learning. The teaching-for-learning model advanced by Clifton F. Conrad, Jason Johnson, and Divya Malik Gupta in Chapter 10 is an inquiry-based framework aimed at helping faculty systematically connect their teaching with student learning. In brief, the model comprises six components that range from identifying course-specific challenges to identifying and testing teaching practices responsive to these challenges that are consonant with the overarching aim of cultivating student learning.

CONCLUSION

For far too long, scholarship on curriculum, teaching, and learning has been placed on the periphery of inquiry in the field of higher education. This is surprising given that all postsecondary institutions in America—community colleges, four-year institutions, and graduate schools—have curricula, faculty who teach, and students who presumably enroll to learn. As the three domains of inquiry reviewed here suggest, scholarship in this field of study is very much needed—not least during a time when the entrepreneurial culture throughout much of higher education invites serious reflection on policies and practices for maintaining loyalty to higher learning.

REFERENCES

Barr, R. B., & Tagg, J. (1995). From teaching to learning: A new paradigm for undergraduate education. *Change, 27*(6), 13–25.

Boyer, E. (1990). *Scholarship Reconsidered: Priorities of the Professoriate*. Princeton, New Jersey: The Foundation for the Advancement of Teaching.

Conrad, C. F. (1978). *The Undergraduate Curriculum: A Guide to Innovation and Reform*. Boulder, Colorado: Westview Press.

Conrad, C. F., & Pratt, A. M. (1983). Making decisions about the curriculum: From metaphor to model. *The Journal of Higher Education, 54*(1), 16–30.

Dressel, P. L. (1971). *College and University Curriculum* (2nd ed.). Berkley, California: McCutchan.

Haworth, J. G., & Conrad, C. F. (1997). *Emblems of Quality: Developing and Sustaining High-Quality Academic Programs*. Boston, Massachusetts: Allyn and Bacon.

Mayhew, L. B., & Ford, J. (1971). *Changing the Curriculum*. San Francisco, California: Jossey-Bass.

6

External Influences on Curriculum

Sociocultural Context

Lisa R. Lattuca and Joan S. Stark

American higher education has experienced a long-term trend toward diversification of institutions, educational missions, students, and academic programs, accompanied by recurring debates about key curricular issues. These debates, spurred by influences both internal and external to colleges and universities, have resulted in significant changes in the educational environment during the relatively short history of higher education in America.

Changes in the nation's economy, in the policies of state governing boards, and in the standards for regional and professional accreditation are a few examples of external influences that have altered higher education curricula. Changes in program resources or alterations in academic missions are among the organizational influences that may require faculty members to revise their academic plans. Additional internal influences stem from changes in faculty expertise or the nature of emerging topics. The academic plan concept acknowledges the complex set of influences that act upon higher education and cause adjustments in the educational environment (see Figure 6.1).

The two types of influences on postsecondary curricula that we have noted—external and internal—are not, of course, independent of each other. For example, we classify accrediting agencies as an influence external to academic programs, while we view instructors' impacts as internal influences. Yet colleges and universities voluntarily (if not enthusiastically) undergo regional and specialized accreditation, and most external examiners are faculty members; the accrediting process is thus strongly influenced by faculty expertise. Accreditation also provides a good illustration of the interaction of external and internal influences and the reciprocal nature of the influences we discuss. We focus this discussion on a single direction of influence—from society (external) to higher education (internal), rather than the reverse—but recognize that colleges shape society, just as society shapes academic plans.

Categorizing the many influences operating on academic plans simplifies discussion and maintains awareness of the varied influences. It also highlights the complexity of the sociocultural environment, reminding us that developing or analyzing academic plans, particularly in the U.S. educational environment, is not a simple task.

A general trend toward diversification of institutional missions, students, academic programs, financial support, and accountability is reflected in changes in curricular purposes, con-

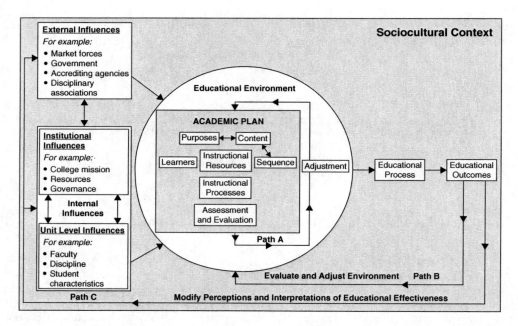

FIGURE 6.1 Academic plans in sociocultural context: external influences on educational environments

tent, and sequence, as well as in instructional process and assessment. A number of key curricular issues surface periodically, but their impact on various elements of the academic plan varies over time. Some have likened this pattern of recurring debate—which has occurred at all levels of American education—to a swinging pendulum (Cuban, 1990; Hansen & Stampen, 1993; Southern Regional Education Board, 1979). Our discussion highlights these patterns as well as variations in these themes.

To place current influences on higher education curricula into historical perspective, we have identified recurring debates about persistent issues, paying particular attention to how these debates have affected the various elements of an academic plan. We emphasize those forces that seem to have influenced the intensity of each debate, providing timelines illustrating periods of significant debate for each issue. Historical perspective helps us to recognize the relationship of current reform efforts to continuing tensions. (A timeline of U.S. curriculum history is available; see Stark & Lattuca, 1997.)

PATTERNS OF CURRICULUM DEBATE

In his classic work, *Curriculum: A History of the American Undergraduate Course of Study Since 1636*, Frederick Rudolph (1977) observed that curricular history is American history, "revealing the central purposes and driving directions of American society" (p. 24). In this chapter, we demonstrate the truth of Rudolph's claim about the impact of societal influences on higher education, focusing on five recurring debates about educational purposes, content, learners, instructional processes, and evaluation. For each of these debates, we review the prevailing influences on colleges and universities, thereby providing a thematic, rather than chronological, curricular history.

Our discussion of educational *purpose* centers on debates about whether undergraduate education should be general or vocationally oriented and whether it should transmit a common view of culture or reflect the variety of cultural backgrounds and interests of students. These debates coincide with a more general trend toward increasing diversity in educational missions and types of institutions.

Our second discussion focuses on external influences that have fostered increasing diversity of *learners*. Although difficult to document, we have identified alternating periods of relatively stronger and weaker emphasis on elitism and access and, perhaps, periodic neglect of the expanding pool of students. Debates about access must be viewed in the context of a long-term trend toward greater access and greater diversity in student enrollments.

Third, we discuss *content*, recalling how different educators have taken up the question of whether the curriculum should be prescribed, either fully or partially, for students. The proliferation of knowledge and changes in the personal characteristics and backgrounds of students have engendered considerable debate between the necessity and desirability of a common foundation of knowledge and the need to respond to social needs. This debate also involves questions of institutional mission and raises the question of the balance between general and specialized education.

Fourth, we examine changes in *instructional process*, describing a relatively few periods of modest experimentation with teaching methods and curricular arrangements at the course, program, and college level. After only modest change thus far, the pace of change in instructional process appears to be escalating as a number of forces—calls for accountability, improvements in educational technologies, funding from government agencies, and further diversification in educational providers (for example, for-profit companies)—result in educational innovations.

Finally, we discuss the relationship of these four debates to periods of emphasis on *evaluation*. Calls for greater accountability have been raised many times in the past, often with the intention of changing the direction or pace of change. Nonetheless, evaluation and adjustment efforts in higher education remain unsystematic.

External influences such as economic trends (for example, recessions and depressions), technological developments (the industrial and information revolutions), globalization, and international or domestic conflicts have produced the most significant undulations in the intensity of these five debates. Relatively speaking, internal influences have spurred less dramatic changes. Meanwhile, the tendency toward greater diversity in curricula continues.

EVOLVING EDUCATIONAL PURPOSES

U.S. college and university curricula gradually changed from educational programs designed with a common purpose in the colonial period—to prepare a select group of young men for the ministry or gentlemanly status—to programs that must prepare students of different ages, genders, social classes, races, and ethnicities for work and life. Changing social needs initially inspired debates about educational purpose and often produced changes in college curricula. Over time these recurring debates also reflected the growing influence of students' diverse backgrounds, interests, and pre-college preparation, as well as differences in educators' judgments about the preservation, transmission, creation, and/or construction of knowledge.

Debates over educational purpose resulted in the evolution of distinctly different types of postsecondary institutions and in the development of institutions with multiple missions. Discussions focusing on the merits of general and specialized education can best be begun by considering three distinct prototypical college missions that had emerged by the end of the 19th century.

Utilitarian Mission

The utilitarian mission was based on the belief that colleges should train citizens to participate in the nation's economic and commercial life. The Morrill Land-Grant Act of 1862 provided the framework for large numbers of state institutions that espoused this mission and stressed the study of agriculture and engineering. By the 1920s, teacher education and other occupational fields such as social work and nursing grew in popularity, and private colleges as well as public ones offered career-oriented programs in business and science. Many state colleges and universities emphasized a mission of practical education and social improvement through economic growth and upward mobility, as they attempted to meet the practical educational needs of their regional constituencies. Despite the early introduction of Harvard Law School in 1817, most colleges and universities did not house professional schools (as we know them today) until early in the 20th century when the prestigious professions of medicine, dentistry, and law joined research universities.

Research Mission

The research university espoused another type of mission, primarily dedicated to the production of new knowledge. Adapted from German universities, this model developed in the mid- to late-1800s as Americans educated abroad returned to the United States to found new institutions. In its purest form, the research mission focused on graduate education, but financial concerns and faculty sentiment convinced universities in the United States to include both graduate and undergraduate programs rather than devote themselves exclusively to research. Research universities tended to attract large numbers of undergraduates due to institutional prestige and substantial resources.

Liberal Arts Mission

The liberal arts mission evolved from earlier forms of classical education that stressed the study of classical languages and literatures. The liberal arts mission, which became prominent just before the turn of the 20th century, emphasized the great artistic, literary, and scientific works of humankind. This mission, and the resulting curriculum, stressed the preservation of knowledge and the improvement of students' abilities to appreciate knowledge and think effectively. These abilities, in turn, were believed to transfer to other tasks and settings, allowing graduates to serve society as productive citizens.

Increasing Diversity of Missions

With the expansion of knowledge, faculty members became increasingly interested in advancing new specializations and less concerned with defending the classical course of study. In the early 1800s, the first academic departments emerged to organize curricula, followed by disciplinary associations that motivated their members to stay on the forefront of knowledge. By the late 1800s, undergraduates, too, could specialize in most colleges, complementing their broad education with a concentration in a single liberal arts field. The last half of the 19th century saw an increase in the number of subjects taught and the emergence of new fields like science and psychology As social and economic needs multiplied and deepened, majors in these new subjects began to focus students' academic programs more closely on future careers. The major field, created in the late 1800s partly to stem the rising tide of student choice, is now an important component of education in all but a handful of four-year institutions.

Although the emergence of majors allowed students to specialize, after 1900 the pendulum swung back from its emphasis on professional and specialized study as faculty groups reacted to the threat of over-specialization. A period of resurgent interest in general education marked the first thirty years of the 1900s (Bell, 1966). The rise of communism and the entrance of the United States into World War I increased awareness of political ferment abroad, and discussions of ideology once again joined technical discussions in college classrooms. During the Great Depression of 1929–1932, students faced with a dismal job market majored in more general fields to enhance their career flexibility.

Mixed Missions

By the mid-1900s most colleges and universities pursued a mixture of the three prototypical missions and continue to do so today. State colleges and universities still emphasize a mission of practical education and social improvement but include elements of liberal education in their academic programs. Independent and denominational colleges (also called private college), which once focused on the classics, also responded to local influences that encouraged specialized occupational programs serving home communities and local employers. The difference between state colleges and independent colleges is often one of emphasis: whereas state colleges use liberal arts education to buttress career programs, many independent institutions add professional and pre-professional majors to supplement liberal arts programs. With less than half of their student enrollment in undergraduate programs, research universities often struggle to balance general and specialized study as different groups within the organization focus on the discovery of new knowledge in their fields of study.

The two-year junior college further diversified institutional missions when it emerged in the early 1900s. Originally designed to provide the academic foundation for students planning to transfer to four-year institutions, public and private two-year colleges soon also provided continuing education, developmental education, skill training in technical education, and community service. After 1950, private junior colleges (never a large number) began to close or merge with four-year institutions, while the number of public two-year colleges grew significantly through the 1960s. Like state colleges and universities, these "community" colleges define service to their communities as part of their mission. They often contract with local businesses to offer professional development courses tailored to their employees' specific needs and provide adult education for populations beyond the age of eligibility for secondary school services. The missions of two-year and four-year colleges overlap somewhat, and thus they compete in many areas, particularly for students who wish to specialize in occupational programs.

The postsecondary landscape also includes various types of for-profit institutions that focus heavily on career preparation. Although structurally and operationally different from traditional two- or four-year colleges, these commercial educational institutions offer associate's, bachelor's, and graduate degrees (as well as non-degree programs) that are tailored to the needs of particular segments of the education market (for example, part-time adult students).

For-profit institutions made their presence known in U.S. higher education in the 1960s, when "proprietary schools" with a purely occupational focus began to seek accreditation so that they might capitalize on federal financial aid programs. At that time, this sector of the higher education enterprise was composed of institutions such as schools of business or cosmetology. The for-profit universe expanded rapidly after the 1990s (Kinser, 2007). Today, for-profit institutions constitute a sizeable proportion of postsecondary institutions in the United States, but only about 40 percent are eligible for federal financial aid through Title IV of the Higher Education

Act, which provides direct funding to students via an array of grants, loans, and work-study opportunities (Tierney & Hentschke, 2007).

The Education Commission of the States identifies three types of for-profit colleges and universities (FPCUs). Enterprise colleges are local, privately owned institutions with small, primarily undergraduate, enrollments. Supersystems are multi-campus organizations with large enrollments that are owned by publicly traded corporations. Finally, Internet institutions are virtual universities that provide online education exclusively. William Tierney and Guilbert Hentschke further distinguish among FPCUs by determining whether they offer certificates and short-term programs or degrees, but note the difficulty of developing fixed categories. Counting for-profit institutions is also complicated by the existence of corporate and virtual universities and the dynamic nature of the market, which spawns hybrid institutions (Kinser, 2007) and which promises to remain volatile for the near future (Tierney & Hentschke, 2007). Kinser (2007) recommends a multidimensional classification scheme that combines geographic scope, ownership, and the highest degree offered by an institution.

Despite variations in markets, funding sources, and structure, the three institutional missions we have discussed—research, liberal arts, and utilitarian preparation—are still broadly applicable and exist in varying proportions in different colleges. For-profit institutions that award bachelor's degrees, for example, may require that students take general education courses in communications and mathematics, even as they emphasize vocational training.

These three missions have spawned a wide variety of subjects that almost defies classification. The scope of subjects taught in two-year and four-year institutions can be grasped by reviewing the U.S. Office of Education coding system that colleges use to report their majors, courses taught, and degrees granted. This comprehensive system, the Integrated Postsecondary Education Data System (IPEDS), classifies and describes courses and programs currently offered in postsecondary schools of all types. Another method of classification, developed in the mid-1970s by the Carnegie Foundation and revised several times, originally classified the institutions themselves by degree level, selectivity and mission. The most recent revision in 2005 additionally uses degree programs, size, and location to classify nearly 4,000 U.S. colleges (Carnegie Foundation for the Advancement of Teaching, 2006).

Short-term certificate programs are also increasingly common in all kinds of institutions, although they tend to be most prominent in the for-profit sector. Tierney and Hentschke (2007) identify two kinds of certificate programs. The first type, which consists of courses added to existing diploma programs to allow students to meet the requirements set by an organization or agency, can be found in a variety of fields and types of institutions (for example, a certificate in cardiopulmonary resuscitation). Stand-alone certificate programs, which are more specialized, prepare individuals to compete for a specific job. They are increasingly common in the information technology field, where computer technicians must complete certificate programs to qualify for examinations that assess specific competencies and thus provide a gateway to employment. Such programs are not included in the IPEDS system because providers that offer information technology certifications do not participate in federal student aid and reporting systems (Adelman, 2000).

DEBATING GENERAL EDUCATION AND SPECIALIZATION

In most four-year colleges, undergraduate students include both general and specialized studies in their degree programs. Debate continues over the balance between these program components and has been intense periodically during the last two hundred years. The varying periods of emphasis on either general education or specialization are illustrated in Figure 6.2.

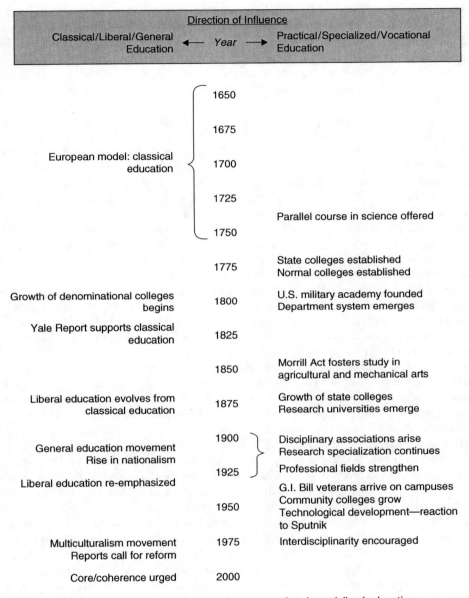

FIGURE 6.2   Periods of emphasis on general and specialized education

General Education

The sheer number of higher education institutions in the United States and the lack of a central agency that coordinates their efforts make it difficult to generalize about postsecondary curricula. The typical four-year college degree consists of 120 credits, and roughly one-third of the credits for a bachelor of arts or bachelor of science is often taken in general education courses, with the remaining two-thirds divided between a major (or specialization) and electives. The two-year college curriculum may also include a general education segment, a major specialization, and some electives, totaling about 60 credits. Thus, many students begin their studies with general education courses intended to provide any or all of the following: (a) a broad base of knowledge and skills thought to be useful to all students in and beyond college, (b) a foundation of skills and knowledge needed for further study, and/or (c) an introduction to different fields of study. But the amounts of general education required for graduation have varied over time and still vary among colleges.

Sometimes the general education a college requires is referred to as the "core curriculum" and is based on the belief that all students should have a common experience or obtain a common foundation of knowledge during college. Few colleges in the United States have an entirely prescribed general education core, but modified core curricula gain ground during the periods when institutions seek to increase the coherence of their general education programs. Various models may include a set of courses (perhaps six to eight) that are required of all students; a single course, perhaps interdisciplinary in nature, required of all; or a set of two or three courses in different disciplines or domains of knowledge that are substantively linked to one another. Most commonly, however, the general education requirements are expressed as "distribution" requirements. In a distributed core, students must fulfill requirements in specified areas but may choose among a range of courses to satisfy those requirements.

Because of the persistent debate about the balance of general and specialized study, considerable efforts have been undertaken to document actual student course patterns resulting from distribution requirements (Adelman, 1990, 1992, 1999, 2004; Ratcliff, 1992; Zemsky, 1989) and the status of curricular components such as general education (Adelman, 2004; Blackburn, Armstrong, Conrad, Didham, & McKune, 1976; Dressel & DeLisle, 1970; Locke, 1989; Ratcliff, Johnson, La Nasa, & Gaff, 2001; Toombs, Amey, & Fairweather, 1989). To summarize this research briefly: in 1967, 43 percent of the courses taken by the average college student were in general education; by 1976, general education requirements had decreased to about 33 percent of a student's program; but by 1988, general education rebounded a bit, accounting for 38 percent of the average student's program. The number of required courses in mathematics has also been documented. In 1967, one-third of all colleges required mathematics as part of general education. By 1974, only 20 percent of colleges required students to study math. The trend reversed itself significantly by 1988, when 65 percent of colleges and universities required the study of mathematics. A recent study in more than five hundred colleges suggested that mathematical requirements have increased again; 88 percent of all responding colleges indicated that they required mathematics or a quantitative reasoning course (Ratcliff, Johnson, La Nasa, & Graff, 2001). The same study indicated that more than 85 percent of institutions required general education courses in the natural and social sciences. Slightly fewer required courses in the humanities (78 percent), fine arts (71 percent), or literature, history, and philosophy (61 percent each). Fewer than half of the five hundred responding institutions reported requirements in foreign language. Despite fluctuations in general education requirements over time, English composition has remained a constant; since 1972 English composition has been the most common course taken by bachelor's degree recipients (U.S. Department of Education, 2004).

Specialization

In four-year college programs, academic specializations are typically of four types: (a) an academic major (intended either to prepare students for graduate school or employment in the same or a related field), (b) a preprofessional major, (c) an interdisciplinary major, or (d) a general education or liberal studies major.

The important concepts of a major field and the methods of inquiry to be taught are determined by the community of scholars in that field. In fields in which there is considerable consensus on key information and methods of inquiry, the undergraduate curriculum tends to be tightly structured; scholars generally agree on concepts, theories, skills, and methods of inquiry and how these should be sequenced. In those fields for which inquiry is more wide-ranging, a more loosely structured undergraduate curriculum results; individual instructors choose what they want to emphasize from a broad range of topics, ideas, and skills. Especially in colleges and universities in which instructors maintain close ties to the disciplinary associations in their fields, the major may reflect key debates among the members of the discipline.

Typically, the undergraduate major follows a sequence in which the student gains progressively more depth of knowledge in a field of study The major typically includes an introductory course (which may double as a general education requirement), a set of intermediate courses, and some advanced courses. It may require a thesis, a senior paper, or some other culminating experience such as a seminar or comprehensive examination that requires demonstration of the ability to synthesize knowledge. Some students who major in an academic discipline plan to continue study in the field at the graduate level, but most seek work after graduation.

Students who begin pursuing professional majors at the undergraduate level (for example, architecture, business, education, engineering, nursing, social work) often practice their future occupations in fieldwork settings as undergraduates. In these fields, some of which require more than four years to complete, the major conveys a knowledge base of skills, attitudes, and behaviors needed for entry into a specific occupation upon receipt of the bachelor's degree. Students' curricular choices are influenced by many factors, but the job market figures prominently. For example, enrollments in education programs declined drastically as the number of teaching jobs decreased in the 1970s and as opportunities simultaneously arose for women in formerly male-dominated fields like business, medicine, and law.

By the late 1990s, nearly 60 percent of all bachelor's degrees in the United States were granted in professional and occupational fields (Brint, 2002). The most common career majors in recent years have been business and management (22 percent of all bachelor's degrees awarded in 2004–2005), education (7 percent), and the visual and performing arts (6 percent) (U.S. Department of Education, 2007). Career majors are even more popular in two-year institutions: in 2004–2005, 18 percent of all associate's degrees were awarded in health professions and clinical sciences; 16 percent in business; 8 percent in engineering and engineering technology; and 5 percent in computer and information sciences. Thirty-five percent of associate's degree recipients majored in the liberal arts and science, general studies, or the humanities (reflecting, in part, the extent to which associate's degree holders plan to transfer to four-year bachelor's programs) (U.S. Department of Education, 2007).

Students may combine two areas of study through a "double major," which typically requires them to complete all the requirements for two separate academic programs. Interdisciplinary majors also permit the study of two or more fields of study, but do not require students to complete separate academic programs. Rather, students either create an "individualized" major, combining courses from two or more fields of their choosing, or pursue a formal interdisciplinary major that draws on the courses and/or faculty from several academic departments. Common interdisciplinary majors include environmental science, international studies, women's studies, American studies, neuroscience, and a variety of ethnic studies programs (for example, Chicano studies and African American studies). Like the disciplinary major, these programs often require students to engage in a culminating experience like a capstone seminar or senior thesis.

Some colleges offer general education or liberal studies majors, which offer greater flexibility and a wider choice of courses than do majors in specific disciplines. A liberal studies major is intended for students who wish to learn about many fields of study and who resist specialization. In some colleges, it is viewed as a catch-all category for students who are undecided about which specific field to pursue in depth, or as an "escape hatch" for unmotivated students. Such negative reaction to the liberal studies major in some colleges provides evidence of how far higher education has moved from a core curriculum to more specialized programs of study.

Some colleges and universities offer preprofessional majors—a set of recommended courses for students intending to pursue graduate-level professional education in fields such as medicine, law, dentistry, and veterinary medicine. Frequently, a special advisor helps students select the appropriate courses and complete their graduate school applications. Students may also prepare for graduate study in such professions by taking relevant courses outside the preprofessional major.

What is called a major specialization in a transfer curriculum in a two-year college may be the approximate equivalent of introductory and intermediate courses in the four-year baccalaureate program in the same field. (Community and for-profit colleges may also offer occupational majors that have no equivalent at the baccalaureate level but that are instead gateways to employment.) Institutions that seek to facilitate the transfer of students from two- to four-year programs develop "articulation" agreements that specify courses that are equivalent at the two- and four-year levels and thus can be transferred for credit. Articulation agreements not only involve administrators who coordinate the process, but instructors who are responsible for aligning course content and syllabi to ensure substantially equivalent educational experiences. In some states, articulation agreements are written into state educational codes (Cohen & Brawer, 2003).

Over more than 350 years, U.S. higher education programs have become both more diversified and more specialized, fragmenting into subfields such as biomedical engineering, supply chain economics, public relations, and advertising, to name a few. Faculty members cite expanding knowledge bases and increasing demand from disciplinary accrediting agencies as unrelenting pressures toward specialized study. Specialization and diversification of academic programs are closely related and both are opposed by advocates of educational breadth who periodically call for greater attention to a broad set of liberal education goals and outcomes (see Figure 6.2).

The three missions—utilitarian, research, and liberal arts—still form the primary basis for the diversity among colleges, but the debate over general and specialized study sometimes occurs within a single institution. For example, the concept of liberal arts as a foundation for life or further study for all college students may pervade the undergraduate programs in many large universities. Here the colleges of arts and sciences provide a general education curriculum intended to complement students' specialized studies in the major. Faculty members in disciplines and fields with tightly prescribed curricula (such as engineering or music) may seek to reduce the proportion of the undergraduate program dedicated to general education requirements to achieve greater specialization. In all kinds of institutions, competition for resources also impinges on the general education program. As programs and colleges are pitted against one another in the budget process, debate about the relative merits of general and specialized study is often viewed in very pragmatic terms.

LEARNERS: AN EMPHASIS ON ACCESS

With very few exceptions, the American colonial colleges educated only a small proportion of the white male populace. In 1850 it is estimated that only 1 percent of the population actually finished college. The rapid rise in bachelor's degrees after records were begun in 1870 is illustrated in Figure 6.3. Since then, an ever-increasing portion of the U.S. population has attended

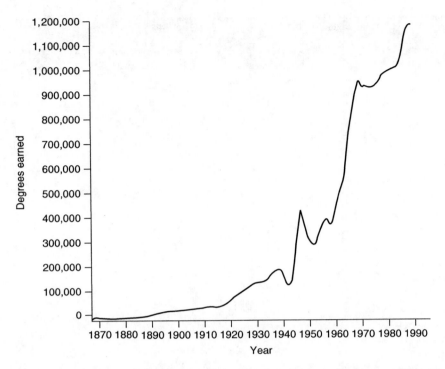

FIGURE 6.3 Bachelor's degrees conferred by U.S. institutions of higher education: 1869–1870 to 1996–1997

Source: Gerald and Hussar (1999); U.S. Bureau of the Census (1975)

college. By 2000, some eight years after most had graduated from high school, 29 percent of the 1988 eighth-grade cohort had earned a bachelor's, master's, or higher (Ph.D. or professional) degree (Ingels, Curtin, Kaufman, Alt, & Chen, 2002). Almost half of the cohort (46 percent) had accumulated some postsecondary credits or earned an associate's degree or certificate. In tracking female City University of New York students twenty and thirty years after they initially entered college, researchers found that 70 percent had earned a postsecondary degree and more than three-fourths of those had earned a bachelor's degree (Attewell & Lavin, 2007). In a similar analysis of data from the National Longitudinal Survey of Youth, which tracked students for twenty years, the same researchers found that 61 percent of students entering college graduated (Attewell & Lavin, 2007).

Opportunity Increases

The Industrial Revolution and the spread of settlement across the continent inspired a number of changes in higher education. The country needed expertise in areas such as surveying and agriculture. An education encompassing these practical subjects appealed to a broader spectrum of the population, and public pressure led to passage of the 1862 Morrill Act, which provided funds for the creation of land-grant universities that would provide the opportunity for every American citizen to receive some form of higher education (Brubacher & Rudy, 1976). In addition, a growing number of families were willing and able to finance a son's education to prepare him for entry into a world of greater opportunity. Figure 6.4 illustrates the periods of emphasis on access.

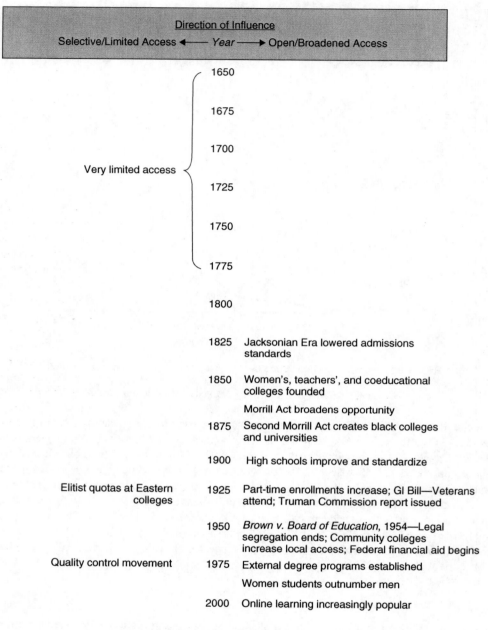

FIGURE 6.4   Periods of emphasis on access

For the first half of the 19th century, women desiring a college education were largely confined to "seminaries," institutions that aimed to prepare women for their future roles as wives and mothers (Lucas, 2006). In the U.S., this changed mid-century with the opening of teachers colleges, women's colleges, and founding of co-educational institutions. Later in the 1800s, some of the leading U.S. women's colleges, many of which evolved from earlier seminaries (for example, Mount Holyoke), were founded (Horowitz, 1993). During the Civil War, significant decreases in male enrollments caused many formerly all-male institutions to encourage women to enroll. After the Civil War, reformist ideals supported the continuation of this trend. By 1860, approximately forty-five colleges and universities, some of which enrolled only female students, offered women the opportunity to earn a degree (Geiger, 2000; Thelin, 2004).

Reforms of the post-Civil War period, and the passage of a second Morrill Act in 1890, which funded the creation of what we now call "historically black colleges and universities" (HBCUs), increased access to higher education for African Americans, although this was accomplished primarily through the creation of segregated institutions. By 1900, all of the southern and border states had state-funded black institutions (Lucas, 2006). However, even as access increased throughout the 19th century, negative assumptions about the suitability of women and blacks, as well as students of lower socioeconomic status, for higher education remained (Lucas, 2006). Although more white men of various social classes sought the education provided by land grants and black institutions, black Americans did not have full access to the types of education provided to white students until well after World War II. A 1917 survey of black higher education suggested that only one of the sixteen black land-grant institutions in the South offered college-level curricula; similarly only thirty-three of nearly one hundred private black colleges provided collegiate-level study (Lucas, 2006).

In 1870 less than 2 percent of the 18- to 24-year-old population in the United States was enrolled in college (Snyder, 1993). In the same year, most of the nation's existing colleges offered preparatory programs for the many students who were not ready for college-level study (Rudolph, 1977). The next period of increased access accompanied the expansion of high school attendance and was fueled by improvements in public high school education. The efforts of the University of Michigan, which developed the first articulation agreements with secondary schools during the 1870s, encouraged standardization of high school curricula. The creation of "standard units" also promoted conformity in the high school course of study, by specifying the amount of time a student had studied a subject. One hundred and twenty hours in one subject area was equivalent to one standard unit of high school credit. Fourteen units were considered to be the minimum academic preparation for college admission (Carnegie Foundation for the Advancement of Teaching, n.d.). As a result, college preparation no longer required private schooling or tutoring.

Improved Preparation Fuels Rapid Growth

Enrollments at colleges and universities in the Eastern United States also swelled with the influx of Jewish immigrants from Europe at the turn of the 20th century (Wechsler, 1977). In the period immediately following World War I, however, many Eastern colleges began to limit the sizes of their entering student cohorts. Newly developed standardized admissions tests intended to ensure adequate preparation allowed institutions to select students based on their test scores. Raising admission standards was a positive step for many institutions, signaling improved educational standards, but at some institutions the standardized tests and other admissions requirements such as assessment of "character" served to limit access (Soares, 2007). For example, "college boards" were first offered by the College Entrance Examination Board, which, according to Nicholas Lemann (2000), was a "clubby association" between a few dozen private schools and colleges with the aim of perfecting the close fit between New England boarding schools and Ivy League colleges (pp. 28–29).

The "Typical" Student Disappears

Most liberal arts colleges enrolled primarily full-time residential students until well after World War II. By mid-century, however, many urban institutions in areas heavily populated by immigrants served commuter and part-time students, establishing large evening divisions to permit the enrollment of working adults. World War II was, however, the most significant catalyst in diversifying college student attendance nationwide. Stimulated by worries about mass unemployment when large numbers of service personnel were demobilized, Congress passed The Servicemen's Readjustment Act of 1944, popularly known as the G.I. Bill. Although the government assumed that only a small number would take advantage of this offer to finance their education, about 2.2 million veterans returned to college with the help of the G.I. Bill. Their enrollment challenged existing visions of the typical student, required massive expansion of higher education, and paved the way for further enrollment growth and student diversity in the following decades. The influx of returning veterans left fewer admission slots for women, however, and women's enrollments declined in the 1950s (Schwartz, 2002). These women were likely to study fields traditionally relegated to them, such as nursing, home economics, and teaching (Goldin, 1992).

Access to higher education became an expectation in the latter half of the 20th century. In a 1947 report entitled *Higher Education for Democracy*, The President's Commission on Higher Education (the Truman Commission) asserted that citizens were "entitled" to higher education regardless of their ability to personally afford it. Reaffirming the usefulness of a college education, the report declared that the nation would benefit when postsecondary education was available to all with the requisite ability (which it estimated at 50 percent of the population). The Commission's report laid the foundation for the Higher Education Act of 1965, which created grant and loan programs that provided financial aid to deserving students with demonstrated financial need. These financial aid programs bolstered college attendance once more and increased students' ability to choose among colleges. The creation of federal financial aid programs also paved the way for federal influence on higher education.

In 1947, the year of the President's Commission report, African American students represented only about 6 percent of all college enrollments in the United States (Lucas, 2006). Access to higher education for African Americans increased following the U.S. Supreme Court's 1954 *Brown v. Topeka Board of Education* decision declaring racial segregation illegal. Desegregation of white institutions in the South accelerated in the years following the decision, sometimes voluntarily and sometimes only following legal action (Wallenstein, 2008). Still, enrollments of black students grew slowly. Between 1960 and 1980, however, after passage of the Higher Education Act, enrollments of African American students in both historically black colleges and universities and predominantly white institutions doubled (Lucas, 2006). Social movements such as the civil rights and women's movements of the 1960s also contributed to the growth and diversification of postsecondary enrollments, encouraging many more women and African American students to enter college. It is only in recent years that African American postsecondary participation rates have been proportional to their representation in the U.S. population. Between 1984 and 2004, minority students had greater growth rates in postsecondary participation than their white counterparts. By 2004, African Americans were the largest minority student population, comprising 13 percent of the total undergraduate student enrollment (Li, 2007).

The number of women undergraduates has increased substantially since the 1960s, and women now constitute more than half of all undergraduate college enrollments. Women also receive almost 60 percent of the associate's degrees awarded and just over half of the more than one million bachelor's degrees awarded annually in the United States. International students also contribute to the diversity of the undergraduate population. In 2006, there were more than 580,000 international students enrolled in U.S. colleges (Institute of International Education, 2007).

New Institutions Appear

By the mid-1900s, the public two-year sector began to expand. Today, most states join with local governmental units to sponsor community colleges that collectively account for more than half of all undergraduate enrollments (Snyder, Tan, & Hoffman, 2006). These colleges (and a few four-year colleges that also grant two-year degrees) now award more than 700,000 associate's degrees annually (*Chronicle of Higher Education Almanac*, 2008). Community colleges account for nearly 40 percent of all enrollments and half of all public college enrollments (Snyder, Tan, & Hoffman, 2006). About 20 percent of students who begin college in a two-year school later enroll in a four-year institution. These students seek to "transfer," or apply the credits they earned in the two-year college to their baccalaureate programs.

Other institutions designed to increase access to college, namely "external degree" colleges or "universities without walls," emerged in the late 1960s to serve adult learners unable to attend formal classes on campuses. This small but distinctive group of colleges, which often award some degree credit for life experiences outside of formal education, typically station faculty in locations convenient to clusters of students. Although these external degree colleges preceded the introduction of computers, by the end of the 20th century substantial numbers of students were enrolled in online education courses and programs using the Internet. For-profit institutions such as the University of Phoenix captured a significant proportion of the adult population seeking credentials and access to employment opportunities. Largely in response to the competition for the growing adult population, public and independent colleges and universities fielded their own distance or online learning programs to serve part-time students. Some created distance learning programs that enroll part-time students as well as residential students seeking flexibility in their course schedules. A few institutions have special units that are dedicated to providing instructional development assistance to instructors developing online courses. In return for supporting these electronic platforms, these units, such as Penn State's World Campus, share the revenues generated through online and hybrid courses with academic programs.

Maintaining Access in the 21st Century

With entitlement and anti-discrimination laws firmly in place in the United States, the years since 1960 can be characterized as a period of particularly strong emphasis on access. Whereas only 5 percent of the population had completed college in 1940; as of 2005, more than 25 percent of individuals in the 25- to 29-year-old age group had earned a bachelor's degree (Snyder, Tan, & Hoffman, 2006).

As of fall 2003, about seventeen million students were enrolled in American collegiate education (Snyder, Tan, & Hoffman, 2006) and nearly thirteen million of these attended public colleges. More than ten million were enrolled in four-year institutions (Snyder, Tan, & Hoffman, 2006), but two-year and community colleges are the largest single segment of higher education. Four in ten undergraduates, that is, about 7.6 million students, attend community colleges (Horn & Nevill, 2006). Although the for-profit sector is also growing, one scenario suggests it will account for one out of ten students by 2015 (Blumenstyk, 2005).

Approximately 40 percent of all students in the United States are over 24 years old (Snyder, Tan, & Hoffman, 2006), and many attend on a part-time basis. Part-time students account for about 60 percent of the undergraduate population in two- and four-year colleges combined (Snyder, Tan, & Hoffman, 2006).

Today, more than two-thirds of all students enrolled in degree-granting institutions in the United States are white. Black students represent just less than 12 percent of graduate and undergraduate enrollments. Hispanic students account for about 10 percent, Asians and Pacific Islanders, 6.5 percent, and American Indians about 1.0 percent of all postsecondary enrollments (U.S. Department of Education, 2005). At four-year institutions (including independent and public institutions and those that award doctoral and master's degrees), about one-quarter of students are minorities, although public two-year institutions enroll more minority students (36 percent) than four-year institutions do. Black and Hispanic students are more likely than other students of color to attend an institution with a high concentration of their own racial/ethnic group. About one-fifth of each of these groups of students attend an institution where they are the majority (U.S. Department of Education, 2005).

Arthur Cohen and Florence Brawer (2003) note that the most rapid change in the two-year college curriculum has been the growth in English as a second language (or ESL) courses. The growth in ESL enrollments reflects the growing diversity of college-going adults in the United States and the growing number of immigrants enrolling in postsecondary education. In 1983, ESL accounted for 30 percent of foreign language enrollments. By 1991, it was over 50 percent and, together with Spanish, accounted for three-quarters of all foreign language credit sections. In 1998, more than half of all two-year colleges offered ESL courses, but students may or may not earn academic credit for them. In some states, state funding and student financial aid policies classify ESL as less-than-college-level work (Cohen & Brawer, 2003, p. 327).

Despite the increasing diversity of U.S. higher education, there are gaps in college achievement. Although the number of historically underrepresented students enrolled has reached record highs, degree attainment levels are considerably higher for white adults than for African Americans and Hispanics. Two-thirds of white Americans in the 25- to 29-year-old age group have attended some college, and about one-third hold a bachelor's degree. In the same age group, only 50 percent of blacks and 30 percent of Hispanics have attended some college, and less than 20 percent of blacks and 10 percent of Hispanic citizens have earned bachelor's degrees. Less than 4 percent of each of these groups has advanced degrees, compared to just over 7 percent of whites (U.S. Census Bureau, 2008). (See Figure 6.5.)

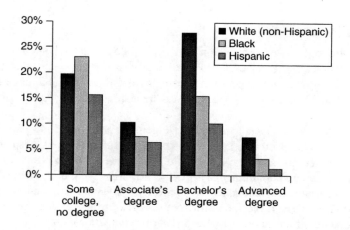

FIGURE 6.5   Degree attainment by race/ethnicity (%), ages 25 to 29
Source: U.S. Census Bureau, 2008

Older and part-time students who live off-campus and are financially independent more commonly attend public two-year colleges, and these students often are ineligible for financial aid. Historically underrepresented students are also disproportionately enrolled in two-year institutions. A student's choice of colleges may be limited by his or her previous academic preparation and success. Because most community colleges have "open door" admissions policies, they are more likely than four-year colleges and universities to offer remedial programs for students who need to develop basic skills in mathematics, writing, reading, or English before or while they enroll in college-level coursework. All public two-year colleges offer at least one remedial course (Kirst, 1998), and about 40 percent of all community college students have taken a remedial course (compared to 28 percent of undergraduates in four-year institutions) (U.S. Department of Education, 2004). In most colleges, enrollment in remedial courses is voluntary, but a few institutions, such as Miami Dade Community College, require students to acquire basic skills before taking courses that require their use.

The sheer number of students in U.S. colleges and universities has caused many to characterize the nation's higher education enterprise as one of "universal" access. This term is somewhat exaggerated since many Americans still do not attend college. External influences, including wars, immigration, desegregation, the shift from an agrarian to a post-industrial society, and various social movements have promoted the diversification of the student population, and the nation has moved steadily from a view of education as a privilege for a few toward an entitlement for citizens of all ages, genders, races, and interests.

CONTENT DEBATES: PRESCRIPTION VS. CHOICE

Curricular choice debates date from the earliest decades of U.S. higher education. Each recurrence yields a temporary victory for one side or the other. New college missions and broader access for diverse students have contributed to the growing variety of courses and programs that colleges and universities offer. This abundance periodically spurs discussions about the extent to which postsecondary institutions should prescribe curricular requirements for their students. Despite this debate's obvious periodicity, it is difficult to separate these discussions from others concerned with the relative virtues of general and specialized education.

Colleges Choose; Students Follow

Today's college students face a daunting array of options compared to the first American students, who lacked the option to choose majors, areas of concentration, or even individual courses. For over fifty years, the colonial colleges offered one program of study, usually incorporating Greek, Latin, Hebrew, rhetoric, logic, moral philosophy (ethics), and natural philosophy (the precursor to what we know as physics).

Colleges gradually responded to a rapidly expanding knowledge base. For example, in 1714 a donation of several hundred new books to Yale University required improvements in mathematics preparation (Rudolph, 1977). Even so, the first mathematics professorship at Yale was not established until 1770. The first real "elective" may have been offered in 1755, when Harvard continued to provide instruction in Hebrew, but no longer required it for graduation.

As new colleges entered the scene, curricular choices expanded somewhat. When it opened in 1754, King's College (now Columbia University), for example, offered courses in commerce and husbandry. By 1776, six of the eight colonial colleges had created professorships in mathematics, a course of study previously neglected, and the study of Newtonian physics was beginning to emerge from natural philosophy. The College of Philadelphia (today the University of Pennsylvania) provided instruction in political science, agriculture, history, and chemistry (Rudolph, 1977). Options of this type, however, did not challenge the assumption that the college, not the student, determined what was to be learned.

New subjects and new institutions were the primary sources of increased choices for students in colonial American colleges. Social and economic changes, however, precipitated more curricular change as the population of a growing nation increasingly questioned the idea that the nation was best served by men significantly familiar with ancient languages and literature but with little knowledge of practical subjects. Colleges gradually introduced subjects such as astronomy, mathematics, engineering, and natural sciences into their curricula. Just before 1800, English supplanted Latin as the language of instruction.

Pressure for Choice Increases

By the early 1800s, prospective and enrolled students, as well as some faculty, were growing dissatisfied with the classical college curriculum, which they perceived to be dated, inflexible, and dull. Colleges first attempted to address student complaints by adjusting the structure of their programs rather than their purpose and content. For example, Harvard offered tutorials and a few electives and began to group students according to ability. The first significant curricular changes came as colleges reluctantly allowed "partial" or "parallel" courses of study in the sciences. Traditionalists viewed these degrees as less prestigious alternatives to the more established requirements of the classical program, but students enrolled nonetheless. In many institutions, students created their own avenues for intellectual pursuits, forming literary and debating societies that enjoyed great popularity.

The "college" system at the University of Virginia, where students chose an organizational unit in which to pursue their studies, represented another early and significant move toward student choice. Once a student at the university enrolled in a particular "college," he had few choices, but the structural subdivision of the university into departments planted the "seeds of the elective system" (Brubacher & Rudy, 1976, p. 99). As other institutions copied this scheme, courses and specializations mushroomed, rendering choice and elective courses possible—and even necessary.

The Yale Report of 1828, which asserted that the classical curriculum provided the only suitable college education, was an extraordinary (although temporary) victory for the conservative faculty forces and a setback for those advocating greater curricular choice. Within a few decades, however, elective reform again emerged as an important topic, even at campuses that had fully subscribed to assertions of the Yale Report. The development of new universities with new missions, such as the land-grant universities, colleges for freed slaves, and coeducational and women's colleges, contributed to the proliferation of new options and fields of study. The Morrill Act encouraged institutions to permit students to choose elective courses, while colleges and universities admitting women added fields such as domestic science, social work, and fine arts, thought to be better suited to women's "gentler" minds and bodies. (See Figure 6.6.)

Debate and Change Intensify

Even as electives became more numerous and evolved into entire new programs, faculty members opposed to choice tried to thwart them—for example, by requiring a higher passing grade for elective courses than for required ones (Brubacher & Rudy, 1976). Each time institutions instituted electives over faculty objections, faculty members resisted.

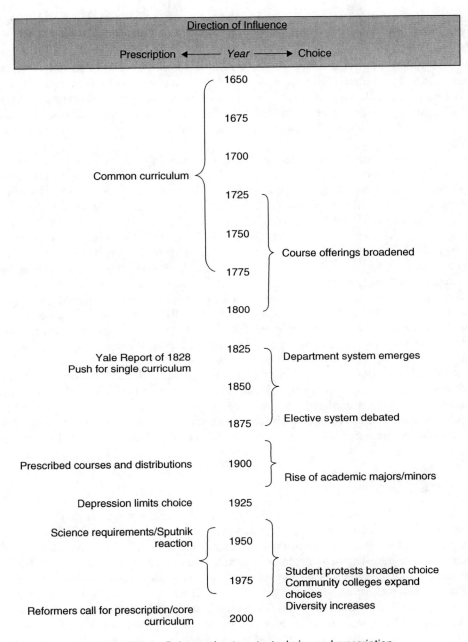

FIGURE 6.6   Debates about content: choice and prescription

The forty-year campaign for the elective system waged between 1869 and 1909 by Charles William Eliot, president of Harvard University, is legendary. Through Eliot's efforts, Harvard abolished all course requirements except English composition by 1897. Yet detractors claimed that the new elective system failed to guide students toward clear and coherent educational programs. An 1898 study at Harvard showed that 55 percent of students elected only elementary courses and nearly three-quarters followed a course of study without any clear focus (Rudolph, 1977). With insufficient guidance, many students avoided pursuing any subject in depth.

Between 1885 and 1905, educators responded to the proliferation of elective courses by shaping the system of general education and academic concentrations that is still common in U.S. colleges and universities. The major system, first introduced in 1885 at Indiana University and put into place at Harvard by 1910, coincided with the rise of specializations. Retreating from the ideology of total choice, the major system sought to remedy the lack of structure and coherence that resulted when colleges eliminated all or most curricular requirements (Rudolph, 1977).

By 1920, the system of the major and general education distribution requirements was widely established. Colleges allowed students to choose an area of specialization but required them to also enroll in a general education program, often structured as a set of "distribution requirements" to be fulfilled by courses in subjects the faculty believed supplied a foundation of common knowledge. Departments specified foundation courses and other requirements for their majors, and then allowed students latitude in filling other credit-hour requirements. In some fields of study, the major was nearly as structured as the prescribed curricula that preceded it.

As the 20th century progressed, so did interest in majors such as business and education, which prepared students for specific careers, and in new majors, such as sociology and psychology, which grew out of existing disciplines like philosophy. As options increased, more educators became concerned that students share a common knowledge of Western culture and values. Spurred by nationalistic sentiments during and following World War I, colleges reintroduced core curricula in the humanities and social science and renewed their emphasis on general education requirements.

In 1957, when the Russian launch of the satellite Sputnik challenged notions of U.S. competitiveness and scientific preparedness, educators responded by establishing rigorous scientific requirements for students in high school and college. Postsecondary institutions strengthened and expanded their general education distribution requirements, including those in laboratory sciences. Colleges and universities frequently used this tactic to prevent students from avoiding laboratory courses.

Students Demand Greater Choice

In the 1960s and 1970s, students became the strongest advocates of greater curricular choice, protesting curricular restrictions by arguing that they faced the draft for the Vietnam War but were denied adult choices on campuses. An increasingly diverse group of students labeled requirements as "establishment"—detrimental to individual development and freedom. Students rejected certification mechanisms such as theses and comprehensive exams as well as curricular prescription. Clifton Conrad and Jean Wyer (1980) described this period as a "virtual free-for-all of the distribution approach" (p. 17). Colleges and universities responded to students who wanted relevant educational programs by experimenting with pass-fail grading options, independent study courses, greater elective choice, and student-designed majors. Buoyed by the civil and women's rights movements, underrepresented women faculty members and their students created programs in women's and black studies.

Despite many concessions to student demands during this turbulent period, the dominant structural features of the curriculum did not change. Most colleges managed to retain, if not fully enforce, programs in general education (required or distributed in groups of courses), a major field of study or combined related studies, and limited electives. As the job market tightened in the 1970s and 1980s, students themselves selected more structured programs in the hope of improving their marketability. As students have become more and more career focused, they have pursued "double majors" and multiple minors to enhance their "credentials."

Whatever curricular constraints students might feel today, the growth in number and variety of programs, majors, and degrees over time has been formidable. As Frederick Rudolph (1977) noted: "It is one thing to describe the curriculum under which Harvard for decade after decade awarded nothing but the B.A.; it is almost an affront to the imagination to be expected to make sense of the almost two hundred different degrees offered by the University of Illinois in 1960" (p. 10). Had Rudolph included the "feeder" community colleges from which students transfer to and from the University of Illinois as well as the university itself, his statement might have been even stronger. The IPEDS includes nearly one hundred categories of subjects, each divided into many subcategories. Traditional programs of study like American history and newly developed specialties like biochemistry exist beside vocational offerings such as refrigeration technology, restaurant management, and horticulture. In some colleges, academic credit is given for life experience, for remedial study, and for career exploration.

Calls for Curricular Coherence

Historically, debates about curricular prescription and choice occupied higher education faculty, administrators, and leaders like President Eliot of Harvard, who supported elective choice, and President John Maynard Hutchins at the University of Chicago, who argued that all students should have a common foundation of knowledge and skills. In the latter quarter of the 1900s, the array of voices grew as additional stakeholders vociferously entered the conversation about curricular content. Originally an internal concern, questions about postsecondary curricula have become more visible as more and more students in the United States attend college and as stakeholders external to higher education institutions, such as employers, legislators, and government officials, have sought to influence college and university curricula.

The 1980s and 1990s saw a wave of reports from blue ribbon committees appointed by state and federal agencies, as well as recommendations from higher education advocacy organizations. These reports (see Table 6.1) assessed the condition of higher education and called for various reforms. The reports that focused primarily on curriculum (for example, Association of American Colleges, 1985; Bennett, 1984; Boyer, 1987; Cheney, 1989; National Institute of Education, 1984; Wingspread Group on Higher Education, 1993) typically decried curricular fragmentation and overspecialization resulting from the lack of coherent general education programs. Although focused on many of the same problems, the authors of these reports arrived at a variety of solutions. William Bennett, chair of the National Endowment for the Humanities, and his successor Lynne Cheney, both published reports that called for greater attention to Western civilization and culture, while the Association of American Colleges called for greater focus on transferable learning skills such as critical thinking and communication.

These reports, particularly Bennett's (1984) "To Reclaim a Legacy," which placed the blame for students' flight from the humanities at the feet of research-oriented and/or ideological faculty, inspired a backlash from critics of the traditional, Eurocentric liberal arts core. Proponents as diverse as educational theorist Henry Giroux (1992) and philosopher and classicist Martha Nussbaum (1997) argued for an education that would prepare students for life in an increasingly diverse nation and world. Although united in their call for greater attention to national and global diversity, these commentators espoused a variety of goals. Some, like Giroux, advocated curricula that would enable students to critique and address social inequities and encourage social transformation. Others, such as feminists like Elizabeth Minnich (1990), sought to redress the distorted view of U.S. history and society resulting from a curriculum that excluded discussion

TABLE 6.1
A Chronology of Critical Reports and Proposals for Reform, 1984–1994

1984	*To Reclaim a Legacy: A Report on the Humanities in Higher Education.* William Bennett, National Endowment for the Humanities.
1984	*Involvement in Learning: Realizing the Potential of American Higher Education.* Study Group on the Condition of Excellence in American Higher Education, National Institute of Education.
1985	*Integrity in the College Curriculum: A Report to the Academic Community.* Task Force of the Association of American Colleges.
1985	*Higher Education and the American Resurgence.* Frank Newman. The Carnegie Foundation for the Advancement of Teaching.
1986	*To Secure the Blessings of Liberty. Report of the National Commission on the Role and Future of State Colleges and Universities.* American Association of State Colleges and Universities.
1986	*Time for Results: The Governors' 1991 Report on Education.* National Governors' Association, Center for Policy Research and Analysis.
1986	*Transforming the State Role in Higher Education.* Education Commission of the States.
1987	*College: The Undergraduate Experience in America.* Ernest L. Boyer. The Carnegie Foundation for the Advancement of Teaching.
1988	*A New Vitality in General Education.* Task Group on General Education. Association of American Colleges.
1988	*Unfinished Design: The Humanities and Social Sciences in Undergraduate Engineering Education.* Joseph S. Johnston, Jr., Susan Shaman, and Robert Zemsky.
1988	*Humanities in America: A Report to the President, the Congress, and the American People.* Lynne V. Cheney. National Endowment for the Humanities.
1988	*Strengthening the Ties That Bind: Integrating Undergraduate Liberal and Professional Study.* Joan S. Stark and Malcolm A. Lowther. Professional Preparation Network, University of Michigan.
1989	*50 Hours: A Core Curriculum for College Students.* Lynne V. Cheney. National Endowment for the Humanities.
1990	*Scholarship Reconsidered: Priorities of the Professoriate.* Ernest L. Boyer. The Carnegie Foundation for the Advancement of Teaching.
1991	*The Challenge of Connecting Learning.* Project on Liberal Learning, Study-in-Depth, and the Arts and Sciences Major. Association of American Colleges.
1991	*Reports from the Fields.* Project on Liberal Learning, Study-in-Depth, and the Arts and Sciences Major. Association of American Colleges.
1992	*Program Review and Educational Quality in the Major.* Project on Liberal Learning, Study-in-Depth, and the Arts and Sciences Major. Association of American Colleges.
1993	*An American Imperative: Higher Expectations for Higher Education.* Wingspread Group on Higher Education. The Johnson Foundation and others.
1994	*Sustaining Vitality in General Education:* Project on Strong Foundations for General Education. Association of American Colleges.

of the experiences of historically underrepresented students and women. Others who focused on economic competitiveness rather than social justice made the case that students must be well prepared for the contemporary, global workplace (Bollinger, 2007).

Another call for curricular reform focuses on the value of interdisciplinary study at the undergraduate and graduate levels. Such calls, although more persistent of late, are not new. During the general education movement after World War I, a number of reformers emphasized interdisciplinary study as a means of connecting the knowledge of the diverse disciplines that comprise general education programs. During the 1960s, the women's studies movement took up the cause, arguing that the traditional academic disciplines provided only partial and limited perspectives from which to view social problems. Viewing interdisciplinarity as the antidote to incomplete understandings of the lives and issues faced by marginalized populations, faculty in these programs encouraged students (and instructors) to critique and expand traditional disciplines. In the late 1980s, a new group of advocates, this time from the sciences and professional fields, grew in force. These proponents of interdisciplinarity asserted that the disciplines in their traditional form were no longer adequate to solving social and scientific problems. They argued that students needed to develop the ability to work in interdisciplinary teams and attack problems from multiple disciplinary viewpoints to spur scientific breakthroughs and innovation. Unlike their predecessors in women's studies, however, science faculty who advocate interdisciplinarity are more likely to believe that students need a strong foundation in the scientific disciplines—rather than simply the ability to critique those disciplines—to advance knowledge (Lattuca, 2001).

INSTRUCTIONAL PROCESS: OCCASIONAL INNOVATIONS

Temporary victories in the debate about content choice and prescription occasionally inspired instructional innovations. In colonial higher education, faculty members typically subscribed to a view of learning as the exercise and discipline of the mind. Students learned through memorization and recitation, as well as through processes of logical disputation. Instructional processes changed somewhat in the middle 1800s as land-grant colleges, with a mission to serve the state and community, focused instruction on improving agricultural and business production. Learning by demonstration and by laboratory practice became common in these fields.

The history of higher education in the United States, however, boasts a few distinct periods of educational experimentation, notably in the 1920s, 1930s, 1960s, and 1990s. Early scientific studies in the psychology of learning, begun by Columbia University professor Edward Thorndike in the early 1900s, stimulated instructional innovation by calling into question the credibility of the mental discipline theory of learning (Bigge & Shermis, 1992). From the field of philosophy, John Dewey and his followers in the field of education argued for the primacy of experience in education, promoting course instruction based on projects, field work, and inquiry, all relevant to the student, rather than memorization and recitation. Rapid enrollment increases following World War II, however, checked the spread of discussion-based courses. The need to teach large numbers of students simultaneously, combined with a faculty reward system that emphasized the importance of research, seemed to cement the lecture as an instructional method. (See Figure 6.7.)

Students Seek Relevance and Freedom

During the experimental years of the 1960s, faculty introduced some alternatives to large lecture classes. Many small colleges experimented with competency-based learning programs like self-paced instruction, which encouraged instructors to specify behavioral objectives (Keller, 1968). During this same period, the demands for "relevance" prompted some colleges to create study arrangements that allowed students to focus on one subject at a time (such as the one-month intensive term, typically during the mid-year break between terms, of the 4-1-4 calendar system). Others combined living and learning experiences in residence halls to foster closer interaction with faculty and a sense of community intended to offset the impersonal nature of large universities. Students also demanded and won new grading systems, such as pass/fail options, and a few experimenting colleges eliminated grades entirely to encourage students to explore new topics without threat of failure. While exciting to faculty and students, many of these experiments were short-lived because they consumed large amounts of faculty time and often limited students' options for transfer or graduate study.

The 1960s also witnessed the founding of several innovative colleges, such as Evergreen State University and Hampshire College. These institutional experiments spawned a considerable literature documenting the efforts and their effects (for example, Smith & McCann, 2001). Arthur Levine (1978) traced some of the sources and results of curricular reforms, concluding that there has been ongoing change in the predominant view of educational purpose and related instructional processes. Since the elements of the academic plan do not operate independently, it is easy to understand why Levine did not distinguish among purposes, content, sequence, and

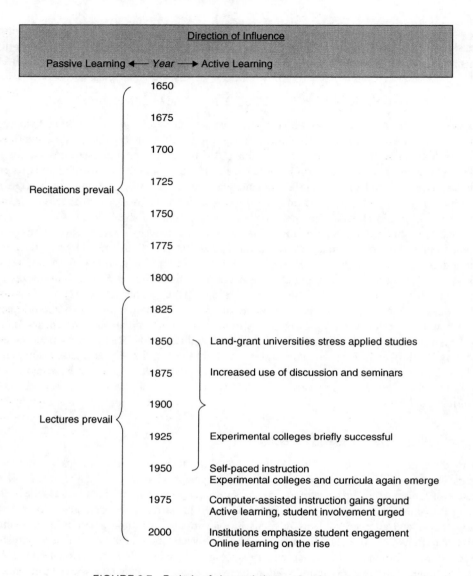

FIGURE 6.7   Periods of change in instructional processes

instructional process. We have added to his summary for the 1960s and 1970s our own assessment of the 1980s through 2000s.

- 1960s—Dominant educational philosophies are education for life (relevance) and education for personal development. Characteristic experiments include new interdisciplinary studies (ethnic studies, environmental studies), reductions in curricular requirements, and customized courses and programs (for example, independent study, student-created majors, pass/fail grading, and experimental colleges).
- 1970s—U.S. colleges and universities become committed to social justice and universal access. Nontraditional students are admitted and, to accommodate them, variable

scheduling, alternatives to courses, off-campus study, credit for experience, and compensatory education are introduced. A strong concern for education and work emerges.

- 1980s—A number of 1940s-era reforms are revived. Curricula move away from electives and toward greater structure in attempts to achieve curricular "coherence." More prescribed distribution requirements emerge, except in two-year colleges, where requirements continue to be reduced. Employers complain that graduates lack basic skills; observers express concerns about educational quality and its measurement and about general education. Decentralization of higher education leads to greater state responsibility and funding for higher education. Experimental colleges and free universities almost disappear.
- 1990s—The catch phrase "student-centered teaching" buoys discussions about instruction. Advocates of active learning and student engagement seek ways to convince faculty of the need for instructional reforms. The emphasis on the quality of teaching gains momentum as a number of accreditation agencies stress the importance of assessment of student learning to demonstrate the quality of a college or university. Online learning begins a rapid ascent as traditional institutions and for-profit educational providers vie for enrollments.
- 2000s—Student-centered teaching becomes "learning centered" as instructional reforms refocus faculty attention on designing curricula and instructional approaches to maximize student learning. Active learning gets a boost with increasing institutional participation in the National Survey of Student Engagement, which collects information about students' involvement in their academic programs. Debates about quality assurance, particularly through general and professional accreditation, take the national stage. Concerns about economic competitiveness and globalization influence calls for educational reforms in the professions. Interdisciplinarity and integration are new watchwords for coherence.

Some innovations from the latter half of the 20th century, notably pass/fail grading, independent study, interdisciplinary area studies, and student-created majors, have endured. Most of the surviving changes, however, are structural rather than philosophical or systemic.

Technological and Instructional Change

Among the educational debates we consider, discussions about instructional processes have been muted, a lifted eyebrow compared to the raised voices generated by purpose, access, and choice. Moreover, most of these discussions about instructional process, as we have noted, occurred internally. Only recently has pressure for reform come from external sources. Today, technological advances appear to have great potential for influencing instruction, as online learning and instructional interfaces like Blackboard™ change the nature of course delivery and student-instructor interactions. These new instructional technologies have the potential to increase significantly both access and student choice.

In fall 2006, online course enrollments reached nearly 3.5 million students, or nearly 20 percent of all enrollments in degree-granting postsecondary institutions in the United States (Allen & Seaman, 2007). More than two-thirds of all higher education institutions offered at least some online offerings in 2006 (Allen, Seaman, & Garrett, 2007). Public institutions were the most likely to offer online education; almost 90 percent of public institutions reported offering at least one online course. Two-year institutions have more online enrollments than all other types of institutions combined (Allen & Seaman, 2007). In fall 2004, half of all institutions offered at least one "blended" course that combined face-to-face and online instruction. Roughly four out of five public institutions offered at least one blended course at the undergraduate level, compared to about a third of independent non-profit institutions, although that gap is beginning to close (Allen

& Seaman, 2007). Private, for-profit institutions are more than twice as likely to offer online rather than blended courses.

Institutional size and mission are strongly correlated with decisions about what kinds of courses to offer. Nearly three-quarters of doctoral/research institutions offered both online and blended courses in 2004, compared to about 30 percent of baccalaureate institutions. The baccalaureate category, often composed of residential colleges, has the least number of schools offering blended or online courses (Allen, Seaman, & Garrett, 2007) and accounts for less than 5 percent of U.S. online enrollments (Allen & Seaman, 2007).

Lecturing and demonstration may remain the predominant instructional method among college and university teachers in face-to-face instruction (Lindholm, Szelényi, Hurtado, & Korn, 2005), but advances in instructional and communications technologies are rapidly changing the nature of student and faculty interaction. Data from the National Survey of Postsecondary Faculty (NSOPF) reveals that from 1994 to 2000, instructors' use of email and Internet resources increased "from a curiosity in one of ten courses in 1994 to a dominant instrument in the majority of courses by 2000" (Schuster & Finkelstein, 2006, p. 110). According to Kenneth C. Green (2002), about one-fourth of all college courses use course management software (for example, to post information, provide links to resources, and/or conduct synchronous or asynchronous discussions).

EVALUATION DEBATES: EMPHASIS ON QUALITY CONTROL

At different points in the history of U.S. higher education, expressions of concern about educational quality and institutional accountability have emanated from society, from educators, and from students. (See Figure 6.8.) Most frequently, however, they come from those who fund higher education—philanthropic foundations, business and industry, and state and federal governments. Although calls for accountability have a financial dimension, they typically emphasize the need for assessment and evaluation to demonstrate educational effectiveness.

Calls for evaluation are often linked with other debates. For example, when educators and government officials believe higher education has overemphasized specialized study, they initiate discussions about the neglect of general education. Conversely, when educational purpose seems divorced from the country's civic and commercial needs, stakeholders argue that college graduates need to improve their mathematical, scientific, and technical knowledge and skills to enable the United States to compete in a global economy. Increased access is linked by some critics to declines in academic rigor and curricular standards. The creation of the land-grant universities with practical programs of study, open-access community colleges, and financial assistance programs all produced some level of backlash. Similarly, the recurring debates about curricular choice are couched as concerns for educational quality and control. Cycles of relaxed curricular requirements to provide more choice for students give way to cycles of tightened requirements to increase "rigor."

Government Funding Begins; Accountability Increases

Throughout U.S. history, sources of funding for higher education have become more heterogeneous and more numerous. Federal support for higher education originally was very small and, despite a few proposals, no "national" university was ever founded. Federal funds were channeled to higher education through special purpose legislation such as the Morrill Land-Grant Act (1862), the Hatch Act (1887), and the Second Morrill Act (1890). With each new federal initiative, record-keeping and evaluation processes developed to ensure that funds were properly

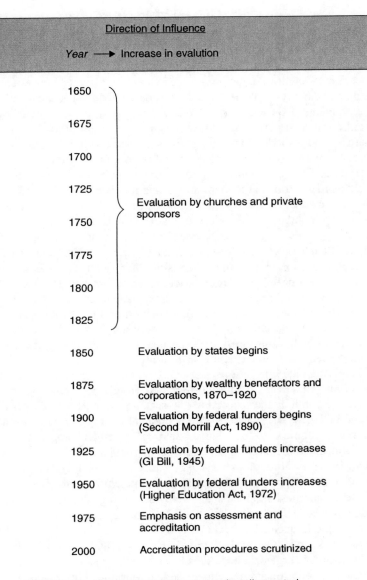

FIGURE 6.8   Emphasis on evaluation and quality control

spent. These factors created the first period of emphasis on quality control in the final decade of the 19th century.

World War II helped forge strong ties between universities and the federal government. Because the nation needed defense research and because it was efficient to use talent and resources already in place, the federal government directly funded research at major universities, an arrangement that continues today through research grants from agencies such as the Department of Defense, the National Institutes for Health, the National Science Foundation, and others. These agencies created systems to ensure effective and legitimate use of funds. The Servicemen's Readjustment Act of 1944 (G.I. Bill) enlisted already existing accrediting agencies to ensure the quality of institutions enrolling veterans whose tuition would be paid with federal entitlements. While the accreditors did not exactly welcome this responsibility, they accepted it because it strengthened their role by placing quality control in the hands of educators (Stark & Associates, 1977).

The National Defense Education Act (1958), and the Higher Education Act (1965) and its subsequent amendments (1968, 1972, and later) continued to spur the development of accountability requirements. Especially after 1972, when new types of students became eligible for financial aid, the federal government took on increased responsibility to monitor many aspects of college activity and responsiveness. Institutions that accept students who have federal financial aid grants and loans are regularly subject to quality-control initiatives.

In the United States, responsibility for operating public systems of higher education rests with the states. States founded the normal schools that later became teachers' colleges, as well as comprehensive colleges with broader missions. Universities initially supported by the Morrill Acts now receive regular appropriations of state and federal funds, although the proportion of such funds is typically a very small percentage of a university's operating budget (National Association of State Universities and Land-Grant Colleges, 1995). With state funding came varying degrees of state coordination and supervision. Many states use state-wide commissions and governing boards to coordinate college missions and programs for efficiency; thus some academic programs are subject to numerous quality control procedures and central reviews. Community colleges are subject as well to local control (usually from their home county or school district). In many states, formal articulation agreements between the community colleges and the four-year state colleges create uniformity in the curriculum by developing guidelines for transferring credits from the sending to the receiving institution.

State-level accountability efforts in the 1980s focused on assessment of student learning, but in the 1990s, a number of states shifted their emphasis to funding, reviewing their funding formulas for public higher education and seeking to link funding to institutional ability to achieve important goals and objectives. Rather than providing institutions with state funds based on other formulae, some states developed "funding for results" programs that awarded funds to public institutions that met performance goals on particular indicators. Others linked funding to achievement indirectly through *performance budgeting*, which considered reports of achievements of public colleges and universities in budget determinations (Burke & Serban, 1997). In the 1990s some states had adopted, some were considering adopting, and some had dropped or suspended performance funding, suggesting a dynamic legislative environment; changes in state governments led to frequent changes in policies.

In 2000, the National Center for Public Policy and Higher Education, an independent, non-profit, and nonpartisan organization, issued its first state-by-state "report card," giving each state an "incomplete" grade for assessment of student learning in postsecondary institutions. The absence of acceptable and comparable data for higher education, the publicity surrounding the state report cards, and the growing popularity of performance-based management elevated performance reporting as the preferred accountability mechanism in public higher education (Burke, 2002; Burke & Minassians, 2002). Performance reports offer a "middle ground" between performance funding and outcomes assessment, allowing states to evaluate higher education on critical issues such as access, quality, affordability, and workforce development, while also permitting many colleges and universities to maintain autonomy over their budgets and expenditures (Burke, 2002).

State funding for independent colleges and universities takes a different form. Some states offer tuition grants to state residents who choose to attend in-state colleges, whether public or independent. Some states provide per-capita funding to independent colleges based on their student enrollments. The result of this heterogeneous funding of all types of colleges and universities is that institutions that had been independent are now quasi-public, and some public institutions are now quasi-independent, garnering much of their revenue from alumni donations, foundations, and corporations that underwrite research (and the faculty and students who conduct it). Governmental control has strengthened with increases in student support and subsidies for academic research. Today, institutions face demands for evaluation and quality control from many sources, although accountability to the federal and state governments may be the most keen.

Concerns About Student Preparation

Academic aptitude and achievement test data show that the academic preparation of students attending college is highly variable. Average scores on college admissions tests such as the SAT and ACT began to decline in the late 1960s and continued to decline through the 1970s. Verbal scores stabilized in the 1980s, but math scores declined even further. In the 1990s, verbal scores were at record lows, but math scores rebounded. Since the mid-1990s, average scores of verbal ability have remained fairly stable, while scores of mathematical ability have continued to rise slowly, even as more and more students take admissions tests (College Board, 2007). High school grades are also on the rise, as are the numbers of students who take a college preparatory curriculum in high school (four years of English and three years of mathematics, science, and social studies). Yet, a 2007 report by ACT, a nonprofit testing organization, found that only one in four of the more than 647,000 ACT-tested students who took a college prep curriculum met all four of ACT'S College Readiness Benchmarks (Redden, 2007). (A student who meets or exceeds an ACT College Readiness Benchmark can be expected to earn a "C" or better in courses like algebra, composition, and biology taken at a four-year college.)

As a result of the variability in high school preparation and basic skills readiness, many four-year institutions require students to take remedial (also known as developmental) education courses in mathematics, writing, or reading before they are admitted or during their first year of college. In some ways, the situation is similar to that facing colleges in the mid-1800s, before the widespread development and standardization of secondary schools. To remedy that problem, many early colleges and universities established their own preparatory divisions for students lacking needed skills.

Today, more than a quarter of all entering first-year students enroll in one or more remedial reading, writing, or mathematics courses. About 20 percent take a remedial math course, compared to 14 percent for writing and 11 percent for reading (Parsad & Lewis, 2003). A government survey of remedial education in degree-granting institutions indicated that more than three-quarters of all two- and four-year institutions offered at least one remedial math, writing, or reading course in fall 2000. Public two-year institutions are more likely than any other type of institution to provide remedial education, enroll more of their entering students in these courses than other kinds of institutions, and report longer than average time periods of student enrollment. More than two-fifths of all public two-year college students took at least one remedial course (Parsad & Lewis, 2003).

Adelman (1999) reported that the type of remedial courses a student takes influences college degree completion. Analyses of longitudinal data from a nationally representative sample indicate that students who take remedial reading are the least likely to complete their bachelor's degrees (39 percent earn their degrees) (Adelman, 1999). In contrast, students who take one or two remedial courses, and do *not* take remedial reading, are much more likely to persist to graduation. Nearly 60 percent of this group of students successfully completed college, compared with

69 percent of students who took no remedial courses (Adelman, 1999). In a study designed to determine whether the lower levels of academic achievement of students in remedial courses were due to the effects of remediation or of pre-existing differences among students, Eric Bettinger and Bridget Terry Long (2004) found that remediation had positive effects on persistence to degree. They estimated that, over five years, math and English remediation reduce a student's chances of stopping out nearly 10 percent and increase the likelihood of completing a baccalaureate degree by 9 percent. Compared to students with similar backgrounds and academic preparation, students in remedial courses obtain better educational outcomes. An analysis of community college students (Bettinger & Long, 2005) similarly revealed some positive outcomes of remediation.

Of the colleges and universities that have compensatory courses, the majority use placement tests, given to all entering first-year students, to identify students in need of remedial education. More than three-quarters of the institutions that have such courses require students to enroll in these courses if their scores on math, writing, or reading placement tests fall below a specified criterion (Parsad & Lewis, 2003). About three-quarters of institutions offering remedial courses award institutional credit for them. However, less than 5 percent give degree credit for these courses, and about 10 percent do not award any credit at all for remedial coursework (Parsad & Lewis, 2003).

State legislation requiring assessment has raised questions about the validity of placement tests (Berger, 1997) and the definition of college-level work (Merisotis & Phipps, 2000). Critics argue that most four-year postsecondary institutions should not offer remedial courses. Underprepared students, they insist, are best served at community colleges whose mission is to provide access to higher education (Ignash, 1997). Cost is also a concern. Opponents argue that remediation education utilizes human and financial resources that might be applied to other institutional priorities, or that public funds should not be used to pay, a second time, to develop academic skills that students should have mastered in high school (Parsad & Lewis, 2003). The number of states that are discouraging four-year institutions from offering remediation education is growing (Jenkins & Boswell, 2002). In 2002, the Board of Regents of City University of New York approved a plan to eliminate most remedial education courses from the system's upper division colleges and to locate these in community colleges or in alternative programs (Hebel, 2003a). Other states have limited the amount of time that a student can be enrolled in remedial courses (Hebel, 2003b).

Pressure for Assessment Mounts

Although educators and the general public tend to believe that students from disadvantaged backgrounds should have equal access to a college education, concerns about the levels of remediation underprepared students need at the postsecondary levels fuel public discussion about the higher education quality. Concerns increased throughout the 1980s, and discussions of quality have continued largely unabated. Increasingly, legislators and government officials are engaged in efforts to scrutinize and improve the performance of colleges and universities.

During the 1980s, most colleges and universities considered various assessment techniques and strategies in an effort to respond to public and policy makers' concerns about quality. In 1989, 70 percent of administrators surveyed reported that their institutions were engaged in some kind of assessment activity—but 40 percent indicated that this was in response to mandates. Only about half of those responding believed that assessment had the potential to improve undergraduate education. Moreover, 70 percent feared that assessment data would be misused by public authorities and agencies (El-Khawas, 1989). By 1992, two-thirds of public institutions reported state-mandated assessment procedures and nearly 60 percent of colleges surveyed had made program or curricular changes as a result of assessment (El-Khawas, 1992).

Institutional responses to public and legislative questions about higher education quality have not, however, quelled concerns. During Congressional hearings on each reauthorization of the Higher Education Act, the emphasis on assessment of student learning and quality assurance mechanisms shifted to high gear. In 2006, U.S. Department of Education Secretary Margaret Spellings convened a blue-ribbon panel that produced a report critical of higher education (U.S. Department of Education, 2006). The Spellings report questioned the value of accreditation as a quality assurance mechanism, arguing that it did not provide useful information on the quality of student learning to the public. As a result, the report concluded, prospective students and their parents have limited ability to choose wisely from among the vast number of the nation's colleges and universities.

Prior to the appointment of the Spellings Commission, accreditors had acknowledged the growing consensus that student learning outcomes should be the ultimate test of the quality of academic programs (Council for Higher Education Accreditation, 2003). The Council for Higher Education Accreditation (CHEA), which recognizes individual accreditation agencies, endorsed assessment of student learning outcomes as one dimension of accreditation, and many regional and professional accreditation agencies had already refocused their criteria, reducing the emphasis on quantitative measures of inputs and resources and requiring judgments of educational effectiveness from measurable outcomes (Volkwein, Lattuca, Caffrey, & Reindl, 2003). A study of the impact of a new set of outcomes-based accreditation criteria in undergraduate engineering programs revealed changes in curriculum and instruction, students' classroom experiences, and student learning before and after the implementation of the new criteria (Lattuca, Terenzini, & Volkwein, 2006). While supporting the use of assessment of student learning as a condition of accreditation, many in the higher education community (including representatives from accrediting agencies, institutions, and higher education advocacy organizations) worried that the reforms sought by the Department of Education threatened to create a new level of federal control on colleges and universities (Basken, 2007). In fact, members of Congress themselves demanded that Secretary Spellings desist from establishing new rules for accreditors until they finished the reauthorization discussions and then prohibited her from doing so in the legislation. Clearly, the accountability debate remains in full swing.

INFLUENCES AND POTENTIAL REFORMS

Historian Frederick Rudolph characterized the curriculum as a battleground for society, a locus and transmitter of values, a social artifact, a reproduction of the national ideology, a reflection of faculty research interests and student desires, a mixture of the cultural and the utilitarian, and sometimes a creature of convenience. The main thesis of Rudolph's (1977) history, and ours, is that curricular history is American history; college and university curricula both reflect societal needs and shape them. This interaction is often pragmatic, as Rudolph suggested, and on occasion the pace of cultural, economic, and technological changes temporarily outstrips the capacity of colleges and universities to respond.

Overall, societal influences have encouraged colleges and universities to expand access and to balance attention to general and specialized education. The mix of internal and external forces operating on curricula, and the relative strengths of those influences, may be changing as a result of new calls for quality control through assessment and external evaluation. The model of the academic plan alerts us to the variety of influences active in the sociocultural environment for education at any given time and enhances our understanding of how these affect curriculum planning.

Our historical overview of recurring curricular debates situates the current set of influences we discuss throughout this book. As societal influences have increased student access and student choice, academic decisions have become more visible and more likely to kindle public debate. Educators are increasingly aware that matters once left to college and university presidents and faculties are being observed by other interested factions. Higher education institutions are responsive to social needs and, consequently, more vulnerable to demands for accountability and quality control.

REFERENCES

Adelman, C. (1990). *A college course map: Taxonomy and transcript data.* Washington, DC: U.S. Department of Education, Office of Educational Research and Improvement.

Adelman, C. (1992). *Tourists in our own land: Cultural literacies and the college curriculum.* Washington, DC: U.S. Department of Education, Office of Educational Research and Improvement.

Adelman, C. (1999). *Answers in the tool box: Academic intensity, attendance pattern, and bachelor's degree attainment.* Washington, DC: National Association on Postsecondary Education, Libraries, and Lifelong Learning

Adelman, C. (2000). A parallel universe: Certification in the information technology guild. *Change, 32*(3), 20–29.

Adelman, C. (2004). *The empirical curriculum: Changes in postsecondary course-taking, 1972–2000.* Washington, DC: U.S. Department of Education.

Allen, I. E., & Seaman, J. (2007). *Online nation: Five years of growth in online learning.* Needham, MA: The Sloan Consortium.

Allen, I. E., Seaman, J., & Garrett, R. (2007). *Blending in: The extent and promise of blended education in the United States.* Needham, MA: Sloan Consortium.

Association of American Colleges. (1985). *Integrity in the college curriculum: A report to the academic community.* Washington, DC: Author.

Attewell, P., & Lavin, D. (2007, July 6). Distorted statistics on graduation rates. *Chronicle of Higher Education, 53*(44), B16.

Basken, P. (2007, June 4.). Final attempt to reach a consensus on new accreditation rules fails [Today's news]. *The Chronicle of Higher Education.* Retrieved June 4, 2007, from http://chronicle.com/daily/2007/2006/2007060402n.htm

Bell, D. (1966). *The reforming of general education: The Columbia College experience in its national setting.* Garden City, NY: Anchor, Doubleday.

Bennett, W. (1984). *To reclaim a legacy: A report on the humanities in higher education.* Washington, DC: National Endowment for the Humanities.

Berger, D. (1997). Mandatory assessment and placement: The view from an English department. In J. Ignash (Ed.), *Implementing effective policies for remedial and developmental education* (pp. 33–41). (New Directions for Community Colleges, No. 100). San Francisco: Jossey-Bass.

Bettinger, E., & Long, B. T. (2004). *Shape up or ship out: The effects of remediation on students at four-year colleges.* Cambridge, MA: National Bureau of Economic Research.

Bettinger, E., & Long, B. T (2005). Remediation at the community college: Student participation and outcomes. In B. L. Bower & K. P. Hardy (Eds.), *From distance education to e-learning: Lessons along the way* (pp. 17–26). (New Directions for Community Colleges, No. 128). San Francisco: Jossey-Bass.

Bigge, M. L., & Shermis, S. S. (1992). *Learning theories for teachers* (5th ed.). New York: HarperCollins.

Blackburn, R. T., Armstrong, E., Conrad, C., Didham, J., & McKune, T. (1976). *Changing practices in undergraduate education: A report prepared for the Carnegie Council on Policy Studies.* Berkeley, CA: Carnegie Foundation for the Advancement of Teaching.

Blumenstyk, G. (2005, November 25). Higher education 2015: For-profit outlook. *The Chronicle of Higher Education, 52*(14), A14.

Bollinger, L. C. (2007, June 1). Why diversity matters [Point of View]. *The Chronicle of Higher Education, 53*(39), B20.

Boyer, E. L. (1987). *College: The undergraduate experience in America.* Princeton, NJ: Carnegie Foundation for the Advancement of Teaching.

Brint, S. (2002). Data on higher education in the United States: Are the existing resources adequate? *American Behavioral Scientist, 45*(10), 1493–1522.

Brubacher, J. S., & Rudy, W. (1976). *Higher education in transition: A history of the American colleges and universities, 1636–1976* (3rd ed., rev. and enl. ed.). New York: Harper & Row.

Burke, J. C. (2002, January/February). Accountability for results—ready or not. *Trusteeship,* 14–18.

Burke, J. C., & Minassians, H. P. (2002). The new accountability: From regulation to results. In J. C. Burke & H. P. Minassians (Eds.), *Reporting higher education results: Missing links in the performance chain* (pp. 5–19). (New Directions for Institutional Research, No. 116). San Francisco: Jossey-Bass.

Burke, J. C., & Serban, A. M. (1997). *Performance funding and budgeting for public higher education: Current status and future prospects* (No. ED41479). Albany, NY: Nelson A. Rockefeller Institute of Government.

Carnegie Foundation for the Advancement of Teaching (n.d.). *The Carnegie unit: What is it?* Retrieved on June 3, 2008, from http://www.carnegiefoundation.org/general/sub.asp?key=17&subkey=1874&topkey=17

Cheney, L. V. (1989). *50 hours: A core curriculum for college students.* Washington, DC: National Endowment for the Humanities.

Chronicle of Higher Education Almanac. (2008, August 29) Degrees awarded by type of institution, 2005–2006. *The Chronicle of Higher Education Supplement, 55*(1), 20.

Cohen, A. M., & Brawer, F. B. (2003). *The American community college* (4th ed.). San Francisco: Jossey-Bass.

College Board. (2007). *2007 College-bound seniors: Total group profile report.* Retrieved November 16, 2007, from http://www.collegeboard.com/prod_downloads/about/news_info/cbsenior/yr2007/national-report.pdf

Conrad, C. F., & Wyer, J. C. (1980). *Liberal education in transition* (AAHE-ERIC Higher Education Research Report No. 3). Washington, DC: American Association for Higher Education.

Council for Higher Education Accreditation. (2003). *Statement of mutual responsibilities for student learning outcomes: Accreditation, institutions, and programs.* Washington, DC: Author.

Cuban, L. (1990). Reforming again, again, and again. *Educational Researcher, 19*(1), 3–13.

Dressel, P. L., & DeLisle, F. H. (1970). *Undergraduate curriculum trends.* Washington, DC: American Council on Education.

El-Khawas, E. (1989). *Campus trends, 1989.* Washington, DC: American Council on Education.

El-Khawas, E. (1992). *Campus trends, 1992.* Washington, DC: American Council on Education.

Geiger, R. L. (2000). *The American college in the nineteenth century* (1st ed.). Nashville, TN: Vanderbilt University Press.

Giroux, H. (1992). *Border crossings: Cultural workers and the politics of education.* New York: Routledge.

Goldin, C. (1992). *The meaning of college in the lives of American women: The past 100 years* (No. 4099). Washington, DC: National Bureau of Economic Research.

Green, K. C. (2002). *The 2002 campus computing survey* [electronic version]. Available from http://www.campuscomputing.net.

Hansen, W. L., & Stampen, J. (1993). Higher education: No better access without better quality. *Higher Education Extension Service Review, 4*(2) 1–15.

Hatch Act of 1887, 7 U.S.C. § 361.

Hebel, S. (2003a, January 3). New York Regents approve CUNY's remediation plan after 3 years of monitoring. *The Chronicle of Higher Education, 49*(17), A30.

Hebel, S. (2003b, February 28). Remedial rolls fall at Cal State. *The Chronicle of Higher Education, 49*(25), A27.

Higher Education Act of 1965, 20 U.S.C.A. § 1070 et seq.

Higher Education Amendment of 1968, Pub L. No. 90–575.

Higher Education Amendment of 1972, Pub. L. No. 92–318.

Horn, L., & Nevill, S. (2006). *Profile of undergraduates in U.S. postsecondary education institutions: 2003–2004. With a special analysis of community college students.* (No. 2006–184). Washington, DC: U.S. Department of Education, National Center for Education Statistics.

Horowitz, H. L. (1993). *Alma mater: Design and experience in the women's colleges from their nineteenth-century beginnings to the 1930s* (2nd ed.). Amherst, MA: University of Massachusetts Press.

Ignash, J. (1997). Who should provide postsecondary remedial/developmental education? In J. Ignash (Ed.), *Implementing effective policies for remedial and developmental education.* (pp. 5–20). (New Directions for Community Colleges, No. 100). San Francisco: Jossey-Bass.

Ingels, S. J., Curtin, T. R., Kaufman, P., Alt, M. N., & Chen, X. (2002). *Coming of age in the 1990s: The eighth-grade class of 1988 12 years later.* (NCES 2002–321). Washington, DC: U.S. Department of Education, National Center for Education Statistics.

Institute of International Education. (2007). *Open doors 2007: Report on international educational exchange.* New York: Institute of International Education.

Jenkins, D., & Boswell, K. (2002, September). *State policies on community college remedial education: Findings from a national survey.* Denver, CO: Education Commission of the States.

Keller, F. S. (1968). Goodbye teacher . . . *Journal of Applied Behavior Analysis, 1*, 76–89.

Kinser, K. (2007, March 30). For-profit institutions need to be classified, too [The Chronicle Review]. *The Chronicle of Higher Education, 53*(30), B9.

Kirst, M. W (1998, September 9). Bridging the remediation gap [Electronic Version]. *Education Week, 18*. Retrieved July 2, 2007, from http://www.stanford.edu/group/bridgeproject/gap/remedgap.pdf.

Lattuca, L. R. (2001). *Creating interdisciplinarity: Interdisciplinary research and teaching among college and university faculty.* Nashville, TN: Vanderbilt University Press.

Lattuca, L. R., Terenzini, P. T, & Vokwein, J. F. (2006). *Engineering change: Findings from a study of the impact of EC2000, final report.* Baltimore, MD: Accreditation Board for Engineering and Technology.

Lemann, N. (2000). *The big test: The secret history of the American meritocracy.* New York: Farrar, Straus and Giroux.

Levine, A. (1978). *Handbook on the undergraduate curriculum.* San Francisco: Jossey-Bass.

Li, X. (2007). *Characteristics of minority-serving institutions and minority undergraduates enrolled in these institutions* (No. 2008–156). Washington, DC: National Center for Education Statistics, U.S. Department of Higher Education.

Lindholm, J. A., Szelényi, K., Hurtado, S., & Korn, W. S. (2005). *The American college teacher: National norms for the 2004–2005 HERI faculty survey.* Los Angeles: Higher Education Research Institute, UCLA.

Locke, L. (1989, July/August). General education: In search of facts. *Change, 21*(4), 20–23.

Lucas, C. J. (2006). *American higher education: A history* (2nd ed.). New York: Palgrave Macmillan.

Merisotis, J., & Phipps, R. (2000). Remedial education in colleges and universities: What's really going on? *The Review of Higher Education, 24*(1), 67–85.

Minnich, E. (1990). *Transforming knowledge.* Philadelphia: Temple University Press.

Morrill Land Grant Act of 1862, Pub. L. No. 37–108, 7 U.S.C. § 301.

Morrill Land Grant Act of 1890 § 841, 7 U.S.C. 322 (1890).

National Association of State Universities and Land-Grant Colleges. (1995). Development of the land-grant system: 1862–1994. Retrieved July 2, 2007, from http://w.nasulgc.org/publications/Land_Grant/Development.htm

National Defense Education Act of 1958. P.L. No. 85–86.

National Institute of Education. (1984). *Involvement in learning: Realizing the potential of American higher education* (Report of the NIE Study Group on the Condition of Excellence in American Higher Education). Washington, DC: U.S. Government Printing Office.

Nussbaum, M. C. (1997). *Cultivating humanity: A classical defense of reform in liberal education.* Cambridge, MA: Harvard University Press.

Parsad, B., & Lewis, L. (2003). *Remedial education at degree-granting postsecondary institutions in fall 2000.* (No. NCES-010). Washington, DC: U.S. Department of Education, National Center for Education Statistics.

Ratcliff, J, L. (1992). What we can learn from coursework patterns about improving the undergraduate curriculum. In J. L. Ratcliff (Ed.), *Assessment and curriculum reform* (pp. 5–22). (New Directions for Higher Education, No. 80). San Francisco: Jossey-Bass.

Ratcliff, J. L., Johnson, D. K., La Nasa, S. M., & Gaff, J. G. (2001). *The status of general education in the year 2000: Summary of a national survey.* Washington, DC: Association of American Colleges & Universities.

Redden, E. (2007, May 16). "College prep" without "college" or "prep" [News]. *Inside Higher Ed.* Retrieved May 16, 2007, from http://www.insidehighered.com/news/2007/2005/2016/act

Rudolph, F. (1977). *Curriculum: A history of the American undergraduate course of study since 1636.* San Francisco: Jossey-Bass.

Schuster, J. H., & Finkelstein, M. J. (2006). *The American faculty: The restructuring of academic work and careers.* Baltimore, MD: The Johns Hopkins University Press.

Schwartz, R. A. (2002). The rise and demise of deans of men. *The Review of Higher Education, 26*(2), 217–239.

Servicemen's Readjustment Act of 1944, Pub. L. No. 85–857, 38 U.S.C. § 1 et seq.

Smith, B. L., & McCann, J. (Eds.). (2001). *Reinventing ourselves: Interdisciplinary education, collaborative learning, and experimentation in higher education.* Boston, MA: Anker Publishing Co.

Snyder, T. (Ed.). (1993). *120 years of American education: A statistical portrait.* Washington, DC: Department of Education, National Center for Education Statistics.

Snyder, T. D., Tan, A. G., & Hoffman, C. M. (2006). *Digest of education statistics, 2005* (No. NCES 2006–030). Washington, DC: U.S. Department of Education, National Center for Education Statistics.

Soares, J. A. (2007). *The power of privilege: Yale and America's elite colleges.* Stanford, CA: Stanford University Press.

Southern Regional Education Board. (1979). The search for general education: The pendulum swings back. *Issues in Higher Education No. 15.* Newsletter of the Southern Regional Education Board, Atlanta, GA.

Stark, J. S., & Associates. (1977). *The many faces of educational consumerism.* Lexington, MA: D. C. Heath.

Stark, J. S., & Lattuca, L. R. (1997). *Shaping the college curriculum: Academic plans in action.* Boston: Allyn & Bacon.

Thelin, J. R. (2004). *A history of American higher education.* Baltimore, MD: Johns Hopkins University Press.

Tierney, W. G., & Hentschke, G. C. (2007). *New players, different game: Understanding the rise of for-profit colleges and universities.* Baltimore, MD: The Johns Hopkins University Press.

Toombs, W., Amey, M., & Fairweather, J. (1989, January 7). *Open to view: A catalog analysis of general education.* Paper presented at the Association of American Colleges, Washington, DC.

U.S. Census Bureau. (2008). *Educational attainment of the population 18 years and over, by age, sex, race, and Hispanic origin: 2007.* Retrieved on July 1, 2008, from http://www.census.gov/population/www/socdemo/education/cps2007.html.

U.S. Department of Education; National Center for Education Statistics. (2004). *The condition of education 2004* (No. NCES 2004–077). Washington, DC: U.S. Government Printing Office.

U.S. Department of Education; National Center for Education Statistics. (2005). *The condition of education 2005* (No. 2005–094). Washington, DC: U.S. Government Printing Office.

U.S. Department of Education. (2006). *A test of leadership: Charting the future of U.S. higher education.* Retrieved November 16, 2007, from http://www.ed.gov/about/bdscomm/list/hiedfuture/reports/final-report.pdf

U.S. Department of Education; National Center for Education Statistics. (2007). *The condition of education 2007* (No. NCES 2007–064). Washington, DC: U.S. Government Printing Office.

Volkwein, J. F., Lattuca, L. R., Caffrey, H. S., & Reindl, T. (2003). What works to ensure quality in higher education institutions. *AASCU/CSHE Policy Seminar on Student Success, Accreditation, and Quality Assurance.* Washington, DC: AASC&U and The Pennsylvania State University.

Wallenstein, P. (2008). *Higher education and the civil rights movement: White supremacy, black southerners, and college campuses.* Gainesville, FL: University Press of Florida.

Wechsler, H. S. (1977). *The qualifying student: A history of selective college admissions in America.* Hoboken, NJ: John Wiley & Sons.

Wingspread Group on Higher Education. (1993, December). *An American imperative: Higher expectations for higher education.* Racine, WI: The Johnson Foundation and others.

Zemsky, R. (1989). *Structure and coherence: Measuring the undergraduate curriculum.* Washington, DC: Association of American Colleges.

7

The Rise of the "Practical Arts"

Steven Brint

The major interpretations of the development of the American university focus on knowledge production and the service faculty provide to society through the generation of new ideas and expert advice (Geiger, 1986, 1993; Kerr, 1964; Veysey, 1965). More recent interpretations have maintained these emphases, while focusing also on the significance of increasing business influence on knowledge production (see, for example, Slaughter and Leslie, 1997). However, if we shift our attention from the research to the teaching activities of the undergraduate college, a different picture takes shape. That picture is of the gradual shrinking of the old arts and sciences core of the university and the expansion of occupational and professional programs.

Students of the urban economy have shown that functions once considered ancillary to the main economic activity of the city often become part of the economic core at a later period. Thus, light manufacturing, legal services, and financial services in New York all grew initially out of the activities surrounding shipping in and out of the port of New York (Hoover and Vernon, 1959). Something analogous has occurred in the City of Intellect. Activities considered ancillary in an earlier age have moved to the center and have become leading engines of growth.

To be sure, the professional studies university has nowhere cast the arts and sciences university entirely in its shadow. The two coexist—and with many complementarities. Indeed, I will argue that one of the more surprising outcomes of the rise of the practical arts is not *how much*, but *how little* has changed, at least at the major research universities that are the main focus of this volume. At the same time, the rise of the practical arts has had important consequences for these universities, quite apart from its effects on the distribution of courses and enrollments. Some of these consequences are predictable, others less so. They include: support for the ethos of student utilitarianism, support for faculty entrepreneurship, and support for "social partnership" models of problem solving. These consequences also include migration of arts and sciences faculty toward professional schools and indeed the migration of whole disciplines toward the professional school model, the increased vulnerability of small arts and sciences disciplines, and increased emphases within colleges of arts and sciences on interdisciplinary program development.

A NEW "PRACTICAL ARTS" CORE?

By the liberal arts, I mean the basic fields of science and scholarship housed in colleges of arts and sciences—physics, chemistry, history, English, political science, and others. By the practical arts, I mean occupational and professional programs often housed in their own schools and colleges—business, engineering, computer science, nursing, education, and other fields oriented to preparing students for careers.

The academic year 1969–70 was the last year in which a majority of American four-year college and university students graduated from arts and sciences fields.[1] Over the next fifteen years, occupational fields gained significantly as compared to arts and sciences fields, with nearly two-thirds of degrees awarded in occupational and professional fields 1985–86.[2] The liberal arts rebounded from their nadir in the mid-1980s, but a decisive majority of degrees have continued to be awarded in occupational fields; in 1997–98, more than 58 percent of bachelors' degrees were awarded in occupational fields. Occupational and professional degrees have long dominated at the postbaccalaureate level (even if the arts and sciences category is expanded to include all doctorate degrees), but today they dominate to a far greater extent than before. In 1970–71, practical arts fields accounted for approximately two-thirds of all graduate degrees; today they account for nearly 80 percent.

At the undergraduate level, the fastest-growing degree fields include a number that barely existed thirty years ago. Protective services and computer and information systems both experienced a tenfold growth between 1970–71 and 1995–96; fitness, recreation, and leisure studies experienced a fivefold growth; and communications grew three times larger. Protective services involve programs for training police and other security personnel. Fitness, recreation, and leisure studies include a variety of programs training people to work in recreational areas or in travel and tourism. Few people in 1970 would have considered these "true" professional fields. Engineering technology—more a technicians' occupation than engineering itself—has doubled in size since 1970–71, as have degrees in public administration and many health professions. Some of these programs are not intrinsically connected to higher education by virtue of the cognitive skills demanded by their work. Instead, their rapid growth indicates that higher education is deeply involved in monitoring potential markets for educated labor.

The first adopters of new occupational programs are typically second-tier research universities that have both the resources and incentives to reach out to incorporate training for emerging white-collar occupations. Institutions such as Florida State University, Wayne State University, and Syracuse University have been among the leaders in the creation of new fields.[3] These institutions have been attentive to occupations of high market demand and acceptable social status that can be constructed, in collaboration with aspiring groups of practitioners, to include all of the institutional forms of academic professionalism—notably, an abstract vocabulary, scholarly journals, and a curriculum that can be accredited. Once a field has been accepted by as few as fifty institutions, its place in the curriculum leading to the baccalaureate degree is likely to be secure (Hashem, 2002).

As Table 7.1 indicates, over the last three decades the fast-growing fields have been occupational in virtually every case. The fastest growing of all has been business, which now accounts for some one-fifth of all undergraduate degrees—up from one-seventh in 1970–71. As Clifford Adelman (1995: 229) observed, business became in the 1980s the "empirical core curriculum." By contrast, over the period only four liberal arts fields grew relative to other fields. Two of these fields—psychology and life sciences—are closely linked to health occupations. The other two are "liberal general studies" and "interdisciplinary studies." These latter two—still quite small in numbers of graduates—illustrate one facet of another interesting trend in academe: the slow and still very limited erosion of disciplinary boundaries in the liberal arts.[4] Performing and visual arts, halfway between liberal and occupational fields, have also grown a little relative to other fields.

Virtually every other liberal arts and sciences field has declined not only in relative but also in absolute terms. It is important to emphasize this point, because the higher education system

TABLE 7.1
Growing, Stable, and Declining Degree Fields, 1970–95

A. Bachelor's Degree Fields

A. Growing fields	B. Stable fields	C. Declining fields
I. Fields with Fewer than 1% of BA/BS Degrees in 1995–96		
Law/Legal Studies	Architecture	Library Science
Transportation-Related Studies	Area/Ethnic Studies	Philosophy/Religious Studies
	Communications Technology	
	Theology	
II. Fields with 1–5% of BA/BS Degrees in 1995–96		
Public Admin./Services	Agricultural Science	English Literature*
Visual/Performing Arts	Home Economics	Physical Sciences*
Communications		Mathematics*
Computer/Info Systems		Foreign Languages/Literature*
Parks/Recreation/Fitness		
Protective Services		
Liberal/General Studies		
Interdisciplinary Studies		
III. Fields with More than 5% of BA/BS Degrees in 1995–96		
Business	Engineering	Education†
Health Professions		Social Science/History†
Psychology		
Biological/Life Sciences		

B. Master's Degree Fields

A. Growing fields	B. Stable fields	C. Declining fields
I. Fields with Fewer than 1% of Master's Degrees in 1995–96		
Communications Tech.	Area/Ethnic Studies	Foreign Languages/
Engineering Tech.	Home Economics	Literature
Law/Legal Studies		Philosophy/Religion
Liberal Studies		
Interdisciplinary/Multidisciplinary Studies		
Parks/Recreation/Fitness		
Protective Services		
II. Fields with 1–5% of Master's Degrees in 1995–96		
Communications	Agriculture/Nat. Resources	Biological/Life Sciences
Computer/Information Sciences	Theology	English Literature
	Visual/Performing Arts	Library Science
Psychology	Architecture	Mathematics
		Physical Sciences
		Social Science/History
III. Fields with More than 5% of Master's Degrees in 1995–96		
Business Administration	Engineering	Education
Health Professions		
Public Administration/Services		

Source: Computed from NCES, 1998.
* Decline in both absolute and relative terms for all four fields.
† Decline in both absolute and relative terms for both fields.

is now substantially larger than it was in 1970–71. More than 1.1 million students graduated with bachelors' degrees in 2000–2001, compared to about 840,000 in 1970–71. Under these circumstances, it is not easy for a field to decline in absolute terms, however poorly it may fare in competition with other fields. So, let me say again with emphasis: *During a period in which the system grew by 50 percent, almost every field which constituted the old arts and sciences core of the undergraduate college was in absolute decline. This includes not only all of the humanities and social sciences (except psychology and economics) but also the physical sciences and mathematics.* One could say that all of the traditional liberal arts fields, except those closely connected to health and business careers, have a receding profile in today's universities.

By contrast, only two professional fields have experienced relative declines: library science and education. An important source of change in education has been the upgrading of standards for teacher training in several states, including California and Massachusetts, where prospective teachers are required to major in an academic discipline and to take courses in education programs only in their fifth year for purposes of certification. For its part, library science has been losing out to computer science for jurisdiction over the organization and distribution of information.

Broadly similar patterns can be described at the masters' and doctoral levels. The growing fields at the masters' level are occupational and professional—with the exception of psychology and the various "blended" programs (such as liberal studies, interdisciplinary and multidisciplinary studies, and ethnic studies), The declining fields are those in the traditional arts and sciences—this time including biological and life sciences. Business administration now rivals education for the top spot in masters' degree production, and the top seven degree-producing fields are now all occupational; indeed, computer science will soon supplant the combined social sciences as the eighth largest field at the masters' level. Because the growing fields at the undergraduate and masters' levels require faculty to teach them, doctoral production closely parallels production at the bachelors' and masters' levels; the same fields growing at the bachelors' level are also growing at the doctoral level.

Beginning during the depressed college labor market of the early 1970s (Freeman, 1976), shifts in enrollments have been encouraged by a vastly larger number of students vying for a less rapidly growing number of good careers. From these new enrollment patterns arises the prevailing wisdom: "[In] recent decades, students . . . have been oriented chiefly toward gaining useful skills and knowledge rather than to membership in a cultural elite" (Trow, 1998: 1), and the familiar but nevertheless arresting statistic showing that the proportion of college freshmen interested in attending college to develop a "meaningful philosophy of life" dropped by 45 percent in the period between 1967 and 1987, while the proportion interested in attending to "become well off financially" grew by 40 percent over roughly the same period (Astin, 1998).

When specific growth fields are considered, theories of postindustrial society fare relatively well, as do theories emphasizing postmaterialist trends in cultural life. The landscape described by the data show the increasing popularity of business and business service fields; the advent of mass computing; and the growth of health fields, entertainment, and other quality-of-life concerns. But to explain the patterns fully postindustrial and postmaterialist theories would require revision to account for the increasing importance of government social control and administrative activities, and for the extension of higher education deeply into fields previously occupied by less well educated technicians and front-line bureaucrats. Far from fading away, occupational fields connected to the state have grown more important. New fields, which would have been considered semiprofessional at best in earlier generations, have also entered higher education.

Changes in enrollments and curricula do not, of course, simply reflect changes in the occupational structure in a one-to-one correspondence. In the first place, access to many professional and managerial occupations is not tightly controlled by the credentialing system. Although they may help, degrees are not required to obtain jobs in such fields as computer science, business management, communications, or even education during periods of teacher shortage. Courses of study connected to these jobs would be significantly more important within colleges and universities if access to them depended in all cases on credentialing in the relevant occupational specialty. In addition, the demand for courses of study among students differs significantly from the demand for college-educated workers among employers. Colleges and universities create their own organizationally based demand through prescription of general education requirements. Some colleges and universities, particularly the more elite schools, also choose to limit occupational/professional degree programs at the undergraduate level. The demand for courses may also be influenced by the difficulty of the field, the intellectual capacities of students, and the psychic satisfactions associated with particular fields of study. Today many fields high in psychic satisfaction are closely connected to student interests in forms of personal expression. In this regard, it is instructive to compare the fate of engineering and the performing arts over the last thirty years. Enrollments in engineering, a high labor demand field, have remained generally stable, while enrollments in performing and visual arts, low labor demand fields, have grown substantially. Similarly, enrollments in psychology programs greatly exceed the market demand for psychologists, therapists, and counselors, and reflect the personal discovery interests of many students.

Nevertheless, the university's relative autonomy from the occupational class structure—its propensity to operate on a set of compatible but distinct principles involving judgments about culturally significant forms of knowledge—has been substantially reduced over the last thirty years. Administrators, at least those outside the elite institutions, no longer assume the unquestioned centrality of scientific and humanistic culture, and the old triumvirate of the natural sciences, the social sciences, and the humanities have all experienced a declining appeal. From an historical perspective, this is a striking change. Only a generation ago, UC Berkeley Professor T. R. McConnell, a well-known consultant and influential commentator on higher education, observed: 'Many of (the) professional schools still do not feel at home in the university, and the university does not feel comfortable with them. . . . When the university and the professional school strengthen and support each other . . . the professional school will not only be 'in the university' but also 'of the university'" (McConnell, Anderson, and Hunter, 1962: 257, 261). Clearly, the "practical arts" have come a long way in a generation—so much so that it is no longer always clear which are the "central and fundamental disciplines" in the eyes of university administrators.

CONSEQUENCES

Occupational and professional programs have moved closer to the center of academic life partly because they have modeled themselves on the arts and sciences—developing similarly abstract vocabularies, similarly illuminating theoretical perspectives, and similarly rigorous conceptual schemes (see, for example, Schlossman and Sedlak, 1988). If the liberal arts have been dethroned, they have been usurped by a claimant whose principles and bearing show striking similarities to those of the previous rulers.

But have the arts and sciences really been dethroned? Survey data suggest some reasons for skepticism. The majority of arts and sciences faculty at American universities do not portray themselves as alienated. Fewer than one in five say that the phrase "at odds with the administration" is "very descriptive" of circumstances at their institutions, and the great majority consider themselves "satisfied" or "very satisfied" with their jobs (Finkelstein, Seal, and Schuster, 1997: 58–59). At Research I universities, arts and sciences faculty are as satisfied as their colleagues in professional schools, and humanities and social sciences faculty are, rather surprisingly, the most satisfied of all.

One reason may be that employment conditions in the arts and sciences have not suffered as much as one might expect given the changing student enrollment patterns. It is true that the proportion of faculty in the arts and sciences has declined relative to the proportion of faculty in occupational and professional programs. Yet at a time in the later 1980s and early 1990s when three-fifths of undergraduate degrees (and three-quarters of graduate degrees) were awarded in professional programs, almost half of new hires continued to be in arts and sciences fields (ibid.: 22). Moreover, adjusting for inflation, tenure-track faculty salaries in the arts and sciences rose in the 1980s and 1990s (Scott and Bereman, 1992), and faculty in all fields have been more likely in recent years than in the 1970s and 1980s to rate their salaries as "good" or "excellent" (Finkelstein, Seal, and Schuster, 1998: 59). Nor have the work conditions of faculty suffered significantly. At both doctoral-granting and research universities, arts and sciences faculty hired in the late 1980s and early 1990s spent somewhat less time teaching than their more senior colleagues—and they taught less at a comparable stage in their careers than their predecessors of an earlier academic generation (ibid.: 65–67).

Differences by Tier and Segment

Even so, the answer to the question, Have the arts and sciences been dethroned? depends on where one looks among the large number of universities in the United States. The Carnegie Foundation classification scheme until recently grouped universities into three major categories: Research Universities, Doctoral-granting Universities, and Comprehensive (or master's-granting) Universities. The rise of the practical arts has led to impressive changes at most of the more than six hundred doctoral and comprehensive institutions. Here enrollments have shifted dramatically toward the practical arts, and liberal arts faculty have in many cases become primarily providers of distribution requirements for students in departments and schools of professional studies. Without the protection of distribution requirements, arts and sciences faculty at institutions such as Central Michigan University, San Jose State University, Sam Houston State University, and the University of Massachusetts-Boston would shrink to a small cadre. At these institutions, senior faculty in the arts and sciences do show comparatively high levels of dissatisfaction. This dissatisfaction may reflect, at least in part, a sense of status incongruity among professors who were trained during a period when the arts and sciences formed the undisputed disciplinary core of the system.

The story is different and more complex, however, in the country's research universities, which are the main focus of this volume. Among the research universities, the movement over time has been in one of two directions—either toward a pattern of many relatively equal parts—the multiversity of Clark Kerr's vision—or toward a continued focus on the arts and sciences as the undergraduate core of the university. Multiversities can be distinguished from liberal arts universities by the number of fields—and particularly the number of applied fields—in which baccalaureate degrees are offered.[5]

Harriet Morgan's (1998) analysis of curricular change between 1966 and 1992 indicates a growth in both the multiversity and the liberal arts university categories. Among research universities, multiversities out-number liberal arts universities by a ratio of approximately two to one. Multiversities are most common among the public land-grant institutions, particularly those in the Midwest, the mountain states, and the South, and in urban private universities serving upwardly mobile student populations. Thus, the University of Arizona, the University of Nebraska, the University of Florida, Temple University, and the University of Cincinnati are examples of multiversities. By contrast, the liberal arts university model predominates among the most prestigious research universities, including both the elite privates and the flagship campuses of the leading public land-grant institutions. The great majority of the fifty leading research universities fall in this category. Duke, Northwestern, UC-Berkeley, the University of Virginia, and Yale all fall in the liberal arts university group.[6] Occupational and professional training is typically highly restricted for undergraduates at these elite universities. This restriction is a consequence of value commitments linked to status, and it ensures that undergraduates focus their professional aspirations on the graduate level.

Quantitative changes in enrollments are only one measure of changing centrality; the more elusive criterion of prestige is another and frequently far more important measure. Undoubtedly the arts and sciences stand at the highest levels of prestige at liberal arts universities, together with graduate schools of business, law, and medicine. Even at multiversities, however, where student enrollments and faculty appointments have increased the quantitative strength of occupational fields, the arts and sciences colleges often rank highest in prestige.

The Continuing Strength of the Arts and Sciences

Some sources of the continuing strength of the arts and sciences at research universities are obvious enough. The distinctive mission of research universities is to conduct research, and the arts and sciences are the original sources of this mission. Among these universities, membership in prestigious organizations such as the Association of American Universities requires demonstration of a well-balanced scholarly and scientific eminence. The natural sciences are a particularly important source both of prestige and revenues for all research universities because of the grants they generate. Support for them seems secure, regardless of trends in undergraduate enrollments. It should be noted too that, even in multiversities, the arts and sciences are an important element in enrollment management. Arts and sciences faculty offer an indispensable array of service courses for students in all fields. In addition, students who do not perform well in fields where projected incomes are high (or do not have interest in these fields) must have some place to go. Some of these destination fields are in the "soft" humanities and social sciences; others are in the schools of the so-called minor professions, such as communications, education, and social work (Glazer, 1974).

Some less obvious reasons also exist for the continued importance, even centrality, of the arts and sciences in research universities. The most consequential of these have to do with the priority placed by professors in all fields on the more purely intellectual side of academic life, and with the disproportionate influence on university governance exercised by administrators and faculty drawn from the arts and sciences. Because these strengths are not always appreciated by contemporary observers of the "market-driven university," I will discuss them at somewhat greater length.

Cultural Prestige.   The university would be a very easy institution to analyze if its only source of strength lay in its connection to high-income occupations. But this is manifestly not the case. The prestige of academic fields reflects their cultural distinction at least as much as their value in the labor market (see Bourdieu, 1984, 1988).

Faculty in the arts and sciences bring attention to the university in ways that are not easily duplicated by faculty in occupational and professional fields. The most prestigious academic bodies are connected to the arts and sciences: the National Academy of Sciences, the American Academy of Arts and Sciences, the American Council of Learned Sciences, the MacArthur and the Guggenheim fellowships. These are the institutions that tend to speak for the values of higher education at the most elite levels. All are dominated by people trained in the arts and sciences. Similarly, studies of intellectual life show that authors of articles in the most prestigious general intellectual periodicals, such as the *New York Review of Books* and the *New York Times Book Review*, are likely to be either journalists or professors in the humanities and social sciences. Faculty in professional fields are not well represented (Brint, 1994: chap. 7). Not surprisingly while public figures rely on technical experts drawn from a variety of fields to help develop and assess policies, they rely almost exclusively on liberal arts faculty and writers influenced by them to define broader themes and to suggest proper contexts for understanding.

Arts and sciences faculty are the university's experts in fundamental forms of analysis, whether in verbal or mathematical expression. Their theoretical and methodological skills encourage the continuing centrality of the liberal arts within the university. They allow for the creation of new knowledge. And they tend, however unevenly, to influence the conduct of research in the professional schools and occupational programs. Law is a rather self-enclosed system, but even many law professors have adopted approaches that combine case analysis with the tools of the humanities and social sciences. Faculty members in other professional schools remain still more dependent on faculty in basic fields. Professors in business rely overwhelmingly on economists and other social scientists for providing theoretical and methodological tools. Professors in engineering draw on the work of physicists and mathematicians for similar reasons. Professors in education meld practitioner knowledge of schools with the tools of the humanities and the social and behavioral sciences. And clinical faculty members in medical schools rely on the knowledge of biologists, microbiologists, and biochemists, who form their basic science faculties. Because they are less deeply involved, in general, in the fundamental theoretical and methodological questions of their disciplines, faculty in the professional schools may enjoy very high standing outside the university, while remaining mindful of the intellectual status of the arts and sciences disciplines, particularly those most closely connected to their work.

Nor would it be wise to underestimate the university's commitment to encouraging students' intellectual development through study of the liberal arts. Many faculty and administrators, including a great many in professional schools, continue to agree with a traditional justification for the centrality of the arts and sciences in undergraduate studies: that they provide superior opportunities for the development of the thinking abilities that mark a broadly capable, rather than simply a technically proficient, mind. These thinking abilities include the capacities to understand logical relations and abstract languages, to make meaningful discriminations, to develop empathy, to appreciate the interplay between the particular and the general, to understand the rhetoric and structure of arguments, to perceive and evaluate context, and to develop skills in building evidence in support of a position. Roger Geiger's conclusion of two decades ago therefore continues to ring true to many faculty and administrators: "[S]haping the intellectual maturation of young people and widening their cultural horizons has traditionally been the strength and the mission of American undergraduate education. . . . If [this source of strength and mission falls into disfavor], the vitality of intellectual life throughout the broad middle of the academic hierarchy will deteriorate badly" (1980: 54).

Participation in Governance. Participation in governance is another less obvious factor that may help to explain the continuing strength of the arts and sciences. We know that the backgrounds of top executives can influence the climate of the firms they lead (Useem, 1989). If this is true in corporations, is it not likely to be true a fortiori in colleges and universities?

The number of college and university presidents from nonacademic backgrounds has grown significantly over the last thirty years, but these top administrators are still primarily recruited from either the arts and sciences or education (American Council of Education, 2000). Doctoral-granting institutions, including research universities, are far more likely than the rest of higher education to have presidents trained in a liberal arts rather than a professional field.[7] The difference a degree field makes should not be overemphasized. All academic leaders are required to assess overall institutional interests—the opportunities, benefits, and costs of moving in one direction or another relative to the actions of their relevant comparison institutions. Nevertheless,

TABLE 7.2
Background of College and University Presidents, 1986 and 1998 (percent)

Field	Public		Private	
	1998	*1986*	*1998*	*1986*
	Doctorate-Granting			
Liberal Arts*	52	60	50	57
Education	9	10	6	12
Religion/Theology	0	0	11	9
Other Professional†	39	30	33	22
	Master's-Granting			
Liberal Arts*	48	50	41	47
Education	28	37	29	30
Religion/Theology	0	1	12	13
Other Professional†	22	12	19	10
	Baccalaureate-Granting			
Liberal Arts*	53	54	44	48
Education	32	26	30	28
Religion/Theology	0	3	10	16
Other Professional†	13	12	17	8

Sources: American Council on Education, 1995: 101, 107; American Council on Education, 2000: 67.
* Liberal arts includes biological sciences, physical sciences, social sciences, humanities, and fine arts.
† Other professional programs include agriculture, engineering, medicine, other health professions, law, and nonspecified professional fields.

within these constraints, it seems likely that disciplinary backgrounds predispose many, and perhaps most, presidents and provosts to see the particular virtues of the fields and colleges closest to their own (compare Kraatz and Zajac, 1998).

Patterns of faculty involvement in governance may be at least equally important. Although the influence of faculty senates is limited today, participation in the political process on campus remains a factor in shaping agendas and policy decisions. By serving on committees and by taking an active role in the politics of university decision-making, arts and sciences faculty put themselves in a position to interact on collegial grounds with administrators, to protect their priorities, and even to help select new university leaders.

Faculty in the arts and sciences may be more likely than those in professional programs to consider the university "theirs" and to participate in academic senate and other governance activities. As a way to begin to test this proposition, I conducted a study of participation as chairs of academic senate standing committees on seven of the University of California's nine campuses, excluding only the San Francisco campus, which is exclusively medical, and the Santa Cruz campus, which has no professional programs. Such a study is only a beginning, but it suggests that the topic deserves further attention. In the three study years (1994–95, 1996–97, and 1998–99), arts and sciences faculty served as chairs on a majority of committees on all seven campuses. These faculty members served as chairs in a significantly higher than expected proportion at four of the seven campuses. On the other campuses, participation was approximately proportionate to the distribution of faculty between liberal arts and professional programs.[8]

New Priorities in the University

In spite of the continuing strength of the arts and sciences, it is clear that some important changes have occurred in the purposes and activities of research universities over the last thirty years. These include: (a) the rise of a utilitarian ethos among students; (b) the rise of faculty and university entrepreneurship; and (c) the extension of "social partnership" models in community relations. To what extent might the rise of the practical arts be related to these developments?

The curricular changes discussed in this chapter show a distinct affinity with each of these developments, but they have been by no means their only or primary cause. In some cases, they have not been a direct cause at all. The following developments show a much more direct relationship to these new priorities of the university:

- College attendance has become the norm rather than the exception; two-thirds of students aged eighteen to twenty-four (and an increasing proportion of older adults) now spend some time studying at a college or university.
- Throughout the 1970s and into the 1980s the relative share of state funding of public universities declined, leading to a markedly greater financial dependence on student tuition and fees, and on private gifts.
- Legislation passed in the early 1980s, particularly the Economic Recovery Act of 1981 and the Bayh-Dole Patent and Trademark Act of 1980, provided incentives for both universities and industries to deepen their collaborative involvements in research.
- The role of "big government" came under ideological attack in the 1970s and early 1980s, opening the way for the rise of smaller-scale collaborative solutions to problems of economic and social development.

Because the rise of the practical arts is but one source of support for the new social and economic priorities of the university, my argument in this section will be based on affinities, not on causality. I will argue that students and faculty in occupational and professional programs provide a constituency of support, and a growing one, for key changes in the university's relation to society, but I will not argue that they have been a direct cause of these developments.

The Ethos of Utilitarianism among Students.   The ethos of utilitarianism can be defined as the tendency of students think of higher education primarily as a means to obtain credentials that will be valuable to them in the labor market. Responses to surveys show that students in occupational and professional programs are more likely than those in the arts and sciences to express utilitarian outlooks. As the data in Table 7.3 indicate, freshmen who expect to declare professional majors are 10 percent more likely than those who expect liberal arts majors to say that "being well off financially" is essential to them. They are more than 10 percent less likely to say that developing a meaningful philosophy of life is essential.

Faculty members teaching in occupational and professional programs tend to support the practical, job-oriented interests of students. They are much more likely than liberal arts faculty to say, for example, that being well off financially is essential or very important to them. They are also significantly more likely to supplement their incomes with outside consulting or consultation with clients and patients.[9]

Entrepreneurial Activities among Faculty.   Higher education scholars have used the term "entrepreneurial" in a variety of ways. I will focus on the efforts of universities and individual faculty to capitalize on research discoveries. These efforts to profit from research include partnership arrangements with industries for support of potentially profitable research, patent and licensing activity, and the creation of faculty and graduate student spin-off firms.

Much of the recent activity in patenting and licensing is concentrated in the applied biomedical sciences. Indeed, these disciplines are the center of many forms of entrepreneurial activity in the university. Studies of university faculty engaging in collaborative research with industry show a compatible but slightly different picture. According to the studies of Wesley Cohen and his colleagues, chemistry and biology are the disciplines most likely to be represented in university-industry research centers (UIRCs). However, if one looks at the disciplines represented at least 10

TABLE 7.3
Attitudes and Activities Related to Dimensions of Materialism and Service, University Freshmen and Faculty, by Academic Discipline Categories, 1998 (percent)

A. Freshmen attitudes*	Being very well off financially is essential or very important	Developing a meaningful philosophy of life is essential	Taking part in community action is very important or essential	Being a community leader is very important or essential
Expect Professional Major†	39%	14%	22%	35%
Expect Liberal Arts Major‡	29%	25%	29%	27%

B. Faculty attitudes/activities	Being well off financially is essential or very important	Spend one hour or more per week on free-lance consulting work	Spend one hour or more per week consulting patients or clients	
Professional Disciplines§	45%	46%	29%	
Liberal Arts Disciplines ‖	33%	32%	10%	

Source: Higher Education Research Institute (1998a, 1998b).
All differences by discipline are significant at p < .05.
* The reported percentages are based on weighting to reflect the distribution of freshmen by expected majors.
† Professional majors include agriculture, business, education, engineering, and health professions.
‡ Liberal arts majors include biological sciences, English, history/political science, humanities, fine arts, mathematics/statistics, physical sciences, and social sciences.
§ Professional disciplines include all departmental affiliations in agriculture and forestry, business, education, engineering, health sciences, and "other technical" disciplines.
‖ Liberal Arts disciplines include all departmental affiliations in biological sciences, English, humanities, fine arts, mathematics and statistics, physical sciences, and social sciences.

percent of the UIRCs in Cohen's sample, professional disciplines, such as engineering and agriculture, outnumber basic science disciplines by two to one (Cohen et al., 1998).[10] (See Table 7.4.)

TABLE 7.4
Disciplines Represented in University-Industry Research Center Research Activities, 1990

	Percent of UIRCs in which discipline is represented in research activities	Number of UIRCs
Natural Science Disciplines		
Chemistry	39	192
Biology	34	169
Physics	24	120
Geology/Earth Sciences	20	91
Mathematics	11	54
Professional Schools/Programs		
Materials Engineering	34	171
Electrical Engineering	32	159
Mechanical Engineering	31	155
Materials Science	29	145
Chemical Engineering	28	137
Computer Science	26	130
Agricultural Sciences	21	106
Civil Engineering	21	103
Medical Sciences	19	93
Industrial Engineering	18	87
Aeronautical/Astronautical Engineering	12	58
Applied Math/Operations Research	12	57
Total N		497

Source: Cohen, Florida, and Goe, 1994: 14.
Note: Only disciplines represented in 10 percent or more of the UIRCs are reported in this table.

Social Partnerships. Less frequently noted has been the rise of community service and social partnership arrangements on campus (Newman, 1985). These activities include "service learning" opportunities and broader institutional commitments to community development. The University of California, Berkeley, for example, currently lists more than three hundred community-serving activities of various types. These activities include: volunteer and charity work and charitable donations; educational outreach activities; research specifically designated as oriented to public service; and community economic development activities. In many research universities, both public and private, community and civic activity extends from relatively large-scale community development and public research activities to "bite-size" programs, such as computer and furniture donations, the provision of extra street-sweeping and "safety ambassadors" in surrounding neighborhoods, and small-scale job training programs for local residents (Brint and Levy, 1999: 183–85).

According to the most recent survey by Campus Compact, five of the top ten "service-learning" disciplines are professional: education, social work, business, communications, and nursing. Two others—psychology and biology—attract many students planning careers in counseling and the health professions (Campus Compact, 1998: 41,197). These data may reflect at least a weak affinity between the ethos of professionalism and the growing significance of social partnership activities in academe. The ethos of professionalism, after all, encourages engagement with practical problem-solving in the world, rather than detachment.

Additional support comes from national faculty data. In 1998 university faculty teaching in professional programs were more likely than their colleagues in the liberal arts to say they spent at least one hour per week on community or public service (71 percent of occupational and professional faculty, compared to 60 percent of liberal arts faculty). They were also more likely to agree strongly that colleges should encourage students to participate in community service activities. Business faculty were more likely than humanities faculty to take these positions, and engineering faculty were more likely than natural science faculty to take them. The differences here are not large, but they are at least mildly supportive of the argument that affinities exist between the rise of the practical arts and university-community partnerships.

New Priorities and Practices in the Liberal Arts

Even at the leading research universities, arts and sciences departments often feel themselves to be under-supported. The temptation is great to consider one's own field under special duress, while others thrive. But mathematics does not prosper while English languishes. The pressure is in fact quite general in the arts and sciences disciplines, and it is connected to the growing significance of the practical arts.

Thus pressure has led to a number of consequences for colleges of arts and sciences. Among the most important of these are: (a) the migration of individual faculty and even whole fields in the direction of professional preparation; (b) the increased vulnerability of the smaller arts and sciences fields; and (c) the growth of interdisciplinary programs in the arts and sciences—a phenomenon likely to become still more important in the future.

Migrations of Faculty and Disciplines. If growth is greater in occupational and professional programs, arts and sciences faculty will have incentives to migrate to those programs, because of the greater number of positions available and sometimes also because of the higher salaries offered. Tables 7.5 and 7.6 examine the academic origins and destinations of faculty in two survey years, 1969 and 1992.[11] The data show that more movement exists in virtually all fields in 1992 than in 1969.

TABLE 7.5
Academic Origins and Destinations, 1969 and 1992 (percent)

I. All Full-time Faculty: 1992

Academic origin: professional	Academic destination			
	Same field	*Other professional**	*Letters and sciences*	*Other fields†*
Agriculture/Home Econ.	59.3	15.0	24.5	1.1
Business	68.6	19.6	10.3	1.5
Education	79.7	8.3	10.9	1.1
Engineering	79.3	8.8	9.7	2.1
Health Sciences	76.3	14.1	8.9	.5
Other Professional	71.2	12.1	15.0	1.7
Academic origin: letters and sciences	*Same field*	*Other letters and sciences*	*Letters and sciences*	*Other fields†*
Fine Arts	89.8	4.1	4.9	1.2
Humanities	85.3	3.8	10.3	.7
Natural Sciences	83.3	2.0	14.4	.3
Social Sciences	83.1	3.8	12.6	.5

II. All Full-time Faculty: 1969

Academic origin: professional	Academic destination			
	Same field	*Other professional**	*Letters and sciences*	*Other fields†*
Business	67.3	17.8	13.7	.3
Education	87.9	2.2	9.6	.2
Engineering	83.1	5.5	9.3	—
Health Sciences	82.9	6.3	9.6	.2
Other Professional	81.2	7.5	9.3	.1
Academic origin: letters and sciences	*Same field*	*Other letters and sciences*	*Letters and sciences*	*Other fields†*
Fine Arts	92.0	2.9	4.2	.1
Humanities	94.1	2.3	3.2	.1
Natural Sciences	90.8	.9	7.8	—
Social Sciences	88.0	3.6	7.8	.2

Sources: Carnegie Foundation for the Advancement of Teaching Faculty Survey, 1969; National Survey of Postsecondary Faculty, 1993.
* "Other Professional" includes architecture and environmental design; city, community, and regional planning; interior design; advertising; communications and communications technologies; law; library science; parks and recreation; theology; protective services; public affairs; and science and engineering technologies. Agriculture and home economics are included in this category in 1969 only.
† "Other Fields" includes all fields otherwise uncategorizable. These include many fields that would at one time have been considered preparation for blue collar or lower white collar occupations, such as industrial arts, construction, personal service, repair, precision production, and transportation-related fields.

In the earlier academic generation, people trained in the arts and sciences were particularly unlikely to move from their home disciplines. But when they did move, they typically moved into professional programs. Today fewer faculty members trained in the arts and sciences remain in their home disciplines, and the amount of increased movement into professional programs is roughly proportionate to this decline in the proportion of those who stay in their home disciplines. Major changes have also occurred among faculty trained in professional schools. In the previous academic generation, people trained in professional programs were also more likely to remain in their home disciplines than they are today. When they did move, they tended to move into associated disciplines in the arts and sciences. For example,

TABLE 7.6
Professional Migration Ratios

	1992	1969
Agriculture/Home Economics	−9.5	NA
Business	+9.3	+4.1
Education	−2.6	−7.4
Engineering	−.9	−3.8
Health Sciences	+5.2	−3.3
Fine Arts	+.8	+1.3
Humanities	+6.5	+.9
Natural Sciences	+12.4	+6.9
Social Sciences	+8.8	+4.2

Note: Professional Migration Ratio = percentage movement into professional − percentage movement into arts and sciences. A positive ratio indicates net movement into professional programs. A negative ratio indicates net movement into arts and sciences.

doctorates in engineering sometimes moved into natural science departments, and doctorates in education sometimes moved into the humanities or social sciences. Today the net movement of doctorates in business and health sciences has been toward other professional programs, while doctorates in education and engineering remain slightly more likely to move into the arts and sciences. But even in the latter cases, the proportion moving into the arts and sciences is now substantially lower than in 1969. Overall, this is a picture of a faculty less anchored to its fields of origin and one that has been increasingly attracted to teaching in occupational and professional programs.[12]

Perhaps more surprising than the migration of individual faculty has been the migration of whole disciplines and specialty areas within disciplines toward professional organization. Perhaps the most notable examples of this trend are psychology and chemistry. Psychology has long been divided between researchers and clinicians, but with the arrival of the licensing of clinical psychologists, the major part of psychology has been transformed into a professional field. Chemists have eschewed occupational licensing, but they increasingly market themselves as a field providing training for positions in chemical-based industries.

Professionalization can also occur through a splitting of tracks within departments and majors. At some institutions economics has become a substitute business major for the great majority of students, while remaining a basic social science field for the minority of students with public policy and academic interests. In sociology, criminology and social welfare tracks are sometimes organized as professional programs, while the major itself remains academic. In political science, public affairs and international relations have become professional tracks at some institutions, while the subdisciplines of political theory, American politics, and comparative politics remain academic.

The Increased Vulnerability of Small Fields. The research thus far on program closings and mergers suggests that the fields most likely to suffer in a competitive environment are those involved in public sector social welfare activities (Gumport, 1993; Morphew, 1998; Slaughter and Silva, 1985). It seems likely that these are not the only fields to face dimmer prospects in an environment in which occupational training programs are increasingly important. Very small fields are likely to be vulnerable, too, unless they are staffed by unusually distinguished faculty or so rare as to be virtually one of a kind.[13] Reliable data do not exist about departmental cutbacks, consolidations, and closings nationwide, but the existing evidence suggests that small departments in area studies and foreign languages have been vulnerable (see, for example, National Council of Area Studies, 1991). The same may be true of some other humanities disciplines. The number of philosophy departments, for example, appears to have declined since the mid-1970s (Philosophy Documentation Center, 1974–95).

In most cases, the issue is not elimination but reduction through attrition and budgetary cutbacks. Administrators can encourage the consolidation of smaller fields by proposing "integrated" majors involving a number of related, small fields. Some small universities with low science enrollments, for example, have adopted integrated natural science majors. Under pressure, scholars in small fields sometimes themselves seek affiliation with larger departments. Thus, archaeologists rarely attempt to make a go of it outside of anthropology departments, and classicists have in some cases transformed themselves into experts in comparative ancient civilizations. Geneticists only rarely attempt to sustain departments separate from other biological sciences (National Center for Educational Statistics, 1998: 285–92).

The Rise of Interdisciplinary Programs.   Statistics on degrees awarded indicate a small to moderate increase in the number of interdisciplinary and multidisciplinary degrees awarded in recent years. These statistics do not do justice to the level of interest in interdisciplinary work in contemporary universities. Many universities, such as the University of Rochester and UCLA, have reorganized their general education curriculum to emphasize the contribution of several disciplines to the understanding of multidisciplinary topics. Foundations, such as the Hewlett Foundation, have provided funds for these "cluster courses." Liberal arts deans throughout the country have been promoting new research umbrella groups and the hiring of faculty who "improve two or three fields rather than one." The new model college searches not for replacements to keep up with specialized fields, but for "synergies" across fields.

To a considerable degree, this remarkable interest in interdisciplinary work reflects a sense that the intellectual excitement lies at the boundaries of fields, rather than in the development of existing disciplinary specialties. The shifting intellectual frontiers in the biological and biomedical sciences and the perceived successes of interdisciplinary "cultural studies" programs have helped to fuel this sense of excitement. But budgetary exigencies may ultimately figure at least as prominently in the thinking of university administrators. As Lynn Hunt has observed, intellectual excitement is but one source of interest in interdisciplinary program development. "[I]nterdisciplinarity may only make the case that humanities faculty are all interchangeable and hence that many are expendable. Interdisciplinarity has tended to weaken the argument for . . . coverage . . . and might thereby facilitate downsizing" (Hunt, 1997: 28).

The ideology of interdisciplinary development substitutes coverage of new topics and approaches for coverage of specialized scholarly fields, the ethos of cross-fertilization for the ethos of specialization, and the politics of coalition-building among groups of enterprising faculty and key administrators for the politics of disciplinary authority. Perhaps this is why many believe that interdisciplinary programs are ultimately more likely to satisfy provosts than professors (Menand, 1997: 214). Yet for institutions focusing scarce resources on developing new professional programs, there may be little choice but to make the most of the current wave of enthusiasm for interdisciplinary work.

CONCLUSION

The sharp shift of student enrollments over the last thirty years from the arts and sciences to occupational programs represents an important change in American higher education. It is reasonable to ask whether these shifts have led the rise of a new "practical arts" core, replacing the old liberal arts and sciences core of the undergraduate college. The answer given in this chapter is that such an outcome is in fact evident at many master's and doctoral-granting institutions, but that the situation is less clear at leading research universities. In these institutions arts and sciences faculty have generally been able to maintain their centrality, due to the cultural prestige of their disciplines and perhaps also their greater propensity to participate in university governance, among other factors.

Nevertheless, some important changes have occurred in the wake of the shift of students toward the practical arts. These include: reinforcement of utilitarianism as the dominant ethos among students; contributions to the acceptability of faculty and university entrepreneurship; and encouragement of collaborative models for the solution of social problems. The rise of the practical arts has also encouraged migrations of faculty and even whole disciplines toward the occupational training fields, created new vulnerabilities among the smaller arts and sciences fields, and intensified interdisciplinary trends in the liberal arts.

As these changes unfold, opinion data suggest that humanists and scientists are more like one another than they are like professional school faculty on some important issues, such as levels of skepticism about administrators' motivations (arts and sciences faculty are more skeptical), support for intellectual over service commitments (arts and sciences faculty are more purely intellectual), and resistance to the ethos of the market (arts and sciences faculty are more resistant). Thus, the division in mentality represented by C. P. Snow's "two cultures" of science and the humanities is now crosscut, in limited but observable ways, by another line of cleavage dividing professors of the liberal and the practical arts. These tensions are one result of a shift in orientation that has allowed the City of Intellect to prosper even as its one-time center has moved to the periphery in some institutions and become but one of several competing nuclei in many others.

NOTES

I would like to thank Andrew Abbott, John Barcroft, Michael E. Brint, Roger L. Geiger, Michael Nacht, Francisco O. Ramirez, Judith Wegener, and David Weiman for comments that improved the quality of this chapter. I would also like to thank Maria Bertero-Barcelo, William Korn, Charles S. Levy, Shoon Lio, Mandy Liu, Harriet P. Morgan, and Mark Riddle for research assistance.

1. I have classified the visual and performing arts as liberal arts fields, and communications as an occupational field. At the graduate level, I have classified both of these fields as occupational. I have also classified virtually all other fields outside the humanities, social sciences, and natural sciences as occupational. These include such large and familiar fields as business, engineering, and education. They also include fields such as agriculture and natural resources, computer and information sciences, and protective services. At the graduate level, I have compared occupational-professional degrees to a combined category of liberal arts and academic research degrees. This comparison makes intuitive sense insofar as we want to look at the hypothesized replacement of the old core of the university, involving basic scholarly and scientific research, with a hypothesized new core of programs preparing students for employment. In the occupational-professional category, I have included all occupationally oriented masters' fields plus all first professional degree programs. In the liberal arts and academic category, I have included all liberal arts masters' fields plus all doctoral fields. The major changes here are adding first professional degree programs—that is, degrees in theology, law, and medical areas—to the occupational-professional category (where they would belong in any event) and placing all research degrees (including those in fields such as business and engineering) as part of the liberal arts-academic research category.

2. 1 will concentrate on degrees awarded rather than enrollments, because of methodological problems surrounding the use of enrollments for comparing fields and change over time. Comparison of enrollments is particularly difficult because educational programs are organized differently at different schools and across fields. Some institutions begin enrollment in a professional college in freshman year, while others begin to count in the junior year. Typically when a program is organized in a separate school or college, enrollments include students in all four years. When the program is organized in a department or a college of arts and sciences, only the junior and senior years are reported. Enrollments are also less reliably reported to NCES than are degrees awarded. A few institutions fail to report

enrollments; therefore, it is necessary to make estimates in order that the totals may take all institutions into account. For a detailed analysis of data on enrollments and degrees from 1970 through 1985, see Bowen and Sosa (1989).

3. Although most new fields begin at nonelite research universities, some new fields with links to prestigious established fields (computer science and legal studies are two examples) begin at more elite institutions (see Hashem, 2002).

4. Note that interdisciplinary studies does not include either area studies or ethnic studies, fields that have remained both small and relatively stable over the twenty-five-year period. Instead, it includes other sorts of interdisciplinary programs, such as Renaissance studies, environmental studies, comparative ancient civilizations, and politics, philosophy, and economics.

5. Based on a cluster analysis of degrees awarded by institution, Morgan (1998: 35–36) defines "multiversities" operationally as institutions offering master's in education and business and law degrees, each of which account for more than 1 percent of degrees granted. In addition, they grant more than 1 percent of baccalaureate degrees in at least twenty-five different fields, eleven of them applied. She defines "liberal arts universities" as institutions granting more than 1 percent of degrees in each of several graduate and professional fields and, with the exception of graduate-level professional education, granting degrees primarily in traditional arts and sciences fields. I will use this empirically based definition of patterns of differentiation among research universities.

6. I am grateful to Harriet P. Morgan for sharing the detailed results of her dissertation research. This section is drawn from an unpublished file of institutions from her cluster analysis of HEGIS/IPEDS degrees awarded data for the years 1966 to 1992. I have cross-classified her findings by Carnegie classification codes to describe changes in research universities during the period.

7. Even in the doctorate-granting institutions, men and women with doctorates in educational management have gained over the last decade in public institutions, moving from 10 to 18 percent of the total number of presidents sampled by the American Council on Education.

8. One can imagine two possible explanations for these findings. One is that the outward looking norms of professional life lead to a relatively lower level of interest in university governance. Another possibility is that busier faculty, whatever their fields, are less able to participate, and less interested. The particularly low level of participation of medical and business school faculty suggests that the second hypothesis may be closer to the mark.

9. Data exist on only one facet of student consumerism—the interests of students in practical, job-related courses of study. The desire of universities to maintain or improve the size and quality of their applicant pool has also greatly encouraged a buyer's market for college amenities. University funds have consequently been poured into recreation centers, food courts, student services, and building up other amenities of the campus and the areas surrounding the campus. On some campuses, the same level of effort may not attach to maintaining the rigor of educational standards, or even to ensuring that libraries are well stocked with books and journals.

10. The Cohen et al. (1994) data are based on a response rate of under 50 percent. Efforts to determine the representativeness of these data involved contacting a sample of nonresponding UIRCs. In comparing the two samples, Cohen and his colleagues found no significant differences in total annual budget, number of research and development projects, and number of companies providing support. However, UIRCs in the sample tended to dedicate significantly greater effort to research and development activities and less effort to education and training and technology transfer activities. Generalizations about national trends must be understood with these sample characteristics taken into account.

11. When examining field mobility data, it is important to keep in mind the extraordinary changes in the distribution of faculty over a generation. In 1969, some two-thirds of the surveyed faculty taught in arts and sciences departments. In 1992, the overall proportion was below 60 percent, and only 50 percent for faculty with "new" and "mid-level" faculty. These changes in the marginal distributions are not highlighted in Table 7.5, but they are an important context for evaluating the data in the table.

12. A comparison of cohorts in the 1993 data suggests that younger doctorates in the arts and sciences have been more likely to move from their home disciplines than senior faculty and that their movement has been in the direction of professional programs at roughly the rate that would be expected given their lesser tendency to stay put in their home disciplines. The patterns of movement among cohorts of doctorates from professional programs are more mixed, however, and seem to depend to a considerable degree on when education schools began to recruit faculty trained in business, health sciences, and other popular professional disciplines.

13. To investigate this possibility further, it might be assumed that fields producing fewer than one in a thousand baccalaureates annually are small and therefore vulnerable. These fields include virtually all area studies programs; botany, ecology, genetics, entomology, and physiology in the biological sciences; Chinese language and literature, Japanese language and literature, Eastern European languages and literatures, Scandinavian and Germanic languages and literatures, Middle Eastern languages and literatures, and classics in the humanities; mathematical statistics, astronomy, astrophysics, atmospheric science, oceanography in the physical sciences; archaeology and urban studies in social science; dance, painting, music history, and music theory and composition in the fine arts.

REFERENCES

Adelman, Clifford. 1995. *A New College Course Map and Transcript Files.* Washington, DC: U.S. Department of Education.

American Council on Education (ACE). 1995. *The American College President: 1995 Edition.* Washington, DC: American Council on Education.

——. 2000. *The American College President: 2000 Edition.* Washington, DC: American Council on Education.

Astin, Alexander W. 1998. "The Changing American College Student: Thirty Year Trends, 1966–1996." *Review of Higher Education* 21: 115–35.

Bourdieu, Pierre. 1984. *Distinction.* Cambridge, MA: Harvard University Press.

——. 1988. *Home Academicus.* Stanford, CA: Stanford University Press.

Bowen, William G., and Julie Ann Sosa. 1989. *Prospects for Faculty in the Arts and Sciences: A Study of Factors Affecting Demand and Supply, 1987 to 2012.* Princeton, NJ: Princeton University Press.

Brint, Steven. 1994. *In an Age of Experts: The Changing Role of Professionals in Politics and Public Life.* Princeton, NJ: Princeton University Press.

Brint, Steven, and Jerome Karabel. 1989. *The Diverted Dream: Community Colleges and the Promise of Educational Opportunity, 1900–1985.* New York: Oxford University Press.

Brint, Steven, and Charles S. Levy. 1999. "Professions and Civic Engagement: Trends in Rhetoric and Practice, 1875–1995." Pp. 163–210 in Theda Skocpol and Morris Fiorina (eds.), *Civic Engagement in American Democracy.* Washington, DC: Brookings Institution.

Campus Compact. 1998. *Service Matters: Engaging Higher Education in the Renewal of America's Communities and American Democracy.* Edited by Michael Rothman. Providence, RI: Campus Compact.

Cohen, Wesley, Richard Florida, Lucien Randazzese, and John Walsh. 1998. "Industry and the Academy: Uneasy Partners in the Cause of Technological Advance." Pp. 171–200 in Roger Noll (ed.), *Challenges to Research Universities,* Washington, DC: Brookings Institution Press.

Duffy, Elizabeth A., and Idana Goldberg. 1998. *Crafting a Class: College Admissions and Financial Aid, 1955–1994.* Princeton, NJ: Princeton University Press.

Finkelstein, Martin J., Robert K. Seal, and Jack H. Schuster. 1998. *The New Academic Generation: A Profession in Transformation.* Baltimore, MD: Johns Hopkins University Press.

Freeman, Richard. 1976. *The Overeducated American.* New York: Academic Press.

Geiger, Roger L. 1980. "The College Curriculum and the Marketplace." *Change* (November/December): 17–23 ff.

——. 1986. *To Advance Knowledge: The Growth of American Research Universities, 1900–1940.* New York: Oxford University Press.

——. 1993. *Research and Relevant Knowledge: American Research Universities since World War II.* New York: Oxford University Press.

Glazer, Nathan. 1974. "The Schools of the Minor Professions." *Minerva* 12: 346–64.

Gumport, Patricia J. 1993. "The Contested Terrain of Academic Program Reduction." *Journal of Higher Education* 64: 284–311.

Hashem, Mazen. 2002. "Academic Knowledge from Elite Closure to Public Catering: The Rise of New Growth Fields in American Higher Education." Unpublished Ph.D. dissertation, Department of Sociology, University of California, Riverside.

Higher Education Research Institute (HERI). 1998a. *The American College Freshman: National Norms for 1998.* Los Angeles: Higher Education Research Institute.

Higher Education Research Institute (HERI). 1998b. *The American College Teacher: National Norms for the 1998–99 HERI Faculty Survey.* Los Angeles: Higher Education Research Institute.

Hoover, Edgar M., and Raymond Vernon. 1959. *Anatomy of a Metropolis.* Cambridge, MA: Harvard University Press.

Hunt, Lynn. 1997. "Democratization and Decline? The Consequences of Demographic Change in the Humanities." Pp. 17–31 in Alvin Kernan (ed.), *What's Happened to the Humanities?* Princeton, NJ: Princeton University Press.

Kerr, Clark. 1964. *The Uses of the University.* New York: Harper Torchbooks.

Kraatz, Matthew, and Edward Zajac. 1998. "Executive Migration and Institutional Change." Unpublished paper, Kellogg School of Management, Northwestern University.

McConnell, T. R., G. Lester Anderson, and Pauline Hunter. 1962. "The University and Professional Education." Pp. 254–78 in Nelson Hardy (ed.), *Education for the Professions.* Chicago: University of Chicago Press.

Menand, Louis. 1997. "The Demise of Disciplinary Authority." Pp. 201–19 in Alvin Kernan (ed.), *What's Happened to the Humanities.* Princeton, NJ: Princeton University Press.

Morgan, Harriet. 1998. "Moving Missions: Organizational Change in Liberal Arts Colleges." Unpublished doctoral dissertation, University of Chicago, Department of Sociology.

Morphew, Christopher. 1998. "The Realities of Strategic Planning: Program Termination at East Central University." Unpublished paper, School of Education, University of Kansas.

National Center for Educational Statistics (NCES). 1998. *Digest of Educational Statistics, 1998.* Washington, DC: Government Printing Office.

National Council of Area Studies Associations. 1991. *Report from the National Council Area Studies Associations.* Stanford CA: National Council of Area Studies Associations.

Newman, Frank M. 1985. *Higher Education and the American Resurgence.* Princeton, NJ: Carnegie Foundation for the Advancement of Teaching.

Philosophy Documentation Center. 1974–1995. *Directory of American Philosophers.* Bowling Green, IN: Bowling Green State University. Series.

Schlossman, Steven L., and Michael Sedlak. 1988. *The Age of Reform in American Management Education.* Los Angeles: Graduate Management Admissions Council.

Scott, Joyce A., and Nancy A. Bereman. 1992. "Competition versus Collegiality: Academe's Dilemma for the 1990s." *Journal of Higher Education* 63: 684–98.

Slaughter, Sheila, and Larry L. Leslie. 1997. *Academic Capitalism: Politics, Policies, and the Entrepreneurial University.* Baltimore, MD: Johns Hopkins University Press.

Trow, Martin. 1998. "From Mass Higher Education to Universal Access: The American Advantage." Unpublished paper presented at the North American and Western European Colloquium on Challenges Facing Higher Education, Glion sur Montaux, France, May 14–16.

Useem, Michael. 1989. *Liberal Education and the Corporation.* New York: Aldine de Gruyter.

Veysey, Laurence R. 1965. *The Emergence of the American University.* Chicago: University of Chicago Press.

8

The Canon Debate, Knowledge Construction, and Multicultural Education

James A. Banks

I review the debate over multicultural education in this chapter, state that all knowledge reflects the values and interests of its creators, and illustrate how the debate between the multicultural-ists and the Western traditionalists is rooted in their conflicting conceptions about the nature of knowledge and their divergent political and social interests. I present a typology that describes five types of knowledge and contend that each type should be a part of the school, college, and university curriculum.

A heated and divisive national debate is taking place about what knowledge related to ethnic and cultural diversity should be taught in the school and university curriculum (Asante, 1991a; Asante & Ravitch, 1991; D'Souza, 1991; Glazer, 1991; Schlesinger, 1991; Woodward, 1991). This debate has heightened ethnic tension and confused many educators about the meaning of multicultural education. At least three different groups of scholars are participating in the canon debate: the Western traditionalists, the multiculturalists, and the Afrocentrists. Although there are a range of perspectives and views within each of these groups, all groups share a number of important assumptions and beliefs about the nature of diversity in the United States and about the role of educational institutions in a pluralistic society.

The Western traditionalists have initiated a national effort to defend the dominance of Western civilization in the school and university curriculum (Gray, 1991; Howe, 1991; Woodward, 1991). These scholars believe that Western history, literature, and culture are endangered in the school and university curriculum because of the push by feminists, ethnic minority scholars, and other multiculturalists for curriculum reform and transformation. The Western traditionalists have formed an organization called the National Association of Scholars to defend the dominance of Western civilization in the curriculum.

The multiculturalists believe that the school, college, and university curriculum marginalizes the experiences of people of color and of women (Butler & Walter, 1991; Gates, 1992; Grant, 1992; Sleeter, personal communication, October 26, 1991). They contend that the curriculum should be reformed so that it will more accurately reflect the histories and cultures of ethnic groups and women. Two organizations have been formed to promote issues related to ethnic and cultural diversity. Teachers for a Democratic Culture promotes ethnic studies and women studies at the university level. The National Association for Multicultural Education focuses on teacher education and multicultural education in the nation's schools.

The Afrocentrists maintain that African culture and history should be placed at the "center" of the curriculum in order to motivate African Americans students to learn and to help all students to understand the important role that Africa has played in the development of Western civilization (Asante, 1991a). Many mainstream multiculturalists are ambivalent about Afrocentrism, although few have publicly opposed it. This is in part because the Western traditionalists rarely distinguish the Afrocentrists from the multiculturalists and describe them as one group. Some multiculturalists may also perceive Afrocentric ideas as compatible with a broader concept of multicultural education.

The influence of the multiculturalists within schools and universities in the last 20 years has been substantial. Many school districts, state departments of education, local school districts, and private agencies have developed and implemented multicultural staff development programs, conferences, policies, and curricula (New York City Board of Education, 1990; New York State Department of Education, 1989, 1991; Sokol, 1990). Multicultural requirements, programs, and policies have also been implemented at many of the nation's leading research universities, including the University of California, Berkeley, Stanford University, The Pennsylvania State University, and the University of Wisconsin system. The success that the multiculturalists have had in implementing their ideas within schools and universities is probably a major reason that the Western traditionalists are trying to halt multicultural reforms in the nation's schools, colleges, and universities.

The debate between the Western traditionalists and the multiculturalists is consistent with the ideals of a democratic society. To date, however, it has resulted in little productive interaction between the Western traditionalists and the multiculturalists. Rather, each group has talked primarily to audiences it viewed as sympathetic to its ideologies and visions of the present and future (Franklin, 1991; Schlesinger, 1991). Because there has been little productive dialogue and exchange between the Western traditionalists and the multiculturalists, the debate has been polarized, and writers have frequently not conformed to the established rules of scholarship (D'Souza, 1991). A kind of forensic social science has developed (Rivlin, 1973), with each side stating briefs and then marshaling evidence to support its position. The debate has also taken place primarily in the popular press rather than in academic and scholarly journals.

VALUATION AND KNOWLEDGE CONSTRUCTION

I hope to make a positive contribution to the canon debate in this chapter by providing evidence for the claim that the positions of both the Western traditionalists and the multiculturalists reflect values, ideologies, political positions, and human interests. Each position also implies a kind of knowledge that should be taught in the school and university curriculum. I will present a typology of the kinds of knowledge that exist in society and in educational institutions. This typology is designed to help practicing educators and researchers to identify types of knowledge that reflect particular values, assumptions, perspectives, and ideological positions.

Teachers should help students to understand all types of knowledge. Students should be involved in the debates about knowledge construction and conflicting interpretations, such as the extent to which Egypt and Phoenicia influenced Greek civilization. Students should also be taught how to create their own interpretations of the past and present, as well as how to identify their own positions, interests, ideologies, and assumptions. Teachers should help students to become critical thinkers who have the knowledge, attitudes, skills, and commitments needed to participate in democratic action to help the nation close the gap between its ideals and its realities. Multicultural education is an education for functioning effectively in a pluralistic democratic society. Helping students to develop the knowledge, skills, and attitudes needed to participate in reflective civic action is one of its major goals (Banks, 1991).

I argue that students should study all five types of knowledge. However, my own work and philosophical position are within the transformative tradition in ethnic studies and multicultural education (Banks, 1988, 1991; Banks & Banks, 1989). This tradition links knowledge, social commitment, and action (Meier & Rudwick, 1986). A transformative, action-oriented curriculum, in my view, can best be implemented when students examine different types of knowledge in a democratic classroom where they can freely examine their perspectives and moral commitments.

THE NATURE OF KNOWLEDGE

I am using knowledge in this chapter to mean the way a person explains or interprets reality. *The American Heritage Dictionary* (1983) defines knowledge as "familiarity, awareness, or understandings gained through experience or study. The sum or range of what has been perceived, discovered or inferred" (p. 384). My conceptualization of knowledge is broad and is used the way in which it is usually used in the sociology of knowledge literature to include ideas, values, and interpretations (Farganis, 1986). As postmodern theorists have pointed out, knowledge is socially constructed and reflects human interests, values, and action (Code, 1991; Foucault, 1972; S. Harding, 1991; Rorty, 1989). Although many complex factors influence the knowledge that is created by an individual or group, including the actuality of what occurred, the knowledge that people create is heavily influenced by their interpretations of their experiences and their positions within particular social, economic, and political systems and structures of a society.

In the Western empirical tradition, the ideal within each academic discipline is the formulation of knowledge without the influence of the researcher's personal or cultural characteristics (Greer, 1969; Kaplan, 1964). However, as critical and postmodern theorists have pointed out, personal, cultural, and social factors influence the formulation of knowledge even when objective knowledge is the ideal within a discipline (Cherryholmes, 1988; Foucault, 1972; Habermas, 1971; Rorty, 1989; Young, 1971). Often the researchers themselves are unaware of how their personal experiences and positions within society influence the knowledge they produce. Most mainstream historians were unaware of how their regional and cultural biases influenced their interpretation of the Reconstruction period until W. E. B. DuBois published a study that challenged the accepted and established interpretations of that historical period (DuBois, 1935/1962).

POSITIONALITY AND KNOWLEDGE CONSTRUCTION

Positionality is an important concept that emerged out of feminist scholarship. Tetreault (1993) writes:

> Positionality means that important aspects of our identity, for example, our gender, our race, our class, our age . . . are markers of relational positions rather than essential qualities. Their effects and implications change according to context. Recently, feminist thinkers have seen knowledge as valid when it comes from an acknowledgment of the knower's specific position in any context, one always defined by gender, race, class and other variables. (p. 139)

Positionality reveals the importance of identifying the positions and frames of reference from which scholars and writers present their data, interpretations, analyses, and instruction

(Anzaldúa, 1990; Ellsworth, 1989). The need for researchers and scholars to identify their ideological positions and normative assumptions in their works—an inherent part of feminist and ethnic studies scholarship—contrasts with the empirical paradigm that has dominated science and research in the United States (Code, 1991; S. Harding, 1991).

The assumption within the Western empirical paradigm is that the knowledge produced within it is neutral and objective and that its principles are universal. The effects of values, frames of references, and the normative positions of researchers and scholars are infrequently discussed within the traditional empirical paradigm that has dominated scholarship and teaching in American colleges and universities since the turn of the century. However, scholars such as Myrdal (1944) and Clark (1965), prior to the feminist and ethnic studies movements, wrote about the need for scholars to recognize and state their normative positions and valuations and to become, in the apt words of Kenneth B. Clark, "involved observers." Myrdal stated that valuations are not just attached to research but permeate it. He wrote, "*There is no device for excluding biases in social sciences than to face the valuations and to introduce them as explicitly stated, specific, and sufficiently concretized value premises*" (p. 1043).

Postmodern and critical theorists such as Habermas (1971) and Giroux (1983), and feminist postmodern theorists such as Farganis (1986), Code (1991), and S. Harding (1991), have developed important critiques of empirical knowledge. They argue that despite its claims, modern science is not value-free but contains important human interests and normative assumptions that should be identified, discussed, and examined. Code (1991), a feminist epistemologist, states that academic knowledge is both subjective and objective and that both aspects should be recognized and discussed. Code states that we need to ask these kinds of questions: "Out of whose subjectivity has this ideal [of objectivity] grown? Whose standpoint, whose values does it represent?" (p. 70). She writes:

> The point of the questions is to discover how subjective and objective conditions together produce knowledge, values, and epistemology. It is neither to reject objectivity nor to glorify subjectivity in its stead. Knowledge is neither value-free nor value-neutral; the processes that produce it are themselves value-laden; and these values are open to evaluation. (p. 70)

In her book, *What Can She Know? Feminist Theory and the Construction of Knowledge*, Code (1991) raises the question, "Is the sex of the knower epistemologically significant?" (p. 7). She answers this question in the affirmative because of the ways in which gender influences how knowledge is constructed, interpreted, and institutionalized within U.S. society. The ethnic and cultural experiences of the knower are also epistemologically significant because these factors also influence knowledge construction, use, and interpretation in U.S. society.

Empirical scholarship has been limited by the assumptions and biases that are implicit within it (Code, 1991; Gordon, 1985; S. Harding, 1991). However, these biases and assumptions have been infrequently recognized by the scholars and researchers themselves and by the consumers of their works, such as other scholars, professors, teachers, and the general reader. The lack of recognition and identification of these biases, assumptions, perspectives, and points of view have frequently victimized people of color such as African Americans and American Indians because of the stereotypes and misconceptions that have been perpetuated about them in the historical and social science literature (Ladner, 1973; Phillips, 1918).

Gordon, Miller, and Rollock (1990) call the bias that results in the negative depiction of minority groups by mainstream social scientists "communicentric bias." They point out that mainstream social scientists have often viewed diversity as deviance and differences as deficits. An important outcome of the revisionist and transformative interpretations that have been produced by scholars working in feminist and ethnic studies is that many misconceptions and partial truths about women and ethnic groups have been viewed from different and more complete perspectives (Acuña, 1988; Blassingame, 1972; V. Harding, 1981; King & Mitchell, 1990; Merton, 1972).

More complete perspectives result in a closer approximation to the actuality of what occurred. In an important and influential essay, Merton (1972) notes that the perspectives of both "insiders" and "outsiders" are needed to enable social scientists to gain a complete view of social reality. Anna Julia Cooper, the African American educator, made a point similar to Merton's when she wrote about how the perspectives of women enlarged our vision (Cooper, 1892/1969, cited in Minnich, 1990, p. viii).

> The world has had to limp along with the wobbling gait and the one-sided hesitancy of a man with one eye. Suddenly the bandage is removed from the other eye and the whole body is filled with light. It sees a circle where before it saw a segment.

A KNOWLEDGE TYPOLOGY

A description of the major types of knowledge can help teachers and curriculum specialists to identify perspectives and content needed to make the curriculum multicultural. Each of the types of knowledge described below reflects particular purposes, perspectives, experiences, goals, and human interests. Teaching students various types of knowledge can help them to better

TABLE 8.1
Types of Knowledge

Knowledge Type	Definition	Examples
Personal/cultural	The concepts, explanations, and interpretations that students derive from personal experiences in their homes, families, and community cultures.	Understandings by many African Americans and Hispanic students that highly individualistic behavior will be negatively sanctioned by many adults and peers in their cultural communities.
Popular	The facts, concepts, explanations, and interpretations that are institutionalized within the mass media and other institutions that are part of the popular culture.	Movies such as *Birth of a Nation, How the West Was Won*, and *Dances With Wolves*.
Mainstream academic	The concepts, paradigms, theories, and explanations that constitute traditional Western-centric knowledge in history and the behavioral and social sciences.	Ulrich B. Phillips, *American Negro Slavery*; Frederick Jackson Turner's frontier theory; Arthur R. Jensen's theory about Black and White intelligence.
Transformative academic	The facts, concepts, paradigms, themes, and explanations that challenge mainstream academic knowledge and expand and substantially revise established canons, paradigms, theories, explanations, and research methods. When transformative academic paradigms replace mainstream ones, a scientific revolution has occurred. What is more normal is that transformative academic paradigms coexist with established ones.	George Washington Williams, *History of the Negro Race in America*; W. E. B. DuBois, *Black Reconstruction*; Carter G. Woodson, *The Mis-education of the Negro*; Gerda Lerner, *The Majority Finds Its Past*; Rodolfo Acuña, *Occupied America: A History of Chicanos*; Herbert Gutman, *The Black Family in Slavery and Freedom 1750–1925*.
School	The facts, concepts, generalizations, and interpretations that are presented in textbooks, teacher's guides, other media forms, and lectures by teachers.	Lewis Paul Todd and Merle Curti, *Rise of the American Nation*; Richard C. Brown, Wilhelmena S. Robinson, & John Cunningham, *Let Freedom Ring: A United States History*.

understand the perspectives of different racial, ethnic, and cultural groups as well as to develop their own versions and interpretations of issues and events.

I identify and describe five types of knowledge (see Table 8.1): (a) personal/cultural knowledge; (b) popular knowledge; (c) mainstream academic knowledge; (d) transformative academic knowledge; and (e) school knowledge. This is an ideal-type typology in the Weberian sense. The five categories approximate, but do not describe, reality in its total complexity. The categories are useful conceptual tools for thinking about knowledge and planning multicultural teaching. For example, although the categories can be conceptually distinguished, in reality they overlap and are interrelated in a dynamic way.

Since the 1960s, some of the findings and insights from transformative academic knowledge have been incorporated into mainstream academic knowledge and scholarship. Traditionally, students were taught in schools and universities that the land that became North America was a thinly populated wilderness when the Europeans arrived in the 16th century and that African Americans had made few contributions to the development of American civilization (mainstream academic knowledge). Some of the findings from transformative academic knowledge that challenged these conceptions have influenced mainstream academic scholarship and have been incorporated into mainstream college and school textbooks (Hoxie, no date; Thornton, 1987). Consequently, the relationship between the five categories of knowledge is dynamic and interactive rather than static (see Figure 8.1).

THE TYPES OF KNOWLEDGE

Personal and Cultural Knowledge

The concepts, explanations, and interpretations that students derive from personal experiences in their homes, families, and community cultures constitute personal and cultural knowledge. The assumptions, perspectives, and insights that students derive from their experiences in their homes and community cultures are used as screens to view and interpret the knowledge and experiences that they encounter in the school and in other institutions within the larger society.

Research and theory by Fordham and Ogbu (1986) indicate that low-income African American students often experience academic difficulties in the school because of the ways that cultural knowledge within their community conflicts with school knowledge, norms, and expectations. Fordham and Ogbu also state that the culture of many low-income African American students is oppositional to the school culture. These students believe that if they

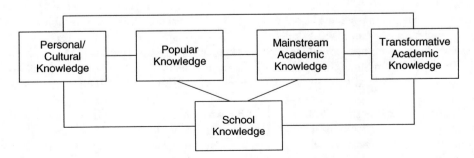

FIGURE 8.1   The interrelationships of types of knowledge. This figure illustrates that although the five types of knowledge discussed in this chapter are conceptually distinct, they are highly interrelated in a complex and dynamic way.

master the knowledge taught in the schools they will violate fictive kinship norms and run the risk of "acting White." Fordham (1988, 1991) has suggested that African American students who become high academic achievers resolve the conflict caused by the interaction of their personal cultural knowledge with the knowledge and norms within the schools by becoming "raceless" or by "ad hocing a culture."

Delpit (1988) has stated that African American students are often unfamiliar with school cultural knowledge regarding power relationships. They consequently experience academic and behavioral problems because of their failure to conform to established norms, rules, and expectations. She recommends that teachers help African American students learn the rules of power in the school culture by explicitly teaching them to the students. The cultural knowledge that many African American, Latino, and American Indian students bring to school conflict with school norms and values, with school knowledge, and with the ways that teachers interpret and mediate school knowledge. Student cultural knowledge and school knowledge often conflict on variables related to the ways that the individual should relate to and interact with the group (Hale-Benson, 1982; Ramírez & Castañeda, 1974; Shade, 1989), normative communication styles and interactions (Heath, 1983; Labov, 1975; Philips, 1983; Smitherman, 1977), and perspectives on the nature of U.S. history.

Personal and cultural knowledge is problematic when it conflicts with scientific ways of validating knowledge, is oppositional to the culture of the school, or challenges the main tenets and assumptions of mainstream academic knowledge. Much of the knowledge about out-groups that students learn from their home and community cultures consists of misconceptions, stereotypes, and partial truths (Milner, 1983). Most students in the United States are socialized within communities that are segregated along racial, ethnic, and social-class lines. Consequently, most American youths have few opportunities to learn firsthand about the cultures of people from different racial, ethnic, cultural, religious, and social-class groups.

The challenge that teachers face is how to make effective instructional use of the personal and cultural knowledge of students while at the same time helping them to reach beyond their own cultural boundaries. Although the school should recognize, validate, and make effective use of student, personal and cultural knowledge in instruction, an important goal of education is to free students from their cultural and ethnic boundaries and enable them to cross cultural borders freely (Banks, 1988, 1991/1992).

In the past, the school has paid scant attention to the personal and cultural knowledge of students and has concentrated on teaching them school knowledge (Sleeter & Grant, 1991a). This practice has had different results for most White middle-class students, for most low-income students, and for most African American and Latino students. Because school knowledge is more consistent with the cultural experiences of most White middle-class students than for most other groups of students, these students have generally found the school a more comfortable place than have low-income students and most students of color—the majority of whom are also low income. A number of writers have described the ways in which many African American, American Indian, and Latino students find the school culture alienating and inconsistent with their cultural experiences, hopes, dreams, and struggles (Hale-Benson, 1982; Heath, 1983; Ramírez & Castañeda, 1974; Shade, 1989).

It is important for teachers to be aware of the personal and cultural knowledge of students when designing the curriculum for today's multicultural schools. Teachers can use student personal cultural knowledge as a vehicle to motivate students and as a foundation for teaching school knowledge. When teaching a unit on the Westward Movement to Lakota Sioux students, for example, the teacher can ask the students to make a list of their views about the Westward Movement, to relate family stories about the coming of the Whites to Lakota Sioux homelands, and to interview parents and grandparents about their perceptions of what happened when the Whites first occupied Indian lands. When teachers begin a unit on the Westward Movement with student personal cultural knowledge, they can increase student motivation as well as deepen their understanding of the schoolbook version (Wiggington, 1991/1992).

Popular Knowledge

Popular knowledge consists of the facts, interpretations, and beliefs that are institutionalized within television, movies, videos, records, and other forms of the mass media. Many of the tenets of popular knowledge are conveyed in subtle rather than obvious ways. Some examples of statements that constitute important themes in popular knowledge follow: (a) The United States is a powerful nation with unlimited opportunities for individuals who are willing to take advantage of them. (b) To succeed in the United States, an individual only has to work hard. You can realize your dreams in the United States if you are willing to work hard and pull yourself up by the bootstrap. (c) As a land of opportunity for all, the United States is a highly cohesive nation, whose ideals of equality and freedom are shared by all.

Most of the major tenets of American popular culture are widely shared and are deeply entrenched in U.S. society. However, they are rarely explicitly articulated. Rather, they are presented in the media and in other sources in the forms of stories, anecdotes, news stories, and interpretations of current events (Cortes, 1991a, 1991b; Greenfield & Cortés, 1991).

Commercial entertainment films both reflect and perpetuate popular knowledge (Bogle, 1989; Cortés, 1991a, 1991b; Greenfield & Cortés, 1991). While preparing to write this chapter, I viewed an important and influential film that was directed by John Ford and released by MGM in 1962, *How the West Was Won.* I selected this film for review because the settlement of the West is a major theme in American culture and society about which there are many popular images, beliefs, myths, and misconceptions. In viewing the film, I was particularly interested in the images it depicted about the settlement of the West, about the people who were already in the West, and about those who went West looking for new opportunities.

Ford uses the Prescotts, a White family from Missouri bound for California, to tell his story. The film tells the story of three generations of this family. It focuses on the family's struggle to settle in the West. Indians, African Americans, and Mexicans are largely invisible in the film. Indians appear in the story when they attack the Prescott family during their long and perilous journey. The Mexicans appearing in the film are bandits who rob a train and are killed. The several African Americans in the film are in the background silently rowing a boat. At various points in the film, Indians are referred to as *hostile Indians* and as *squaws.*

How the West Was Won is a masterpiece in American popular culture. It not only depicts some of the major themes in American culture about the winning of the West; it reinforces and perpetuates dominant societal attitudes about ethnic groups and gives credence to the notion that the West was won by liberty-loving, hard-working people who pursued freedom for all. The film narrator states near its end, "[The movement West] produced a people free to dream, free to act, and free to mold their own destiny."

Mainstream Academic Knowledge

Mainstream academic knowledge consists of the concepts, paradigms, theories, and explanations that constitute traditional and established knowledge in the behavioral and social sciences. An important tenet within the mainstream academic paradigm is that there is a set of objective truths that can be verified through rigorous and objective research procedures that are uninfluenced by human interests, values, and perspectives (Greer, 1969; Kaplan, 1964; Sleeter, 1991). This empirical knowledge, uninfluenced by human values and interests, constitute a body of objective truths that should constitute the core of the school and university curriculum. Much of this objective knowledge originated in the West but is considered universal in nature and application.

Mainstream academic knowledge is the knowledge that multicultural critics such as Ravitch and Finn (1987), Hirsch (1987), and Bloom (1987) claim is threatened by the addition of content about women and ethnic minorities to the school and university curriculum. This knowledge reflects the established, Western-oriented canon that has historically dominated university research and teaching in the United States. Mainstream academic knowledge consists of the theories and interpretations that are internalized and accepted by most university researchers, academic societies, and organizations such as the American Historical Association, the American Sociological Association, the American Psychological Association, and the National Academy of Sciences.

It is important to point out, however, that an increasing number of university scholars are critical theorists and postmodernists who question the empirical paradigm that dominates Western science (Cherryholmes, 1988; Giroux, 1983; Rosenau, 1992). Many of these individuals are members of national academic organizations, such as the American Historical Association and the American Sociological Association. In most of these professional organizations, the postmodern scholars—made up of significant numbers of scholars of color and feminists—have formed caucuses and interest groups within the mainstream professional organizations.

No claim is made here that there is a uniformity of beliefs among mainstream academic scholars, but rather that there are dominant canons, paradigms, and theories that are accepted by the community of mainstream academic scholars and researchers. These established canons and paradigms are occasionally challenged within the mainstream academic community itself. However, they receive their most serious challenges from academics outside the mainstream, such as scholars within the transformative academic community whom I will describe later.

Mainstream academic knowledge, like the other forms of knowledge discussed in this chapter, is not static, but is dynamic, complex, and changing. Challenges to the dominant canons and paradigms within mainstream academic knowledge come from both within and without. These challenges lead to changes, reinterpretations, debates, disagreements and ultimately to paradigm shifts, new theories, and interpretations. Kuhn (1970) states that a scientific revolution takes place when a new paradigm emerges and replaces an existing one. What is more typical in education and the social sciences is that competing paradigms coexist, although particular ones might be more influential during certain times or periods.

We can examine the treatment of slavery within the mainstream academic community over time, or the treatment of the American Indian, to identify ways that mainstream academic knowledge has changed in important ways since the late 19th and early 20th centuries. Ulrich B. Phillips's highly influential book, *American Negro Slavery*, published in 1918, dominated the way Black slavery was interpreted until his views were challenged by researchers in the 1950s (Stampp, 1956). Phillips was a respected authority on the antebellum South and on slavery. His book, which became a historical classic, is essentially an apology for Southern slaveholders. A new paradigm about slavery was developed in the 1970s that drew heavily upon the slaves' view of their own experiences (Blassingame, 1972; Genovese, 1972; Gutman, 1976).

During the late 19th and early 20th centuries, the American Indian was portrayed in mainstream academic knowledge as either a noble or a hostile savage (Hoxie, 1988). Other notions that became institutionalized within mainstream academic knowledge include the idea that Columbus discovered America and that America was a thinly populated frontier when the Europeans arrived in the late 15th century. Frederick Jackson Turner (Turner, 1894/1989) argued that the frontier, which he regarded as a wilderness, was the main source of American democracy. Although Turner's thesis is now being highly criticized by revisionist historians, his essay established a conception of the West that has been highly influential in American mainstream scholarship, in the popular culture, and in schoolbooks. The conception of the West he depicted is still influential today in the school curriculum and in textbooks (Sleeter & Grant, 1991b).

These ideas also became institutionalized within mainstream academic knowledge: The slaves were happy and contented; most of the important ideas that became a part of American civilization came from Western Europe; and the history of the United States has been one of constantly expanding progress and increasing democracy. African slaves were needed to transform the United States from an empty wilderness into an industrial democratic civilization. The American Indians had to be Christianized and removed to reservations in order for this to occur.

Transformative Academic Knowledge

Transformative academic knowledge consists of concepts, paradigms, themes, and explanations that challenge mainstream academic knowledge and that expand the historical and literary canon. Transformative academic knowledge challenges some of the key assumptions that mainstream scholars make about the nature of knowledge. Transformative and mainstream academic knowledge is based on different epistemological assumptions about the nature of knowledge, about the influence of human interests and values on knowledge construction, and about the purpose of knowledge.

An important tenet of mainstream academic knowledge is that it is neutral, objective, and was uninfluenced by human interests and values. Transformative academic knowledge reflects postmodern assumptions and goals about the nature and goals of knowledge (Foucault, 1972; Rorty, 1989; Rosenau, 1992). Transformative academic scholars assume that knowledge is not neutral but is influenced by human interests, that all knowledge reflects the power and social relationships within society, and that an important purpose of knowledge construction is to help people improve society (Code, 1991; S. Harding, 1991; hooks & West, 1991; King & Mitchell, 1990; Minnich, 1990). Write King and Mitchell: "Like other praxis-oriented Critical approaches, the Afrocentric method seeks to enable people to understand social reality in order to change it. But its additional imperative is to transform the society's basic ethos" (p. 95).

These statements reflect some of the main ideas and concepts in transformative academic knowledge: Columbus did not discover America. The Indians had been living in this land for about 40,000 years when the Europeans arrived. Concepts such as "The European Discovery of America" and "The Westward Movement" need to be reconceptualized and viewed from the perspectives of different cultural and ethnic groups. The Lakota Sioux's homeland was not the West to them; it was the center of the universe. It was not the West for the Alaskans; it was South. It was East for the Japanese and North for the people who lived in Mexico. The history of the United States has not been one of continuous progress toward democratic ideals. Rather, the nation's history has been characterized by a cyclic quest for democracy and by conflict, struggle, violence, and exclusion (Acuña, 1988; Zinn, 1980). A major challenge that faces the nation is how to make its democratic ideals a reality for all.

Transformative academic knowledge has a long history in the United States. In 1882 and 1883, George Washington Williams (1849–1891) published, in two volumes, the first comprehensive history of African Americans in the United States, *A History of the Negro Race in America From 1619 to 1880* (Williams, 1982–1983/1968). Williams, like other African American scholars after him, decided to research and write about the Black experience because of the neglect of

African Americans by mainstream historians and social scientists and because of the stereotypes and misconceptions about African Americans that appeared in mainstream scholarship.

W. E. B. DuBois (1868–1963) is probably the most prolific African American scholar in U.S. history. His published writings constitute 38 volumes (Aptheker, 1973). DuBois devoted his long and prolific career to the formulation of new data, concepts, and paradigms that could be used to reinterpret the Black experience and reveal the role that African Americans had played in the development of American society. His seminal works include *The Suppression of the African Slave Trade to the United States of America, 1638–1870*, the first volume of the Harvard Historical Studies (DuBois, 1896/1969). Perhaps his most discussed book is *Black Reconstruction in America: An Essay Toward a History of the Part Which Black Folk Played in the Attempt to Reconstruct Democracy in America, 1860–1880*, published in 1935 (1935/1962). In this book, DuBois challenged the accepted, institutionalized interpretations of Reconstruction and emphasized the accomplishments of the Reconstruction governments and legislatures, especially the establishment of free public schools.

Carter G. Woodson (1875–1950), the historian and educator who founded the Association for the Study of Negro Life and History and the *Journal of Negro History*, also challenged established paradigms about the treatment of African Americans in a series of important publications, including *The Mis-education of the Negro*, published in 1933. Woodson and Wesley (1922) published a highly successful college textbook that described the contributions that African Americans have made to American life, *The Negro in Our History*. This book was issued in 10 editions.

Transformative Scholarship Since the 1970s

Many scholars have produced significant research and theories since the early 1970s that have challenged and modified institutionalized stereotypes and misconceptions about ethnic minorities, formulated new concepts and paradigms, and forced mainstream scholars to rethink established interpretations. Much of the transformative academic knowledge that has been produced since the 1970s is becoming institutionalized within mainstream scholarship and within the school, college, and university curricula. In time, much of this scholarship will become mainstream, thus reflecting the highly interrelated nature of the types of knowledge conceptualized and described in this chapter.

Only a few examples of this new, transformative scholarship will be mentioned here because of the limited scope of this chapter. Howard Zinn's *A People's History of the United States* (1980); *Red, White and Black: The Peoples of Early America* by Gary B. Nash (1982); *The Signifying Monkey: A Theory of African-American Literacy Criticism* by Henry Louis Gates, Jr. (1988); *Occupied America: A History of Chicanos* by Rodolfo Acuña (1988); *Iron Cages: Race and Culture in 19th-Century America* by Ronald T. Takaki (1979); and *The Sacred Hoop: Recovering the Feminine in American Indian Traditions* by Paul Gunn Allen (1986) are examples of important scholarship that has provided significant new perspectives on the experiences of ethnic groups in the United States and has helped us to transform our conceptions about the experiences of American ethnic groups. Readers acquainted with this scholarship will note that transformative scholarship has been produced by both European-American and ethnic minority scholars.

I will discuss two examples of how the new scholarship in ethnic studies has questioned traditional interpretations and stimulated a search for new explanations and paradigms since the 1950s. Since the pioneering work of E. Franklin Frazier (1939), social scientists had accepted the notion that the slave experience had destroyed the Black family and that the destruction of the African American family continued in the post–World War II period during Black migration to and settlement in northern cities. Moynihan (1965), in his controversial book, *The Negro*

Family in America: The Case for National Action, used the broken Black family explanation in his analysis. Gutman (1976), in an important historical study of the African American family from 1750 to 1925, concluded that "despite a high rate of earlier involuntary marital breakup, large numbers of slave couples lived in long marriages, and most slaves lived in double-headed households" (p. xxii).

An important group of African and African American scholars have challenged established interpretations about the origin of Greek civilization and the extent to which Greek civilization was influenced by African cultures. These scholars include Diop (1974), Williams (1987), and Van Sertima (1988, 1989). Cheikh Anta Diop is one of the most influential African scholars who has challenged established interpretations about the origin of Greek civilization. In *Black Nations and Culture,* published in 1955 (summarized by Van Sertima, 1989), he sets forth an important thesis that states that Africa is an important root of Western civilization. Diop argues that Egypt "was the node and center of a vast web linking the strands of cultures and languages; that the light that crystallized at the center of this early world had been energized by the cultural electricity streaming from the heartland of Africa" (p. 8).

Since the work by Diop, Williams, and Van Sertima, traditional interpretations about the formation of Greek civilization has been challenged by Bernal (1987–1991), a professor of government at Cornell University. The earlier challenges to established interpretations by African and African Americans received little attention, except within the African American community. However, Bernal's work has received wide attention in the popular press and among classicists.

Bernal (1987–1991) argues that important aspects of Greek civilization originated in ancient Egypt and Phoenicia and that the ancient civilization of Egypt was essentially African. Bernal believes that the contributions of Egypt and Phoenicia to Greek civilization have been deliberately ignored by classical scholars because of their biased attitudes toward non-White peoples and Semites. Bernal has published two of four planned volumes of his study *Black Athena.* In Volume 2 he uses evidence from linguistics, archeology and ancient documents to substantiate his claim that "between 2100 and 1100 B.C., when Greek culture was born, the people of the Aegean borrowed, adapted or had thrust upon them deities and language, technologies and architectures, notions of justice and polis" from Egypt and Phoenicia (Begley, Chideya, & Wilson, 1991, p. 50). Because transformative academic knowledge, such as that constructed by Diop, Williams, Van Sertima, and Bernal, challenges the established paradigms as well as because of the tremendous gap between academic knowledge and school knowledge, it often has little influence on school knowledge.

School Knowledge

School knowledge consists of the facts, concepts, and generalizations presented in textbooks, teachers' guides, and the other forms of media designed for school use. School knowledge also consists of the teacher's mediation and interpretation of that knowledge. The textbook is the main source of school knowledge in the United States (Apple & Christian-Smith, 1991; Goodlad, 1984; Shaver, Davis, & Helburn, 1979). Studies of textbooks indicate that these are some of the major themes in school knowledge (Anyon, 1979, 1981; Sleeter & Grant, 1991b): (a) America's founding fathers, such as Washington and Jefferson, were highly moral, liberty-loving men who championed equality and justice for all Americans; (b) the United States is a nation with justice, liberty, and freedom for all; (c) social class divisions are not significant issues in the United States; (d) there are no significant gender, class, or racial divisions within U.S. society; and (e) ethnic groups of color and Whites interact largely in harmony in the United States.

Studies of textbooks that have been conducted by researchers such as Anyon (1979, 1981) and Sleeter and Grant (1991b) indicate that textbooks present a highly selective view of social reality, give students the idea that knowledge is static rather than dynamic, and encourage students to master isolated facts rather than to develop complex understandings of social reality. These studies also indicate that textbooks reinforce the dominant social, economic, and power arrangements within society. Students are encouraged to accept rather than to question these arrangements.

In their examination of the treatment of race, class, gender, and disability in textbooks, Sleeter and Grant (1991b) concluded that although textbooks had largely eliminated sexist language and had incorporated images of ethnic minorities into them, they failed to help students to develop an understanding of the complex cultures of ethnic groups, an understanding of racism, sexism and classism in American society, and described the United States as a nation that had largely overcome its problems. Sleeter & Grant write:

> The vision of social relations that the textbooks we analyzed for the most part project is one of harmony and equal opportunity—anyone can do or become whatever he or she wants; problems among people are mainly individual in nature and in the end are resolved. (p. 99)

A number of powerful factors influence the development and production of school textbooks (Altbach, Kelly, Petrie, & Weis, 1991; FitzGerald, 1979). One of the most important is the publisher's perception of statements and images that might be controversial. When textbooks become controversial, school districts often refuse to adopt and to purchase them. When developing a textbook, the publisher and the authors must also consider the developmental and reading levels of the students, state and district guidelines about what subject matter textbooks should include, and recent trends and developments in a content field that teachers and administrators will expect the textbook to reflect and incorporate. Because of the number of constraints and influences on the development of textbooks, school knowledge often does not include in-depth discussions and analyses of some of the major problems in American society, such as racism, sexism, social-class stratification, and poverty (Anyon, 1979, 1981; Sleeter & Grant, 1991b). Consequently, school knowledge is influenced most heavily by mainstream academic knowledge and popular knowledge. Transformative academic knowledge usually has little direct influence on school knowledge. It usually affects school knowledge in a significant way only after it has become a part of mainstream and popular knowledge. Teachers must make special efforts to introduce transformative knowledge and perspectives to elementary and secondary school students.

Teaching Implications

Multicultural education involves changes in the total school environment in order to create equal educational opportunities for all students (Banks, 1991; Banks & Banks, 1989; Sleeter & Grant, 1987). However, in this chapter I have focused on only one of the important dimensions of multicultural education—the kinds of *knowledge* that should be taught in the multicultural curriculum. The five types of knowledge described above have important implications for planning and teaching a multicultural curriculum.

An important goal of multicultural teaching is to help students to understand how knowledge is constructed. Students should be given opportunities to investigate and determine how cultural assumptions, frames of references, perspectives, and the biases within a discipline influence the ways the knowledge is constructed. Students should also be given opportunities to create knowledge themselves and identify ways in which the knowledge they construct is influenced and limited by their personal assumptions, positions, and experiences.

I will use a unit on the Westward Movement to illustrate how teachers can use the knowledge categories described above to teach from a multicultural perspective. When beginning the unit, teachers can draw upon the students' personal and cultural knowledge about the Westward Movement. They can ask the students to make a list of ideas that come to mind when they think of "The West." To enable the students to determine how the popular culture depicts the West, teachers can ask the students to view and analyze the film discussed above, *How the West Was Won*. They can also ask them to view videos of more recently made films about the West and to make a list of its major themes and images. Teachers can summarize Turner's frontier theory to give students an idea of how an influential mainstream historian described and interpreted the West in the late 19th century and how this theory influenced generations of historians.

Teachers can present a transformative perspective on the West by showing the students the film *How the West Was Won and Honor Lost*, narrated by Marlon Brando. This film describes how the European Americans who went West, with the use of broken treaties and deceptions, invaded the land of the Indians and displaced them. Teachers may also ask the students to view segments of the popular film *Dances With Wolves* and to discuss how the depiction of Indians in this film reflects both mainstream and transformative perspectives on Indians in U.S. history and culture. Teachers can present the textbook account of the Westward Movement in the final part of the unit.

The main goals of presenting different kinds of knowledge are to help students understand how knowledge is constructed and how it reflects the social context in which it is created and to enable them to develop the understandings and skills needed to become knowledge builders themselves. An important goal of multicultural education is to transform the school curriculum so that students not only learn the knowledge that has been constructed by others, but learn how to critically analyze the knowledge they master and how to construct their own interpretations of the past, present, and future.

Several important factors related to teaching the types of knowledge have not been discussed in this chapter but need to be examined. One is the personal/cultural knowledge of the classroom teacher. The teachers, like the students, bring understandings, concepts, explanations, and interpretations to the classroom that result from their experiences in their homes, families, and community cultures. Most teachers in the United States are European American (87%) and female (72%) (Ordovensky, 1992). However, there is enormous diversity among European Americans that is mirrored in the backgrounds of the teacher population, including diversity related to religion, social class, region, and ethnic origin. The diversity within European Americans is rarely discussed in the social science literature (Alba, 1990) or within classrooms. However, the rich diversity among the cultures of teachers is an important factor that needs to be examined and discussed in the classroom. The 13% of U.S. teachers who are ethnic minorities can also enrich their classrooms by sharing their personal and cultural knowledge with their students and by helping them to understand how it mediates textbook knowledge. The multicultural classroom is a forum of multiple voices and perspectives. The voices of the teacher, of the textbook, of mainstream and transformative authors—and of the students—are important components of classroom discourse.

Teachers can share their cultural experiences and interpretations of events as a way to motivate students to share theirs. However, they should examine their racial and ethnic attitudes toward diverse groups before engaging in cultural sharing. A democratic classroom atmosphere must also be created. The students must view the classroom as a forum where multiple perspectives are valued. An open and democratic classroom will enable students to acquire the skills and abilities they need to examine conflicting knowledge claims and perspectives. Students must become critical consumers of knowledge as well as knowledge producers if they are to acquire the understandings and skills needed to function in the complex and diverse world of tomorrow. Only a broad and liberal multicultural education can prepare them for that world.

NOTES

This chapter is adapted from a paper presented at the conference "Democracy and Education," sponsored by the Benton Center for Curriculum and Instruction, Department of Education, The University of Chicago, November 15–16, 1991, Chicago, Illinois. I am grateful to the following colleagues for helpful comments on an earlier draft of this chapter: Cherry A. Cortés, McGee Banks, Carlos E, Geneva Gay, Donna H. Kerr, Joyce E. King, Walter C. Parker, Pamela L. Grossman, and Christine E. Sleeter.

REFERENCES

Acuña, R. (1988). *Occupied America: A history of Chicanos* (3rd ed.). New York: Harper & Row.

Alba, R. D. (1990). *Ethnic identity: The transformation of White America.* New Haven, CT: Yale University Press.

Allen, P. G. (1986). *The sacred hoop: Recovering the feminine in American Indian traditions.* Boston: Beacon Press.

Altbach, P. G., Kelly, G. P., Petrie, H. G., & Weis, L. (Eds.). (1991). *Textbooks in American Society.* Albany, NY: State University of New York Press.

The American heritage dictionary (1983). New York: Dell.

Anyon, J. (1979). Ideology and United States history textbooks. *Harvard Educational Review, 49,* 361–386.

Anyon, J. (1981). Social class and school knowledge. *Curriculum Inquiry, 11,* 3–42.

Anzaldúa, G. (1990). Haciendo caras, una entrada: An introduction. In G. Anzaldúa (Ed.), *Making face, making soul: Haciendo caras* (pp. xv–xvii). San Francisco: Aunt Lute Foundation Books.

Apple, M. W., & Christian-Smith, L. K. (Eds.). (1991). *The politics of the textbook.* New York: Routledge.

Aptheker, H. (Ed.). (1973). *The collected published works of W. E. B. Dubois* (38 Vols.). Millwood, NY: Kraus.

Asante, M. K. (1991a). The Afrocentric idea in education. *The Journal of Negro Education, 60,* 170–180.

Asante, M. K. (1991b, September 23). Putting Africa at the center. *Newsweek, 118,* 46.

Asante, M. K., & Ravitch, D. (1991). Multiculturalism: An exchange. *The American Scholar, 60,* 267–275.

Banks, J. A. (1988). *Multiethnic education: Theory and practice* (2nd ed.). Boston: Allyn & Bacon.

Banks, J. A. (1991). *Teaching strategies for ethnic studies* (5th ed.). Boston: Allyn & Bacon.

Banks, J. A. (1991/1992). Multicultural education: For freedom's sake. *Educational Leadership, 49,* 32–36.

Banks, J. A., & Banks, C. A. M. (Eds.). (1989). *Multicultural education: Issues and perspectives.* Boston: Allyn & Bacon.

Begley, S., Chideya, F., & Wilson, L. (1991, September 23). Out of Egypt, Greece: Seeking the roots of Western civilization on the banks of the Nile. *Newsweek, 118,* 48–49.

Bernal, M. (1987–1991). *Black Athena: The Afroasiatic roots of classical civilization* (Vols. 1–2). London: Free Association Books.

Blassingame, J. W. (1972). *The slave community: Plantation life in the Antebellum South.* New York: Oxford University Press.

Bloom, A. (1987). *The closing of the American mind.* New York: Simon & Schuster.

Bogle, D. (1989). *Toms, coons, mulattoes, mammies & bucks: An interpretative history of Blacks in American films* (new expanded ed.). New York: Continuum.

Butler, J. E., & Walter, J. C. (1991). (Eds.). *Transforming the curriculum: Ethnic studies and women studies.* Albany, NY: State University of New York Press.

Cherryholmes, C. H. (1988). *Power and criticism: Poststructural investigations in education.* New York: Teachers College Press.

Clark, K. B. (1965). *Dark ghetto: Dilemmas of social power.* New York: Harper & Row.

Code, L. (1991). *What can she know? Feminist theory and the construction of knowledge.* Ithaca, NY: Cornell University Press.

Cooper, A. J. (1969). *A voice from the South.* New York: Negro Universities Press. (Original work published 1982)

Cortés, C. E. (1991a). Empowerment through media literacy. In C. E. Sleeter (Ed.), *Empowerment through multicultural education.* Albany: State University of New York Press.

Cortés, C. E. (1991b). Hollywood interracial love: Social taboo as screen titillation. In P. Loukides & L. K. Fuller (Eds.), *Beyond the stars II: Plot conventions in American popular film* (pp. 21–35). Bowling Green, OH: Bowling Green State University Press.

Delpit, L. D. (1988). The silenced dialogue: Power and pedagogy in educating other people's children. *Harvard Educational Review, 58,* 280–298.

Diop, C. A. (1974). *The African origin of civilization: Myth or reality?* New York: Lawrence Hill.

D'Souza, D. (1991). *Illiberal education: The politics of race and sex on campus.* New York: Free Press.

DuBois, W. E. B. (1962). *Black reconstruction in America 1860–1880: An essay toward a History of the part which Black folk played in the attempt to reconstruct democracy in America, 1860–1880.* New York: Atheneum. (Original work published 1935)

DuBois, W. E. B. (1969). *The suppression of the African slave trade to the United States of America, 1638–1870,* Baton Rouge, LA: Louisiana State University Press. (Original work published 1896)

Ellsworth, E. (1989). Why doesn't this feel empowering? Working through the repressive myths of critical pedagogy. *Harvard Educational Review, 59,* 297–324.

Farganis, S. (1986). *The social construction of the feminine character.* Totowa, NJ: Russell & Russell.

FitzGerald, F. (1979). *America revised: History schoolbooks in the twentieth century.* New York: Vintage.

Fordham, S. (1988). Racelessness as a factor in Black students' school success: Pragmatic strategy or Pyrrhic victory? *Harvard Educational Review, 58,* 54–84.

Fordham, S. (1991). Racelessness in private schools: Should we deconstruct the racial and cultural identity of African-American adolescents? *Teachers College Record, 92,* 470–484.

Fordham, S., & Ogbu, J. (1986). Black students' school success: Coping with the burden of 'acting White.' *The Urban Review, 18,* 176–206.

Foucault, M. (1972). *The archaeology of knowledge and the discourse on language.* New York: Pantheon.

Franklin, J. H. (1991, September 26). Illiberal education: An exchange. *New York Review of Books, 38,* 74–76.

Frazier, E. F. (1939). *The Negro family in the United States.* Chicago: University of Chicago Press.

Gates, H. L., Jr. (1988). *The signifying monkey: A theory of African-American literary criticism.* New York: Oxford University Press.

Gates, H. L., Jr. (1992). *Loose canons: Notes on the culture wars.* New York: Oxford University Press.

Genovese, E. D. (1972). *Roll Jordan roll: The world the slaves made.* New York: Pantheon.

Giroux, H. A. (1983). *Theory and resistance in education.* Boston: Bergin & Garvey.

Glazer, N. (1991, September 2). In defense of multiculturalism. *The New Republic,* 18–21.

Goodlad, J. I. (1984). *A place called school: Prospects for the future.* New York: McGraw-Hill.

Gordon, E. W. (1985). Social science knowledge production and minority experiences. *Journal of Negro Education, 54,* 117–132.

Gordon, E. W., Miller, F., & Rollock, D. (1990). Coping with communicentric bias in knowledge production in the social sciences. *Educational Researcher, 14*(3), 14–19.

Grant, C. A. (Ed.). (1992). *Research and multicultural education: From the margins to the mainstream.* Washington, DC: Falmer.

Gray, P. (1991, July 8). Whose America? *Time, 138,* 12–17.

Greenfield, G. M., & Cortés, C. E. (1991). Harmony and conflict of intercultural images: The treatment of Mexico in U.S. feature films and K-12 textbooks. *Mexican Studies/Estudios Mexicanos, 7,* 283–301.

Greer, S. (1969). *The logic of social inquiry.* Chicago: Aldine.

Gutman, H. G. (1976). *The Black family in slavery and freedom 1750–1925.* New York: Vintage.

Habermas, J. (1971). *Knowledge and human interests.* Boston: Beacon.

Hale-Benson, J. E. (1982). *Black children: Their roots, culture, and learning styles* (rev. ed.). Baltimore: John Hopkins University Press.

Harding, S. (1991). *Whose science? Whose knowledge? Thinking from women's lives.* Ithaca, NY: Cornell University Press.

Harding, V. (1981). *There is a river: The Black struggle for freedom in America.* New York: Vintage.

Heath, S. B. (1983). *Ways with words: Language, life and work in communities and classrooms.* New York: Cambridge University Press.

Hirsch, E. D., Jr. (1987). *Cultural literacy: What every American needs to know.* Boston: Houghton Mifflin.

hooks, b., & West, C. (1991). *Breaking bread: Insurgent Black intellectual life.* Boston: South End Press.

Howe, I. (1991, February 18). The value of the canon. *The New Republic,* 40–47.

Hoxie, F. E. (Ed.). (1988). *Indians in American history.* Arlington Heights, IL: Harlan Davidson.

Hoxie, F. E. (no date). *The Indians versus the textbooks: Is there any way out?* Chicago: The Newberry Library, Center for the History of the American Indian.

Kaplan, A. (1964). *The conduct of inquiry: Methodology for behavioral science.* San Francisco: Chandler.

King, J. E., & Mitchell, C. A. (1990). *Black mothers to sons: Juxtaposing African American literature with social practice.* New York: Lang.

Kuhn, T. S. (1970). *The structure of scientific revolutions* (2nd ed.). Chicago: University of Chicago Press.

Labov, W. (1975). *The study of nonstandard English.* Washington, DC: Center for Applied Linguistics.

Ladner, J. A. (Ed.). (1973). *The death of White sociology.* New York: Vintage.

Meier, A., & Rudwick, E. (1986). *Black history and the historical profession 1915–1980.* Urbana, IL: University of Illinois Press.

Merton, R. K. (1972). Insiders and outsiders: A chapter in the sociology of knowledge. *The American Journal of Sociology, 78,* 9–47.

Milner, D. (1983). *Children and race.* Beverly Hills, CA: Sage.

Minnich, E. K. (1990). *Transforming knowledge.* Philadelphia: Temple University Press.

Moynihan, D. P. (1965). *The Negro family in America: A case for national action.* Washington, DC: U.S. Department of Labor.

Myrdal, G. (with the assistance of R. Sterner & A. Rose). (1944). *An American dilemma: The Negro problem in modern democracy.* New York: Harper.

Nash, G. B. (1982). *Red, White and Black: The peoples of early America.* Englewood Cliffs, NJ: Prentice-Hall.

New York City Board of Education. (1990). *Grade 7, United States and New York state history: A multicultural perspective.* New York: Author.

New York State Department of Education. (1989, July). *A curriculum of inclusion* (Report of the Commissioner's Task Force on Minorities: Equity and excellence). Albany, NY: The State Education Department.

New York State Department of Education. (1991, June). *One nation, many peoples: A declaration of cultural interdependence.* Albany, NY: The State Education Department.

Ordovensky, P. (1992, July 7). Teachers: 87% White, 72% women. *USA Today,* p. 1A.

Philips, S. U. (1983). *The invisible culture: Communication in classroom and community on the Warm Springs Indian Reservation.* New York: Longman.

Phillips, U. B. (1918). *American Negro slavery.* New York: Appleton.

Ramírez, M., III, & Castañeda, A. (1974). *Cultural democracy, bicognitive development and education.* New York: Academic Press.

Ravitch, D., & Finn, C. E., Jr. (1987). *What do our 17-year-olds know? A report on the first national assessment of history and literature.* New York: Harper & Row.

Rivlin, A. M. (1973). Forensic social science. *Harvard Educational Review, 43,* 61–75.

Rorty, R. (1989). *Contingency, irony, and solidarity.* New York: Cambridge University Press.

Rosenau, P. M. (1992). *Post-modernism and the social sciences: Insights, inroads, and intrusions.* Princeton, NJ: Princeton University Press.

Schlesinger, A., Jr. (1991). *The disuniting of America: Reflections on a multicultural society.* Knoxville, TN: Whittle Direct Books.

Shade, B. J. R. (Ed.). (1989). *Culture, style and the educative process.* Springfield, IL: Thompson.

Shaver, J. P., Davis, O. L., Jr., & Helburn, S. W. (1979). The status of social studies education: Impressions from three NSF studies. *Social Education, 43,* 150–153.

Sleeter, C. E. (1991). (Ed.). *Empowerment through multicultural education.* Albany: State University of New York Press.

Sleeter, C. E., & Grant, C. A. (1987). An analysis of multicultural education in the United States. *Harvard Educational Review, 57,* 421–444.

Sleeter, C. E., & Grant, C. A. (1991a). Mapping terrains of power: Student cultural knowledge versus classroom knowledge. In C. E. Sleeter. (Ed.), *Empowerment through multicultural education* (pp. 49–67). Albany: State University of New York Press.

Sleeter, C. E., & Grant, C. A. (1991b). Race, class, gender and disability in current textbooks. In M. W. Apple & L. K. Christian-Smith (Eds.), *The politics of textbooks* (pp. 78–110). New York: Routledge.

Smitherman, G. (1977). *Talkin and testifyin: The language of Black America.* Boston: Houghton Mifflin.

Sokol, E. (Ed.). (1990). *A world of difference: St. Louis metropolitan region, preschool through grade 6, teacher/student resource guide.* St. Louis: Anti-Defamation League of B'nai B'rith.

Stampp, K. M. (1956). *The peculiar institution: Slavery in the ante-bellum South.* New York: Vintage.

Takaki, R. T. (1979). *Iron cages: Race and culture in 19th-century America.* Seattle, WA: University of Washington Press.

Tetreault, M. K. T. (1993). Classrooms for diversity: Rethinking curriculum and pedagogy. In J. A. Banks & C. A. M. Banks (Eds.), *Multicultural education: Issues and perspectives* (2nd ed.) (pp. 129–148). Boston: Allyn & Bacon.

Thornton, R. (1987). *American Indian holocaust and survival: A population history since 1492.* Norman: University of Oklahoma Press.

Turner, F. J. (1989). The significance of the frontier in American history. In C. A. Milner II (Ed.), *Major problems in the history of the American West* (pp. 2–21). Lexington, MA: Heath. (Original work published 1894)

Van Sertima, I. V. (Ed.). (1988). *Great Black leaders: Ancient and modern.* New Brunswick, NJ: Rutgers University, Africana Studies Department.

Van Sertima, I. V. (Ed.). (1989). *Great African thinkers: Vol. 1. Cheikh Anta Diop.* New Brunswick, NJ: Transaction Books.

Wiggington, E. (1991/1992). Culture begins at home. *Educational Leadership, 49,* 60–64.

Williams, C. (1987). *The destruction of Black civilization: Great issues of a race from 4500 B.C. to 2000 A.D.* Chicago: Third World Press.

Williams, G. W. (1968). *History of the Negro Race in America from 1619 to 1880: Negroes as slaves, as soldiers, and as citizens* (2 vols.). New York: Arno Press. (Original work published 1892 & 1893).

Woodson, C. G. (1933). *The Mis-education of the Negro.* Washington, DC: Associated Publishers.

Woodson, C. G., & Wesley, C. H. (1922). *The Negro in our history.* Washington, DC: Associated Publishers.

Woodward, C. V. (1991, July 18). Freedom and the universities. *The New York Review of Books, 38,* 32–37.

Young, M. F. D. (1971). An approach to curricula as socially organized knowledge. In M. F. D. Young (Ed.), *Knowledge and control* (pp. 19–46). London: Collier-Macmillan.

Zinn, H. (1980). *A people's history of the United States.* New York: Harper & Row.

9

The Learning College

Creating a New Architecture for Community Colleges

Terry O'Banion

A Learning Revolution is spreading rapidly through all sectors of education, and the community college has become the most visible crucible in which the concepts and practices of this revolution are being forged. First articulated in the early 1990s by Robert Barr, John Tagg, and George Boggs as a new Learning Paradigm, this fresh approach to educational reform leads educators away from fixing educational problems by the process of adding on a new program, new staff, and more technology to a traditional core of programs and services. The new approach suggests that the old models of education are no longer functional and that they even stand in the way of changes that would substantially improve student learning. Pat Cross (1984) has recognized the problem for many years: "After some two decades of trying to find answers to the question of how to provide education for all the people, I have concluded that our commitment to the lock-step, time-defined structures of education stands in the way of lasting progress" (p. 171).

The basic concepts of the Learning Revolution were best expressed in the work of the Wingspread Group on Higher Education (1993): "Putting learning at the heart of the academic enterprise will mean overhauling the conceptual, procedural, curricular, and other architecture of postsecondary education on most campuses." These two key concepts—(a) place learning first (b) by overhauling the traditional architecture of education—charted a new direction for educational reform and launched a revolution in the way we think about the core business and basic structures of education.

It was not difficult to "place learning first," at least in the language of education. Many educational institutions began embracing the language of "learning," and community colleges were among the early adopters. Ironically, mission and value statements had to be revised to make explicit that learning was the central purpose, the institution's first priority. Deans of Instruction became Vice-Presidents for Learning. The accrediting associations pressed for colleges to identify and measure learning outcomes. Colleges claimed to be Learning Organizations creating Learning Communities for their students and for their staffs. Strategic plans were revised to include the core principles of the Learning College. Learning became the mantra of educational reform throughout the 1990s.

Earnest and eager to "place learning first" in every policy, program, practice, and in the way they use their personnel, the early leaders of the Learning Revolution found it relatively easy to change the language of education. However, they began to run into problems reflected in Roger Moe's (1994) keen observation that "Higher education is a thousand years of tradition wrapped in a hundred years of bureaucracy." It was the second key concept of the Learning Revolution— "overhauling the traditional architecture of education"—that was the real challenge.

The traditional architecture of education was designed in an earlier time to meet the needs of an agrarian and an industrial economy; it was not designed to improve and expand student learning. At the end of the 1800s, schools were based on an agricultural economy that accommodated the needs of farmers who depended on their children to work on the farms. Schools were designed to end in the middle of the afternoon so that students could be home before dark to milk the cows, gather the eggs, and feed the hogs. School closed down for the summer to allow students to attend to major farm chores: harvesting crops, tilling new land, building barns, and repairing tools and fences. "Everyone recognizes it (the academic calendar) for what it is: a relic of an agrarian society in which all able-bodied men and women were needed in the fields at certain times of the year" (Lovett, 1995, p. B1).

When the nation changed in the 1920s and 1930s from an agricultural to an industrial economy, the old school structure remained as the foundation but was updated and streamlined to fit the new industrial organizational model. "Scientific management" and hierarchical organization, the bedrock principles of bureaucracy, were introduced in the schools, in part to socialize youth in the virtues of order and discipline. More importantly, the modern factory, pioneered by Henry Ford in the production of automobiles, appealed to educators as an ideal model on which to structure the schools. Organize students into groups of 35 and move them through 55-minute periods of instruction in a 16-week term; the school bell echoed the factory whistle that kept everything moving on time. "America's schools still operate like factories, subjecting the raw material (students) to standardized instruction and routine inspection" (Alvin and Heidi Toffler, 1995, p. 13).

Today, this inherited architecture of education places great limits on a system struggling to redefine and transform itself into a learning-centered enterprise, one that can continually deepen learning and improve student success. The school system, from K to Gray, is time-bound, place-bound, bureaucracy-bound, and role-bound. These bonds must be broken and a new, more fluid architecture created that places learning first and enables the institution to become ever smarter and better at improving its outcomes if the Learning Revolution is to come to full fruition. The Wingspread Group on Higher Education (1993) defined the Learning Revolution and pointed the way for ensuring its success: "The nation that responds best and most rapidly to the educational demands of the Age of the Learner will enjoy a commanding international advantage in the pursuit of both domestic tranquility and economic prosperity. To achieve these goals for our country, we must educate more people and educate them far better. *That will require new ways of thinking*" (p. 7, Italics added).

NEW WAYS OF THINKING

The 12 Vanguard Learning Colleges in the League for Innovation's Learning College Project have been struggling with new ways of thinking about how to implement the concepts called for in the Learning Revolution—concepts expressed in the Learning Paradigm and the core principles of the Learning College. They have been particularly interested in exploring how to "overhaul the traditional architecture of education" so they could more substantively "place learning first" and improve it. Beginning in January of 2000, the Vanguard Learning Colleges agreed to work together over a three-year period to create new architectural forms that would allow them to place learning as their first priority. Teams from the 12 colleges have met for intensive seminars for the past three summers and in special sessions at the League's annual conference on innovations. In addition, the colleges have shared an active network of communication facilitated through the Learning College Web site at www.league.org. Some promising "new ways of thinking" about an architecture to support learning are beginning to emerge from the work of these colleges. The early outlines of this new architecture—new practices and key questions—in five selected areas will be of interest to many colleges struggling to implement the Learning Revolution.

DEPARTMENTAL STRUCTURES

Community colleges inherited the departmental/divisional structures for organizing faculty into discipline groups from the universities. Some educators believe that such an organizing structure serves to reinforce the culture of the discipline guilds over larger institutional values, especially community college values that may be different in some important ways from the values of the university. One example is that by organizing around disciplines, the vocational faculty and the liberal arts faculty in community colleges tend to be isolated from one another when they need to forge curriculum and instructional alliances to enhance student learning.

In the 1960s, a number of new community colleges experimented with an organizational architecture designed to enhance communication across faculty disciplines. The Novato Campus of the College of Marin (California) organized faculty into "Houses" that represented a very broad view of the knowledge and skills the college valued. At Santa Fe Community College (Florida), faculty were organized into "Units" of 16. Each unit included representatives from a wide range of disciplines. The unit's leader attended to the needs of members and guided them in the creation of a community that addressed larger institutional values that, at Santa Fe, were quite different from those of other community colleges. Faculty met in discipline groups when they needed to select textbooks, agree on common assessment, and make curriculum decisions, but their primary physical and philosophical commitment was to the "Unit."

Cascadia Community College (Washington) is currently organizing its faculty and staff around four fundamental learning outcomes. Learning Outcome Teams (LOTs), involving all faculty, staff, and administration are the funded units that create college initiatives and projects, act as communication outlets, and select their own methods and priorities for insuring that students achieve the desired outcome. Creating such a structure is easier when a college is new, but it can be done even in established colleges. Sir Sandford Fleming College (Ontario) eliminated the traditional departmental structure and created six new "Centres of Specialization" managed by faculty teams. The centers are organized around natural resources, community development and health, law and justice, management and business studies, interdisciplinary studies, and applied computing and information technology. The new structure was supported by the faculty union, and both management and the union agree that, to date, the new model is working extremely well.

If a college wished to continue with a discipline-oriented structure, how would it be organized to best represent new fields of knowledge while enhancing cross-disciplinary communication? How can technology enhance the communication required in some disciplines without organizing the entire college around disciplines? Is it necessary to organize faculty and staff into any kind of groupings? Why? And, if so, how could they be organized to best meet the rationale posed in the answer to why? Is there an organizational structure for faculty and staff that would communicate that a college is truly learning centered and that would insure a focus on improving learning?

THE WORKLOAD FORMULA

The bureaucracy-bound historical architecture has created one of the most limiting practices in educational culture with the concept of the workload formula. The long shadow of education's adaptation to the industrial economy is clearly evident in the formula that the best way to use faculty resources is to assign full-time faculty to teach five courses a semester as their *load*, an apt term for this inefficient and educationally ineffective practice. All other faculty assignments are keyed to this formula. Many faculty are permitted to teach one or two courses more as an "overload." This practice of allowing faculty to teach an "overload" raises very serious but unaddressed questions about the validity of the load concept—or at least the formula that five courses represent tasks truly equivalent to at least a 40-hour work week. Some faculty are released from teaching one or more courses to do other things, and the time assigned is based on the workload formula. Part-time faculty are hired and assigned to teach courses according to the workload formula when there are not enough full-time faculty to teach all the courses offered.

The fact that the workload formula is so deeply embedded in the culture of most educational institutions is testimony to the value placed on institutional efficiency over improving and expanding learning for students. How faculty time is allocated is more important than student time. If institutions placed a priority on learning they would design many variations in terms of structures to accommodate student needs. Indeed, many institutions experiment with such variations as independent study, learning communities, service learning, cooperative education, etc.; but the workload formula is ever present to cast its long and restrictive shadow over these innovations.

The workload formula enslaves faculty in a structured system in which they do not often have opportunities to contribute their greatest talents and creativity to the educational enterprise. The innovators have adapted to the system. Like the "A" students who have learned to negotiate the traditional architecture, faculty innovators have learned to be subversive and cunning in getting around the system. They do this in order to create environments that work better for learning. If the workload formula was changed faculty would not have to waste their energies working around its limiting structures; what could faculty accomplish in their roles as the facilitators of learning if they were freed from the workload formula?

Since education has been such a labor-intensive enterprise, there will be no major reforms and little increased productivity on the part of the faculty until we free ourselves from the tyranny of the workload formula. We need to change the conversation from "my load, my classes, my students" to "How can we realign our resources to improve and expand learning for our students?" We begin by defining resources not on the basis of a formula that *assumes* full-time faculty load equals learning produced in students. We do it by determining what we want our students to learn and then figuring out how to use the vast resources available to us: classified staff, students, community volunteers, administrators, educators in other institutions, technology, full-time faculty, and part-time faculty. Ask the faculty what ways other than teaching five classes they can identify to make a significant contribution to improving and expanding learning.

If the number of classes or number of students is not the basis for faculty contributions to the educational enterprise, how is the learning they produce to be calculated? Need this be calculated at the individual faculty or staff member level? What kind of architecture is needed to implement the concept of the faculty member as a "manager of learning"? What kinds of creative alliances would emerge in the institution to accommodate the needs of the "boundless" faculty? If the roles of learning facilitators are to be determined by the needs of the students, what implications does such a practice have for workload? What kind of architecture can support clearly defined learning facilitator roles that are based on clearly defined student learning needs?

THE GRADING SYSTEM

The grading system of A through F is one of the most powerful elements of the historical architecture of education. Grades begin to stamp a person's value in the early years of schooling and accumulate weight with each passing (or failing!) year. Eventually grades are pooled into a grade point average (GPA) and stick with the student, like the Scarlet Letter, for the rest of his or her life. The GPA influences participation in athletics and social events, plays a key role in determining high school graduation and admission to college, influences decisions regarding scholarships and financial aid, and becomes an issue in social standing and parental approval. Grades are the coin of the realm as sectors of education trade in student lives for the good of society.

It is a little discouraging, therefore, when we come to understand that "The course grade is an inadequate report of an inaccurate judgment by a biased and variable judge of the extent to which a student has attained an undefined level of mastery of an unknown proportion of an indefinite material" (Dressel, 1983, p. 1). No wonder that two teachers grading the same piece of work cannot agree on the grade to be assigned. Teachers receive little or no training in assessment and the grading process and, thus, may assign grades as a measure of punctuality, a measure of gain or growth, a measure of place in a distribution, a measure of dishonesty, a measure of extra work, a measure of attendance, a measure of writing skill, a measure of motivation or perseverance, a measure of social class, a measure of political statement, or as a measure of the teacher's health or emotional state the day a grade is assigned. Pooling grades from various courses—an A in Russian literature has as much value as an A in Volleyball—from various teachers to create a grade point average creates a witches' brew of which we would rather not know the specific origins of the ingredients.

Educators generally agree that grades are a poor measure of what a student knows and understands about a body of knowledge, and there have been numerous attempts to redress the wrong by creating alternative systems of proficiencies, competencies, skills, standards, or outcomes. There is a great deal of attention focused on these alternatives at the moment as educational leaders and critics call for a "culture of evidence" to replace a culture that assumes learning takes place because something has been taught. A League for Innovation project captures this rising tide of concern in a project that assists 16 community colleges in defining learning outcomes, teaching learning outcomes, assessing learning outcomes, and documenting learning outcomes. Accrediting associations are embedding the concept of "learning outcomes" deeply into revised accreditation processes, laying the foundation for a new educational architecture that places learning first.

How can we create a common understanding and a common system for documenting what a student has learned during his or her formal schooling? Can we agree on learning outcomes for every planned educational experience, on ways to determine levels of proficiency for the outcomes, on ways to assess the acquisition of the outcomes? How can we strike a balance between the supposed efficiency of the GPA and the cumbersome lists of skills achieved at some level of proficiency? How do we measure what a student knows in contrast to what a student can do with that knowledge? What responsibility does the student have in participating in this process that is so important to future success?

LATE REGISTRATION

Almost every institution of higher education in the country engages every term in a practice that plays havoc with the goal of creating an effective learning environment for students—late registration. The practice emerged to provide opportunities for students and for the institution. During the late registration period, usually the first week of class of a 16-week term, students are allowed, with some restrictions at some colleges, to change class schedules as they seek more accommodating times, more useful courses, and better teachers.

In some cases, students may be seeking easier courses or teachers. For the institution, the purpose is to increase the number of enrolled students and hence revenue through a funding formula based on full-time equivalent students or average daily attendance: the more students, the more money. Late registration is an educationally ineffective architecture deeply embedded in the culture of institutions of higher education.

Faculty abhor late registration—and with good reason. Most faculty recognize that the first day of class may be the most important as they begin to create an expectation and a climate to entice students to master the course. Faculty give careful consideration to orienting students, welcoming students, creating a sense of class community, providing course overviews, introducing themselves and their perspectives, and making beginning assignments—all on the first day and in the first week. This initial groundwork early in the term is the key to subsequent success for many students, but the preparation process is constantly interrupted by the comings and goings of late registering students. Thus, many teachers do not even try to use the first day and the first week in any substantive way, and often dismiss students from class early. In these situations there develops a cynical collusion between both students and the faculty member that communicates that learning is really not very important at this institution. A climate of cynicism begins to pervade the institution as faculty realize that administrators are more interested in head count and the increased income than they are in supporting faculty efforts to create an effective learning environment.

What can colleges do to market registration as an opportunity that ends the day before the first class begins? What compromises can faculty and administrators make to ensure that the institution enrolls the maximum number of students who wish to register but does so in time to take advantage of the special arrangements faculty create for the first day and first week of class? How can the late registration issue be addressed as an opportunity for students to take responsibility for improving and expanding their own learning?

TIME-BOUND ARTIFACTS

The class hour, the three-hour credit course, the semester or quarter term, and the school year are the building blocks of an architecture created for agricultural and industrial economies. They may have been useful building blocks in earlier times and understandings of our mission, but today they are impediments to creating the most powerful learning environments possible.

Recognizing that schools suffer from a time-bound mentality, the U.S. Department of Education, in 1992, appointed a national commission to study the issue. Addressing the time issue primarily in K-12 schools, the commission noted "Unyielding and relentless, the time available in a uniform six-hour day and a 180-day year is the unacknowledged design flaw in American education. By relying on time as the metric for school organization and curriculum, we have built the learning enterprise on a foundation of sand" (National Education Commission on Time and Learning, 1994, p. 8).

Herding groups of students through one-hour sessions five days a week in high schools and three days a week in college flies in the face of everything known about what works to improve and expand learning. No one believes that 30 different students arrive at the appointed hour ready to learn in the same way, on the same schedule, all in rhythm with each other and the teacher. The National Education Commission on Time and Learning concluded, "Learning in America is a prisoner of time. For the past 150 years, American public schools have held time constant and let learning vary . . . Time is learning's warden" (1994, p. 7).

The time framework is particularly pernicious when it is extended to credit hours per course. "The vast majority of college courses have three or four hours of credit. Isn't it a coincidence of cosmic proportions that it takes exactly the same billable unit of work to learn the plays of Shakespeare and differential calculus? Or maybe the guest has been amputated to fit the bed"

(Peters, 1994, p. 23). The National Education Commission on Time and Learning reports that "no matter how complex or simple the school subject—literature, shop, physics, gym, or algebra—the schedule assigns each an impartial national average of 51 minutes per class period, regardless of how well or poorly students comprehend the material" (1994, p. 7).

The unit of measure must be changed to reflect mastery instead of time in the seat, recognizing what is universally understood: human beings learn at different rates. Students should not have to serve time in schools. Students able to learn fast are held back and bored. Students needing more time are denied it. School time should be redesigned to serve the learning needs of students.

What time-free alternatives can colleges create to better serve the learning needs of students? How can entrance and exit competencies be used to design a time-free architecture? How can technology be used to free students and teachers from the old time-bound architecture? How does a college maintain some time-bound structures that work for some students and create time-free structures that work for other students?

CONCLUSION

These five examples are but the tip of the iceberg of the challenges colleges face in overhauling the architecture of education to place learning first and to embarking on the path of creating ever more powerful learning experiences and environments. The old architecture restricts what works for learning in every nook and cranny of the institution—in the governance and management structures, in the divisions between instruction and student services, in the buildings constructed in earlier times, in the design of student seats and faculty desks, in the dominance of the lecture, in the academic policies: the residue of "a thousand years of tradition wrapped in a hundred years of bureaucracy" (Moe, 1994, p. 1).

If we can, however, begin redesigning our inherited architecture one brick at a time we may begin to learn the skills and attitudes necessary to creating a new architecture. In the process, we may discover that the pieces are connected in such a way that changing one brick affects many others. We will need to be agile to ensure that dislodging one brick does not bring the entire house down on our heads. We may need to create temporary structures to hold up a sagging program until we can fortify the new architecture. As we put on our hard hats and enter the danger zones, we must keep in mind that the purpose is not just the destruction of the old but the creation of the new for one reason: improving and expanding learning and success for our students.

REFERENCES

Cross, K. P. (November 1984). The rising tide of school reform reports. *Phi Delta Kappan.*

Dressel, P. (1983). Grades: One more tilt at the windmill. In A. W. Chickering (Ed.), *Bulletin*, Memphis State University Center for the Study of Higher Education.

Lovett, C. (November 24, 1995). Small steps to achieve big changes. *The Chronicle of Higher Education.*

Moe, R. (January 1994). Cited in Armajani, B. et al. *A model for the reinvented higher education system: State policy and college learning.* Denver: Education Commission of the States.

National Education Commission on Time and Learning (April 1994). *Prisoners of time.* Washington, D. C.: U. S. Government Printing Office.

O'Banion, T. (Fall 1995). Community colleges lead a learning revolution. *Educational Record, 76*(4), 23–27.

Peters, R. (November/December 1994). Some snarks are boojums: Accountability and the end(s) of higher education. *Change.*

Toffler, A. & Toffler, H. (March/April 1995). Getting set for the coming millennium. *The Futurist.*

Wingspread Group on Higher Education. (1993). *An American imperative: Higher expectations for higher education.* Racine, WI: The Johnson Foundation.

10

Teaching-for-Learning (TFL)

A Model for Faculty to Advance Student Learning

Clifton F. Conrad, Jason Johnson, and Divya Malik Gupta

Those of us who teach at colleges and universities have at least one thing in common regardless of differences among our fields of study and the courses we teach: there are well-worn paths between our offices and the classrooms in which we teach, and we can each trace much of our growth as teachers to the thoughts and feelings we have had while traveling those paths. Approaching the classroom, we often review our plans and make last-minute adjustments. Returning to the office, we reflect on what transpired in class. Sometimes we are filled with the spirited satisfaction of knowing that we helped to advance our students' learning. Other times, frustrated or pleasantly surprised by having experienced the unexpected yet again, we try to make sense of what happened and begin to consider the implications for future classes. Such is the dance of teaching and learning.

While college and university teaching has traditionally been a relatively private matter, accountability initiatives in the last few decades have emphasized the importance of student learning outcomes and drawn attention to the fact that little has been done to intentionally prepare faculty to teach. In turn, the last few years have seen robust conversation about teaching and learning; scholarly journals and other volumes contain scores of promising ideas for how teaching, assessment, and learning can be improved, and small-scale campus initiatives of every sort boldly pursue large-scale change. Nevertheless, the vast majority of us who teach at colleges and universities are left to persist with our own devices. When we do feel compelled to turn to the literature for guidance, we are reminded about how much is known about teaching, learning, and assessment, respectively, and yet how little is known about their interrelationships. In short, scholarly work in this area has still not produced a widely-accepted—much less widely accessible—model that systematically connects teaching and assessment practices with student learning.

In this chapter, we advance a model that can at once serve as a guide for individual teachers and extend the substantial work underway on the scholarship of teaching and learning. Specifically, we introduce Teaching-for-Learning (TFL), an inquiry-based approach to enhancing the learning of all students through systematically connecting teaching practices, assessment practices, and student learning experiences in light of course-specific challenges. This focus on course-specific challenges is the principal distinction between TFL and classic instructional design models; in contrast to those models, TFL invites teachers to view course challenges not as friction in a well-oiled input–throughput–output model of instructional design but as the fuel for helping teachers to ensure teaching-for-learning along the bumpy roads that teachers confront in their everyday lives. As we elaborate in our discussion of the definition and scope of TFL, we propose that TFL invites faculty to recognize and address the ongoing "mystery of teaching" through a dynamic framework for constantly replenishing their teaching practices to enrich the learning of all students.

We begin by reviewing recent scholarship on teaching, learning, and assessment and then define TFL and its six major components. We then illustrate through a vignette how TFL can be used by teachers in their everyday practice and conclude with a brief discussion of the possibilities of TFL for enhancing the learning of all students. In so doing, we propose that TFL is best viewed as a heuristic device that can be used by individual faculty, by those who support faculty in instructional training and development, and by researchers who wish to test and improve TFL.

SCHOLARSHIP OF TEACHING AND LEARNING

Ernest Boyer's *Scholarship Reconsidered: Priorities of the Professoriate* (1990) provided the foundation for the movement termed the Scholarship of Teaching and Learning (SoTL). Circulated by the Carnegie Foundation for the Advancement of Teaching as a part of its CASTL (Carnegie Academy for the Scholarship of Teaching and Learning) initiative, this text is but one of the Carnegie Foundation's dozens of publications that are concerned with recasting the concept of "scholarship" in such a way that legitimates professors' research on teaching and learning in their own classrooms (e.g., Glassick et al. 1997; Huber 2005; Huber and Hutchings 2005; Huber and Morreale 2002; Hutchings 2000, 2002). Further evincing the influence of CASTL and SoTL are the many offices, centers, and initiatives using the "scholarship of teaching and learning" moniker at colleges and universities, including several holding no formal affiliation with the CASTL initiative. As Huber and Morreale noted, "The scholarship of teaching and learning in higher education currently belongs to no single national association and has no unique campus address" (2002, p. 1).

The rapid growth of the scholarship of teaching and learning has also brought forth a profusion of ideas accompanied by an explosion of new terminology. As classrooms have come to be viewed more and more as "laboratories for learning" as predicted by Cross (1996, p. 5), we have been presented with a variety of ways for viewing teaching, learning, and assessment— and a growing collection of categories and sub-categories. There have been numerous ideas for addressing various dimensions of learning: learning styles (Lewthwaite and Dunham 1999), problem-based learning (Jones 2002; Savin-Baden 2000), active learning (Johnson and Malinowski 2001), alternative learning approaches (Scovic 1983), and taxonomies of learning objectives (Bloom et al. 1956; Krathwohl 2002). Aspects of teaching such as teacher research (Cochran-Smith and Lytle 1999), teaching practices (Nilson 2003), action research (Collins and Spiegel 1995; Marion and Zeichner 2001), inquiry-based teaching and learning (Brew 2003), scientific teaching (Handelsman et al. 2004), and teaching and research (Jenkins et al. 2002) have likewise been advanced. Especially in the last few years, assessment has become increasingly prominent as scholars have addressed formative evaluation (Smith 2001), classroom research (Cross 1996; Cross and Steadman 1996), and student evaluation of teaching (Bastick 2001).

Scholars have also advanced a wide range of specific strategies and techniques for individual faculty to use in their courses—such as classroom assessment techniques (Angelo and Cross 1993), strategies for adventurous and critical thinking (Barell 1995), technology-based teaching strategies (Palaskas 2002) and learning-centered assessment (Huba and Freed 2000). Discipline-specific approaches have also been developed to advance teaching, learning, and assessment across many areas of knowledge, ranging from medicine (Anderson 1999) to statistics (Kirk 2002) to Spanish (Cabedo-Timmons 2002) to psychology (McCann et al. 2001). And, of course, journals in the field of higher education have presented sustained conversations about teaching, learning, and assessment. In the last ten volumes of *Innovative Higher Education* alone, no less than 110 articles can be found with emphases on teaching (e.g., Hansen 1998; Justice et al. 2007; McDaniel and Colarulli 1997), learning (e.g., Ash and Clayton 2004; Cross 1999; Rogers et al. 2001), or assessment (e.g., Beaman 1998; C. B. Myers and S. M. Myers 2007; Quarstein and Peterson 2001). Inquiry related to teaching, learning, and assessment is no less prominent in the other leading journals in the field of higher education (e.g., Colbeck et al. 2000; Fairweather 2005; Lattuca et al. 2004; Wright 2005).

In summary, there is a rapidly growing body of promising ideas regarding approaches, strategies, and techniques for enhancing teaching, learning, and assessment. The sheer volume of this work can be taken as evidence of what Barr and Tagg (1995) observed in their oft-cited *Change* magazine article: higher education is in the midst of a "paradigm shift" as its aims, structures, and theories are moving from being instruction-centered to being learning-centered. Perhaps needless to say, this shift has produced conceptual overlaps, competing ideas, and a flood of terms and phrases that, overall, provide a wellspring of ideas through which faculty may sift and winnow.

The flip side of having such an abundance of ideas for teaching, learning, and assessment is having to make sense of these ideas in practice. Put simply, how do these three domains of literature stand in relation to one another conceptually and how should they be operationalized in practice? Faculty are currently left to intuit or infer an answer to these questions as they attempt to make sense of the complex web that constitutes the scholarship of teaching and learning. To address this lacuna, we advance Teaching-for-Learning (TFL)—a model to help orient faculty to basic principles and practices drawn from the scholarship of teaching and learning (though without the element of *doing* the scholarship of teaching and learning) and guide them in a systematic process of exploring and testing teaching and assessment practices to achieve course learning goals.

TEACHING-FOR-LEARNING (TFL): DEFINITION AND SCOPE

Teaching-for-Learning (TFL) is a systematic and inclusive model for teachers to explore and test teaching and assessment practices in order to ensure learning experiences that enhance the learning of all students. The model places teachers in an investigative role and allows them to draw from their background, skills, and dispositions to advance their own "theories-in-practice" within the context of their discipline or field of study, course goals, learning environment, and student population. In advancing TFL, we invite readers to scrutinize it, test it, and modify it as appropriate within the context of their courses, their students, and their respective learning contexts.

Before turning to the model itself, it is important to elaborate on the definition and scope of TFL, particularly in relation to the extant literature. To begin with, a signature contribution of the scholarship of teaching and learning movement has been its characterization of teaching as an inquiry-based activity. As the movement has evolved, Hutchings and Shulman (1999) have drawn a meaningful distinction in the ongoing scholarship of teaching and learning, namely, between the "scholarship of teaching" and "scholarly teaching"—with the latter focused on teaching to enhance student learning and the former focused more broadly on developing and disseminating knowledge about teaching and learning while, at the same time, enhancing student learning. As an inquiry-based model, TFL may be used by faculty to share their findings with a scholarly audience—as in the "scholarship of teaching." That said, such external concerns are secondary to TFL's primary focus on student learning—that is, teaching for the sake of learning. Unlike "scholarly teaching," which precludes by definition "scholarship of teaching," TFL does not draw such a boundary.

Because TFL neither fits squarely within nor precludes the existing rubrics of "scholarly teaching" and the "scholarship of teaching," we propose that it be viewed as a generic model with generative potential. We suggest that TFL is generic because it reflects what we see as a genre that has emerged in the teaching, learning, and assessment literature. Indeed, we developed the TFL model in our review of these texts, identifying and giving expression to points of convergence regarding teaching, learning, and assessment. In other words, TFL— a heuristic model—stands as both an interpretation of extant texts and a guide for further interpretation. We suggest that TFL is generative because the simple, dynamic, and inclusive approach of the model builds capacity for continuous experimentation and discovery grounded in the experiences of individual faculty. To illustrate, TFL can be thought of as a model which facilitates professors' ongoing experiences in what Parker Palmer observed as the "mystery" of teaching:

> Good teachers dwell in the mystery of good teaching until it dwells in them. As they explore it alone and with others, the insight and energy of mystery begins to inform and animate their work. They discover and develop methods of teaching that emerge from their own integrity—but they never reduce their teaching to technique.
>
> (Palmer 1990, p. 11)

In light of the notion of faculty "living the mystery" of teaching, we make a distinction between TFL and other models which also explicitly advocate a systematic approach to teaching, learning, and assessment. For example, Diamond (1998) described in great detail a two-phase systematic design model consisting of "project selection and design" and "production, implementation, and evaluation" (p. 17). Although TFL is not wholly dissimilar in comparison to Diamond's emphasis on engaging in a step-wise process of developing goals and identifying ways to reach and evaluate them, it differs significantly from his and other models informed by systems and quality approaches (e.g., Cornesky 1993; Dick et al. 2001) in two major ways. First, TFL is primarily animated by *classroom experiences* (both anticipated and unanticipated), including teachers' experiences, students' experiences, and the interaction among them rather than by a "vision" (Shulman 1998) and other instructional design "inputs" that are associated with systems models. Second, whereas systems models are usually focused on the whole of a course, TFL can be used not only for planning a course at the outset but also for mid-course adjustments (e.g., course modules spanning multiple class sessions, a single class session, a portion of a single class session) made by faculty in response to unfolding classroom experiences. We elaborate on these qualities as we explicate the major components of the TFL model in the section that follows.

THE TEACHING-FOR-LEARNING MODEL

Six components make up the Teaching-for-Learning model. Figure 10.1 is a diagrammatic representation of these six components.

Identifying Course-Specific Challenges

Arguably the most important component of the TFL approach is identifying the major challenges that need to be addressed in a course. As teachers we usually know what we expect our students

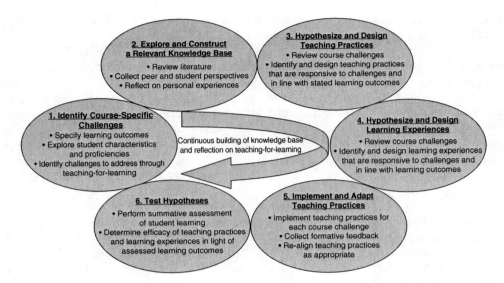

FIGURE 10.1   Teaching-for-Learning. A systematic approach for teachers to identify and enact—through exploring and testing—teaching practices that enrich learning experiences leading to the enhancement of learning for all students.

to achieve in terms of learning by the end of a course; but more often than not, we give relatively little thought to what invisible hindrances—and missed opportunities—might come along the way. TFL begins by urging us to identify and articulate the major challenges we need to address within our course—challenges that might arise from factors as varied as the learning environment, diverse student demographics, and course content. This emphasis on the early identification of challenges encourages us to work backwards from the learning goals we have set for our students and anticipate the factors that could hinder attainment. In effect, TFL explicitly reminds us of the need to make a direct connection between our teaching and our students' learning by identifying and addressing the impediments that may militate against closing the gap between the two.

Because they not only give direction to the teacher in designing the course but also provide a foundation for assessing student learning, identifying specific learning outcomes expected of all students is a critical initial step in TFL. Learning outcomes may range from the mastery of a specific skill to the understanding of a concept to the cultivation of greater appreciation for a particular way-of-knowing. In identifying learning goals, it is important not only that they reflect teacher expectations for the course; they should also be in alignment with the mission, purpose, and culture of the program in which the course is nested.

A follow-up step in the process of identifying key course-specific challenges is teacher exploration of the backgrounds and characteristics of students in the course—collectively and, insofar as possible, individually—in concert with entry-level assessment of their subject matter proficiency. Alternatively, teachers might choose to begin the TFL process by exploring student characteristics and establishing learning goals based on a preliminary judgment of their proficiency. Put simply, studying the student population invites the teacher to begin thinking about potentially valuable learning experiences and teaching practices that seem likely to match the needs of a diverse student group. Optimum learning experiences for a heterogeneous student cohort will likely differ from a cohort of a more homogenous group of students. An enhanced understanding of the student population can also provide a foundation for subsequent assessment of student learning.

Anchored in the context of student learning goals and an understanding of the backgrounds, characteristics, and subject matter expertise of students in the course, faculty members can begin to identify specific challenges that may hinder the achievement of the intended learning outcomes. These may include a lack of students' preparation for certain course expectations, limited time available to teach content matter, or even the instructor's own struggle with specific subject matter. The challenges that have been identified provide the foundation for TFL, for the remainder of the TFL process is centered on the identification of teaching practices that will help foster learning experiences consonant with each of the challenges specified.

Constructing a Knowledge Base

Developing a foundation of knowledge is an important part of the inquiry-based TFL process: what is known about teaching, learning, and assessment can go a long way in helping faculty systematically connect teaching and learning. To take but one example, the literature on Classroom Research (Cross and Steadman 1996)—with its focus on "how students learn" and attendant classroom challenges—can be a valuable resource. By drawing in part on such literature and then testing it within the context of their courses, TFL is a tool that encourages individual faculty to navigate systematically through myriad teaching techniques advanced in the literature in order to enhance the learning of all of their students.

To construct a knowledge base, the teacher, guided by the course-specific challenges identified, explores potentially effective learning experiences in light of student diversity in background and learning styles, reflects on alternative teaching practices for cultivating these experiences, and considers alternative approaches to assessing the teaching and learning in the course. As suggested earlier, reviewing the literature on teaching, learning, and assessment both across and within disciplines and fields of study can help a teacher construct a knowledge base for TFL. For example, an enormous amount of research has been done on learning styles and learner needs in the fields of psychology, education, and engineering. One might also draw from research in such fields as educational psychology which have identified and explored the efficacy of diverse teaching and instructional styles in varying circumstances. And, of course, peers and colleagues can be a valuable source of ideas as can one's own reflections on previous teaching experiences.

To be sure, most faculty members do not have the time and energy to explore directly the literatures on teaching, learning, and assessment. Fortunately, most colleges and universities now have faculty development offices with highly-skilled faculty developers who have easy access to the literature and, in our experiences, can be of great assistance to faculty in developing a knowledge base. Underscoring the generative potential of TFL, we encourage faculty to seek out faculty development experts. The reality of implementing the TFL model almost requires their services and expertise.

Hypothesizing and Designing Relevant Learning Experiences

Based on literature reviews and perspectives from peers and students as well as knowledge of student characteristics, the teacher then identifies and designs learning experiences that seem most conducive to addressing the major course challenges and, in turn, achieving the intended learning outcomes for the student population. Learning experiences—which deserve explicit attention lest they be overlooked—represent the ways in which students are engaged (e.g., memorizing, thinking, reasoning, applying, doing) or otherwise. In short, the teacher hypothesizes relationships between learning experiences and outcomes, choosing those experiences that seem most likely to match the intended learning goals and course challenges. TFL invites faculty to recognize the salience of identifying and designing learning experiences that help link teaching with learning. These learning experiences provide the means through which TFL strives to accomplish the end-goal: enhanced learning outcomes. The focus on learning experiences encourages faculty as teachers-qua-researchers to deliberate over the ways in which students learn and what specifically can be done to bring about such learning. They guide the selection and use of teaching practices that we think will foster experiences that enhance learning.

Designing learning experiences is at the heart of the TFL process because it is these experiences—shaped by teaching practices—that influence what students learn. To be sure, the teacher must be mindful that some learning experiences may work better for certain students than others and hence a variety of experiences may have to be created in order to address the needs of all students. TFL encourages teachers to learn about their students and consciously think about experiences and teaching practices. In short, TFL encourages faculty members to acknowledge and respond to varied learning styles, abilities, and interests among students and seeks to create a range of experiences that may facilitate the learning of a diverse student body.

Hypothesizing and Designing Teaching Practices

Having identified course-specific challenges and designed learning experiences aimed at addressing those challenges, teachers can now explore relationships between teaching practices and students' learning experiences. More precisely, this involves the teacher selecting (from the knowledge base constructed) teaching practices most likely to lead to learning experiences which will enhance learning. To illustrate, in order to strengthen students' writing skills (course challenge), a teacher might hypothesize that employing small group discussions (teaching strategy) to share students' in-class writing would encourage them to apply their critical thinking and analytic skills (learning experience) which, in turn, will help them attain the desired learning outcome.

As Palmer (1998) has suggested, "good teaching" cannot be reduced to technique; in his words, good teaching also comes from the "identity and integrity" of the teacher. In selecting teaching practices in the TFL model, it is important to reflect not only on teaching techniques per se but also on "who" the teacher is as a person. Selection of teaching practices should be in alignment with one's own personality and disposition.

Implementing and Adapting Teaching Practices

Once learning experiences have been identified and teaching practices have been selected, teaching practices are implemented. Formative assessment—ongoing assessment of both teaching practices and students that, in turn, provides information to guide instruction and improve student performance—provides the teacher with insight into the effectiveness of teaching practices as well as ideas for adjustments in teaching practices. Such assessment may be carried out directly through students' feedback and testing students and/or indirectly through observations of students' engagement in class and responses to teaching practices. In turn, teaching practices are adapted as appropriate.

Hypotheses-Testing

Until this point in the TFL process, the teacher will have made two hypotheses for each course challenge, namely, that the selected learning experiences will lead to desired learning outcomes and that the selected teaching practices will enhance the selected learning experiences. Hypotheses-testing is the final stage in the TFL process whereby the teacher explores the efficacy of the various teaching practices. Summative assessment—a conclusive evaluation to record student achievement and gauge student learning in light of the entry-level assessment carried out at the beginning of the course—is then carried out.

The teacher may invite student feedback on the effectiveness of teaching strategies used in the course and can then decide if the methods should be adopted for future use or if they need to be modified. If a teaching strategy is found appropriate for meeting a particular challenge, the teacher can add this learning to her knowledge base and begin again with another challenge and teaching method; alternatively, the experiment may be tried again with another teaching strategy or learning experience for the same challenge. Of course, TFL can be used by teachers to address multiple learning outcomes and/or challenges at the same time.

ENGAGING IN TEACHING-FOR-LEARNING: A VIGNETTE

She began this first session of her qualitative methods course as she always had, namely, by briefly discussing her learning outcomes with her students in order to identify any major course-specific challenges that she might need to address. In order to get a sense of her students' backgrounds and other notable characteristics, she asked them to indicate why they enrolled in the course and what they expected to learn from it. Without exception, every student in the class communicated that they were there to learn "methodologically correct" qualitative research techniques. She understood, of course, that they likely had come to embrace this goal for many reasons, not the least of which was because "technique" was a predominant concern in courses elsewhere in the school and, indeed, the field at large. Yet, for these same reasons she was deeply troubled because she believed that spirited engagement with ideas was the hallmark of exemplary inquiry and ought to trump methodology concerns, per se. As she communicated in several of her learning outcomes for the course, she expected students to identify and crystallize meaningful problems to guide their inquiry and to "seize their own voice" throughout their research.

After reflecting on that first night of class, she determined that the most formidable challenge she faced was to get her students to place ideas at the center of their inquiry and to seize ownership of their inquiry by developing and maintaining fidelity to a meaningful research question that had both personal and professional significance. She considered the option of entering the next class meeting with a plan to engage in a single didactic and passionate commentary; but she suspected that such an approach would either be seen as a footnote to her earlier presentation of class objectives, as an annoyance, or both. Instead, she began to explore and construct a relevant knowledge base to address this challenge. After discussing the matter with several colleagues, including two faculty developers, the best idea they could come up with was to have class members form "research groups" in which they were asked to generate an agreed-upon research question and approach to answering it. The animating intent of having the students do this was to demonstrate that determining the appropriateness of a research question and methodology is as much a matter of satisfying groups of individuals as it is a matter of adhering to transcendent truths.

In the first few weeks of the course, she remained conscious of the challenge she had identified at the outset and made a variety of efforts to modify the direction of the conversation in subtle ways and not to allow the exclusively technique-centered sensibilities of the first week continue to dominate the classroom discourse. The harsh reality was that provisional project proposals from the students showed her that she was hardly making a dent, for they were heavy on methods and light on the ideas and messy complications associated with conducting meaningful research.

She then turned to major texts and the most recent journal articles regarding graduate education in an attempt to identify promising practices she might implement. She didn't find much that she could use; neither the literature nor her peers had many promising suggestions.

However, by sheer coincidence she then came across a chapter in a book on research that caught her attention. Entitled "The Challenge of Framing a Problem: What is your Burning Question" (Harter 2006), the chapter was written in first person and in lively and invitational prose that communicated the importance of taking ownership of a research question at once meaningful to self and others. After reading the chapter, she hypothesized that the metaphor of the "burning question" might help individuals—and groups—to take ownership of their inquiry, beginning with their research question. Consonant with that metaphor, she asked each research group to reorganize their group "learning experiences" around developing and maintaining fidelity to their burning question. More specifically, she asked each group to come up with their burning question and, in turn, to conduct their inquiry in the spirit of the metaphor.

As she engaged in implementing and adapting her teaching practices in light of the challenge that she had identified that first night of the course, she solicited a great deal of informal feedback on the impact of the "burning question" intervention. Somewhat to her surprise, the chapter and the metaphor seemed to be doing more than she could have ever imagined in terms of encouraging students to personally invest in the pursuit of ideas as much as they were focused on technique and methodological rules and procedures. And in class, she found herself using the burning question approach (she was mindful that it, too, could simply become another "rule" if it were not treated as a metaphor) as they reflected on various research studies that they read during the term.

She was able further to test her hypothesis on the occasion of reviewing her students' final papers. While she did not use an experimental design, she did compare students' in-class presentations of their final papers and the papers themselves with those of other qualitative research classes she had taught previously. To her delight, the group papers were among the best she had ever received; and in the class presentations students communicated an ownership of their problems with a passion she had rarely seen before. In short, the evidence strongly suggested that the simple intervention of a "reading," in concert with inviting students to apply the message of that reading throughout their research project, had made a significant difference in her students' learning. To come full circle, students consistently placed ideas at the center of their inquiry through seizing ownership and developing and maintaining fidelity to a meaningful research question that had personal as well as professional significance. Moreover, the papers displayed a fierce intellectuality and rigor in comparison to many previous classes. She was delighted with some unexpected outcomes: students were more imaginative, self-directed, curious, and engaged inquirers than had often been the case in her previous classes.

CONCLUSION

Triggered by the identification of course-specific challenges in light of intended learning outcomes and student characteristics, we advance TFL as an inclusive and dynamic approach in the search for teaching and assessment practices to enhance the learning of all students. More specifically, TFL invites faculty to engage in a dynamic process of constructing a knowledge base, designing learning experiences and teaching practices, hypothesizing their effect on students' learning experiences (and, in turn, learning outcomes), applying these teaching practices within the course and testing their effectiveness in enhancing student learning.

TFL is inclusive of what have traditionally been discrete areas of research and innovations in practice. While most approaches found in the literature focus mainly on teaching, learning, or assessment, TFL incorporates all three of these domains in concert with other elements that are salient in the literature: student characteristics and learning styles, learning experiences, teaching practices, and assessment techniques. Moreover, the model is inclusive because it represents both teachers and learners, perhaps most importantly by encouraging teachers to select teaching practices in concert with their students' needs as well as their own personality and disposition. And not insignificantly, the model encourages teachers to explore and test a wide range of so-called "best practices"—not only those advanced in the literature but also those suggested by colleagues and peers as well as those drawn from their own experiences—for enhancing student learning.

TFL invites faculty to engage in the dynamic process of teaching-for-learning and continuously revitalize their teaching in ways that ensure student learning in widely differing contexts—including learning environment, diversity in student populations, and course learning goals. As higher education continues to change, experimentation and innovation in our teaching and learning practices will clearly be needed for the foreseeable future. The TFL model provides a heuristic model for faculty members to reexamine their teaching in order to determine what teaching practices are meaningfully contributing to student growth and development and what alternative teaching practices might be introduced within the context of the ever-changing challenges that we face in teaching-for-learning.

REFERENCES

Anderson, M. B. (1999). In progress: Reports of new approaches in medical education. *Academic Medicine*, 74, 561–618.

Angelo, T. A., & Cross, K. P. (1993). *Classroom assessment techniques: A handbook for college teachers* (2nd ed.). San Francisco, CA: Jossey-Bass.

Ash, S. L., & Clayton, P. H. (2004). The articulated learning: An approach to guided reflection and assessment. *Innovative Higher Education*, 29, 137–154.

Barell, J. (1995). *Teaching for thoughtfulness: Classroom strategies to enhance intellectual development* (2nd ed.). White Plains, NY: Longman.

Barr, R. B., & Tagg, J. (1995). From teaching to learning: A new paradigm for undergraduate education. *Change*, 27(6), 13–25.

Bastick, T. (2001, August). *Relationships between in-course alignment indicators and post-course criteria of quality teaching and learning in higher education.* Paper presented at the Biennial Meeting of the European Association for Research in Learning and Instruction, Fribourg, Switzerland.

Beaman, R. (1998). The unquiet . . . even loud, andragogy! Alternative assessment for adult learners. *Innovative Higher Education*, 23, 47–59.

Bloom, B. S., Engelhart, M. D., Furst, E. J., Hill, W. H., & Krathwohl, D. R. (1956). *Taxonomy of educational objectives: The classification of educational goals. Handbook 1: Cognitive domain.* New York, NY: David McKay.

Boyer, E. (1990). *Scholarship reconsidered: Priorities of the professoriate.* Princeton, NJ: The Carnegie Foundation for the Advancement of Teaching.

Brew, A. (2003). Teaching and research: New relationships and their implications for inquiry-based teaching and learning in higher education. *Higher Education Research & Development*, 22, 3–18.

Cabedo-Timmons, G. (2002). *Teaching Spanish subject matters to college students in the USA.* Macomb, IL: Western Illinois University. (ERIC Document Reproduction Service no. ED468881)

Cochran-Smith, M., & Lytle, S. L. (1999). The teacher research movement: A decade later. *Educational Researcher*, 28, 15–25.

Colbeck, C. L., Cabrera, A. F., & Terenzini, P. T. (2000). Learning professional confidence: Linking teaching practices, students' self-perceptions, and gender. *The Review of Higher Education*, 24, 173–191.

Collins, A., & Spiegel, S. A. (1995). *So you want to do action research?* Retrieved October 29, 2004, from Eisenhower National Clearinghouse (ENC) website: http://www.enc.org/professional/learn/research/journal/science/document.shtm?input=ENC-002432-2432.

Cornesky, R. (1993). *The quality professor: Implementing TQM in the classroom*. Madison, WI: Magna Publications.

Cross, K. P. (1996). Classroom research: Implementing the scholarship of teaching. *American Journal of Pharmaceutical Education*, 60, 402–407.

Cross, K. P. (1999). What do we know about students' learning, and how do we know it? *Innovative Higher Education*, 23, 255–270.

Cross, K. P., & Steadman, M. H. (1996). *Classroom research: Implementing the scholarship of teaching*. San Francisco, CA: Jossey-Bass.

Diamond, R. M. (1998). *Designing and assessing courses and curricula: A practical guide*. San Francisco, CA: Jossey-Bass.

Dick, W., Carey, L., & Carey, J. (2001). *The systematic design of instruction*. New York, NY: Longman.

Fairweather, J. S. (2005). Beyond the rhetoric: Trends in the relative value of teaching and research in faculty salaries. *Journal of Higher Education*, 76, 401–422.

Glassick, C., Huber, M. T., & Maeroff, G. I. (1997). *Scholarship assessed: A special report on faculty evaluation*. San Francisco, CA: Jossey-Bass.

Handelsman, J., Ebert-May, D., Beichner, R., Bruns, P., Chang, A., DeHaan, R., et al. (2004). Scientific teaching. *Science*, 304, 521–522.

Hansen, E. J. (1998). Creating teachable moments . . . and making them last. *Innovative Higher Education*, 23, 7–26.

Harter, S. (2006). The challenge of framing a problem: What is your burning question? In C. F. Conrad & R. Serlin (Eds.), *The SAGE handbook on research in education: Engaging ideas and enriching inquiry* (pp. 331–348). Thousand Oaks, CA: SAGE.

Huba, M. E., & Freed, J. E. (2000). *Learner-centered assessment on college campuses*. Needham Heights, MA: Allyn and Bacon.

Huber, M. T. (2005). *Balancing acts: The scholarship of teaching and learning in academic careers*. Washington, DC: The American Association for Higher Education and The Carnegie Foundation for the Advancement of Teaching.

Huber, M., & Hutchings, P. (2005). *The advancement of learning: Building the teaching commons*. San Francisco, CA: Jossey-Bass.

Huber, M. T., & Morreale, S. (2002). *Disciplinary styles in the scholarship of teaching and learning: Exploring common ground*. Washington, DC: The American Association for Higher Education and The Carnegie Foundation for the Advancement of Teaching.

Hutchings, P. (Ed.) (2000). *Opening lines: Approaches to the scholarship of teaching and learning*. Princeton, NJ: The Carnegie Foundation for the Advancement of Teaching.

Hutchings, P. (2002). *Ethics of inquiry: Issues in the scholarship of teaching and learning*. Menlo Park, CA: The Carnegie Foundation for the Advancement of Teaching.

Hutchings, P., & Shulman, L. E. (1999). The scholarship of teaching: New elaborations, new developments. *Change*, 31(5), 10–15.

Jenkins, A., Breen, R., Lindsay, R., & Brew, A. (2002). *Re-shaping higher education: Linking teaching and research*. London, England: Kogan Page.

Johnson, M. C., & Malinowski, J. C. (2001). Navigating the active learning swamp: Creating an inviting environment for learning. *Journal of College Science Teaching*, 31, 172–177.

Jones, E. A. (2002). Myths about assessing the impact of problem-based learning on students. *Journal of General Education*, 51, 326–334.

Justice, C., Rice, J., Warry, W., Inglis, S., Miller, S., & Sammon, S. (2007). Inquiry in higher education: Reflections and directions on course design and teaching methods. *Innovative Higher Education*, 31, 201–214.

Kirk, R. E. (2002, August). *Teaching introductory statistics: Some things I have learned*. Paper presented at the Annual Conference of the American Psychological Association, Chicago, IL.

Krathwohl, D. R. (2002). A revision of Bloom's taxonomy: An overview. *Theory into Practice*, 41, 212–218.

Lattuca, L. R., Voigt, L. J., & Fath, K. Q. (2004). Does interdisciplinarity promote learning? Theoretical support and researchable questions. *Review of Higher Education, 28*, 23–48.

Lewthwaite, B. J., & Dunham, H. P. (1999, February*). Enriching teaching scholarship through learning styles.* Paper presented at the Annual Meeting of the American Association of Colleges for Teacher Education, Washington, DC.

Marion, R., & Zeichner, K. (2001). *Practitioner resource guide for action research.* Oxford, OH: National Staff Development Council. (ERIC Document Reproduction Service no. ED472207)

McCann, L. I., Perlman, B., & De Both, T. L. (2001). Instructor evaluations of introductory psychology teaching techniques. *Teaching of Psychology, 28*, 274–276.

McDaniel, E. A., & Colarulli, G. C. (1997). Collaborative teaching in the face of productivity concerns: The dispersed team model. *Innovative Higher Education, 22*, 19–36.

Myers, C. B., & Myers, S. M. (2007). Assessing assessment: The effects of two exam formats on course achievement and evaluation. *Innovative Higher Education, 31*, 227–236.

Nilson, L. B. (2003). *Teaching at its best: A research-based resource for college instructors.* Boston, MA: Anker.

Palaskas, T. A. (2002). Model for selecting technology mediated teaching strategies. *Educational Technology, 42*(6), 49–54

Palmer, P. J. (1990). Good teaching: A matter of living the mystery. *Change, 22*(1), 11–16. January.

Palmer, P. J. (1998). *The courage to teach: Exploring the inner landscape of a teacher's life.* San Francisco, CA: Jossey-Bass.

Quarstein, V. A., & Peterson, P. A. (2001). Assessment of cooperative learning: A goal-criterion approach. *Innovative Higher Education, 26*, 59–77.

Rogers, G., Finley, D., & Kline, T. (2001). Understanding individual differences in university undergraduates: A learner needs segmentation approach. *Innovative Higher Education, 25*, 183–196.

Savin-Baden, M. (2000). *Problem-based learning in higher education: Untold stories.* London, England: Society for Research into Higher Education.

Scovic, S. P. (1983, April). *What are "alternative learning approaches" and do they work?* Paper presented at the National School Boards Association Convention, San Francisco, CA.

Shulman, L. S. (1998). Course anatomy: The dissection and analysis of knowledge through teaching. In P. Hutchings (Ed.), *The course portfolio: How instructors can examine their teaching to advance practice and improve student learning* (pp. 5–12). Washington, DC: American Association for Higher Education.

Smith, R. A. (2001). Formative evaluation and the scholarship of teaching and learning. In C. Knapper & P. Cranton (Eds.), *Fresh approaches to the evaluation of teaching* (pp. 51–62). *New directions for teaching and learning,* vol. 88. San Francisco, CA: Jossey Bass.

Wright, M. (2005). Always at odds? Congruence in faculty beliefs about teaching at a research university. *Journal of Higher Education, 76*, 331–353.

III

STUDENTS

Laura I. Rendón, Section Editor

A recent Pew Research Center study (Fry, 2009) indicated that college enrollments hit an-all time high in Fall 2008, fueled mainly by growth in the community college sector. Moreover, data from the U.S. Department of Education (2009) show that enrollments in degree-granting institutions increased by 14% between 1987 and 1997. However, college student enrollments grew at a faster rate (26%), from 14.5 million in 1997 to 18.2 million in 2007. Also reported are increases in full-time enrollments; a larger share of female undergraduates; an expected increase in the number of older students; and increased enrollments for Latino, Asian American/Pacific Islander, and African American students. Clearly, the changing and now quite diverse profile of American college students will create new opportunities and challenges for higher education researchers, faculty, administrators, and policymakers.

The five chapters focusing on college students in this section are of import not only because they were written by formidable scholars who have achieved national distinction for their intellectual contributions to the field, but also because this scholarship has impacted state, federal, and institutional policy and practice. Additionally, these researchers have offered rich theoretical perspectives that scholars and practitioners should consider when working with diverse student populations. Collectively, their work provides future direction for the study of college students in increasingly diverse and complex postsecondary educational settings. The five chapters offer interesting viewpoints on the evolution of theory, student success and institutional accountability, as well as race and the benefits of student diversity. Several chapters in this section disrupt widely-held assumptions about college access and student persistence.

INTERROGATING THE ASSUMPTION THAT ONLY STUDENTS ARE RESPONSIBLE FOR THEIR SUCCESS

Popular frameworks derived from earlier research on undergraduates focus primarily on students taking responsibility for their own success. More recent theoretical perspectives have shifted to include the role of institutions in supporting and fostering affirming educational environments that enable success for diverse student populations. For example, Linda Serra Hagedorn, Scott Cypers, and Jaime Lester (in Chapter 12), as well as Laura I. Rendón, Romero E. Jalomo, and Amaury Nora (in Chapter 13), explain that some researchers such as Tinto (1987) employed an interactional model where students were conceptualized as continuously interacting with institutional, academic, and social communities to become incorporated (or integrated). The degree to which a student became academically and socially integrated into campus life supposedly determined her or his success in college. A somewhat similar viewpoint was presented by Astin (1984), who introduced a theory of student involvement theory that included psychological and behavioral dimensions of time-spending and the quality of student effort in educational exercises. While it may not have been the researchers' intention when developing these theories, student responsibility for getting involved and accessing the academic and social resources of the institution tended to be the primary foci.

In the mid-1990s, several researchers (e.g., Terenzini et al., 1994; Rendón, 1994) contributed important modifications to student integration and involvement theories. Here, the authors of Chapter 13 do not discount the importance of involvement and interactions with the campus, but note that many first-generation and low-income students find it difficult to get involved. They argue that many colleges are set up to facilitate involvement for dominant populations and unlike affluent students, non-traditional undergraduates often find it difficult to negotiate the values, structures, and norms of higher education to their academic and personal advantage.

INCLUDING INSTITUTIONAL RESPONSIBILITY AS A KEY FACTOR TO PROMOTE STUDENT SUCCESS

In Chapter 11, George D. Kuh focuses on student engagement to represent "the time and effort students devote to activities that are empirically linked to desired outcomes of college *and* what institutions do to induce students to participate in these activities." Kuh, apparently recognizing the limitations of focusing solely on a student's actions and behaviors as the only way to explain success, appropriately added institutional responsibility as an important factor in the student success equation. In other words, it is not only students who are responsible for their engagement, but postsecondary educators and administrators also share the responsibility for student success, learning, and development. Kuh discusses the importance of the National Survey on Student Engagement (NSSE) and the Community College Survey of Student Engagement (CCSSE), widely-employed instruments that assess how students spend their time and how well institutions are doing in addressing students' needs. In the community college sector of higher education, student transfer has remained an important topic of study. Authors in Chapter 12 underscore the importance of advising and academic assistance to help community college transfer students take transfer-level courses in a transfer-focused curriculum, complete remedial work as quickly as possible, and remain continuously enrolled in order to increase their chances of actually transferring.

Rendón's (1994) theory also emphasized the importance of the institution in taking the initiative to support students with a process she termed *academic and interpersonal validation*. Using primarily low-income and first-generation students' voices to illuminate the college experience, Rendón discovered that these undergraduates found it difficult to get involved in college on their own. Rather than citing their personal involvement in college as a key to their success, students focused on the active role that agents such as faculty, peers, coaches, advisors, and family members played in initiating contact with them early in their college experiences. Validation helped these students believe they could be successful in college and that they were valuable members of the campus community. Students also saw that someone believed in and was willing to care for them. This sort of academic and interpersonal validation is especially critical for students who often do not even know what questions to ask or how to seek and negotiate engagement opportunities when they arrive on campus.

The key role of the institution is again highlighted in Chapter 15 by Shaun R. Harper and Sylvia Hurtado, who underscore the importance of collecting data on campus racial climates. They describe the role that educators and administrators should play in enacting espoused institutional values concerning diversity, assessing the racialized experiences of undergraduate student populations (including White undergraduates), and implementing practices and policies that help transform campuses into welcoming spaces where productive cross-racial learning is deliberately facilitated. Similarly, Patricia Gurin, Eric L. Dey, Sylvia Hurtado, and Gerald Gurin (in Chapter 14) emphasize the importance of affirmative action policies and institutional diversity efforts, not only to increase college access, but also to foster students' academic and social development.

VIEWING RACE AS AN IMPORTANT FACTOR IN STUDYING STUDENTS AND INSTITUTIONS

It was only in the 1980s that higher education researchers began to focus on issues related to race in their studies of college students. In the 1960s, social scientists tended to view members of racial/ethnic minority groups as inferior, deviant, and self-destructive—their only salvation would be to adopt the group norms and cultural patterns of the white, dominant society, which required a process of assimilation (de Anda, 1984; Hurtado, 1997). As such, theories of college student development and retention were largely based on white student populations. Furthermore, these studies tended to stress that people, not institutions, were the focus of persistence problems. Consequently, solutions were proposed to "fix" the person, but not to address systemic inequities that existed within institutions.

In this section on college students, some authors advocate a movement away from deficit-oriented and assimilationist models that perceive individuals from minority groups as inferior. These scholars also target institutions as the location for change. For example, Harper and Hurtado reviewed numerous post-1992 studies on students' experiences with race and campus racial climates. Among the key themes that emerged from 15 years of research is the marginality and isolation minority students often feel on predominantly white college campuses, as well as their desire for greater cultural representation. Participants in the study also wanted their institutions to move from rhetoric to action. In other words, it is one thing for institutions to articulate that they care about students of color and wish to support them, but more desirable was for institutional agents to actually provide the academic, social, and financial support necessary to more strongly connect minority students to the campus. Harper and Hurtado also identified the benefits associated with campus climates that facilitate cross-racial engagement; they explain how White students and students of color benefit from cross-racial interactions.

The importance of race is also underscored in Chapter 14, which examines the benefits of cross-racial engagement and having a diverse student body. Gurin, Dey, Hurtado, and Gurin focus on the educational purposes and benefits of diversity. The findings and conclusions from this research were carefully reviewed all the way to the Supreme Court as it debated whether or not colleges and universities could employ race-conscious strategies in college admissions. At stake in using race as a "plus factor" to admit students to college was maintaining a diverse student body and providing access to students who were not well represented in American higher education. The momentous 2003 *Grutter v. Bollinger* and *Gratz v. Bollinger* Supreme Court rulings were partially informed by scholarship that provided empirical evidence to show that "education is enhanced by extensive and meaningful informal interracial interaction, which depends on the presence of significantly diverse student bodies."

CONCLUSION

To varying degrees the chapters in this section call for educators and campus leaders to engage in institutional change and transformation. For example, Kuh makes clear how NSSE and CSSE data can be used to improve the quality of the undergraduate experience. Hagedorn, Cypers, and Lester call for an overhaul in student advising practices at community colleges, while Gurin, Dey, Hurtado, and Gurin underscore the importance of institutions working to expand the "presence of diverse students and a pedagogy that facilitates learning in a diverse environment." Rendón, Jalomo, and Nora argue that while theory development is important, institutions must also attend to making "transformative shifts in governance, curriculum development, in- and out-of-class teaching and learning, student programming, and other institutional dimensions that affect students on a daily basis." Finally, in promoting institutional audits of campus climates to determine a need for change, Harper and Hurtado cite Eckel and Kezar (2003) who "defined transformation as the type of change that affects the institutional culture, is deep and pervasive, is intentional, and occurs over time" (p. 20). Clearly, scholars who authored chapters in this section thought broadly and deeply about what it would take for institutions to respond in a fashion that moves away from routine acts that do little or nothing to equitably confer rich educational outcomes upon diverse populations of college students.

REFERENCES

Astin, A. W. (1984). Student involvement: A developmental theory for higher education. *Journal of College Student Personnel*, *12*, 297–308.

de Anda, D. (1984). Bicultural socialization: Factors affecting the minority experience. *Social Work*, *29*(2), 101–107.

Eckel, P. D., & Kezar, A. J. (2003). *Taking the Reins: Institutional Transformation in Higher Education.* Westport, Connecticut: Praeger.

Fry, R. (2009). *College Enrollment Hits All Time High, Fueled by Community College Surge.* Washington, DC: Pew Research Center, Social and Demographic Trends Project.

Gratz v. Bollinger, 123 S. Ct. 2411 (2003).

Grutter v. Bollinger, 123 S. Ct. 2325 (2003).

Hurtado, A. (1997). Understanding multiple group identities: Inserting women into cultural transformations. *Journal of Social Issues*, *53*(2): 299–328.

Rendón, L. I. (1994). Validating culturally diverse students: Toward a new model of learning and student development. *Innovative Higher Education*, *19*(1), 23–32.

Terenzini, P. T., Rendón, L. I., Upcraft, L., Millar, S., Allison, K., Gregg, P., & Jalomo, R. (1994). The transition to college: Diverse students, diverse stories. *Research in Higher Education*, *35*(1), 57–73.

Tinto, V. (1987). *Leaving College: Rethinking the Causes and Cures of Student Departure.* Chicago, Illinois: University of Chicago Press.

U.S. Department of Education. (2009). *Digest of Education Statistics, 2008.* Washington, DC: National Center for Education Statistics.

11

What Educators and Administrators Need to Know About College Student Engagement

George D. Kuh

In a 1992 *Calvin and Hobbs* cartoon (Watterson), 6-year-old Calvin asks his teacher whether he is being adequately prepared for the challenges of the 21st century. He wants to know if he will have the skills and competencies that will allow him to succeed in a tough, global economy. In response, the teacher suggests he start working harder because what he will get out of school depends on how much effort he puts into it. Calvin ponders this advice for a moment and says, "Then forget it."

The exchange between Calvin and his teacher gets right to the point about what matters to student learning and personal development. Indeed, one of the few unequivocal conclusions from *How College Affects Students* (Pascarella & Terenzini, 2005) is that the amount of time and energy students put forth—student engagement—is positively linked with the desired outcomes of undergraduate education. Unfortunately, Calvin's response is all too common, if not according to what students say, then by what they do or do not do.

In this chapter, I summarize the role and contributions of the scholarship and institutional research about student engagement and its relevance for student development professionals and others committed to enhancing the quality of the undergraduate experience. The presentation is organized into four major sections. First, I briefly describe the evolution of the student engagement concept and explain its importance to student development. Then, I summarize findings from research studies about the relationships between student engagement and selected activities including participation in high-impact practices, employment, and some other experiences of relevance to the current generation of undergraduates. Next, I discuss some topics that warrant additional investigation to better understand how to further potential and utility of student engagement research and institutional policies and practices that the findings suggest. I close with some observations about the implications of student engagement research for student affairs professionals and others on campus committed to improving the quality of undergraduate education.

MEANING, EVOLUTION, AND IMPORTANCE OF STUDENT ENGAGEMENT

Student engagement represents the time and effort students devote to activities that are empirically linked to desired outcomes of college *and* what institutions do to induce students to participate in these activities (Kuh, 2001, 2003, 2009). The meaning and applications of this definition of student engagement have evolved over time to represent increasingly complex understandings of the relationships between desired outcomes of college and the amount of time and effort students invest in their studies and other educationally purposeful activities (Kuh, 2009; Wolf-Wendel, Ward, & Kinzie, 2009). For example, building on Tyler's "time on task" concept (Merwin, 1969), Pace (1980, 1984) developed the College Student Experiences Questionnaire (CSEQ) to measure "quality of effort" to identify the activities that contributed to various dimensions of student learning and personal development. His research across three decades (1960 to 1990) showed that students gained more from their studies and other aspects of the college experience when they devoted more time and energy to certain tasks that required more effort than others—studying, interacting with their peers and teachers about substantive matters, applying their learning to concrete situations and tasks in different contexts, and so forth (Pace, 1984, 1990).

Astin (1984) further fleshed out and popularized the quality of effort concept with his "theory of involvement," which highlighted the psychological and behavioral dimensions of time on task and quality of effort. His landmark longitudinal studies about the impact of college on students empirically demonstrated the links between involvement and a range of attitudinal and developmental outcomes (Astin, 1977, 1993). Astin was a major contributor to the widely cited *Involvement in Learning* report (National Institute of Education, 1984) which underscored the importance of involvement to student achievement and such other valued outcomes as persistence and educational attainment (Astin, 1999).

In that same decade, after an invitational conference of scholars and educators held at the Wingspread Conference Center in Wisconsin, Chickering and Gamson (1987) distilled the discussions about the features of high-quality teaching and learning settings into seven good practices in undergraduate education: (a) student–faculty contact, (b) active learning, (c) prompt feedback, (d) time on task, (e) high expectations, (f) respect for diverse learning styles, and (g) cooperation among students. Each of these represents a different dimension of engagement.

Since then, numerous scholars have contributed scores of papers addressing different features of student engagement variously defined (e.g., time on task, quality of effort, involvement) and their relationship to various desired outcomes of college (e.g., Braxton, Milem, & Sullivan, 2000; Pascarella, 1985; Pascarella & Terenzini, 2005; Pike, 2006a, 2006b; Tinto, 1987, 1993). These outcomes include cognitive development (Astin, 1993; Kuh, 1993, 1995; Pascarella, Seifert & Blaich, 2009; Pascarella & Terenzini, 2005); psychosocial development, self-esteem, and locus of control (Bandura, Peluso, Ortman, & Millard, 2000; Chickering & Reisser, 1993); moral and ethical development (Jones & Watt, 1999; Liddell & Davis, 1996); and persistence (Berger & Milem, 1999).

In addition, virtually every reform report since *Involvement in Learning* emphasized to varying degrees the important link between student engagement and desired outcomes of college (e.g., Association of American Colleges and Universities [AAC&U], 2002, 2005, 2007; American College Personnel Association, 1994; Education Commission of the States,1995; Joint Task Force on Student Learning, 1998; Keeling, 2004; National Association of State Universities and Land Grant Colleges, 1997; National Commission on the Future of Higher Education, 2006; Wingspread Group on Higher Education, 1993).

Some have understandably and correctly sounded cautionary notes about whether the assumptions on which the engagement construct rest apply more to full-time, traditional-age, and residential students, and less to students from historically underserved groups (Bensimon, 2007; Harper & Quaye, 2008). The bulk of the empirical research suggests that students from different backgrounds all generally benefit from engaging in effective educational practices, although conditional effects apply, meaning that some students benefit more than others from certain activities (Pascarella & Terenzini, 2005). As explained in more detail later, some research shows that engagement has compensatory effects on grades and persistence for students who most need a boost to performance because they are not adequately prepared academically when they start college (Cruce, Wolniak, Seifert, & Pascarella, 2006; Kuh, Cruce, Shoup, Kinzie, & Gonyea, 2008; National Survey of Student Engagement [NSSE], 2007; Pascarella & Terenzini, 2005).

In the 1990s, a second feature of student engagement began to receive more attention—how the institution allocates its resources and arranges its curricula, other learning opportunities, and support services to encourage students to participate in activities positively associated with persistence, satisfaction, learning, and graduation (Kuh, 2001; Kuh, Schuh, Whitt, & Associates, 1991; Kuh, Kinzie, Schuh, Whitt, & Associates, 2005). What the institution does to foster student engagement can be thought of as a margin of educational quality—sometimes called value added—and something a college or university can directly influence to some degree (Kuh, 2009). Using student engagement as an indicator of quality was prompted by questions about whether colleges and universities were using their resources effectively to foster student learning in general and to enhance success of students from increasingly diverse backgrounds (Kuh, Kinzie, Buckley, Bridges, & Hayek, 2007).

Other related factors also compelled institutions to pay attention to student engagement. By the end of the 1990s, regional accrediting agencies and their counterparts in the disciplines required that institutions show evidence that they were assessing student outcomes and aspects of the campus environment associated with these outcomes and were using this information to improve student learning and success (Ewell, 2008). At the same time, building frustration with the amount of attention given to rankings based on institutional resources compelled scholars and educational leaders to find a more promising, responsible way to measure quality that could also be used to improve teaching and learning. The argument was that credible, actionable information about how students spent their time and what institutions emphasized in terms of student performance could tell an accurate, comprehensive story of students' educational experiences and be a powerful lever for institutional improvement (Ewell & Jones, 1996; Gonyea & Kuh, 2009).

As the calls for accountability became more frequent and occasionally strident (National Commission on the Future of Higher Education, 2006), some leaders championed systematic approaches to demonstrate that institutions were taking seriously their responsibility for student learning. They include:

- the Voluntary System of Accountability sponsored by the Association of Public and Land-Grant Universities and American Association of State Colleges and Universities and its College Portrait which features data on learning outcomes (McPherson & Shulenburger, 2006);
- the Council of Independent Colleges, which encourages its member institutions to use standardized and locally developed instruments to document student learning; and
- the National Association of Independent Colleges and Universities' U-CAN Web site, where colleges and universities can present selected information about costs, the student experience, and other information.

All of these efforts encourage or require that student engagement data be incorporated in some meaningful way.

Taken together, the combination of decades of empirical findings documenting the importance of student engagement such as the seven good practices in undergraduate education and the press on institutions to be more accountable for student learning and its improvement led to the development of the widely used NSSE in 1999 (Kuh, 2009). Building on the acceptance and widespread use of NSSE in the United States and Canada, other instruments based on the engagement premise were developed for use by two-year colleges (Community College Survey of Student Engagement), law schools (Law School Survey of Student Engagement), faculty (Community College Faculty Survey of Student Engagement, Faculty Survey of Student Engagement), and beginning college students (Beginning College Survey of Student Engagement for four-year schools, Survey of Entering Student Engagement for Community Colleges). The High School Survey of Student Engagement collects data about the extent to which high school students engage in a range of productive learning activities. Other instruments also gather information related to some aspects of student engagement. In addition to the CSEQ and its partner tool for students starting college, the College Student Expectations Questionnaire (CSXQ), the best known are the Cooperative Institutional Research Program's Entering Student Survey and its follow-up version, the College Senior Survey (Astin, 1993). By design, the NSSE, Community College Survey of Student Engagement (CCSSE), and their counterparts have demonstrated that student engagement can be reliably measured across large numbers of institutions and that the results from these instruments can be used by faculty and staff to improve the undergraduate experience.

Scores of articles, chapters, books, and reports have generated a treasure trove of insights into how and why engagement is important to a high quality undergraduate experience in the first decade of the twenty-first century (e.g., Astin & Sax, 1998; Carini, Kuh, & Klein, 2006; Community College Survey of Student Engagement, 2006, 2007, 2008; Gellin, 2003; Greene, Marti, & McClenney, 2008; Hurtado, Dey, Gurin, & Gurin, 2003; Hu & Kuh, 2003; Kinzie, Thomas, Palmer, Umbach, & Kuh, 2007; Klein, Kuh, Chun, Shavelson, & Benjamin, 2005; Kuh 2001, 2003, 2008; Kuh & Pascarella, 2004; NSSE, 2000, 2001, 2002, 2003, 2004, 2005, 2006, 2007, 2008; Nelson Laird, & Kuh, 2005; Nelson Laird, Shoup, Kuh, & Schwarz, 2008; Outcalt & Skewes-Cox, 2002; Pascarella et al., 2006; Pike, 2003, 2006a, 2006b; Pike & Kuh, 2005, 2006; Pike, Kuh, & Gonyea, 2003, 2007; Pike, Smart, Kuh, & Hayek, 2006; Umbach & Kuh, 2006; Zhao, Carini, & Kuh, 2005; Zhao & Kuh, 2004; Zhao, Kuh, & Carini, 2005).

This work helped to firmly root student engagement into the higher education lexicon and to feature the construct in policy discussions, the scholarly and institutional research literatures, and the popular media in the United States. In addition, questionnaires based on NSSE are being used in Australia, New Zealand, and South Africa (Coates, 2008; Strydom, Mentz, & Kuh, in press). Other countries such as China, Macedonia, and Spain also have experimented with instruments adapted from NSSE, making the engagement phenomenon worldwide.

SELECTED RESEARCH FINDINGS

This section addresses to two key questions about student engagement:

1. What is the evidence that the commonly used engagement measures are valid and reliable? and
2. Who benefits from engagement and why?

Reliability and Validity of Engagement Measures

Precollege characteristics such as academic achievement represented by ACT or SAT scores are strong predictors of first-year grades and persistence. However, once college experiences are taken into account—living on campus, enrollment status, working off campus, and so forth—the effects of precollege characteristics and experiences diminish considerably. As explained, the college experiences that matter most to desired outcomes are those that engage students at high levels in educationally purposeful activities. These are the focus of the most widely used student engagement instrument, the NSSE. Its psychometric properties, including reliability and validity, are acceptable, especially when aggregated across multiple institutions (Kuh, 2001, 2002; Pike, 2006a, 2006b).

For example, reliability studies were conducted for the first five administrations of NSSE including the first two field tests in 1999 (Kuh, 2002). The reliability coefficient (Cronbach alpha) for the twenty-two NSSE college activity items representing student engagement behaviors was .85. Student responses to these questions were relatively normally distributed, with generally acceptable skewness and kurtosis estimates. The fifteen NSSE gains in educational and personal growth items had an alpha coefficient of .90 and were also normally distributed. In addition, different approaches have been used to measure the stability of NSSE measures at both the institution and student levels (Kuh, 2002), and the results indicate that NSSE data are relatively stable. To illustrate, Spearman rho correlations of institutional benchmark scores from different years range from .74 to .93. These benchmarks, described in more detail in Appendix A, are academic challenge, active and collaborative learning, student–faculty interaction, enriching educational experiences, and supportive campus environment. The test–retest correlation for all items for students who completed NSSE twice during the same administration period was a respectable .83 (Kuh, 2002).

Institution-specific analysis sometimes produce factor structures different than the five benchmarks or clusters of effective educational practices that NSSE uses to report its findings (e.g., Gordon, Ludlum, & Hoey 2006). Even so, higher scores on the NSSE, the CCSSE, the CSEQ, and other engagement-related tools generally are positively associated with various self-reported and institutionally reported measures of achievement, satisfaction, and persistence as well as objective outcome measures as shown later (Astin, 1993; Kuh et al., 2008; Pascarella et al., 2009; Pascarella & Terenzini, 2005), providing evidence of predictive and concurrent validity.

The most definitive study so far examining the relationships between student engagement and some of the essential learning outcomes described by such organizations as the AAC&U (2007) is the Wabash National Study of Liberal Arts Education. Using a multi-institutional sample and a pretest–posttest longitudinal design, Pascarella et al. (2009) found that, net of student background characteristics, the type of institution attended, and other college experiences, one or more of the NSSE measures of good practices in undergraduate education consistently predicted development during the first college year on multiple objective measures of student development, including effective reasoning and problem solving, well-being, inclination to inquire and lifelong learning, intercultural effectiveness, leadership, moral character, and integration of learning. At the institutional level, NSSE measures were positively linked with these liberal arts outcomes even after controlling for precollege measures of the outcomes.

Consistent with the pattern of findings reported by Pascarella et al., (2009), Pike, Kuh, McCormick, & Ethington (2007) found that all five NSSE engagement clusters of effective educational practice were significantly and positively related with students' self-reported cognitive and noncognitive gains in learning and development. As the authors explained, this finding is somewhat surprising; when regressing an outcome measure on a set of moderately intercorrelated variables, as with engagement measures, suppressor effects frequently reverse the directions of the observed relationships (Ethington, Thomas, & Pike, 2002). This did not happen, however, which suggests that the various engagement measures make unique, positive contributions to student learning and development.

Three independent studies have validated the CCSSE's use of student engagement as a proxy for student academic achievement and persistence. Across all three inquiries, CCSSE benchmarks consistently exhibited positive links with key outcome measures such as persistence and academic achievement (McClenney, Marti, & Adkins, 2006).

Who Benefits From Engagement and Why

One implication of these studies is that the greatest impact on learning and personal development during college seems to be a function of institutional policies and practices that induce higher levels of engagement across various kinds of in-class and out-of-class educationally purposeful activities (Kuh et al., 2005; Pascarella & Terenzini, 2005). In addition, the effects of engagement are generally in the same positive direction for all students, including those from different racial and ethnic backgrounds, those first in their families to attend college, and those who are less well prepared for college (Greene et al., 2008; Kuh, 2003; Pace 1990). At the same time, the greatest effects of college experiences are conditional, meaning that some students benefit more than others from certain activities (Pascarella & Terenzini, 2005).

For example, Hu and Kuh's (2002) study of student engagement at baccalaureate granting institutions and Greene, Marti, and McClenney's (2008) research into student engagement in two-year colleges found an effort–outcome gap for African-American students. That is, African-American students report spending more time studying than their White counterparts, but earn lower grades. At the same time, there is evidence that engagement has compensatory effects. That is, although exposure to effective educational practices generally benefits all students, the effects on first-year grades and persistence are even greater for lower ability students and students of color compared with White students (Kuh et al., 2008). The compensatory effect of engagement has been noted by others (Cruce et al., 2006; Pascarella & Terenzini, 2005), suggesting that institutions should seek ways to channel student energy toward educationally effective activities, especially for those who start college with two or more "risk" factors, such as being academically underprepared, first in the family to go to college, or from low-income backgrounds. Unfortunately, students from these groups are less likely to participate in high-impact activities during college (Kuh, 2008a), the next topic to be discussed.

High-Impact Activities.   The AAC&U's LEAP project (2007) calls for more consistent, widespread use of effective educational practices, featuring ten potentially "high-impact practices" that make a claim on student time and energy in ways that channel student effort toward productive activities and deepen learning. They include first-year seminars, learning communities, writing-intensive courses, common intellectual experiences, service learning, diversity experiences, student–faculty research, study abroad, internships and other field placements, and senior capstone experiences. For example, Zhao and Kuh (2004) found that students with a learning community experience, defined as "some formal program where groups of students take two or more classes together," were substantially more engaged in all the other educationally effective activities represented by NSSE benchmarks compared with their counterparts who had not participated in such a program. In other words, learning community students interacted more with faculty and diverse peers, studied more, and engaged more frequently in higher order mental activities such as synthesizing material and analyzing problems. They also reported gaining more from their college experience. Moreover, the differences favoring learning community students persisted through the senior year, suggesting that this experience—which most students have in their first college year—continued to positively affect students throughout their college years.

Probing more deeply into the nature of high impact activities and the characteristics of students who do them, Kuh (2008a) found that they seem to have very strong direct effects on engagement, including a NSSE scale of deep learning (see Nelson Laird et al., 2008). This is consistent with what Pike, Kuh, and McCormick (2008) found with regard to the learning community experience. Rather than having direct effects on student learning, participating in a learning community seems to boost student engagement which, in turn, leads to a host of positive educational outcomes. Similarly, the relationships among learning community participation, student engagement, and learning outcomes seem to vary according to characteristics of the institution and how the learning community is structured (NSSE, 2007). For example, after controlling for where students live (on or off campus) and other factors such as gender, major, and year in school, students in learning communities report higher levels of academic challenge and contact with faculty when instructors create assignments that require students integrate across the multiple courses associated with the learning community (NSSE, 2007). In addition, whereas first-year participants in a learning community who were required to live on campus together reported more positive views of the quality of social life and more contact with faculty, they did not engage more often in other ways nor did they report greater gains on NSSE outcomes. Furthermore, Pike et al. (2008) found that learning-community participation was not directly related to gains in learning and development; rather, participating in a learning community was related to levels of student engagement that were, in turn, related to gains in learning and development. Also, learning communities seem to be less positively related with student engagement at larger and more selective institutions, but more positively related with student engagement at institutions with a strong arts and science emphasis. Thus, "a simple inoculation model in which learning community membership has a direct, linear effect on student learning does not adequately explain the complex interactions of learning community design, student characteristics, and institutional settings" (Pike et al., 2008, p. 30).

Similarly, Gonyea (2008) found that studying abroad not only had a positive impact on various dimensions of student development as frequently asserted (Lewin, 2009), but also was related to increased levels of engagement after the experience in the senior year. These positive findings are especially noteworthy because, in addition to controlling for student and institutional characteristics, the analysis also controlled for such self-selection effects as predispositions to engage and to report greater gains after the first year of college. In other words, although students who studied abroad had higher grades, better educated parents, and devoted more effort to educationally purposeful activities in the first year of college compared with their counterparts who did not study abroad, study abroad participants were even more engaged after returning from their time away from the campus.

What faculty think and value makes a difference with regard to the likelihood that students will participate in educationally effective practices (Kuh, Chen, & Nelson Laird, 2007; Umbach & Wawrzynski, 2005), including high-impact practices (Kuh, 2008a). That is, the greater the number of faculty members at a given school who say it is important that students at their institution do a particular activity before they graduate (such as study abroad, participate in a learning community, or have a capstone seminar), the greater the number of students who actually participate in the activity (Kuh, 2008a). For example, on a campus where the average faculty member believes participating in a learning community is just somewhat important, only three percent of first-year students become involved in this activity. In contrast, at institutions where the typical faculty member agrees that learning communities are very important, fifty-five percent of first-year students participate. This also holds for student participation and the importance faculty place on culminating senior experiences, research with a faculty member, and study abroad. For each activity, an increase of one category in the average importance faculty place on the activity—from somewhat important to important or important to very important—corresponds to about a twenty percent increase in student participation. Apparently, when large numbers of faculty and staff at an institution agree on the merit of an activity, members of the campus community are more likely to devote their own time and energy to it as well as provide resources to support it, all of which increases the likelihood that the activities will be available to large numbers of students and that the campus culture encourages student participation in the activities. This view is consistent with the concept of institutional commitment student welfare posited by Braxton, Hirschy, and McClendon (2004). Although similar information is not, to my knowledge, available for the views of student affairs professionals, it stands to reason that what they value can also have an indirect, positive effect on student participation in high-impact activities.

Women in Science, Mathematics, Engineering and Technology (SMET).   Disproportionately low numbers of women persist in SMET majors. Contrary to what might be expected, Zhao et al. (2005) found that females in the various SMET majors were as or more engaged in effective educational practices as their male counterparts. Particularly noteworthy is that female SMET majors were at least as or more satisfied with their collegiate experience and they also viewed their campus environment more favorably than did their male counterparts. In stark contrast with the commonly held notion that SMET fields are often inhospitable to women, these findings are consistent with other research suggesting that women tend to thrive in college when they survive initial entry into technical fields (Huang, Taddese, & Walter, 2000; Spade & Reese, 1991). In other words, even if the climate for women SMET majors remains "chilly," many women today seem to be able to persist and succeed by putting forth more academic effort. However, even though women in SMET majors spent more time reading and studying and less time relaxing and socializing, they reported lower gains in quantitative, analytical, and work-related skills (Zhao et al., 2005). Perhaps women majoring in traditionally male-dominated fields underestimate their collegiate educational accomplishments to a greater extent than do men (Beyer, 1999, 2002; Beyer & Bowden, 1997). If so, the Zhao et al. findings may understate the higher levels of engagement of women in SMET fields. In any case, why women majors in SMET fields must expend more effort to realize the same benefits as men is worrisome and warrants additional investigation.

Engagement at Minority-Serving Institutions (MSI).   Attending an MSI seems to have salutary effects in terms of engagement (Bridges, Kinzie, Nelson Laird, & Kuh, 2008). The insights from the MSIs and other schools in the Documenting Effective Educational Practices (DEEP) project (Kuh et al., 2005), a study of twenty four-year colleges with higher than predicted graduation rates and NSSE scores, are especially instructive for understanding what these institutions do and how they foster student success. Integrating NSSE results with DEEP data produced three patterns of findings that distinguished MSIs from other institutions: high levels of student–faculty interaction, perceptions that the campus environment is supportive of students' academic and social needs, and a network of intrusive educationally effective policies and practices (Bridges et al., 2008). Students interacted more frequently with faculty and staff at HBCUs and also at Hispanic Serving Institutions, especially after student background characteristics were controlled for the latter. This finding lends credence to the common belief that faculty and staff at MSIs are not only integral to fostering student success, but may also provide more support to their students than their counterparts at predominantly White campuses. In addition, after controlling for differences in student background characteristics, participating in effective educational practices at MSIs seemed to compensate for some of the documented student academic preparation and resource inequalities that exist between MSIs and PWIs (Benitez, 1998).

As Bridges et al. explained, student–faculty interaction and supportive campus climate appear to be critical to cultivating the third distinguishing feature—the web of policies and practices that induce students to take part in various demonstrably effective educational activities;

indeed, some MSIs such as Fayetteville State University and Winston-Salem State University require students to do so. These programs and practices are not independent of, but exist and are effective because they bring faculty and students into more frequent, meaningful contact, particularly around structured curricular components such as small freshman seminars linked to academic departments or to advising. All this suggests that MSIs are especially effective when they cultivate a culture of affirmation, aspiration, and achievement buttressed by widespread use of effective educational practices.

Engagement at a Distance.   Chen, Gonyea, and Kuh (2008) found that distance learners—defined as those who took all their courses on-line in a given academic year—generally scored higher on the student engagement and outcomes measures than their campus-based counterparts (see also NSSE [2008]). For example, distance learners reported higher levels of academic challenge and reflective thinking—a component of deep learning as defined by Nelson Laird et al. (2008). They also reported that they gained more in practical competence and in personal and social development, and they were generally more satisfied with their educational experiences. First-year distance learners reported interacting more with faculty and engaging more in enriching educational experiences, such as participating in a learning community and independent study. Senior distance learners perceived the learning environment to be more supportive than their campus-based counterparts and reported greater gains in practical competence, personal and social development, as well as in general education. In only one area of engagement—active and collaborative learning—were distance learners significantly less involved. To a nontrivial degree, the results favoring distance education students may be a function of age and maturity. That is, although older distance learners were much less likely to participate in active and collaborative learning and had fewer enriching experiences and less contact with faculty, they were more engaged in deep learning activities, reported greater gains in practical competence and generation education, and were also more satisfied overall with their educational experiences.

Precollege Dispositions, Expectations, and Student Engagement.   The CSXQ and the Beginning College Student Survey of Student Engagement asks first-year students as they are starting college about their academic and extracurricular involvements in high school as well as the importance they place on participating in educationally purposeful activities in the first year of college (Kuh, 2005; Kuh et al., 2005). Dispositions to engage are important because they influence students' willingness to engage in different activities during college. First tested in 2008, the Survey of Entering Student Engagement for two-year college students focuses on the first three weeks of college and assesses practices that are likely to engage and encourage students to persist to attain their educational goals.

Studies using the Beginning College Student Survey of Student Engagement–NSSE and CSXQ–CSEQ generally show that first-year students expect to do more during the first year of college than they actually do (Gonyea, Kuh, Kinzie, Cruce, & Nelson Laird, 2006; Kuh, 2005; Kuh et al., 2005; NSSE, 2007, 2008). For example, about three fifths expected to spend more than fifteen hours a week studying, but only two fifths did so (Kuh et al., 2005). Put another way, they study two to six hours less per week on average than they thought they would when starting college. Even so, nine of ten first-year students expected to earn grades of B or better, while spending only about half the amount of time preparing for class that faculty say is needed to do well. Three of ten first-year students reported working just hard enough to get by.

The shortfall between expectations and behavior extends to life outside the classroom as well; most entering students expected to participate in co-curricular activities, but thirty-two percent spent no time in these activities during their first year. In this same vein, between forty and fifty percent of first-year students never used career planning, financial advising, or academic tutoring services. In some areas, students do pretty much what they thought they would. One area is relaxing and socializing where one quarter of students said they would spend more than fifteen hours per week with twenty-seven percent actually doing so. More than half predicted they would have little contact with their instructors outside the classroom and, sadly, this became the case (NSSE, 2005). At two-year colleges, after the first three weeks of class, thirty-two percent of students were unaware that their institution had academic skills labs for their use; twenty-seven percent did not know about tutoring or financial aid advising (Center for Community College Student Engagement, 2009). More than one third never met with an academic advisor (CCSSE, 2007).

Disposition is not destiny, however; some students who do not expect to interact with faculty frequently do so; the same is true for participating in active and collaborative learning activities. This suggests, that "wellcrafted first-year experience programs and individual effort can allow students to exceed expectations" (NSSE, 2008, pp. 17–18).

Employment and Engagement. Working during college is now the norm for undergraduates in the United States (King, 1998). Nearly half of full-time first-year students and three quarters of seniors attending four-year colleges and universities responding to the 2008 NSSE reported working for pay. The numbers were even higher for part-time students, with seventy-six percent of first-year students and eighty-four percent of seniors doing so. Among first-generation students, one fifth of full-time first-years and two fifths of full-time seniors worked more than twenty hours per week. At two-year colleges, fifty-seven percent of all students worked more than twenty hours per week (CCSSE, 2007).

McCormick, Moore, and Kuh (in press) found that, surprisingly, working either on or off campus was positively related to several dimensions of student engagement, especially for full-time students. As with previous research (Astin, 1993; Pascarella & Terenzini, 2005), those who worked on campus generally benefitted more than their counterparts who worked off campus. For example, full-time students who worked on campus for up to ten hours per week had slightly higher self-reported grades, whereas those working more than twenty hours per week on campus had slightly lower grades. The grade point average penalty was about twice as much for the same amount of work off campus. Heavy work commitments on or off campus seemed to dampen engagement for part-time students. In addition, net of student and institutional characteristics, working off campus, and students' perceptions of the campus environment were negatively related. However, some of the stronger positive effects on engagement were for full-time students working more than twenty hours per week on campus. The greatest net engagement advantage was for students who reported working both on and off campus. This was a relatively small group about which more must be learned. Given the positive relationships between work and several measures of student engagement and between engagement and selected educational outcomes, the benefits of work during college seem to be mediated by student engagement.

Consistent with the findings of McCormick et al., Pike, Kuh, and McKinley (2009) found that a substantial proportion of students worked more than twenty hours per week, with many employed both on and off campus. Although working during college had variable effects on grades depending on where, whether, and how much a student worked, those students who worked part time on campus had significantly higher grades than students who did not work, students who worked off campus, or students working more than twenty hours per week. For first-year students, working more than twenty hours a week was negatively related with grades; however, seniors with part-time jobs off campus tended to have higher grade point averages than students who did not work. Moreover, seniors who worked more than twenty hours per week did not differ significantly from seniors who did not work in terms of their academic achievement. When the mediating relationships among work, grades, and student engagement were taken into account, even working more than twenty hours a week was positively related to seniors' grades. Although students who worked more hours tended to spend less time preparing for class, working on or off campus did not seem to negatively affect other forms of engagement. In fact, working students reported higher levels of active and collaborative learning, perhaps because their jobs provided them with opportunities to apply what they are learning. In addition, students who worked part time on campus also had substantially more interaction with faculty members. Pike et al. (2009) tentatively concluded that student engagement plays a mediating role on work and grades, which could be interpreted perhaps as a compensatory effect of engagement on grades. They also pointed out that it is possible that seniors with higher grades work more hours; in other words, working itself does not necessarily lead to higher grades.

Taken together, these studies suggest that some of the shibboleths and conclusions about the negative effects of work on student achievement from earlier studies may no longer hold. Indeed, employment may provide opportunities for students to practice and become more competent in collaboration and teamwork, skills that are needed to function effectively in the twenty-first century work environment (AAC&U, 2007).

WHAT MORE DO WE NEED TO LEARN ABOUT STUDENT ENGAGEMENT?

Although much is known about the nature and extent of the effects of student engagement for different groups of students on a variety of outcome measures, much is left to discover and better understand. In this section I raise five questions, the answers to which would be instructive to future efforts to promote student engagement and success in college.

What Are the Key Factors and Features of Student Participation in Different Activities That Lead to Differential Outcomes?

Although engagement, achievement, satisfaction, and persistence are positively linked, the strength of these relationships varies as demonstrated by the review of the selected research findings just presented. Many engaged students leave college prematurely, and some who seem by standard measures to be disengaged complete the baccalaureate degree in timely fashion. Equally important, compared with White students, many students of color expend more time and energy on some activities but report benefitting less, including earning lower grades (Greene et al., 2008; Hu & Kuh, 2002). Some of these equivocal or disappointing findings may be due to differences in learning productivity on the part of the student (Hu & Kuh, 2003)—the ability to optimally convert the amount of time one spends on task into the desired outcome whether it be grades or something else of value. Another plausible explanation is that how an educational practice is implemented varies considerably. For example, learning communities take different forms (Inkelas, Brower, Crawford, Hummel, Pope, & Zeller, 2004; Inkelas & Weisman, 2003; NSSE 2007), as do approaches to study abroad (Lewin, 2009), supervising student–faculty research (Boyd & Wesemann, 2009), or the timing, duration, and structure of internships and other field placements such as student teaching. Even within a single campus, service learning or capstone courses can look very different within or between majors. Some are more effective than others in terms of fostering student engagement and desired outcomes (Kuh, 2008a; NSSE, 2007), and we need to learn more about how their various features affect aspects of student engagement and outcomes (Swaner & Brownell, 2009). Finally, the most widely used measure of engagement,

NSSE, is a short questionnaire and cannot measure all the behaviors and institutional conditions that may influence engagement. As Astin framed the challenge:

> We have not done enough work on the varieties of engagement and what kinds of involvement are positive, or related. For example, political involvement is negatively involved with retention, and satisfaction, it's not a uniformly positive experience. [We need to] look at exceptions and think about why some forms of involvement are negatively related to development.
>
> (cited in Wolf-Wendel et al., 2009)

What Is the Cost of Demonstrably Effective Educational Practices Relative to Other Approaches?

High-impact activities seem to have unusually powerful effects on all students. Given the cost-conscious environment, studies are needed to determine their cost–benefit ratios, taking into account whether students who participate in them are more likely to persist and graduate.

The additional revenues realized from tuition and other fees from students who stay in school could offset what may be marginally higher costs of some of these practices, such as making available a small writing- or inquiry-intensive first-year seminar for every student and subsidizing study away experiences.

Knowing the costs of high-impact practices and student success interventions such as mentoring programs and early warning systems could help institutional decision makers to decide whether to reallocate resources and invest in them.

Under What Conditions, If Any, Can Institutions Systematically Alter Students' Dispositions to Engage?

Students start college predisposed to perform or behave in certain ways (Pascarella, 2001). As noted, many students do less than they expected in terms of participating in educationally effective activities. But some students also do more. Because the standard NSSE and CCSSE administrations are cross-sectional, in the absence of precollege measures it is not possible to infer with a high level of confidence the influence of the institution on engagement independent of student background and predilections (Astin & Lee, 2003). We need to discover how institutions can productively use such tools as the Beginning College Student Survey of Student Engagement, the CSXQ, the Survey of Entering Student Engagement, and the Cooperative Institutional Research Program with other information to identify students who are more or less disposed to engage and design pre- and early college socialization experiences to induce them to take part in beneficial activities.

What Are the Distinctive Features of Engagement in On-Line Environments?

The results are promising in terms of the merits of distance learning, but they also beg additional questions. For example, do distance learners interpret the meaning of engagement questions the same way that campus-based students do? Or do some questions take on different meanings in different contexts? Are the effects on such outcomes as intellectual gains, persistence, and personal and social development of student–faculty interactions and active and collaborative learning activities more or less powerful in the on-line environment? Answers to these questions and others are needed to ensure that on-line programs are at least comparable to and even outperform campus-based programs and provide high-quality educational opportunities for students who otherwise might be excluded from postsecondary education.

How Can Student Engagement Instruments Be Used Responsibly for Benchmarking, Assessment, Accountability, and Improvement?

Up until the turn of this century, the results of student engagement studies were generally low stakes in that they were typically used internally, sometimes for improvement purposes, but often just for institutional research. Occasionally the results were shared externally with accreditors, but rarely with others. In large part, it was hard to stimulate interest in such information without a frame of reference such as having the results from comparable questions from multiple institutions with similar missions and characteristics. As noted near the beginning of this chapter, a confluence of factors in the late 1990s increased interest on the part of stakeholders both on and off campus in student engagement and related data about the student experience. The development of the NSSE and the CCSSE was in large part intended to respond to these conditions. Their widespread use along with other tools made it possible to compare institutional performance on these measures, although not always to the extent some groups preferred (National Commission on the Future of Higher Education, 2006).

Improvement, transparency, and accountability are desirable ends. Every year, additional examples are discovered about how institutions are using their student engagement results to improve the quality of the undergraduate experience (e.g., Kinzie & Pennipede, 2009) and more are needed, especially illustrations of how and to what ends campuses "close the loop"—demonstrate the changes that the institution has made in response to its student engagement results and the impact of these changes on student engagement and learning outcomes.

At the same time, we must be vigilant to ward off misuse or misinterpretation of student engagement results that can lead to problematic and unacceptable outcomes (Kuh, 2007a). Although some thoughtful work has been done to help guide appropriate use of student engagement results for various purposes (Borden & Pike, 2008; McCormick, 2009), systematic monitoring of such uses are needed to avoid, for example, simplifying student experience and institutional performance by comparing schools on only one or two indicators or presuming schools with high graduation rates have high engagement scores. To illustrate, an institution can have a high graduation rate, but low engagement and unacceptable educational outcomes. "Strong performance on engagement, achievement, and graduation measures are certainly not mutually exclusive, but each says something different about institutional performance and student development" (Kuh, 2007a, p. 33).

IMPLICATIONS FOR STUDENT AFFAIRS

The student affairs profession has long embraced various iterations of the student engagement construct. Indeed, "engaging students in active learning" is one of the principles of good practice in student affairs (Blimling, Whitt, & Associates, 1999). Elsewhere, I and others have discussed what student affairs professionals can do with others on campus to promote higher levels of student engagement (Kinzie & Kuh, 2004; Kuh 2007b, 2008b, in press; Kuh et al., 2005, 2007; Manning, Kinzie, & Schuh, 2006). Here I offer some observations about what student affairs professionals can do to help their institutions use student engagement data to promote student success.

The first step is to make certain various constituents become familiar with what the student engagement construct represents and its empirical and conceptual foundations, which is the focus of this chapter. Especially important is that faculty, student affairs professionals, and institutional leaders agree as to who shares the responsibility for student engagement. Until recent years, the dominant institutional philosophy was that the student had to adjust to the institution to succeed.

As student populations have become more diverse and participation in postsecondary education became all but universal, policy makers and institutional leaders increasingly recognized that institutions must also change teaching and learning approaches and cultivate campus cultures that welcome and affirm students as well as faculty and staff from historically underrepresented backgrounds (Kuh, 2007b). Simply put, engagement is a two-way street. Both institutions and students have roles to play in creating the conditions for engagement and for taking advantage of engagement opportunities. Each campus must determine the most appropriate balance.

At high-performing colleges and universities, student affairs staff collaborate with others to periodically collect and review data about the effectiveness of policies and practices with an eye toward insuring that what is enacted is of acceptable quality and consistent with the institution's espoused priorities and values (Kuh et al., 2005). Such examinations are sometimes triggered by self-studies to prepare for a regional accreditation visit. Others may be prompted by institutional strategic priorities. For example, the University of Michigan conducted several major studies between the mid-1980s and 2000 to monitor the impact of initiatives intended to improve the quality of the undergraduate experience (Kuh et al., 2005).

Deciding what to measure is critical because whatever student affairs collects data about is what the division of student affairs will probably report and, perhaps, even target resources for. Along with student engagement data, other commonly used indicators of success to which student affairs should attend include course completion rates, success rates of developmental coursework and supplemental instruction, student retention and graduation rates, transfer student success, student satisfaction, student personal and professional development, and citizenship. Another critical step is making sure the programs that research show to be potentially to be high impact (Kuh, 2008a) actually are having the desired effects. One of the reasons so many college impact studies show equivocal or mixed findings is because the program or practice being evaluated was not implemented effectively.

Many campuses know a good deal about their first-year students and graduating seniors, those students who are highly involved in leadership positions, and those who struggle academically and socially. Not enough is known about the all-but-invisible majority with whom most student affairs staff have little or no contact. Many of these students leave college without completing their degree, including some who are only a semester or two away from fulfilling graduation requirements. The students at greatest risk of leaving college sometime after the second year are almost identical in terms of demographic characteristics to those who leave before that point. It is essential that student affairs extend its data collection to the experiences of students that span all the years of baccalaureate study. One promising approach are the Web-based templates that allow student affairs staff to send electronic prompts to students to encourage them to take advantage of institutional resources and report on their use of the resources.

The ability to leverage significant institutional change to increase student success will be severely limited unless student affairs has adequate data systems to use to evaluate its performance and that of students with different characteristics and backgrounds, such as race/ethnicity, gender, socioeconomic status, first-generation status, and transfer status. By identifying the gaps between the expectations that different groups of students have for college and their level of engagement at different points in the first year of college, student affairs professionals can help institutions target their efforts to create educationally effective programs for new students (Miller, Bender, Schuh, & Associates, 2005; Upcraft, Gardner, & Barefoot, 2005). Another way student affairs professionals can enhance student engagement and success is by championing and themselves consistently using what the research shows are effective educational practices. To have the optimal impact, these practices must be implemented at a high level of quality. At too many institutions, only small numbers of students take part in high-impact activities and, as noted, even fewer students from historically underrepresented groups participate. Student affairs could take the lead in monitoring student participation in these and other effective educational activities—akin to what Hurtado (2007) called "the opportunity structure"—and work with academic administrators and faculty colleagues to find ways to scale them up to create enough opportunities so that every student has a real chance to participate.

This would go a long way to helping those students who most need it to compensate for shortcomings in their academic preparation as well as cultivate a campus culture that fosters student success. In addition to the high-impact activities identified by the AAC&U (2007) and described by Kuh (2008a), students do other things during college that likely confer similar benefits—writing for the student newspaper, working in an office or program on campus, participating in an honors program, being a leader for a student organization or campus committee, and playing intercollegiate athletics to name a few. But these opportunities—with the exception of working on campus—too often are limited to small numbers of students, especially on large campuses.

Campus employment is a target of opportunity in this regard. Working on campus could become a developmentally powerful experience for more students if student affairs professionals who supervise students in their employ intentionally created some of the same conditions that characterize the high-impact activities Kuh (2008a) described. For example, bringing small groups of students together monthly to discuss what they are learning on the job and how it relates to their studies would give students practice in reflecting on and integrating these experiences. Most traditional-age undergraduates—especially first- and second-year students—do not often or ever do this on their own, and all would benefit from hearing their peers talk about these important aspects of their college life. Initial discussions about these matters will predictably be replete with sometimes awkward silences. But after a few sessions, students will have had enough practice to do more of this without too much prompting. And this is, after all, the kind of experience that helps students to develop the capacity for deep, integrative learning, the gateway to a lifetime of continuous learning and personal development.

A FINAL WORD

Student engagement and its historical antecedents—time on task, quality of effort, and involvement—are supported by decades of research showing positive associations with a range of desired outcomes of college. Engaging in educationally purposeful activities helps to level the playing field, especially for students from low-income family backgrounds and others who have been historically underserved. Moreover, engagement increases the odds that any student—educational and social background notwithstanding—will attain his or her educational and personal objectives, acquire the skills and competencies demanded by the challenges of the twenty-first century, and enjoy the intellectual and monetary advantages associated with the completion of the baccalaureate degree. At the same time, there are limits to what student affairs professionals and faculty can realistically do to help students overcome years of educational disadvantages.

Although the engagement construct is widely accepted and used today, in the future more complex iterations of the underlying properties will emerge. These new conceptualizations and operationalizations will more precisely identify the teaching and learning conditions that are even more effective for helping increasingly diverse students acquire the knowledge, dispositions, skills, and competencies demanded by future circumstances. Over the past twenty-five years, student affairs professionals have traditionally been among the first on campus to acknowledge, embrace, and attempt to apply research-based innovative practices. To meet our obligations to students and institutions, it is imperative the student affairs professionals remain open to alternative interpretations of what at this moment in time seem to be near-paradigmatic understandings of what matters to student success and enthusiastically welcome evidence that points to other, better ways to define and measure student engagement.

APPENDIX A. NSSE BENCHMARKS

The benchmarks are based on forty-two key questions from the National Survey of Student Engagement (NSSE) that capture many of the most important aspects of the student experience. These student behaviors and institutional features are some of the more powerful contributors to learning and personal development.

Level of Academic Challenge

Challenging intellectual and creative work is central to student learning and collegiate quality. Colleges and universities promote high levels of student achievement by emphasizing the importance of academic effort and setting high expectations for student performance.

- Preparing for class (studying, reading, writing, rehearsing, etc., related to academic program)
- Number of assigned textbooks, books, or book-length packs of course readings
- Number of written papers or reports of twenty pages or longer; number of written papers or reports of between five and nineteen pages; and number of written papers or reports of fewer than five pages
- Coursework emphasizing analysis of the basic elements of an idea, experience or theory
- Coursework emphasizing synthesis and organizing of ideas, information, or experiences into new, more complex interpretations and relationships
- Coursework emphasizing the making of judgments about the value of information, arguments, or methods
- Coursework emphasizing application of theories or concepts to practical problems or in new situations
- Working harder than you thought you could to meet an instructor's standards or expectations
- Campus environment emphasizing time studying and on academic work

Active and Collaborative Learning

Students learn more when they are intensely involved in their education and asked to think about what they are learning in different settings. Collaborating with others in solving problems or mastering difficult material prepares students for the messy, unscripted problems they will encounter daily during and after college.

- Asked questions in class or contributed to class discussions
- Made a class presentation
- Worked with other students on projects during class
- Worked with classmates outside of class to prepare class assignments
- Tutored or taught other students
- Participated in a community-based project as part of a regular course
- Discussed ideas from your readings or classes with others outside of class (students, family members, co-workers, etc.)

Student–Faculty Interaction

Students learn firsthand how experts think about and solve practical problems by interacting with faculty members inside and outside the classroom. As a result, their teachers become role models, mentors, and guides for continuous, life-long learning.

- Discussed grades or assignments with an instructor
- Talked about career plans with a faculty member or advisor
- Discussed ideas from readings or classes with faculty members outside of class
- Worked with faculty members on activities other than coursework (committees, orientation, student-life activities, etc.)
- Received prompt feedback from faculty on your academic performance (written or oral)
- Worked with a faculty member on an outside research project

Enriching Educational Experiences

Complementary learning opportunities in in- and out-of-class augment academic programs. Diversity experiences teach students valuable things about themselves and others. Technology facilitates collaboration between peers and instructors. Internships, community service, and senior capstone courses provide opportunities to integrate and apply knowledge.

- Participating in co-curricular activities (organizations, publications, student government, sports, etc.)
- Practicum, internship, field experience, co-op experience, or clinical assignment
- Community service or volunteer work
- Foreign language coursework
- Study abroad
- Independent study or self-designed major
- Culminating senior experience (comprehensive exam, capstone course, thesis, project, etc.)
- Serious conversations with students of different religious beliefs, political opinions, or personal values
- Serious conversations with students of a different race or ethnicity
- Using electronic technology to discuss or complete an assignment
- Campus environment encouraging contact among students from different economic, social, and racial or ethnic backgrounds
- Participate in a learning community or some other formal program where groups of students take two or more classes together

Supportive Campus Environment

Students perform better and are more satisfied at colleges that are committed to their success and cultivate positive working and social relations among different groups on campus.

- Campus environment provides the support you need to help you succeed academically
- Campus environment helps you cope with your non-academic responsibilities (work, family, etc.)
- Campus environment provides the support you need to thrive socially

- Quality of relationships with other students
- Quality of relationships with faculty members
- Quality of relationships with administrative personnel and offices

REFERENCES

American College Personnel Association (ACPA). (1994). The student learning imperative. Retrieved December 5, 2007, from http://www.myacpa.org/sli_delete/sli.htm

Association of American Colleges and Universities (AAC&U). (2002). *Greater expectations: A new vision for learning as a nation goes to college*. Retrieved November 15, 2006, from http://www.greaterexpectations.org

Association of American Colleges and Universities (AAC&U). (2005). *Liberal education outcomes: A preliminary report on student achievement in college*. Washington, DC: Author.

Association of American Colleges and Universities (AAC&U). (2007). *College learning for the new global century: A report from the National Leadership Council for Liberal Education and America's Promise*. Washington, DC: Author.

Astin, A. W. (1977). *Four critical years*. San Francisco: Jossey-Bass.

Astin, A. W. (1984). Student involvement: A developmental theory for higher education. *Journal of College Student Development, 25*, 297–308.

Astin, A. W. (1993). *What matters in college? Four critical years revisited*. San Francisco: Jossey-Bass.

Astin, A. W. (1999, March/April). *Involvement in Learning* revisited. *Journal of College Student Development*. Retrieved May 9, 2008, from http://findarticles.com/p/articles/mi_qa3752 /is_199909

Astin, A. W., & Lee, J. (2003). How risky are one-shot cross-sectional assessments of undergraduate students? *Research in Higher Education, 44*, 657–672.

Astin, A. W., & Sax, L. (1998). How undergraduates are affected by service participation. *Journal of College Student Development, 39*, 251–263.

Bandura, A., Millard, M., Peluso, E. A., & Ortman, N. (2000). Effects of peer education training on peer educators: Leadership, self-esteem, health knowledge, and health behaviors. *Journal of College Student Development, 41*, 471–478.

Benitez, M. (1998). Hispanic-serving institutions: Challenges and opportunities. *New Directions for Higher Education, 102*, 57–68.

Bensimon, E. M. (2007). The underestimated significance of practitioner knowledge in the scholarship on student success. *Review of Higher Education, 30*, 441–469,

Berger, J. B., & Milem, J. F. (1999). The role of student involvement and perceptions of integration in a causal model of student persistence. *Research in Higher Education, 40*, 641–664.

Beyer, S. (1999). Gender differences in the accuracy of grade expectancies and evaluations. *Sex Roles, 41*, 279–296.

Beyer, S. (2002). The effects of gender, dysphoria, and performance feedback on the accuracy of self-evaluations. *Sex Roles, 47*, 453–464.

Beyer, S., & Bowden, E. M. (1997). Gender differences in self-perceptions: Convergent evidence from three measures of accuracy and bias. *Personality and Social Psychology Bulletin, 23*, 157–172.

Blimling, G. S., Whitt, E. J., & Associates (1999). *Good practice in student affairs: Principles to foster student learning*. San Francisco: Jossey-Bass.

Borden, V. M. H., Pike, G. R. (Eds). (2008). *Assessing and accounting for student learning: Beyond the Spellings Commission. New Directions for Institutional Research Assessment Supplement 2007*. San Francisco: Jossey-Bass.

Boyd, M. K., & Wesemann, J. L. (Eds.). (2009). *Broadening participation in undergraduate research: Fostering excellence and enhancing the impact*. Washington, DC: Council on Undergraduate Research.

Braxton, J. M., Hirschy, A. S., & McClendon, S. A. (2004). *Understanding and reducing college student departure*. ASHE-ERIC Higher Education Report, Vol. 30, No. 3. Washington DC: School of Education and Human Development, The George Washington University.

Braxton, J. M., Milem, J. F., & Sullivan, A. S. (2000). The influence of active learning on the college student departure process: Toward a revision of Tinto's theory. *Journal of Higher Education, 71*, 569–590.

Bridges, B.K., Kinzie, J., Nelson Laird, T.F., & Kuh, G.D. (2008). Student engagement and student success at minority serving institutions. In M. Gasman, B. Baez, and C.S. Turner (Eds.), *Interdisciplinary approaches to understanding minority institutions*. Albany, NY: SUNY Press.

Carini, R. M., Kuh, G. D., & Klein, S. P. (2006). Student engagement and student learning: Testing the linkages. *Research in Higher Education, 47*, 1–32.

Center for Community College Student Engagement. (2009). *Imagine success: Engaging entering students (2008 SENSE field test findings)*. Austin, TX: The University of Texas at Austin, Community College Leadership Program.

Chen, D. P., Gonyea, R. M., & Kuh, G. D. (2008). Learning at a distance: Engaged or not? *Innovate: Journal of Online Education* [serial online], *4*(3). Retrieved from http://innovateonline.info/index.php?view=article&id=438&action=login

Chickering, A. W., & Gamson, Z. F. (1987). Seven principles for good practice in undergraduate education. *AAHE Bulletin*, March, 3–7.

Chickering, A. W., & Reisser, L. (1993). *Education and identity.* San Francisco: Jossey-Bass.

Coates, H. (2008). *2008 Australasian student engagement report*. Melbourne: Australian Council for Educational Research.

Community College Survey of Student Engagement (CCSSE). (2006). *Act on fact: Using data to improve student success.* Austin, TX: University of Texas at Austin, Community College Leadership Program.

Community College Survey of Student Engagement (CCSSE). (2007). *Committing to student engagement: Reflections on CCSSE's first five years*. Austin, TX: University of Texas at Austin, Community College Leadership Program.

Community College Survey of Student Engagement (CCSSE). (2008). *High expectations and high support: Essential elements of engagement.* Austin, TX: University of Texas at Austin, Community College Leadership Program.

Cruce, T., Wolniak, G. C., Seifert, T. A., & Pascarella, E. T. (2006). Impacts of good practices on cognitive development, learning orientations, and graduate degree plans during the first year of college. *Journal of College Student Development, 47*, 365–383.

Education Commission of the States. (1995). *Making quality count in undergraduate education*. Denver, CO: Education Commission of the States.

Ethington, C. A., Thomas, S. L., & Pike, G. R. (2002). Back to the basics: Regression as it should be. In J. C. Smart (Ed.), *Higher education: Handbook of theory and research* (Vol. 17, pp. 267–287). Dordrecht, The Netherlands: Springer.

Ewell, P. T. (2008). *US accreditation and the future of quality assurance: A tenth anniversary report from the Council on Higher Education Accreditation*. Washington, DC: CHEA Institute for Research and Study of Accreditation and Quality Assurance.

Ewell, P. T., & Jones, D. P. (1996). *Indicators of "good practice" in undergraduate education: A handbook for development and implementation*. Boulder, CO: National Center for Higher Education Management Systems.

Gellin, A. (2003). The effect of undergraduate student involvement on critical thinking: A meta-analysis of the literature, 1991–2000. *Journal of College Student Development, 44*, 746–762.

Gonyea, R.M. (2008, November). *The impact of study abroad on senior year engagement*. Paper presented at the annual meeting of the Association for the Study of Higher Education, Jacksonville, FL.

Gonyea, R.M., & Kuh, G.D. (2009). *Using NSSE in institutional research. New Directions for Institutional Research*, No 141. San Francisco: Jossey-Bass.

Gonyea, R. M., Kuh, G. D., Kinzie, J., Cruce, T., & Nelson Laird, T. (2006, November). *The influence of high school engagement and pre-college expectations on first-year student engagement and self-reported learning outcomes at liberal arts institutions*. Paper presented at the annual meeting of the Association for the Study of Higher Education, Anaheim, California.

Gordon, J., Ludlum, J., & Hoey, J.J. (2006, May). *Validating the National Survey of Student Engagement against student outcomes: Are they related?* Paper presented at the Annual Forum of the Association for Institutional Research, Chicago, IL.

Greene, T. G., Marti, C. N., & McClenney, K. (2008). The effort-outcome gap: Differences for African-American and Hispanic community college students in student engagement and academic achievement. *Journal of Higher Education, 79*, 513–539.

Harper, S. R., & Quaye, S. J. (2008). *Student engagement in higher education: Theoretical perspectives and practical approaches for diverse populations.* London: Routledge.

Hu, S., & Kuh, G. D. (2002). Being (dis)engaged in educationally purposeful activities: The influence of student and institutional characteristics. *Research in Higher Education, 43*, 555–576.

Hu, S., & Kuh, G. D. (2003). A learning productivity model for estimating student gains during college. *Journal of College Student Development, 44*, 185–203.

Huang, G., Taddese, N., & Walter, E. (2000). *Entry and persistence of women and minorities in college science and engineering education.* Report No. NCES 2000–601. Washington, DC: National Center for Education Statistics.

Hurtado, S. (2007). The sociology of the study of college impact. In P. Gumport (Ed.), *The sociology of higher education: Contributions and their contexts.* Baltimore: The Johns Hopkins University Press.

Hurtado, S., Dey, E. L., Gurin, P. Y., & Gurin, G. (2003). College environments, diversity, and student learning. In J.C. Smart (Ed.), *Higher education: Handbook of theory and research* (Vol. XVIII, pp. 145–189). Dordrecht, The Netherlands: Kluwer.

Inkelas, K. K., & Weisman, J. L. (2003). Different by design: An examination of student outcomes among participants in three types of living-learning programs. *Journal of College Student Development, 44*, 335–368.

Inkelas, K. K., Brower, A. M., Crawford, S., Hummel, M., Pope, D., & Zeller, W. L. (2004). National Study of Living-Learning Programs: 2004 report of findings. Retrieved July 11, 2009, from http://www.live-learnstudy.net/images /NSLLP_2004_Final_Report.pdf

Joint Task Force on Student Learning. (1998). Powerful partnerships: A shared responsibility for learning. Retrieved from http://www.myacpa.org/pub/documents/taskforce.pdf

Jones, C. E., & Watt, J. D. (1999). Psychosocial development and moral orientation among traditional-aged college students. *Journal of College Student Development, 40*, 125–132.

Keeling, R. P. (Ed.). (2004). *Learning reconsidered: A campus-wide focus on the student experience.* Washington, DC: National Association of Student Personnel Administrators & American College Personnel Association.

King, J. E. (1998, May 1). Too many students are holding jobs for too many hours. *Chronicle of Higher Education*, p. A72.

Kinzie, J., & Pennipede, B. S. (2009). Converting engagement results into action. In R. Gonyea and G. Kuh (Eds.), *Using student engagement data in institutional research. New Directions for Institutional Research*, No. 141 (pp. 83–96). San Francisco: Jossey-Bass.

Kinzie, J., & Kuh, G. D. (2004). Going DEEP: Learning from campuses that share responsibility for student success. *About Campus, 9*(5), 2–8.

Kinzie, J. L., Thomas, A. D., Palmer, M. M., Umbach, P. D., & Kuh, G. D. (2007). Women students at coeducational and women's colleges: How do their experiences compare? *Journal of College Student Development, 48*, 145–165.

Klein, S. P., Kuh, G. D., Chun, M., Shavelson, R., & Benjamin, R. (2005). An approach to measuring cognitive outcomes across higher education institutions. *Research in Higher Education, 46*, 251–276.

Kuh, G. D. (1993). In their own words: What students learn outside the classroom. *American Educational Research Journal, 30*, 277–304.

Kuh, G. D. (1995). The other curriculum: Out-of-class experiences associated with student learning and personal development. *Journal of Higher Education, 66*, 123–155.

Kuh, G. D. (2001). Assessing what really matters to student learning: Inside the National Survey of Student Engagement. *Change, 33*(3), 10–17, 66.

Kuh, G. D. (2002). *The National Survey of Student Engagement: Conceptual framework and overview of psychometric properties.* Bloomington: Indiana University, Center for Postsecondary Research. Retrieved July 11, 2009, from http://nsse.iub.edu /html/pubs.cfm?action=&viewwhat=Journal%20Article,Book %20Chapter,Report,Research%20Paper

Kuh, G. D. (2003). What we're learning about student engagement from NSSE. *Change, 35*(2), 24–32.

Kuh, G. D. (2005). Student engagement in the first year of college. In Upcraft, L. M., Gardner, J. N., & Barefoot, B. O. (Eds.), *Challenging and supporting the first-year student.* San Francisco: Jossey-Bass.

Kuh, G. D. (2007a). Risky business: Promises and pitfalls of institutional transparency. *Change, 39*(5), 30–35.

Kuh, G. D. (2007b). Success in college. In P. Lingenfelter (Ed.), *More student success: A systemic solution.* Boulder, CO: State Higher Education Executive Officers.

Kuh, G. D. (2008a). *High-impact educational practices: What they are, who has access to them, and why they matter.* Washington, DC: Association of American Colleges and Universities.

Kuh, G. D. (2008b). Diagnosing why some students don't succeed. *The Chronicle of Higher Education, 55*(16), A72.

Kuh, G. D. (2009). The National Survey of Student Engagement: Conceptual and empirical foundations. In R. Gonyea and G. Kuh (Eds.), *Using student engagement data in institutional research. New Directions for Institutional Research,* No. 141 (pp. 5–20). San Francisco: Jossey-Bass.

Kuh, G. D. (in press). Student success in college: What student affairs can do. In J. Schuh, S. Jones, & S. Harper (Eds.), *Student services: A handbook for the profession* (5th ed.). San Francisco: Jossey-Bass.

Kuh, G. D., Chen, D. P., & Nelson Laird, T. F. (2007). Why teacher-scholars matter: Some insights from FSSE and NSSE. *Liberal Education, 93*(4), 40–45.

Kuh, G. D., Cruce, T. M., Shoup, R., Kinzie, J., & Gonyea, R. M. (2008). Unmasking the effects of student engagement on college grades and persistence. *Journal of Higher Education, 79,* 540–563.

Kuh, G. D., Gonyea, R. M., & Williams, J. M. (2005). What students expect from college and what they get. In T. Miller, B. Bender, J. Schuh, & Associates, *Promoting reasonable expectations: Aligning student and institutional thinking about the college experience.* San Francisco: Jossey-Bass/National Association of Student Personnel Administrators.

Kuh, G. D., Kinzie, J., Buckley, J. A., Bridges, B. K., & Hayek, J. C. (2007). *Piecing together the student success puzzle: Research, propositions, and recommendations.* ASHE Higher Education Report, 32(5). San Francisco: Jossey-Bass.

Kuh, G. D., Kinzie, J., Schuh, J. H., Whitt, E. J., & Associates (2005). *Student success in college: Creating conditions that matter.* San Francisco: Jossey-Bass.

Kuh, G. D., & Pascarella, E. T. (2004). What does institutional selectivity tell us about educational quality? *Change, 36*(5), 52–58.

Kuh, G. D., Schuh, J. H., Whitt, E. J., & Associates (1991). *Involving colleges: Successful approaches to fostering student learning and personal development outside the classroom.* San Francisco: Jossey-Bass.

Liddell, D. L., & Davis, T. L. (1996). The measure of moral orientation: Reliability and validity evidence. *Journal of College Student Development, 37,* 485–493.

Lewin, R. (Ed.), (2009). *The handbook of practice and research in study abroad: Higher education and quest for global citizenship.* New York: Routledge and Association of American Colleges and Universities.

McClenney, K., Marti, C. N., & Adkins, C. (2006). *Student engagement and student outcomes: Key findings from CCSSE validation research.* Austin, TX: University of Texas at Austin, Community College Leadership Program.

McCormick, A. M. (2009). Toward reflective accountability: Using NSSE for accountability and transparency. In R. Gonyea & G. Kuh (Eds.), *Using student engagement data in institutional research. New Directions for Institutional Research,* No. 141 (pp. 97–106). San Francisco: Jossey-Bass.

McCormick, A. C., Moore, J. V., III, & Kuh, G. D. (In press). Working in college: Its relationship to student engagement and educational outcomes. In L. W. Perna (Ed.), *Understand the working college student: Implications for policy, administrators, academic affairs, and institutional support.* Sterling, VA: Stylus.

McPherson, P., & Shulenburger, D. (2006, August). *Toward a public universities and colleges Voluntary System of Accountability for undergraduate education (VSA): A NASULGC and AASCU discussion draft.* Washington, DC: NASULGC.

Manning, K., Kinzie, J., & Schuh, J. H. (2006). *One size does not fit all: Traditional and innovative models of student affairs practice.* New York: Routledge.

Merwin, J. C. (1969). Historical review of changing concepts of evaluation. In R. L. Tyler (Ed.), *Educational evaluation: New roles, new methods.* The 68th Yearbook of the National Society for the Study of Education, Part II. Chicago: University of Chicago Press.

Miller, T., Bender, B., Schuh, J. H., & Associates (2005). *Promoting reasonable expectations: Aligning student and institutional thinking about the college experience.* San Francisco: Jossey-Bass/National Association of Student Personnel Administrators.

National Association of State Universities and Land Grant Colleges. (1997). *Returning to our roots: The student experience.* Washington, DC: Author.

National Commission on the Future of Higher Education. (2006). *A test of leadership: Charting the future of U.S. higher education.* Washington, DC: US Department of Education. Retrieved September 4, 2008, from http://www.ed.gov/about/bdscomm/list/hiedfuture/reports/final-report.pdf

National Institute of Education. (1984). *Involvement in learning.* Washington, DC: US Department of Education.

National Survey of Student Engagement (NSSE). (2000). *The NSSE 2000 Report: National benchmarks of effective educational practice.* Bloomington: Indiana University Center for Postsecondary Research.

National Survey of Student Engagement (NSSE). (2001). *Improving the college experience: National benchmarks for effective educational practice.* Bloomington: Indiana University Center for Postsecondary Research.

National Survey of Student Engagement (NSSE). (2002). *From promise to progress: How colleges and universities are using student engagement results to improve collegiate quality.* Bloomington: Indiana University Center for Postsecondary Research.

National Survey of Student Engagement (NSSE). (2003). *Converting data into action: Expanding the boundaries of institutional improvement.* Bloomington: Indiana University Center for Postsecondary Research.

National Survey of Student Engagement (NSSE). (2004). *Student engagement: Pathways to collegiate success.* Bloomington: Indiana University Center for Postsecondary Research.

National Survey of Student Engagement (NSSE). (2005). *Student engagement: Exploring different dimensions of student engagement.* Bloomington: Indiana University Center for Postsecondary Research.

National Survey of Student Engagement (NSSE). (2006). *Engaged learning: Fostering success of all students.* Bloomington: Indiana University Center for Postsecondary Research.

National Survey of Student Engagement (NSSE). (2007). *Experiences that matter: Enhancing student learning and success.* Bloomington: Indiana University Center for Postsecondary Research.

National Survey of Student Engagement (NSSE). (2008). *Promoting engagement for all students: The imperative to look within.* Bloomington: Indiana University Center for Postsecondary Research.

Nelson Laird, T. F., Chen, P. D., & Kuh, G. D. (2008). Classroom practices at institutions with higher than expected persistence rates: What student engagement data tell us. In J. M. Braxton (Ed.), *The role of the classroom in college student persistence.* San Francisco: Jossey-Bass.

Nelson Laird, T. F., & Kuh, G. D. (2005). Student experiences with information technology and their relationship to other aspects of student engagement. *Research in Higher Education, 46,* 211–233.

Nelson Laird, T. F, Shoup, R., Kuh, G. D., & Schwarz, M. J. (2008). The effects of discipline on deep approaches to student learning and college outcomes. *Research in Higher Education, 49,* 469–494.

Outcalt, C. L., & Skewes-Cox, T. E. (2002). Involvement, interaction, and satisfaction: The human environment at HBCUs. *The Review of Higher Education, 25,* 331–347.

Pace, C. R. (1980). Measuring the quality of student effort. *Current Issues in Higher Education, 2,* 10–16.

Pace, C. R. (1984). *Measuring the quality of college student experiences. An account of the development and use of the college student experiences questionnaire.* Los Angeles: Higher Education Research Institute.

Pace, C. R. (1990). *The undergraduates: A report of their activities and college experiences in the 1980s.* Los Angeles: Center for the Study of Evaluation, UCLA Graduate School of Education.

Pascarella, E. T. (1985). College environmental influences on learning and cognitive development: A critical review and synthesis. In J. C. Smart (Ed.), *Higher education: Handbook of theory and research, Vol. 1* (pp.1–62). New York: Agathon.

Pascarella, E. T. (2001). Using student self-reported gains to estimate college impact: A cautionary tale. *Journal of College Student Development, 42,* 488–492.

Pascarella, E. T., Cruce, T., Wolniak, G. C., Kuh, G. D., Umbach, P. D., Hayek, J. C., et al. (2006). Institutional selectivity and good practices in undergraduate education. *Journal of Higher Education, 77,* 251–285.

Pascarella, E. T., Seifert, T. A., & Blaich, C. (2009). *Validation of the NSSE Benchmarks and deep approaches to learning against liberal arts outcomes.* Iowa City: University of Iowa Center for Research on Undergraduate Education.

Pascarella, E. T., & Terenzini, P. T. (2005). *How college affects students: A third decade of research.* San Francisco: Jossey-Bass.

Pike, G. R. (2003). Membership in a fraternity or sorority, student engagement, and educational outcomes at AAU public research universities. *Journal of College Student Development, 44,* 369–382.

Pike, G. R. (2006a). The dependability of NSSE scalets for college and department-level assessment. *Research in Higher Education, 47,* 177–195.

Pike, G. R. (2006b). The convergent and discriminant validity of NSSE scalet scores. *Journal of College Student Development, 47,* 551–564.

Pike, G. R., & Kuh, G. D. (2005). First- and second-generation college students: A comparison of their engagement and intellectual development. *Journal of Higher Education, 76,* 276–300.

Pike, G. R., & Kuh, G. D. (2006). Relationships among structural diversity, informal peer interactions and perceptions of the campus environment. *Review of Higher Education, 29,* 425–450.

Pike, G. R., Kuh, G. D., & Gonyea, R. M. (2003). The relationship between institutional mission and students' involvement and educational outcomes. *Research in Higher Education, 44,* 241–261.

Pike, G.R., Kuh, G. D., & Gonyea, R. M. (2007). Evaluating the rationale for affirmative action in college admissions: Direct and indirect relationships between campus diversity and gains in understanding diverse groups. *Journal of College Student Development, 48,* 166–182.

Pike, G. R., Kuh, G. D., & McCormick, A. M. (2008, November). *Direct, indirect, and contingent relationships between participating in a learning community and educational outcomes.* Paper presented at the annual meeting of the Association for the Study of Higher Education, Jacksonville, Florida.

Pike, G. R., Kuh, G. D., McCormick, A. C., & Ethington, C. A. (2007). *If and when money matters: Direct and indirect relationships between expenditures and student learning.* Paper presented at the annual meeting of the Association for the Study of Higher Education, Louisville, KY.

Pike, G. R., Kuh, G. D., & McKinley, R. (2009). First-year students' employment, engagement, and academic achievement: Untangling the relationship between work and grades. *NASPA Journal, 45,* 560–582.

Pike, G. R., Smart, J. C., Kuh, G. D., & Hayek, J. C. (2006). Educational expenditures and student engagement: When does money matter? *Research in Higher Education, 47,* 847–992.

Spade, J. Z., & Reese, C. A. (1991). We've come a long way, maybe: College students' plans for work and family. *Sex Roles, 24,* 309–321.

Strydom, J. F., Mentz, M., & Kuh, G. D. (in press). Maximising success in higher education: The case for student engagement in South Africa. *Acta Academica.*

Swaner, L. E., & Brownell, J. E. (2009). *Outcomes of high impact practices for underserved students: A review of the literature.* Washington, DC: Association of American Colleges and Universities.

Tinto, V. (1987). *Leaving college: Rethinking the causes and cures of student attrition.* Chicago: University of Chicago Press.

Tinto, V. (1993). *Leaving college: Rethinking the causes and cures of student attrition* (2nd ed.). Chicago: University of Chicago Press.

Umbach, P.D., & Kuh, G.D. (2006). Student experiences with diversity at liberal arts colleges: Another claim for distinctiveness. *Journal of Higher Education, 77,* 169–192.

Umbach, P. D., & Wawrzynski, M. R. (2005). Faculty do matter: The role of college faculty in student learning and engagement. *Research in Higher Education, 46*, 153–184.

Upcraft, L. M., Gardner, J. N., & Barefoot, B. O. (Eds.). (2005). *Challenging and supporting the first-year student.* San Francisco: Jossey-Bass.

Watterson, B. (1992, March 30). *Calvin and Hobbs.* Universal Press Syndicate.

Wingspread Group on Higher Education. (1993). *An American imperative: Higher expectations for higher education.* Racine, WI: The Johnson Foundation.

Wolf-Wendel, L., Ward, K., & Kinzie, J. (2009). A tangled web of terms: The overlap and unique contribution of involvement, engagement, and integration to understanding college student success. *Journal of College Student Development, 50*, 407–428.

Zhao, C-M., Carini, R. M., & Kuh, G. D. (2005). Searching for the peach blossom Shangri-la: Student engagement of men and women SMET majors. *Review of Higher Education, 28*, 503–525.

Zhao, C-M., & Kuh, G. D. (2004). Adding value: Learning communities and student engagement. *Research in Higher Education, 45*, 115–138.

Zhao, C-M., Kuh, G. D., & Carini, R. M. (2005). A comparison of international student and American student engagement in effective educational practices. *Journal of Higher Education, 76*, 209–231.

12

Looking in the Rearview Mirror

Factors Affecting Transfer for Urban Community College Students

Linda Serra Hagedorn, Scott Cypers, and Jaime Lester

For more than a century, American community colleges have served as a beacon of postsecondary access for those less likely to attend college. The mission statements of almost all community colleges include their role in the transfer function—allowing students to begin college at two-year institutions to be followed by transfer to four-year colleges or universities. Thus, a major role of community colleges is to be an "access bridge" to other levels of postsecondary education. Despite a concerted emphasis on transfer, the transfer rates of community college students remain problematically low. Estimates in the large Los Angeles Community College District (LACCD), the site of the research reported in this chapter, indicate that only 5–8% of the student population transfer to four-year institutions (LACCD, 2001). The inexact estimate of transfer is due in part to the lack of a uniform definition of transfer (Bradburn & Hurst, 2001). Therefore, there is general consensus that transfer rates are much lower than optimal. Actual transfer rates are almost impossible to ascertain due to the complex nature of tracking student progress through multiple institutions and across large spans of time (Hagedorn, 2004a; Harbin, 1997; Helm, & Cohen, 2001; Surette, 2001).

Despite low transfer rates, community college students generally express high academic aspirations. Hagedorn (2004a) and others have noted that despite modest GPAs, low college placement, and obstacles along the postsecondary path, community college students generally have very high aspirations that often include graduate study. Therefore, although community colleges still claim transfer as a main function, and community college students declare aspirations to transfer, only low numbers of students actually do transfer. While previous research has struggled to create an appropriate definition for transfer (Banks, 1990) and has explored factors affecting the transfer and retention of community college students (Hagedorn, 2004b), the current study is unique in its retrospective approach. Analyzed were the transcript records of former community college students who have transferred. This chapter identified those factors that have actually helped or hindered students to transfer. This work, informed by two frameworks, introduces a new theory of student transfer.

TRANSFER RESEARCH: THE CLASSIC APPROACH IN HIGHER EDUCATION RESEARCH

Much of the research on community college transfer applies popular theories of integration and student departure (Tinto, 1993; Pascarella & Terenzini, 1983). These studies claim that student academic progress is highly influenced by the levels of a student's integration into higher education institutions. Tinto introduced the dual integration of academic and social integration. Academic integration is often associated with good grades, positive interactions with faculty, and other activities directly related to the academic college experience. In contrast, social integration refers to contact with peers and involvement of a social nature with college activities and student groups (Tinto, 1993). Because the distinction between academic and social integration is oftentimes artificial and overlapping, many studies use similar measures under both headings. For example, Braxton, Milem, and Sullivan (2000) have defined interaction with faculty as social integration while other studies have classified such interactions as academic integration. Despite differences in operationalizing behaviors and terminology, integration theory remains a widely adopted framework for examining community college student persistence.

Tinto's classic work (1975) cites precollege and background characteristics that work to indirectly impact persistence by affecting educational expectations and commitment. Although Tinto did not specify the exact precollege characteristics, subsequent studies by a number of researchers have noted that parental education, high school grades, ethnicity, and socioeconomic status have been potent predictors of persistence (Cabrera, Nora, & Casteaneda, 1993; Nora, 1987; Nora & Rendon, 1990). Most studies that use the integration model include student characteristics as inputs. Other external (outside of the college) variables that have been found useful when examining student persistence include hours of work, finances, and family problems (Bean & Metzner, 1985; Cabrera, Nora, & Casteaneda, 1993).

Since transferring from the community college to a four-year institution is an act of system persistence, these theories are often stretched to explain transfer behaviors and outcomes. Studies examining social and academic integration among community college students have reported mixed results. In an integration-based examination of student persistence at two-year colleges, Bers and Smith (1991) found that students' educational objectives, precollege characteristics (age, gender, ethnicity, etc.), and employment status were more predictive than the social and academic integration. This finding supports the work of Voorhees (1987) who also disputed the importance of social and academic integration in student persistence. Rather, Voorhees reported that gender, intent to leave, and purpose for enrolling significantly predicted persistence. Nora and Rendon (1990), however, found supporting evidence concluding that the integration model predicted predisposition to transfer. In response to the contradictory evidence that integration models predict student persistence among community college students, Napoli and Wortman (1996) conducted a meta-analysis that examined integration among two-year student populations. They found that academic and social integration played a significant role in student persistence. Social integration was more significant for students that involved a term-to-term persistence rather than a year-to-year measure, concluding that a term-to-term measure was more appropriate for the community college population. Clearly, the act of transfer is a behavior linking persistence from one institution to the enrollment of another that can be interpreted as persistence in the system of higher education.

RATIONAL CHOICE THEORY

With its roots in sociology and economics, rational choice theory posits that individuals base their choices on a cost-benefit analysis of alternatives. For example, a student may decide to transfer based on a comparison of the cost of the four-year institution and the relative "payoffs" after completing the degree. Simply put, each individual must weigh the costs (measured in monetary terms as well as time and opportunity costs) of college against the expected lifetime dividends. Rational choice theory has been used to explore a number of factors within the higher education literature, including issues of persistence (McPherson & Schapiro, 1998; Massy, 1996; McIntyre, 1987), college selection (Heller, 1999; Kane, 1995; St. John, 1994), and major selection/educational attainment (Storen & Arnesen, 2007; Jonsson, 1999). Much of the research using rational choice with college selection has examined the integral role that financial aid plays in the decision of if and where to attend college (Heller, 1999; Kane, 1995; St. John, 1994).

Rational choice is also applicable to transfer. Students must weigh the gains associated with additional education, additional costs, and adapting to a new environment. In California, the community colleges have historically charged a marginal tuition. For the time period of the current study, tuition ranged from $6 to $26 a unit. However, the tuition charges at four-year universities were considerably higher. Thus, in terms of financial decisions, transferring typically involves moving from low cost institutions to higher cost institutions.

McIntyre (1987) examined college choice in California presupposing that choice to transfer is determined by a number of supply and demand variables including individual career goals, cost of community colleges related to alternatives, and financial and academic capabilities. Results indicated that choice to attend a community college and subsequently transfer was affected by individuals' goals not related to financial resources and the cost of college. In a cost-benefit analysis in the Netherlands, Beekhoven, De Jong, and Van Hout (2002) noted three mechanisms which can impact student persistence. These mechanisms included family income, social costs, and students' subjective belief in their personal abilities. Higher class status lead to more resources and lower social costs while self-efficacy in academic abilities increased the odds of student persistence. They found that education level of parents, time students expect they need to complete their studies, and perceived likelihood to success all predicted academic success.

In summary, both of these frameworks potentially provide a useful lens to examine community college student transfer. In this study, we are informed by each framework and introduce a combined theory of student transfer.

COMMUNITY COLLEGE STUDENT TRANSFER

Studies examining student transfer have cast a wide net to capture the factors that predict success. In essence, however, the factors can be reduced to two categories (a) institutional (related to the community college or the desired transfer college or university); and (b) intraindividual (pertaining to the student and his/her environment, history, or other life aspect for which institutions have no control).

Institutional Factors

The institutional perspective places culpability on the community colleges as helping or hindering student transfer. Institutional barriers to creating a convenient course schedule, lack of faculty involvement, insufficient information regarding transfer requirements, and poor academic advising have all been noted as institutional factors that create barriers to student transfer. In addition, institutions have also been cited for racism or not understanding the cultural needs of underrepresented minority students including tracking minority students who aspire to transfer to vocational courses.

Several institutional factors have been directly linked to the success or failure of transfer students. In an examination of credit transfer from community colleges to four-year institutions, Kinnick and others (1997) found that students often lose course credit due to their enrollment in nontransfer courses. Often enrollment in noncredit courses may be due to lack of available academic advising. Addressing the role of faculty members in student transfer, Cejda (1998) examined an alternative articulation agreement between two-year institutions and a liberal arts college that recently changed its curriculum to be more "transfer-friendly." Transfer students under the new curriculum performed better academically and were more likely to receive a bachelor's degree.

Intraindividual Factors

In contrast to the institutional factors that help or hinder student transfer, several intraindividual factors have been identified that are related to student transfer. Students' lack of academic preparation, familiarity with higher educational systems, and financial pressures are cited as the dominant reasons for low transfer rates. Financial burdens such as shouldering increasingly large loan debt (Zamani, 2001), issues with poor quality advisement, and inadequate levels of preparedness are but a few examples of the barriers that students encounter (Helm & Cohen, 2001).

Using the High School and Beyond database, Lee and Frank (1990) designed a path diagram to explore the student characteristics that facilitate transfer. The five constructs used in the model were student background, high school academic behavior and outcomes, community college academic behavior, and probability of transfer. Results indicated that successful transfers were more likely to be of a higher social class, White, male, have higher test scores, have a high GPA from high school, and to have high educational aspirations (Lee & Frank, 1990). In addition, Lee and Frank note that stronger parental interest in academic pursuits, enrollment in a math course in high school, and high school grades all predict student transfer. Similarly Carlan and Byxbe (2000) found that GPA, choice of major, and race also impacted academic performance among transfer students once they transferred to a four-year institution. The importance of mathematics and intent to transfer were also confirmed in a study of student transfer among Hispanic students (Kraemer, 1995).

Although some of the research is contradictory when exploring the factors affecting transfer, there is general consensus that successful articulation of coursework between the community colleges and the four-year institutions is at the heart of a seamless transfer experience for students (California Community Colleges System [CCCO], 2002). Despite the knowledge that taking the "right" courses prepares students to transfer, rarely has any study closely examined the community college transcript records of students to verify the veracity of this notion. One study conducted using data from a community college in California did find that remedial course taking impacted bachelor's degree attainment (Jones & Lee, 1992).

METHOD

TRUCCS Project

This retrospective examination of the factors that influence transfer for community college students is conducted as part of the Transfer and Retention of Urban Community College Students (TRUCCS) Project. TRUCCS is a five-year initiative to study the goals, success, and academic patterns of community college students. TRUCCS seeks to identify the factors that promote success of different types of community college students, specifically within an urban setting, the Los Angeles Community College District (LACCD).

Sample

The sample for this study was drawn from 5,000 students from the nine campuses of the Los Angeles Community College District (LACCD). The LACCD is one of the largest districts in the country as well as being one of the most highly diverse with respect to ethnicity, socioeconomic status, and native language. The initial sample of community college students consisted of all students who answered a 47-item questionnaire during the spring semester of 2001. The questionnaire included an optional release form to allow enrollment records as well as other college files to be used for purposes of research. The release stated that enrollment and other college records would include all enrollments in the LACCD—past, present, and future. Sampling was performed through a stratified sampling of 241 classrooms that reflected the remedial and college level distribution of students. More specifically, the sampling relied heavily on three levels of English courses (two levels below transfer, one level below transfer, and transfer level); plus a smaller number of occupational programs stratified by gender, other courses, learning communities, and traditional gateway courses. The validity of the sampling design was assessed by comparing the sample to the entire LACCD population on a number of factors, including ethnicity, primary language, and age and deemed representative of the district's population (Hagedorn, Maxwell, & Moon, 2002). The questionnaire was developed to reflect issues specific to community college students based on the extant literature (Bean & Metzner, 1985; Bers & Smith, 1991; de los Santos & Wright, 1990; Hagedorn & Castro, 1999; McCormick & Carroll, 1997; Moss & Young, 1995).

In addition to the initial survey, two follow-up surveys were sent in hardcopy through the mail as well as made available online in 2002 and 2004. An attempt was made to contact all non-responders by telephone and, when successful, to immediately administer a shorter version of the survey on the phone. The combination of follow-up questionnaires, telephone contacts, and continuing enrollments at the LACCD resulted in our knowledge of postsecondary enrollment of 85% of the original sample.

In the fall of 2003 all participants in the initial survey were checked against records from the National Loan Clearinghouse to determine transfer. In the fall of 2005, the names were again checked against national Right to Know records. Students reported as enrolled in a four-year institution during either of these sweeps were coded as transfer. The type of institution (i.e., state school, research university, for-profit, etc.) was also duly noted.

Analyses

Within this study we employ a range of descriptive and statistical analyses under the umbrella heading of transcript analysis. Transcript analysis is a process of coding and aggregating data elements to quantify and measure student actions and consequences (Hagedorn, 2005). Unlike questionnaire or interview data, student records are not subject to student memory or truthfulness (Adelman, 1999) and, thus, are measures that can be assumed to be without error.

Codings and Definitions

Remediation Levels.   Three levels of remedial courses were identified in terms of content knowledge, difficulty and relationship to four-year colleges as follows:

Level 0: There exist no prerequisites to enter the course and the course is designed to teach the students the necessary skills to be successful in Level 1 courses and beyond.

Level 1: There may be a prerequisite to join the course and the course is designed at a basic skills level aiding the student to master the basic skills needed to be successful in the advanced level courses.

Level 2: There exists a prerequisite to enroll in the course and the course is beyond the basic understanding of the core concepts. Usually the course itself is indicated with the title of intermediate. However, the course does not provide transfer credit to either the University of California or California State University systems, so is not at the advanced transfer level.

Level 3: The course provides transfer credits and is considered a college level course.

Course Success Ratios.   Successful completion of courses was measured by the course success ratio. This ratio is formed by a denominator consisting of the number of credits in which a student enrolled and did not drop prior to the add and drop period (or census date). The numerator consists of those credits resulting when the grade of A, B, C, or P (pass) was earned.

$$\frac{\text{\# Courses with the grade of A, B, C, or P}}{\text{\# of courses of enrollment}}$$

IGETC Modules.   IGETC is an acronym used in California for the Intersegmental General Education Transfer Curriculum (pronounced I-Get-C). IGETC is the statewide articulation agreement between the California Community Colleges and the state's public four-year universities. The state has identified five distinct areas, each consisting of modules of several courses that when passed with a grade of "C" or better, generally satisfy the lower division education requirements of the public university system. At the time of these analyses, there are five modules for transfer to the California State University System (CSU). The modules are:

English
Math
Physical and biological sciences
Arts and humanities
Social and behavioral sciences

Determination.   There is generally a relationship between a student's academic performance and level of determination. We included a 5-item scale (alpha coefficient of .7807) from the TRUCCS survey to measure student determination. Specifically, the following items were measured on a 5-point Likert scale:

I am very determined to reach my goals.
It is important for me to finish courses in program of studies.
I am satisfied when I work hard to achieve my goals.
I expect to do well and earn good grades.
I keep trying even when I am frustrated by a task.

Data Analysis

We analyzed transcripts to ascertain grades, course completion, course taking patterns, transfer readiness and other indicators of success. In this manuscript, we provide a complete descriptive profile of these transfer students along with more inferential data mining techniques. Our work included stepwise discriminant analysis to isolate the factors that best differentiate those that transferred from those that did not. Discriminant analysis is a multivariate statistical technique highly useful to study mutually exclusive groups and to isolate the best "discriminating variables" (Klecka, 1980). We choose to use the stepwise procedure because our work at this time is emergent and exploratory. We acknowledge that by using the stepwise approach the variables entering the equation have been selected due to their ability to yield maximum discrimination. While we employ an *a priori* alpha level of .01, we also acknowledge that our findings may not reflect the true alpha error rate due to the sheer number of tests performed by the stepwise procedure.

Table 12.1 provides a breakdown of the sample by the demographics of gender, age, and ethnicity as well as the results of chi-square analyses for these comparisons. In this instance the chi-square, a nonparametric test of statistical significance, tests the assumption that different groups transfer at the same rates. While we note no differences by gender, we do report that younger students as well as African American and Asians were more overrepresented among those that transferred. Hispanic students were underrepresented in the transfer population.

Table 12.2 provides a simple comparison of means of the two groups: those that transferred and those that did not. A pattern of higher academic success clearly emerges indicating that those who transferred had higher math and English placement scores, GPAs, and success ratios. In addition, those that transferred were more transfer ready as measured by IGETC modules.

In Table 12.3, we provide information regarding the proportion of students passing specific "gatekeeper" and "gateway" courses. Specifically, we separated the file by transfer (yes or no) and report the percentage of students passing specific types of courses. Note large differences in the proportions of students passing the courses illustrated in the table.

Table 12.4 has two purposes. First, it indicates the most popular institutions of transfer and the number of students attending each. Secondly, it provides a breakdown by receiving institution as sorted by the community college GPA. Only cells with more than one individual were included in the table. The table is also sorted by highest to lowest community college GPA.

Table 12.5 provides information pertaining to the discriminant analysis using transfer to a four-year institution (yes or no) as the criterion. Specifically shown are the variables or predictors

TABLE 12.1
Demographic Variables by Transfer Status

Demographic variable	Number of people and percentage that did not transfer from LACCD (N = 3290)	Number of people and percentage that transferred to a BA granting institution (N = 411)	Chi square results
Gender			
Female	1952 (59.3%)	249 (60.6%)	$p > .05$
Male	1338 (40.7%)	162 (39.4%)	
Age			
Younger than 30	2412 (73.3%)	359 (87.3%)	$p < .01*$
30 and older	878 (26.7%)	52 (12.7%)	
Ethnicity			
African American	426 (12.9%)	73 (17.8%)	$p < .01*$
Asian	373 (11.3%)	61 (14.8%)	
Caucasian	369 (11.3%)	48 (11.7%)	
Hispanic	1711 (52.0%)	166 (40.4%)	
Other	411 (12.5%)	63 (15.3%)	

* Notes statistical significance.

TABLE 12.2
Descriptive Statistics—Non-transfer and Transfer Students (Non-transfers = 3,038; Transfers = 407)

	Non-transfer mean (SD)	Transfer mean (SD.)	
Cumulative GPA	2.44 (7.99)	2.94 (596)	*
Number of IGETC modules completed	1.38 (1.29)	3.79 (1.19)	*
Number of semesters	9.71 (5.44)	9.54 (4.24)	ns
Total CSU IGETC success ratio (areas 1 through 5)	.654 (.290)	.833 (.181)	*
Number of CSU transfer level courses attempted	7.97 (6.86)	11.49 (6.32)	*
Total courses attempted	26.85 (15.85)	29.53 (12.34)	*
Number of CSU transfer level courses passed	5.89 (5.54)	9.62 (5.39)	*
Total courses passed	19.11 (12.298)	24.35 (9.66)	*
Success ratio in CSU transfer courses	.70 (.28)	.845 (.162)	*
Success ratio in all courses attempted	.699 (.217)	.834 (.150)	*
Ratio of CSU transfer courses to total courses attempted	.282 (.174)	.392 (.152)	*
Average number of courses per semester of enrollment	2.80 (.847)	3.20 (.822)	*
English placement score	1.43 (.892)	1.66 (.913)	*
Mathematics placement score	.741 (.854)	1.22 (.991)	*
Total English courses attempted	4.62 (3.46)	4.17 (.253)	ns
Number of Level 3 English passes	1.08 (1.06)	1.90 (1.04)	*
Total English success ratio	.679 (.319)	.833 (.226)	*
Total math courses attempted	3.88 (2.71)	4.15 (2.61)	*
Number of Level 0 math attempts	2.07 (1.70)	1.78 (1.71)	*
Number of Level 3 math passes	.424 (.897)	1.36 (1.43)	*
Success ratio math total	.555 (.359)	.7512 (.284)	*
Transfer math index (total number of transfer level math/total number of math)	.535 (.291)	.634 (.304)	*
Transfer English index (total number of transfer English courses/total English courses)	.532 (.263)	.658 (.264)	*
SES—Highest occupational status score of parent	53.067 (26.367)	54.827 (27.268)	ns
Continuity index	.812 (.244)	.831 (.208)	ns

* p < .01.

TABLE 12.3
Proportion of Students Passing Who Selected "Gateway" and "Gatekeeper" Courses

Course	Did not transfer (%)	Transferred (%)
Chemistry	11.3	23.1
Economics	15.3	30.4
Psychology	42.3	59.12
Calculus	1.38	9.49
Statistics	4.35	17.5
Biology	19.8	48.7
Physics	3.1	12.9

that entered and did not enter the analysis in the final step of the stepwise procedure. There were 347 transfers and 2,690 nontransfers included in this final analysis. The final Wilk's Lambda was .848 (11, 1, 3035; $p < .0001$) with a chi-square of 498.357 ($df = 11$, $p < .0001$). Due to the dichotomous outcome of transfer (yes or no), there is one discriminant function. The Eigenvalue was .179 and the canonical correlation was .389. While statistically significant, these measures indicate only a moderate difference between those who transferred and those who did not. This difference is reflected in the group centroids where nontransfer is at −.152 and transfer is at 1.177. Figures 12.1 through 12.3 provide a visual to understand the utility of discriminant analysis. Because this is a two-group analysis, only one discriminant function was produced. Figure 12.1 provides a boxplot of the entire sample by the discriminant function score. Note that while there

TABLE 12.4
GPA of Transfers by Receiving Institution

Institution	N	Mean GPA
UC-Berkeley	2	3.7
UC-San Diego	2	3.7
University of Southern California	15	3.5
UC-Los Angeles	34	3.4
CSU-Fullerton	6	3.3
San Francisco State University	2	3.3
CA State Polytechnic	6	3.2
UC-Irvine	10	3.1
CSU-Los Angeles	26	3.0
UC-Santa Barbara	6	3.0
UC-Riverside	3	2.9
CSU-Dominguez Hills	27	2.8
CSU-Long Beach	16	2.8
Mt. Saint Marys	6	2.8
San Diego State University	3	2.8
CSU-Northridge	72	2.7
Chapman University	2	2.7
University of Phoenix	11	2.7
San Jose State University	2	2.6
University of Nevada-Vegas	2	2.5

TABLE 12.5
Variables that Entered and Did Not Enter the Discriminant Equation

Variables in the analysis	Variables not in the analysis
Transfer Readiness: Number of IGETC modules completed	Student Gender
Time: Number of semesters of enrollment at the community college	Number of transfer courses taken
Transfer ratio: Proportion of transfer level courses to all courses taken	Highest level of English taken
Transfer math index: Proportion of transfer level mathematics to all mathematics courses taken	Ethnicity: minority/non-minority English as native language
Transfer English index: Proportion of transfer level English to all English courses taken	SES-Highest occupational status score by parent
Total success ratio: Proportion of courses passed with a "C" or better	
Continuity index: Measure of continuous enrollment	
Enrollment intensity: Average number of courses taken each semester average	
Student age	
Determination	
Math intensity: Highest level of mathematics taken	

is definite symmetry to the graph, that it is not anchored at 0. More students were nontransfers than transfers. Figure 12.2 provides the function graph of only those who did not transfer. Note that the bulk of the scores are in the negative region (scores less than 0). On the other hand, Figure 12.3 provides the graph of those who did transfer. Note that in Figure 12.3, the bulk of scores are to the right of 0 indicating likelihood of transfer.

The standardized canonical discriminant function coefficients are provided in Table 12.6. These coefficients assess the relative strength of the predictors as compared to each other. Note that by far, the strongest predictor is completion of the IGETC modules or the California transfer readiness curriculum. Also of importance is the continuity index (less continuity yields less transfer prediction), and the transfer math index (less math transfer courses yields less transfer prediction).

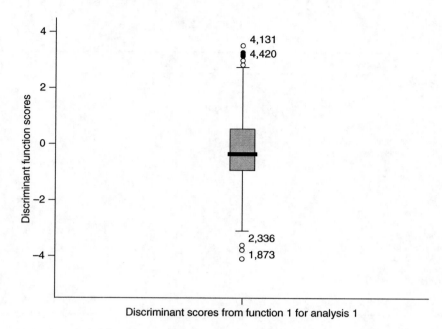

FIGURE 12.1   Boxplot of discriminant scores

Table 12.7 provides the structure matrix or discriminant loadings indicating the relation between the function and the variable. The scores clearly lead to an academic intensity function as predominant.

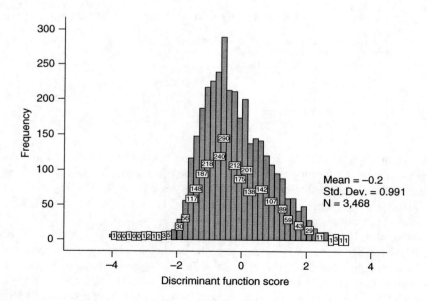

FIGURE 12.2   Non transfers by discriminant score

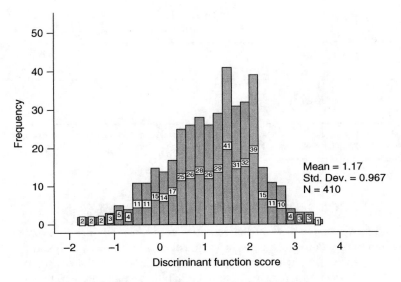

FIGURE 12.3   Transfers by discriminant score

TABLE 12.6
Standardized Canonical Discriminant Function Coefficients

	Function
Student age	−.148
Transfer readiness	.735
Total success ratio	.234
Transfer ratio	.128
Time (# of semesters)	−.253
Enrollment intensity	.159
Highest math	.106
Continuity index	−.225
Transfer math index	.120
Transfer English index	.159
Determination	.130

TABLE 12.7
Structure Matrix

	Function
	1
Transfer readiness	.811
Total success ratio	.514
Number of transfer courses passed[a]	.498
Transfer ratio	.438
English transfer ratio	.380
Highest math	.366
Enrollment intensity	.323
Math transfer ratio	.247
Highest English[a]	.226
Student age	−.216
Determination[a]	.168
Minority/Non-minority[a]	−.161
SES: Highest occupational score between mother and father[a]	.076
Continuity index	.040

TABLE 12.7
(Continued)

| | Function |
	1
English as native language[a]	−.029
Time (number of semesters)	−.012
Gender[a]	−.009

Note: Pooled within-groups correlations between discriminating variables and standardized canonical discriminant functions. Variables ordered by absolute size of correlation within function.

a This variable not used in the analysis.

CONCLUSIONS AND POLICY IMPLICATIONS

This study is a retrospective view of the activities and transcript files that separated approximately 400 community college students who transferred to a four-year institution from those of a larger sample of students who similarly expressed a desire to transfer and, to date, have not transferred. We freely admit that desire to transfer may not be an appropriate way to categorize "transfer possible" students. However, for the purpose of this chapter, we wanted to be as inclusive as possible in order to isolate those practices of students who desire to transfer yet do not transfer from those who successfully achieve their goals.

While female students predominate the community college enrollments, we found that they were no more likely to transfer than their male counterparts. But as expected, transfer is highly related to age such that older students find it more difficult to actually transfer, even if they have an expressed desire to do so. This finding is unfortunate in that previous studies using the TRUCCS data has revealed that older students perform better academically than their younger classmates (Hagedorn, 2004b, 2005).

Each community college district has its unique population. The largest ethnic group at the Los Angeles Community College District is Hispanic. Despite many programs to assist specifically Hispanic students (Hagedorn & Cepeda, 2004), they do not transfer in equal proportions to their representation.

Table 12.2 provided the means, standard deviations, and results of *t*-test comparisons across a number of outcomes for the transfers and nontransfers. While no causation can be attributed to these figures, the reader should note the obvious differences between these two groups of students. Immediately evident is the difference in academic preparation. Transfers had higher English and math placement scores but did not come from higher socioeconomic families (as measured by highest occupational status score of parent).

But performance at the community college appears highly important. Students who transferred had completed more transfer course modules (IGETC) and passed 18% more courses successfully. Furthermore, they were more likely to be more engaged as evidenced by the higher average number of courses per semester.

The exploration of gateway and gatekeeper courses revealed big differences between the transfer and nontransfer group. Those who transferred were about twice as likely to have passed a chemistry, economics, or biology course. While few students took calculus, statistics or physics, note that transfers were four times more likely to pass a statistics or physics class and almost seven times more likely to pass calculus.

Transfer data on students were obtained through data supplied by the Student Right to Know Data and the National Student Clearinghouse. Interestingly, while the list of receiving institutions was very high ($n=65$), many of the institutions only received one student. Furthermore, there were large differences in the average GPA when viewed by receiving institution. Students with the highest GPAs attended selective research universities like the University of California at Berkeley, Los Angeles, or San Diego.

The discriminant analysis revealed that transfer readiness was the most differentiating factor. While it may come as no surprise that being prepared to transfer is the best predictor of transfer, the sheer magnitude of this item truly shouts the simplicity and importance of this statement. Students who transferred took the courses that were designated to open the transfer door. Earlier work at these same campuses, however, revealed that the vast majority of students desiring to transfer had very little to no knowledge of the IGETC sequences (Hagedorn & Garcia, 2004). Another important predictor of transfer was the success ratio. Again, it is simplistic to say transfers were more likely to successfully complete the courses in which they enrolled, but obviously this is the case. Transfers also had higher transfer math and English indices indicating that they were less likely to be entrenched in remedial/developmental courses. Time, or number of semesters, was a negative predictor. Therefore, students who spent many semesters at the college were less likely to eventually transfer. Another significant predictor was the continuity index. This measure of continuous enrollment or lack of idle semesters was also a strong discriminator between those who transferred and those who did not.

The structure matrix is clear and unmistakable. When it comes to unlocking the transfer door, academics and academic persistence are the keys. The simplicity of our findings makes policy implications equally uncomplicated. Students in the Los Angeles Community College District who desire to transfer should be advised and assisted to take transfer level courses within the IGETC specified curriculum. They should progress through the remedial/developmental work as quickly as possible and should remain continuously enrolled through completion of the transfer-ready sequence. While this directive is simple and supported by our findings, the reality of the district is less pliable. Our findings promote strong and consistent academic advising. Yet the district has few advisors (ratios can be as high as 2,000 students per advisor). Further, in a district where the vast majority of students attend college part-time in the evenings, evening and weekend advising is almost nonexistent.

Tinto (2006) advocates implementing new policies based on the accumulation of research surrounding issues of retention and transfer. Based on these findings as well as other studies by the TRUCCS Research Team, the policies of advising and assisting students would likely benefit from an overhaul. Rather than have advising exist as a separate entity, it is suggested that it be more enmeshed with the classroom experience. Advisors and other administrators must come to terms with the fact that many students will not seek them out. In the absence of convenient advising, students will turn to their peers for advice or will just try to figure it all out themselves. Periodic visits to classrooms by advisors (especially classes that meet in the evenings and weekends) would bring advice to the student. Information regarding the IGETC curriculum should be widely and repetitively dispensed. There are excellent Web sites (http://www.assist.org, and http://igetc.org/) to assist students to understand and to follow the IGETC curriculum. But these Web sites are only valuable if students are aware of them and use them. Flyers, posters, or other means of dissemination announcing the Web sites should be made available to students.

Another viable alternative for academic advising to meet the need and current landscape of community colleges would be to demand student participation in academic advising through interactive Web based systems. Demanding that students complete an online counseling experience prior to first enrollment would ensure that students successfully understand the pathway to transfer and possible obstacles on the transfer path prior to enrolling in their first class.

It is also important to note that academic course progression and completion played a greater role than personality characteristics in discriminating between those students that transfer and those that did not. This lends further credence to the importance of proper advising to insure student success.

Finally, those who wish to help students navigate the community college as a bridge to transfer and the bachelor's degree must acknowledge that community college is an academic experience. While endeavors to assist students to be more engaged in college life and to enjoy their experiences may be positive, they are hollow if not accompanied by intensive academic support and consistent advising services. We must acknowledge that transfer rates are lower than optimal and that many students are not succeeding. The roots of the problems are academic, and only academic solutions will make a difference.

REFERENCES

Adelman, C. (1999). *Answers in a toolbox: Academic intensity, attendance patterns, and bachelor's degree attainment*. Washington, DC: U.S. Department of Education, Office of Educational Research and Improvement.

Banks, D. L. (1990). Why a consistent definition of transfer? An ERIC review. *Community College Review*, *18*(2), 47–53.

Bean, J. P. & Metzner, B. S. (1985). A conceptual model of nontraditional undergraduate student attrition. *Review of Educational Research*, *55*(4), 485–540.

Beekhoven, S., De Jong, U., & Van Hout, H. (2002). Explaining academic progress via combining concepts of integration theory and rational choice theory. *Research in Higher Education*, *43*(5), 577–600.

Bers, T. H. & Smith, K. E. (1991). Persistence of community college students: The influence of student intent and academic and social integration. *Research in Higher Education*, *32*(5), 539–556.

Bradburn, E. M. & Hurst, D. G. (2001). Community college transfer rates to 4-year institutions using alternative definitions of transfer. *Education Statistics Quarterly*, *3*(3), 119–125.

Braxton, J. M., Milem, J. F., & Sullivan, A. S. (2000). The influence of active learning on the college student departure process. *The Journal of Higher Education*, *71*(5), 569–590.

Cabrera, A. F., Nora, A., & Castaneda, M. B. (1993). College persistence. Structural equations modeling. Test of an integrated model of student retention. *Journal of Higher Education*, *64*(2), 122–139.

California Community Colleges Chancellor's Office (CCCO). (2002). *Transfer capacity and readiness in the California community colleges: A progress report to the legislature*. Report prepared by Student Services and Special Programs Division and the Technology, Research, and Information Systems Division.

Carlan, P. E. & Byxbe, F. R. (2000). The promise of humanistic policing: Is higher education living up to societal expectation? *American Journal of Criminal Justice*, *24*(2), 235–246.

Cejda, B. D. (1998). Faculty collaboration and competency-based curriculum agreements: Meaningful links in transfer education. *Michigan Community College Journal of Research and Practice*, *4*(1), 69.

de los Santos, A. G. & Wright, I. (1990). Maricopa's swirling students: Earning one-third of Arizona State's bachelor's degrees. *Community, Technical, and Junior College Journal*, *60*(6), 32–34.

Hagedorn, L. S. (2004a). The American community college student: Transcript stories and course completion. *Journal of University Management: Practice and Analysis*, *2*(30), 90–101.

Hagedorn, L. S. (2004b). The role of urban community colleges in educating diverse populations: The case of the Los Angeles community college district. In B. V. Laden (Ed.), *Serving minority populations: New directions for community colleges* (pp. 21–34). San Francisco: Jossey-Bass.

Hagedorn, L. S. (January/February 2005). Square pegs: Adult students and their "fit" in postsecondary institutions. *Change*, 22–29.

Hagedorn, L. S. & Castro, C. R. (1999). Paradoxes: California's experience with reverse transfer students. In B. K. Townsend (Ed.), *Understanding the impact of reverse transfer students on community colleges* (Summer, 1999 ed., Vol. 106, pp. 15–26). San Francisco: Jossey-Bass.

Hagedorn, L. S. & Cepeda, R. (2004). Serving Los Angeles: Urban community colleges and educational success among Latino students. *Community College Journal of Research and Practice, 28*(3), 199–212.

Hagedorn, L. S. & Garcia, H. (2004, November). *Transfer center stories: A mission, a plan, or missed opportunities?* Kansas City, MO: Association for the Study of Higher Education.

Hagedorn, L. S., Maxwell, W. E., & Moon, H. S. (2002). *Research on urban community college transfer and retention: The Los Angeles TRUCCS project.* Report to the U.S Department of Education.

Harbin, C. E. (1997). A survey of transfer students at four-year institutions serving a California community college. *Community College Review, 25*(2), 21–40.

Heller, D. E. (1999). The effects of tuition and state financial aid on public college enrollment. *The Review of Higher Education, 23*(1), 65–89.

Helm, P. K. & Cohen, A. M. (2001). Leadership perspectives on preparing transfer students. *New Directions for Community Colleges,* 114, 99–103.

Jones, J. C. & Lee, B. S. (1992). Moving on: A cooperative study of student transfer. *Research in Higher Education,* 33, 125–140.

Jonsson, J. O. (1999). Explaining sex differences in educational choice: An empirical assessment of a rational choice model. *European Sociological Review, 15*(4), 391–404.

Kane, T. (1995). *Rising public college tuition and college entry: How well do public subsidies promote access to college?* National Bureau of Economic Research Working Paper 5164, Cambridge, MA.

Kinnick, M. K., et al. (1997, May). *Student transfer and outcomes between community college and a university in an urban environment.* Paper presented at the annual forum of the Association for Institutional Research, Orlando, FL.

Klecka, W. R. (1980). Discriminant analysis. *Sage university paper series on quantitative applications in the social sciences, 07–019.* Newbury Park, CA: Sage.

Kraemer, B. A. (1995). Factors affecting Hispanic student transfer behavior. *Research in Higher Education, 36*(3), 303–322.

Lee, V. E. & Frank, K. A. (1990). Students' characteristics that facilitate the transfer from two-year to four-year colleges. *Sociology of Education, 63*(3), 178–193.

Los Angeles Community College District. (2001). Retrieved January 25, 2005, from http://marlin.laccd.edu/research/home.htm.

Massy, W. F. (Eds.). (1996). *Resource allocation in higher education.* Ann Arbor, MI: University of Michigan Press.

McCormick, A. C. & Carroll, C. D. (1997). NCES 97–266, Transfer behavior among beginning postsecondary students: 1989–94. (ERIC Document Reproduction Service No. 408929)

McDonough, P. M. (1997). *Choosing colleges: How social class and schools structure opportunity.* Albany, NY: State University of New York Press.

McIntyre, C. (1987). Assessing community college transfer performance. *Research in Higher Education, 27*(2), 142–162.

McPherson, M. S. & Schapiro, M. O. (1998). *The student aid game: Meeting need and rewarding talent in American higher education.* Princeton, NJ: Princeton University Press.

Moss, R. L. & Young, R. B. (1995). Perceptions about the academic and social integration of underprepared students in an urban community college. *Community College Review, 16*(4), 47–61.

Napoli, A. R. & Wortman, P. M. (1996). A meta-analytic examination of the relative importance of academic and social integration among community college students. *Journal of Applied Research in the Community College, 4*(1), 5–21.

Nora, A. (1987). Determinants of retention among Chicago college students: A structural model. *Research in Higher Education, 26*(1), 31–59.

Nora, A. & Rendon, L. I. (1990). Determinants of predisposition to transfer among community college students: A structural model. *Research in Higher Education, 31*(3), 235–255.

Rendon, L. T. & Matthews, T. B. (1989). Success of community college students. *Education and Urban Society, 21,* 312–327.

Rendon, L. & Nora, A. (1987). Hispanic students: Stopping the leaks in the pipeline. *Educational Record, 69*(1), 79–85.

St. John, E. P. (1994). *Prices, productivity, and investment: Assessing financial strategies in higher education*. ASHE-ERIC Higher Education Report Number 3. Washington, DC: The George Washington University.

Storen, L. A. & Arnesen, C. A. (2007). Women's and men's choice of higher education—what explains the persistent sex segregation in Norway? *Studies of Higher Education, 32*(2), 253–275.

Surette, B. J. (2001). Transfer from two-year to four-year college: An analysis of gender differences. *Economics of Education Review, 20*(2), 151–163.

Tinto, V. (1975). Dropout from higher education: A theoretical synthesis of recent research. *Review of Educational Research, 45*, 89–125.

Tinto, V. (1993). *Leaving college: Rethinking the causes and cures of student attrition* (Rev. ed.). Chicago: University of Chicago Press.

Tinto, V. (2006). Research and practice of student retention: What next? *Journal of College Student Retention, 8*(1), 1–19.

Vorhees, R. A. (1987). *Leaving college: Rethinking the causes and cures of student attrition*. Chicago: The University of Chicago Press.

Zamani, E. M. (2001). Institutional responses to barriers to the transfer process. *New Directions for Community Colleges, 114*, 15–24.

13

Theoretical Considerations in the Study of Minority Student Retention in Higher Education

Laura I. Rendón, Romero E. Jalomo, and Amaury Nora

Research on college student persistence is by now voluminous. Much of this research is based on testing and validating Vincent Tinto's (1975, 1987, 1993) highly acclaimed model of student departure. The basic premise of Tinto's model is that social and academic integration are essential to student retention. Tinto's model (especially the 1975 and 1987 versions) has certainly provided a workable and testable foundation for analyzing the multiple factors involved with student departure, particularly employing quantitative methods. Quantitative researchers such as Nora and Cabrera (1996) note that there is sufficient empirical evidence establishing the validity of Tinto's (1975, 1987) model of student persistence. Others have modified and improved the model utilizing diverse study populations at different higher education institutions (Nora 1987; Nora, Attinasi, and Matonak 1990; Rendón 1982; Nora and Rendón 1990; Cabrera, Nora, and Castañeda 1992; Nora and Cabrera 1993, 1996; Cabrera et al. 1992; Pavel 1992; Cabrera and Nora 1994; Pascarella and Terenzini 1991; Pascarella 1980; Terenzini, Lorang, and Pascarella 1981). Yet, more remains to be done.

Braxton, Sullivan, and Johnson's (1997) assessment of Tinto's theory (based on the 1975 version) found that, in the aggregate, assessment of empirical evidence regarding thirteen of Tinto's primary propositions indicated only partial support for the theory. The researchers cited problems with empirical internal consistency in multi-institutional or single-institutional assessments, in both residential and commuter universities, and across female and male college students. Further, Tierney (1992), Attinasi (1989, 1994), and Kraemer (1997) have questioned the validity of the model to fully and appropriately capture the experiences of nonwhite students, given that the model is based on an assimilation/acculturation framework.

It is worthy at this point to note the linkage between Tinto's interactionalist theory and the assimilation/acculturation perspective. Interactionalist theory is concerned with the impact of person- and institution-related characteristics on a particular phenomenon (Caplan and Nelson 1973; Braxton, Sullivan, and Johnson 1997). Tinto (1993) notes that his persistence model is an "interactional system" (p. 136) in which both students and institutions (through social and educational communities) are, over time, continually interacting with one another in a variety of formal and informal situations. Key to the interactionalist view is that persistence is contingent on the extent to which students have become incorporated (integrated) into the social and academic communities of the college.

Interactionalist theory may be linked to the acculturation/assimilation perspective that was prevalent during the 1960s when social scientists from various fields studied how members of minority groups became integrated into the dominant white society. It was believed that minority individuals were engaged in a self-perpetuating cycle of poverty and deprivation and that they could avoid societal alienation by becoming fully absorbed (assimilated) or adapted (acculturated) into the dominant culture (Hurtado 1997). Assimilation required a process of separation, a cultural adaptation that required minority individuals to break away from their traditions, customs, values, language, etc., in order to find full membership in the predominantly white American society. However, during the 1970s and 1980s critics contested this perspective, citing problems such as the use of mainstream cultural norms as evaluative criteria, as well as the problematic assumption that minority group norms and cultural patterns were inferior, deviant, and self-destructive when compared to those of the majority culture (de Anda 1984).

Along these lines, Caplan and Nelson (1973) provided important distinctions between person-centered and situation-centered problems, noting that the way a problem was identified gave way to specific solutions. For example, researchers focusing on person-centered problems would focus on individual characteristics as the root of the issue and the target of the solution, while ignoring situationally relevant factors. In the case of studying why minority cultures experience alienation, a person-centered definition would identify the pathology as residing with minority group characteristics. Conversely, Caplan and Nelson noted that situation-centered problems have a system change orientation. Here, the context in which individuals operate is examined and remedies are proposed to change the system.

Once in effect and legitimated, irrespective of their validity, these definitions resist replacement by other definitions or perspectives. For example, the idea that minority students are not motivated to learn or have low expectations has been around for decades and ignores how systemic inequities, racism, and discrimination have worked against minority populations. Within the past twenty years there has been greater emphasis on examining the interactions among individuals and systems. Yet Caplan and Nelson's (1973) view that to the extent that problem definitions conform to and reinforce dominant cultural myths and clichés, as indeed most definitions must in order to become widely accepted, their change or replacement will be stubbornly resisted. People tend to conform to public definitions and expectations, even when there are doubts regarding their accuracy.

Because interactionalist retention theory adheres to some of the basic premises of the acculturation/assimilation framework, such as separation and incorporation, several researchers have challenged the way these processes have been conceptualized in relation to explaining minority student retention in college. In particular, the assumption that minority students must separate from their cultural realities and take the responsibility to become incorporated into colleges' academic and social fabric in order to succeed (with little or no concern to address systemic problems within institutions or to the notion that minority students are often able to operate in multiple contexts) becomes central to the critique of Tinto's student departure model.

At the same time, emerging scholarship that is beginning to take root not only in education but in fields such as psychology, anthropology, and sociology is revolutionizing the way we conceptualize different phenomena and the selection of empirical tools to guide this understanding (Hurtado 1997; Rosaldo 1989). For example, Hurtado (1997) explains that much feminist research advocates a multidisciplinary and multimethod approach that is nonhierarchical (i.e., one dominant group is not favored over another) and reflexive (i.e., invites critique and further analysis). Given these developments, we believe that revisionist models and theory refinements are needed. Also needed are new models that consider the key theoretical issues associated with the experiences of minority students in higher education.

It is important to note that researchers (primarily white) began studying student retention prior to the time that minorities had become a critical mass on college campuses. Few minority students resulted in small sample sizes or total exclusion from the samples. Consequently, much of the most widely acclaimed research guiding theories of students' transitions to college, departure, involvement, and learning was often based on white male students (Tierney 1992; Belenky et al. 1986). This research produced a monolithic view of students devoid of issues of race/ethnicity, culture, gender, politics, and identity (Hurtado 1997).

The research on minority college students is relatively young, and the majority focuses on African American and Hispanic (primarily Mexican American) students. Especially fertile territory is research on American Indians, Asians, Pacific Islanders, Filipinos, Puerto Ricans, Cubans, and immigrant students from Asia and Central and South America. As our society becomes more multicultural and complex, the experiences of multiracial students will merit careful investigation. In the 1970s only a few studies, such as Gurin and Epps (1975) and Olivas (1979), focused on minority students. Only within the past fifteen years have researchers, many of them nonwhite, begun to study minority students (Nora and Cabrera 1994; Nora and Rendón 1988, 1990; Rendón 1982, 1994; Jalomo 1995; Tierney 1992, 1993; Wright 1988; Allen 1984; Ogbu 1978, 1987; Thomas 1984; Harvey and Williams 1989; Attinasi 1989; Fleming 1984; Nettles et al. 1985; London 1978, 1989; Weis 1985; Hurtado and Garcia 1994; Kraemer 1997; Nora, Attinasi, and Matonak 1990; Cabrera, Nora, and Castañeda 1993; Lowe 1989; Melchior-Walsh 1994; Galindo and Escamilla 1995; Gandara 1993; Wycoff 1996; Valadez 1996; Mow and Nettles 1990). This relatively new research not only lifts the knowledge base of student retention and development theories, it advances policy and practice and calls to question the predominant ways of structuring student development services employing research that included few, if any, minority students.

Much of the research that provides important modifications to the problem definition, introduces new variables to the retention equation, and attempts to refine traditional paradigms of student retention is scattered and unconnected. Consequently, a new, coherent vision of minority student persistence has failed to evolve. Researchers and practitioners alike tend to view issues related to the retention of minority students as similar, if not identical, to those of majority students. What transpires is an almost universally entrenched view that Tinto's (1975, 1987) departure model, with all of its assumptions, is complete, appropriate, and valid for all students regardless of their varied ethnic, racial, economic, and social backgrounds. To his credit, Tinto (1993) elaborates on the importance of supportive student communities for students of color and adult students who may experience difficulties making the transition to college and becoming incorporated. Tinto (1993) also notes the need to build inclusive campuses, explaining that "to be fully effective, college communities, academic and social, must be inclusive of all students who enter" (p. 187). Yet researchers such as Hurtado (1997) would argue that linear models based on an assimilation/acculturation framework leave many questions unanswered, especially with regard to multiple group identifications and how both minority and majority groups change when they come into contact with each other.

PURPOSE

The purpose of this chapter is to (1) provide a critical analysis of Tinto's student departure theory (1975, 1987, 1993) with a specific focus on the separation and transition stage, (2) critique Tinto's concepts of academic and social integration, and (3) present future directions designed to take retention theory to a higher level. The main concern is not whether the Tinto theory works for minority students. Rather, the emphasis is on the kind of theoretical foundation and methodological approaches that are needed to more fully understand and facilitate the retention process for minority students in an increasingly complex and multiracial institutional environment. Our critique is not meant to assault or discredit the work of researchers who have devoted their careers to studying how students become engaged in college. Rather, we offer alternative perspectives that seek a similar aim: to more fully understand student retention in college. We believe scholars ought to periodically reassess their work and how they apply their empirically based perspectives to new contexts in order to advance knowledge. Indeed, even the ideas advanced here should be taken further, and we encourage researchers to do so.

THEORETICAL CONSIDERATIONS IN TINTO'S STUDENT DEPARTURE MODEL

Tinto's (1975, 1987, 1993) model of student departure has been extensively employed to study how majority and minority students become academically and socially integrated into institutional life. To help develop his theory on student departure, Tinto employed the rites-of-passage framework of Dutch anthropologist Arnold Van Gennep (1960). Van Gennep was concerned with the movement of individuals and societies over time and the rituals designed to move individuals from youth to adulthood in order to ensure social stability. To facilitate a discussion of theoretical issues on the concepts of separation, as well as academic and social integration, a brief summary of Van Gennep's theory is presented.

Conceptual Issues in Van Gennep's Rites of Passage

The rites of passage as described by Van Gennep (1960) included a three-phase process of separation, transition, and incorporation. In stage one, separation, the individual became separated from past associations and a decline occurred in interactions with members of the group from which the individual originated. Specific ceremonies marked outmoded views and norms of the old group. In stage two, transition, the individual began to interact in new ways with members of the new group in which membership was being sought. Rituals such as isolation, training, and ordeals were used to facilitate separation, which ensured that the individual acquired the knowledge and skills of the new group. In the third stage, incorporation, the individual took on new patterns of interaction with members of the new group and established competent membership. Though able to interact with members of the old group, individuals now did so only as members of the new group. In this stage individuals became fully integrated into the culture of the new group (Tinto 1987). Tinto stressed that it was "possible to envision the process of student persistence as functionally similar to that of becoming incorporated in the life of human communities" (p. 94).

How generalizable are Van Gennep's perspectives and assumptions when studying minority college students? First, let us consider the concept of separation and the ways some scholars have interpreted the theory. One of the assumptions scholars have made is that individuals should disassociate themselves from their native cultural realities in order to assimilate into college life. The assumption made is that an individual's values and beliefs rooted in his or her cultural background must be abandoned to successfully incorporate the values and beliefs not only of the institution but of the majority population upon which they are based. Only in this way can an individual student become integrated into the new environment. According to this assumption, minority students must reconcile the fact that they must leave the old world behind in order to find full membership in the new college world, since the two are distinctly different. A second assumption is that there is one "dominant" culture and that in order to succeed, members of minority cultures should become more similar to this dominant culture. A third assumption is that it will be relatively easy to find membership and acceptance in the new college world and that individuals who become integrated will have little or no contact with members of their old groups. Indeed, the hallmark of Tinto's (1993) revised model is that students should find social and intellectual communities to attain membership and receive support. Even students who initially resist separation will later determine that leaving their groups to succeed in college is appropriate and necessary. These assumptions are not entirely correct. Alternative views that challenge the three aforementioned assumptions are presented next.

A Critical Analysis of the Assumption of Separation

Scholars investigating how minority students make the transition to college should be familiar with the concepts of biculturalism and dual socialization, which challenge the assumption of separation. In addition, scholars should note the problematic issues in relation to the assumption of a dominant culture and the membership assumption.

The Concept of Biculturalism.   While conducting an ethnographic study of poverty and Afro-Americans in a large northern city, Charles A. Valentine (1971) found that accepted cultural deficit and difference models of the time neglected and obscured important elements of the Afro-American culture. Referring to cultural deficit models as an alternative to analyze nonmainstream cultures, the researcher argued that "any theory of class or racial deficits of biological origin is quite undemonstrable, indeed scientifically untestable, in an ethically plural and structurally discriminatory society" (p. 138). While not negating cultural distinctions between black and mainstream cultures, Valentine (1971) observed: "The central theoretical weakness of the 'difference model' is an implicit assumption that different cultures are necessarily competitive alternatives, that distinct cultural systems can enter human experience only as mutually exclusive alternatives, never as intertwined or simultaneously available repertoires" (p. 141). Valentine cited cultural difference models as incorrect and harmful when employed for establishing new educational policies and programs.

As an alternative to predominant cultural difference models, Valentine (1971) proposed the employment of a bicultural educational model. The researcher argued that since many blacks were simultaneously committed to both black and mainstream cultures, the two were not mutually exclusive of each other. Rather, blacks could be simultaneously socialized in two different cultures. He relied on the findings of Steven Polgar (1960), who had earlier found that individuals living on an Indian reservation regularly went through a process he termed "biculturation." Biculturation occurred when individuals were simultaneously enculturated and socialized in two different ways of life. In Polgar's example teenage Mesquakie boys experienced a contemporary form of their traditional Amerindian lifeways and mainstream Euro-American culture.

Valentine (1971) used Polgar's (1960) research to expand the concept of biculturation, the ability of a minority individual to step in and out of the repertoires of two cultures that were seen as distinct and separate (de Anda 1984; see Figure 13.1). For Valentine, biculturation helps explain how people learn and practice both the mainstream culture and ethnic cultures at the same time. He indicates: "the Black community is bicultural in the sense that each Afro-American ethnic segment draws upon a distinctive repertoire of standardized Afro-American group behavior and, simultaneously, patterns derived from the mainstream cultural system of Euro-American deviation. Socialization into both systems begins at an early age, continues throughout life, and is generally of equal importance in most individual lives" (Valentine 1971, p. 143). The

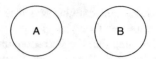

A = Majority Culture

B = Minority Culture

FIGURE 13.1   Two separate cultures
Source: de Anda, 1984

concept of bitculturalism seriously challenges the first two assumptions (noted earlier) of the separation stage.

The Concept of Dual Socialization.   Diane de Anda (1984) elaborates on Valentine's (1971) concept of biculturation, citing six factors that affect biculturalism: (1) the degree of over-lap of commonalty between the two cultures with regard to norms, values, beliefs, perceptions, and the like; (2) the availability of cultural translators, mediators, and models; (3) the amount and type (positive or negative) of corrective feedback provided by each culture regarding attempts to produce normative behavior; (4) the conceptual style and problem-solving approach of the minority individual and their mesh with the prevalent or valued styles of the majority culture; (5) the individual's degree of bilingualism; and (6) the degree of dissimilarity in physical appearance from the majority culture, such as skin color and facial features (p. 102). Unlike Valentine, she indicates that the bicultural experience was possible not because the two cultures were totally disparate, but because there was some overlap between the two cultures (see Figure 13.2). For de Anda, "dual socialization is made possible and facilitated by the amount of overlap between two cultures. That is, the extent to which an individual finds it possible to understand and predict successfully two cultural environments and adjust his or her behavior according to the norms of each culture depends on the extent to which these two cultures share common values, beliefs, perceptions, and norms for prescribed behaviors" (p. 102). In short, de Anda's model is not about individual separation from an old world in search of membership in a new one. Instead, de Anda argues that converging the two worlds could allow individuals to function more effectively and less stressfully in both worlds. This requires changing, indeed transforming, the academic and social culture of institutions of higher education to accommodate culturally diverse students.

Kuh and Whitt (1988) suggest that culture, in the context of higher education, could be described as a "social or normative glue" that is defined by the shared values and beliefs that exist within a college or university while serving four general purposes: (1) conveying a sense of identity; (2) facilitating commitment to an entity, such as the college or peer group, other than

A = Majority Culture

B = Minority Culture

C = Shared Values and Norms

FIGURE 13.2   Biculturation
Source: de Anda, 1984

self; (3) enhancing the stability of a group's social system; and (4) providing a sense-making device that guides and shapes behavior (p. 10). In addition, the researchers propose that the culture of a college or university defines, identifies, and legitimates authority in educational settings. However, they caution that institutions may, perhaps even unwittingly, have "properties deeply embedded in their cultures that make it difficult for members of historically underrepresented groups to prosper socially and environmentally" (p. 15). In cases such as this, students already potentially at risk often find themselves decidedly at odds with prevailing social and cultural norms on campus.

Dual socialization does not occur naturally in a college environment that contains values, conventions, and traditions that are alien to first-generation students, many of whom are minority. Jalomo (1995) substantiates de Anda's dual socialization model in a study of Latino community college students who had completed their first semester. For these students the transition was not linear. Rather, Latino students were found to operate in multiple contexts: the Latino culture, comprised of four subcultures (family, work, barrio, and gang); and the prevailing culture of the community colleges they attended. In the study, students who conveyed difficulty in their transition to college spoke of the growing incongruence between their native environment and the newly encountered college arena. These students indicated that they had maneuvered a number of social domains in their native environment while attempting to meet the growing demands associated with college life. Upon transiting to college, Latinos experienced the downside and upside of college attendance. They expressed some tension and loss associated with separation, although at the same time they experienced excitement at learning new things and making new college friends. They also experienced culture clash as a result of the differences between their home lives and the world of college. To diminish this disjuncture, Jalomo proposes that individuals not totally separate but instead be supported to transit between two cultures.

Levy-Warren (1988) provides additional perspectives to the concept of separation. In analyzing disruptions that people experience in separating from their cultures of origin (culture loss, culture shock), Levy-Warren indicates that the passage involves cultural dislocation and relocation, a disjunctive process that is both internal and external. The internal level involves identity formation—an individual is shedding a part of the self and assuming a new, redefined identity. The external level is the actual move from one geographical location to another and involves the loss of familiar objects and people. Cultural relocation may be highly traumatic if the move is made before the individual has established mental representations of culture. That is, individuals must be able to distinguish differences between their own world and the new world. Consequently, Rendón (1996) argues that rather than asking students to disassociate themselves from their culture, they should be assisted to make modifications in their relationships. The passage to college needs to be gradual, giving students time to slowly break away and move toward healthy individualization.

Theoretically, the concept of dual socialization seriously challenges the assumptions of separation. In addition, there are retention policy considerations. Navigating two landscapes, one of which is almost entirely different from home realities, requires both individual and institutional responsibility. To this end, the critical role of the institution cannot be overstated, yet is often diminished in retention and involvement studies. Tinto highlights the importance of the classroom as a learning community in his 1993 model. However, as noted earlier, Tinto's revised model has yet to gain widespread attention of the higher education research community. Connecting the world of the student to the world of college means that students must be able to find animate and inanimate objects in the new college culture that might evoke a sense of comfort that originates in their early cultural upbringing. That is why events and programs such as Black History Month, Women's Studies, and Cinco de Mayo celebrations are so important. Converging two worlds requires the use of cultural translators, mediators, and role models to (1) provide information and guidance that can help students decipher unfamiliar college customs and rituals, (2) mediate problems that arise from disjunctions between students' cultural traits and the prevailing campus culture, and (3) model behaviors that are amenable with the norms, values, and beliefs of the majority and minority cultures (Jalomo 1995; Rendón 1996; de Anda 1984).

The Assumption of a Dominant Culture.   Tierney's (1992) critique of the Tinto model substantiates de Anda's convergence perspective. Tierney argues that Tinto did not consider an important point in Van Gennep's theory. The point was that Van Gennep uses the term *ritual* to speak of rites of passage within the same specific culture, i.e., some Indian cultures have puberty rituals designed specifically for girls and others specifically for boys. Here, the ritual is nondisruptive. However, Tinto employs the use of *ritual* in a way that "individuals from one culture, such as Apache, are to undergo a ritual in another culture, such as Anglo" (p. 609). In this case the transition constitutes a disjuncture—in effect, students from a minority culture enter a majority world that is vastly different from their sociocultural realities.

However, in his 1993 revised model Tinto argues that the majority of colleges are made up of several, if not many, communities or "subcultures." Rather than conforming to one dominant culture in order to persist, students would have to locate at least one community in which to find membership and support. Further, Tinto notes that membership does not require a full sharing of values. Instead, only some degree of consensus is necessary. Consequently, Tinto explains that the use of the term *membership* is more applicable than *integration*. Of course, safe havens and enclaves have their benefits and drawbacks. One of their key benefits is that they help students break down the institution into manageable parts. However, special communities and programs do not address the real challenge of today's institutions: the total transformation of colleges and universities from monocultural to multicultural institutions. This requires more convergence between the minority student's world and the college world. Further, Hurtado (1997) notes that research based on assimilation/acculturation views group contact as unidirectional in nature (i.e., the ethnic group changes to reflect the mainstream/dominant/white group). Hurtado argues that "this type of approach effectively blocks the possibility that cultural contact can indeed bring change in both the minority and majority groups" (p. 305). In some areas of the nation and in some colleges and universities, minorities are the majority or are rapidly on their way to acquiring majority status. While white students have normally been viewed as the dominant or majority group, future research will have to take into account how group identities and power relationships are changing and the overall impact on student persistence.

The Membership Assumption.   It is also important for scholars to consider that de Anda's concept of "dual socialization—where individuals both develop and sustain membership in new and old cultures—has been the reality of behavior for most Americans who maintain an ethnic identity while coexisting within the dominant culture. In short, many minority students are not likely to give up their affiliations and lose contact with their cultural groups in order to find membership in a new college world. Just as many Latino immigrants maintain extensive and frequent contact with Mexico (Hurtado 1997), many minority students experience multiple associations with their own cultures and their new college realities. Tierney (1992) indicates that American Indian students value group membership over the individualized process of separation. In many Latino cultures separation is often not a viable option, as family is a source of rootedness and strength. This view that both minority and majority groups coexist and actually hold similar attitudes, values, and perceptions has been obliquely (indirectly) established by Nora and Cabrera (1996). Within this context, similarities between white and nonwhite students were noted in attitudes regarding the influence of family, perceptions of discrimination on campus, and educational goals and commitments. Nora and Cabrera's (1996) research validates de Anda's (1984) notion that groups (or minorities) do not need to break all ties with past communities in order to attain membership status in a new or an alien culture, as in the case of minority students who retain their sense of identity and cultural values while integrating in a predominately majority educational environment.

Moreover, the membership option often represents a false choice given the lack of acceptance of racial/ethnic minorities in many dimensions of college life. In fact, many minorities leave college due to "cultural assaults" (Zambrana 1988) to their sense of identity and self-esteem that lead to stress and tension. Though some students may leave, others may exhibit differential patterns of behavior. Some will become subservient to the codes of others, and others may deny their cultural heritage. Still others will manage to turn a negative into a positive—developing a strong sense of ethnic consciousness, i.e., pride in their cultural heritage and awareness of racism, discrimination, sexism, and elitism prevalent in higher education systems (Zambrana 1988).

While more research is needed to substantiate the multiple varieties of external and internal group memberships and their impact on retention, research has substantiated the view that different forms of encouragement and support from family and friends from the students' past communities not only continue to influence students during college enrollment but are instrumental in affecting persistence. These associations negate discriminatory experiences, enhance the social and academic integration of students, and positively affect students' commitments to earning a college degree (Nora and Cabrera 1993, 1996; Nora et al. 1996; Nora, Kraemer; and Itzen 1997; Cabrera, Nora, and Castañeda 1993; Cabrera et al. 1992).

THEORETICAL CONSIDERATIONS REGARDING ACADEMIC/SOCIAL INTEGRATION

Separation and transition are the initial processes associated with Tinto's student retention model. The next stage involves incorporation in institutional life. Tinto (1987) notes that "eventual persistence requires that individuals make the transition to college and become incorporated into the ongoing social and intellectual life of the college" (p. 126). Incorporation is analogous to integration. The term "integration can be understood to refer to the extent which the individual shares the normative attitudes and values of peers and faculty in the institution and abides by the formal and informal structural requirements for membership in that community or in the subgroups of which the individual is a part" (Pascarella and Terenzini 1991, p. 51). To learn more about how incorporation came about, Tinto turned to French sociologist Emile Durkheim (1951) and the study of suicide. Durkheim was interested in the character of the social environment, including social and intellectual characteristics, and its relationship to individual behavior, such as suicide. To draw an analogy between suicidal and dropout behavior, Tinto employed Durkheim's view of "egotistical suicide." Individuals who committed egotistical suicide were unable to become socially or intellectually integrated within communities of society. As noted earlier, interactionalist theory, when used to study minority student retention, has been called into question given that some of the theory's premises are based on an assimilation/acculturation framework.

Problems with the Use of an Acculturation/Assimilation Framework

Hurtado (1997) notes that during the 1960s an assimilation framework was the impetus of research on ethnicity, especially for Mexican Americans. Since assimilation was contingent on the minority group becoming incorporated into the life of the majority group, assimilation scales were developed to measure the quickest and most efficient ways to assimilate immigrants. In

1964 Gordon advanced the notion that individuals could be highly acculturated in one group but remain unassimilated in other dimensions of society. In short, biculturality became a viable option. But the assimilation/acculturation framework had multiple problems, which are listed below.

Focus on Academic Failure as Opposed to Success.   Hurtado (1997) indicates that assimilation/acculturation research has focused on the left tail of the normal distribution curve, "that is, it has focused on cultural adaptations that are not particularly healthy, ones for which the only solutions are to assimilate to the dominant mainstream or spend a lifetime of psychological and social alienation" (p. 312). Some of the recent research (primarily within the past five to ten years) has called for a focus and examination of a variety of adaptations leading to academic success in addition to the repository of traditional research approaches examining academic failure (Hurtado and Garcia 1994).

Exclusion of Contextual and Historical Forces.   Zambrana (1988) notes that during the 1960s and 1970s studies on racial/ethnic communities were in large part descriptive and ahistorical. These descriptions were in line with the cultural deficit model that emphasized the problems or "deficiencies" within these communities, for the most part pathological and disruptive. It was believed that these deficits led to a self-perpetuating cycle of poverty and deprivation. When applied to education, the cultural deficit model suggests that cultural patterns of marginalized groups are essentially inferior and predispose students within those groups to poor academic performance; de Anda (1984) notes that the discrediting of the cultural deficit model led to the ascendance of the cultural difference model that emphasized the uniqueness of each minority culture. An inherent assumption with both of these models was that upward mobility and acculturation were possible to the extent that minority groups approximated the values and norms of the dominant society. However, a model known as "internal colonialism" (Almaguer 1974; Blauner 1972) argued that cultural adaptations of ethnic/racial groups were due more to the organization of economics, labor, and power in the capitalist way the nation was structured than to differences in traits between minority and majority groups. As such, groups that had the experience of conquest were subject to race discrimination in every dimension of organized society, including education (Hurtado 1997).

In her review of cultural studies, Zambrana (1988) notes that "the most limiting aspect of the majority of studies has been their neglect of the relationship of racial/ethnic groups to the social structure" (p. 63). The lives of racial/ethnic minorities are shaped by social forces such as racism, sexism, and discrimination. Yet many researchers tend to view people of color as if they have all the options and privileges of white, middle-class Americans, when this is not often the case.

Lack of Focus on Systemic Barriers.   Rather than focusing on systemic issues in the lives of oppressed people, most past researchers employing an assimilation/acculturation framework have tended to focus on perceived cultural traits or differences (i.e., poor motivation, academic deficiencies) as the source of a group's ability or inability to succeed and be upwardly mobile. This view suggests that students who possess or adopt mainstream cultural norms are capable of moving farther along the educational pipeline than those who lack these cultural traits (Nieto 1996). In opposition to this view, more recent educational research has documented that systemic barriers such as tracking, low expectations, and funding inequities, among others, play a critical role in hindering the educational achievements of ethnic/racial minorities (Oakes 1985; Brint and Karabel 1989; Nieto 1996). Nonetheless, perceptions of minority student inferiority persist to this day and have even been used as a rationale to place restrictions on college access for minorities.

Failure to Challenge Theoretical Assumptions and Paradigms.   Even when minorities are studied, researchers often fail to challenge the philosophical assumptions made in traditional paradigms that are often grounded or developed from studies based on full-time, traditional-age, residential, middle-class, white, male students and/or fail to consider current research that presents a more comprehensive and contextual view of minority student lives and educational experiences. The lack of a grounded historical perspective has led to the frequent omission of minority groups, or else they are identified as a source of their group's problems (a deficit perspective). Myths and stereotypes continue to prevail for racial and ethnic groups simply because there is a void in the incorporation of roles, characteristics, and perceptions of these subgroups. Many times variables are operationally defined in the same manner for all groups involved, thus excluding any cultural or racial differences in perceptions and attitudes. Rather than conducting culturally and racially based studies that can uncover new variables and that can offer insightful and meaningful findings to transform institutional structures that preclude academic success for minority students, invisible hierarchies are left intact. In these cases, minority students are measured simply by scales that reveal their level of acculturation and integration, or lack thereof (Zambrana 1988; Hurtado 1997).

Failure to Connect Theory to Practice.   In his 1993 theory review Tinto acknowledges the importance of policy-relevant research and the importance of the institution in enhancing retention. When theoretical propositions are not compared across different subgroups or when diverse and culturally driven theoretical views are not incorporated in retention studies, institutional policies and practices cannot truly detect or address differences among student groups. Theories developed without using minority student perspectives and/or without "member checks" from the field may miss important details and nuances about the connection between student cultural realities and collegiate experiences. Tierney (1992) elaborates: "The search for an understanding about why students leave college is not merely of theoretical interest; if a model may be built that explains student departure then it may be possible for colleges to retain students" (p. 604).

CONCEPTUAL ISSUES IN INTERACTIONALIST THEORY

There are at least three conceptual problems with social/academic interactionalist theory as used in Tinto's (1975, 1987, 1993) student departure model.

Individual Responsibility as Opposed to Institutional Responsibility

The first conceptual problem is overemphasis on individual responsibility for change and adaptation. In 1987 Tinto emphasized the following points:

> The problems associated with separation and transition to college are conditions that, though stressful, need not in themselves lead to departure. It is the individual's response to those conditions that finally determines staying or leaving. Though external assistance may make a difference, it cannot do so without the individual's willingness to see the adjustments through.
>
> (p. 98)

> To adapt Durkheim's work to the question of individual departure from institutions of higher education we must move to a theory of individual behavior.
>
> (p. 105)

> To move to a theory of individual suicide, and therefore to a theory of individual departure, one

has to take account of the personal attributes of individuals which predispose them to respond to given situations or conditions with particular forms of behavior.

(p. 109)

While Tinto (1987) does indicate that "differences in institutional rates of departure may arise out of discernible differences in the structure of institutional academic and social systems" (p. 107), the overall tone of social/academic integration theory is that individuals, not the system, are responsible for departure. Elaborating on this point, Tierney (1992) argues that social integrationists tend to use anthropological terms in an individualist, rather than a collective, manner. Individuals attend college, become integrated or not, leave or stay, fail or succeed. Absent from the traditional social integrationist view are the distinctions among cultures; differences among students with regard to class, race, gender, and sexual orientation; and the role of group members and the institution in assisting students to succeed.

Nora, Kraemer, and Itzen (1997) and Nora and Cabrera (1993) argue that current quantitative models must include factors that are able to differentiate among racial and ethnic groups or must include measurement approaches (and techniques) that provide indicators of constructs that reflect racial, ethnic, and cultural differences. In a study of student persistence at an exclusively Hispanic two-year institution Nora, Kraemer, and Itzen (1997) employed a different and more culturally sensitive set of items that more closely reflected the manner in which the study's Hispanic students became integrated on their campus. In doing so, the researchers reduced misspecification in the model. The researchers elaborate: "The measures of academic integration used to form the scale not only [represented] possible academic interest and involvement with faculty and staff, but . . . also [reflected] those circumstances (both financial and academic) that [were] prevalent among [the] Hispanic group" (p. 15).

Problems Associated with the Concept of Student Involvement

While interactionalist theory is concerned with the interaction among individuals and institutions, involvement is the mechanism through which student effort is engaged in the academic and social lives of the college. Tinto explains that the 1993 model is "at its core, a model of educational communities that highlights the critical importance of student engagement or involvement in the learning communities of the college" (1993, p. 132). Consequently, it becomes important to address problematic issues related to the involvement dimension implicit in the Tinto model.

Alexander Astin's (1985) theory of student involvement is perhaps the most widely adopted college impact model of student development. According to involvement theory, "the individual plays a central role in determining the extent and nature of growth according to the quality of effort or involvement with the resources provided by the institution" (Pascarella and Terenzini 1991, p. 51). Astin's involvement theory is based on the Freudian notion of cathexis, in which individuals invest psychological energy in objects outside themselves such as friends, families, schooling, jobs, and the like. Astin (1984) defines involvement as "the amount of energy that the student devotes to the academic experience" (p. 27). Indeed, research indicates that the more time and energy students devote to learning and the more intensely they engage in their own education, the greater the achievement, satisfaction with educational experiences, and persistence in college (Pascarella and Terenzini 1991; Tinto 1987).

While both Tinto and Astin would agree that the institution plays an important role in facilitating involvement, and in fact Tinto's 1993 revised model emphasizes this point, practitioners have concentrated on the aspect of individual responsibility. The result is that practitioners have resorted to offering programs to help students get involved but have not focused on active outreach to students. Consequently, few dropout-prone students actually get involved. If practitioners accept the cultural separation assumption without understanding its inherent trauma for nontraditional students, then practitioners will tend to see involvement as a relatively easy task since they will also assume that all students, regardless of background, are ready, willing, and able to get involved.

Researchers who have studied nontraditional students (Terenzini et al. 1994; Rendón 1994; Jalomo 1995) have contributed important findings and modifications to involvement theory. While the importance of involvement cannot be negated, these researchers note that many students, especially nontraditional students, find it difficult to get involved. Important differences between traditional and nontraditional students were not explained in the original conception of student involvement theory. Traditional students often come from upper- to middle-class backgrounds, are predominantly white, and come from families in which at least one parent has attended college and the expectation of college attendance is well established. For traditional students college attendance is a normal rite of passage and a part of family tradition. Consequently, they are more likely to understand and manipulate the values, traditions, and practices of college to their academic advantage. Involvement theory does not emphasize the fact that most two- and four-year colleges are set up to facilitate involvement for traditional students.

On the other hand, nontraditional students often come from working-class backgrounds, are older, work at least part-time, and are predominantly minority and first-generation—the first in their families to attend college (Rendón 1994; Terenzini et al. 1993; Jalomo 1995). Jalomo's (1995) study of Latino first-year community college students found that involvement was difficult for students who found the transition to college troublesome or whose background characteristics did not "fit" the traditional student profile found on most college campuses today. Table 13.1 portrays the characteristics of students who found college involvement difficult. Moreover, Jalomo (1995) found that students required the assistance of cultural translators, mediators, and role models in order to survive or succeed in their first semester in college.

Rendón (1994) found that validation, as opposed to involvement, had transformed nontraditional students into powerful learners. While it is likely that most white and traditional students can become involved on their own in an institutional context that merely affords

TABLE 13.1
Characteristics of Latino Students Who Found It Difficult to Get Involved in Their Community College

Married students with family obligations
Single parents
Students who have been out of school for some time
Students who are the first in their families to attend college
Students who never liked high school or who were rebellious in high school
Students who have had negative experiences with former teachers or administrative staff in elementary and secondary schools
Students who were not involved in academic activities or student groups during high school
Students who did not participate in school-based social activities or student programs during high school
Students who are afraid or feel out of place in the mainstream college culture
Students who have had negative interactions with college faculty or administrative staff
Students who have a hard time adjusting to the fast pace of college
Students who take evening courses when little or no services are available
Students who lack the financial resources to take additional courses or participate in campus-based academic and social activities in college

Source: Jalomo 1995

involvement opportunities (i.e., tutoring centers, clubs and organizations, extracurricular activi-ties), nontraditional students expect active outreach and intervention in order to become involved. Rendón explains: "It appears that nontraditional students do not perceive involvement as *them* taking the initiative. They perceive it when someone takes an active role in assisting them" (p. 44).

Presenting a model of validation, Rendón (1994) notes that what had transformed nontra-ditional students into powerful learners and persisters were incidents in which some individual, either inside or outside class, had validated them. Validating agents made use of interpersonal and academic validation. Validating agents took an active interest in students. They provided encouragement for students and affirmed them as being capable of doing academic work and supported them in their academic endeavors and social adjustment. The critical role of the insti-tution and its agents is underscored in Rendón's validation model. The role of the institution is not simply to offer involvement opportunities, but to take an active role in fostering validation. Faculty, counselors, coaches, and administrators take the initiative to reach out to students and design activities that promote active learning and interpersonal growth among students, faculty, and staff (Rendón 1994).

Focus on the Negative Impact of the External Community

A third conceptual problem with interactionalist theory is that external forces and cultures are seen as distinct and having mainly a negative impact on student involvement. Tinto (1987) acknowledges that family and culture may play an important part in student decisions to depart from college. However, what Tinto (1987) stresses (and what scholars and practitioners are likely to emphasize) is that "in some situations, external social systems may work counter to the demands of institutional life. When the academic and social systems of the institution are weak, the countervailing external demands may seriously undermine the individual's ability to persist on completion" (p. 108). Even in his 1993 revised model, Tinto argues that external ele-ments are secondary to those in college, conditioning but not determining the character of the experience on campus. Researchers have validated some of the negative effects of the external environment. For example, Terenzini et al. (1993) found that "friends who did not attend college could complicate the transition by anchoring students to old networks of friends and patterns of behavior rather than allowing them to explore and learn about their new college environment" (p. 5). Similarly, parents who feel anxious about students leaving home may function as liabilities. Nora et al. (1996) found that minority students who needed to work off-campus for financial reasons were 36 percent more likely to drop out of college than those who did not. Moreover, researchers found that female students, as opposed to male students, who were required to leave campus immediately after class to help care for family members were 83 percent more likely to withdraw.

However, not everything external is a liability. For example, Terenzini et al. (1993) found that precollege friends performed a "bridge function," providing support and encouragement. And with few exceptions, students named family members when asked "Who are the most important people in your life right now?" Jalomo (1995) found that there were more out-of-class agents helping students to make connections on campus than in-class agents. Clearly, much more research is needed to assess the positive and negative influences of the external environment and how students negotiate external influences, not only during the first year of college but through-out the student's collegiate experience.

TAKING RETENTION THEORY TO A HIGHER LEVEL

The conceptual issues presented in this chapter, based both on empirical evidence and conceptual critiques, substantiate that Tinto's college student retention theory needs to be taken to an even higher level of theoretical development. Tinto has done this through extensions and refinements of his theory (Braxton, Sullivan, and Johnson 1997). However, Attinasi (1989, 1994) and Tierney (1992) would likely go as far as rejecting the theory and building another that is capable of reflecting subtle processes (particularly cultural and political and emerging from qualitative analysis) involved in persistence. We believe that with all that is now known about student retention, it is quite possible that a totally new theory is needed to take Tinto's theory to a different level. Moreover, knowledge from disciplines other than education can also be used to develop new theoretical perspectives regarding student retention. For example, Hurtado (1997) has developed a "social engagement model [that] takes into account gender as well as other significant social identities like ethnicity/race, class, and sexuality to study how groups change as they come into contact with each other" (p. 299).

Employing a social psychology perspective, Hurtado (1997) advocates that understanding cultural transformations in an increasingly complex and multicultural society, as in the case when students from one group enter the sphere of social engagement of another group, requires not an assimilation/acculturation framework, but a social engagement model. Hurtado (1994) has employed a social engagement framework to study the participation of Latino parents in school. Hurtado's analysis of Latino parents' participation in school is quite similar to how one might analyze college student retention.

For example, research findings illustrate that working-class Latino students are not as likely to get involved in the academic and social domains of the college as often as whites do. Engagement is usually defined as participating in clubs and organizations, meeting with faculty in and out of class, etc. Hurtado would argue that this narrow definition of student engagement is predominately based in the dominant group's perspective and not from the Latino students' view of what is possible and desirable for them. Indeed, Rendón (1994), Jaloino (1995), and Terenzini et al. (1994) have found that involvement is not easy for nontraditional students from working-class backgrounds and that both in- and out-of-class validation were essential to their engagement and persistence. Validation is a powerful, interactive process involving a student and a validating agent. Much of the validation occurred out of class (with friends, parents, spouses, etc.), substantiating that there are other forms of engagement that can have a positive impact on persistence. These researchers employed qualitative methods that allowed students to express who and what was making a difference in their academic lives and why this was so.

If these researchers had relied only on an assimilation/acculturation framework (i.e., narrowly measuring student traits that restricted minority group involvement), then they most likely would have reached the following conclusions:

1. Latino students from working-class backgrounds are not as academically and socially integrated in college as are white students, leading to their higher dropout rate.
2. Traditional, primarily white students from upper- and middle-class backgrounds are more engaged in college than Latino students, which accounts for their higher levels of educational adjustment and attainment.
3. Consequently, we need to encourage working-class Latino students to avail themselves of services and opportunities that can increase their college retention rates. Further, because white students score the highest on scales of college involvement, they are the models all students should emulate.

An assimilation/acculturation framework would not allow Latino students to contribute their own perceptions and definitions of all that constitutes integration. Nor would their definitions influence the views of white students. We would also not be able to discuss the internal variations of each group, i.e., there are Hispanic students who exhibit very high achievement and engagement levels, and there are white students who do not. Many studies may not capture much of the variability in withdrawal decisions because of the misspecification of important constructs. Findings may turn out to be statistically significant, even though very little of the variance is explained. In these cases what may be most interesting is not what was statistically significant. Rather, the most important finding could be that there are other multiple, unaccounted factors that may be influencing retention.

Hurtado (1997) explains that a social engagement model, which has at its core a definitional approach to differences in social adaptations, would yield different results. Besides standard measures of college integration, there would be measures that allowed different groups of students to provide their own definitions of what they consider to be engagement and why. It could very well be that Latino students would report that they considered cultural activities, external relationships with family and friends, and race-based programs as essential and vital to their personal and academic development. Students could also identify the systemic barriers to integration. Similarities among the different ethnic/racial groups in terms of engagement and barriers related to involvement could also be identified. These variables could then be incorporated into quantitative models for statistical testing. Strategies for facilitating in- and out-of-class involvement for *both* minority and majority students could be generated from these findings. The key issue is that the sole use of an acculturation/assimilation framework to study retention does not go far enough.

Taking existing retention/involvement theory to a more sophisticated level will require a thorough, thoughtful, and critical analysis of all the quantitative and qualitative data that have been generated to date. Rather than operate in isolation, quantitative and qualitative researchers should be open to each other's methods, share findings, and probe further into the meaning of their results. We should also be open to theory developments in fields other than education. Multimethod approaches to the study of retention are likely to lift the current corpus of college persistence research. In short, we believe that the future of college student retention research offers exciting and viable possibilities both to uncover the dynamics involved in retention and to use data to shape practice and policy.

CONCLUSION

Researchers employing quantitative models based on Tinto's (1975, 1987) depiction of student persistence have conceptually advanced some of the factors and interrelationships postulated in Tinto's model (i.e., Nora and Cabrera 1993, 1996; Nora et al. 1996; Cabrera and Nora 1995; Cabrera, Nora, and Castañeda 1992, 1993). Qualitative studies also provide some support to Tinto's propositions (Terenzini et al. 1993; Jalomo 1995). But while traditional theories of student retention and involvement have been useful in providing a foundation for the study of persistence, they need to be taken further, as much more work needs to be done to uncover race, class, and gender issues (among others) that impact retention for diverse students in diverse institutions. Certainly, the theoretical issues regarding separation, transition, and incorporation presented in this chapter provide avenues for conducting future research. Yet we stress that the ideas presented here are intended to go beyond stirring intellectual discussion that will lift theory and research.

Minority students are altering the nature of higher education in many ways. Over the past twenty years we have witnessed dramatic changes in the classroom and the curriculum (with the inclusion of ethnic/racial perspectives and the use of learning communities), in student services (with race-based programs), and in faculty and staff composition, among other areas. While we believe that theory building is important, out of scholarly discussions and research should come advances in the development and dramatic transformation of academic and student services. Assuming that good social scientists are also caring humanitarians, the goal of student retention research transcends making conceptual modifications in theoretical models. In the end, students will elect to stay or leave college not so much because of a theory, but because college and university faculty and administrators have made transformative shifts in governance, curriculum development, in- and out-of-class teaching and learning, student programming, and other institutional dimensions that affect students on a daily basis. Consequently, connecting retention research to field practitioners and policy makers in new and creative ways that involve collaborative relationships and mutual learning experiences can take student retention research to a whole new level of theoretical accuracy and applicability.

REFERENCES

Allen, W. R. 1984. Race consciousness and collective commitments among black students on white campuses. *Western Journal of Black Studies* 8 (3): 156–166.

Almaguer, T. 1974. Historical notes on Chicano oppression: The dialectics of racial and class domination in North America. *Aztlán* 5 (1–2): 27–56.

Astin, A. 1984. Student involvement: A developmental theory for higher education. *Journal of College Student Personnel* 12 (July): 297–308.

Astin, A. 1985. *Achieving educational excellence: A critical assessment of priorities and practices in higher education.* San Francisco: Jossey-Bass.

Attinasi, Jr., L. 1989. Getting in: Mexican Americans' perceptions of university attendance and the implications for freshman year persistence. *Journal of Higher Education* 60 (3): 247–277.

Attinasi, Jr., L. 1994. Is going to college a rite of passage? Paper presented at the annual meeting of the American Research Association, New Orleans, La.

Belenky, M., B. Clinchy, N. Goldberger, and J. Tarule. 1986. *Women's ways of knowing.* New York: Basic Books, Inc.

Blauner, R. 1972. *Racial oppression in America.* New York: Harper & Row.

Braxton, J. M., A. V. S. Sullivan, and R. M. Johnson. 1997. Appraising Tinto's theory of college student departure. In J. C. Smart (ed.), *Higher education: A handbook of theory and research,* vol. 12, pp. 107–164. New York: Agathon Press.

Brint, S., and J. Karabel. 1989. *The directed dream: Community colleges and the promise of educational opportunity in America, 1900–1985.* New York: Oxford University Press.

Cabrera, A. F, and A. Nora. 1994. College students' perceptions of prejudice and discrimination and their feelings of alienation. *Review of Education, Pedagogy, and Cultural Studies* 16: 387–409.

Cabrera, A. F, A. Nora, and M. B. Castañeda. 1992. The role of finances in the student persistence process: A structural model. *Research in Higher Education* 33 (5): 571–594.

Cabrera, A. F, A. Nora, and M. B. Castañeda. 1993. College persistence: Structural equations modeling test of an integrated model of student retention. *Journal of Higher Education* 64 (2): 123–139.

Cabrera, A. F, M. B. Castañeda, A. Nora, and D. Hengstler. 1992. The convergent and discriminant validity between two theories of college persistence. *Journal of Higher Education* 63 (2): 143–164.

Caplan, N., and S. Nelson. 1973. The nature and consequences of psychological research on social problems. *American Psychologist* 28 (3): 199–211.

de Anda, D. 1984. Bicultural socialization: Factors affecting the minority experience. *Social Work* 29 (2): 101–107.

Durkheim, E. 1951. *Suicide: A study in sociology.* Edited by G. Simpson. Translated by J. A. Spaulding and E. Simpson. Originally published in 1897. Glencoe, Ill.: The Free Press.

Fleming, J. 1984. *Blacks in college*. San Francisco: Jossey-Bass.

Galindo, R., and K. Escamilla. 1995. A biographical perspective on Chicano educational success. *The Urban Review* 27 (1).

Gandara, P. 1993. *Choosing higher education: The educational mobility of Chicano students*. Report to the Latina/Latino Policy Research Program, California Policy Seminar. (ERIC Document Reproduction Service No. ED 374 942).

Gordon, M. M. 1964. *Assimilation in American life: The role of race, religion, and national origins*. New York: Oxford University Press.

Gurin, P., and E. Epps. 1975. *Black consciousness, identity and achievement*. New York: John Wiley & Sons.

Harvey, W. B., and L. Williams. 1989. Historically black colleges: Models for increasing minority representation. *Journal of Black Studies* 21 (3): 238.

Hurtado, A. 1997. Understanding multiple group identities: Inserting women into cultural transformations. *Journal of Social Issues* 53 (2): 299–328.

Hurtado, A., and E. Garcia. 1994. The educational achievement of Latinos: Barriers and successes. Santa Cruz: Regents of the University of California.

Jalomo, R. 1995. *Latino students in transition: An analysis of the first-year experience in community college*. Ph.D. diss., Arizona State University, Tempe.

Kraemer, B. A. 1997. The academic and social integration of Hispanic students into college. *Review of Higher Education* 20: 163–179.

Kuh, G., and E. Whitt. 1988. *The invisible tapestry: Culture in American colleges and universities*. ASHE-ERICD Higher Education Report.

Levy-Warren, M. H. 1988. Moving to a new culture: Cultural identity, loss, and mourning. In Bloom-Fesback & Associates (eds.), *The psychology of separation and loss*. San Francisco: Jossey-Bass.

London, H. 1978. *The culture of a community college*. New York: Praeger.

London, H. 1989. Breaking away: A study of first generation college students and their families. *American Journal of Education* 97 (February): 144–170.

Lowe, M. (1989). *Chicano students' perceptions of their community college experience with implications for persistence: A naturalistic inquiry*. Ph.D. diss., Arizona State University, Tempe.

Melchior-Walsh, S. 1994. *Sociocultural alienation: Experiences of North American Indian students in higher education*. Ph.D. diss., Arizona State University, Tempe.

Mow, S., and M. Nettles. 1990. Minority student access to, and persistence and performance in, college: A review of the trends and research literature. In J. C. Smart (ed.), *Higher education: A handbook of theory and research*, vol. 6, pp. 35–105. New York: Agathon Press.

Nettles, M., C. Gosman, A. Thoeny, and B. Dandrige. 1985. *The causes and consequences of college students' attrition rates, progression rates and grade point averages*. Nashville, Tenn.: Higher Education Commission.

Nieto, S. 1996. *Affirming diversity: The sociopolitical context of multicultural education*. 2d ed. New York: Longman.

Noel, L., R. Levitz, and D. Saluri. 1985. *Increasing student retention: Effective programs and practices for reducing the dropout rate*. San Francisco: Jossey-Bass.

Nora, A. 1987. Determinants of retention among Chicano college students: A structural model. *Research in Higher Education* 26 (1): 31–59.

Nora, A., and A. F. Cabrera. 1993. The construct validity of institutional commitment: A confirmatory factor analysis. *Research in Higher Education* 34 (2): 243–262.

Nora, A., and A. F. Cabrera. 1996. The role of perceptions of prejudice and discrimination on the adjustment of minority students to college. *Journal of Higher Education* 67 (2): 119–148.

Nora, A., and L. I. Rendón. 1988. Hispanic students in community colleges: Reconciling access with outcomes. In L. Weis (ed.), *Class, race, and gender in U.S. education*, pp. 126–143. New York: State University Press.

Nora, A., and L. I. Rendón. 1990. Determinants of predisposition to transfer among community college students: A structural model. *Research in Higher Education* 31: 235–255.

Nora, A., L. Attinasi, and A. Matonak. 1990. Testing qualitative indicators of precollege factors in Tinto's attrition model: A community college student population. *Review of Higher Education* 13 (3): 337–356.

Nora, A., B. Kraemer, and R. Itzen. 1997. Factors affecting the persistence of Hispanic college students. Paper presented at the annual meeting of the Association for the Study of Higher Education, November.

Nora, A., A. F. Cabrera, L. Hagedorn, and E. T. Pascarella. 1996. Differential impacts of academic and social experiences on college-related behavioral outcomes across different ethnic and gender groups at four-year institutions. *Research in Higher Education* 37 (4): 427–452.

Oakes, J. 1985. *Keeping track. How schools structure inequality*. New Haven, Conn.: Yale University Press.

Ogbu, J. U. 1978. *Minority education and caste: The American system in cross-cultural perspective*. New York: Academic Press.

Ogbu, J. U. 1987. Variability in minority school performance: A problem in search of an explanation. *Anthropology and Education Quarterly* 18 (4): 312–334.

Olivas, M. 1979. *The dilemma of access: Minorities in two year colleges*. Washington, D.C.: Howard University Press.

Pascarella, E. T. 1980. Student-faculty informal contact and college outcomes. *Review of Educational Research* 50: 545–595.

Pascarella, E., and P. Terenzini. 1991. *How college affects students: Findings and insights from twenty years of research*. San Francisco: Jossey-Bass.

Pavel, M. 1992. The application of Tinto's model to a Native American student population. Paper presented at the annual meeting of the Association for the Study of Higher Education in November.

Polgar, S. 1960. Biculturation of Mesquakie teenage boys. *American Anthropologist* 62: 217–235.

Rendón, L. I. 1982. *Chicano students in south Texas community colleges: A study of student—and institution-related determinants of educational outcomes*. Ph.D. diss., University of Michigan, Ann Arbor.

Rendón, L. 1. 1994. Validating culturally diverse students: Toward a new model of learning and student development. *Innovative Higher Education* 19 (1): 23–32.

Rendón, L. I., and R. O. Hope. 1996. *Educating a new majority*. San Francisco: Jossey-Bass.

Rosaldo, R. 1989. *Culture and truth: The remaking of social analysis*. Boston: Beacon Press.

Terenzini, P., K. Allison, P. Gregg, R. Jalomo, S. Millar, L. I. Rendón, and L. Upcraft. 1993. *The transition to college: Easing the passage. A summary of the research findings of the Out-of-Class Experiences Program*. University Park, Pa.: National Center on Postsecondary Teaching, Learning, & Assessment.

Terenzini, P., L. I. Rendón, L. Upcraft, S. Millar, K. Allison, P. Gregg, and R. Jalomo. 1994. The transition to college: Diverse students, diverse stories. *Research in Higher Education* 35 (1): 57–73.

Thomas, G. E. 1984. *Black college students and factors influencing their major field choice*. Atlanta: Southern Education Foundation.

Tierney, W. 1992. An anthropological analysis of student participation in college. *Journal of Higher Education* 63 (6): 603–618.

Tierney, W. 1993. *Building communities of difference: Higher education in the 21st century*. Westport, Conn.: Bergin & Garvey.

Tinto, V. 1987. *Leaving college: Rethinking the causes and cures of student departure*. Chicago: University of Chicago Press.

Tinto, V. 1993. *Leaving college: Rethinking the causes and cures of student attrition*. Chicago: University of Chicago Press.

Valadez, J. 1996. Educational access and social mobility. *Review of Higher Education* 19 (4): 391–409.

Valentine, C. A. 1971. Deficit, difference, and bicultural models of Afro-American behavior. *Harvard Educational Review* 41 (2): 137–157.

Van Gennep, A. 1960. *The rites of passage*. Translated by M. B. Vizedom and G. 1. Caffee. Chicago: University of Chicago Press.

Weis, L. 1985. *Between two worlds: Black students in an urban community college.* Boston: Routledge and Kegan Paul.

Wright, B. 1988. For the children of the infidels?: American Indian education in the colonial colleges. *American Indian Culture and Research Journal* 12: 1–14.

Wycoff, S. 1996. Academic performance of Mexican-American women: Sources of support that serve as motivating variables. *Journal of Multicultural Counseling and Development* 24 (July): 146–155.

Zambrana, R. E. 1988. Toward understanding the educational trajectory and socialization of Latina women. In T. McKenna and F. I. Ortiz (eds.), *The broken web: The educational experience of Hispanic American women,* pp. 61–77. Claremont, Calif.: The Tomás Rivera Center.

14

Diversity and Higher Education

Theory and Impact on Educational Outcomes

Patricia Gurin, Eric L. Dey, Sylvia Hurtado, and Gerald Gurin

Educators in U.S. higher education have long argued that affirmative action policies are justified because they ensure the creation of the racially and ethnically diverse student bodies essential to providing the best possible educational environment for students, white and minority alike. Yet until recently these arguments have lacked empirical evidence and a strong theoretical rationale to support the link between diversity and educational outcomes. As Jonathan Alger, former counsel for the American Association of University Professors, argues: "The unfinished homework in the affirmative action debate concerns the development of an articulated vision—supported by a strong evidentiary basis—of the educational benefits of racial diversity in higher education" (1998, p. 74). This suggests not only that educators must clarify the conceptual link between diversity and learning in educational practice, but also that educational researchers play a key role in providing evidence on whether diversity contributes to achieving the central goals of higher education. The purpose of this chapter is both to provide a theory of how diversity can be linked to educational outcomes in higher education and to test this theory using national data and data from students at the University of Michigan—an institution that has faced affirmative action legal challenges.

In the 1978 case *Regents of the University of California v. Bakke*, U.S. Supreme Court Justice Lewis Powell wrote the pivotal opinion, arguing that the "atmosphere of 'speculation, experiment and creation'—so essential to the quality of higher education—is widely believed to be promoted by a diverse student body. . . . It is not too much to say that the nation's future depends upon leaders trained through wide exposure to the ideas and mores of students as diverse as this Nation of many peoples" (p. 2760).[1] Since the *Bakke* decision, the educational benefits of diversity as a compelling governmental interest have provided the primary justification for affirmative action at selective institutions across the country.[2] However, the diversity argument has not been supported in all lower court cases since the original *Bakke* decision. For example, in *Hopwood v. University of Texas*, the Fifth Circuit Court of Appeals denied that diversity has any impact on educational experience: "The use of race, in and of itself, to choose students simply achieves a student body that looks different. Such a criterion is no more rational on its own terms than would be choices based upon the physical size or blood type of applicants" (*Hopwood*, 1996, p. 950). If this statement were true, there would be no basis for arguing that there was a compelling interest in a racially/ethnically diverse student body. However, such a conclusion flies in the face of the role that race and ethnicity have played in our polity and society. As Victor Bolden, David Goldberg, and Dennis Parker point out, "No constitutional compromise was required over blood type; no civil war was fought and no Southern Manifesto signed over physical size" (1999, p. 27).

Since the *Hopwood* decision, courts across the country have produced conflicting rulings on diversity as a compelling governmental interest. In *Smith v. University of Washington Law School* (2001), the Ninth Circuit Court of Appeals affirmed the district court's ruling that *Bakke* is still good law and stands for the proposition that educational diversity can be a compelling governmental interest that justifies race-sensitive admissions programs. In *Johnson v. Board of Regents of the University of Georgia* (2001), the Eleventh Circuit Court of Appeals declined to rule on the question of whether diversity is a compelling governmental interest but struck down the University of Georgia's admissions policy on the grounds that it was not "narrowly tailored" to that interest. In two cases involving the University of Michigan, one challenging its undergraduate admissions and the other its law school admissions, two different rulings on diversity as a compelling governmental interest were given at the district court level. In *Gratz v. Bollinger, et al.* (2000), the court ruled on summary judgment in favor of the University of Michigan, upholding its current undergraduate admissions policy and finding that diversity was a compelling governmental interest that justified the policy. In *Grutter v. Bollinger, et al.* (2002), the court held that the educational benefits of diversity are not a compelling state interest, and even if they were, the law school's policy was not "narrowly tailored" to the interest of diversity. Both cases were appealed to the Sixth Circuit Court of Appeals, which heard arguments in December 2001. This court overturned the lower court decision in *Grutter*, deciding in favor of the university and setting the stage for an appeal to the U.S. Supreme Court.[3] It is clear from these now-famous higher education cases that the question of whether *Bakke* is still good law and whether diversity is a compelling state interest justifying the use of race-sensitive admissions policies remains controversial. It is also clear that diversity is the primary basis for arguing the constitutionality of using race as one of many factors in college admission, and thus research on *whether* and *how* diversity might affect education is of crucial legal and practical importance.

It is important to explain how higher education might expose students to racial and ethnic diversity, since they may experience it in several ways. First, students attend colleges with different levels of racial/ethnic diversity in their student bodies. This has been termed *structural diversity*, or the numerical representation of diverse groups (Hurtado, Milem, Clayton-Peterson, & Allen, 1999). Although structural diversity increases the probability that students will encounter others of diverse backgrounds, given the U.S. history of race relations, simply attending an ethnically diverse college does not guarantee that students will have the meaningful intergroup interactions that social psychologist Gordon Allport (1954) suggested in his classic book, *The Nature of Prejudice*, are important for the reduction of racial prejudice. For this reason, a second definition of racial/ethnic diversity is important, one that involves both the *frequency* and the *quality* of intergroup interaction as keys to meaningful diversity experiences during college, or what we term *informal interactional diversity*. Although these informal interactions with racially diverse peers can occur in many campus contexts, the majority of them occur outside of the classroom. Such interactions may include informal discussions, daily interactions in residence halls, campus events, and social activities (antonio, 1998; Chang, 1996). Finally, a third form of diversity experience includes learning about diverse people (content knowledge) and gaining experience with diverse peers in the classroom, or what we term *classroom diversity*. We contend that the impact of racial/ethnic diversity on educational outcomes comes primarily from engagement with diverse peers in the informal campus environment and in college classrooms. Structural diversity is a necessary but insufficient condition for maximal educational benefits; therefore, the theory that guides our study is based on students' actual engagement with diverse peers.

Recent reviews of educational research, as well as summaries of new studies, present an emerging body of scholarship that speaks directly to the benefits of a racially/ethnically diverse postsecondary educational experience (Hurtado et al., 1999; Milem & Hakuta, 2000; Orfield, 2001; Smith, 1997). The evidence for the diversity rationale for affirmative action has come from four approaches to research:

1. students' subjective assessments of the benefits they receive from interacting with diverse peers (e.g., Orfield & Whitla, 1999);
2. faculty assessments about the impact of diversity on student learning or on other outcomes related to the missions of their universities (e.g., Maruyama, Moreno, Gudeman, & Marin, 2000);
3. analyses of monetary and nonmonetary returns to students and the larger community in terms of graduation rates, attainment of advanced and professional degrees that prepare students to become leaders in underserved communities, personal income or other post-college attainment that results from attending highly selective institutions where affirmative action is critical to achieving diversity (e.g., Bowen & Bok, 1998; Bowen, Bok, & Burkhart, 1999; Komaromy et al., 1997);
4. analyses tying diversity experience during the college years to a wide variety of educational outcomes (Astin, 1993a, 1993b; Chang, 1996; Chang, Witt-Sandis, & Hakuta, 1999; Hurtado, 2001; Pascarella, Edison, Nora, Hagedorn, & Terenzini, 1996; Terenzini, Rendon et al., 1994; Terenzini, Springer, Pascarella, & Nora, 1994).

It is important to note that, across these different approaches and different samples of students and faculty, researchers have found similar results showing that a wide variety of individual, institutional, and societal benefits are linked with diversity experiences.

The research reported here is an example of the fourth approach in which we compare how different types of diversity experiences are associated with differences in educational outcomes among students from different racial and ethnic backgrounds. We first present the theoretical foundation for the educational value of racial/ethnic diversity, and then we examine the effects of two kinds of diversity experiences—diversity in the formal classroom and in the informal campus environment—on different educational outcomes.

THEORETICAL FOUNDATIONS FOR THE EFFECT OF DIVERSITY

Racial and ethnic diversity may promote a broad range of educational outcomes, but we focus on two general categories. Learning outcomes include active thinking skills, intellectual engagement and motivation, and a variety of academic skills. Democracy outcomes include perspective-taking, citizenship engagement, racial and cultural understanding, and judgment of the compatibility among different groups in a democracy. The impact of diversity on learning and democracy outcomes is believed to be especially important during the college years because students are at a critical developmental stage, which takes place in institutions explicitly constituted to promote late adolescent development.

The Critical Importance of Higher Education

In essays that profoundly affected our understanding of social development, psychologist Erik Erikson (1946, 1956) introduced the concept of identity and argued that late adolescence and early adulthood are the unique times when a sense of personal and social identity is formed. Identity involves two important elements: a persistent sameness within oneself and a persistent sharing with others. Erikson theorized that identity develops best when young people are given a psychosocial moratorium—a time and a place in which they can experiment with different social roles before making permanent commitments to an occupation, to intimate relationships, to social and political groups and ideas, and to a philosophy of life. We argue that such a moratorium should ideally involve a confrontation with diversity and complexity, lest young people passively make commitments based on their past experiences, rather than actively think and make decisions informed by new and more complex perspectives and relationships.

Institutions of higher education can provide an opportunity for such a psychosocial moratorium, thus supporting young adults through this identity development stage. Residential colleges and universities provide many students with an opportunity to experiment with new ideas, new relationships, and new roles. Peer influences play a normative role in this development, and students are able to explore options and possibilities before making permanent adult commitments. Yet not all institutions of higher education serve this developmental function equally well (Pascarella & Terenzini, 1991). Higher education is especially influential when its social milieu is different from students' home and community background and when it is diverse and complex enough to encourage intellectual experimentation and recognition of varied future possibilities. We maintain that attending college in one's home environment or replicating the home community's social life and expectations in a homogeneous college that is simply an extension of the home community impedes the personal struggle and conscious thought that are so important for identity development.

Sociologist Theodore Newcomb's classic study of students at Bennington College (1943) supported Erikson's assertion that late adolescence is a time to determine one's relationship to the sociopolitical world and affirmed the developmental impact of the college experience. Newcomb's study demonstrated that political and social attitudes—what Erikson would call one aspect of social identity—are quite malleable in late adolescence and that change occurred particularly in those students to whom Bennington presented new and different ideas and attitudes. Peer influence was critical in shaping the attitudinal changes that Newcomb documented. Follow-ups with these students showed that the attitudes formed during the college experience were quite stable, even twenty-five (Newcomb, Koenig, Flacks, & Warwick, 1967) and fifty years later (Alwin, Cohen, & Newcomb, 1991).

Developmental theorists emphasize that discontinuity and discrepancy spur cognitive growth. Jean Piaget (1971, 1975/1985) termed this process *disequilibrium*. Drawing on these theories, psychologist Diane Ruble (1994) offers a model that ties developmental change to life transitions such as going to college. Transitions are significant because they present new situations about which individuals know little and in which they will experience uncertainty. The early phase of a transition, what Ruble calls construction, is especially important, since people have to seek information in order to make sense of the new situation. Under these conditions individuals are likely to undergo cognitive growth unless they are able to retreat to a familiar world. Ruble's model gives special importance to the first year of college, since it is during this time that classroom and social relationships discrepant from students' home environments become especially important in fostering cognitive growth.

Writing long before the controversies about diversity and affirmative action became politically important or were studied academically, Erikson, Newcomb, and Piaget were not making an explicit case for racial/ethnic diversity. Nonetheless, their arguments about the significance of discontinuity and the power of a late adolescence/early adulthood moratorium provide a strong theoretical rationale for the importance of bringing students from varied backgrounds together to create a diverse and complex learning environment.

Campus environments and policies that foster interaction among diverse students are discontinuous from the home environments of many American students. Because of the racial separation that persists in this country, most students have lived in segregated communities before coming to college. The work of Gary Orfield and associates documents a deepening segregation in U.S. public schools (Orfield, 2001; Orfield, Bachmeier, James, & Eitle, 1997; Orfield & Kurlaender, 1999; Orfield & Miller, 1998). This segregated precollege educational background means that many students, White and minority alike, enter college without experience with diverse peers. Colleges that diversify their student bodies and institute policies that foster genuine interaction across race and ethnicity provide the first opportunity for many students to learn from peers with different cultures, values, and experiences. Genuine interaction goes far beyond mere contact and includes learning about difference in background, experience, and perspectives, as well as getting to know one another individually in an intimate enough way to discern common goals and personal qualities. In this kind of interaction—in and out of the classroom—diverse peers will learn from each other. This can be viewed as extending the traditional conception of a liberal education as one "intended to break down the narrow certainties and provincial vision with which we are born" (Association of American Colleges and Universities, 1985, p. 22).

Learning Outcomes

As educators, we might expect that a curriculum that deals explicitly with social and cultural diversity and a learning environment in which diverse students interact frequently with one another would affect the content of what is learned. However, based on the recent social psychological research that we discuss below, we consider the less obvious notion that features of the learning environment affect students' modes of thought. In this study we hypothesize that a curriculum that exposes students to knowledge about race and ethnicity acquired through the curriculum and classroom environment and to interactions with peers from diverse racial and ethnic backgrounds in the informal college environment will foster a learning environment that supports active thinking and intellectual engagement.

Research in social psychology over the past twenty years has shown that active engagement in learning and thinking cannot be assumed (Bargh, 1997). This research confirms that much apparent thinking and thoughtful action are actually automatic, or what psychologist Ellen Langer (1978) calls mindless. To some extent, mindlessness is the result of previous learning that has become so routine that thinking is unnecessary. Instead, scripts or schemas that are activated and operate automatically guide these learned routines. Some argue that mindlessness is necessary because there are too many stimuli in the world to which to pay attention. It is more efficient for us to select only a few stimuli or, better still, to go on automatic pilot—to be what some people call cognitive misers (Fiske, 1993; Hilton & von Hippel, 1996).

Psychologist John Bargh (1997) reviews both historical and recent research evidence showing that automatic psychological processes play a pervasive role in all aspects of everyday thinking. He concludes that automatic thinking is evident not only in perceptual processes (such as categorization) and in the execution of perceptional and motor skills (such as driving and typing), but that it is also pervasive in evaluation, emotional reactions, determination of goals, and social behavior itself. Bargh uses the term *preconscious* to describe processes that act as mental servants to take over from conscious, effortful thinking. One of our tasks as educators is to interrupt these automatic processes and facilitate active thinking in our students.

In one early study indicating the pervasiveness of automatic thinking, Langer (1978) described the many positive psychological benefits that people derive from using active, effortful, conscious modes of thought. She also argued that such thinking helps people develop new ideas and ways of processing information that may have been available to them but were simply not often used. In several experimental studies, she showed that such thinking increases alertness and greater mental activity, which fosters better learning and supports the developmental goals of higher education.

What are the conditions that encourage effortful, mindful, and conscious modes of thought? Langer (1978) contends that people will engage in such modes of thought when they encounter a situation for which they have no script or when the environment demands more than their current scripts provide, such as an encounter discrepant with their past experience. These conditions are similar to what sociologist Rose Coser (1975) calls complex social structures—situations where we encounter people who are unfamiliar to us, when these people challenge us to think or act in new ways, when people and relationships change and thus produce unpredictability, and when people we encounter hold different expectations of us. Coser shows that people who function within complex social structures develop a clearer and stronger sense of individuality and a deeper understanding of the social world.[4]

The specific environmental features that Langer and Coser suggest will promote mental activity are compatible with cognitive-developmental theories. In general, those theories posit that cognitive growth is fostered by discontinuity and discrepancy (as in Piaget's notion of disequilibrium). To learn or grow cognitively, individuals need to recognize cognitive conflicts or contradictions, situations that, as psychologist Diane Ruble (1994) argues, then lead to a state of uncertainty, instability, and possibly anxiety (see also Acredolo & O'Connor, 1991; Berlyne, 1970; Doise & Palmonaari, 1984). Ruble states:

> Such a state may occur for a number of reasons. . . . It may be generated either internally via the recognition of incompatible cognitions or externally during social interaction. The latter is particularly relevant to many types of life transitions, because such transitions are likely to alter the probability of encountering people whose viewpoints differ from one's own.
>
> (1994, p. 171)

Racial and ethnic diversity in the student body and university efforts to foster opportunities for diverse students to interact and learn from each other in and out of the classroom offer college students who have grown up in the racially segregated United States the very features that these theories suggest will foster active thinking and personal development. These features include:

- novelty and unfamiliarity that occurs upon the transition to college
- opportunities to identify discrepancies between students with distinct pre-college social experiences[5]

A White student, evaluating a course on intergroup relations that one of the authors taught at the University of Michigan, conveys the importance of these facets of diversity:

> I come from a town in Michigan where everyone was white, middle-class and generally pretty closed-down to the rest of the world, although we didn't think so. It never touched us, so I never questioned the fact that we were "normal" and everyone else was "different." Listening to other students in the class, especially the African American students from Detroit and other urban areas just blew me away. We only live a few hours away and yet we live in completely separate worlds. Even more shocking was the fact that they knew about "my world" and I knew nothing about theirs. Nor did I think that this was even a problem at first. I realize now that many people like me can go through life and not have to see another point of view, that somehow we are protected from

it. The beginning for me was when I realized that not everyone shares the same views as I, and that our different experiences have a lot to do with that.

One of our primary goals was to discover whether such encounters with diversity contribute to learning outcomes, not only among students at the University of Michigan but also among those attending a variety of four-year institutions across the country. A second key goal was to understand the extent to which these same diversity experiences contribute to the development of the skills and dispositions that students will need to be leaders in a pluralistic democracy.

Democracy Outcomes

From the time the founding fathers debated what form U.S. democracy should take—representational or directly participatory—education has been seen as the key to achieving an informed citizenry. In the compromise they reached involving both representation and broad participation, education was the mechanism that was to make broad participation possible. Benjamin Barber (1998) argues that it was Jefferson, certainly no advocate of diversity, who most forcefully argued that broad civic participation required education: "It remained clear to Jefferson to the end of his life that a theory of democracy that is rooted in active participation and continuing consent by each generation of citizens demands a civic pedagogy rooted in the obligation to educate all who would be citizens" (p. 169). To be sure, Jefferson was talking about education for those he defined as the body of citizens and not for the many who were not citizens at that time.

If education is the very foundation of democracy, how do experiences with racial/ethnic diversity affect the process of learning to become citizens? We contend that students educated in diverse institutions will be more motivated and better able to participate in an increasingly heterogeneous and complex society. In *Democratic Education in an Age of Difference*, Richard Guarasci and Grant Cornwell (1997) concur, claiming that "community and democratic citizenship are strengthened when undergraduates understand and experience social connections with those outside of their often parochial 'autobiographies,' and when they experience the way their lives are necessarily shaped by others" (p. xiii).

However, the compatibility of diversity and democracy is not self-evident. Current critics of multicultural education worry that identities based on race, ethnicity, gender, class, and other categorizations are inimical to the unity needed for democracy. Yet the tension between unity and diversity, however politically charged, is not new in the United States.

In *Fear of Diversity*, Arlene Saxonhouse (1992) describes how the pre-Socratic playwrights as well as Plato and Aristotle dealt with the fear that "differences bring on chaos and thus demand that the world be put into an orderly pattern" (p. x). While Plato envisioned a city in which unity and harmony would be based on the shared characteristics of a homogeneous citizenry, Aristotle recognized the value of heterogeneity and welcomed the diverse. Saxonhouse writes: "Aristotle embraces diversity as the others had not. . . . The typologies that fill almost every page of Aristotle's *Politics* show him uniting and separating, finding underlying unity and significant differences" (p. 235). Aristotle advanced a political theory in which unity could be achieved through differences and contended that democracy based on such a unity would be more likely to thrive than one based on homogeneity. What makes democracy work, according to Aristotle, is equality among citizens (admittedly, in his time only free men, not women or slaves) who hold diverse perspectives and whose relationships are governed by freedom and rules of civil discourse. It is a multiplicity of perspectives and discourses in response to the inevitable conflicts that arise when citizens have differing points of view, not unanimity, that help democracy thrive (Pitkin & Shumer, 1982).

Diversity, plurality, equality, and freedom are also implied in Piaget's theory of intellectual and moral development. He argues that children and adolescents can best develop a capacity to understand the ideas and feelings of others—what he calls perspective-taking—and move to a more advanced stage of moral reasoning when they interact with peers who have different points of view. Both differing perspectives and equality in relationships are important for intellectual and moral development (Piaget, 1965). In a homogeneous environment in which young people are not forced to confront the relativity or limitations of their point of view, they are likely to conform to a single perspective defined by an authority. In a hierarchical environment in which young people are not obliged to discuss and argue with others on an equal basis, they are not likely to do the cognitive and emotional work that is required to understand how other people think and feel. These cognitive and emotional processes promote the moral development needed to make a pluralistic democracy work.

In the United States, however, common conceptions of democracy do not treat difference as being compatible with unity. In general, popular understandings of democracy and citizenship take one of two forms: 1) a liberal individualist conception in which citizens participate by voting for public servants to represent them and by other individual acts, and 2) a direct participatory conception in which people from similar backgrounds who are familiar with each other come together to debate the common good, as in the New England town meeting. Both of these conceptions privilege individuals and similarities rather than groups and differences.

The increasingly heterogeneous U.S. population challenges these popular conceptions of democracy. Consequently, we are now facing cultural, academic, and political debates over the extent to which American democracy can survive increasing heterogeneity and group-based social and political claims. Yet, it is clear that an ethnic hierarchy or one-way assimilation, both of which call for muting differences and cultural identities, is much less likely to prevail than in the past (Fredrickson, 1999).

The theories of Aristotle and Piaget both suggest that difference and democracy can be compatible. The conditions deemed important for this compatibility include the presence of diverse others and diverse perspectives, equality among peers, and discussion according to rules of civil discourse. We hypothesize that these conditions foster the orientations that students will need to be citizens and leaders in the postcollege world: perspective-taking, mutuality and reciprocity, acceptance of conflict as a normal part of life, capacity to perceive differences and commonalties both within and between social groups, interest in the wider social world, and citizen participation.

METHOD

Samples

We tested our theory using two longitudinal databases—one from the University of Michigan and one from a national sample of college students—that would allow us to parallel our analysis as closely as possible. The Michigan Student Survey (MSS) was initiated to monitor students' response to the University of Michigan's diversity focus. This focus was the result of the Michigan Mandate, a major initiative designed both to reaffirm the centrality of diversity to the university's institutional mission and to directly address racial concerns that arose on campus during the late 1980s. The MSS database is a single-institution survey of students who entered the University of Michigan in 1990 and a follow-up survey four years later. The Michigan sample examined here included 1,129 White students, 187 African American students, and 266 Asian American students. (Native American and Latino/a students were not included due to their small sample sizes.) The MSS concluded its data collection three years before the affirmative action lawsuits were filed against the University of Michigan.

The Michigan data were particularly useful in examining the effects of experiences with racial/ethnic diversity on student outcomes. For most of its students the University of Michigan's racial and ethnic diversity create the discrepancy, discontinuity, and disequilibrium that may produce the active thinking and intellectual engagement that educators demand. At the time the MSS was conducted, 92 percent of White students and 52 percent of African American students came to the University of Michigan from segregated communities. As groups, only Asian American and Latino/a students came to the University having lived and gone to school in environments where they were not in the majority. Thus, the university's conscious effort to help students experience diversity in and out of the classroom provide the very features that foster active, conscious, and effortful thinking.

The second dataset came from the Cooperative Institutional Research Program (CIRP), a national survey conducted by the Higher Educational Research Institute at UCLA. The CIRP included 11,383 students from 184 institutions who were surveyed upon entering college in 1985 and again four years later (see Astin, 1993b, for administration details). The national sample included 216 African American, 496 Asian American, 206 Latino/a, and 10,465 White students attending predominantly White, four-year institutions. (Native Americans were not included due to their small sample size.) In order to parallel important controls and analyses of the CIRP with those of the Michigan dataset, we selected only students in their fourth year (1989) who participated in the four-year follow-up and in a subsequent nine-year follow-up survey. This was done to control for the level of segregation of the students' neighborhood before they entered college (a key retrospective question included only in the nine-year follow-up). The CIRP is the largest national dataset that incorporates questions about diversity that can be used to study students' educational outcomes longitudinally. The survey was conducted during an era when there were numerous racial incidents on college campuses and racial climates were highly variable according to student reports (Hurtado, 1992).

Although developed for a wide range of educational purposes, the CIRP longitudinal study was the closest national parallel to data collected locally at the University of Michigan. By examining these two datasets, we were able to identify broad patterns of educational benefits both within a single institution and across varying institutional contexts. These patterns suggest that our findings at the University of Michigan were not an anomaly but generalizable to many types of campuses. In both the national and institutional studies we used parallel controls for student demographic characteristics that could influence involvement in diversity experiences and the learning and democracy outcomes, as well as controls for pretest measures of most of the educational outcomes. Therefore, we focus here on the effects of diversity experiences on student outcomes, controlling for relevant student background characteristics and institutional characteristics, which are pertinent in the national, multi-institutional analyses.

Measures

Tables 14.1 and 14.2 show the independent and dependent measures employed in both the multi- and single-institution analyses. These are described as control variables, institutional characteristics (for the multi-institutional sample), diversity experiences, and educational outcomes. Many of the measures were constructed as indices, with alpha reliabilities shown in these tables.

Control Variables. Table 14.1 shows that the two studies included comparable measures of control variables: ethnic/racial composition of the high school and of the precollege neighborhood, gender, high school cumulative grade point average, total SAT scores, and parental education as a measure of the student's socioeconomic background.[6] While these are not of primary substantive interest, they are important considerations in the analyses because they represent the previous choices, preferences, and experiences of students that, unless taken into account, could have influenced the outcomes and caused an overestimation of the effects of experiences with diversity. In instances where the measures of the expected outcomes were also available on the entrance questionnaire, the entrance measures were included as control variables.

In the national study we also controlled for institutional features that might foster classroom and informal diversity experiences and/or the educational outcomes of interest in this study. In all multi-institutional analyses, we controlled for the percentage of minority enrollments in order to distinguish the effects of classroom and informal diversity interactions from the mere presence of diverse students on campus. We also controlled for two additional diversity-related institutional features obtained from faculty responses. One is an index of academic emphasis on diversity, obtained by asking faculty to assess how much they emphasize diversity in their teaching, research, and writing. The second index represents institutional emphasis on diversity, measured by faculty perceptions of the priority the institution placed on diversity. These measures have been used in previous studies (for reliability indices see Astin, 1993b; Dey, 1991; Hurtado, 1992). Finally, in *all* analyses of the national data we controlled for characteristics of institutions that are typically controlled for in multi-institutional studies such as the CIRP: whether the school is private or public, a university or a four-year college, and the selectivity of the institution (Pascarella & Terenzini, 1991).[7]

Diversity Experiences.   Although different questions were asked in the two studies, each provided measures of both classroom and informal interactional diversity. In the Michigan Student Study, classroom diversity was measured in the 1994 fourth-year survey using two questions. One question asked students to assess the extent to which they had been exposed in classes to "information/activities devoted to understanding other racial/ethnic groups and inter-racial ethnic relationships." The other asked students if they had taken a course during college that had an important impact on their "views of racial/ethnic diversity and multiculturalism."

Classroom diversity involves more than just exposure to content about racial and ethnic groups. In the MSS, students' answers likely referred to classes that exposed them to racially/ethnically diverse students as well as to curriculum content. In 1994, when these students were seniors, they had to have taken a course that met the Race and Ethnicity Requirement (R&E) for which the Literature, Sciences, and Arts College had approved 111 courses. We obtained the racial/ethnic distribution of students in those courses for 1993–1994, the year that the MSS gathered senior data. Two-thirds of these courses had enrolled between 20 percent and 80 percent students of color. Consequently, there is a strong probability that the majority of classes White students were referring to in the MSS measure of classroom diversity included at least 20 percent students of color.

The CIRP asked fourth-year students if they had taken an ethnic studies course in college. Enrollment data for these courses were not available; however, there is no reason to believe that the ethnic studies courses attracted fewer students of color than the R&E courses did at the University of Michigan, unless one of the institutions fell into the group of colleges with very little diversity—a factor that we controlled for using institutional enrollment data.

Exposure to diverse peers, however, does not only occur in college classrooms. For this reason, experiences with informal interactional diversity were measured in both studies. In the CIRP, this experience was measured by an index summarizing responses to three questions asked in 1989 about the extent to which students, over their college years, had socialized with someone

TABLE 14.1
Measures of Independent Variables in the Analysis

Control Variables	CIRP Data	Michigan Student Study (MSS)
Student Background:		
Gender (female)	Dichotomous measure	Dichotomous measure
SAT scores	Obtained on entrance survey	Obtained from Michigan Registrar
Cumulative high school GPA	Obtained on entrance survey	Obtained from Michigan Registrar
Parents' education level	Obtained on entrance survey	Measured on entrance/senior survey
Racial composition of the high school	Not available at entrance, but similar items captured on the 9-year follow-up survey	Measured on entrance survey
Racial composition of the neighborhood	Not available at entrance, but similar items captured on the 9-year follow-up survey	Measured on entrance survey
Pretests on selected measures*	Measured on entrance survey	Measured on entrance survey
Institutional Characteristics:		
Selectivity of the college	Average SAT of entering freshmen	Not applicable—institutional characteristics are a constant for all students
Private/public control	Dichotomous measure	
University/four-year college	Dichotomous measure	
Percentage students of color (African Americans, Latino/as, Native Americans, and Asian Americans)	Derived from IPEDS data on student enrollment for each institution	
Faculty diversity emphasis	Aggregate measure of faculty incorporation of information on women and racial/ethnic groups into research, readings for courses, and writing **	No faculty level data were collected
Institutional emphasis on diversity	Aggregate measure of faculty responses to institutional diversity priorities **	No faculty level data were collected
Diversity Experiences:		
Informal interaction	Index of items (α = .561): attended cultural awareness workshop, discussed racial issues, and socialized with a person of a different race	Index of four items (α = .780): amount of contact with students from other racial groups, proportion of six best friends from other racial groups, positive interaction with diverse peers
Classroom diversity	Enrollment in an ethnic studies course	Index of two items (α = .507): exposure in classes to information/activities devoted to understanding other racial groups, and enrollment in a course that had an impact on views on racial/ethnic diversity
Diversity events/dialogues	Not available	Index of six items (α = .612): number of multicultural events attended and participation in a dialogue group

* Dependent measures with pretests at entrance shown in Table 14.2
** Derived from faculty survey at participating institutions, reported in Astin (1993b)

from a different racial/ethnic group, had discussed racial issues, and had attended a racial/cultural awareness workshop. In the MSS, an index summarizing responses to several questions asked in 1994 was used to measure informal interaction. Two questions probed the positive quality of inter-racial/interethnic interactions in college, asking students how much such interactions had involved "meaningful and honest discussions about race and ethnic relations" and "sharing of personal feelings and problems." Another asked students to describe the gender, geographical home residency, and race/ethnicity of their "six closest friends at Michigan." For this measure we coded for the number of friends who were not of the students' own racial/ethnic group. The last question focused on quantity rather than quality, asking how much contact they had at Michigan with racial/ethnic groups other than their own. For White students we included contact with African American, Asian American, and Latino/a students, and for African American and Asian American students we included contact with White students in this measure of informal interactional diversity.[8]

In the Michigan Student Study, we also assessed experience with diversity through the number of multicultural campus events students had attended and whether they had participated in intergroup dialogues during college. The multicultural campus events were Hispanic Heritage Month, Native American Month, the annual Pow Wow, Asian American Awareness Week, a Martin Luther King Jr. Symposium, and Black History Month. Intergroup dialogues are also offered on the Michigan campus within various courses. These dialogues involve weekly sessions of structured discussion between an equal number of members (usually seven or eight) from each of two identity groups (Arab/Jewish, Anglo/Latino/a, men/women, African American/White, Native American/Latino/a, and others). The students discuss contentious issues that are relevant to their particular groups. The goals of the dialogues are four-fold: 1) to discern differences and commonalties in perspectives between and within the groups; 2) to incorporate readings on intergroup relations in their discussions; 3) to learn how to deal with conflict; and 4) to define one action that the two groups can take in coalition with each other. Participation in these multicultural events and intergroup dialogues comprise an index that includes both knowledge content and interaction with diverse others.

Learning Outcome.   Table 14.2 shows the outcome measures in the study. The theory linking diversity to learning outcomes led us to focus on measures of active thinking and engagement in learning. In the CIRP, intellectual engagement included self-rated aspirations for postgraduate education, the drive to achieve, intellectual self-confidence, and the importance placed on original writing and creating artistic works. The other learning outcome in the CIRP, academic skills, included self-rated academic ability, writing ability, and listening ability, as well as self-reported change in general knowledge, analytic and problem-solving skills, ability to think critically, writing skills, and foreign language skills.

In the MSS, we had available a measure that directly represented the active thinking that we hypothesize is promoted by experiences with diversity. This measure includes seven items from a longer scale, which is correlated with this seven-item measure at .81 (Fletcher, Danilovics, Fernandez, Peterson, & Reeder, 1986). They define their scale as the motivation to understand human behavior, a preference for complex rather than simple explanations, and the tendency to think about underlying processes involved in causal analysis. It has both discriminant and convergent validity and is not related to the tendency to answer questions in a socially desirable way. It is related, as it should be, to a measure of a similar construct developed by John Cacioppo and Richard Petty (1982) of an individual need for cognition, defined as the need to understand and explain the world and the enjoyment of thinking. Examples of the items in our seven-item measure are: "I take people's behavior at face value" (reverse coding), "I enjoy analyzing reasons for behavior," and "I prefer simple rather than complex explanations" (reverse coding). Because the same questions were included in the entrance questionnaire and used as controls in our regression analyses, diversity effects can be construed as affecting active thinking. The other learning outcome measure in the MSS, intellectual engagement and motivation, asked students to assess the extent to which they had "gained a broad, intellectually exciting education at Michigan" and how satisfied they were with "the intellectual quality and challenge of classes."

Democracy Outcomes.   According to the theory outlined here, students who had the most experience with diversity during college would be more motivated and better able to participate in an increasingly heterogeneous democracy. To participate effectively, students need to understand

TABLE 14.2
Measures of Dependent Variables

	CIRP Data	Michigan Student Study (MSS)
Learning Outcomes:		
Active thinking	Not available	Index (α = .797) of four complex thinking items and three socio-historical thinking items based on Fletcher's measure of Attributional Complexity (1986, 1990), correlated with total scale .81.*
Intellectual engagement and motivation	Index of items (α = .613): self-ratings of drive to achieve and self-ratings of intellectual self-confidence; degree aspirations in 1989; interest in attending graduate school; importance of writing original works and creating artistic works*	Index of two items (α = .650): gained a broad, intellectually exciting education at Michigan, and satisfaction with intellectual quality and challenge of classes.
Academic skills	Index of items (α = .657): self-change assessments in general knowledge, analytical/problem-solving skills, ability to think critically, writing skills, foreign language skills, and self-ratings of academic ability, writing, and listening ability*	Not available
Democracy Outcomes:		
Citizenship engagement	Index of items (α = .752): importance of influencing the political structure, influencing social values, helping others in difficulty, involvement in cleaning up the environment, and participation in community action programs*	Not available
Compatibility of difference and democracy	Not available	Index of five items (α = .583): belief that diversity is non-divisive; perceived commonality in life values with groups other than one's own *
Perspective-taking	Not available	Index (α = .684) of four items of Davis's scale (1983), correlated with total scale .85*
Racial/cultural engagement	Index of items: self-change in cultural awareness and appreciation, and acceptance of persons from different races (α = .700)	Single item: learned about other racial/ethnic groups during college

* Pretest also available used as control at entrance to college

and consider multiple perspectives that are likely to exist when people of different backgrounds interact, to appreciate the common values and integrative forces that incorporate differences in the pursuit of the broader common good, and to understand and accept cultural differences that arise in a racially/ethnically diverse society.

In the CIRP data, citizenship engagement is a measure of students' motivation to participate in activities that affect society and the political structure. These activities include "influencing the political structure," "influencing social values," "helping others in difficulty," "being involved in programs to clean up the environment," and "participating in a community action program." Racial and cultural understanding is assessed by students' self-ratings of how much they had changed in "cultural awareness and appreciation" and "acceptance of persons from different races/cultures" since entering college.

The MSS included three measures of democracy outcomes. One outcome, perspective-taking, refers directly to the tendency to consider other people's points of view. This four-item index comes from a longer scale of empathy that was developed by Mark Davis (1983), with which the MSS index is correlated at .85. An example is "I sometimes find it difficult to see things from the other person's point of view" (reversed). The Davis scale is internally reliable and has both discriminant and convergent validity. The second MSS measure, racial/cultural engagement, is a one-item question asking students how much they have learned during college "about the contributions to American society of other racial/ethnic groups."

A third MSS democracy measure was developed to ascertain student views about the compatibility of difference and democracy. Critics of diversity and multicultural education assert that an emphasis on groups rather than individuals and on differences between groups creates division on college campuses and threatens the very fabric of democracy. If that were true, students who had experienced the most classroom and informal interactional diversity would perceive only differences rather than commonalties and would believe that difference is inimical to democracy. Our questions directly challenged these beliefs. Commonality in values was assessed at the time of entrance to the University of Michigan and again four years later by asking students how much difference in "values in life—like values about work and family" they perceived between their own racial/ethnic group and other groups. Perception of nondivisiveness was measured by asking how much students agreed/disagreed with four statements (also used in Gurin, Peng, Lopez, & Nagda, 1999). Examples are: "The University's commitment to diversity fosters more intergroup division than understanding" and "The University's emphasis on diversity means I can't talk honestly about ethnic, racial, and gender issues." These items were scored so that high scores indicate that difference is nondivisive. The commonality in values and perception of nondivisiveness measures were combined into a compatibility of difference and democracy index (see Table 14.2 for construction of measures for different groups).

Self-Assessments. All of these measures required students to assess themselves. Self-assessments are credible and widely accepted methods of measuring educational outcomes. For example, in a review of the research on a variety of possible indicators of college outcomes, the National Center for Higher Education Management Systems concluded that self-reported data on academic development and experiences have moderate to high potential as proxies for a national test and as possible indicators for decision making in higher education (Ewell & Jones, 1993). In addition, in their major review of over 2,600 studies on the impact of college on students, Ernest Pascarella and Patrick Terenzini (1991) found that self-assessments are positively correlated with standard tests of achievement and serve quite well as indicators of college outcomes.[9]

GRE scores were not used as a measure of learning outcomes for two reasons: 1) student performance on the SAT (already in the analysis as a control variable) was correlated at .85 with the GRE, and 2) including only students who had taken the GRE in their fourth year of college would have substantially reduced the sample of students within each of the racial/ethnic groups and skewed the analytical sample with extremely high-ability students. College grades were not selected as a measure of learning primarily because grades inadequately capture the active thinking and intellectual engagement we were attempting to test. The meaning of grades also varies substantially from institution to institution, major to major, and course to course. This was particularly evident in the institution with which we were most familiar, where some departments grade on a curve and other departments have no standard method.

ANALYSES

Multiple regression analyses were performed using the two datasets. We conducted regression analyses on the multi-institutional CIRP data to explore the relationships between two types of diversity (classroom and informal interactional diversity) and the four dependent variables (intellectual engagement, academic skills, citizenship engagement, and racial/cultural engagement). Separate regressions were fit for African American, Asian American, Latino/a, and White students in the national study. Regressions were also conducted on the MSS data to explore the relationships between three types of diversity experiences (interactional diversity, classroom diversity, and events/dialogues) and the five dependent variables (active thinking, intellectual engagement, compatibility of differences, perspective-taking, and racial/cultural engagement). Again, separate regressions were run for three student groups in the MSS: African American, Asian American, and White.

Given our primary interest in the effects of informal interaction and classroom diversity measures on the outcomes described above, the regressions were structured in a blocked hierarchical regression to provide information on how these variables relate to the outcome measures after first controlling for student background characteristics (including entrance pretest measures where available) and institutional characteristics found in the CIRP data. After these statistical controls were applied, the effect of each diversity experience variable was first considered as the sole diversity predictor and then simultaneously with other diversity experiences in the entire predictive model.[10] We conducted both kinds of analyses because students who have the most experience with diversity also tend to have the most informal interaction with peers from different backgrounds. We were interested in *both* the total and net effects of each type of diversity experience. Finally, variation in sample size of each of the groups necessitated reporting a wide range of significance tests—using the traditional significance levels (.05, .01, and .001) to evaluate results for the very large sample of White students, and adding the significance level of .10 for the much smaller samples of students of color.

RESULTS

As noted in the methods section, we examined the effects of each type of diversity experience in two ways—its individual impact, ignoring the other kinds of diversity experiences, and its net impact, controlling for the other kinds of diversity experiences. In the national study and the Michigan study, both sets of analyses show that diversity experiences had robust effects on educational outcomes for all groups of students, although to varying degrees.

Learning Outcomes

Table 14.3 summarizes the results for both the Michigan and the national study of the effects of diversity experiences on learning outcomes. The first set of columns (Model 1) provides the zero-order correlations showing the size of the maximal possible effect of diversity experiences. Model 1 also shows the standardized betas for each diversity experience when it is entered as the sole diversity predictor, along with the various control variables. The second set of columns (Model 2) gives the standardized betas for each diversity experience when it is entered simultaneously with the other diversity experience(s), again, after statistically removing the effects of the various control variables. Finally, the third set of columns gives the amount of variance that is explained by the entire model, including the control variables and the amount of variance that is attributable specifically to all the diversity experiences.

We predicted that diversity experiences would have a positive relationship with the learning outcomes. In both the national study and the MSS, this prediction was consistently supported. As shown in Table 14.3 and described in more detail below, one kind of diversity experience or another was significantly related to each of the learning outcomes, even after adjusting for individual students' differences upon entering college that might have predisposed them to participate, or not, in diversity experiences on their campuses. Moreover, with all but one exception, when there was a statistically significant relationship between diversity experience and learning outcomes, the observed effect was universally positive for each of the groups of students we studied.

In the national study, informal interactional diversity was especially influential in accounting for higher levels of intellectual engagement and self-assessed academic skills for all four groups of students (Table 14.3). The impact of classroom diversity was also statistically significant and positive for White students and for Latinos/as. The effects of classroom diversity disappeared for Asian American students when we examined the net effect, controlling for the simultaneous effect of informal interaction. One statistically significant negative result emerged for African American students in the analyses that tested the net effect of classroom diversity on self-assessed academic skills.

It is important to note in Table 14.3 that, when both types of diversity were simultaneously used as predictors with the national data, the effect of informal interactional diversity was nearly always maintained and was considerably larger than the effect of classroom diversity. This was true for all four groups of students, except in the comparative effects of the two kinds of diversity on intellectual engagement among Latino/a students.

A reason for the relatively greater effects of informal interactional diversity in the national data might come in part from the fact that it was measured by three indicators, while classroom diversity was represented by only one question that asked about enrollment in an ethnic studies course. Conclusions about relative importance are affected by properties of particular measures of various concepts. Still, at the very least, these analyses show that actual interaction with diverse others was an influential aspect of the educational experiences of the students in the national sample.

The Michigan study provided both a broader measure of classroom diversity and two types of informal interactional diversity measures. One measure, the amount and quality of interaction with diverse peers, was conceptually comparable to the informal interactional measure in the national study. It is important to point out, however, that the Michigan measure is unique in that it assesses both the quality and the quantity of interaction with diverse peers. It includes students' assessments of how many positive personal interactions they had with peers from racial/ethnic backgrounds different from their own. The other, a measure of participation in multicultural events and intergroup dialogues, takes advantage of our knowledge of diversity experiences within the student environment at the University of Michigan.

In the Michigan study, all three kinds of diversity experiences were influential for at least one of the groups, and for at least one measure of learning outcomes. This may simply indicate that students of color respond differently to opportunities for diversity experiences and have distinct interaction patterns that affect different outcomes. The most consistent effects were found for White students. All three kinds of diversity experiences were significantly related to higher levels of active thinking scores in the senior year, controlling for levels of active thinking in the freshman year among White students. In addition, both classroom diversity and events/dialogues were significantly related to intellectual engagement for this group. The results show clearly that the largest effects came from campus-facilitated diversity activities, namely classroom diversity and multicultural events, and intergroup dialogues held on campus (the dialogues facilitate interaction among an equal number of diverse peers). For Asian American students, classroom diversity also fostered both of the learning outcomes.

For African American students in the Michigan study, classroom diversity was the only predictor that had a statistically significant effect on both learning outcomes. The other two diversity experiences were related to one of each of these learning outcomes: events/dialogues participation was statistically related to intellectual engagement in the Model 1 regression; informal interaction was statistically related to intellectual engagement in Model 2.

Democracy Outcomes

We also predicted that diversity experiences would help students develop the skills to participate and lead in a diverse democracy. The results of both studies support this prediction for all groups of students. Some kind of diversity experience was related to each of the democracy outcomes, even after adjusting for individual differences on measures of most of these outcomes at the time students entered college. (See Table 14.4 and the description of results that follows.)

In the national study, informal interactional diversity was significantly related to both citizenship engagement and racial/cultural engagement for all four groups. This was also true of the effect of classroom diversity on democracy outcomes for White students. In contrast, the effects of classroom diversity were more group-specific for students of color and, on the whole, classroom diversity had less consistent effects for these students. The major finding, however, is that informal interaction was the key for fostering democracy outcomes for all groups in the national study.

In the Michigan study all three types of diversity experiences had significant positive effects on the compatibility of difference and the racial/cultural engagement outcomes for White students. White students who had the greatest amount of informal interactional diversity and experience with diversity in the classroom most frequently believed that difference is compatible with democracy and were the most engaged with racial/cultural issues. These two diversity experiences also significantly affected White students' perspective-taking.

For African American and Asian American students in the Michigan study, the impact of the three diversity experiences was less consistent. Among both groups, informal interaction with diverse peers was associated with an understanding that difference and democracy can be compatible. Further, classroom diversity had a positive effect on racial and cultural engagement for both groups. Participation in multicultural events and intergroup dialogues only had a significant effect on perspective-taking among African Americans. Among Asian Americans these activities were related to two of the democracy outcomes (Model 1), although the net effect of this kind of diversity was no longer statistically significant when the other kinds of diversity were taken into account (Model 2).

Summary

Several conclusions can be drawn from the results. First, an important feature of our analyses is the consistency of results across both the national and Michigan studies. Second, in the national study informal interactional diversity was influential for all groups and more influential than classroom diversity. Third, of the many analyses we conducted, all but one that had a significant effect confirmed our prediction of a positive relationship between diversity experiences and educational outcomes as posited in our theory. Fourth, with few exceptions, the separate diversity effects remained statistically significant after controlling for the other diversity experiences in Model 2.[11]

Finally, Tables 14.3 and 14.4 show that the whole models (including the precollege background controls, initial measures of senior-year outcomes, where available, diversity experience measures, and, in the national study, measures of institutional characteristics) explain between 3 percent and 49 percent of the variance across both studies, across the various groups of students,

TABLE 14.3

Effect of Diversity Experiences on Learning Outcomes

A. CIRP National Study

	Model 1				Model 2		Percent variance explained	
	As sole diversity predictor							Attributable to both diversity measures
	Informal interaction		Classroom diversity		Informal interaction controlling for classroom diversity	Classroom diversity controlling for informal interaction	Whole model	
	Zero-order correlation	Beta	Zero-order correlation	Beta	Beta	Beta		
Whites								
Intellectual engagement	.230	.130***	.095	.057***	.123***	.026**	26.2%	1.5%
Academic skills	.243	.168***	.115	.075***	.159***	.035***	14.7%	2.5%
African American								
Intellectual engagement	.149	.146**	.014	-.040	.166**	-.083	24.0%	2.4%
Academic skills	.196	.175**	-.021	-.072	.206**	-.126 *	16.1%	3.9%
Asian American								
Intellectual engagement	.218	.170***	.044	.078*	.161***	.038	28.9%	2.6%
Academic skills	.199	.134**	.078	.072*	.124**	.042	15.4%	1.7%
Latino								
Intellectual engagement	.147	.138*	.116	.157*	.096	.126*	31.7%	2.8%
Academic skills	.241	.258***	.178	.205**	.212*	.135*	21.5%	7.0%

Model 1

B. Michigan Student Study

| | As sole diversity predictor | | | | | | Model 2 | | | Percent variance explained | |
| | Interactional diversity | | Classroom diversity | | Events/Dialogues | | Informal interaction controlling for classroom diversity and Events/Dialogues | Classroom diversity controlling for informal interaction and Events/Dialogues | Events/dialogues controlling for informal interaction and classroom diversity | | Attributable to the three diversity measures |
	Zero-order correlation	Beta	Zero-order correlation	Beta	Zero-order correlation	Beta	Beta	Beta	Beta	Whole model	
White students											
Active thinking	.174	.100***	.348	.196***	.321	.176***	.054*	.158***	.130***	43.2%	5.3%
Intellectual engagement	.053	.084	.121	.112***	.119	.108***	.018	.090**	.086****	3.2%	1.9%
African American students											
Active thinking	.064	.019	.258	.211*	.086	-.052	.022	.227**	.227**	42.3%	5.1%
Intellectual engagement	.157	.117	.151	.169*	.121	.126**	.166*	.168*	.168*	9.3%	6.6%
Asian American students											
Active thinking	.179	.077	.374	.256***	.207	.060	.102*	.291***	.291***	48.9%	8.1%
Intellectual engagement	.093	.086	.158	.156**	.002	.001	.087	.361**	.161**	4.3%	3.0%

Note: In the MSS, Betas shown control for student characteristics; in the CIRP, the Betas shown control for student characteristics, institutional characteristics, and (where available) for measures of the outcomes taken at time of entrance to college. p<.10=~, p<.05=*, p<.01=**, and p<.001=***

TABLE 14.4
Effect of Diversity Experiences on Democracy Outcomes

A. CIRP National Study	Model 1				Model 2		Percent variance explained	
	As sole diversity predictor				Informal interaction controlling for classroom diversity	Classroom diversity controlling for informal interaction		Attributable to both diversity measures
	Informal interaction		Classroom diversity				Whole model	measures
	Zero-order correlation	Beta	Zero-order correlation	Beta	Beta	Beta		
Whites								
Citizenship engagement	.372	.301***	.211	.138***	.282***	.070***	20.2%	7.8%
Racial/cultural engagement	.350	.337***	.200	.164***	.314***	.083***	4.3%	10.2%
African American								
Citizenship engagement	.335	.328***	.138	.121**	.319***	.035	25.1%	9.3%
Racial/cultural engagement	.269	.251***	.097	.040	.258***	−.027	5.4%	5.6%
Asian American								
Citizenship engagement	.342	.272***	.138	.066	.271***	.001	18.8%	6.3%
Racial/cultural engagement	.375	.365***	.211	.185***	.341**	.100*	8.5%	12.6%
Latino								
Citizenship engagement	.383	.311***	.334	.214***	.270***	.134*	28.1%	9.1%
Racial/cultural engagement	.330	.313***	.175	.142*	.298***	.044	5.3%	8.5%

B. Michigan Student Study

	Model 1						Model 2			Percent variance explained	
	As sole diversity predictor						Informal interaction controlling for classroom diversity and Events/ Dialogues	Classroom diversity controlling for informal interaction and Events/ Dialogues	Events/ dialogues controlling for informal interaction and classroom diversity		Attributable to the three diversity measures
	Interactional diversity		Classroom diversity		Events/ Dialogues					Whole model	
	Zero-order correlation	Beta	Zero-order correlation	Beta	Zero-order correlation	Beta	Beta	Beta	Beta		
White Students											
Compatibility of differences	.178	.156***	.142	.129***	.259	.233***	.105**	.082*	.195***	10.6%	7.4%
Perspective-taking	.167	.090**	.185	.123***	.143	.048	.077***	.117**	.003	28.7%	2.0%
Racial/cultural engagement	.172	.172***	.316	.300***	.197	.186***	.120***	.261***	.096***	16.0%	11.1%
African American Students											
Compatibility of differences	.230	.270*	.279	.251**	-.113	-.079	.262*	.233*	-.098	20.5%	11.2%
Perspective-taking	.158	.138	.088	-.052	.236	.207*	.150	-.072	.212*	30.4%	6.1%
Racial/cultural engagement	.049	.107	.338	.352***	.048	.042	.098	.365***	-.026	16.9%	13.8%
Asian American Students											
Compatibility of differences	.198	.193*	.087	.088	.161	.163*	.197*	.056	.142	11.1%	6.2%
Perspective-taking	.061	.056	.040	.069	.048	.006	.048	.085	-.024	33.6%	0.8%
Racial/cultural engagement	-.009	-.047	.359	.350***	.178	.170**	-.045	.320***	.071	15.0%	11.8%

Note: In the MSS, Betas shown control for student characteristics; in the CIRP, the Betas shown control for student characteristics, institutional characteristics, and (where available) for measures of the outcomes taken at time of entrance to college. p < .10 = ~, p < .05 = *, p < .01 = **, and p < .001 = ***

and across the various outcome measures. More important, however, is the amount of variance that is attributable to diversity experiences. In the national study, the two diversity experiences explained between 1.5 percent and 12.6 percent of the variance in the different educational outcomes for the four groups. In the Michigan study, the three diversity experiences explained between 1.9 percent and 13.8 percent of the variance across the educational outcomes of the three groups.

The size of these effects is commonly viewed in social science as highly consequential for policy, especially when outcomes and predictors are likely to be measured with substantial random error, as they typically are in studies of college impact. It is widely known that the kinds of processes and outcomes of interest here are difficult to measure with high precision and that measurement error diminishes effect size. Given that the dependent variables in the CIRP analyses were multiple-item scales with calculated reliability estimates, we replicated the analyses for each of the racial/ethnic groups in the national study after applying the standard attenuation correction. In each instance, the results were consistent with those presented here, but with larger regression coefficients and an enhanced level of explained variance. For example, the coefficients and degree of predictability associated with the White student analyses were roughly one-third larger in the attenuation-corrected analyses.

DISCUSSION

The results of these longitudinal analyses show, as our theory predicts, that the actual experiences students have with diversity consistently and meaningfully affect important learning and democracy outcomes of a college education. Diversity experiences explain an important amount of variance in these outcomes. These effects are quite consistent across the various outcomes, across the national and single institutional studies, and across the different groups of students.

Is Curriculum Enough?

Some opponents of affirmative action advance the view that the educational benefits of diversity can be achieved without the presence of racially/ethnically diverse peers (*Hopwood*, 1996). Since content about race/ethnicity can be introduced into courses even at institutions with minimal student diversity, it was especially important for our research to explore whether informal interaction with diverse peers had significant effects independent of the effects of classroom diversity. In the national study, informal interaction remained statistically significant in all but one test when classroom diversity was added as a control. We also found that informal interaction with diverse peers was consistently influential on all educational outcomes for all four groups of students and, with one exception, that the effect of informal interaction was larger than that of classroom diversity.

In the Michigan study, the unique contribution of significant informal interaction effects remained on democracy outcomes when the other diversity experiences were added as controls, and were actually more consistent on learning outcomes in Model 2 than in Model 1. The results for White students show that the effects of the three different kinds of diversity experiences are more comparable to each other than was true in the national study, and the results for African American and Asian American students show a fairly differentiated picture of effects. While classroom diversity carried greater weight in some cases and informal interactional diversity or events/dialogues in others, we could not conclude that the presence of racially/ethnically diverse peers is irrelevant to the diversity benefits for any of these groups of students. Moreover, as pointed out earlier, classroom diversity at the University of Michigan nearly always involves the presence of diverse students as well as exposure to curriculum content addressing diversity. The success of these curricular initiatives is facilitated by the presence of diverse students and a pedagogy that facilitates learning in a diverse environment. In conclusion, we find that education is enhanced by extensive and meaningful informal interracial interaction, which depends on the presence of significantly diverse student bodies.

In the introduction to this chapter, we laid out a theoretical rationale for why actual experience with diversity provides the process through which the presence of diverse peers affects the education of all students. The results of our research support this rationale across both studies and for all groups of students. Still, in the months immediately following the *Gratz v. Bollinger* and *Grutter v. Bollinger* trials in district court, opponents of affirmative action began to argue that diversity experience is irrelevant legally and that the only evidence relevant to these cases would have to show that the percentage of minority students on a campus has a direct effect on educational outcomes. An *amicus* brief filed on behalf of the plaintiffs in these Michigan lawsuits claims that Justice Powell defined diversity in his opinion in the *Bakke* case simply as the percentage of minority students on a campus. While the interpretation of what Justice Powell said is, of course, up to the courts, his statement includes a long passage quoting William Bowen, then president of Princeton University, on how "a great deal of learning occurs informally . . . through interactions among students" (*Regents*, 1978, p. 312). Justice Powell's use of Bowen's statement indicates that Powell understood that actual interaction with diverse peers is a major component of the effects of diversity.

The conclusion that the racial diversity of a campus operates *through* students' experiences is powerfully supported by the research reported here. It is also supported by a developing body of research on diversity that demonstrates the significant impact of interactions with diverse peers (Chang, 1999; Hurtado, 2001; Pascarella et al., 1996). At a more general level, higher education researchers have noted the critical importance of students' college experiences in their personal development. In a review of the impact of college on students, Pascarella and Terenzini (1991) note that structural features of institutions (size, control, selectivity, percentage of minority students, etc.) generally have only an indirect influence on students—their effects being mediated through the experiences students have in the institution's general environment. If it were true that increasing the number of minority students on a campus must *by itself be sufficient* for achieving desired educational outcomes, then having good buildings, high faculty salaries, and good libraries would all be sufficient to ensure a good education. No one with the responsibility for educating students would make such an argument, precisely because the nature of educational activities and the extent to which the students make use of these resources are crucial for achieving an excellent education. Thus, a diverse student body is clearly a resource and a necessary condition for engagement with diverse peers that permits higher education to achieve its educational goals.

Diversity enables students to perceive differences both within groups and between groups and is the primary reason why significant numbers of students of various groups are needed in the classroom. The worst consequence of the lack of diversity arises when a minority student is a token in a classroom. In such situations, the solo or token minority individual is often given undue attention, visibility, and distinctiveness, which can lead to greater stereotyping by majority group members (Kanter, 1977). These effects of the solo or token situation are well-documented in the research literature (Lord & Saenz, 1985; Mellor, 1996; Sekaquaptewa & Thompson, 2002; Spangler, Gordon, & Pipkin, 1978; Thompson & Sekaquaptewa, 2002; Yoder, 1994). Research shows that individuals become more aware of within-group variability when the minority group is not too small relative to the majority group (Mullen & Hu, 1989; Mullen & Johnson, 1993), and that individuals have more complex views of members of other groups when relative group size is not greatly imbalanced (Mullen, Rozell, & Johnson, 2000).

The results of our research also support the conclusion of an *amicus* brief filed on behalf of the University of Michigan by General Motors:

> Diversity in academic institutions is essential to teaching students the human relations and analytic skills they need to thrive and lead in the work environments of the twenty-first century. These skills include the abilities to work well with colleagues and subordinates from diverse backgrounds; to view issues from multiple perspectives; and to anticipate and respond with sensitivity to the needs and cultural differences of highly diverse customers, colleagues, employees, and global business partners.
>
> (Brief of General Motors, 2000, p. 2)

Significant Features of the Research

Four features of this research give it particular importance in the continuing debate about education and diversity. First, we have offered a theoretical rationale for the impact of diversity, whereas much of the testimony offered in previous court cases in higher education has been largely anecdotal. Second, the consistency of the results across both a national study of multiple institutions and a single institution provides significant support for our theoretical rationale. This kind of cross-validation is not always possible and in this instance increases confidence in our conclusions. Third, having both a national and a single institutional study protects against inappropriate generalizations that might have been made had only one study been available for this research. For example, we might have generalized from the national study that informal interactional diversity is always more important than classroom diversity, whereas the Michigan study calls for a more nuanced conclusion. Fourth, the longitudinal nature of both studies, in which many of the same measures were taken at entrance to college and four years later, made it possible to talk about an effect of diversity with some assuredness. In most of the analyses reported here it was possible to control for students' scores on the outcome measures when they entered college. This is a traditional method of assessing effects in studies of college students and allows us to conclude that diversity experiences had an impact on active thinking and intellectual engagement and on the orientations and sentiments that students will need to become leaders in a diverse democracy.

Other control variables that we employed in all analyses also address, at least partially, the selectivity problem—that certain kinds of students might be predisposed to take courses that deal with race and ethnicity and to interact with students from varied backgrounds. For example, it is plausible that students who entered college with greater exposure to diverse peers because they lived in racially heterogeneous neighborhoods and attended heterogeneous high schools might seek diversity experiences in college. We were able to control for this because we had measures of neighborhood and high school racial composition in both studies. The control for initial position on the outcome measures also minimizes selectivity to some extent. It adjusts for the possibility that students already intellectually engaged and motivated to be active thinkers—or students already committed to participate in citizenship activities and to understand the perspectives of other people when they enter college—might choose to take diversity courses and to seek relationships with diverse students. A careful reader will know, however, that the controls for these predisposing influences do not remove all sources of selection bias. Our approach does not control for correlated error in the predisposing and outcome measures, and correlated error may bring about selection bias. This is a limitation in the study, although in the Michigan data we have attempted to further reduce selection bias in another way. We were able to demonstrate an effect of classroom diversity for students who did not choose to take race and ethnicity courses but were required to do so for college graduation. As we have already noted, undergraduates in the College of Literature, Sciences, and the Arts, who comprise 70 percent of the Michigan study sample, are required to take at least one course that addresses issues of race/ethnicity. This requirement significantly decreases the likelihood that selection bias could explain the effects of experience with classroom diversity in the Michigan study results.

Implications for Practice

In the post–civil rights era and beyond, higher education leaders set the vision to create in their institutions a microcosm of the equitable and democratic society we aspire to become. The admission of a more racially/ethnically diverse student body is an important starting point in realizing this vision. Classroom diversity, diversity programming, opportunities for interaction, and learning across diverse groups of students in the college environment now constitute important initiatives to enhance the education of all students.[12] The results of this research not only support the curricular initiatives that introduce diversity into college courses, but also suggest that more attention should be given to the types of experiences students have with diverse peers inside and outside the classroom. Both the theory and findings indicate that individual students benefit when they are engaged with diverse peers; however, as a society we have provided no template for interaction across racial/ethnic groups and such interaction cannot be taken for granted in the college environment. Helping faculty develop a pedagogy that makes the most of the diverse perspectives and student backgrounds in their classrooms can foster active thinking, intellectual engagement, and democratic participation. In addition, colleges and universities should provide a supportive environment in which disequilibrium and experimentation can occur by increasing interaction among diverse peers and help faculty and students manage conflict when individuals share different points of views. (See Gurin, Nagda, and Lopez, in press; Lopez, Gurin, and Nagda, 1998; and Nagda, Gurin, and Lopez, in press, for analyses of the effects of the Intergroup Relations, Community and Conflict Program, a program at the University of Michigan explicitly designed to accomplish these pedagogical and learning goals.) Given the evidence from higher education research on the impact of peer groups (Astin, 1993b; Kuh, 1993; Pasacarella & Terenzini, 1991), student affairs administrators may understand best the power of peer group interaction for student learning and development. However, in order to foster citizenship for a diverse democracy, educators must intentionally structure opportunities for students to leave the comfort of their homogeneous peer group and build relationships across racially/ethnically diverse student communities on campus.

NOTES

1. Justice Lewis Powell is quoting, in part, the U.S. Supreme Court's decision in *Keyshian v. Board of Regents* (1967).
2. The Supreme Court has not acted on affirmative action in higher education admissions since the *Bakke* case in 1978. In that case, Justice Powell wrote the defining opinion. Controversy exists with respect to how many justices joined him in arguing that race could be used as one of many factors in admissions provided that the institution could show that it was being used to achieve racial/ethnic diversity, that diversity was a compelling governmental interest, and that the method of achieving diversity was "narrowly tailored" to meet that interest. Narrow tailoring means that race is used no more than is necessary to achieve diversity and that it is only one of many factors being used. Justice Powell argued that diversity is a compelling interest, though of course there are debates about what he meant by diversity. These arguments are part of the legal dispute now being heard in the courts in two cases involving the University of Michigan (*Gratz v. Bollinger, et al.*, 2002; *Grutter v. Bollinger, et al.*, 2002).
3. As of this writing, the Court has not ruled in *Gratz*. The Center for Individual Rights, representing the plaintiff, Barbara Grutter, has appealed the Sixth Circuit Court decision in the law school case to the U.S. Supreme Court.

4. Similar ideas have been offered by sociologists Melvin Kohn and Carmi Schooler (1978) in a series of classic papers delineating features of work environments that produce "intellectual flexibility." They found that work that involves tasks requiring workers to think and make judgments is an important determinant of intellectual flexibility. Workers who are less closely supervised and thus have to think about what they are doing demonstrate more thoughtful response patterns.

5. Connecting racial and ethnic diversity to multiple perspectives does *not* mean that students from a particular group have identical perspectives. Our point is not to argue that all members of a particular racial/ethnic group are the same due to some inherent, essential, and probably biological quality. Our argument is the exact opposite of such a group-based and stereotypical assumption. As Jonathan Alger (1998) stresses, the import of diversity comes from the range of similarities and differences within and among racial groups.

6. Parental education level was the only socioeconomic status (SES) proxy common to both the national and Michigan datasets. It is important to note that measures of parental education have been used in previous CIRP studies as part of a latent SES construct in confirmatory factor analyses using samples of diverse students, with father's education loading at .79 and mother's education loading at .86 (Hurtado, Dey, & Trevino, 1994).

7. We ran preliminary analyses using a Hierarchical Linear Modeling (HLM) approach, but the results obtained were not substantially different from those produced by models based on a traditional linear model approach. Moreover, an analysis of diagnostic statistics (such as the intraclass correlation coefficient) did not suggest that it would be productive to consistently employ the HLM approach. Therefore, we proceeded with the multiple regression analysis.

8. The MSS queried students of color about their interactions with other groups of color, but in this chapter we emphasize the major racial divide in the United States between Whites and groups of color. The complexities of interactions among different groups of color require separate treatment because they cannot be given the depth of analysis they deserve within this chapter.

9. Further evidence for the validity of using self-reports comes from a study (Anaya, 1999) that analyzed data from a subsample of the students who had taken the GRE, drawn from the CIRP cohort analyzed here. Anaya's results show that similar substantive conclusions can be made using GRE scores and using students' self-assessments of their learning.

10. Analyses testing for statistical interaction effects among the diversity experiences and outcomes did not produce a significant increase in the variance explained in the additive regression model. Therefore, we focus here on the main effects of the diversity experiences.

11. In the national study, 82 percent of the separate diversity effects were still statistically reliable when the two diversity experiences were considered simultaneously. When the three diversity experiences were considered simultaneously in the Michigan Student Study data, three of the separate diversity effects were no longer statistically reliable, *and* two additional net effects were statistically significant.

12. Over 60 percent of institutions have added some type of diversity course requirement to their general education program.

REFERENCES

Acredolo, C., & O'Connor, J. (1991). On the difficulty of detecting cognitive uncertainty. *Human Development, 34,* 204–223.

Alger, J. R. (1998). Unfinished homework for universities: Making the case for affirmative action. *Washington University Journal of Urban and Contemporary Law, 54,* 73–92.

Allport, G. (1954). *The nature of prejudice.* Cambridge, MA: Addison-Wesley.

Alwin, D. F., Cohen, R. I., & Newcomb, T. L. (1991). *Political attitudes over the life span.* Madison: University of Wisconsin Press.

Anaya, G. (1999). College impact on student learning: Comparing the use of self-reported gains, standardized test scores, and college grades. *Research in Higher Education, 40,* 499–526.

antonio, a. (1998). *The impact of friendship groups in a multicultural university.* Unpublished doctoral dissertation, University of California, Los Angeles.

Association of American Colleges and Universities. (1985). Integrity in the college curriculum. Washington, DC. Author.

Astin, A. W. (1993a). Diversity and multiculturalism on campus: How are students affected? *Change, 25*(2), 44–49.

Astin, A. W. (1993b). *What matters in college?* San Francisco: Jossey-Bass.

Barber, B. R. (1998). *A passion for democracy.* Princeton, NJ: Princeton University Press.

Bargh, J. A. (1997). The automaticity of everyday life. *Advances in Social Cognition, 10,* 2–48.

Berlyne, D. E. (1970). Children's reasoning and thinking. In P. H. Mussen (Ed.), *Carmichael's manual of child psychology* (vol. 1, pp. 939–981). New York: Wiley.

Bolden, V. A., Goldberg, D. T., & Parker, D. D. (1999). Affirmative action in court: The case for optimism. *Equity and Excellence in Education, 3*(2), 24–30.

Bowen, W. G., & Bok, D. (1998). *The shape of the river: Long-term consequences of considering race in college and university admissions.* Princeton, NJ: Princeton University Press.

Bowen, W. G., Bok, D., & Burkhart, G. (1999). A report card on diversity: Lessons for business from higher education. *Harvard Business Review, 77,* 138–149.

Brief of General Motors Corporation as amicus curiae in support of defendants, Gratz v. Bollinger, et al., 122 F.Supp.2d 811 (2000).

Cacioppo, J. T., & Petty, R. E. (1982). The need for cognition. *Journal of Personality and Social Psychology, 42,* 116–131.

Chang, M. J. (1996). *Racial diversity in higher education: Does a racially mixed student population affect educational outcomes?* Unpublished doctoral dissertation, University of California, Los Angeles.

Chang, M. J. (1999). Does diversity matter? The educational impact of a racially diverse undergraduate population. *Journal of College Student Development, 40,* 377–395.

Chang, M. J., Witt-Sandis, D., Hakuta, K. (1999). The dynamics of race in higher education: An examination of the evidence. *Equity and Excellence in Education, 32*(2), 12–16.

Coser, R. (1975). The complexity of roles as a seedbed of individual autonomy. In L. A. Coser (Ed.), *The idea of social structure: Papers in honor of Robert K. Merton* (pp. 85–102). New York: Harcourt Brace Jovanovich.

Davis, M. H. (1983). Measuring individual differences in empathy: Evidence for a multidimensional approach. *Journal of Personality and Social Psychology, 44,* 113–126.

Dey, E. L. (1991). *Perceptions of the college environment: An analysis of organizational, interpersonal, and behavioral influences.* Unpublished dissertation, University of California, Los Angeles.

Doise, W., & Palmonari, A. (Eds.). (1984). *Social interaction in individual development.* New York: Cambridge University Press.

Erikson, E. (1946). Ego development and historical change. *Psychoanalytic Study of the Child, 2,* 359–396.

Erikson, E. (1956). The problem of ego identity. *Journal of American Psychoanalytic Association, 4,* 56–121.

Ewell, P. T., & Jones, D. P. (1993). Actions matter: The case for indirect measures in assessing higher education's progress on the national education goals. *Journal of General Education, 42,* 123–148.

Fiske, S. T. (1993). Social cognition and social perception. *Annual Review of Psychology, 44,* 155–194.

Fletcher, G. J. O., Danilovics, P., Fernandez, G., Peterson, D., & Reeder, G. D. (1986). Attributional complexity: An individual differences measure. *Journal of Personality and Social Psychology, 51,* 875–884.

Fredrickson, G. M. (1999). Models of American ethnic relations: An historical perspective. In D. Prentice & D. Miller (Eds.), *Cultural divides: The social psychology of intergroup contact* (pp. 23–45). New York: Russell Sage.

Gratz v. Bollinger, et al., 122 F.Supp.2d 811 (2000).

Grutter v. Bollinger, et al., 137 F. Supp.2d 821 (E.D. Mich. 2001), rev'd, 288 F.3d 732 (6th Cir. 2002).

Gurin, P., Nagda, R., & Lopez, G. (in press). Preparation for citizenship. *Journal of Social Issues.*

Gurin, P., Peng, T., Lopez, G., & Nagda, B. R. (1999). Context, identity, and intergroup relations. In D. Prentice & D. Miller (Eds.), *Cultural divides: The social psychology of intergroup contact* (pp. 133–172). New York: Russell Sage.

Guarasci, R., & Cornwell, G. H. (Eds.). (1997). *Democratic education in an age of difference: Redefining citizenship in higher education.* San Francisco: Jossey-Bass.

Hilton, J. L., & von Hippel, W. (1996). Stereotypes. In J. T. Spence, J. M. Darley, & D. J. Foss (Eds.), *Annual Review of Psychology* (vol. 47, pp. 237–271). Palo Alto, CA: Annual Reviews.

Hopwood v. University of Texas, 78 F.3d 932 (5th Cir., 1996), cert. Denied, 518 U.S. 1033.

Hurtado, S. (1992). Campus racial climates: Contexts for conflict. *Journal of Higher Education, 63,* 539–569.

Hurtado, S. (2001) Linking diversity and educational purpose: How diversity affects the classroom environment and student development. In G. Orfield (Ed.), *Diversity challenged: Evidence on the impact of affirmative action* (pp. 187–203). Cambridge, MA: Harvard Education Publishing Group and The Civil Rights Project at Harvard University.

Hurtado, S., Dey, E. L., & Trevino, J. G. (1994, April). *Exclusion or self-segregation? Interaction across racial/ethnic groups on campus.* Paper presented at the annual meeting of the American Educational Research Association, New Orleans.

Hurtado, S., Milem, J., Clayton-Pederson, A., & Allen, W. (1999). *Enacting diverse learning environments: Improving the climate for racial/ethnic diversity in higher education.* San Francisco: Jossey-Bass.

Johnson v. Board of Regents of the University of Georgia, 263 F.3d. 1234 (11th Cir. 2001).

Kanter, R. M. (1977). Some effects of proportions on group life: Skewed sex ratios and responses to token women. *American Journal of Sociology, 82,* 965–990.

Keyshian v. Board of Regents, 385 U.S. 589 (1967).

Kohn, M. L., & Schooler, C. (1978). The reciprocal effects of the substantive complexity of work and intellectual flexibility: A longitudinal assessment. *American Journal of Sociology, 84*(1), 24–52.

Komaromy, M., Grumbach, K., Drake, M., Vranizan, K., Lurie, N., Keane, D., & Bindman, A. B. (1997). The role of Black and Hispanic physicians in providing health care for underserved populations. *New England Journal of Medicine, 334,* 1305–1310.

Kuh, G. D. (1993). In their own words: What students learn outside the classroom. *American Educational Review Journal, 30,* 277–304.

Langer, E. J. (1978). Rethinking the role of thought in social interaction. In J. Harvey, W. Ickes, & R. Kiss (Eds.), *New directions in attribution research* (vol. 3, pp. 35–38). Hillsdale, NJ: Erlbaum.

Lopez, G. E., Gurin, P., & Nagda, B. A. (1998). Education and understanding structural causes for group inequalities. *Political Psychology, 19,* 305–329.

Lord, C. G., & Saenz, D. S. (1985). Memory deficits and memory surfeits: Differential cognitive consequences of tokenism for tokens and observers. *Journal of Personality and Social Psychology, 49,* 918–926.

Maruyama, G., Moreno, J. F., Gudeman, R. W., & Marin, P. (2000). *Does diversity make a difference? Three research studies on diversity in college classrooms.* Washington, DC: American Council on Education.

Mellor, S. (1996). Gender composition and gender representation in local unions: Relationships between women's participation in local office and women's participation in local activities. *Journal of Applied Psychology, 80,* 706–720.

Milem, J., & Hakuta, K. (2000). The benefits of racial and ethnic diversity in higher education. In D. J. Wilds (Ed.), *Minorities in higher education, 1999–2000, seventeenth annual status report* (pp. 39–67). Washington, DC: American Council on Education.

Mullen, B., & Hu, L. (1989). Perceptions of ingroup and outgroup variability: A meta-analytic integration. *Basic Applied Social Psychology, 25,* 525–559.

Mullen, B., & Johnson C. (1993). The determinants of differential group evaluations in distinctiveness-based illusory correlations in stereotyping. *British Journal of Social Psychology, 32,* 253–304.

Mullen, B., Rozell, D., & Johnson, C. (2000). Ethnophaulisms for ethnic immigrant groups: Cognitive representation of the minority and the foreigner. *Group Processes and Intergroup Relations, 3,* 5–24.

Nagda, R., Gurin, P., & Lopez, G. (in press). Transformative pedagogy for democracy and social justice. *Race, Ethnicity, and Education.*

Newcomb, T. L. (1943). *Personality and social change: Attitude formation in a student community.* New York: Dryden Press.

Newcomb, T. L., Koenig, K. E., Flacks, R., & Warwick, D. P. (1967). *Persistence and change: Bennington College and its students after 25 years*. New York: John Wiley & Sons.

Orfield, G. (Ed.). (2001). *Diversity challenged: Evidence on the impact of affirmative action*. Cambridge, MA: Harvard Education Publishing Group.

Orfield, G., Bachmeier, M., James, D. R., & Eitle, T. (1997). Deepening segregation in American public schools: A special report from the Harvard Project on School Desegregation. *Equity and Excellence in Education, 30*(2), 5–24.

Orfield, G., & Miller, E. (Eds.). (1998). *Chilling admissions: The affirmative action crisis and the search for alternatives*. Cambridge, MA: Harvard Education Publishing Group and The Civil Rights Project at Harvard University.

Orfield, G., & Kurlaender, M. (1999). In defense of diversity: New research and evidence from the University of Michigan. *Equity and Excellence in Education, 32*(2), 31–35.

Orfield, G., & Whitla, D. (1999). *Diversity and legal education: Student experiences in leading law schools*. Cambridge, MA: The Civil Rights Project at Harvard University.

Pascarella, E. T., Edison, M., Nora, A., Hagedorn, L. S., & Terenzini, P. T. (1996). Influences on students' openness to diversity and challenge in the first year of college. *Journal of Higher Education, 67*, 174–195.

Pascarella, E. T., & Terenzini, P. T. (1991). *How college affects students*. San Francisco: Jossey-Bass.

Piaget, J. (1965). *The moral judgement of the child*. New York: Free Press.

Piaget, J. (1971). The theory of stages in cognitive development. In D. R. Green, M. P. Ford, & G. B. Flamer (Eds.), *Measurement and Piaget* (pp. 1–111). New York: McGraw-Hill.

Piaget, J. (1985). *The equilibration of cognitive structures: The central problem of intellectual development*. Chicago: University of Chicago Press. (Original work published 1975)

Pitkin, H. F., & Shumer, S. M. (1982). On participation. *Democracy, 2*, 43–54.

Regents of the University of California v. Bakke, 438 U.S. 312, 98 S. Ct. 2760 (1978).

Ruble, D. (1994). Developmental changes in achievement evaluation: motivational implications of self-other differences. *Child Development, 65*, 1095–1110.

Saxonhouse, A. (1992). *Fear of diversity: The birth of political science in ancient Greek thought*, Chicago: University of Chicago Press.

Sekaquaptewa, D., & Thompson, M. (2002). The differential effects of solo status on members of high and low status groups. *Personality and Social Psychology Bulletin, 28*, 694–707.

Smith, D. G. (1997). *Diversity works: The emerging picture of how students benefit*. Washington, DC: Association of American Colleges and Universities.

Smith v. University of Washington Law School, 233 F.3d 1188 (9th Cir. 2000) cert. Denied 532 U.S. 1051 (2001).

Spangler, E., Gordon, M. A., & Pipkin, R. M. (1978). Token women: An empirical test of Kanter's hypothesis. *American Journal of Sociology, 84*, 160–170.

Terenzini, P. T., Rendon. L. I., Upcraft, M. L., Millar, S. B., Allison, K. W., Gregg, P. L., & Jalomo, R. (1994). The transition to college: Diverse students, diverse stories. *Research in Higher Education, 35*(1), 57–73.

Terenzini, P. T., Springer, L., Pascarella, E. T., & Nora, A. (1994*). The multiple influences of college on students' critical thinking skills.* Paper presented at the annual meeting of the Association for the Study of Higher Education, Tucson, AZ.

Thompson, M., & Sekaquaptewa, D. (2002). When being different is detrimental: Solo status and the performance of women and racial minorities. *Analyses of Social Issues and Public Policy, 2*, 183–203.

Yoder, J. D. (1994). Looking beyond numbers: The effects of gender status, job prestige, and occupational gender-typing on tokenism processes. *Social Psychology Quarterly, 57*, 150–159.

15

Nine Themes in Campus Racial Climates and Implications for Institutional Transformation

Shaun R. Harper and Sylvia Hurtado

Administrators at two universities were probably less than excited about the news coverage their campuses received on April 27, 2006. Although they were located in different regions of the country, various indicators of racism and racial/ethnic minority student discontent were apparent at both institutions. On one campus in the Northeast, four alarming headlines and racerelated stories were printed on the front page of the student newspaper. An incident in which a campus police officer made racist remarks to three African American female students was juxtaposed with the story of a philosophy professor suing the university for demoting him from department chair because he reported to the dean of his college that students had been racially harassed and discriminated against by his faculty colleagues. The third front-page article described a letter sent to the administration by Hillel, the Jewish student organization, demanding an apology and other concessions for the unfair cancellation of a student art exhibit on campus. Among their requests, Hillel student board members asked the university to conduct "an investigation into the discrimination, racism, and intimidation" one of their members experienced in his interactions with the art gallery director.

A protest at the Office of the President organized by Black Caucus and the LGBT (lesbian, gay, bisexual, and transgender) student organization the day before was described in the final story. Protestors said they were insulted that staff members locked the office door and the president walked by refusing to address their concerns. Therefore, they slid a letter under the door, chanted outside on megaphones, and subsequently posted a video of the entire protest on YouTube.com. The protest was in response to what students perceived to be insufficient punishment against the women's head basketball coach, a White woman, who allegedly interrogated a Black female player about her sexual orientation, repeatedly threatened to dismiss the student from the team if it was discovered that she was in fact a lesbian, and eventually demanded that the player leave the team. While this story appears to be more about sexual orientation than race, Black Caucus members were especially disturbed that this happened to an African American woman who was probably not the first or only player the coach suspected was gay. Perhaps institutional leaders believed these were isolated incidents that coincidentally occurred around the same time, hence there being no formal assessment of the campus racial climate following this day of problematic news coverage.

With support from the president and provost, the second university commissioned an audit of its campus racial climate. The day after a public presentation of preliminary findings from the audit, a reporter from the city newspaper wrote an article with a bold headline indicating the institution had received "a poor racial report card." The story included a summary of the auditor's findings and this quote from an African American male sophomore: "It is not a sensitive community for Black students. If I stay, the only reason will be to help effect change." The article was also retrieved by the Associated Press and reprinted in newspapers across the nation. Unlike at the first university, administrators on this campus felt public pressure to respond to the problems that had been exposed and were expected to use findings from the racial climate audit to guide institutional change. Within one year, the midwestern school hired a chief diversity officer, crafted a memorandum of understanding with the local chapter of the National Association for the Advancement of Colored People to improve the campus racial climate, organized a conference to examine the status of racial/ethnic minority male students, and pursued more purposefully the recruitment of a diverse faculty, among other efforts. The audit clearly raised institutional consciousness about the realities of race on campus and revealed racial toxins that had long existed but remained unaddressed.

These two predominantly White institutions (PWIs) had similar responses to racial issues on campus. Although the second university was forced to change after having been embarrassed in the local and national press, it is highly unlikely that the audit was the first indicator of racial turbulence on campus. Instead, there had been signals such as those at the first institution that had been disregarded, either intentionally or inadvertently. Unfortunately, such incidents and subsequent responses are not atypical.

In this chapter, we synthesize fifteen years of research about campus racial climates and present nine themes that emerged from a multi-institutional qualitative study we conducted. The primary goal here is to illuminate trends that persist on many college and university campuses, especially those that are predominantly White. At the end of the chapter, we use perspectives on transparency and organizational change to frame our implications for institutional transformation.

POST-1992 RESEARCH ON CAMPUS RACIAL CLIMATES

"The Campus Racial Climate: Contexts of Conflict" (Hurtado, 1992) is the most widely cited study on this topic. Results were derived from the Cooperative Institutional Research Program (CIRP) fourth-year follow-up survey, a nationally representative longitudinal study of college students in the late 1980s. Among the most salient findings was that approximately one in four survey respondents perceived considerable racial conflict on their campuses; this proportion was even higher at four-year institutions that were large, public, or selective. When racial conflict was present on campus, few students were convinced that fostering racially diverse learning environments was a high institutional priority. Racial/ethnic minority students were more likely to believe espoused institutional commitments to multiculturalism when racial tension was low. Hurtado also found that White students were less likely than Blacks and Latinos to perceive racial tension on their campuses, as most believed racism was no longer problematic in society. Furthermore, she concluded that racial tension is probable in environments where there is little concern for individual students, which is symptomatic of many large PWIs that enroll several thousand undergraduates.

The Hurtado study has been reprinted in books and frequently cited by scholars who have written about racial realities on college campuses over the past fifteen years. Given the problematic nature of the results presented in this landmark study, we retrieved and analyzed empirical research studies that have since been published in education and social sciences journals to determine how campus racial climates have evolved since 1992. Although considerable effort has been devoted to studying various topics concerning racial/ethnic minority undergraduates at PWIs, we reviewed only journal articles that focused on the racialized experiences of college students and campus racial climates. Also excluded are climate studies regarding racial/ethnic minority faculty and other underrepresented populations (such as LGBT and low-income students), conceptual pieces, literature reviews, unpublished conference papers, dissertations and theses, legal proceedings, reports, and books (with one exception: Feagin, Vera, and Imani, 1996). Findings from studies that have been published since 1992 can be divided into three categories: (1) differential perceptions of campus climate by race, (2) racial/ethnic minority student reports of prejudicial treatment and racist campus environments, and (3) benefits associated with campus climates that facilitate cross-racial engagement. Studies in which these findings have emerged as well as the methods and samples on which they are based are presented in Table 15.1. Seventy-one percent of the articles we reviewed are based on quantitative methods, and only one qualitative study (Solórzano, Ceja, and Yosso, 2000) was conducted at multiple institutions. Also apparent is that too few researchers have explored how Asian American and Native American students experience campus racial climates. What follows is a brief synopsis of recurring findings within each thematic cluster of studies.

Differential Perceptions of Campus Climate by Race

Researchers have consistently found that racial/ethnic minority students and their White peers who attend the same institution often view the campus racial climate in different ways. For example, racial/ethnic minorities in Rankin and Reason's study (2005) perceived campus climates as more racist and less accepting than did White survey respondents. Similarly, D'Augelli and Hershberger (1993) noted, "Almost all of the sampled African American students reported having borne the brunt of racist remarks and most assumed that African Americans would be mistreated on campus" (p. 77). White students in their study did not report similar experiences and expectations. Nora and Cabrera (1996) found that Whites and racial/ethnic minorities alike perceived the campus climate negatively, reported discrimination from faculty, and recognized insensitivity in the classroom. However, White students' perceptions were weaker on all three measures and not necessarily attributable to race. While both White and Black participants in Cabrera and Nora's study (1994) felt alienated in various ways on campus, racial prejudice and discrimination was the predominant source of such feelings among the latter group.

Radloff and Evans (2003) linked perceptual differences to their participants' home communities. That is, the White students they interviewed grew up in predominantly White neighborhoods and thus had limited firsthand exposure to racism prior to college. Cabrera and others (1999) found that perceptions of racial prejudice had greater effects on Black students' levels of institutional commitment in comparison to their White counterparts who had also experienced various forms of discrimination. Multiple studies have shown that Black students report lower levels of satisfaction with racial climates and perceive differential treatment on the basis of race more frequently than do their Asian American, Latino, Native American, and White peers (Ancis, Sedlacek, and Mohr, 2000; Cabrera and Nora, 1994; Hurtado, 1992; Suarez-Balcazar and others, 2003). These differences are not just in perceptions but also in the way racial/ethnic minority students experience PWIs.

TABLE 15.1

Clusters of Post-1992 Research Studies on Student Experiences with Race and Campus Racial Climates

Authors	Research Design	Sites	Sample (N)	Respondents/Participants
Differential perceptions of campus climate by race				
Ancis, Sedlacek, and Mohr (2000)	Quantitative	Single	578	Asian American, Black, Latino, and White students
Cabrera and Nora (1994)	Quantitative	Single	879	Asian American, Black, Latino, and White students
Cabrera and others (1999)	Quantitative	Multiple	1,454	Black and White students
D'Augelli and Hershberger (1993)	Quantitative	Single	146	Black and White students
Eimers and Pike (1997)	Quantitative	Single	799	Asian American, Black, Latino, Native American, and White students
Helm, Sedlacek, and Prieto (1998)	Quantitative	Single	566	Asian American, Black, Latino, and White students
Johnson-Durgans (1994)	Quantitative	Single	2,957	Black and White students
Nora and Cabrera (1996)	Quantitative	Single	831	Asian American, Black, Latino, Native American, and White students
Radloff and Evans (2003)	Qualitative	Single	27	Black and White students
Rankin and Reason (2005)	Quantitative	Multiple	7,347	Asian American, Black, Latino, Native American, and White students
Suarez-Balcazar and others (2003)	Quantitative	Single	322	Asian American, Black, Latino, and White students
Racial/ethnic minority student reports of prejudicial treatment and racist campus environments				
Davis and others (2004)	Qualitative	Single	11	Black students
Diver-Stamnes and LoMascolo (2001)	Qualitative	Single	153	Asian American, Black, Latino, Native American, and White students
Feagin, Vera, and Imani (1996)	Qualitative	Single	77	Black students and Parents
Fries-Britt and Turner (2001)	Qualitative	Single	15	Black students
Hurtado (1994a)	Quantitative	Multiple	510	Black and Latino students
Hurtado (1994b)	Quantitative	Multiple	859	Latino students
Hurtado and Carter (1997)	Quantitative	Multiple	272	Latino students
Hurtado, Carter, and Spuler (1996)	Quantitative	Multiple	203	Latino students
Lewis, Chesler, and Forman (2000)	Qualitative	Single	75	Asian American, Black, Latino, and Native American students
Smedley, Myers, and Harrell (1993)	Quantitative	Single	161	Asian American, Black, and Latino students
Solórzano, Ceja, and Yosso (2000)	Qualitative	Multiple	34	Black students
Swim and others (2003)	Mixed	Single	51	Black students
Turner (1994)	Qualitative	Single	32	Asian American, Black, Latino, and Native American students and faculty
Benefits associated with campus climates that facilitate cross-racial engagement				
antonio (2004)	Qualitative	Single	18	Asian American, Black, Latino, and White students
antonio and others (2004)	Mixed	Multiple	357	White students
Chang (1999)	Quantitative	Multiple	11,680	Asian American, Black, Latino, and White students
Chang (2001)	Quantitative	Single	167	Asian American, Black, Latino, and White students
Chang, Astin, and Kim (2004)	Quantitative	Multiple	9,703	Asian American, Black, Latino, and White students
Chang, Denson, Sáenz, and Misa (2006)	Quantitative	Multiple	19,667	Asian American, Black, Latino, Native American, and White students
Gurin, Dey, Hurtado, and Gurin (2002)	Quantitative	Multiple	12,965	Asian American, Black, Latino, and White students
Levin, van Laar, and Sidanius (2003)	Quantitative	Single	1,215	Asian American, Black, Latino, and White students
Milem, Umbach, and Liang (2004)	Quantitative	Single	536	White students
Pike and Kuh (2006)	Quantitative	Multiple	42,588	Asian American, Black, Latino, and White students
Sáenz, Ngai, and Hurtado (2007)	Quantitative	Multiple	4,380	Asian American, Black, Latino, and White students

Minority Student Reports of Prejudicial Treatment and Racist Campus Environments

The second cluster of studies, half of them qualitative, offer insights into how racial/ethnic minority students experience race and racism on predominantly White campuses. Consistent with the pre-1992 literature (Allen, 1988; Fleming, 1984; Loo and Rolison, 1986; Nettles, Thoeny, and Gosman, 1986), the research reviewed here consistently calls attention to the isolation, alienation, and stereotyping with which these students are often forced to contend on campuses where they are not the majority. Perhaps the title of Caroline Sotello Viernes Turner's article, "Guests in Someone Else's House: Students of Color" (1994), best characterizes a feeling that is shared among many at most PWIs. In their study of racial/ethnic minority first-year students, Smedley, Myers, and Harrell (1993) discovered that racial conflict and race-laden accusations of intellectual inferiority from White peers and faculty engendered stresses beyond those generally associated with attending a highly selective university; they also found these stresses were most pronounced among Black students. While similar research has focused mostly on undergraduates, Hurtado (1994a) confirmed that Black and Latino graduate students are not immune to the deleterious effects of campus racial climates.

In their study of Latino student transition to college, Hurtado, Carter, and Spuler (1996) suggested, "Even the most talented Latinos are likely to have difficulty adjusting if they perceive a climate where majority students think all minorities are special admits [and] Hispanics feel like they do not 'fit in.' . . . Students may internalize these climate observations, presumably because these are more difficult to identify or sanction than overt forms of discrimination" (p. 152). Reportedly, experiences with racial discrimination and perceptions of racial/ethnic tension complicated the participants' first- and second-year transitions. Beyond the first year, Hurtado and Carter (1997) found that perceptions of racial hostility had negative effects on Latino students' sense of belonging in the junior year of college. In another study (Hurtado, 1994b), 68 percent of the high-achieving Latino students surveyed felt their peers knew very little about Hispanic culture, which significantly increased the participants' feelings of racial/ethnic tension and reports of discriminatory experiences on campus.

Feagin, Vera, and Imani's study (1996) appears to be the first to involve both Black students and parents in an examination of the campus racial climate. Situated at a public university in the Southeast, the participants were well aware of the institution's racist history and the reputation it had garnered for being racially toxic. And the students described the confrontations they had with White peers and faculty, the absence of cultural space they could call their own, barriers to successfully navigating the institution, and the constant burden of disproving racist stereotypes regarding their academic abilities. Fries-Britt and Turner (2001) described how Black students' confidence in their academic abilities is often eroded by stereotypes regarding their intellectual inferiority and presumed entry to universities because of affirmative action.

Black undergraduates participating in a research study by Swim and others (2003) wrote in diaries each time (if at all) they experienced racism or perceived something on their campuses to be racist over a two-week period. Thirty-six percent documented unfriendly looks and skeptical stares from White students and faculty, 24 percent chronicled derogatory and stereotypical verbal remarks directed toward them, 18 percent kept a log of bad service received in the dining hall and other facilities on campus, and 15 percent noted other assorted incidents. The students attributed all of this negative treatment to racism. Solórzano, Ceja, and Yosso (2000) found that when Black students experience racial microaggressions (subtle verbal, nonverbal, or visual insults), they begin to feel academically and socially alienated in spaces where such oppression occurs, and as a defense mechanism they create their own academic and social counterspaces (ethnic enclaves that offer shelter from the psycho-emotional harms of racial microaggressions). While the worth of ethnic culture centers, minority student organizations, and other counterspaces has been empirically proven in recent studies (Guiffrida, 2003; Harper and Quaye, 2007; Patton, 2006; Solórzano and Villalpando, 1998), a reality is that they often limit interactions between White students and racial/ethnic minorities.

Benefits Associated with Campus Climates That Facilitate Cross-Racial Engagement

Findings from studies in the third cluster are relatively consistent. Researchers have recently furnished a large body of empirical evidence to confirm the educational merit of deliberately creating racially diverse college campuses. Much of this evidence was used in support of testimony for the University of Michigan affirmative action cases (*Gratz* v. *Bollinger* and *Grutter* v. *Bollinger*). These studies verify that students who attend racially diverse institutions and are engaged in educationally purposeful activities that involve interactions with peers from different racial/ethnic backgrounds come to enjoy cognitive, psychosocial, and interpersonal gains that are useful during and after college (antonio and others, 2004; Chang, 1999, 2001; Chang, Astin, and Kim, 2004; Chang, Denson, Sáenz, and Misa, 2006; Gurin, Dey, Hurtado, and Gurin, 2002; Pike and Kuh, 2006).

Exposure to diverse perspectives during college could interrupt longstanding segregation trends in society. Students (especially Whites) who engage meaningfully with peers from different backgrounds and diverse perspectives both inside and outside college classrooms are unlikely to remain isolated within their own racial/ethnic communities (Sáenz, Nagi, and Hurtado, 2007), which is believed to be sustainable in environments (such as residential neighborhoods) after college (Milem, Umbach, and Liang, 2004). In contrast to those who maintained racially homogeneous friendships, undergraduates (especially first-year students) with friends outside their race held fewer biases about and expressed less anxiety toward racially different others at the end of college (Levin, van Laar, and Sidanius, 2003). Participants in antonio's study on friendship grouping (2004) agreed their campus was racially segregated and could describe the range of racially homogeneous groups that existed. Despite this, many selected best friends based on those with whom they interacted most in the first year of college, not on the basis of race. These findings illustrate the importance of institutional intent in creating spaces and opportunities for meaningful cross-racial engagement, especially for students who are newcomers to an institution.

A MULTICAMPUS QUALITATIVE STUDY OF RACIAL CLIMATES

Solórzano, Ceja, and Yosso's article (2000) appears to be the only published qualitative study of racial climates based on data collected from more than one institution. It should be noted that their sample was composed exclusively of Black students. To explore the realities of race more deeply, we used qualitative research methods at five PWIs located in three different geographical regions of the country; two campuses were in rural towns and the others in urban areas. In light of Hurtado's finding (1992) that institutional size affects perceptions of the campus racial climate, only large institutions were included in this study. On average, White students composed 73 percent of the undergraduate populations on these campuses. The primary goals were to pursue a deeper understanding of how contemporary cohorts of students experience campus racial climates in the three areas consistently noted in the literature, while searching for additional themes that have not been captured as fully in previous research.

Focus groups were facilitated with 278 Asian American, Black, Latino, Native American, and White students across the five campuses. The composition of each focus group was racially homogeneous (for example, only Native Americans in one and Latinos exclusively in another).

Administrators in academic affairs, student affairs, and multicultural affairs assisted in participant recruitment by sending mass e-mail invitations to all undergraduates from each of the racial/ethnic minority populations on the campus; each White participant led a major campus organization such as student government. In addition to interviews with students, one additional focus group was facilitated with staff persons (mostly entry- and midlevel professionals) from academic affairs, student affairs, and multicultural affairs at each institution. Interestingly, only five of the forty-one staff participants were White, even though we never specified a preference for racial/ethnic minorities who worked at the institutions.

Each focus group session was audiorecorded and later transcribed. The interview transcripts were analyzed using the NVivo Qualitative Data Analysis Software Program. Several techniques prescribed by Miles and Huberman (1994) and Moustakas (1994) were systematically employed to analyze the data collected in this study. The analyses led to the identification of nine recurring themes, which are presented in the next section. To ensure the trustworthiness of the data, we shared our findings in public forums on each campus where participants were invited to deny or confirm our syntheses of what they reported in focus groups about the racial climate, a technique referred to as "member checks" (Lincoln and Guba, 1986). Patton (2002) noted that participants with seemingly unpopular or minority points of view might not feel empowered to offer divergent perspectives in focus groups and subsequently may decide against reporting something different or controversial, a trend better known as "focus group effect." This certainly could have been the case in this study and is therefore acknowledged as a limitation. Using a different sampling and participant recruitment technique for White students, while justified below, is another noteworthy shortcoming.

Each of the five campuses in this study had its own context-specific challenges with race and racism, which are not discussed here to keep the institutions' identities anonymous. Instead, we present and summarize nine common racial realities across the institutions.

Cross-Race Consensus Regarding Institutional Negligence

Racial/ethnic minorities and White students alike expressed frustration with the incongruence of espoused and enacted institutional values concerning diversity. "The university has diversity plastered everywhere, but I have yet to see any real evidence of it," one focus group participant commented. Many were also disappointed with the lofty expectation that they would magically interact across racial difference on their own. A White student told of growing up on a ranch in Texas where he had not interacted with anyone outside his race prior to enrolling at the university. Regarding the initiation of conversations with racial/ethnic minorities on the campus, he asked: "Why should I be expected to know how to do this on my own? And the university expects us to talk about something as sensitive as racism without helping us. This is unrealistic and actually unfair." Other students wanted and needed assistance, structure, and venues in which to meaningfully engage with racially different peers, but they found little guidance from educators and administrators. Consequently, almost all of the students interviewed deemed their institutions negligent in the educational processes leading to racial understanding, both inside and outside the classroom.

Race as a Four-Letter Word and an Avoidable Topic

Participants, including the staff persons interviewed, spoke of the infrequency with which race-related conversations occurred on their campuses. Put simply, race remained an unpopular topic and was generally considered taboo in most spaces, including classes other than ethnic studies. At one institution, a midlevel staff member shared: "We don't talk about race on this campus because this state has long struggled with racial issues that trace back to slavery. So the political climate is such that the university would get into trouble with the state legislators if we talked too much about race." Students also referenced city and state political norms in their comments about the silencing of topics related to racism and racial injustice. "This campus is a microcosm of [this town] when it comes to running away from anything that even smells like race. It is just something we never talk about here, and most people are okay with that." Many participants recognized the contradiction inherent in expecting students to interact across racial lines on campuses where race is deliberately unacknowledged in classrooms and other structured venues.

Self-Reports of Racial Segregation

Like the students in antonio's study (2004), participants here were well aware of the segregation on their campuses. Few encountered difficulty naming spaces where evidence of racial segregation could be found. Chief among them was fraternity row. In fact, one Black student referred to this segregated space as "Jim Crow Row," as he reflected on fraternity parties and other events to which he had been denied access, perceivably due to his race. At the conclusion of a focus group at another institution, the participants led a guided tour through various "ethnic neighborhoods" (as they called them) in the campus dining hall, where racial segregation was visibly apparent. Beyond observable segregation trends on the campuses, most students we interviewed personally confessed to having few (if any) friends from different racial/ethnic backgrounds. Several White participants expressed an interest in building friendships with others but said they did not know how. By her own admission, a White female student leader was embarrassed that she had not even noticed until the focus group discussion that all of her close friends were White. In some instances, White students attributed their lack of engagement with racial/ethnic minority peers to the existence of minority student organizations. "If we did not have the Black frats, our chapters would have more diverse members," an Interfraternity Council president claimed. Worth acknowledging here is that only twenty-nine students held membership in the four Black fraternities on this particular campus.

Gaps in Social Satisfaction by Race

White and Asian American students often expressed feelings of social satisfaction at the five institutions and found it difficult to identify aspects of the campus environment they would change. Because all the White participants were student leaders, the universality of this finding should be interpreted with caution. While not as satisfied as the White and Asian American students, Latinos and Native Americans mostly expressed gratitude for having been afforded the opportunity to matriculate at the various campuses. Their expectations for the provision of stronger social support appeared to be modest in comparison to those of their Black peers. It should be noted that Native American undergraduates were less than half of 1 percent of the undergraduate student populations on four of the campuses we studied. In one focus group, a Latina first-year student began with an enthusiastic description of the benefits associated with attending such a prestigious university, but hearing stories from others ignited consciousness of just how little social support she had been afforded at the institution. At every university, Black students expressed the highest degrees of dissatisfaction with the social environment.

Reputational Legacies for Racism

One logical explanation for Black student displeasure was the bad reputations that preceded the universities they attended. Some entered their institutions expecting to experience racism.

"My parents, sister, aunt, and just about every African American in my home town couldn't understand why I came here. They told me to go to [a black college] because this place is so racist," one woman shared. In each focus group, other Black students told similar stories of how they had been warned about the racist environments they would encounter. "Kanye West said George W. Bush does not care about Black people. Well, it is obvious [this institution] does not care about Black people, and we have known this for a few generations now." Like the students and parents in Feagin, Vera, and Imani's study (1996), Black undergraduates interviewed for this study described how negatively their institutions were viewed within Black communities across the state because of historical exclusionary admissions practices. Many Black students withdrew prematurely in the past, and those who managed to persist through degree attainment often returned to their home communities with stories of the racism they had endured. Although this was found only among Black students in the study, its salience and consistency across the five campuses makes it noteworthy.

White Student Overestimation of Minority Student Satisfaction

White student leaders were selected because they were thought to be most likely to have interacted with racial/ethnic minority peers in the student organizations they led. Moreover, we suspected they were positioned to offer more meaningful appraisals of the campus racial climates because of their levels of political leadership on the campuses. Focus groups with these participants were always conducted after those with racial/ethnic minority students. The White students were most satisfied with the social environments, and they erroneously assumed their Black, Latino, and Native American peers experienced the institutions this same way. They reported that racial/ethnic minority student engagement in mainstream campus organizations was low, but for some reason those students were thought to be equally satisfied with their college experiences. When asked about the basis of their assumptions, the White participants often responded with, "I don't know . . . I just figured everyone loves it here." Because there was so little structured and meaningful interaction across races, student leaders who were presumed to have understood the general pulse of the campus were generally unaware of the disparate affective dispositions their racial/ethnic minority peers held toward the institutions.

The Pervasiveness of Whiteness in Space, Curricula, and Activities

Beyond ethnic and multicultural centers on the five campuses, Asian American, Black, Latino, and Native American students found it difficult to identify other spaces on campus in which they felt shared cultural ownership. White interests were thought to be privileged over others, which many racial/ethnic minorities viewed as inconsistent with institutional claims of inclusiveness. These perceptions are perhaps best illustrated in this quote from a sophomore student: "Everything is so White. The concerts: White musicians. The activities: catered to White culture. The football games: a ton of drunk White folks. All the books we read in class: White authors and viewpoints. Students on my left, right, in front and in back of me in my classes: White, White, White, White. I feel like there is nothing for us here besides the [cultural] center, but yet [this university] claims to be so big on diversity. That is the biggest white lie I have ever heard." Other participants also critiqued the isolation of ethnic culture to a single center, office, or academic major. Although Asian American students generally appeared to be as satisfied as their White peers, even they expressed a desire for greater cultural representation.

The Consciousness-Powerlessness Paradox among Racial/Ethnic Minority Staff

Nearly 88 percent of the staff persons we interviewed were racial/ethnic minorities. Interestingly, they were fully aware of the degree to which minority students were disadvantaged and dissatisfied on the five campuses. They also knew about the extent to which racial segregation existed. Much of what the students shared in focus groups was confirmed (mostly without prompting) in interviews with the staff. One of the five White staff participants asserted, "Everyone around this table knows how segregated students are, but we never talk about it. It is the sort of thing that will piss the upper administration off and make them leery of you for raising the issue." Despite their consciousness of the realities of race, most indicated a reluctance to publicly call attention to these trends for fear of losing their jobs or political backlash. "I feel bad for what the young brothers and sisters go through here, but there is only so much I can do since I have only been here two years," a Latino academic advisor explained. Staff persons would complain to each other and privately strategize with students but felt powerless in voicing observations to senior administrators and White colleagues. Fear of being seen as troublemakers who were always calling attention to racism compelled many to remain silent.

Unexplored Qualitative Realities of Race in Institutional Assessment

In every focus group on each of the five campuses, student participants (Whites and racial/ethnic minorities alike) indicated that it was the first time any institutional effort was made to inquire about the qualitative realities of their racialized experiences. "You're the first person to ask us these kinds of questions" was a common remark. Furthermore, the White student leaders said no one, including their student organization advisors, had ever asked them questions about minority student engagement and satisfaction or the frequency with which they interacted with peers who were racially different. Reportedly, the institutional research offices had not conducted any formal climate assessments. Likewise, informal queries from faculty and administrators were also uncommon. "If they truly cared, they would have asked us about these things before now," a Native American male senior believed.

IMPLICATIONS FOR INSTITUTIONAL TRANSFORMATION

The 2006 report of the commission appointed by U.S. Department of Education Secretary Margaret Spellings to explore needed areas of improvement in higher education called for more transparency regarding student learning outcomes on college and university campuses. Merely reporting outcomes, however, keeps the source of racial inequities undisclosed and does not result in better, more inclusive climates for learning. The consistency of results from fifteen years of empirical research, along with the nine themes that emerged in our study, make clear the need for greater transparency regarding racial realities in learning environments at PWIs. Even when cues are readily available (for example, a newspaper with four front-page articles related to racial injustice), the realities of race are typically made transparent only when there is a highly publicized, racially motivated incident or when embarrassing findings from an external auditor are made public.

Consistent with Kezar and Eckel's recommendation (2002a), we suggest that administrators, faculty, and institutional researchers proactively audit their campus climates and cultures to determine the need for change. As indicated in many of the nine themes, racial realities remained undisclosed and unaddressed in systematic ways on college campuses. As long as administrators espouse commitments to diversity and multiculturalism without engaging in examinations of campus climates, racial/ethnic minorities will continue to feel dissatisfied, all students will remain deprived of the full range of educational benefits accrued through cross-racial engagement, and certain institutions will sustain longstanding reputations for being racially toxic environments.

Eckel and Kezar (2003) defined *transformation* as the type of change that affects the institutional culture, is deep and pervasive, is intentional, and occurs over time. Accordingly, deep change reflects a shift in values (for example, from espoused to enacted) and assumptions that underlie daily operations (for example, the flawed expectation that cross-racial interactions will magically occur on their own). Pervasiveness indicates that change is felt across the institution in the assumptions and daily work of faculty, staff, and administrators. For example, the Black culture center on a campus cannot improve an institution's external reputation if professors routinely perpetuate racist stereotypes in classrooms. Also, racial/ethnic minority students will continue to feel like "guests in someone else's house" if student activities offices fail to sponsor programs that reflect the diverse cultures represented on a campus. Intentionality in constructing culturally affirming environments and experiences that facilitate the cultivation of racially diverse friendship groups must substitute passivity and negligence. As previous research has established, these racial climate issues have consequences for student outcomes (Hurtado, Milem, Clayton-Pedersen, and Allen, 1998). For example, attention to diversity in the curriculum and cocurriculum, particularly in the first two years of college, results in student development along many dimensions of complex thinking and social cognitive growth (Hurtado, 2005).

Eckel and Kezar (2003) also distinguished transformation from other types of change, including adjustments that continually happen in academia that are neither pervasive nor deep, such as showing a one-hour video on respecting diversity at new student orientation; isolated change that may be deep but limited to one unit or program area, as when an ethnic studies department offers a cluster of elective courses on race; or far-reaching change that affects many across the institution but lacks depth, as with a policy regarding the symbolic inclusion of an equal opportunity statement on letterhead and all hiring materials. Moreover, Kezar and Eckel (2002b) found that senior administrative support, collaboration, and visible action are among the core elements requisite for transformational change in higher education. While administrative leadership on its own is insufficient, our findings make clear that entry- and midlevel professionals, especially racial/ethnic minorities, often feel silenced and powerless to transform campus racial climates.

In their 2005 study, Kezar and Eckel interviewed thirty college presidents who had been engaged in organizational change with a significant emphasis on the success of racial/ethnic minority students. The presidents used a strategy of dialogue and discussion in the appraisal of their own and their institutions' commitments to diversity, while holding various stakeholders accountable for aligning efforts with stated institutional values and priorities. If this is to occur on other campuses, race cannot remain an avoidable topic. For instance, if accountability for student learning is a high priority, dialogue and strategic efforts must be directed toward addressing undercurrents of racial segregation that inhibit the rich learning that occurs in cross-racial engagement. Likewise, faculty and staff in academic affairs, student affairs, multicultural affairs, and other units on campus should be challenged to consider their roles as accomplices in the cyclical reproduction of racism and institutional negligence.

Despite fifteen years of racial climate research on multiple campuses, the themes of exclusion, institutional rhetoric rather than action, and marginality continue to emerge from student voices. Conducting a climate study can be symbolic of institutional action, only to be filed away on a shelf. We advocate that data gathered through the ongoing assessment of campus racial climates guide conversations and reflective examinations to overcome discomfort with race, plan for deep levels of institutional transformation, and achieve excellence in fostering racially inclusive learning environments.

REFERENCES

Allen, W. R. "Black Students in U.S. Higher Education: Toward Improved Access, Adjustment, and Achievement." *Urban Review,* 1988, *20*(3), 165–188.

Ancis, J. R., Sedlacek, W. E., and Mohr, J. J. "Student Perceptions of Campus Cultural Climate by Race." *Journal of Counseling and Counseling Development,* 2000, *78,* 180–185.

antonio, a. l. "When Does Race Matter in College Friendships? Exploring Men's Diverse and Homogeneous Friendship Groups." *Review of Higher Education,* 2004, *27*(4), 553–575.

antonio, a. l., and others. "Effects of Racial Diversity on Complex Thinking in College Students." *Psychological Science,* 2004, *15*(8), 507–510.

Cabrera, A. F., and Nora, A. "College Students' Perceptions of Prejudice and Discrimination and Their Feelings of Alienation: A Construct Validation Approach." *Review of Education/Pedagogy/Cultural Studies,* 1994, *16*(3), 387–409.

Cabrera, A. F., and others. "Campus Racial Climate and the Adjustment of Students to College: A Comparison Between White Students and African American Students." *Journal of Higher Education,* 1999, *70*(2), 134–160.

Chang, M. J. "Does Racial Diversity Matter? The Educational Impact of a Racially Diverse Undergraduate Population." *Journal of College Student Development,* 1999, *40*(4), 377–395.

Chang, M. J. "Is It More Than About Getting Along? The Broader Educational Relevance of Reducing Students' Racial Biases." *Journal of College Student Development,* 2001, *42*(2), 93–105.

Chang, M. J., Astin, A. W., and Kim, D. "Cross-Racial Interaction Among Undergraduates: Some Consequences, Causes and Patterns." *Research in Higher Education,* 2004, *45*(5), 529–553.

Chang, M. J., Denson, N., Sáenz, V., and Misa, K. "The Educational Benefits of Sustaining Cross-Racial Interaction Among Undergraduates." *Journal of Higher Education,* 2006, *77*(3), 430–455.

D'Augelli, A. R., and Hershberger, S. L. "African American Undergraduates on a Predominantly White Campus: Academic Factors, Social Networks, and Campus Climate." *Journal of Negro Education,* 1993, *62*(1), 67–81.

Davis, M., and others. "'A Fly in the Buttermilk': Descriptions of University Life by Successful Black Undergraduate Students at a Predominately White Southeastern University." *Journal of Higher Education,* 2004, *75*(4), 420–445.

Diver-Stamnes, A. C., and LoMascolo, A. F. "The Marginalization of Ethnic Minority Students: A Case Study of a Rural University." *Equity and Excellence in Education,* 2001, *34*(1), 50–58.

Eckel, P. D., and Kezar, A. J. *Taking the Reins: Institutional Transformation in Higher Education.* Westport, Conn.: Praeger, 2003.

Eimers, M. T., and Pike, G. R. "Minority and Nonminority Adjustment to College: Differences or Similarities?" *Research in Higher Education,* 1997, *38*(1), 77–97.

Feagin, J. R., Vera, H., and Imani, N. *The Agony of Education: Black Students at White Colleges and Universities.* New York: Routledge, 1996.

Fleming, J. *Blacks in College: A Comparative Study of Students' Success in Black and White Institutions.* San Francisco: Jossey-Bass, 1984.

Fries-Britt, S. L., and Turner, B. "Facing Stereotypes: A Case Study of Black Students on a White Campus." *Journal of College Student Development,* 2001, *42*(5), 420–429.

Gratz v. *Bollinger,* 123 2411 (S. Ct. 2003).

Grutter v. *Bollinger,* 124 35 (S. Ct. 2003).

Guiffrida, D. A. "African American Student Organizations as Agents of Social Integration." *Journal of College Student Development,* 2003, *44*(3), 304–319.

Gurin, P., Dey, E. L., Hurtado, S., and Gurin, G. "Diversity and Higher Education: Theory and Impact on Educational Outcomes." *Harvard Educational Review,* 2002, *72*(3), 330–366.

Harper, S. R., and Quaye, S. J. "Student Organizations as Venues for Black Identity Expression and Development Among African American Male Student Leaders." *Journal of College Student Development,* 2007, *48*(2), 127–144.

Helm, E. G., Sedlacek, W. E., and Prieto, D. O. "The Relationship Between Attitudes Toward Diversity and Overall Satisfaction of University Students by Race." *Journal of College Counseling,* 1998, *1,* 111–120.

Hurtado, S. "The Campus Racial Climate: Contexts of Conflict." *Journal of Higher Education,* 1992, *63*(5), 539–569.

Hurtado, S. "Graduate School Racial Climates and Academic Self-Concept Among Minority Graduate Students in the 1970s." *American Journal of Education,* 1994a, *102*(3), 330–351.

Hurtado, S. "The Institutional Climate for Talented Latino Students." *Research in Higher Education,* 1994b, *35*(1), 21–41.

Hurtado, S. "The Next Generation of Diversity and Intergroup Relations Research." *Journal of Social Issues,* 2005, *61*(3), 595–610.

Hurtado, S., and Carter, D. F. "Effects of College Transition and Perceptions of the Campus Racial Climate on Latino College Students' Sense of Belonging." *Sociology of Education,* 1997, *70*(4), 324–345.

Hurtado, S., Carter, D. F., and Spuler, A. "Latino Student Transition to College: Assessing Difficulties and Factors in Successful College Adjustment." *Research in Higher Education,* 1996, *37*(2), 135–157.

Hurtado, S., Milem, J. F., Clayton-Pedersen, A., and Allen, W. R. "Enhancing Campus Climates for Racial/Ethnic Diversity: Educational Policy and Practice." *Review of Higher Education,* 1998, *21*(3), 279–302.

Johnson-Durgans, V. D. "Perceptions of Racial Climates in Residence Halls Between African American and Euroamerican College Students." *Journal of College Student Development,* 1994, *35*(4), 267–274.

Kezar, A. J., and Eckel, P. D. "The Effect of Institutional Culture on Change Strategies in Higher Education: Universal Principles or Culturally Responsive Concepts?" *Journal of Higher Education,* 2002a, *73*(4), 435–460.

Kezar, A. J., and Eckel, P. D. "Examining the Institutional Transformation Process: The Importance of Sensemaking, Interrelated Strategies, and Balance." *Research in Higher Education,* 2002b, *43*(3), 295–328.

Kezar, A. J., and Eckel, P. D. *Leadership Strategies for Advancing Campus Diversity: Advice from Experienced Presidents.* Washington, D.C.: American Council on Education, 2005.

Levin, S., van Larr, C., and Sidanius, J. "The Effects of Ingroup and Outgroup Friendships on Ethnic Attitudes in College: A Longitudinal Study." *Group Processes and Intergroup Relations,* 2003, *6*(1), 76–92.

Lewis, A. E., Chesler, M., and Forman, T. A. "The Impact of 'Colorblind' Ideologies on Students of Color: Intergroup Relations at a Predominantly White University." *Journal of Negro Education,* 2000, *69*(1), 74–91.

Lincoln, Y., and Guba, E. G. "But Is It Rigorous? Trustworthiness and Authenticity in Naturalistic Evaluation." In D. William (ed.), *Naturalistic Evaluation.* New Directions for Program Evaluation, no. 30. San Francisco: Jossey-Bass, 1986.

Loo, C. M., and Rolison, G. "Alienation of Ethnic Minority Students at a Predominantly White University." *Journal of Higher Education,* 1986, *57*(1), 58–77.

Milem, J. F., Umbach, P. D., and Liang, C.T.H. "Exploring the Perpetuation Hypothesis: The Role of Colleges and Universities in Desegregating Society." *Journal of College Student Development,* 2004, *45*(6), 688–700.

Miles, M. B., and Huberman, A. M. *Qualitative Data Analysis: An Expanded Sourcebook.* (2nd ed.) Thousand Oaks, Calif.: Sage, 1994.

Moustakas, C. *Phenomenological Research Methods.* Thousand Oaks, Calif.: Sage, 1994.

Nettles, M. T., Thoeny, A. R., and Gosman, E. J. "Comparative and Predictive Analyses of Black and White Students' Achievement and Experiences." *Journal of Higher Education,* 1986, *57*(3), 289–318.

Nora, A., and Cabrera, A. F. "The Role of Perceptions of Prejudice and Discrimination on the Adjustment of Minority Students to College." *Journal of Higher Education,* 1996, *67*(2), 119–148.

Patton, L. D. "The Voice of Reason: A Qualitative Examination of Black Student Perceptions of Black Culture Centers." *Journal of College Student Development,* 2006, *47*(6), 628–644.

Patton, M. Q. *Qualitative Research and Evaluation Methods.* (3rd ed.) Thousand Oaks, Calif.: Sage, 2002.

Pike, G. R., and Kuh, G. D. "Relationships Among Structural Diversity, Informal Peer Interactions, and Perceptions of the Campus Environment." *Review of Higher Education,* 2006, *29*(4), 425–450.

Radloff, T. D., and Evans, N. J. "The Social Construction of Prejudice Among Black and White College Students." *NASPA Journal,* 2003, *40*(2), 1–16.

Rankin, S. R., and Reason, R. D. "Differing Perceptions: How Students of Color and White Students Perceive Campus Climate for Underrepresented Groups." *Journal of College Student Development,* 2005, *46*(1), 43–61.

Sáenz, V. B., Nagi, H. N., and Hurtado, S. "Factors Influencing Positive Interactions Across Race for African American, Asian American, Latino, and White College Students." *Research in Higher Education,* 2007, *48*(1), 1–38.

Smedley, B. D., Myers, H. F., and Harrell, S. P. "Minority-Status Stresses and the College Adjustment of Ethnic Minority Freshmen." *Journal of Higher Education,* 1993, *64*(4), 434–452.

Solórzano, D., Ceja, M., and Yosso, T. J. "Critical Race Theory, Racial Microaggressions, and Campus Racial Climate: The Experiences of African American College Students." *Journal of Negro Education,* 2000, *69*(1), 60–73.

Solórzano, D., and Villalpando, O. "Critical Race Theory: Marginality and the Experience of Students of Color in Higher Education." In C. A. Torres and T. R. Mitchell (eds.), *Sociology of Education: Emerging Perspectives.* Albany: State University of New York Press, 1998.

Suarez-Balcazar, Y., and others. "Experiences of Differential Treatment Among College Students of Color." *Journal of Higher Education,* 2003, *74*(4), 428–444.

Swim, J. K., and others. "African American College Students' Experiences with Everyday Racism: Characteristics of and Responses to These Incidents." *Journal of Black Psychology,* 2003, *29*(1), 38–67.

Turner, C.S.V. "Guests in Someone Else's House: Students of Color." *Review of Higher Education,* 1994, *17*(4), 355–370.

U.S. Department of Education. *A Test of Leadership, Charting the Future of U.S. Higher Education: A Report of the Commission Appointed by Secretary of Education Margaret Spellings.* Washington, D.C.: U.S. Department of Education, 2006.

IV

ORGANIZATIONS, LEADERSHIP AND GOVERNANCE

Adrianna J. Kezar, Section Editor

These are interesting and challenging times that face administrators in higher education. On the one hand, there are issues regarding assessment, accountability, academic capitalism, the decline of shared governance, corporate management, loss of public trust, and greater responsiveness to public concerns. On the other hand, there are challenges and opportunities regarding changing demographics, technology, globalization, and increasing competition. To add further complexity, there are teams and other collaborative forms of leadership, the resurgence of unions, and calls to save shared governance. Not to be daunting, it is important to note that each historical time period has its challenges and opportunities in higher education. Administrators in the 1960s focused on student riots, faculty radicalization, demands for more democratic campus structures, and rising enrollments, while in the 1980s campus leaders faced the challenge of returning adult students, predicted declining enrollments, decreasing state budget contributions, and the beginning of government calls for accountability. Today's challenges are unraveling some of the distinctive features that have long characterized higher education institutions in the U.S.

As a result, many of the foundational principles that helped administrators understand the organization, governance, and leadership of higher education are increasingly less relevant. For example, shared governance has been a hallmark of the decision-making process in higher education for decades. Shared governance is a traditional process within colleges and universities that involves different stakeholders, especially faculty with expertise in an area like curriculum, in the planning, management, and direction setting of the campus. While trustees have formal authority within colleges and universities, they typically delegate considerable authority to the college president and other senior administrators. Through shared governance, the administration involves faculty, staff, and students as part of decision-making processes. In the past, this decentralized form of decision making and campus operations was seen as appropriate within an organization that had strong professional expertise, often termed a professional bureaucracy (Mintzberg, 1979).[1] However, in more contemporary settings, shared governance has declined on many campuses; more corporate boards and administrators have centralized decision making and are increasingly excluding faculty and staff in the process.

We are at a time where colleges and universities are hybrid organizations—part professional bureaucracy and part corporate entity. Therefore, it is important to understand foundational concepts such as shared governance, professional bureaucracy, dual systems of authority (between faculty and the administration), tenure, and academic freedom that are central to the administration and governance of American colleges and universities. The first two chapters in this section speak to foundational and historic organizational principles. The third chapter helps to interpret organizational culture that is relevant to the direction a college and university organization takes in its future. The fourth chapter focuses on organizational change, a key activity that administrators engage during this time of uncertainty and challenge. Lastly, the fifth chapter examines a particular challenge facing all campuses: how to be more inclusive of women and minorities as well as issues of organizational discrimination.

In Chapter 16, Robert Birnbaum introduces several important foundational concepts that have helped generations of new administrators understand how to be leaders on college campuses. The first point that Birnbaum makes is that colleges and universities are distinctive from other organizations such as corporations, hospitals, or even other nonprofits. He reminds us that higher education organizations have distinctive characteristics that make it difficult for administrators to be successful when applying business principles to colleges and universities. For example, top-down and authoritative leadership from presidents and administrators is often met with resistance on college campuses where shared governance and professional autonomy are valued aspects of the culture. Few organizations have longtime employees such as tenured faculty, who can stay on the campus for their entire careers.

Birnbaum highlights shared governance as one characteristic that makes colleges truly distinctive organizations. His chapter explains the roles of trustees, administrators, and faculty in a complex system of governance, and the tensions that arise when several groups have authority and control within an organization. Birnbaum also describes how colleges and universities have complex and ambiguous missions and goals, as well as how power is extremely diffuse among a variety of different subgroups. All of these characteristics create what he describes as constraints on leaders to enact change, make decisions, and operate in ways that people may see as effective. His chapter calls on leaders to support and facilitate the work of others, rather than attempt to directly control their behaviors. Supportive leadership, rather than micro-management, he argues, would likely be a better method for success within this type of ambiguous and complex environment.

Within a professional organization where multiple groups have expertise, administrators should ask themselves: How can I support faculty to create the best teaching and learning environments possible? How can I help faculty to become curricular leaders? How can I help staff to become educators wherever students are—the library, residence halls, or in out-of-class activities? Birnbaum reminds aspiring administrators that these distinctive characteristics of colleges (governance, professional staff, long-time employees, and disbursed power) help determine success or failure. Those who are unaware of the distinctive characteristics of colleges and universities will likely become victims to misunderstanding them.

J. Douglas Orton and Karl E. Weick (in Chapter 17) also review one of the underlying foundational concepts of colleges and universities: loose coupling. Whether you work in a Historically Black University, a technical college, or a regional comprehensive institution, the campus operates within the principles of a loosely coupled system. Loose coupling refers to the fact that colleges and universities are made up of many interdependent units and divisions that have a fair degree of autonomy and operate differently from more bureaucratic or tight systems. There are many different units throughout the campus and they often operate both autonomously and may even have distinctive missions; yet they also work in concert toward an overarching goal. The parts work together, but only loosely. Loosely coupled systems tend to be more spontaneous and indeterminate. Colleges and universities are inherently loosely coupled because of the ambiguity in a decision-making environment that develops because of the professional status of faculty and a dual system of control (where both faculty and administrators have power). Loose coupling also occurs because the production of knowledge is extremely complex and does not lend itself to more bureaucratic forms of organization.

Orton and Weick explain the causes of loose coupling, the different types of loose coupling within organizations (intentions and actions versus activities), the effects of loose coupling (more decentralization and behavioral discretion), outcomes of loose coupling (buffering individuals from the external environment and greater effectiveness), and ways to compensate for loose coupling through enhanced leadership, focused attention, and shared values. Loose coupling has both positive and negative consequences. For example, a positive element of loosely coupled systems is that different subunits can adopt innovations because the units are not closely linked. However, centralized efforts to create change are met with greater resistance. For every positive quality in a loosely coupled system, there are also dysfunctions that leaders encounter (just as there are in any system). Birnbaum's chapter also highlights the qualities of a loosely coupled system through a discussion of the different campus subgroups, the governance system, and the challenges and opportunities leaders face. When read together, the first two chapters in this section can help explain some of the underlying dynamics that make colleges and universities distinctive organizations.

In their book, *Academic Capitalism and the New Economy*, Slaughter and Rhoades (2004) describe the move to a more corporatized and commercialized college culture. They specifically document how the external political and economic environment has shifted in the last 30 years toward supporting higher education as an instrument of revenue generation for the state through research and development dollars. Increasingly, colleges and universities receive fewer government funds and are expected to generate their own revenues; many have become focused on fundraising rather than educational mission. Consequently, governance on some campuses has become centralized to a few administrators and trustees, as the market is more competitive and decisions need to be made quickly to adapt within the competitive environment. Shared governance may exist in name on many campuses, but increasingly, faculty members have less input on decisions, compared to 40 years ago.

Some commentators claim that these changes are inevitable, but others like Slaughter and Rhoades (2004) suggest that this is merely an ideology that is being promoted and corporatization and commercialization is a choice, not inevitability. This shift uproots many of the classic principles that have undergirded the understanding of the organization of colleges and universities and the resultant leadership and governance. In fact, the shift toward academic capitalism questions whether governance will be a meaningful part of colleges in the future. Perhaps trustees and select administrators will make all decisions in the near future, similar to for-profit institutions. With more than half the faculty being non-tenure track now, the academy is fast moving toward this new corporate structure. Kezar (2004) and other scholars have suggested that a more corporatized environment will affect higher education's ability to serve the public good. By the public good, I mean that higher education has long had goals that more broadly serve society, such as increasing access for underrepresented groups and creating knowledge that is freely distributed, rather than the specific institutional objectives. As state funding for higher education declines, it becomes more difficult for institutions to serve the public good as they focus on the bottom line.

An important work that can help new administrators to understand their campus—whether it has a more traditional structure (operating under principles of shared governance and loose coupling) or in more corporate environment (operating under hierarchy, deskilled workers or managed professionals)—is William G. Tierney's chapter in this book. As Birnbaum notes, colleges and universities represent unique organizational types and possess distinctive organizational cultures. While Birnbaum focuses on more global typologies of culture (such as being bureaucratic, collegial, political, or anarchical), Tierney helps administrators think about their campuses as a distinctive and unique culture and to see the important role that culture plays in the leadership of a campus. In Chapter 18, he encourages administrators to see themselves as anthropologists who are trying to analyze their campus to understand what holds the place together and makes it distinctive. Also emphasized is that each campus has an overarching culture, but different units and subunits have their own subcultures, hence analyses need to be done at many levels. Tierney notes, "Effective administrators are well aware that they can take a given action in some institutions but not in others." He suggests several areas that an administrator can analyze in order to best understand the culture—environment, mission, socialization, information, strategy, and leadership. Through a detailed example, leaders learn the art and science of cultural analysis that can help them with hard tasks, such as cutting funds during difficult times. Understanding culture means being able to develop solutions that work within that environment.

Within this challenging environment with more competition, pressures to be accountable, and the need to respond to a variety of external forces (e.g., shifting demographics and new technologies), leaders need to be able to effectively change campuses. In Chapter 19, Adrianna J. Kezar and Peter D. Eckel focus on creating transformational change that helps campus administrators better understand the key strategies needed to improve campus operations. This chapter connects to Tierney's work by demonstrating how creating meaningful change requires knowledge of the institutional culture and modifying strategies to fit into established norms of the campus. While change often involves shifting or changing the culture, the way leaders go about the process of change should be aligned with the culture, even as it alters that culture. Kezar and Eckel's chapter also reflects principles articulated by Birnbaum, in that effective change requires working through the shared governance process and engaging the full leadership capacity of faculty, staff, and students on campus. The principle of robust design (a flexible shared vision) also highlights the importance of including others in the change process. Instead of administrators creating a vision for change from the top down, they develop a broad idea that is altered as faculty, staff, and other stakeholders are brought into the change process. This model demonstrates that administrators play a key role in change and how collaboratively engaging other stakeholders can propel campuses forward.

One major change that campuses are addressing is how to create a positive organizational climate for women and historically underrepresented groups. In Chapter 20, Barbara K. Townsend explores the ways community colleges have historically addressed climate—through examining representation patterns, equal pay, and equal opportunity for promotion. She also critiques discourse patterns (values and assumptions) that need to be changed to push campuses toward their goals of creating less discriminatory and more inclusive environments. The main discourse pattern she examines is the deficit language applied to women and minorities; although Townsend's chapter is situated in the community college context, similar discourse patterns exist about these groups in four-year institutions. Townsend argues that policies and institutional structures alone may not change the climate if the underlying assumption that women and underrepresented minorities are deficient remains unchallenged. She highlights the work of Chesler and Crowfoot (2000), which reviews institutional discrimination and racism in higher education, to help explain why less progress has been made on campuses than expected given ongoing efforts to create organizational change. Even as scholars like Townsend push for greater inclusion, the drive to compete, generate revenue, and increase prestige is increasingly pushing this important goal to the side, particularly as the United States emerges from a worldwide recession.

CONCLUSION

Instinctively, I feel campus governance and leadership are gradually moving in the wrong direction. While shared governance may no longer be possible in a competitive and global environment, surely administrators still need to understand and be connected to the educational mission. Likewise, faculty and staff professionals need to play some role in the decision-making and leadership of the campus. The struggle is to figure out what the appropriate structures and processes are, and not allow a purely corporate model to take over American higher education. While the classic professional bureaucracy may need to shift and loose coupling does present some problems, there are distinctive advantages (e.g., academic freedom, autonomy, and input from workers closest to the educational mission) that are lost as we move to a new culture of academic capitalism with its corporate structure, commercialization and focus on revenue generation, and predominance of market priorities over educational values.

NOTE

1. While there is not space to put in all the classic documents about colleges and universities as organizations, Henry Mintzberg's (1979) book on the professional bureaucracy is an important source that readers should review. Mintzberg notes that professional organizations have skilled workers that possess a lot of training and take responsibility for their work. They require less oversight and vertical and hierarchical administrative practice is not needed. Instead, more decentralization, coordination, and communication across the organization is the task of the administrator who connects the activities and units across the organization. The administrator's role is to support professionals who control their own work. Administrators lead *with* faculty to make decisions collectively.

REFERENCES

Chesler, M. A., & Crowfoot, J. (2000). Racism in higher education: An organizational analysis. In M. C. Brown II (Ed.), *Organization and Governance in Higher Education* (5th ed., pp. 436–469). Boston, Massachusetts: Pearson.

Kezar, A. J. (2004). Obtaining integrity? Reviewing and examining the charter between higher education and society. *The Review of Higher Education*, 27(4), 429–459.

Mintzberg, H. (1979). *The Structuring of Organizations: A Synthesis of the Research*. New York: Prentice-Hall.

Slaughter, S., & Rhoades, G. (2004). *Academic Capitalism and the New Economy: Markets, State, and Higher Education*. Baltimore, Maryland: Johns Hopkins University Press.

16

Problems of Governance, Management, and Leadership in Academic Institutions

Robert Birnbaum

American colleges and universities are the most paradoxical of organizations. On the one hand, it has been said that "they constitute one of the largest industries in the nation but are among the least businesslike and well managed of all organizations" (Keller, 1983, p. 5). On the other hand, many believe that our institutions of higher education exhibit levels of diversity, access, and quality that are without parallel. At a time when American business and technology suffer an unfavorable trade deficit and are under siege from foreign competition, our system of higher education maintains a most favorable "balance of trade" by enrolling large numbers of students from other countries. Our system remains the envy of the world.

The apparent paradox that American colleges and universities are poorly run but highly effective is easily resolved if either or both of these judgments are wrong. But what if they are both right? Such a state of affairs would lead to several interesting speculations. For example, it might be that the success of the system has come about *in spite of* bad management, and that if management could somehow be improved, the system could be made even more effective than it is today. Or it might be that, contrary to our traditional expectations, at least in colleges and universities, management and performance are not closely related. If this is true, then improvements in management might not yield comparable benefits in organizational accomplishment. Or, strangest of all, it might be that to at least some extent our colleges and universities are successful *because* they are poorly managed, at least as *management* is often defined in other complex organizations. If this is true, then attempts to "improve" traditional management processes might actually diminish rather than enhance organizational effectiveness in institutions of higher education. This book is in large part an exploration of these possibilities.

The concept that best reflects the ways in which institutions of higher education differ from other organizations is *governance*, and I shall use it extensively in this chapter. There is no single and generally accepted definition of governance; it has been variously discussed in terms of structures, legal relationships, authority patterns, rights and responsibilities, and decision-making processes. I shall use the word *governance* in a very broad way to refer to the structures and processes through which institutional participants interact with and influence each other and communicate with the larger environment. A governance system is an institution's answer—at least temporarily—to the enduring question that became a plaintive cry during the campus crisis of the late 1960s and early 1970s: "Who's in charge here?"

PROBLEMS OF GOVERNANCE

The authority to establish a college or university belongs to the state, which exercises it by forming through statute, charter, or constitutional provision an institution with a corporate existence and a lay governing board. An uncomplicated view of governance need go no further than this fact, because legally the governing board *is* the institution (Glenny and Dalglish, 1973). But the reality of governance today is much different from what this strict legal interpretation would suggest. In fact, "decision making is spread among trustees, presidents, and faculty, and although the legal status of the trustees has not changed, there is ambivalence about how much power they should have" (Carnegie Foundation for the Advancement of Teaching, 1982, p. 72).

Trustees and Faculty

In earlier times, institutions were small, trustees were clergymen, and administration and faculty might consist of a president and a handful of tutors. Boards could—and often did—exercise the full authority that they legally possessed. Governance was not an issue; it was the will of the board. But as institutions became more complex, boards delegated de facto authority to presidents. And as the faculty became more professionalized during the early part of the twentieth century, much authority on many campuses, particularly in curriculum and academic personnel matters, was further delegated to faculties. Some reached the point where "the faculty . . . tend to think of themselves as being the university. This leaves the board of trustees with little authority over the [major] function of the university, instruction" (Besse, 1973, p. 109).

As a result, different campus constituencies now assert their claim to primacy in areas over which boards retain legal obligations and responsibilities. Radical remedies to clarify governance rights have occasionally been suggested. One such suggestion argued that the board should take back from the faculty authority for the curriculum, since the board has full legal responsibility for all aspects of the institution (Ruml and Morrison, 1959). More recently it has been suggested that trustees consider simplifying governance by stripping all campus groups of governance prerogatives except insofar as they might be granted as a privilege by the president acting as the board's exclusive agent (Fisher, 1984). Proposals such as these cannot be taken seriously, but more moderate and responsible calls for greater trustee involvement in governance are increasing (Carnegie Foundation for the Advancement of Teaching, 1982).

Tensions between trustees and faculty are not new. Probably the most outspoken observer and critic of this conflict was Thorsten Veblen ([1918] 1957), whose 1918 book *The Higher Learning in America* railed against the effects of boards of trustees increasingly made up of businessmen whose interest was focused on efficiency and who did not understand the unique nature of the academic enterprise. In their view, he said, "the university is conceived as a business house dealing in merchantable knowledge, placed under the governing hand of a captain of erudition, whose office it is to turn the means at hand to account in the largest feasible output" (Veblen, [1918] 1957, p. 62). In contrast, said Veblen, scholars pursue their work individually, each in his or her own way. It is not amenable to the orderly and systematic procedures of the administrator and cannot be reduced to the bottom line of a balance sheet. The administrative role is not to govern scholars but rather to serve as their assistants and cater to their idiosyncratic needs. To the extent that this is not done, the university will lose effectiveness, because "a free hand is the first and abiding requisite of scholarly and scientific work" (p. 63). Veblen's acerbic comments set forth the governance issue clearly if simplistically: shall the university be controlled by trustees and administrators or by faculty?

The answer to this question is important, because faculty and lay trustees have different backgrounds and values. Approximately 40 percent of all board members are businesspeople ("College Governing Boards," 1986), who are more likely than faculty to see their institutions as comparable to business firms in their structure and authority patterns and to support ideas of "top-down" management. Trustees are also likely to have a lesser understanding and support of principles of academic freedom than do faculty and are more likely than faculty to believe that certain academic decisions do not require faculty involvement. In general, "trustees differ markedly from those occupying the academic positions 'beneath' them. In terms of political party affiliation and ideology, and attitudes about higher education, the trustees are generally more conservative than the faculty" (Hartnett, 1969, p. 51).

Administrators and Faculty

The days of amateur administration when faculty temporarily assumed administrative positions and then returned to the classroom are long since over at most institutions. As institutions become larger and more complex, knowledge of legal precedents, federal regulations, management information systems, student financial aid procedures, grant and contract administration, and many other areas of specialized expertise is needed to accomplish many administrative tasks. Faculty and administrators fill different roles, encounter and are influenced by different aspects of the environment, and have different backgrounds. The increasing numbers and importance of managers at all levels have led to the "administered university" (Lunsford, 1970, p. 91), in which administrators are separated from the rest of the university. As a consequence, university executives and faculty form separated and isolated conclaves in which they are likely to communicate only with people similar to themselves. The use of more sophisticated management techniques can make things even worse. "In a context in which faculty members are less privileged and in which they often feel oppressed beneath the weight of administrative authority, the innovations wrought by the new devices of management may widen the gulf between faculty and administration and thus intensify the antagonism, latent and overt, which has traditionally existed between the administrative and the academic cultures" (Rourke and Brooks, 1964, p. 180).

Administration and management can become so complex that even those faculty who are interested in governance may not have the time or the expertise to fully understand the processes of decision making or resource acquisition and allocation that are at the heart of many governance issues. Because of these changes, administrators become identified in the faculty mind with red tape, constraints, and outside pressures that seek to alter the institution. They come to be seen by the faculty as ever more remote from the central academic concerns that define the institution. Faculty in turn come to be seen by the administration as self-interested, unconcerned with controlling costs, or unwilling to respond to legitimate requests for accountability.

Normative Statements on Governance

It might be thought that uncertainty and conflict concerning governance roles and procedures could be moderated by authoritative statements that enunciate the elements of sound practice. Several important normative statements of this kind exist, perhaps the most influential of which is the "Joint Statement on Government of Colleges and Universities" (American Association of University Professors, 1984) published in 1967. The document articulated the concept of governance as a shared responsibility and joint effort involving all important constituencies of the academic community, with the weight given to the views of each group dependent on the specific issues under discussion. In particular, while recognizing the legal authority of the board and the president, the document identified the faculty as having primary responsibility for the fundamental areas of curriculum, instruction, faculty status, and the academic aspects of student life. The term *primary responsibility* was specifically defined to mean that "the governing board and president . . . should concur with the faculty judgment except in rare instances and for compelling reasons which should be stated in detail" (p. 109). This appears to give the de facto authority of the faculty more weight than the de jure authority of the board in those areas that in fact define the institution—what shall be taught, who shall teach, and who shall study. In the eyes of some, this muddled the problem further rather than clarifying solutions.

A major problem with the "Joint Statement"—as well as with the content of other normative statements—is that while it presents positions of high principle that can be endorsed by many campus constituencies, it is less successful in identifying the specific structures and processes that would implement these principles. The behavioral implications of the statement are unclear and can be interpreted in quite different ways. The statement has also been criticized for failing to describe how governance *really* functions in many institutions, for assuming that governance is characterized by shared aims and values without giving proper weight to the conflict and competition that exist between constituencies, and for ignoring the ways in which the external environment affects governance (Mortimer and McConnell, 1978). The "Joint Statement" is thus seen by some as an academic Camelot—devoutly to be wished for but not achievable by mere mortals.

The "Joint Statement" has another weakness, which has been less widely noticed: it does not fully appreciate the differences between various kinds of institutions. The diversity of American higher education is reflected in significant differences in such critical matters as purpose, size, sponsorship, tradition, and values. Policies appropriate and fruitful for one type of institution may be harmful for another. Recommendations of policies that treat *"the* faculty" or *"the* administration" as alike in all institutions (and that speak as if these groups were monolithic within institutions) ignore the reality that the background and expectations of faculty and administrators at community colleges and at research universities, for example, might well produce very different approaches to governance.

PROBLEMS OF ORGANIZATION

Dualism of Controls

If a college is compared to a business firm, it is possible to consider the confused relationships between boards, administration, and faculty that we have just discussed as reflecting disorganization, willfulness, or the pursuit of self-interest in preference to college interests. Corson (1960) was among the first observers to ascribe a different cause when he identified the administration of colleges and universities as presenting "a unique dualism in organizational structure" (p. 43). Corson saw the university as including two structures existing in parallel: the conventional administrative hierarchy and the structure through which faculty made decisions regarding those aspects of the institution over which they had jurisdiction. This dual system of control was further complicated by the fact that neither system had consistent patterns of structure or delegation. The faculty governance structure on every campus was different, and each administration seemed to "have been established to meet specific situations in particular institutions or to reflect the strengths and weaknesses of individuals in various echelons" (p. 45).

The two control systems not only were structurally separate but were based on different systems of authority as well (Etzioni, 1964). In most business organizations, major goal activities are directed and coordinated by a hierarchy of administrators who decide questions such as what products should be made, in what number, and with what characteristics. Those higher in rank rely on administrative authority, derived from their position in the organizational structure, to direct the activities of others. These organizations also have need for experts who are not involved in coordinating the institution's goal activities. These experts rely on professional authority to provide specialized knowledge and judgment in one or more professional areas. Their judgments are individual acts that are not governed by the directives of others.

Administrative authority is predicated on the control and coordination of activities by superiors; professional authority is predicated on autonomy and individual knowledge. These two sources of authority are not only different but in mutual disagreement. In business organizations, the administrative line officers direct the primary goal activities of the institution, and the staff professionals provide secondary support activities and knowledge. Conflict caused by the incompatibility of administrative and professional authority is resolved by recognizing the supremacy of administrative authority. But in professional organizations, such as colleges and universities, the resolution is far more problematic. These organizations have staffs composed predominantly of professionals who produce, apply, preserve, or communicate knowledge (Etzioni, 1964) and who are also responsible for setting organizational goals and maintaining standards of performance (Scott, 1981). Etzioni suggests that "although administrative authority is suitable for the major goals activities in private business, in professional organizations administrators are in charge of secondary activities; they administer *means* to the major activity carried out by professionals. In other words, to the extent that there is a staff-line relationship at all, professionals should hold the major authority and administrators the secondary staff authority" (p. 81). This reversal of the patterns seen in other settings makes the organization of colleges and universities difficult to understand.

Mission and Management

Clarity and agreement on organizational mission are usually considered a fundamental principle for establishing systems of accountability. It is commonly stated that "in a business corporation there is always one quantifiable measure of performance . . . the rate of earnings on the capital invested. Because dollar profits are both the objective of the activity and the measure of performance, the operation of the company is keyed to accountability for the profit achieved" (Besse, 1973, p. 110). This relationship between performance and profit can then be translated into systems for identifying responsibility, measuring costs, and preparing periodic reports and analyses.

Although it is too simple to say that the mission of a business enterprise is to make money, that assertion contains an underlying truth that to a great extent provides a clarity of purpose and an integration of management that are absent in higher education. As colleges and universities become more diverse, fragmented, specialized, and connected with other social systems, institutional missions do not become clearer; rather, they multiply and become sources of stress and conflict rather than integration. The problem is not that institutions cannot identify their goals but rather that they simultaneously embrace a large number of conflicting goals (Gross and Grambsch, 1974).

There is no metric in higher education comparable to money in business, and no goal comparable to "profits." This is so in part because of disagreement on goals and in part because neither goal achievement nor the activities related to their performance can be satisfactorily quantified into an educational "balance sheet." Does a core curriculum produce more liberally educated students than a program built on the great books? Should a college measure its performance by the percentage of students who graduate, the percentage who get jobs, the percentage who are satisfied, or the percentage who participate in civic activities? The accountability techniques of the business corporation are of little benefit to the educational purposes of higher education.

Lack of clarity and agreement on institutional goals and mission has equally important effects on organization and management. The list of legitimate institutional missions is a lengthy one, but the problem can be seen in a consideration of only the three commonly articulated missions of teaching, research, and service. Each of these three missions is likely to rely on different structures for its effective implementation. For example, while the academic department may serve as the focus for teaching, funded research is based primarily on the activities of individual faculty members and requires different, and incompatible, management systems, budgeting processes, and organizational units. At the same time, the central coordination that supports service activities not only often operates outside existing faculty units but also conflicts with traditional notions of faculty autonomy and academic freedom (Perkins, 1973a). Teaching, research, and service are interrelated and mutually reinforcing production processes in the higher education system as a whole. However, on many campuses these activities are performed by different people operating within overlapping yet competing structures. Most faculty have their primary affiliation with either an academic department that supports their teaching, an institute within which they engage in research, or an extension division or other unit that provides community service. Few are affiliated with all three. No single organizational design can optimize all legitimate organizational interests; a structure that provides the most effective support for research, for example, will be quite different from a structure that seeks to closely integrate undergraduate teaching activities.

Although some have suggested that higher education institutions could be managed more effectively if their missions were clarified, this has proved to be impossible to do in larger and more complex organizations. A more sensible suggestion might be to redefine management so that it can function usefully within a context of conflicting objectives. Given the differences in the clarity of goals, we should not be too surprised to find that effective management in colleges and universities would differ from that seen in business firms.

Power, Compliance, and Control

Power is the ability to produce intended change in others, to influence them so that they will be more likely to act in accordance with one's own preferences. Power is essential to coordinate and control the activities of people and groups in universities, as it is in other organizations. There are many ways of thinking about power. One influential typology has identified five kinds of power in social groups: coercive power, reward power, legitimate power, referent power, and expert power (French and Raven, 1959). Coercive power is the ability to punish if a person does not accept one's attempt at influence. Reward power is the ability of one person to offer or promise rewards to another or to remove or decrease negative influences. Legitimate power exists when both parties agree to a common code or standard that gives one party the right to influence the other in a specific range of activities or behaviors and obliges the other to comply. A major source of legitimate power in our society is the acceptance of a hierarchical authority structure in formal groups. Referent power results from the willingness to be influenced by another because of one's identification with the other. Expert power is exercised when one person accepts influence from another because of a belief that the other person has some special knowledge or competence in a specific area.

The exercise of power may cause alienation, and responses by faculty and others to various forms of power in institutions of higher education may pose problems for their organization and administration. Coercive power always alienates those subject to it. The use of reward power or legitimate power may or may not produce alienation, depending on the circumstances and the expectations of those subject to it. Neither referent power nor expert power results in alienation.

Different forms of power are typically used in different kinds of organizations, and they have different effects on the responses of organizational participants. One approach has identified coercive, utilitarian, and normative organizations as representing three major patterns (Etzioni, 1961). Coercive organizations, such as prisons, rely predominantly on the punishments and threats of coercive power, and they produce alienated involvement of participants. Utilitarian organizations, such as business firms, emphasize reward power and legitimate power to control participants. People calculate the costs and benefits of involvement in order to decide whether or not to participate. Normative organizations, such as colleges and universities, rely on referent and expert power that is less likely to cause alienation and that produces committed participants who are influenced through the manipulation of symbols. This does not mean that faculty are indifferent to money, or that they will not become disaffected if they do not consider their salaries to be reasonable. But it is true that faculty members on many campuses are likely to be influenced more by internalized principles of academic freedom and ethical behavior, and by communications from colleagues who are seen as sharing their values, than by salary increases or threats of administrative sanctions.

The means by which faculty behavior can be influenced are therefore very different from what would be effective in traditional business firms emphasizing utilitarian power. Trying to control faculty by offering material benefits, such as money, or by giving orders might affect their behavior but at the same time would increase their alienation and decrease the effectiveness of normative power. The autonomous focus of professional authority and the unwillingness of professionals to accept administrative authority require that higher education take a different approach to the problems of management and governance.

INSTITUTIONAL AND ORGANIZATIONAL CONSTRAINTS

Many factors have increasingly limited the discretion and flexibility of academic leaders (Commission on Strengthening Presidential Leadership, 1984). Some of these factors develop as institutions interact with other institutions in their environments, while some arise within the institution itself. Environmental constraints include more federal and state controls, greater involvement by the courts in academic decision making, more layers of governance, particularly in institutions that are part of statewide systems, fewer opportunities for growth and consequently for changes accompanying growth, questions of the importance of the missions of higher education, less acceptance of authority in general, and fewer potential applicants and therefore greater responsiveness to the student market. Within institutions themselves, constraints to leadership arise from greater involvement by faculties in academic and personnel decisions, faculty collective bargaining, greater goal ambiguity, greater fractionation of the campus into interest groups, leading to a loss of consensus and community, greater involvement by trustees in campus operations, and increased bureaucracy and specialization among campus administrators. The dual system of authority, the expectation of participation as an element of shared authority, the linkages of faculty with groups external to the campus—these and related factors already noted severely limit the influence of administrators.

Institutions and Environments

Institutions must be responsive to their environments to survive, and the responses made by colleges and universities have had profound effects on their governance structures and processes.

The number and pervasiveness of these environmental forces have increased almost exponentially at many institutions over the past decades. Two examples showing the effects of external sources of support and power serve to illustrate the problem in different ways.

The confusion in governance that results when both faculty and administration lose the ability to understand and control the processes of their institutions was noted over a quarter of a century ago (Mooney, 1963). The loss of faculty control is related to increased institutional size and complexity and the division of faculty into different departments, committees, and other units. This fractionation prevents the development of a holistic faculty perspective. The loss of administrative control is related to the presence of external funding and control agencies that bypass and weaken institutional administration. As a consequence, neither faculty nor administration feels able to take command, since neither group fully understands the enterprise or has control of enough of its resources. As individuals and groups lose their ability to affect their institution through the implementation of positive and constructive programs, they increasingly tend to assert their influence and status by acting as veto blocs, thus increasing institutional conservatism. The result, says Clark Kerr (1982, p. 30), is more commitment "to the status quo—the status quo is the only solution that cannot be vetoed." The same forces that limit the power of faculty groups affect deans and presidents as well, so that the power of administrators in many cases is determined by their right to block programs they consider unwise or improper (Bok, 1983, p. 85).

The major external force limiting institutional autonomy is the exercise of increased authority by the states. The growth of the public sector of higher education during the past quarter century, as well as support in some states of nonpublic institutions, has led to increased state funding of—and therefore concern for—the programs and management of both public and independent colleges and universities. Coordinating or consolidated governing boards in almost all states exercise increasing influence over matters reserved in the past to the campus. Other state executive or legislative agencies become involved in program review, administrative operations, budgeting, and planning. The rationale often offered is the need for public accountability, but the consequence is often chaos and confusion (Carnegie Foundation for the Advancement of Teaching, 1982). Individual institutions become part of larger regional or statewide systems in which single boards have authority for several campuses and not enough time or energy to become familiar with any of them. As the locus of influence moves from the campus to the state, public-sector presidents may find themselves becoming more like middle managers than campus leaders. Faculty may respond to increased centralization of control by centralizing their own participation through processes of collective bargaining that often ritualize disruptive conflict. The loss of ability to exert local influence leads to mutual scapegoating by faculty and administration, end runs to state offices that further reduce administrative authority, and a diminished sense of both campus responsibility and accountability. The sense of powerlessness comes not just from the recognition of one's own limited ability to exert influence upward but also from the realization that those higher in the organization cannot exert much upward influence either.

Decentralization

The centralization of authority at levels above the campus has influenced the distribution of influence at many institutions in two quite different ways. Institutions have become more administratively centralized because of requirements to rationalize budget formats, implement procedures that will pass judicial tests of equitable treatment, and speak with a single voice to powerful external agencies. At the same time, increased faculty specialization and decreased administrative authority have fostered decentralization of educational decision making at many institutions, which leads to further faculty specialization and continued reduction of administrative authority. As faculty become more specialized, they assert their expertise as a requirement for designing curriculum and assessing the qualifications of colleagues. Particularly in larger and more complex institutions, schools or departments become the locus of decision making, sometimes reinforced by an "every tub on its own bottom" management philosophy that makes these subunits responsible for their own enrollment and financial affairs as well. In such cases, the larger institution may become an academic holding company, presiding over a federation of quasi-autonomous subunits. Unable to influence the larger institution, faculty retreat into the small subunit for which they feel affinity and from which they can defend their influence and status.

Inflexibility of Resources

The ability of groups to significantly influence their campus through participation in governance is severely constrained by both the paucity of resources available and the short-term difficulties in internally reallocating those resources that do exist. Some important intangible campus resources, such as institutional prestige or attractiveness to students or to potential donors, are tied into networks of external relationships that are virtually impossible to change in the short run and difficult to alter even over long periods of time. Internally, the personnel complement on most campuses is largely fixed through tenure and contractual provisions, program change is constrained by faculty interests and structures as well as facilities limitations, and yearly planning begins with the largest share of the budget precommitted. In the public sector, institutions are subject to state personnel, purchasing, and construction regulations, as well as budget management restrictions that make certain expenditures impossible even when resources are available. But resources are not always available, and when last year's expenditures exceed this year's projected income, major changes are rare. Even on campuses that stress rational planning and budgeting, opportunities for short-term effects are minimal. For example, one relatively wealthy institution found that its extensive planning program accounted for less than 6 percent of the variance in the budget over ten years. An observer commented that "it may be hard to believe that any effort above a minimal level is justifiable" but added that "since so much of the budget is virtually fixed, especially in the short run, the small portion that is free to vary assumes tremendous importance" (Chaffee, 1983, p. 402).

Confusion of Organizational Levels

Organizations can be thought of as composed of three levels of responsibility and control—technical, managerial, and institutional (Thompson, 1967). In colleges or universities, the technical level includes the research, teaching, and service responsibilities carried out primarily by the faculty. The responsibility of the organization's institutional level, which in higher education is represented by boards of trustees and presidents, is to ensure that the organization is able to respond appropriately to the uncertainty of external social forces. The managerial level is represented by the administration, which is charged with mediating between these two levels and buffering the faculty and researchers who make up the technical core against disruption caused by problems in the acquisition of funding, fluctuations in student enrollments, or governmental interference.

Organizations are presumed to be most effective when the institutional level specializes in coping with uncertainty and the technical level specializes in functioning effectively in conditions of certainty. This specialization is not uncommon in business organizations in which senior officers are responsible for monitoring the environment (Katz and Kahn, 1978, p. 4). But in higher education, distinctions among the three levels can be difficult if not impossible to maintain, particularly in certain types of colleges and universities. For example, there are institutions in which faculty (technical level) are also members of the board of trustees (institutional level). At many institutions, faculty are expected by tradition as well as law (*NLRB* v. *Yeshiva University*, 444 U.S. 672 [1980]) to exercise responsibilities for personnel and for program that in other types of organizations would be considered managerial. Faculty in some types of institutions, through their professional associations, funded research, and consulting activities, often have direct access to major actors and resources in the environment and so bypass the managerial level. And major participants may sequentially (or simultaneously) be both administrators and faculty and therefore participants in both the managerial and technical levels, while the products of the technical level as alumni may become trustees at the institutional level. There are probably few organizations in our society in which someone who is a member of the union bargaining team one day can become the organizational president the next, but it has happened in higher education!

Distinctions among the institutional, managerial, and technical levels are clearer in some institutions than in others (church-related institutions or community colleges, for example). This should make the technical core more rational and management able to be more bureaucratized without creating problems. Other organizations, such as research universities, have technical cores that resist rationality and separation from the environment; faculty engaged in state-of-the-art research often cannot determine their research plans in advance, and they must keep in constant communication with colleagues and funding agencies. In such situations, arbitrary bureaucratic boundaries would be disruptive.

Cosmopolitans and Locals: Prestige and Rank

The growing professionalism and specialization of faculty have tended to create faculty orientations to their institutions and to their disciplines that can be considered across a continuum. The two polar types have been referred to as "cosmopolitans" and "locals" (Gouldner, 1957). Cosmopolitans are faculty whose peers are colleagues across the country—or the world—who share their specialized scholarly interests. They tend to do research and publish, to find their rewards and satisfactions in their disciplinary activities, and to use their institutions as bases for their external activities. Cosmopolitans are less likely to be concerned with parochial campus issues and would tend to think of themselves primarily as independent professionals and scholars and secondarily (if at all) as faculty members at a particular university. Locals, on the other hand, are faculty whose major commitments are to their campuses. They tend to be integrated into the life of the campus community, to focus their attention on teaching, and to be concerned with and participate in institutional activities. They might think of themselves primarily as faculty members at a particular university and secondarily (if at all) as independent professionals and scholars.

The proportions on a faculty of cosmopolitans and locals can have a major effect on campus governance and patterns of influence. In traditional business organizations, prestige and rank are synonymous. The president at the top of the pyramid has both the greatest degree of prestige and the highest status (or rank) in the organization. A vice-president has less prestige and rank than the president but more than a subordinate officer. The organization confers both rank and prestige, and they are mutually reinforcing.

In higher education, however, prestige and rank may not be identical. While the institution may confer rank, prestige may be conferred by professional groups outside the university. A senior department chairperson may have less prestige (and peer influence) than an assistant professor who has just won a national award; a dean with a strong record of scholarship may be more influential with faculty than a vice-president for academic affairs. Particularly in institutions with large proportions of cosmopolitans, the conflicts between rank and prestige may weaken administrative authority and increase the difficulties in coordinating activities.

Other Organizational Differences

A number of organizational principles that differentiate colleges and universities from other organizations have already been suggested; there are other differences as well. If a "typical" business organization and "typical" university were compared, the university would exhibit less specialization of work activities (assistant professors and full professors do essentially the same things), a greater specialization by expertise ("unnecessary" history professors cannot be assigned to teach accounting when enrollments shift), a flatter hierarchy (fewer organizational levels between the faculty "workers" and the chief executive), lower interdependence of parts (what happens in one academic department is likely to have little effect on another), less control over "raw materials" (particularly in public institutions where student admission is nonselective), low accountability (because the administrative hierarchy and control system is less involved in directing goals activities), and less visible role performance (faculty usually carry out their professional teaching responsibilities unseen by either administrators or other professionals).

The differences between academic institutions and business firms are significant enough that systems of coordination and control effective in one of these types of organization might not have the same consequences in the other. In particular, it might be expected that colleges and businesses might require different approaches to leadership.

THE PROBLEM OF LEADERSHIP

Our common notions of leadership arise from the perception that the success of business organizations depends on the directives of hard-driving, knowledgeable, and decisive executives. There are those who also see colleges and universities as the long shadows of great leaders or who assert that "our future rests on the bold, decisive leadership of college and university presidents nationwide" (Fisher, 1984, p. 11). On the other hand, it has been said that "the view of the university as the shadow of a strong president is unrealistic now, however, if indeed it was ever accurate" (Walker, 1979, p. 118) and even that "the presidency is an illusion" (Cohen and March, 1974, p. 2).

How important are administrative leaders to college and university performance? Do presidents make a difference? Because of what we think we see in business organizations, and what experts say about leaders in higher education, questions such as these may appear foolish. Lists identify the 100 most effective presidents ("The 100 Most Effective . . .," 1986), and blue-ribbon panels argue that "strengthening presidential leadership is one of the most urgent concerns on the agenda of higher education" (Commission on Strengthening Presidential Leadership, 1984, p. 102). Leadership is treated as something identifiable, tangible, measurable, and efficacious. From the way we talk, it appears that we know what leadership is and how it should be practiced. Fine tuning may be required, of course, but the problems of higher education would presumably diminish if only leaders would be willing to exercise leadership—or if we would have the courage to replace them with others who would.

Calling for leadership is easy. But despite thousands of essays, research studies, and other scholarly and practical works, the fact remains that little is actually known about the phenomenon we refer to as "leadership." There is still no agreement on how leadership can be defined, measured, assessed, or linked to outcomes, and "no clear and unequivocal understanding exists as to what distinguishes leaders from nonleaders, and perhaps more important, what distinguishes effective leaders from ineffective leaders" (Bennis and Nanus, 1985, p. 4).

Leadership Theories

Most studies of leadership have taken place in business organizations, the military, and governmental agencies, with little attention given to higher education. The study of leadership is even more difficult in colleges and universities than in other settings because of the dual control systems, conflicts between professional and administrative authority, unclear goals, and the other unique properties of professional, normative organizations. In particular, the relationship between those identified as leaders and those whom they presume to lead is problematic. Some theoretical approaches assert that leadership can be understood only in the context of "followership." But in higher education, there is a strong resistance to leadership as it is generally understood in more traditional and hierarchical organizations; in particular, in most institutions it may be more appropriate to think of faculty as constituents than as followers.

Five basic approaches to studying organizational leadership are found in the literature (for summaries, see, for example, Yukl, 1981; Bass, 1981; Hollander, 1985). They include *trait theories*, which identify specific characteristics that are believed to contribute to a person's ability to assume and successfully function in a leadership position; *power and influence theories*, which attempt to understand leadership in terms of the source and amount of power available to leaders and the manner in which leaders exercise influence over followers through either unilateral or reciprocal interactions with them; *behavioral theories*, which study leadership by examining activity patterns, managerial roles, and behavioral categories of leaders—that is, considering what it is that leaders actually do; *contingency theories*, which emphasize the importance of situational factors such as the nature of the task or the external environment in understanding effective leadership; and *symbolic and cultural theories*, which assume that leadership is a social attribution that permits people to cognitively connect outcomes to causes and thereby make sense of an equivocal, fluid, and complex world.

Social Exchange Theory

One orientation to leadership particularly suited to higher education is known as social exchange theory. The theory posits that there is a reciprocal relationship whereby leaders provide needed services to a group in exchange for the group's approval and compliance with the leader's demands. In essence, the group agrees to collectively reduce its own autonomy and to accept the authority of the leader in exchange for the rewards and benefits (social approval, financial benefits, competitive advantage) the leader can bring them. Leaders are as dependent on followers as followers are on leaders.

Leaders accumulate power through their offices and their own personalities to the extent that they produce the expected rewards and fairly distribute them and lose power to the extent that they do not. This suggests that effectiveness as a leader depends on either fulfilling the expectations of followers by being a transactional leader or changing those expectations by being a transformational leader (Burns, 1978; Bennis and Nanus, 1985). The transactional leader meets the needs of followers and emphasizes means; the transformational leader emphasizes ends and taps the motivations of followers to lead them to new and better values in the support of intended change. Neither form, says Burns, should be confused with what commonly passes for leadership—"acts of oratory, manipulation, sheer self-advancement, brute coercion, . . . conspicuous position-taking without followers or follow through, posturing on various stages, . . . authoritarianism" (Burns, 1978, p. 427).

This caveat is important. It illuminates a common cognitive bias that leads us to base judgments about leaders on the extent to which they have characteristics that make them *look* like leaders. The old joke states the qualifications for college president as "white hair for that look of experience and hemorrhoids for that look of concern." As is true of many jokes, there is an important core of reality in this one that suggests that the effects of leadership may rely as much on our preconceptions and biases as on the observed outcomes that are clearly the consequences of leadership behavior.

Leadership as Symbol

Symbolic, cognitive, or cultural theories (see, for example, Deal and Kennedy, 1982; Cohen and March, 1974; Schein, 1985; Sergiovanni and Corbally, 1984; Weick, 1979) view organizations as systems of belief and perception in which reality is invented, not discovered. From this perspective, the role of leaders in business organizations is to "manage" the organizational culture. But the professional nature of colleges and universities may make the management of culture difficult if not impossible, and the role of leaders may therefore be more symbolic than real. Presidents may have relatively little influence over outcomes when compared with other forces that affect organizational functioning.

The possibility that leadership in its traditional sense may play only a minor role in the life of most colleges and universities most of the time is difficult to accept. We have developed highly romanticized, heroic views of leadership—what leaders do, what they are able to accomplish, and the general effects they have on our lives. One of the principal elements in this romanticized conception is the view that leadership is a central organizational process and the premier force in the scheme of organizational events and activities. It amounts to what might be considered a faith in the potential if not in the actual efficacy of people identified as leaders (Meindl, Ehrlich, and Dukerich, 1985). Cognitive biases allow us to see the "evidence" of the effects of leadership even when it does not exist. For example, work groups that are arbitrarily told that they have been successful at a task are more likely to perceive that they have had good leadership than groups that have been arbitrarily told that they have failed (Staw, 1975). Extreme (good or bad) performance of an organization is likely to lead to a preference to use leadership as an explanation even in the absence of any supporting data (Meindl, Ehrlich, and Dukerich, 1985). And it has been proposed that merely focusing someone's attention on a potential cause (and who is more likely to be visible and thought of than the president?) will affect the extent to which it is perceived as the cause (Nisbett and Ross, 1980). Findings such as these suggest that administrative leadership may be in part a product of social attributions. By creating roles that we declare will provide leadership to an organization, we construct the attribution that organizational effects are due to leadership behavior (Pfeffer, 1977). This allows us to simplify and make sense of complex organizational processes that would otherwise be impossible to comprehend (Meindl, Ehrlich, and Dukerich, 1985). In some ways, it is perhaps as sensible to say that successful organizational events "cause" effective administrators as it is to say that effective administrators "cause" successful events.

In many situations, presidential leadership may not be real but rather may be a social attribution. This can happen because of the tendency of campus constituents to assign to a president the responsibility for unusual institutional outcomes because the leader fills a role identified as that of leader, because presidents are very visible and prominent, because presidents spend a great deal of time doing leaderlike things (such as engaging in ceremonial and symbolic activities), and because we all have the need to believe in the effectiveness of individual control. Leaders, then, are people believed by followers to have caused events. "Successful leaders," says Pfeffer

(1977, p. 110), "are those who can separate themselves from organizational failures and associate themselves with organizational successes."

Leadership and Environments

Comparing traditional notions of leadership to those that come out of the symbolic or cognitive approach puts us in a rather difficult situation. Those who call for the strengthening of presidential leadership recognize the high quality of current presidents (Commission on Strengthening Presidential Leadership, 1984), and yet the best appear not to be good enough. The primary factors affecting leadership may be found not in the presidents themselves but rather in the constraints that exist in the environment within which administrators function. Good times seem to call forth strong leaders. The late nineteenth century is seen now as a time of giants who founded or expanded great institutions (although it might have been difficult in 1890 to predict exactly who these giants would appear to have been in 1990). Similarly, the early 1960s saw an extraordinary number of campus leaders who were skillful in directing new construction and burgeoning enrollments. But, as has been pointed out, administrators then had an easy job, and "by traditional standards, administrative effectiveness was almost universal. Enrollments were increasing, revenues were growing, innovations in the form of new and experimental programs were common. . . . Of course, the problem with traditional standards of administrator effectiveness is that criteria such as those listed above are largely a product of environmental forces and beyond administrative control" (Whetten and Cameron, 1985, p. 35).

Unfortunately, leadership appears in short supply in bad times, such as during eras of decline or of student unrest. In the late 1960s, for example, presidents faced with campus disruptions were criticized for not calling in the police as frequently as they were for calling them, and for calling them either too soon or too late. Presidents were castigated for ineffective leadership even though post hoc suggestions proposing how one president could have succeeded were precisely the explanations given on another campus for why a president failed.

Presidential influence is constrained by many factors, and many aspects of institutional functioning do not appear to depend on who the president happens to be (Birnbaum, forthcoming c). But this does not mean that presidents are unimportant. Complex social organizations cannot function effectively over the long term without leaders to coordinate their activities, represent them to their various publics, and symbolize the embodiment of institutional purpose. Moreover, if these leaders are to avoid conspicuous failure, they must have a high level of technical competence, an understanding of the nature of higher education in general and the culture of the individual institution in particular, and skills required to effectively interact with external constituencies. These are uncommon traits, but the processes of presidential selection function in a manner that makes it likely that successful candidates by and large will usually possess them (Birnbaum, forthcoming b). There may be little relationship between institutional functioning and presidential actions, but this does not necessarily mean that presidents are too weak; it could equally well be used to argue that presidents in general are quite good but that they are generally homogeneous in their effectiveness. This may in part be because the training and socialization of a new president are likely to be similar to those of the predecessor president, as well as to those of other persons who could plausibly have been considered for that specific vacancy. In general, most presidents do the right things, and do them right, most of the time; they properly fulfill the requirements of their roles even if they are unlikely to leave a distinctive mark on their institution.

THE NATURE OF ACADEMIC ORGANIZATION—A SUMMARY

Because most institutions of higher education lack a clear and unambiguous mission whose achievement can be assessed through agreed upon quantifiable measures such as "profits," the processes, structures, and systems for accountability commonly used in business firms are not always sensible for them. Many college and university managers do not exercise primary control over the curriculum, faculty recruitment or promotion, or the methods of teaching, major processes of production that in business firms would be fundamental managerial prerogatives. Issues of governance are clouded at least in part because "there is no center of authority analogous to the owners of the corporation, to the cabinet member, governor or mayor" (Corson, 1979, p. 7). The authority of various constituencies to participate in or make decisions is often unclear and frequently contested.

Although it is tempting to consider a college or university, in view of its corporate existence, as being comparable in many ways to a business corporation, the differences between the two are striking. In addition to matters already discussed, it has been noted (Kerr and Gade, 1986) that business firms, unlike institutions of higher education, have no tenured faculty members, face no criticisms from employees shielded by the principles of academic freedom, and have no alumni. The boards of business firms are likely to include large numbers of corporate officers and to be controlled by the corporate administration. The business firm can make and remake decisions constantly without the need for full consultation. In short, as Baldridge, Curtis, Ecker, and Riley (1978, p. 9) have put it, "the organizational characteristics of academic institutions are so different from other institutions that traditional management theories do not apply to them. Their goals are more ambiguous and diverse. They serve clients instead of processing materials. Their key employees are highly professionalized. They have unclear technologies based more on professional skills than on standard operating procedures. They have 'fluid participation' with amateur decision makers who wander in and out of the decision process. As a result, traditional management theories cannot be applied to educational institutions without carefully considering whether they will work well in that unique academic setting."

Common ideas about the efficacy of strong and decisive leadership may have some validity in business firms that are hierarchical and goal directed and in which subordinates expect to receive directives from superiors. But leaders in higher education are subject to internal and external constraints that limit their effectiveness and may make their roles highly symbolic rather than instrumental.

REFERENCES

American Association of University Professors. *Policy Documents and Reports, 1984 Edition.* Washington, D.C.: American Association of University Professors, 1984.

Baldridge, J. V., Curtis, D. V., Ecker, G., and Riley, G. L. *Policy Making and Effective Leadership: A National Study of Academic Management.* San Francisco: Jossey-Bass, 1978.

Bass, B. M. *Stogdill's Handbook of Leadership.* New York: Free Press, 1981.

Bennis, W., and Nanus, B. *Leaders: The Strategies for Taking Charge.* New York: Harper & Row, 1985.

Besse, R. M. "A Comparison of the University with the Corporation." In J. A. Perkins (ed.), *The University as an Organization.* New York: McGraw-Hill, 1973.

Bok, S. *Secrets: On the Ethics of Concealment and Revelation.* New York: Random House, 1983.

Burns, J. M. *Leadership.* New York: Harper & Row, 1978.

Carnegie Foundation for the Advancement of Teaching. *The Control of the Campus: A Report on the Governance of Higher Education.* Washington, D.C.: Carnegie Foundation for the Advancement of Teaching, 1982.

Chaffee, E. E. "The Role of Rationality in University Budgeting." *Research in Higher Education*, 1983, *19*, 387–406.

Cohen, M. D., and March, J. G. *Leadership and Ambiguity: The American College President.* New York: McGraw-Hill, 1974.

"College Governing Boards." *Chronicle of Higher Education*, Feb. 12, 1986, p. 27.

Commission on Strengthening Presidential Leadership. *Presidents Make a Difference.* Washington, D.C.: Association of Governing Boards of Universities and Colleges, 1984.

Corson, J. J. *Governance of Colleges and Universities.* New York: McGraw-Hill, 1960.

Corson, J. J. "Management of the College or University: It's Different." Topical Paper no. 16, Center for the Study of Higher Education, University of Arizona, June 1979.

Deal, T. E., and Kennedy, A. K. *Corporate Cultures: The Rites and Rituals of Organizational Life.* Reading, Mass.: Addison-Wesley, 1982.

Etzioni, A. *A Comparative Analysis of Complex Organizations.* New York: Free Press, 1961.

Etzioni, A. *Modern Organizations.* Englewood Cliffs, N.J.: Prentice-Hall, 1964.

Fisher, J. L. "Presidents Will Lead—If We Let Them." *AGB Reports*, July/Aug. 1984, pp. 11–14.

French, J.R.P., Jr., and Raven, B. "The Bases of Social Power." In D. Cartwright (ed.), *Studies in Social Power.* Ann Arbor: Institute for Social Research, University of Michigan, 1959.

Glenny, L. A., and Dalglish, T. K. "Higher Education and the Law." In J. A. Perkins (ed.), *The University as an Organization*, New York: McGraw-Hill, 1973.

Gouldner, A. W. "Cosmopolitans and Locals: Toward an Analysis of Latent Social Roles." *Administrative Science Quarterly*, 1957, *2*, 281–307.

Gross, E., and Grambsch, P. V. *Changes in University Organization, 1964–1971.* New York: McGraw-Hill, 1974.

Hartnett, R. T. *College and University Trustees: Their Backgrounds, Roles, and Educational Attitudes.* Princeton, N.J.: Educational Testing Service, 1969.

Hollander, E. P. "Leadership and Power." In G. Lindzey and E. Aronson (eds.), *The Handbook of Social Psychology.* (3rd ed.) New York: Random House, 1985.

Katz, D., and Kahn, R. L. *The Social Psychology of Organizations.* (2nd ed.) New York: Wiley, 1978.

Keller, G. *Academic Strategy: The Management Revolution in American Higher Education.* Baltimore, Md.: Johns Hopkins University Press, 1983.

Kerr, C. "Postscript 1982." *Change*, Oct. 1982, pp. 23–31.

Kerr, C., and Gade, M. L. *The Many Lives of Academic Presidents: Time, Place, and Character.* Washington, D.C.: Association of Governing Boards of Universities and Colleges, 1986.

Lunsford, T. F. "Authority and Ideology in the Administered University." In C. E. Kruytbosch and S. L. Messinger (eds.), *The State of the University: Authority and Change.* Beverly Hills, Calif.: Sage, 1970.

Meindl, J. R., Ehrlich, S. B., and Dukerich, J. M. "The Romance of Leadership." *Administrative Science Quarterly*, 1985, *30*, 78–102.

Nisbett, R., and Ross, L. *Human Inference: Strategies and Shortcomings of Social Judgment.* Englewood Cliffs, N.J.: Prentice-Hall, 1980.

Perkins, J. A. "Organization and Functions of the University." In J. A. Perkins (ed.), *The University as an Organization.* New York: McGraw-Hill, 1973.

Pfeffer, J. "The Ambiguity of Leadership." *Academy of Management Review*, 1977, *2*, 104–119.

Rourke, F. E., and Brooks, G. E. "The 'Managerial Revolution' in Higher Education." *Administrative Science Quarterly*, 1964, *9*, 154–181.

Ruml, B., and Morrison, D. H. *Memo to a College Trustee.* New York: McGraw-Hill, 1959.

Schein, E. H. *Organizational Culture and Leadership: A Dynamic View.* San Francisco: Jossey-Bass, 1985.

Scott, W. R. *Organizations: Rational, Natural, and Open Systems.* Englewood Cliffs, N.J.: Prentice-Hall, 1981.

Sergiovanni, T. J., and Corbally, J. E. (eds.). *Leadership and Organizational Culture.* Urbana: University of Illinois Press, 1984.

Staw, B. M. "Attribution of the Causes of Performance: A New Alternative Explanation of Cross-Sectional Research on Organizations." *Organizational Behavior and Human Performance*, 1975, *13*, 414–432.

Thompson, J. D. *Organizations in Action.* New York: McGraw-Hill, 1967.

Veblen, T. *The Higher Learning in America.* New York: Sagamore Press, 1957. (Originally published 1918.)

Walker, D. E. *The Effective Administrator: A Practical Approach to Problem Solving, Decision Making, and Campus Leadership.* San Francisco: Jossey-Bass, 1979.

Weick, K. E. *The Social Psychology of Organizing.* (2nd ed.) Reading, Mass.: Addison-Wesley, 1979.

Whetten, D. A., and Cameron, K. S. "Administrative Effectiveness in Higher Education." *Review of Higher Education*, 1985, *9*, 35–49.

Yukl, G. A. *Leadership in Organizations.* Englewood Cliffs, N.J.: Prentice-Hall, 1981.

17

Loosely Coupled Systems

A Reconceptualization

J. Douglas Orton and Karl E. Weick

The concept of organizations as loosely coupled systems is widely used and diversely understood. The concept has a rare combination of face validity, metaphorical salience, and cutting-edge mysticism, all of which encourage researchers to adopt the concept but do not help them to examine its underlying structure, themes, and implications. Like a linguistic Trojan horse, the loose coupling concept has preceded loose coupling theory into the various strongholds of organizational studies.

Because the concept has been underspecified, its use has generated controversy. Researchers who oppose the concept on the basis of its imprecision have watched as more and more researchers adopt it. Researchers who advocate the concept on the basis of its face validity have watched it become unrecognizable. Researchers who are in the middle have often used the concept hesitantly, convinced that it fits the phenomena they study, but uncertain about its meaning. These problems become even more apparent when loose coupling is compared with four other organizational perspectives that were published about the same time as Weick's (1976) article on educational organizations as loosely coupled systems: transaction cost economics (Williamson, 1975), institutional theory (Meyer & Rowan, 1977), population ecology theory (Hannan & Freeman, 1977), and resource dependence theory (Pfeffer & Salancik, 1978). Each of these four perspectives has a more distinctive paradigm, a more compact theory, and more empirical support than is true of loose coupling.

Researchers who invoke the concept of loose coupling generally cite one of three definitions. Glassman (1973) wrote that loose coupling is present when systems have either few variables in common or the variables they have in common are weak (p. 73). Weick (1976) defined loose coupling as a situation in which elements are responsive, but retain evidence of separateness and identity (p. 3). Later, he wrote that loose coupling is evident when elements affect each other "suddenly (rather than continuously), occasionally (rather than constantly), negligibly (rather than significantly), indirectly (rather than directly), and eventually (rather than immediately)" (Weick, 1982a, p. 380). Few researchers have questioned the meaning behind these statements.

On the surface, these underspecifications and the contradictions they have created may seem like social science run amok. However, as Levine (1985) argued, underspecified formulations often serve as a vehicle through which investigators can work on difficult conceptual problems.

This seems to have been true of writing about loose coupling, and such an argument would explain why the notion is widely used, despite its apparent ambiguity.

This chapter has two objectives. The first is to organize the diverse literature on loose coupling. While reviewing this literature, we were disappointed to find that the concept has been applied to simpler organizational puzzles than originally intended. Thus, the second goal is to redirect research on loose coupling toward more difficult, yet potentially more useful, interpretations.

In studying approximately 300 works that invoke the concept of loose coupling, five relatively distinct voices were noted: causation, typology, effects, compensations, and organizational outcomes. To attain the first goal of organizing the loose coupling literature, most of the chapter is devoted to discussions of these five voices and their recurring arguments. Once the voices are established, they are linked in a preliminary theory of the loosely coupled system. To attain the second goal of directing loose coupling research, the chapter begins with a discussion of the underlying loose coupling puzzle. Throughout the essay we explain how each of the five voices drifts away from the puzzle, and we conclude with suggestions on how researchers can focus more directly on explaining the puzzle.

THE UNDERLYING PUZZLE

The basic problem being addressed when people struggle to grasp the nature of loose coupling was first identified by Thompson (1967). He argued that although organizational forms are designed to deal with inherent contradictions, the language of organizational scholars does not allow them to capture this reality. Organizations appear to be both determinate, closed systems searching for certainty and indeterminate, open systems expecting uncertainty. Faced with these "incompatible concepts," and with "the fact that our culture does not contain concepts for simultaneously thinking about rationality and indeterminateness" (Thompson, 1967, p. 10), people simplify their analyses either by ignoring uncertainty to see rationality or by ignoring rational action to see spontaneous processes.

Thompson's contribution was to see that one way to preserve both rationality and indeterminacy in the same system is to separate their locations. He treated the technical core as a closed, rational system that eliminated uncertainty; the institutional level as an open system that "faced up to uncertainty" and permitted "the intrusion of variables penetrating from the outside"; and the managerial level as a system that "mediated" between the two extremes (p. 12).

Loose coupling has proven to be a durable concept precisely because it allows organizational analysts to explain the simultaneous existence of rationality and indeterminacy without specializing these two logics in distinct locations. Loose coupling suggests that any location in an organization (top, middle, or bottom) contains interdependent elements that vary in the number and strength of their interdependencies. The fact that these elements are linked and preserve some degree of determinacy is captured by the word *coupled* in the phrase *loosely coupled*. The fact that these elements are also subject to spontaneous changes and preserve some degree of independence and indeterminacy is captured by the modifying word *loosely*. The resulting image is a system that is simultaneously open and closed, indeterminate and rational, spontaneous and deliberate. If a person selectively attends to the determinacy that exists among some elements, he or she will describe the interdependence as a tightly coupled system. That characterization is partly inaccurate because not all elements and linkages are affected and parts of the system remain loose and open. If a person selectively attends to the openness, independence, and indeterminate links among some elements, he or she will describe what amounts to a decoupled system. That characterization, too, is incomplete and inaccurate because parts of the system remain coupled and closed.

Thus, the concept of loose coupling allows theorists to posit that any system, in any organizational location, can act on both a technical level, which is closed to outside forces (coupling produces stability), and an institutional level, which is open to outside forces (looseness produces flexibility).

The image that *should* emerge from this discussion is the following. If there is neither responsiveness nor distinctiveness, the system is not really a system, and it can be defined as a *noncoupled* system. If there is responsiveness without distinctiveness, the system is tightly coupled. If there is distinctiveness without responsiveness, the system is decoupled. If there is both distinctiveness and responsiveness, the system is loosely coupled. This general image is described here as the dialectical interpretation of loose coupling.

The image that more commonly *does* emerge from uses of the loose coupling concept is much simpler. Loose coupling is typically portrayed as the endpoint of a scale that extends from tightly coupled to loosely coupled. Tightly coupled systems are portrayed as having responsive components that do not act independently, whereas loosely coupled systems are portrayed as having independent components that do not act responsively. This image is described here as the unidimensional interpretation of loose coupling.

Researchers who invoke the concept of loose coupling have not yet made a distinction between the unidimensional and dialectical interpretation of the concept. Consequently, the loose coupling literature contains confusing mixtures of the two interpretations. For example, Rubin (1979) drew on dialectical interpretations to portray universities as loosely coupled systems. From this portrayal, she derived the unidimensional proposition that it should be easy for universities, because they are loosely coupled systems, to eliminate unwanted departments. Yet, when studying five state universities, she found that departments were difficult to eliminate because of ties among faculty members. She concluded by dismissing the notion that universities are loosely coupled systems and argued that researchers should pay attention to patterns of loose and tight coupling. Within one article, then, the concept of loose coupling was described in terms of dialectical theory, a unidimensional proposition, dialectical findings, unidimensional dismissal, and dialectical suggestions for further research.

One reason that the distinction between the unidimensional and dialectical interpretation has not been made is that no reviews of the loose coupling literature have been published. Instead, what have been written are documents that approximate reviews, including several unpublished qualifying examinations and dissertations (Beekun, 1988b; Cude, 1989; Taylor, 1983), a few retrospective assessments of the concept (Firestone, 1985; Weick, 1986, 1989), occasional translations of the concept across disciplinary boundaries (Dane, 1985; Gummer, 1982), a typology of loose coupling presented at a conference (Clark, Astuto, & Kuh, 1983), and the summary of a seminar on loosely coupled systems (Gibson, 1977). Because few of these works are widely available, organizational researchers have had to construct idiosyncratic interpretations of the concept, its general propositions, and its operationalizations. A straightforward review of the loose coupling literature may be the easiest way to free theorists to consider puzzles such as the one highlighted in this section.

THE VOICE OF CAUSATION

The voice of causation is the first voice used in this chapter to review the loose coupling literature. Researchers who use the causation-seeking voice neither advocate nor condemn loose coupling as a management tool. In a relatively dispassionate way, they look for process and variance theories that help to explain why some systems are loosely coupled and others are not. This causation-seeking voice is structured around three recurring explanations for what causes loose coupling: causal indeterminacy, fragmentation of the external environment, and fragmentation of the internal environment.

Causal Indeterminacy

Several researchers have suggested that causal indeterminacy causes loose coupling. Causal indeterminacy refers to unclear means-ends connections, which are explored in writings on bounded rationality, selective perception, uncertainty, ambiguity, and intangibility of production materials. For example, Orton and Weick (1988, p. 14) argued that because people have bounded rationality (e.g., limited information-processing capabilities, memories that obscure details, and short attention spans) they notice different parts of their surroundings, will tune out different parts at different times, and will process different parts at different speeds. As a result of the idiosyncratic worlds formed under these conditions, people will find it difficult to coordinate their actions and will share few variables or weak variables, all of which leads to loose coupling.

Glassman (1973) portrayed loose coupling as a problem of selective perception: "If the observer is not looking at or understanding the operation of variables involved in coupling then his conceptual system will show a looser coupling than exists in the real world" (p. 85). According to Glassman, the perception of loose coupling is most likely when observation time is limited, the number of observable variables is decreased, and the instruments for measuring variables are weakened.

Researchers also have observed how uncertainty can create causal indeterminacy, which can then create loose coupling (Weick, 1976, p. 4). For example, Faulkner and Anderson (1987) studied the effects of uncertainty on governance structures by analyzing the credits of 2,430 films released between 1965 and 1980. Unclear links between means ("capitalization, choice of creative elements, and marketing strategies"; p. 885) and ends ("economic and critical outcomes"; p. 884) were created by variance in the content and composition of artistic work, variance in the rates of investment flows, and variance in stochastic demand; this lack of clarity was heightened by diverse, uncertain, and imperfectly perceived markets. Under these uncertain conditions, loosely coupled project-based teams were created.

In a similar vein, March (1987) argued that ambiguity causes loose coupling, and he identified four ambiguities that are inherent in decision environments: (a) the preferences of decision makers are unstable and unpredictable over time; (b) problems, solutions, and actions are unrelated to each other; (c) self-interested reason is subordinated to occasionally obsolescent traditions; and (d) information is used primarily to create meaning out of previous decisions. March suggested that these ambiguities create loose coupling between information activities and decision activities.

Additionally, Clark (1983) wrote that the loosely coupled structure of universities is an inevitable consequence of their primary production material: knowledge.

> [A]n academic system works with materials that are increasingly specialized and numerous, knowledge-intensive and knowledge-extensive, with a momentum of autonomy. This characterization applies most strongly to advanced systems, but even the most retarded systems will be based on a half-dozen or more distinct bundles of knowledge that have their own internal logics and an inherent bent toward autonomy.
>
> (p. 16)

Fragmented External Environment

Fragmentation of a system's external environment, a second recurring cause of loose coupling, typically takes one of two forms: dispersed stimuli or incompatible expectations. Fragmentation that takes the form of dispersed stimuli explains such diverse concepts as geographic dispersion, specialized market niches, and varied demands on the system. For example, Chase and Tansik (1983) wrote that customer contact increases the need for decoupling the activities within the organization. Manning (1979) demonstrated that the constant stream of diverse emergency calls to police organizations diminished the effects of hierarchical coordination by creating internal differentiation among operators, dispatchers, and officers. Manning argued that geographical dispersion and multiple possible stimuli require information structures that can simultaneously filter and respond to an environment of callers.

Fragmentation that takes the form of incompatible expectations has been illustrated by Meyer and Rowan (1977), who argued that schools must somehow reconcile incompatibilities between institutional pressures and technical pressures. They noted that organizations respond to this contradiction by buffering, building gaps between, loosely coupling, or decoupling formal structures from actual work activities in order to maintain "ceremonial conformity" (p. 341). In addition, support for Meyer and Rowan's decoupling thesis has been found in studies of hospitals (Covaleski & Dirsmith, 1983), courts (Hagan, Hewitt, & Alwin, 1979), and prisons (Thomas, 1984).

Fragmented Internal Environment

A third recurring source of loose coupling is the fragmentation of the internal environment, which can take a variety of forms. For example, Pfeffer (1978) suggested that organizations "are loosely coupled, in part, because few participants are constantly involved or care about every dimension of the organization's operations" (p. 37). Additionally, Boynton and Zmud (1987) observed that professionals who work with information systems face increased loose coupling between subunits when personal computers are dispersed throughout organizations. Sunesson (1985) suggested that "street-level bureaucracies" (p. 243) lead to loose coupling between goals and actions, whereas Raghunathan and Beekun (1989) proposed that the ownership coupling patterns of multinational corporations are a function of the maturity and cultural diversity of subsidiaries. Finally, Thomas (1983) described the Chicago Eight trial as a competition for control of proceedings and meanings that created loose couplings between judicial practices and the ideological premises of due process.

In summary, this voice often preserves a dialectical interpretation, as is evident in work on project-based teams over time (Faulkner & Anderson, 1987), interactions between judicial practices and due process principles (Thomas, 1983), and police organizations' joint tasks of filtering and responding to emergency calls (Manning, 1979). However, this voice also drifts from a dialectical interpretation when investigators portray loose coupling as *decoupling* (e.g., Chase & Tansik, 1983; Meyer & Rowan, 1977). When loose coupling is portrayed as decoupling, the diminished emphasis on connectedness, responsiveness, and interdependence dissolves the dialectic.

THE VOICE OF TYPOLOGY

The voice of typology is the second voice used in this chapter to review the loose coupling literature. Similar to researchers who use the voice of causation, researchers who use the voice of typology are not directly concerned with the value of loose coupling as a management tool. The voice of typology emphasizes descriptive clarity as a precursor to causal clarity. Such researchers see loose coupling as an analytical language, rather than as a set of causal propositions. Consequently, this voice is structured around different types of loose coupling, rather than its causes or effects.

Working in the voice of typology, we identify the eight most frequently recurring types of loose coupling: loose coupling among individuals, among subunits, among organizations, between hierarchical levels, between organizations and environments, among ideas, between activities, and between intentions and actions.

Studies of loose coupling in which the individual is the unit of analysis are illustrated by Beekun's (1988a) network analysis of a multiplayer organization game, Hedberg's (1984) use of loose coupling as a design criterion in a steelworks, Schall's (1983) description of an investment division, Keidel's (1984) description of baseball teams, and Hagan, Hewitt, and Alwin's (1979) study of relationships within the judicial system.

Researchers also have considered a wide range of structural elements that are above the individual level and below the organizational level; in this chapter, these elements are categorized as *subunits*. Bemuse the concept of loose coupling was first empirically grounded in educational organizations, one of the most frequently studied subunits has been the school classroom (Deal & Celotti, 1980; Murphy & Hallinger, 1984; Weick, 1976). Researchers have also considered the loose coupling between functional departments. For example, they have studied groups of telephone operators, dispatchers, and officers in a police organization (Manning, 1979); information systems departments and the rest of the organization (Boynton & Zmud, 1987); nursing subunits and physicians and paramedical subunits of hospitals (Leatt & Schneck, 1984); and business units (Gupta, 1984; Horwitch & Thietart, 1987).

Many studies have been conducted on the third type of loose coupling, loose coupling between organizations. For example, Provan (1983) differentiated five types of organizations of organizations: coalitions, participatory federations, independent federations, mandated federations, and intraorganizational systems (p. 83). Although Provan rank-ordered these interorganizational organizations from loosely coupled (coalition) to tightly coupled (intraorganizational system), loose coupling has been documented within each of these organizational types. Bygrave (1988) studied the coupling in co-investment coalitions of venture capitalists. Covaleski, Dirsmith, and Jablonsky (1985) described a loosely coupled network of state geriatric service agencies. Luke, Begun, and Pointer (1989) described independent "quasi firms" in the hospital industry. Kaplan (1982) described an intervention into a loosely coupled federation of state agencies that shared a mandated common funding source. Finally, Raghunathan and Beekun (1989) discussed the varying looseness of ownership patterns of multinational corporations.

The fourth type of loose coupling, loose coupling that occurs between hierarchical levels, also has received attention. Firestone (1985) and his colleagues documented loose coupling between hierarchical levels in schools through a "school assessment survey," which measured coupling on five vertical dimensions: vertical communications, centralization on instruction matters, centralization on resource matters, support by the principal, and goal consensus (p. 12). In keeping with this theme, Gamoran and Dreeben (1986) also studied the influence of principals on classroom activity. Similarly, Ouchi (1978) studied the transmission of behavioral control and output control between hierarchical levels in department stores.

In a different approach to loose coupling between hierarchical levels, Covaleski and Dirsmith (1983) studied how the structural separations implied by Meyer and Rowan's (1977) version of institutional theory could be translated into the freedom of nurses from the intrusion of cost controls. Covaleski and Dirsmith suggested that effective nurse administrators alternately adopt "budget masks" (for communications with hospital administrators) and professional "clan masks" (for communications with nurses), and they inferred that loose coupling between hierarchical levels occurs when people are willing and able to speak different languages to different levels.

A fifth type of loose coupling, loose coupling between organizations and environments, also has been described (e. g., Beekun & Ginn, 1988; Weick, 1979, p. 178). Other examples include

Manning (1982), who described semiotic loose coupling between a police communication system and an environment of people making emergency phone calls. He reported that dramatic phone calls are "conventionalized" (p. 234) and frozen (p. 235) into rigidly defined crime codes by police operators, and he defined the telephone operators' task as one of processing, decoding, classifying, encoding, and transforming the calls into the code, language, or perspective of the organization. Therefore, by changing the information as it crosses the boundaries into the organization, police communication systems (a) maintain the integrity, consistency, and autonomy of their organizations and (b) loosen the couplings between the organization and its environment.

Frequently, researchers are concerned with the actions, events, or sequences within organizations, rather than specific entities or levels (Weick, 1979, p. 236). Such studies are categorized in this chapter as demonstrations of loose coupling between activities, and one example of this type of analysis is the study of loose coupling between problems and choices. Cohen, March, and Olsen's (1972) article focused on the loose coupling between problems and choice:

> A major feature of the garbage can process is the uncoupling of problems and choices. Although decision making is thought of as a process for solving problems, that is often not what happens. Problems are worked upon in the context of some choice, but choices are made only when the shifting combinations of problems, solutions, and decision makers happen to make action possible.
>
> (p. 16)

This puzzle, in various permutations, including loose coupling between information gathering and decision making, has been revisited many times by March and his colleagues (Cohen & March, 1974; Feldman & March, 1982; March, 1987; March & Olsen, 1976; March & Simon, 1958, p. 176).

Several theorists have explored loose coupling between ideas contained in accounts, goals, and ideologies. For example, Gaertner and Ramnarayan (1983) discussed four types of accounts that can be loosely coupled: auditing (performing within a framework for an external audience), implementation (performing within a framework for an internal audience), integration (setting the framework for an internal audience), and legitimation (setting the framework for an external audience). Bussigel, Barzansky, and Grenholm (1986) found that not only were goals in some medical schools incompatible, inconsistent, and indirectly related, but the relationships between these goals also were vaguely articulated. In addition, Meyerson and Martin (1987) suggested that ideologies can be loosely coupled (p. 634).

The final type of loose coupling, that is, loose coupling between intentions and actions, is described through the following examples. An unpublished manuscript by Salancik (1975) on loose coupling between intentions and actions serves as an anchor for several ideas, including loose coupling between planning and implementation (Withane, 1984), official structures and negotiated orders (Thomas, 1983, 1984), and structural facades and technical cores (Meyer & Rowan, 1977). Similarly, Hagan, Hewitt, and Alwin (1979), who studied loose coupling between the structural facades and technical cores of judicial systems, argued that societal demands for individualized justice were grafted onto the American judicial system in the early 20th century in the form of probation officers' presentencing recommendations (p. 597). These authors further demonstrated that the judicial system has kept parole officers decoupled from a more efficiency-oriented judge-prosecutor subsystem that rewards guilty pleas.

In summary, this voice can also preserve the dialectical interpretation of loose coupling. The dialectical interpretation is most evident when the typology captures descriptions of ongoing actions, for example, nurse administrators adopting masks (Covaleski & Dirsmith, 1983), police operators conventionalizing emergency phone calls (Manning, 1982), and judicial systems decoupling parole officers' recommendations from sentencing decisions (Hagan, Hewitt, & Alwin, 1979). However, this voice drifts from the dialectical interpretation when the typology captures descriptions of static entities, for example, when sports teams, schools, or geriatric services networks are labeled as loosely coupled systems (Keidel, 1984; Murphy & Hallinger, 1984; Covaleski, Dirsmith, & Jablonsky, 1985).

THE VOICE OF DIRECT EFFECTS

Researchers who use the voice of direct effects are the strongest advocates of loose coupling as a management strategy. The voice's theme is, "loose coupling has specific effects and the effects are desirable." The three most frequently recurring direct effects are modularity, requisite variety, and discretion.

For example, Page-Jones (1980) encouraged software designers to attain "modularity" (p. 102) through loose coupling:

> The first way of measuring design quality we'll explore is *coupling*, the degree of interdependence between two modules. Our objective is to minimize coupling; that is, to make modules as independent as possible. . . . *Low* coupling between modules signifies a well-designed system.
>
> (pp. 101, 103)

Page-Jones suggested that modularity is attained by the elimination of unnecessary relationships, by reducing the number of necessary relationships, and by using loose couplings instead of tight couplings. To differentiate loose couplings from tight couplings, he proposed a continuum of couplings between software modules, ranging from "loose, or good" to "tight, or bad" (p. 103). As the tightness of couplings increases, the modularity (p. 102) of the system decreases. Page-Jones referred to high coupling as "pathological coupling" because it "brings us back to the mess of nonmodular coding" (p. 114). Other studies by Perrow (1984) and Cude and Browning (1989) have identified similarities between machine modularity and modularity in human systems.

The second direct effect of loose coupling, requisite variety, also has been analyzed by organizational scholars. Weick (1976) proposed that loosely coupled systems could more accurately register their environments through requisite variety. (A system has requisite variety to the extent that its elements serve as a medium that can register inputs with accuracy.) Additionally, registering improves when elements become more numerous and the constraints among them weaken (Heider, 1959; Orton, 1988).

The final direct effect of loose coupling, discretion, can be broken into two forms: behavioral discretion and cognitive discretion. *Behavioral discretion* is the capacity for autonomous action. March (1987) suggested that ambiguity creates loose coupling between information activities and decision activities and that this loose coupling creates autonomy for information gatherers. Vaughan (1982), writing for a law review audience, suggested a more specific type of behavioral discretion—freedom to make external alliances for illegal purposes. She cited loosely coupled systems as an organizational form which obscures subunit activities from the monitoring of top management. Acccording to her, as top management's ability to monitor subunit activities decreases, the subunits are more likely to "engage in a fraudulent transaction with another organization" because "no countervailing intraorganizational authority can prevent or control the unlawful behavior" (Vaughan, 1982, pp. 1394–1395).

In contrast to behavioral discretion, *cognitive discretion* is the freedom to perceive or construct an idiosyncratic meaning. For example, Manning (1982) described the process through which police organizations create semiotic worlds, which are distinct from the communities these organizations are intended to serve. This process is facilitated by an expectation that Weick, Gilfillan, and Keith (1973) described as the *presumption of logic.* These authors proposed that when people are about to confront an indeterminate set of events, they often presume that the events will have made sense and then act as if the events are sensible and determinate, which often makes the set of events determinate in the process. The process unfolds like a generic self-fulfilling prophecy. Having presumed that the events follow a logic of some sort, these people act with confidence and implant a logic that confirms their prescription.

In summary, the voice of direct effects preserves the dialectical interpretation of loose coupling when it frames loose coupling as a counterrational concept. The voice of direct effects has always been dependent on a prevailing, rational, Weberian emphasis on structures that increase determinacy. One important example is found in the abstract to Weick's (1976) loose coupling article, which begins, "In contrast to the prevailing image. . . ." (p. 3). Additionally, when researchers such as Manning (1982) describe how connectedness (police responsiveness to phone calls) can be explained as disconnectedness (idiosyncratic semiotic worlds), they are grounding the voice of direct effects in a larger context that expects connectedness. As theorists' concepts of loose coupling have matured, the counterrational tone has softened, but so too has the dialectical tone. When researchers remove the concept of loose coupling from the rational background that it attacks, the voice of direct effect drifts toward a unidimensional interpretation (e.g., Page-Jones, 1980; Vaughan, 1982), highlighting modularity, requisite variety, and discretion, while ignoring interaction, requisite integration, and control.

THE VOICE OF COMPENSATIONS

Theorists who use the voice of compensations try to restore a dialectic to the concept of loose coupling. The voice's theme is "loose coupling is an unsatisfactory condition that should be reversed." The voice of compensations is most visible in the educational administration literature, where researchers have had to redefine the role of educational administrators based on recurrent findings that schools are loosely coupled systems (Firestone, 1985). Researchers working in the voice of compensations search for nonobvious sources of order that administrators can use to influence dispersed organizations. The three most frequently recurring managerial strategies are enhanced leadership, focused effort, and shared values.

Enhanced Leadership

Some theorists view the management of loosely coupled systems as a problem and call for "stronger" leadership. For example, Murphy and Hallinger (1984) argued that loose coupling research described "what is" and school effectiveness research described "what can be" (p. 10). They wrote that loose coupling research implies that organizational levels and components have limited influence on other organizational levels and components because of "the presence of multiple and often conflicting goals" and "the lack of a clear instructional technology" (p. 7). Murphy and Hallinger (1984) also stated that in contrast to loose coupling, "the teacher effectiveness literature portrays schools as possessing a clearly defined technology or means to reach goals" (p. 8). The solution, according to these authors, is strong leadership that unifies goals and clarifies technology (pp. 9–10).

Other researchers have suggested that loose coupling calls for subtle leadership. For example, Boynton and Zmud (1987) counseled information systems professionals who, because of the dispersal of computer technology, will find themselves in more loosely coupled systems, to try "to simultaneously provide centralized direction and coordination while recognizing the value of increased discretion" (p. 62). Similarly, Weick (1982b) counseled educational administrators to be more attentive to the "glue" that holds loosely coupled systems together: "since channels are unpredictable, administrators must get out of the office and spend lots of time one on one—both to remind people of central visions and to assist them in applying these visions to their own activities" (p. 676). Therefore, this one-on-one or subtle leadership implies sensitivity to diverse system components (Kaplan, 1982) and the ability to control systems through conversation (Gronn, 1983, p. 20).

Focused Attention

A second form of compensation is to focus attention on specific relations in the system. For example, Peters (1978) wrote that "small step strategies" within "vast, loosely linked systems" may produce more effective, efficient, interesting, varied, and thoughtful organizational changes (p. 49). In addition, researchers have described several ways in which individuals can compensate for loose coupling by carefully selecting targets, controlling resources, and acting forcefully.

Glatthorn (1981) emphasized the careful selection of targets when he described a process through which a successful curriculum change could be attained in a loosely coupled system: map what is currently taught, reduce the curriculum to structured and basic information, and provide flexibility for teachers to adapt the curriculum (p. 112). Generalizing from this strategy, managers can change the behavior of subordinates in loosely coupled systems if they build on subordinates' ongoing behavior, focus only on controllable and essential behaviors, and provide the freedom for subordinates to adapt the behavior to local needs.

The use of resource control as a compensation for loose coupling has been illustrated by Gamoran and Dreeben (1986) in their study of school administrators. They found, in a year-long study of 13 classes in 7 schools, that the allocation of time to reading activities, the provision of particular curricular materials, and the grouping of students each had a significant effect on children's reading ability. Gamoran and Dreeben interpreted their findings as evidence of administrator influence on classroom activity.

Specific targets, such as curriculum materials and resource flows, do not have to be "correctly" selected to serve as compensations for loose coupling. Forceful action itself can often create orderly contingencies among events that then remove some indeterminacy. Self-fulfilling prophecies are an example of this process, but the more general formulation is that people can enact regularities into their environment (Smircich & Stubbart, 1985; Weick, 1979). People who disagree about causation can reestablish some determinacy either by voting for a subset of factual premises, which they will treat as binding, or by manipulating the environment (Hedberg, Nystrom, & Starbuck, 1976) so that it contains explicit cause-effect ties on which they can agree.

Shared Values

Use of shared values is a third means to compensate for loose coupling. This form of compensation is especially crucial because it often constitutes the sole remaining basis that holds together a loosely coupled system. If organizations are determinate means-ends structures for attaining preferred outcomes, and if loose coupling is produced by uncertainties about these means-ends structures (Thompson, 1967, p. 134), then agreement about preferences is the only source of order that is left. Reaffirmation of shared values in the face of loose coupling has been emphasized by such authors as Deal (1985), Ouchi (1978, 1980), and Meyer and Rowan (1977).

For example, Deal (1985) wrote that administrators should use tight cultural couplings to counteract loose couplings between policies and actions. He suggested that administrators should build stronger cultures through the analysis of history, the identification of heroes and hero-ines, the enhancement of ceremonies and rituals, and the cultivation of stories and storytellers. Similarly, Ouchi (1978) argued that control loss between hierarchical levels leads to modularity and discretion (p. 283), which is compensated for by a clan orientation (Ouchi, 1980, 1981).

Meyer and Rowan (1977) suggested that the cohesive force that keeps decoupled organizations from becoming anarchies is "the logic of confidence and good faith" (p. 358). This logic emphasizes ceremonial management, considerations of face, the twin assumptions that people are performing their tasks correctly and that "things are as they seem," all of which allow decoupled structures to continue operation.

In summary, this voice preserves a dialectical interpretation when it builds on the premise that looseness on some dimensions should be complemented by coupling on other dimensions. Gamoran and Dreeben (1986) accepted the concept of diminished direct control by principals, which fuels a search for alternative sources of control. Researchers who use this voice drift away from the dialectical interpretation when they reject looseness as a legitimate organizational form. When researchers try to replace looseness with coupling, they assume the dialectic away (e.g., Lutz, 1982; Murphy & Hallinger, 1984).

THE VOICE OF ORGANIZATIONAL OUTCOMES

Researchers who use the voice of organizational outcomes try to predict and measure the effects that loose coupling has on the performance of organizations. Because of the causal distance between loose coupling and organizational outcomes, the voice of organizational outcomes requires the consideration of more independent variables than does the voice of direct effects. The outcome voice, consequently, is less forceful than the voice of direct effects in advocating loose coupling as a managerial strategy, and it focuses on five organizational outcomes: persistence, buffering, adaptability, satisfaction, and effectiveness.

Persistence

Persistence, a general term referring to stability, resistance to change, and continued operation, is discussed frequently as an organizational outcome of loose coupling. For example, Glassman (1973) presented 13 examples, from varying levels of system complexity, of loose couplings that create persistence. Persistence is also evident in the reduced responsiveness of an organization. Wilson and Corbett (1983) found empirical support, emphasized by Firestone (1985), for the idea that tightly coupled systems are more conducive to systemwide change than loosely coupled systems. In addition, Meyerson and Martin (1981) noted that managers were unable to plan, predict, control, or change a loosely coupled system. Finally, Hagan, Hewitt, and Alwin (1979) demonstrated that parole officers evoke little response from judges; Kaplan (1982) suggested that interventionists can only evoke short-term responses from federations; and Deal and Celotti (1980) noted that communities are not always able to evoke responses from loosely coupled schools.

Buffering

Buffering is a second outcome of loose coupling (Thompson, 1967). Weick (1976) suggested that loosely coupled systems seal off and prevent the spread of problems, an ability that Schoonhoven (1986) saw as desirable in space stations. One proposed benefit of modularity in software design is that it reduces the occurrence of ripple effects, for example, a bug in one module appearing as a symptom in another module (Page-Jones, 1980, p. 102).

Three studies have demonstrated that buffering in loosely coupled systems is partial, rather than complete. Although Perrow (1984) idealized loose coupling as a solution to the dangers of tight coupling, evidence in his analysis of the Three Mile Island accident indicated that loose coupling was part of the cause of the Three Mile Island accident: Three warnings that conceivably could have prevented the accident were not communicated to the plant engineers (Perrow, 1981). In a similar vein, Rubin (1979) found that five state universities could not easily terminate departments, which she interpreted as evidence that the universities were characterized by patterns of tight and loose couplings, rather than simply loose couplings. Finally, Cameron, Kim, and Whetten (1987) found that although administrators in loosely coupled systems could buffer their subordinates from turbulence, they could not buffer them from decline (p. 236).

Adaptability

Whereas persistence and buffering imply adaptation to change through neutralizing the impact of the change, another outcome of loose coupling, adaptability, implies assimilation and accommodation of the change (Weick, 1979, p. 120). In the literature on loose coupling, three types of adaptability have been suggested: experimentation, collective judgment, and dissent.

To cope directly with conditions such as apparent causal indeterminacy, people often "act to expose the conditions for acting; causal relationships in the environment or in the interface between learner and environment are gradually untangled" (Hedberg, 1981, p. 4). Actions that untangle causality are what is meant by experimentation. Hedberg (1984) argued that the design of a steelworks should respond to workers' desires for more local information, exploration (p. 53), leaning, self-design, experimentation, reflection (p. 57), "a right to curiosity" (p. 58), local learning, and local solutions (p. 64). Confirming Hedberg's link between loose coupling and experimentation, Manning (1979) argued that loosely coupled police officers were better able to find solutions to complex problems than tightly coupled police officers, and Perrow (1984) argued that if complex technologies were more loosely coupled, operators would be able to find solutions through exploratory problem solving.

Collective judgment, another form of adaptability, was described by Thompson and Tuden (1959). They argued that when loose coupling takes the form of disagreement on means-ends relationships (causal indeterminacy), the system coheres if there is still agreement on preferences (shard values). Thompson and Tuden referred to this combination as the *judgment* decision-making strategy. The structural form which corresponds to a judgment decision strategy is represented by a self-governing voluntary group, a form often called a *collegium* (Thompson, 1967, p. 200). The collegium promotes wise choice because people who have equal influence, equal information, and a decision scheme of majority rule are able to apply multiple perspectives to situations and combine their perspectives to create a collective judgment. Because of the relative advantages of the loosely coupled form in creating collective judgment, it is not surprising that collegium forms such as the judiciary (e.g., Hagan, Hewitt, & Alwin, 1979), universities (e.g., Rubin, 1979), and voluntary associations (e.g., Golembiewski, 1979) are heavily represented in loose coupling literature.

A third type of adaptability, the preservation of dissent, is preserved and generated in loosely coupled systems through cultural insurance (Weick, 1976) and unified diversity (Eisenberg, 1984). Nemeth (1986) argued that minority influence helps systems adapt to complex problems because it intensifies cognitive effort by the majority. Nemeth and Staw (in press) demonstrated through a review of literature on minority influence that the strain for uniformity threatens dissent and restricts adaptability, creativity, and survival. Eisenberg (1984) wrote that ambiguity facilitates "unified diversity" because people retain multiple understandings while believing their understanding is singular and shared. The result is an increased likelihood of adaptability.

Satisfaction

Loose coupling also appears to have implications for job satisfaction because it affects efficacy, conflict, security, and social contacts. First, some investigators have argued that loose coupling fosters self-determination and a sense of efficacy (Weick, 1976). In part, this may be because the setting of objectives is easier on a localized level (Chase & Tansik, 1983). Second, researchers have noted that loosely coupled systems often reduce conflict between system elements because in these situations such elements are not required to agree, interact with, or adapt to each other, creating fewer occasions for conflict (Deal & Celotti, 1980; Meyer & Rowan, 1977). Third, researchers have suggested that loosely coupled systems create a haven of psychological safety in which deviance and experimentation are protected (Meyerson & Martin, 1987, p. 636). Finally, Jones (1984) proposed that loosely coupled, horizontally differentiated, or self-contained subunits create a perception of smaller group size, which he hypothesized would increase task visibility, monitoring, and social exchange among employees. Although self-determination, reduced conflict, psychological safety, and deepened social interaction are generally considered as contributors to higher satisfaction, loose coupling can also generate loneliness (Deal & Celotti, 1980), which detracts from satisfaction.

Effectiveness

If an organization is persistent, buffered, and adaptable, and has satisfied employees, is it effective? Some researchers emphasize organizational outcomes of loose coupling that suggest ineffectiveness (e.g., Lutz, 1982; Murphy & Hallinger, 1984), whereas others emphasize outcomes that suggest effectiveness (e.g., Covaleski & Dirsmith, 1983). The debate over the effectiveness of loose coupling is pervasive, woven throughout many discussions of loose coupling. For example, a few investigators have addressed effectiveness directly by considering productivity, market share, return on investment (ROI), efficiency, and "excellence" as organizational outcomes.

On a group level, Birnbaum (1981) found that research groups composed of members who agreed on the overall goals of the research project, but had diverse academic training and affiliations, were more productive on some dimensions than groups composed of members with less diverse academic training and affiliations.

On a business-unit level, Horwitch and Thietart (1987) conducted a PIMS data analysis that tested the effects of three types of coupling on ROI (a measure of short-term effectiveness) and market share (a measure of long-term effectiveness). These authors found (a) that loose coupling (e.g., no shared market) is often compensated for (e.g., by shared facilities) to create effectiveness and (b) that different contexts require different coupling patterns. Beekun and Ginn (1988) reported similar findings in hospitals' extra-organizational linkages: Different strategic types (analyzer, defender, reactor, prospector) imply their own optimal coupling gestalts for attaining efficiency and effectiveness. Therefore, effectiveness, from a strategy perspective, is attained by conforming to the coupling patterns dictated by a combination of environment and strategy (Raghunathun & Beekun, 1989).

On a general organizational level, Peters and Waterman (1982) argued that simultaneous loose-tight coupling helped create "excellence." More specifically, they argued that employee autonomy, experimentation, and innovation can be facilitated through a strongly held set of shared values.

In summary, researchers who use this voice preserve the dialectical interpretation of loose coupling when they begin with a unidimensional interpretation of loose coupling and end by concluding that researchers should use a dialectical interpretation. For example, according to Rubin (1979), universities have a limited ability to eliminate departments, and researchers should continue to study patterns of loose and tight coupling. Cameron, Kim, and Whetten (1987, p. 236) found that loose coupling can protect organizations from some effects of decline, but not from others. Theorists who use this voice weaken the dialectical interpretation when they begin and end with a unidimensional interpretation of loose coupling (e.g., Kuplan, 1982).

A PRELIMINARY MODEL OF LOOSE COUPLING THEORY

The five voices reviewed in the previous section can be combined to form a simple, sequential model. In Figure 17.1, we present a preliminary model of loose coupling theory, built on the presentation conventions of causal modeling (Jöreskog & Sörbom, 1986).

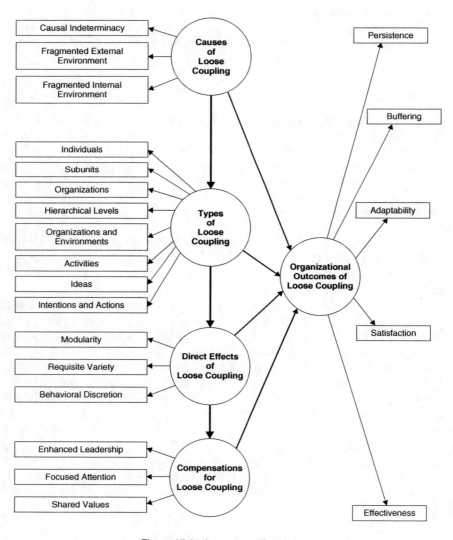

Figure 17.1 Loose coupling theory

The switch from five voices to five latent-variable-like constructs changes the discussion in several ways. First, the intricate interactions among the voices/variables are represented as simple sequentiality. Second, each variable now appears to have the same weight, although different voices are stronger in different contexts. Third, the single model implies a much higher degree of consensus than actually exists among loose coupling researchers; researchers who use different voices would portray the model differently. Despite all these simplifications, the model compactly summarizes past thinking on loose coupling. Additionally, although not formally presented as propositions, each arrow in the model is a proposed causal relationship.

CONCLUSIONS

In general, the review of the loose coupling literature presented here supports Thompson's (1967) assertion that organization theorists find it difficult to think simultaneously about rationality and indeterminacy. For each of the five voices, loose coupling is often reduced to a unidimensional variable, a simplification that should be resisted. The following section explains how researchers can avoid that simplification.

Within organization theory, there are many unidimensional variables but few dialectical concepts. Dialectical concepts are rare because they are difficult to build. Loose coupling, for example, is the product of many years of effort by organization theorists to combine the contradictory concepts of connection and autonomy. Burns and Stalker (1961) assigned connectedness to the mechanistic organization and autonomy of components to the organic organization. Thompson (1967) moved these two forces inside one system by combining the concepts of open systems (connected to environmental forces) and closed systems (independent of environmental forces). Lawrence and Lorsch (1967) provided another organizational resolution to the connected autonomous paradox by arguing that differentiation could be compensated for by the creation of integrating mechanisms such as liaisons or cross-functional committees. The dialectical interpretation of loose coupling builds on and extends these arguments by juxtaposing both forces, simultaneously, within the same system (Das, 1984).

If loose coupling is maintained as a dialectical concept, it can illuminate the answers to several organizational puzzles that have eluded organization theorists.

The first puzzle involves the definition of *organization*. Most definitions of organization consist of at least two components: (a) a source of order which consolidates, unifies, or coalesces diverse elements or fragments and (b) elements or fragments, which are consolidated, unified, or coalesced by a source of order. When researchers define organizations as monolithic corporate actors, they overemphasize order and underemphasize elements; when researchers define organizations as mere aggregates of individuals, they overemphasize elements and underemphasize order. If researchers begin with richer definitions of organization, they will arrive at more accurate findings and conclusions. If the loose coupling concept can be maintained in its dialectical form, and if it can help researchers begin studies with more subtle and intricate definitions of organizations, it can raise the quality of organizational research.

A second potential contribution of loose coupling is its use in the measurement and interpretation of interpretive systems (Daft & Weick, 1984). A loosely coupled system is a good vehicle for registering objectives outside itself, but is itself an elusive object to understand. Thus, in a loosely coupled system, what is most likely to be socially constructed is the system itself, not the world it faces. This raises an interesting issue because it suggests that analysts know and understand least well the vehicles that are most effective at sensing. The property that makes them good sensors is the very same property that has made them indistinct objects. A corollary to these ideas is that organization theory currently may be skewed toward the study of organizations that are least able to interpret their environments. The concept of loose coupling, when maintained in its dialectical form, should be a useful tool in identifying, measuring, and understanding interpretive systems.

A third puzzle that the loose coupling concept may help theorists to understand is the fluidity, complexity, and social construction of organizational structure. Loose coupling may be able to do for the study of organizational structure what bounded rationality did for the study of decision making (Simon, 1976). By recognizing and explaining how decisions are made by humans with limited interest, time, and energy, Simon required studies of decision making to move into more subtle, more detailed, and more enigmatic directions. The concept of loose coupling, with its recognition of numerous structural dimensions, its emphasis on simultaneous coupling and decoupling, and its portrayal of structures as malleable through managerial intervention, similarly forces researchers to move more deeply into the human workings which underlie organizational structure. In the same way that bounded rationality has led researchers to study the processes of decision making, rather than merely the outcomes, loose coupling may lead researchers to study structure as something that organizations do, rather than merely as something they have.

For researchers to begin to solve puzzles such as these, it is essential that the concept of loose coupling remain dialectical, rather than unidimensional. The following suggestions are means by which the simplification of unidimensionality can be avoided.

Research methodologies that encourage researchers to parse dialectical concepts into unidimensional variables should be avoided. The frequently pursued direct effect, X causes Y, is still the social science ideal. The numerous, more complicated forms of this relationship have been considered as disappointing approximations to the ideal. Within this netherworld of approximations to direct effects, there are several ways to represent dialectical concepts. One of the simplest is the translation of bipolar variables to two-variable matrices (Bobko, 1985). Another technique is to regress a concept onto contradictory independent variables, which was used in Figure 17.1 to combine decoupling (types of loose coupling) and coupling (compensations for loose coupling). A third technique is the use of deviation-regulating loops, in which variables shift values as the cycle progresses (Maruyama, 1963; Orton & Weick, 1988). To preserve the dialectical interpretation of loose coupling, researchers must continue to transform methodology to serve theory, rather than transforming theory to serve methodology.

The concept of loose coupling is simplified when researchers use it for flat, static descriptions, rather than detailed, dynamic descriptions. Weick (1979, p. 44) argued that nouns focus attention on reified objects, whereas verbs focus attention on dynamic processes. Researchers who see systems as static objects to be labeled ("this is a loosely coupled system") are less likely to capture loose coupling than are researchers who *see* systems as an arena for complex, ongoing processes ("loose coupling in this system occurs when . . ."). The dialectical interpretation of loose coupling can be strengthened when researchers look closely at the processes within systems. For example, ethnographies, case studies, and systematic observations (Manning, 1979, 1982; Rubin, 1979; Thomas, 1984) are methodologies that seem to encourage this careful analysis, whereas questionnaires and casual observations (Firestone, 1985; Lutz, 1982) are methodologies that seem to discourage it. The relevant criterion is familiarity: Will researchers describe the processes within the system or will they simply categorize systems? To preserve the dialectical interpretation, greater familiarity with a few systems is currently more valuable than lesser familiarity with many.

The third way to drift away from the unidimensional interpretation is to ignore the presence of connectedness within organizations. From a Weberian bureaucratic perspective, the recurring surprise is that organizations routinely exhibit looseness (Corwin, 1981). From a decoupling perspective, the recurring surprise is that organizations routinely exhibit coupling. When researchers enter organizations expecting to find little that is coupled (e.g., Orton, 1989), they are surprised to find that organizational members spend most of their time thinking about structural connections, rather than structural disconnections. Theorists who err on the side of overemphasizing the presence of disconnectedness in organizations need little exposure to organizations before they begin to speak about patterns of couplings and decouplings, instead of just decouplings (Meyer, 1980; Rubin, 1979).

Researchers also drift away from the dialectical interpretation by making imprecise general statements, as in the following argument: (a) "loosely coupled systems are supposed to be more effective than tightly coupled systems," (b) "General Motors is more loosely coupled than Ford," (c) "Ford has been more profitable in recent years," therefore, (d) "tightly coupled systems may be more effective than loosely coupled systems." To state that an organization is a loosely coupled system is the beginning of a discussion, not the end. What elements are loosely coupled? What domains are they coupled on? What domains are they decoupled on? What are the characteristics of the couplings and decouplings? Researchers who invoke the concept of loose coupling can avoid simplifying it by specifying their assumptions more precisely.

The last way in which researchers drift away from the dialectical interpretation of loose coupling is to describe it as managerial failure. The easiest way to remedy this situation is to observe a set of organizations that are routinely labeled as loosely coupled systems: schools, universities, hospitals, police organizations, and judicial systems. These forms are not failed bureaucracies, but distinct organizational forms. As Grandori (1987) noted, "A system in which everybody can do everything and in which the links between various parts do not necessarily have to follow given interdependence relationships but are virtually interchangeable and separable is a concept that organization theory had previously treated primarily in terms of peer groups. Indeterminists coined the phrase *loosely coupled systems* to define complex organizations that have this feature" (pp. 93–94). Some organizations fit Grandori's description better than others. The reason it is important to focus on these organizations is that such organization members are more likely to have thought deeply about interactions between couplings and decouplings, their interactions are more salient, and observers are more likely to categorize the interactions as characteristics of loosely coupled systems.

To assert that a system is loosely coupled is to predicate specific properties and a specific history to the system, rather than an absence of properties.

REFERENCES

Beekun, R. I. (1988a) *Toward a contingency framework of coupling: A conceptual and quantitative approach.* Unpublished doctoral dissertation, University of Texas at Austin.

Beekun, R. I. (1988b) *Dimensionalizing and measuring loose coupling: A conceptual and quantitative approach.* Unpublished manuscript.

Beekun, R. I., & Ginn, G. O. (1988) *The impact of organizational strategy upon external coupling and performance.* Unpublished manuscript.

Birnbaum, P. H. (1981) Integration and specialization in academic research. *Academy of Management Review*, 24, 487–503.

Bobko, P. (1985) Removing assumptions of bipolarity: Towards variation and circularity. *Academy of Management Review*, 10, 99–108.

Boynton, A. C., & Zmud, R. W. (1987) Information technology planning in the 1990's: Directions for practice and research. *MIS Quarterly*, 11, 59–71.

Burns, T., & Stalker, G. M. (1961) *The management of innovation.* London: Tavistock.

Bussigel, M., Barzansky, B., & Grenholm, G. (1986) Goal coupling and innovation in medical schools. *The Journal of Applied Behavioral Science*, 22, 425–441.

Bygrave, W. D. (1988) The structure of the investment networks of venture capital firms. *Journal of Business Venturing*, 3, 137–157.

Cameron. K. S., Kim, M. U., & Whetten, D. A. (1987) Organizational effects of decline and turbulence. *Administrative Science Quarterly*, 32, 222–240.

Chase, R. B., & Tansik, D. A. (1983) The customer contact model for organization design. *Management Science*, 29, 1037–1050.

Clark, B. R. (1983) *The higher education system: Academic organization in cross-national perspective.* Berkeley: University of California Press.

Clark, D. L., Astuto, T., & Kuh, G. (1983) *Strength of coupling in the organization and operation of colleges and universities.* Paper presented at the American Educational Research Association Convention, Montreal.

Cohen, M. D., & March, J. G. (1974) *Leadership and ambiguity.* New York: McCraw-Hill.

Cohen, M. D., March, J. G., & Olsen, J. P. (1972) A garbage can model of organizational choice. *Administrative Science Quarterly*, 17, 1–25.

Corwin, R. G. (1981) Patterns of organizational control and teacher militancy: Theoretical continuities in the idea of "loose coupling." In R. G. Corwin (Ed.), *Research in the sociology of education and socialization* (Vol. 2, pp. 261–291). Greenwich, CT: JAI Press.

Covalaski, M. A., & Dirsmith, M. W. (1983) Budgeting as a means for control and loose coupling. *Accounting, Organizations, and Society*, 8, 323–340.

Covaleski, M. A., Dirsmith, M. W., & Jablonsky, S. F. (1985) Traditional and emergent theories of budgeting: An empirical analysis. *Journal of Accounting and Public Policy*, 4, 277–300.

Cude, R. L. (1989) *A model of loose communication coupling in organizations.* Unpublished manuscript, University of Texas at Austin.

Cude, R. L., & Browning, L. D. (1989) *A comparison of loose coupling theory in technical and managerial literature.* Unpublished manuscript. The University of Texas at Austin.

Daft, R. L., & Weick, K. E. (1984) Toward a model of organizations as interpretation systems. *Academy of Management Review*, 9, 284–295.

Dane, E. (1985) Managing organizational relationships in continuing education programs: Is loose coupling the answer? *Administration in Social Work*, 9(3), 83–42.

Das, T. K. (1984) Discussion note: Portmanteau ideas for organizational theorizing. *Organization Studies*, 5, 261–267.

Deal, T. E. (1985) The symbolism of effective schools. *The Elementary School Journal*, 85, 601–620.

Deal, T. E., & Celotti, L. D. (1980, March) How much influence do (and can) educational administrators have on classrooms? *Phi Delta Kappan*, 471–473.

Eisenberg, E. M. (1984) Ambiguity as strategy in organizational communication. *Communication Monographs*, 51, 227–242.

Faulkner, R. R., & Anderson, A. B. (1987) Short-term projects and emergent careers: Evidence from Hollywood. *American Journal of Sociology*, 92, 879–909.

Feldman, M. S., & March, J. G. (1982) Information in organizations as signal and symbol. *Administrative Science Quarterly*, 26, 171–186.

Firestone, W. A. (1985) The study of loose coupling: Problems, progress, and prospects. In A. Kerckhoff (Ed.), *Research in sociology of education and socialization* (Vol. 5, pp. 3–30). Greenwich, CT: JAI Press.

Gaertner, G. H., & Ramnarayan, S. (1983) Organizational effectiveness: An alternative perspective. *Academy of Management Review*, 8, 97–107.

Gamoran, A., & Dreeben, R. (1986) Coupling and control in educational organizations: An explication and illustrative comparative test. *Administrative Science Quarterly*, 31, 612–632.

Gibson, D. V. (Ed.) (1977) *Seminars on organizations at Stanford University* (Vol. 4). Stanford, CA: Stanford University, Organizational Research Training Program, Department of Sociology.

Glassman, R. B. (1973) Persistence and loose coupling in living systems. *Behavioral Science*, 18, 83–98.

Glatthorn, A. A. (1981) Curriculum change in loosely coupled systems. *Educational Leadership*, 19, 110–113.

Golembiewski, R. T. (1979) Perspectives on the growth and development of organizations: SPSA as a specific case of choice and transition. *The Journal of Politics*, 41, 335–360.

Grandori, A. (1987) *Perspectives on organization theory.* Cambridge, MA: Ballinger.

Gronn, P. C. (1983) Talk as work: The accomplishment of school administration. *Administrative Science Quarterly*, 28, 1–21.

Gummer, B. (1982) Organized anarchies, loosely coupled systems, and adhocracies: Current perspectives on organizational design. *Administration in Social Work*, 8(3), 5–15.

Gupta, A. K. (1984) Contingency linkages between strategy and general manager characteristics: A conceptual examination. *Academy of Management Review*, 9, 399–412.

Hagan, J., Hewitt, J. D., & Alwin, D. F. (1979) Ceremonial justice: Crime and punishment in a loosely coupled system. *Social Forces*, 58, 506–527.

Hannan, M. T., & Freeman, J. (1977) The population ecology of organizations. *American Journal of Sociology*, 82, 929–964.

Hedberg, B. (1981) How organizations learn and unlearn. In P. C. Nystrom & W. H. Starbuck (Eds.), *Handbook of organizational design* (Vol. 1, pp. 1–27). New York: Oxford University Press.

Hedberg, B. (1984) Career dynamics in a steelworks of the future. *Journal of Occupational Behaviour*, 5, 53–69.

Hedberg, B. L. T., Nystrom, P. C., & Starbuck, W. H. (1976) Camping on seesaws: Prescriptions for a self-designing organization. *Administrative Science Quarterly*, 21, 41–65.

Heider, F. (1959) Thing and medium. *Psychological Issues*, 1, 1–34.

Horwitch, M., & Thietart, R. A. (1987) The effect of business interdependencies on product R & D-intensive business performance. *Management Science,* 33, 178–197.

Jones, G. R. (1984) Task visibility, free riding, and shirking: Explaining the effect of structure and technology on employee behavior. *Academy of Management Review*, 9, 684–695.

Jöreskog, K. G., & Sörbom, D. (1986) *LISREL VI: Analysis of linear structural relationships by maximum likelihood, instrumental variables, and least squares methods* (4th ed.). Mooresville, IN: Scientific Software.

Kaplan, R. E. (1982) Intervention in a loosely organized system: An encounter with non-being. *The Journal of Applied Behavioral Science*, 18, 415–432.

Keidel, R. W. (1984) Baseball, football, and basketball: Models for business. *Organizational Dynamics*, 12(3), 4–18.

Lawrence, P. R., & Lorsch, J. W. (1967) Differentiation and integration in complex organizations. *Administrative Science Quarterly*, 12, 1–47.

Leatt, P., & Schneck, R. (1984) Criteria for grouping nursing subunits in hospitals. *Academy of Management Journal*, 27, 150–165.

Levine, D. N. (1985) *The flight from ambiguity.* Chicago: University of Chicago.

Luke, R., Begun, G. W., & Pointer, D. D. (1989) Quasi firms: Strategic interorganizational forms in the health care industry. *Academy of Management Review*, 14, 9–19.

Lutz, F. W. (1982) Tightening up loose coupling in organizations of higher education. *Administrative Science Quarterly*, 27, 653–669.

Manning, P. K. (1979). *Semiotics and loosely coupled organizations.* Revised version of a paper presented to the Southern Sociological Society, Atlanta.

Manning, P. K. (1982) Producing drama: Symbolic communication and the police. *Symbolic Interaction*, 5, 223–241.

March, J. G. (1987) Ambiguity and accounting: The elusive link between information and decision making. *Accounting, Organizations, and Society*, 12, 153–168.

March, J. G., & Olsen, J. P. (Eds.) (1976) *Ambiguity and choice in organizations.* Bergen, Norway: Universitetsforlaget.

March, J. G., & Simon, H. A. (1958) *Organizations.* New York: Wiley.

Maruyama, M. (1963) The second cybernetics: Deviation-amplifying mutual causal processes. *American Scientist*, 51, 164–179.

Meyer, A. D. (1980) *Operationalizing loose coupling: From metaphor to prediction*. Unpublished manuscript, School of Business Administration, University of Wisconsin-Milwaukee.

Meyer, J. W., & Rowan, B. (1977) Institutionalized organizations: Formal structure as myth and ceremony. *American Journal of Sociology*, 83, 340–363.

Meyerson, D., & Martin, J. (1987) Cultural change: An integration of three different views. *Journal of Management Studies*, 24, 623–647.

Murphy, J. A., & Hallinger, P. (1984) Policy analysis at the local level: A framework for expanded investigation. *Educational Evaluation and Policy Analysis*, 6, 5–13.

Nemeth, C. J. (1986) Differential contributions of majority and minority influence. *Psychological Review*, 93, 23–32.

Nemeth, C. J., & Staw, B. M. (in press) The trade-offs of social control and innovation within groups and organizations. In L. Berkowitz (Ed.), *Advances in experimental social psychology* (Vol. 22). New York: Academic Press.

Orton, J. D. (1988) *Group design implications of requisite variety*. Unpublished manuscript, University of Michigan.

Orton, J. D. (1989) *Structuring the Ford White House: A microsociological archival ethnography*. Unpublished manuscript, University of Michigan.

Orton, J. D., & Weick, K. E. (1988) *Toward a theory of the loosely coupled system*. Working Paper No. 586, University of Michigan, School of Business Administration, Division of Research, Ann Arbor, MI.

Ouchi, W. G. (1978) Coupled versus uncoupled control in organizational hierarchies. In M. W. Meyer & Associates (Eds.), *Environments and organizations* (pp. 264–289). San Francisco: Jossey-Bass.

Ouchi, W. G. (1980) Markets, clans, and hierarchies. *Administrative Science Quarterly*, 25, 129–141.

Ouchi, W. G. (1981) *Theory Z: How American business can meet the Japanese challenge*. Reading, MA: Addison-Wesley.

Page-Jones, M. (1980) *The practical guide to structured systems design*. New York: Yourdon Press.

Perrow, C. (1981) Normal accident at Three Mile Island. *Society*, 18(5), 17–26.

Perrow, C. (1984) *Normal accidents: Living with high-risk technologies*. New York: Basic Books.

Peters, T. J. (1978) Some applications of the loose coupling approach in managerial/organizational consulting practice. [Summarized by R. J. Bies] In D. V. Gibson (Ed.), *Seminars on organizations at Stanford University* (Vol. 4, pp. 46–50). Stanford, CA: Organizational Research Training Program, Department of Sociology.

Peters, T. J., & Waterman, R. H., Jr. (1982) *In search of excellence: Lessons from America's best-run companies*. New York: Warner Books.

Pfeffer, J. (1978) The micropolitics of organizations. In M. W. Meyer & Associates (Eds.), *Environments and organizations* (pp. 29–50). San Francisco: Jossey-Bass.

Pfeffer, J., & Salancik, G. R. (1978) *The external control of organizations*. San Francisco: Harper & Row.

Provan, K. G. (1983) The federation as an interorganizational linkage network. *Academy of Management Review*, 8, 79–89.

Raghunathan, S. P., & Beekun, R. I. (1989) *Intra-MNC ownership structures: A coupling perspective*. Unpublished manuscript, Temple University, Philadelphia.

Rubin, I. S. (1979) Retrenchment, loose structure, and adaptability in the university. *Sociology of Education*, 52, 211–222.

Salancik, G. R. (1975) *Notes on loose coupling: Linking intentions to actions*. Unpublished manuscript, University of Illinois, Urbana-Champaign.

Schall, M. S. (1983) A communication-rules approach to organizational culture. *Administrative Science Quarterly*, 28, 559–581.

Schoonhoven, C. B. (1986) Sociotechnical considerations for the development of the space station: Autonomy and the human element in space. *The Journal of Applied Behavioral Science*, 22, 271–286.

Simon, H. A. (1976) *Administrative behavior* (3rd ed.). New York: Free Press.

Smircich, L., & Stubbart, C. (1985) Strategic management in an enacted world. *Academy of Management Review*, 10, 724–736.

Sunesson, S. (1985) Outside the goal paradigm: Power and structural patterns of non-rationality. *Organization Studies,* 6, 229–249.

Taylor, P. D. (1983) *The use of qualitative methods in search of loose coupling within a complex public agency.* Unpublished doctoral dissertation, University of Texas at Austin.

Thomas, J. (1983) Justice as interaction: Loose coupling and mediations in the adversary process. *Symbolic Interaction,* 6, 243–260.

Thomas, J. (1984) Some aspects of negotiated order, loose coupling, and mesostructure in maximum security prisons. *Symbolic Interaction,* 7, 213–231.

Thompson, J. D. (1967) *Organizations in action: Social science bases of administrative theory.* New York: McGraw-Hill.

Thompson, J. D., & Tuden, A. (1959) Strategies, structures, and processes of organizational decision. In J. D. Thompson, P. B. Hammond, R. W. Hawkes, B. H. Junker, & A. Tuden (Eds.), *Comparative studies in administration.* Pittsburgh, PA: The University of Pittsburgh Press.

Vaughan, D. (1982) Toward understanding unlawful organizational behavior. *Michigan Law Review,* 80, 1377–1402.

Weick, K. E. (1976) Educational organizations as loosely coupled systems. *Administrative Science Quarterly,* 21, 1-19.

Weick, K. E. (1979) *The social psychology of organizing* (2nd ed.). Reading, MA: Addison-Wesley.

Weick, K. E. (1982a) Management of organizational change among loosely coupled elements. In P. S. Goodman & Associates (Eds.), *Change in organizations* (pp. 375–408). San Francisco: Jossey-Bass.

Weick, K. E. (1982b, June) Administering education in loosely coupled schools. *Phi Delta Kappan,* 673–676.

Weick, K. E. (1986, December) The concept of loose coupling: An assessment. *AERA Organizational Theory Diologue,* 8–11.

Weick, K. E. (1989) Loose coupling: Beyond the metaphor. *Current Contents,* 20(12), 14.

Weick, K. E., Gilfillan, D. P., & Keith, T. (1973) The effect of composer credibility on orchestra performance. *Sociometry,* 36, 435–462.

Williamson, O. E. (1975) *Markets and hierarchies: Analysis and anti-trust implications.* New York: Free Press.

Wilson, B. L., & Corbett, H. D. (1983) Organization and change: The effects of school linkages on the quantity of implementation. *Educational Administration Quarterly,* 19(4), 85–104.

Withane, S. (1984) Changing patterns of local administration in Sri Lanka: Loose coupling between planning and implementation. *Canadian Journal of Developmental Studies,* 5, 243–255.

18

Organizational Culture in Higher Education

Defining the Essentials

William G. Tierney

Within the business community in the last ten years, organizational culture has emerged as a topic of central concern to those who study organizations. Books such as Peters and Waterman's *In Search of Excellence* [37], Ouchi's *Theory Z* [33], Deal and Kennedy's *Corporate Cultures* [20], and Schein's *Organizational Culture and Leadership* [44] have emerged as major works in the study of managerial and organizational performance.

However, growing popular interest and research activity in organizational culture comes as something of a mixed blessing. Heightened awareness has brought with it increasingly broad and divergent concepts of culture. Researchers and practitioners alike often view culture as a new management approach that will not only cure a variety of organizational ills but will serve to explain virtually every event that occurs within an organization. Moreover, widely varying definitions, research methods, and standards for understanding culture create confusion as often as they provide insight.

The intent for this chapter is neither to suggest that an understanding of organizational culture is an antidote for all administrative folly, nor to imply that the surfeit of definitions of organizational culture makes its study meaningless for higher education administrators and researchers. Rather, the design of this chapter is to provide a working framework to diagnose culture in colleges and universities so that distinct problems can be overcome. The concepts for the framework come from a year-long investigation of organizational culture in American higher education.

First, I provide a rationale for why organizational culture is a useful concept for understanding management and performance in higher education. In so doing, I point out how administrators might utilize the concept of culture to help solve specific administrative problems. The second part of the chapter considers previous attempts to define culture in organizations in general, and specifically, in colleges and universities. Third, a case study of a public state college highlights essential elements of academic culture. The conclusion explores possible avenues researchers might examine in order to enhance a usable framework of organizational culture for managers and researchers in higher education.

THE ROLE OF CULTURE IN MANAGEMENT AND PERFORMANCE

Even the most seasoned college and university administrators often ask themselves, "What holds this place together? Is it mission, values, bureaucratic procedures, or strong personalities? How does this place run and what does it expect from its leaders?" These questions usually are asked in moments of frustration, when seemingly rational, well-laid plans have failed or have met with unexpected resistance. Similar questions are also asked frequently by members new to the organization, persons who want to know "how things are done around here." Questions like these seem difficult to answer because there is no one-to-one correspondence between actions and results. The same leadership style can easily produce widely divergent results in two ostensibly similar institutions. Likewise, institutions with very similar missions and curricula can perform quite differently because of the way their identities are communicated to internal and external constituents and because of the varying perceptions these groups may hold.

Institutions certainly are influenced by powerful, external factors such as demographic, economic, and political conditions, yet they are also shaped by strong forces that emanate from within. This internal dynamic has its roots in the history of the organization and derives its force from the values, processes, and goals held by those most intimately involved in the organization's workings. An organization's culture is reflected in what is done, how it is done, and who is involved in doing it. It concerns decisions, actions, and communication both on an instrumental and a symbolic level.

The anthropologist, Clifford Geertz, writes that traditional culture, "denotes a historically transmitted pattern of meanings embodied in symbols, a system of inherited conceptions expressed in symbolic forms by means of which [people] communicate, perpetuate, and develop their knowledge about and attitudes toward life" [25, p. 89]. Organizational culture exists, then, in part through the actors' interpretation of historical and symbolic forms. The culture of an organization is grounded in the shared assumptions of individuals participating in the organization. Often taken for granted by the actors themselves, these assumptions can be identified through stories, special language, norms, institutional ideology, and attitudes that emerge from individual and organizational behavior.

Geertz defines culture by writing, "Man is an animal suspended in webs of significance he himself has spun. I take culture to be those webs, and the analysis of it to be therefore not an experimental science in search of law, but an interpretive one in search of meaning" [25, p. 5]. Thus, an analysis of organizational culture of a college or university occurs as if the institution were an interconnected web that cannot be understood unless one looks not only at the structure and natural laws of that web, but also at the actors' interpretations of the web itself. Organizational culture, then, is the study of particular webs of significance within an organizational setting. That is, we look at an organization as a traditional anthropologist would study a particular village or clan.

However, not unlike traditional villagers, administrators often have only an intuitive grasp of the cultural conditions and influences that enter into their daily decision making. In this respect they are not unlike most of us who have a dim, passive awareness of cultural codes, symbols, and conventions that are at work in society at large. Only when we break these codes and conventions are we forcibly reminded of their presence and considerable power. Likewise, administrators tend to recognize their organization's culture only when they have transgressed its bounds and severe conflicts or adverse relationships ensue. As a result, we frequently find ourselves dealing with organizational culture in an atmosphere of crisis management, instead of reasoned reflection and consensual change.

Our lack of understanding about the role of organizational culture in improving management and institutional performance inhibits our ability to address the challenges that face higher education. As these challenges mount, our need to understand organizational culture only intensifies. Like many American institutions in the 1980s, colleges and universities face increasing complexity and fragmentation.

As decision-making contexts grow more obscure, costs increase, and resources become more difficult to allocate, leaders in higher education can benefit from understanding their institutions as cultural entities. As before, these leaders continue to make difficult decisions. These decisions, however, need not engender the degree of conflict that they usually have prompted. Indeed, properly informed by an awareness of culture, tough decisions may contribute to an institution's sense of purpose and identity. Moreover, to implement decisions, leaders must have a full, nuanced understanding of the organization's culture. Only then can they articulate decisions in a way that will speak to the needs of various constituencies and marshal their support.

Cultural influences occur at many levels, within the department and the institution, as well as at the system and state level. Because these cultures can vary dramatically, a central goal of understanding organizational culture is to minimize the occurrence and consequences of cultural conflict and help foster the development of shared goals. Studying the cultural dynamics of educational institutions and systems equips us to understand and, hopefully, reduce adversarial relationships. Equally important, it will enable us to recognize how those actions and shared goals are most likely to succeed and how they can best be implemented. One assumption of this chapter is that more often than not more than one choice exists for the decision-maker; one simple answer most often does not occur. No matter how much information we gather, we can often choose from several viable alternatives. Culture influences the decision.

Effective administrators are well aware that they can take a given action in some institutions but not in others. They are less aware of why this is true. Bringing the dimensions and dynamics of culture to consciousness will help leaders assess the reasons for such differences in institutional responsiveness and performance. This will allow them to evaluate likely consequences before, not after they act.

It is important to reiterate that an understanding of organizational culture is not a panacea to all administrative problems. An understanding of culture, for example, will not automatically increase enrollments or increase fund raising. However, an administrator's correct interpretation of the organization's culture can provide critical insight about which of the many possible avenues to choose in reaching a decision about how to increase enrollment or undertake a particular approach to a fund-raising campaign. Indeed, the most persuasive case for studying organizational culture is quite simply that we no longer need to tolerate the consequences of our ignorance, nor, for that matter, will a rapidly changing environment permit us to do so.

By advocating a broad perspective, organizational culture encourages practitioners to:

- consider real or potential conflicts not in isolation but on the broad canvas of organizational life;
- recognize structural or operational contradictions that suggest tensions in the organization;
- implement and evaluate everyday decisions with a keen awareness of their role in and influence upon organizational culture;
- understand the symbolic dimensions of ostensibly instrumental decisions and actions; and
- consider why different groups in the organization hold varying perceptions about institutional performance.

Many administrators intuitively understand that organizational culture is important; their actions sometimes reflect the points mentioned above. A framework for organizational culture will provide administrators with the capability to better articulate and address this crucial foundation for improving performance.

Thus far, however, a usable definition of organizational culture appropriate to higher education has remained elusive. If we are to enable administrators and policy makers to implement effective strategies within their own cultures, then we must first understand a culture's structure and components. A provisional framework will lend the concept of culture definitional rigor so that practitioners can analyze their own cultures and ultimately improve the performance of their organizations and systems. The understanding of culture will thus aid administrators in spotting and resolving potential conflicts and in managing change more effectively and efficiently. However, if we are to enable administrators and researchers to implement effective strategies within their own cultures, then we first must make explicit the essential elements of culture.

CULTURAL RESEARCH: WHERE HAVE WE BEEN

Organizations as Cultures

Ouchi and Wilkins note: "Few readers would disagree that the study of organizational culture has become one of the major domains of organizational research, and some might even argue that it has become the single most active arena, eclipsing studies of formal structure, of organization-environment research and of bureaucracy" [34, pp. 457–58].

Researchers have examined institutions, organizations, and subunits of organization as distinct and separate cultures with unique sets of ceremonies, rites, and traditions [30, 32, 38, 49]. Initial attempts have been made to analyze leadership from a cultural perspective [3, 39, 43, 45]. The role of cultural communication has been examined by March [28], Feldman and March [22], and Putnam and Pacanowsky [41], Trujillo [50], Tierney [46], and Pondy [40]. Organizational stories and symbols have also been investigated [17, 18, 29, 47].

Recent findings indicate that strong, congruent cultures supportive of organizational structures and strategies are more effective than weak, incongruent, or disconnected cultures [7, 27]. Moreover, the work of numerous theorists [5, 26, 31, 42] suggests that there is an identifiable deep structure and set of core assumptions that may be used to examine and understand culture.

Colleges and Universities as Cultures

Numerous writers [11, 21] have noted the lack of cultural research in higher education. Dill has commented: "Ironically the organizations in Western society which most approximate the essential characteristics of Japanese firms are academic institutions. They are characterized by lifetime employment, collective decision making, individual responsibility, infrequent promotion, and implicit, informal evaluation" [21, p. 307]. Research in higher education, however, has moved toward defining managerial techniques based on strategic planning, marketing and management control.

Higher education researchers have made some attempts to study campus cultures. Initially, in the early 1960s the study of culture primarily concerned student cultures [2, 6, 12, 19, 35, 36]. Since the early 1970s Burton Clark has pioneered work on distinctive colleges as cultures [13], the role of belief and loyalty in college organizations [14], and organizational sagas as tools for institutional identity [15]. Recent work has included the study of academic cultures [1, 23, 24], leadership [8, 10, 48], and the system of higher education as a culture [4, 16]. Thus, a foundation has been prepared on which we can build a framework for studying culture in higher education.

A CULTURAL FRAMEWORK: WHERE WE MIGHT GO

Anthropologists enter the field with an understanding of such cultural terms as "kinship" or "lineage." Likewise, productive research depends on our being able to enter the field armed with equally well defined concepts. These terms provide clues for uncovering aspects of organizational culture as they also define elements of a usable framework. Necessarily then, we need to consider what cultural concepts can be utilized by cultural researchers when they study a college or university. This chapter provides an initial attempt to identify the operative cultural concepts and terms in collegiate institutions.

The identification of the concepts were developed through the analysis of a case study of one institution. By delineating and describing key dimensions of culture, I do not presume to imply that all institutions are culturally alike. The intense analysis of one institution provides a more specific understanding of organizational culture than we presently have and presumably will enable researchers to expand upon the framework presented here.

Of the many possible avenues that exist for the cultural researcher to investigate, Table 18.1 outlines essential concepts to be studied at a college or university. That is, if an anthropologist conducted an in-depth ethnography at a college or university and omitted any mention of institutional mission we would note that the anthropologist had overlooked an important cultural term.

Each cultural term occurs in organizational settings, yet the way they occur, the forms they take, and the importance they have, differs dramatically. One college, for example, might have a history of formal, autocratic leadership, whereas another institution might operate with an informal, consensually oriented leader. In order to illustrate the meaning of each term I provide examples drawn from a case study of a public institution identified here as "Family State College." The data are drawn from site visits conducted during the academic year 1984–85. Participant observation and interviews with a random sample of the entire college community lend "thick

TABLE 18.1
A Framework of Organizational Culture

Environment:	How does the organization define its environment?
	What is the attitude toward the environment?
	(Hostility? Friendship?)
Mission:	How is it defined?
	How is it articulated?
	Is it used as a basis for decisions?
	How much agreement is there?
Socialization:	How do new members become socialized?
	How is it articulated?
	What do we need to know to survive/excel in this organization?
Information:	What constitutes information?
	Who has it?
	How is it disseminated?
Strategy:	How are decisions arrived at?
	Which strategy is used?
	Who makes decisions?
	What is the penalty for bad decisions?
Leadership:	What does the organization expect from its leaders?
	Who are the leaders?
	Are there formal and informal leaders?

description" [25] to the analysis. Each example highlights representative findings of the college community.

Family State College

"The intensity of an academic culture," writes David Dill, "is determined not only by the richness and relevance of its symbolism for the maintenance of the professional craft, but by the bonds of social organization. For this mechanism to operate, the institution needs to take specific steps to socialize the individual to the belief system of the organization. . . . The management of academic culture therefore involves both the management of meaning and the management of social integration" [21, p. 317]. Family State College offers insight into a strong organizational culture and exemplifies how administrators at this campus utilize the "management of meaning" to foster understanding of the institution and motivate support for its mission.

In dealing with its environment Family State College has imbued in its constituents a strong feeling that the institution has a distinctive purpose and that the programs reflect its mission. By invigorating old roots and values with new meaning and purpose, the president of Family State has largely succeeded in reconstructing tradition and encouraging a more effective organizational culture. As with all executive action, however, the utilization, strengths, and weaknesses of a particular approach are circumscribed by institutional context.

Environment

Founded in 1894, Family State College exists in a fading industrial town. The institution has always been a career-oriented college for the working class in nearby towns and throughout the state. "I came here," related one student, "because I couldn't afford going to another school, and it was real close by." Fifty percent of the students remain in the local area after graduation, and an even higher percentage (80 percent) reside in the state. In many respects the city of Family and the surrounding area have remained a relatively stable environment for the state college due to the unchanging nature of the working-class neighborhoods. An industrial arts professor explained the town-gown relationship: "The college has always been for the people here. This is the type of place that was the last stop for a lot of kids. They are generally the first generation to go to college and college for them has always meant getting a job."

When Family State's president arrived in 1976, he inherited an institution in equilibrium yet with a clear potential to become stagnant. The institution had low visibility in the area and next to no political clout in the state capital. Family State was not a turbulent campus in the late 1970s; rather, it was a complacent institution without a clear direction. In the past decade the institutional climate has changed from complacency to excitement, and constituents share a desire to improve the college.

The college environment provided rationales for change. Dwindling demand for teachers required that the college restructure its teacher-education program. A statewide tax that eliminated "nonessential" programs in high schools reduced the demand for industrial arts at Family State. New requirements by state hospitals brought about a restructured medical-technology program. The college's relationship to its environment fostered a close identification with its working-class constituency and prompted change based on the needs of a particular clientele.

Mission

Individuals spoke of the mission of the college from one of two angles: the mission referred either to the balance between career-oriented and liberal arts programs or to the audience for whom the college had been founded—the working class. Although people spoke about the mission of the college in terms of both program and clientele, the college's adaptations concerned programmatic change, not a shift in audience. That is, in 1965 the college created a nursing program that easily fit into the mission of the college as a course of study for working-class students. An industrial-technology major is another example of a program that responded to the needs of the surrounding environment and catered to the specified mission of the institution. Rather than alter or broaden the traditional constituency of the institution, the college tried to create new curricular models that would continue to attract the working-class student to Family State.

As a consequence, the college continues to orient itself to its traditional clientele—the working people of the area. The city and the surrounding area have remained a working-class region throughout the college's history; the town has neither prospered and become middle class nor has it faded into oblivion. Continuing education programs and the courtship of adult learners have broadened the clientele of the college while maintaining its traditional, working-class constituency.

The president frequently articulates his vision of the institutional mission in his speeches and writing. One individual commented: "When I first came here and the president said that 'we're number one' I just thought it was something he said, like every college president says. But after [you're here] awhile you watch the guy and you see he really believes it. So I believe it too." "We are number one in a lot of programs," said the president. "We'll go head to head with a lot of other institutions. Our programs in nursing, communication, and industrial technology can stack up against any other state college here. I'd say we're the best institution of this kind in the state."

Presidential pronouncements of excellence and the clear articulation of institutional mission have a two-fold import. First, institutional mission provides the rationale and criteria for the development of a cohesive curricular program. Second, the president and the other organizational participants have a standard for self-criticism and performance. All too often words such as "excellence" can be so vague that they have no measurable meaning. Family State however, can "stack up against any other state college." That is, rather than criterion-referenced performance measures such as standardized tests and achievement levels of incoming students, Family State College has standards of excellence that are consistent with the historic mission of state colleges.

Socialization

One individual who had recently begun working at the college noted: "People smiled and said hello here. It was a friendly introduction. People said to me, 'Oh, you'll really love it here.' It was that wonderful personal touch. When they hire someone here they don't want only someone who can do the job, but someone who will also fit in with the personality of the place." One individual also noted that, soon after he arrived, the president commented on how well he did his work but was worried that he wasn't "fitting in" with the rest of the staff. What makes these comments interesting is that they are about a public state college. Such institutions often have the reputation of being impersonal and bureaucratic, as opposed to having the "personal touch" of private colleges.

A student commented: "If a student hasn't gotten to know the president in a year then it's the student's damn fault. Everybody sees him walking around here. He's got those Monday meetings. He comes to all the events. I mean, he's really easy to see if you've got something you want to talk to him about. That's what's special about Family. How many places can a student get to know the president? We all call him 'Danny' (not to his face) because he's so familiar to us." The student's comment is particularly telling in an era of declining enrollments. One reason students come to the school, and one reason they stay at Family, is because the entire institution reflects concern and care for students as personified by the president's open door and the easy accessibility of all administrators.

Information

People mentioned that all segments of the institution were available to one another to help solve problems. Every Monday afternoon the president held an open house where any member of the college community could enter his office and talk to him. All segments of the community used the vehicle. As one administrator reported: "That's sacred time. The president wants to know the problems of the different constituencies. People seem to use it. He reflects through the open house that he really cares."

The president also believes in the power of the written word, especially with respect to external constituencies. It is not uncommon to read about Family State or the president in the local press. A survey done by the college discovered that the local citizenry had a positive, working knowledge of the president and the college. The president attends a multitude of local functions, such as the chamber of commerce and United Way meetings, and civic activities. He also invites the community onto the college campus.

Although mailings and written information are important vehicles for sharing information with external constituencies, oral discourse predominates among members of the institution. Internal constituencies appear well informed of decisions and ideas through an almost constant verbal exchange of information through both formal and informal means. Formal means of oral communication include task forces, executive council meetings, and all-college activities. At these gatherings individuals not only share information but also discuss possible solutions to problems or alternatives to a particular dilemma.

The president's communicative style percolates throughout the institution. Information from top administrators is communicated to particular audiences through weekly meetings of individual departments. One vice president described the process: "The president's executive staff meets once a week and we, in turn, meet with our own people. There's lots of give and take. The key around here is that we're involved in a process to better serve students. Open communication facilitates the process. God help the administrator or faculty member who doesn't work for students."

Informal channels of communication at Family State are an equally, if not more important means for sharing and discussing ideas as well as developing an esprit de corps. The president hosts several functions each year at his house near campus. He brings together disparate segments of the college community, such as different faculty departments, for a casual get-together over supper, brunch, or cocktails. "This is like a family," explained the president. "Too often people don't have the time to get together and share with one another food and drink in a pleasant setting."

It is not uncommon to see many different segments of the institution gathered together in public meeting places such as the cafeteria or a lounge. In discussions with faculty, staff, and administrators, many people showed a working knowledge of one another's tasks and duties and, most strikingly, the student body.

Throughout the interviews individuals consistently mentioned the "family atmosphere" that had developed at the college. As one individual noted: "Everything used to be fragmented here. Now there's a closeness."

Strategy

Family State's decision-making process followed a formal sequence that nevertheless accommodated informal activity. Initiatives often began at the individual or departmental level, as with proposals to create a new program. Eventually the new program or concept ended up in the College Senate—composed of faculty, students, and administration. A subcommittee of the senate decided what action should be taken and recommended that the idea be accepted or defeated. The senate then voted on the issue. Once it had taken action, the next step was presidential—accept the proposal, veto it, or send it back to the senate for more analysis. The final step was approval by the Board.

Formalized structures notwithstanding, a strictly linear map of decision analysis would be misleading. Most often the administration made decisions by widespread discussion and dialogue. "It's participative decision making," commented one individual. The president's decisions existed in concrete, but individuals saw those decisions as building blocks upon which further, more participative decisions were made. "The key around here," observed one administrator, "is that we're involved in a process to better serve students. Open communication facilitates the process."

Although, as noted, the college has adapted to its environment, the college did not rely solely on adaptive strategy. The president noted: "I don't believe that an institution serves its culture well if it simply adapts. The marketplace is narrow and changes quickly." Instead, the administration, particularly the president, has brought about change through an interpretive strategy based on the strategic use of symbols in the college and surrounding environment.

Chaffee defines interpretive strategy as ways that organizational representatives "convey meanings that are intended to motivate stakeholders" [9, p. 94]. Interpretive strategy orients metaphors or frames of reference that allow the organization and its environment to be understood by its constituents. Unlike strategic models that enable the organization to achieve goals or adapt to the environment, interpretive strategy proceeds from the understanding that the organization can play a role in creating its environment. Family State's president accentuates process, concern for the individual as a person, and the central orientation of serving students. He does so through several vehicles, foremost among them being communication with constituencies and the strategic use of space and time.

The president's use of space is an important element in his leadership style and implementation of strategy. He frequently extends his spatial domain beyond the confines of the college campus and into the city and surrounding towns. Conversely, invitations to the community to attend events at the college and utilize the library and other facilities have reduced spatial barriers with a city that otherwise might feel excluded. Informal gatherings, such as suppers at the president's house, or luncheons at the college, have brought together diverse constituencies that otherwise have little reason to interact with one another. Moreover, the president has attended to the physical appearance of the institution, making it an effective symbol to his constituencies that even the grounds demand excellence and care.

The president's symbolic use of space sets an example emulated by others. His open-door policy, for example, permeates the institution. Administrators either work in open space areas in full view of one another or the doors to their offices are physically open, inviting visits with colleagues, guests, or more importantly, students. The openness of the president's and other administrators' doors creates an informality throughout the college that fosters a widespread sharing of information and an awareness of decisions and current activities.

The president is also a visible presence on the campus. He spends part of every day walking throughout the institution for a casual inspection of the grounds and facilities. These walks provide a way for people to talk with him about matters of general concern and enable him to note something that he may not have seen if he had not walked around the campus. Administrators, too, interact with one another and with students not only in their offices but on the other's "turf." "The atmosphere here is to get to know students," said one administrator, "see them where they are, and not have a host of blockades so students feel as if they are not listened to."

The discussion of communication and space has made reference to time. The president continually integrates formal and informal interactions with his constituencies. According to his secretary and a study of the presidential calendar, about one and one-half hours per day are scheduled as "free time" that he uses as he sees fit—for reading, writing, or perhaps walking around the campus.

The president regularly schedules meetings with his executive circle or individuals such as the treasurer. The meetings revolve around both a mixture of formal agenda-like items and ideas or problems that either the president or his lieutenants feel they have. Although his schedule is generally very busy, it is not difficult to see the president. His secretary makes his appointments. She notes that if a faculty member or administrator asked to see the president, she would schedule an appointment when he was available in the very near future. Students, too, can see the president, but his secretary generally tries to act as a gatekeeper to insure that the students really need to see the president and not someone else.

Leadership

The president's awareness of patterns and styles of communication and his conscious use of time and place are perhaps best illustrated by a meeting we had during one of our site visits to Family State. We waited in the president's outer office with the director of institutional research.

The door swung open and the president walked out to greet us. He said: "I'm sorry for being late. I knew about your appointment and had planned to be back here on time, but I was walking around the campus for forty-five minutes, and just at the last minute I made a detour to check out the cafeteria, to see how things were going. I met a guy down there who works in the kitchen and he and I have always said we should play cribbage some time (he's a cribbage player) and wouldn't you know he had a board with him today and he asked me to play. So I did. He beat me too. So I wasn't doing anything very presidential in being late for you. I was just walking around the campus on this beautiful day, and playing cribbage in the kitchen with a friend."

The president's disclaimer notwithstanding, his actions are presidential in that they develop and reinforce an institutional culture. His effective use of symbols and frames of reference, both formally and informally, articulates the college's values and goals and helps garner support from faculty, students, staff, and the community. This should not imply, however, that presidents should necessarily spend their time walking around campus or playing cribbage with the kitchen help. What is effective at one institution is unlikely to work at another. Nevertheless, the role of symbolic communication that we witness on this campus, buttressed by tangible, constructive change, provides valuable clues about effectiveness and organizational culture.

Tying the Framework Together

People come to believe in their institution by the ways they interact and communicate with one another. The ongoing cultural norms of Family State foster an implicit belief in the mission of the college as providing a public good. In this sense, staff, faculty members, and administrators all feel they contribute to a common good—the education of working-class students. When individuals apply for work at Family State, they are considered not only on the basis of skill and qualifications but also on how they will fit into the cultural milieu. Socialization occurs rapidly through symbols such as open doors, the constant informal flow of communication punctuated by good-natured kidding, access throughout the organization, dedication to hard work, and above all, commitment to excellence for students. When people speak of their mission, they speak of helping people. Members of the college community work from the assumption that an individual's actions do matter, can turn around a college, and can help alter society.

Belief in the institution emerges as all the more important, given an unstable economic and political environment. The district in which the college resides has little political clout, and consequently the institution is not politically secure. Rapidly shifting employment patterns necessarily demand that the institution have program flexibility. Although the college has created programs such as medical technology and communication/media, it has not made widespread use of adaptive strategy.

"The strength of academic culture," states David Dill, "is particularly important when academic institutions face declining resources. During these periods the social fabric of the community is under great strain. If the common academic culture has not been carefully nurtured during periods of prosperity, the result can be destructive conflicts between faculties, loss of professional morale, and personal alienation" [21, p. 304]. Family State College exemplifies a strong organizational culture. Further, the academic culture nurtures academic excellence and effectiveness.

It is important to reiterate, however, that all effective and efficient institutions will not have similar cultures. The leadership exhibited by the president at Family State, for example, would fail miserably at an institution with a different culture. Similarly, the role of mission at Family State would be inappropriate for different kinds of colleges and universities. The rationale for a cultural framework is not to presume that all organizations should function similarly, but rather to provide managers and researchers with a schema to diagnose their own organizations.

In providing a provisional framework for the reader, I have neither intended that we assume the different components of the cultural framework are static and mutually exclusive, nor that an understanding of organizational culture will solve all institutional dilemmas. If we return to the Geertzian notion of culture as an interconnected web of relationships, we observe that the components of culture will overlap and connect with one another. In the case study, for example, the way the leader articulated organizational mission spoke both to the saga of the institution as well as its leadership.

How actors interpret the organizational "web" will not provide the right answers to simplistic choices. Rather, a cultural analysis empowers managers with information previously unavailable or implicit about their organization which in turn can help solve critical organizational dilemmas. As with any decision-making strategy, all problems cannot be solved simply because an individual utilizes a particular focus to an issue. For example, a specific answer to whether or not tuition should be raised by a particular percentage obviously will not find a solution by understanding culture. On the other hand, what kind of clientele the institution should have, or what its mission should be as it adapts to environmental change are critical issues that speak to the costs of tuition and demand cultural analysis.

CONCLUSION: WHERE DO WE GO FROM HERE?

Many possible avenues await the investigation of organizational culture. This chapter has provided merely the essential terms for the study of academic culture. A comprehensive study of organizational culture in academic settings will demand increased awareness of determinants such as individual and organizational use of time, space, and communication. In this case study, we observed the president's formal and informal uses of different cultural concepts. Individuals noted, for example, how they were well-informed of administrative decisions and plans primarily through informal processes. Evidence such as the president's casual conversations with administrators or walking around the campus were effective examples of the informal use of time. Further work needs to be done concerning the meaning and effective use of formality and informality with regard to time, space, and communication.

I have used the term "organizational culture" but have made no mention of its subsets: subculture, anticulture, or disciplinary culture. An investigation of these cultural subsets will provide administrators with useful information about how to increase performance and decrease conflict in particular groups. We also must investigate the system of higher education in order to understand its impact on individual institutions. For example, state systems undoubtedly influence the culture of a public state college in ways other than budgetary. A study of the influence of states on institutional culture appears warranted.

Each term noted in Table 18.1 also demands further explication and analysis. Indeed, the concepts presented here are an initial attempt to establish a framework for describing and evaluating various dimensions of organizational culture. Developing such a framework is an iterative process that should benefit from the insights of further research endeavors. An important research activity for the future will be the refinement and extension of this framework. The methodological tools and skills for such cultural studies also need elaboration.

By developing this framework and improving ways of assessing organizational culture, administrators will be in a better position to change elements in the institution that are at variance with the culture. This research will permit them to effect orderly change in the organization without creating unnecessary conflict. Moreover, the continued refinement of this framework will permit research to become more cumulative and will help foster further collaborative efforts among researchers.

REFERENCES

1. Becher, T. "Towards a Definition of Disciplinary Cultures." *Studies in Higher Education,* 6 (1981), 109–22.
2. Becker, H. S. "Student Culture." In *The Study of Campus Cultures,* edited by Terry F. Lunsford, pp. 11–26. Boulder, Col.: Western Interstate Commission for Higher Education, 1963.
3. Bennis, W. "Transformative Power and Leadership." In *Leadership and Organizational Culture*, edited by T. J. Sergiovanni and J. E. Corbally, pp. 64–71. Urbana, Ill.: University of Illinois Press, 1984.
4. Bourdieu, P. "Systems of Education and Systems of Thought." *International Social Science Journal,* 19 (1977), 338–58.
5. Burrell, G., and G. Morgan. *Sociological Paradigms and Organizational Analysis.* London: Heinemann, 1979.
6. Bushnell, J. "Student Values: A Summary of Research and Future Problems." In *The Larger Learning,* edited by M. Carpenter, pp. 45–61. Dubuque, Iowa: Brown, 1960.
7. Cameron, K. S. "Measuring Organizational Effectiveness in Institutions of Higher Education." *Administrative Science Quarterly,* 23 (1987), 604–32.
8. Chaffee, E. E. *After Decline, What? Survival Strategies at Eight Private Colleges.* Boulder, Col.: National Center for Higher Education Management Systems, 1984.
9. ——."Three Models of Strategy." *Academy of Management Review,* 10 (1985), 89–98.
10. Chaffee, E. E., and W. G. Tierney. *Collegiate Culture and Leadership Strategy.* New York: Macmillan, forthcoming.
11. Chait, R. P. "Look Who Invented Japanese Management!" *AGB Quarterly,* 17 (1982), 3–7.
12. Clark, B. R. "Faculty Culture." In *The Study of Campus Cultures*, edited by Terry F. Lunsford, pp. 39–54. Boulder, Col.: Western Interstate Commission for Higher Education, 1963.

13. Clark, B. R. *The Distinctive College.* Chicago, Ill.: Aldine, 1970.
14. —— "Belief and Loyalty in College Organization." *Journal of Higher Education,* 42 (June 1971) , 499–520.
15. —— "The Organizational Saga in Higher Education." In *Readings in Managerial Psychology,* edited by H. Leavitt. Chicago, Ill.: University of Chicago Press, 1980.
16. Clark B. R. (ed.) *Perspectives in Higher Education.* Berkeley, Calif.: University of California Press, 1984.
17. Dandridge, T. C. "The Life Stages of a Symbol: When Symbols Work and When They Can't." In *Organizational Culture,* edited by P. J. Frost, L. F. Moore, M. R. Louis, C. C. Lundberg, and J. Martin, pp. 141–54. Beverly Hills, Calif.: Sage, 1985.
18. Dandridge, T. C., I. Mitroff, and W. F. Joyce. "Organizational Symbolism: A Topic to Expand Organizational Analysis." *Academy of Management Review,* 5 (1980), 77–82.
19. Davie, J. S., and A. P. Hare. "Button-Down Collar Culture." *Human Organization,* 14 (1956), 13–20.
20. Deal, T. E., and A. A. Kennedy. *Corporate Cultures: The Rites and Rituals of Corporate Life.* Reading, Mass.: Addison-Wesley, 1982.
21. Dill, D. D. "The Management of Academic Culture: Notes on the Management of Meaning and Social Integration." *Higher Education,* 11 (1982), 303–20.
22. Feldman, M. S., and J. G. March. "Information in Organizations as Signal and Symbol." *Administrative Science Quarterly,* 26 (1981), 171–86.
23. Freedman, M. *Academic Culture and Faculty Development.* Berkeley, Calif.: University of California Press, 1979.
24. Gaff, J. G., and R. C. Wilson. "Faculty Cultures and Interdisciplinary Studies." *Journal of Higher Education,* 42 (March 1971), 186–201.
25. Geertz, C. *The Interpretation of Cultures.* New York: Basic Books, 1973.
26. Koprowski, E. J. "Cultural Myths: Clues to Effective Management." *Organizational Dynamics,* (1983), 39–51.
27. Krakower, J. Y. *Assessing Organizational Effectiveness: Considerations and Procedures.* Boulder, Col.: National Center for Higher Education Management Systems, 1985.
28. March, J. G. "How We Talk and How We Act: Administrative Theory and Administrative Life." In *Leadership and Organizational Culture,* edited by T. J. Sergiovanni and J. E. Corbally, pp. 18–35. Urbana, Ill.: University of Illinois Press, 1984.
29. Mitroff, I. I., and R. H. Kilmann. "Stories Managers Tell: A New Tool for Organizational Problem Solving." *Management Review,* 64 (1975), 18–28.
30. ——. "On Organizational Stories: An Approach to the Design and Analysis of Organizations through Myths and Stories." In *The Management of Organization Design,* edited by R. H. Kilmann, L. R. Pondy, and D. P. Slevin, pp. 189–207. New York: North Holland, 1976.
31. Mitroff, I. I., and R. Mason. "Business Policy and Metaphysics: Some Philosophical Considerations." *Academy of Management Review,* 7 (1982), 361–70.
32. Morgan, G., P. J. Frost, and L. R. Pondy. "Organizational Symbolism." In *Organizational Symbolism,* edited by L. R. Pondy, P. J. Frost, and T. C. Dandridge. Greenwich, Conn.: JAI Press, 1983.
33. Ouchi, W. G. "Theory Z: An Elaboration of Methodology and Findings." *Journal of Contemporary Business,* 11 (1983), 27–41.
34. Ouchi, W. G., and A. L. Wilkins. "Organizational Culture." *Annual Review of Sociology,* 11 (1985), 457–83.
35. Pace, C. R. "Five College Environments." *College Board Review,* 41 (1960), 24–28.
36. ——. "Methods of Describing College Cultures." *Teachers College Record,* 63 (1962), 267–77.
37. Peters, T. J., and R. H. Waterman. *In Search of Excellence.* New York: Harper and Row, 1982.
38. Pettigrew, A. M. "On Studying Organizational Cultures." *Administrative Science Quarterly,* 24 (1979), 570–81.
39. Pfeffer, J. "Management as Symbolic Action: The Creation and Maintenance of Organizational Paradigms." *Research in Organizational Behavior,* 3 (1981), 1–52.

40. Pondy, L. R. "Leadership is a Language Game." In *Leadership: Where Else Can We Go,* edited by M. McCall and M. Lombardo, pp. 87–99. Durham, N.C.: Duke University Press, 1978.
41. Putnam, L. L., and M. E. Pacanowsky (eds.) *Communication and Organizations: An Interpretive Approach.* Beverly Hills, Calif.: Sage, 1983.
42. Quinn, R. E., and J. Rohrbaugh. "A Competing Values Approach to Organizational Effectiveness." *Public Productivity Review,* 5 (1981), 122–40.
43. Schein, E. H. "The Role of the Founder in Creating Organizational Culture." *Organizational Dynamics,* 12 (1983), 13–28.
44. ———. *Organizational Culture and Leadership.* San Francisco: Jossey-Bass, 1985.
45. Smircich, L., and G. Morgan. "Leadership: The Management of Meaning." *Journal of Applied Behavioral Science,* 18 (1982), 257–73.
46. Tierney, W. G. "The Communication of Leadership." Working paper. Boulder, Col.: National Center for Higher Education Management Systems, 1985.
47. ———. "The Symbolic Aspects of Leadership: An Ethnographic Perspective." *American Journal of Semiotics,* in press.
48. ———. *The Web of Leadership.* Greenwich, Conn.: JAI Press, forthcoming.
49. Trice, H. M., and J. M. Beyer. "Studying Organizational Cultures through Rites and Ceremonials." *Academy of Management Review,* 9 (1984), 653–69.
50. Trujillo, N. "'Performing' Mintzberg's Roles: The Nature of Managerial Communication." In *Communication and Organizations: An Interpretive Approach,* edited by L. L. Putnam and M. E. Pacanowsky. Beverly Hills, Calif.: Sage, 1983.

19

The Effect of Institutional Culture on Change Strategies in Higher Education

Universal Principles or Culturally Responsive Concepts?

Adrianna J. Kezar and Peter D. Eckel

The array of challenges that higher education faces today is virtually unparalleled when compared to any other point in U.S. history. The litany of changes is familiar to those in the field of higher education: financial pressure, growth in technology, changing faculty roles, public scrutiny, changing demographics, competing values, and the rapid rate of change in the world both within and beyond our national boarders. The changes many institutions face have accelerated beyond tinkering; more campuses each year attempt to create comprehensive (or transformational) change. Yet, change strategies have not been exceedingly helpful in their capacity to guide institutions, and we know even less about how to facilitate major, institutionwide change.

The current change literature in higher education provides mostly generalized strategies about what is effective: a willing president or strong leadership, a collaborative process, or providing rewards (Roberts, Wren, & Adam, 1993; Taylor & Koch, 1996). This broad writing may mask information helpful to advance institutional change on a specific campus. "Achieving buy-in" or "communicating effectively" can seem very empty to institutional leaders and higher education scholars. Can this strategy be used at every institution and in the same way? The assumptions behind this approach are that each strategy is enacted similarly on each campus and that nuance and context do not much matter. Broad change strategies are presented as uniform, universal, and applicable.

As an alternative, some scholars of organizations suggest that meaningful insight to understand the change process comes from context-based (micro-level) data (Bergquist, 1992). Context-based data help the change agent to understand why and under what circumstances strategies work at a particular institution at a particular time. The difficulty of working at the micro-level is becoming too specific and idiosyncratic to be of much help to others. As Hearn noted, the first and fundamental proposition we can stress about change is so simple as to seem banal or deflating, "it depends" (Hearn, 1996). Idiosyncratic observations are often of little use to practitioners. The challenge is to chart a middle ground and identify findings informative at a level that can be used to guide change processes. This task is challenging, because markers that one might use to determine the level of detail or the appropriate level of abstraction are not readily apparent.

One solution to charting meaningful middle ground is through a cultural perspective. Organizational research in the 1980s illustrated the impact of culture on many aspects of organizational life (Peterson & Spencer, 1991). Yet, there have been few empirical studies examining how institutional culture affects change processes and strategies. The assumption from the organizational literature is that culture will be related to the change process; specifically, change processes can be thwarted by violating cultural norms or enhanced by culturally sensitive strategies (Bergquist, 1992). This study attempts to fill the gap in the literature, moving beyond generalized principles of change, by adopting a two-tiered cultural framework to examine the effect of institutional culture on change strategies across six institutions. The two research questions addressed are: (1) is the institutional culture related to the change process, and how is it related? and (2) are change processes thwarted by violating cultural norms or enhanced by culturally sensitive strategies? The two theories adopted for exploring the relationship of culture and change are Bergquist's (1992) four academic cultures and Tierney's (1991) individual institutional culture framework. The dual level of analysis offers a multiple-lens perspective that is better suited to understand complex organizational phenomena (Birnbaum, 1988; Bolman & Deal, 1991).

Analyses of the six institutions (three are presented as detailed case examples) engaged in change processes over a four-year period through case study methodology (interviews, document analysis, and observation) are presented, examining five core change strategies: senior administrative support, collaborative leadership, robust design (vision), staff development, and visible actions. In addition to demonstrating a relationship between institutional culture and change, the results support several assumptions from cultural theory, including the significance of culturally appropriate strategies, the importance of examining multiple layers of culture (enterprise, institutional, group), and the possibility of predicting which strategies will be more important. This study challenges conventional notions about change processes; namely, that one can follow a general principle or approach and not be aware of how distinct organizational cultures impact the process. Its findings suggest the need for practitioners to become cultural outsiders in order to observe their institutional patterns. The Bergquist and Tierney cultural frameworks provide initial templates for this analysis.

UNDERSTANDING ORGANIZATIONAL CULTURE AND CHANGE: A REVIEW

Six main categories of change theories[1] exist throughout a multidisciplinary literature, including biological, teleological, political, life cycle, social cognition, and cultural. (For detailed descriptions of these various models please see: Burns, 1996; Collins, 1998; Levy & Murray, 1986; Morgan, 1986; Sporn, 1999; Van de Ven & Poole, 1995). Biological (unplanned change) and teleological models (planned change) have received the most attention in higher education and have the longest histories; most recently biological models were used in a major study by Sporn (1999) and teleological models in a study by Eckel, Hill, and Green (1998). Biological and teleological models tend to produce the generalized change strategies noted in the introduction as problematic (Burns, 1996; Collins, 1998). Political models also have a long history but have been critiqued for their inability to provide solutions for organizational participants in facilitating or reacting to the change process (Burns, 1996; Collins, 1998; Van de Ven & Poole, 1996). Researchers have recently touted cultural and social cognitive theories for their sophistication in illustrating complexity in showing the ambiguity, context based nature, and human aspects of the change process (Collins, 1998). This study attempted to examine the promise of cultural theories to understand change within the higher education context, because they are mostly unexplored, yet show great potential. The researchers also assumed that comprehensive change, the type focused on in this study, might best be examined through a framework in which values and beliefs are a focus because major alterations to an organization usually impact underlying belief systems (Schein, 1985).

This next section provides the context for the study by briefly reviewing the evolution of cultural approaches to studying organizations and the implications of the culture literature for this study. Next, a review of the extant literature on institutional culture and change in higher education is presented. Lastly, the theoretical frameworks guiding this study of culture (Tierney and Bergquist) and change (Lindquist) are reviewed.

Organizational Culture

In the 1980s, organizational researchers across various disciplines began examining the role of culture within organizational life (Morgan, 1986; Schein, 1985; Smirich & Calas, 1982) and then connected it to effectiveness (Tichy, 1983) and central processes (i.e., leadership, governance) of the organization (Schein, 1985). Culture shifted from being used as a descriptive device to becoming linked with improvement and success. Higher education followed that pattern. Early research used culture to illustrate that campuses had unique cultures from other types of institutions, describing the myths and rituals of colleges, and student and faculty subcultures (see Clark, 1970; Lunsford, 1963; Riesman, Gusfield, & Gamson, 1970). Several later studies on higher education linked institutional culture with organizational success (Chaffee & Tierney, 1988; Peterson, Cameron, Jones, Mets, & Ettington, 1986). Further studies demonstrated the way that different cultures shaped various institutional functions including governance (Chaffee & Tierney, 1988), leadership (Birnbaum, 1988), and planning (Hearn, Clugston, & Heydinger, 1993; Leslie & Fretwell, 1996).

Two links between culture and change have been made in the higher education literature. The first set of literature suggests that institutions need to have a "culture" that encourages change (Curry, 1992). The goal of this body of research is to determine the aspects of culture or type of culture that need to be fostered to promote institutional change (Schein, 1985). The second set of ideas suggests that culture or key institutional elements that shape culture, i.e., vision or mission, are modified as a result of the change process (Chaffee & Tierney, 1988; Eckel, Hill, & Green, 1998; Guskin, 1996). In other words, the outcome of change is a modified culture (Schein, 1985). The research presented here pursues a third path, investigating the ways in which culture shapes an institution's change processes or strategies. It is the modifying element rather than the subject of the modification.

Conceptual Frameworks for Studying the Effect of Culture on Change Strategies

Within this study, we define culture as "the deeply embedded patterns of organizational behavior and the shared values, assumptions, beliefs, or ideologies that members have about their organization or its work" (Peterson & Spencer, 1991, p. 142). Culture provides meaning and context for a specific set of people (Bergquist, 1992; Schein, 1985). Other scholars suggest nuances to this broad definition. For example, some view it as a variable (such as corporate culture), while others see it as a fundamental metaphor for a specific type of organization (see Morgan, 1986). Some researchers conceptualize culture as strong and congruent, or weak and incongruent (see Tierney, 1988); others merely note that cultures vary, without assigning a value to different cultures (see Bergquist, 1992; Martin, 1992). With these nuances in mind, culture is conceptualized within this study as a fundamental metaphor, emerging as a composite of many different levels—the enterprise, the institution, the subgroup (faculty, administrators), and the individual levels (Martin, 1992). The researchers assumed that cultures differ and that they are not necessarily negative or positive; nor are multiple cultures or fragmented cultures necessarily to be avoided.

This study adopts two conceptual frameworks of culture: (1) Bergquist's institutional archetypes of culture and (2) Tierney's unique institutional culture. First, the inquiry builds on Bergquist's (1992) work on institutional culture. Bergquist focuses on archetypes by which numerous institutions might be categorized and described.[2] He hypothesized (yet never empirically tested) that different change strategies would be needed and appropriate within the four different academic culture archetypes that reflect any higher education institution—collegial culture, managerial culture, developmental culture, and negotiating culture.[3] The *collegial culture* arises primarily from the disciplines of the faculty. It values scholarly engagement, shared governance and decision making, and rationality, whereas the *managerial culture* focuses on the goals and purposes of the institution and values efficiency, effective supervisory skills, and fiscal responsibility. This contrasts with the *developmental culture*, which is based on the personal and professional growth of all members of the collegiate environment. Lastly, the *negotiating culture* values the establishment of equitable and egalitarian policies and procedures, valuing confrontation, interest groups, mediation, and power. Bergquist illustrated how the managerial culture, for example, might hinder an institution's ability to change structures, whereas a collegial culture was better equipped to modify institutional structures because there was greater trust.

Although Bergquist's framework provides one lens for examining the effect of institutional culture on change strategies, these institutional cultural archetypes can mask many of the complexities of individual institutional cultures. This study adopts a second conceptual framework to explore the ways in which culture affects change processes within unique institutions. The Tierney framework includes the following six categories: environment, mission, socialization, information, strategy, and leadership. Analysis consists of examining each category in depth, asking such questions as, how is the mission defined and articulated? Is it used as a basis for decisions? What constitutes information and who has it? Or how are decisions arrived at and who makes them? This approach assumes that the values, beliefs, and assumptions of an institution are reflected in its processes and artifacts. By examining the key elements suggested by Tierney (1991), the researcher develops a clearer picture of the institutional culture.

When using both frameworks together, they provide a more powerful lens than when using only one in helping to interpret and understand culture. The archetypes provide a ready framework for institutions unfamiliar with cultural analysis; the framework establishes patterns for them to identify. The Tierney lens provides a sophisticated tool for understanding the complexities of unique institutions. Although Tierney's framework is an important framework, it may be more difficult for practitioners to use readily. Thus, both frameworks were used in this study; the dual level of analysis offers a multiple-lens perspective better suited to understand complex organizational phenomena (Birnbaum, 1988; Bolman & Deal, 1991).

Framework for Studying Change

The change under investigation in this study is comprehensive change; it is defined as change that is pervasive, affecting numerous offices and units across the institution; deep, touching upon values, beliefs and structures, is intentional, and occurs over time (Eckel et al., 1998). To study the effect of culture on the change process, it is important to focus on a type of institutional change that was neither isolated in a particular unit nor affected only the surface of the institution. Lindquist's (1978) work on change, one of the most comprehensive sets of change strategies found in the higher education literature, was used as a change strategy framework for the study. Bergquist also used Lindquist's framework in his speculation of the impact of culture on change. The applicability of Lindquist's approach was recently tested on a broader set of institutions undertaking change (he only examined liberal arts institutions), and the following core change strategies emerged (Kezar & Eckel, in press):

1 *Senior administrative support*, refers to individuals in positional leadership providing support in terms of value statements, resources, or new administrative structures.
2 *Collaborative leadership*, defined as a process where the positional and nonpositional individuals throughout the campus are involved in the change initiative from conception to implementation.
3 *Robust design*, a more complex and less well known term than vision; it is adopted from the work of Eccles and Nohria (1992). Leaders develop a "desirable" and flexible picture of the future that is clear and understandable and includes set goals and objectives related to the implementation of that picture. The picture of the future and the means to get there are flexible and do not foreclose possible opportunities.
4 *Staff development*, a set of programmatic efforts to offer opportunities for individuals to learn certain skills or knowledge related to issues associated with the change effort.
5 *Visible actions*, refers to advances in the change process that are noticeable. Activities must be visible and promoted so that individuals can see that the change is still important and is continuing. This is an important strategy for building momentum within the institution.

These five core strategies contain sets of substrategies; for example senior administrative support is related to incentives, change in governance structures, and providing support structures. Because it is not the intent of this chapter to investigate the specific strategies for change, please see Kezar and Eckel (in press) for a detailed discussion of the core strategies and substrategies. These strategies are identified here to provide a framework through which the investigation of culture and its relationship to the strategies for change can proceed.

In summary, the following diagram illustrates the relationships among the various concepts reviewed and used to frame the study:

Bergquist's cultural + archetypes	Tierney's individual → institutional culture	Change strategies
Collegial culture	Environment	Senior administrative support
Managerial culture	Mission	Collaborative leadership
Developmental culture	Socialization	Robust design
Negotiating culture	Information	Staff development
	Strategy	Visible actions
	Leadership	

Each institution in the study will be examined using the four elements of Bergquist's cultural archetype in addition to Tierney's six characteristics that define unique individual institutional culture. These two cultural frameworks will then be explored in relation to the way the change process occurred at all six institutions along the five core strategies.

RESEARCH DESIGN AND METHODOLOGY

Case Selection Criteria

This study is based on six institutions participating in the ACE Project on Leadership and Institutional Transformation; the project included 23 institutions. The project focused on understanding the process of institutional transformation. A subset of six institutions was identified through purposeful sampling utilizing four criteria: (1) they made the most progress on their identified change agendas; (2) they had the capacity and willingness to collect detailed data on change strategies and institutional culture; (3) they represented different institutional types; and (4) they had similar change initiatives. The six institutions in the study included one research university, three doctoral-granting universities, a liberal arts college, and a community college. Because institutional type has been related to Bergquist's cultural archetypes (Bergquist, 1992; Birnbaum, 1992), various institutional types were purposefully examined. As noted previously, all of the institutions were engaged in intentional comprehensive change. But to ensure additional consistency across cases, institutions were selected that had similar change initiatives; i.e., they were all working to transform teaching and learning. Thus, differences in strategies would be associated with cultural differences, rather than related to diffuse change agendas.

Data Collection and Analysis

In order to examine the effect of organizational culture on change and to move beyond the broad generalizations in the literature, an ethnographic approach was adopted. The project was a five-and-a-half year initiative on institutional transformation; the reported data were collected in years one through four. Participant-observers from each institution provided data on a semesterly basis in response to open-ended questionnaires and at biannual project meetings. Outside researchers visited each campus twice a year for the first three years and once during the fourth year. Researchers additionally collected and analyzed internal institutional documents.

Data analysis was conducted through three different approaches. First, theme analysis of the change strategies was conducted, using Lindquist's framework, examining ways each strategy was enacted on that campus. Categorical analysis was used to search for micro and macro themes (Miles & Huberman, 1994). Second, researchers developed institutional culture profiles of all six institutions based on the Bergquist and Tierney frameworks for examining institutional culture.[4] This analysis resulted in the example profiles provided in the results section. Third, Bergquist's and Tierney's frameworks were applied to the data to identify whether institutional culture patterns could be identified in the change strategies. Variations from the cultural lens were also noted. Emergent themes were identified and negotiated between the two reviewers. After the analysis was completed, the profiles of institutional culture, change strategies, and the relationship between the two conditions were sent to the site visit researchers (other than the lead researchers) to confirm interpretations of institutional culture and to have outsiders check the themes that emerged.

Due to space constraints, profiles of three sample institutions are presented to illustrate the relationship of institutional culture and change strategies common to all six institutions. These three were selected because they represent three different types of institutions (a research university, a doctoral university, and a community college), they illustrate three different Bergquist cultural archetypes (developmental, managerial, and collegial), and they had the most and the richest data to best capture their culture and change strategies.

Limitations

First, because institutions self-selected to be part of the project from which this subsample was taken, they may not represent the range of institutions undergoing comprehensive change. Second, although we attempted to identify institutions with similar change initiatives, there were small variations in their agendas. Finding institutions engaging in identical change efforts is almost impossible. Third, since much of the data are self-reported they may be biased to reflect success.

RESULTS

This section is organized as follows: (1) descriptions of the three highlighted institutions, introducing the institutions, their change initiatives, and their cultures; and (2) presentations of the way the cultures have a bearing on institutional change strategies. Because the intent of this study is to understand the effect of culture on specific change strategies, the results are organized by each of the five core change strategies. Space limitations prevent a detailed description of the institutions and all the ways that institutional culture manifests itself across all five core change strategies. It is hoped that the summary tables and results section provide some of the key data to make these institutions real for the reader. Each of the five tables focuses on one change strategy, describing the way the strategy emerged at all three institutions. The notation "B" or "T" next to each theme reflects the way it related to the Bergquist or Tierney frameworks.

Institutional Profiles

Informal Trusting University (ITU) is a public doctoral university located in a small Midwestern town. It enrolls approximately 18,000 students, of whom over half are women. Close to 90% of its students come from within its state, and 1% are international; approximately 40% live on campus. The university has seven academic colleges and a graduate school with over 870 full-time faculty. Included among the colleges are architecture, business, fine arts, communications, and applied sciences and technology. Its 100-year history is that of a teacher's college developing into a doctoral university. It is endeavoring to integrate technology into the core of the teaching and learning process. This initiative had the ambitious goal of having the entire faculty involved in rethinking their courses and curricula around infusing technology to enrich the undergraduate student experience.

At ITU, both the organizational culture and change strategies used reflect the developmental culture in Bergquist's typology. The mission and faculty socialization strongly supported the importance of learning; at one time the institution defined itself as a "premier teaching university." Bergquist noted that many developmental cultures tend to have a strong focus on teaching. The leadership process on developmental campuses tends to be facilitative and strongly collaborative, as was the case at ITU. Developmental campuses like ITU also tend to share information widely, because it is critical to growth.

From a Tierney perspective, ITU's institutional culture is best characterized by the terms informal and trusting. Although a sense of trust is likely to develop within the developmental culture, it is stronger than described in Bergquist's framework. Trust at ITU appears to result from the long and stable leadership created by having the same president and provost for over 15 years, the large number of long-term dedicated employees (over 60% have only worked under the current president and provost), and the strong connection between the campus and its community. The institution also is run exceedingly informally. For example, the institution does not have a strategic planning process, and institutional direction is set informally and communicated through a series of conversations between the president, the provost, and various key stakeholders. ITU's policies and practices were developed locally in departments and colleges, were modified frequently, and lacked uniformity. Although some campus decision-making structures are in place, such as a faculty senate, there appears to be little reliance on them as the primary decision-making venues. Much of the business of the campus happens around a lunch table, in the hallways, or through various different meetings. People who work at ITU are likely to know each other well, for many interact both within the workplace and outside of it in the local community.

Responsible and Self-Reflective Community College (RSCC) is a multi-campus community college of approximately 54,000 students, located outside a major Southern metropolitan area. It serves two of the fastest growing counties in the state. Founded in the late 1960s, close to 70% of RSCC students enroll in credit courses, and over 60% of its students are enrolled in at least one developmental course. The average age of its credit students is 25. The college ranks fourth in the nation in the number of A.A. and A.S. degrees it awards. It has 326 full-time faculty and approximately 1,100 part-time instructors. Last year, it generated over $8 million in federal and state grants. It is attempting to shift from a teaching- or faculty-centered institution to a more learning-centered one, a process that the institution views as a major transformation in the ways it conducts its business. If successful, institutional leaders note that the structures, processes, pedagogies, and beliefs will change dramatically.

The culture at RSCC is best classified as managerial, using Bergquist's framework. It is characterized by strong senior administrative directive, driven by goals, plans, and assessment, is cognizant of outside forces pressing the institution, strives to meet customer needs, and frequently experiences clashes in values between faculty and administrators.

However, there are many ways that this campus is different from the managerial archetype. RSCC has a strong commitment to student learning, which pervades this large and complex four-campus college, and we therefore label it "responsible." RSCC's responsible culture is not simply driven by managerial accountability, but a deeply human desire to help. RSCC also is strongly introspective. Central administrators force introspection by the types of questions they ask faculty and the heads of the four campuses. Faculty and administrators also spend significant time discussing "the way we do things around here" and how to improve those practices. Institutional leaders note that the environment is changing and seek to effect change on campus that will align it with these external shifts. Information and data are collected not only to assess college goals, but also to understand institutional identity. There was a strong desire across the campus to understand RSCC students and their needs and, additionally, to understand who RSCC is and how it works. Staff development through workshops such as managing personal transformations (based on personal introspection) provide additional self-reflective mechanisms.

Autonomous Insecure University (AIU) is a private research university, located in a major urban area on the Eastern seaboard. It has seven academic colleges, including a law school, and a school for continuing education. It has approximately 13,000 undergraduate and 6,000 graduate students, and close to 750 full-time faculty. Close to 85% of new students live on campus, and 55% come from out of state. Its expected tuition and fees for new students is approximately $20,000. It is attempting to re-craft its general education program. Its agenda for change will lead to a profound shift in the campus' thinking about the purposes and structures of general education and in the strategies to actualize the new general education objectives, disseminating to all faculty responsibility for the goals of general education.

AIU manifests Bergquist's collegial culture. Colleges and schools are highly independent; the institution is focused on research and the disciplines. One of AIU's main goals is striving to move up in the traditional academic rankings. Academic affairs issues and priorities dominate governance, and decision making occurs at the department and school levels.

Through the Tierney lens, the autonomous nature of AIU far exceeds that described within the collegial archetype. The change initiative itself—to reexamine the general education curriculum, its structure and its purposes, as well as its modes of delivery—results from a history of high fragmentation across the extremely autonomous schools and colleges and a poor accreditation review. The institution is private, which may contribute to the high level of autonomy, as it is neither part of a system nor dependent on state funds, but is responsible for its own resources in a continually shrinking fiscal environment. Central administrators, in the past, have had a high turnover rate, leaving colleges and schools responsible for their own continuity of purposes and for providing their own direction. Many people in the highly academic city where it is located view it as a low-status institution. New faculty are quickly socialized to learn that they work at a less prestigious institution. AIU has recently gone through a downturn in enrollment, creating significant financial distress at the university, which included laying off academic staff. Its insecurity was additionally reinforced and heightened by the poor accreditation review.

Change Strategies

Having briefly described the cultures of the three institutions through both the Bergquist and Tierney frameworks, the following discussion is framed around the five core change strategies. The intent of this organization is to present examples that highlight the different ways each distinct culture appears to shape the application of each change strategy.

Senior administrative support. Senior administrative support concerns itself with the way senior administrators can facilitate change through resources, structures, and so on. This strategy varied across the three campuses discussed here. A summary of the variations in senior administrative support across the three institutions is found in Table 19.1.

At ITU senior administrative support appeared in the background of the change efforts and consisted primarily of providing needed resources and facilities regarding technology. Senior administrators also continually reminded the campus of the importance of technology and computer competency, but they were laissez faire in the direction of the initiatives. At managerial oriented RSCC, the senior administration provided very visible project leadership: developing the plan and a conceptual model to drive campus transformation, coordinating the leadership team, facilitating and coordinating communication among the four campuses, and securing external resources and reallocating internal ones. RSCC also created a new position, vice president for transformation, to help facilitate the campus' efforts. At collegial AIU, the provost and his administrative staff designed the overall process and oversaw it from a distance but moved much of the key decision making to the faculty of each college. Senior administrative support took the role of launching the efforts and then providing resources and creating accountability mechanisms. They were fairly absent from shaping decisions directly and worked intentionally to stay out of the way. All decisions were pushed down to the college.

Although Bergquist's archetypes were partially helpful in explaining the way senior administrative support emerged, the Tierney individual-level cultural analysis, provided additional insight. ITU differed from the developmental culture in the way senior administrative support emerged; for example, no governance structures were altered or support mechanisms established. Within the developmental culture Bergquist predicted that leaders would establish many support mechanisms to facilitate change; governance structures were typically altered to assure inclusiveness and formal communication vehicles were typically established. Yet, within this informal environment, people, not processes or structures were the core support. Furthermore,

TABLE 19.1
Senior Administrative Support Strategies by Institution

Informal, Trusting University (Developmental)	Responsible, Self-Reflective Community College (Managerial)	Autonomous, Insecure University (Collegial)
Provide resources[B]	Formal communication[B]	Top-down plan, turned over to units[B]
In the background[B]	Sr. admin. actively involved and center of communication[B]	College-level focus[B]
Provide opportunities and support[B]	Securing funding[B]	Respected faculty promoted to VP to oversee related change area[B]
Informal communication[T]	Coordinate leadership team[B]	Develop mechanisms to work with colleges[B]
Few changes to governance or structures[T]	Developed new structures to facilitate communication and decision making[B]	College-level incentives as key support[B]
Facilitate indirectly[T]	VP for Transformation hired from outside[B]	Saw outside influences as interference, not help[B]
External forces encourage and coalesce community[T]	Provide incentives through central structure[B]	Outside influence important to facilitate change[T]
Remind campus of importance[T]	Frame external forces to motivate (threat)[B]	Colleges involved in grant-writing process, money as central[T]
	Develop conceptual framework[T]	Few changes to governance or structures[T]
		Cross-functional teams[T]
		Public deadlines and discussions[T]

Note: B refers to Bergquist Framework; T refers to Tierney Framework

the informal communication around lunch tables and in hallways with senior leaders was the ideal process rather than the more deliberate communication mechanisms established within typical developmental cultures. The insecure culture of AIU seemed linked to the reliance on incentives as a major strategy for change. It appeared that incentives became the primary way that senior administrators could develop a sense of efficacy among insecure faculty. Thus, the unique culture of AIU seemed to alter the central processes needed for change from those offered in Lindquist's framework. Incentives became more important than senior administrative support, which was the general pattern on other campuses. Table 19.1 presents the different manifestations of senior administrative support.

Collaborative leadership. Lindquist's change framework suggests that leadership at the top alone is insufficient and that change requires collaborative leadership from throughout the institution, particularly from the faculty. Collaborative leadership was a natural element of the developmental culture of ITU, where decisions and much of the action was pushed out to individual academics and departments. Mechanisms for collaborative leadership were already established through informal information networks and cross-departmental groups that met on a regular basis to discuss improvements. Developing people's leadership capacities and tapping their creativity had been a long-term philosophy for the current administration.

This manifestation was quite a contrast from RSCC, where the managerial culture had not historically created mechanisms for collaborative leadership. Cross-campus input was foreign to RSCC, thus several different committees were established by central administrators to tap leadership across the college. One of the first big steps in sharing leadership was to help people understand that they could now shape institutional direction and that their leadership was welcome. To promote shared leadership, twelve collegewide forums and campus structured dialogues were held in order to capture the good ideas from the faculty and staff. To demonstrate their willingness to share leadership, central administrators started writing "draft" on all documents and encouraged written and electronic comments throughout the change process.

AIU reflected the collegial culture in its approach to collaborative leadership by tapping its decentralized bureaucracy. Deans and chairs were expected to take leadership within their various units. The senior administrators delegated leadership to them and encouraged them to get faculty involvement and ownership in key unit decisions. Many key decisions and valuable solutions to institutional problems were made in cross-functional task forces that brought together faculty and staff from different units. AIU also learned that the term "draft" needed to be placed on documents until there was official approval from each college. On a few occasions a document was sent out without one or two schools' official approval, which led to great disruption.

Examining these institutions through the lens of their individual cultures, collaborative leadership was enacted in distinctive ways. The trusting and informal environment of ITU shaped involvement; campus leaders did not need to invite participation or develop channels for communication, and there was no need to work through troubled relations on campus. Within most managerial cultures, the level of participation that RSCC obtained at their dialogues, forums, and voluntary action teams would be unheard of. The reason so many people attended the meetings was their commitment to students. This sense of responsibility made them attend meetings where they were not sure if they would be heard, events that might simply be a waste of time. Also, RSCC's focus on self-reflection seemed to make communication a core strategy; the forums and dialogues took on a distinctive form with people expressing feelings, beliefs, and interpretations. Collaboration on this campus meant people needed to understand each other and themselves. Another helpful insight through the Tierney framework is the way in which AIU's autonomous culture related to collaborative leadership. Few institutions would "truly" delegate responsibility solely to the colleges and schools for the change initiative. But, at AIU, this was the only way to successfully achieve faculty ownership and participation. Many other initiatives had failed because they had not been attuned to this aspect of the culture on AIU's campus. Several faculty noted that this respect for the nature of collaborative leadership is what made this particular initiative succeed.

Robust design. This concept is an extension of Lindquist's ideas modified with the work of Eccles and Nohria (1992). It suggests that a flexible vision is needed, one that does not foreclose future opportunities. ITU, with its developmental culture, epitomizes the flexibility inherent in the concept of robust design. Institutional leaders had no overall grand scheme for change; instead they established a process that launched a series of uncoordinated, yet broadly linked change efforts. Decisions and ideas emerged at the local, departmental level, often informally. The few planning documents evolved at the local level (within programs and departments) were for local use. The vision and "real" plan for the future regarding technology and the educational experience was in each individual's head or within the strategy of each department. Even new promotion and tenure criteria that reflected the institution's technology goals were left to the design of each unit to best fit their specific intellectual contexts.

The managerial culture of RSCC, which gravitated toward having a mandated vision and clear plan, at first had difficulty in creating a strategy characterized by robust design. After a slow start, the change leaders developed mechanisms by which they could be more flexible and yet stay visionary. The message behind labeling every document with the word "draft" was an artifact of a new flexible mindset. The leadership team also incorporated the comments and feedback from the various campus dialogues and feedback sessions in ways that continued to leave future options open. Outside pressures, in particular concerning performance indicators, also helped to promote the change design.

TABLE 19.2
Collaborative Leadership Strategies by Institution

Informal, Trusting University (Developmental)	Responsive, Self-Reflective Community College (Managerial)	Autonomous, Insecure University (Collegial)
Individual initiative, no central initiation[B]	Collaboration foreign to the campus; needed outreach and invited participation[B]	Faculty ownership of initiative key to success[B]
Individual unit-level invitation[B]	Cross-site planning team representing all groups[B]	Campuswide committee to gain involvement across campus[B]
Part of the long-time philosophy[B]	Invited to comment on notes; action teams asked for volunteers[B]	Formal newsletter; Faculty Center for communication[B]
Trust; positive working relations[B]	Realized importance of communication—12 structured dialogues[B]	Draft until colleges were able to provide feedback[B]
No formal structure[T]	"Draft" on everything sent out from central source[B]	Forum to discuss relationships among different colleges— historically tension between some disciplines[B]
All individuals realize process involved authentic opportunity for communication[T]	Forums to discuss relationships between groups[B]	Cross-unit interest groups to assure all of faculty voice included; older students involved as well[T]
Decentralized efforts[T]	Had to provide stipends to get participation[B]	Delegation of all key decisions[T]
No new collaborative mechanisms[T]	Consensus of collegewide vision based on responsibility to student[T]	Used fear of being behind competition as motivator for involvement[T]
Loose cross-unit teams[T]	Public reflection of college purposes[T]	
	Comprehensive leadership development program for self-reflection[T]	

Note: B refers to Bergquist Framework; T refers to Tierney Framework.

AIU's collegial culture was evident in its strategies to create robust design. Members of the campus immediately rejected the initial plan developed by the president as too restrictive and unwarranted. The responsibility for designing and implementing the change then shifted to the college/school level. The design was created to allow for flexibility at the departmental level. For example, the central administrators created a master document tracking aspects of the plan that had been delegated to the colleges and departments, yet central administrators allowed each unit to create the specifics to meet institutional goals. Careful communication, always in writing, existed between the various levels of the organization related to the design of the change process. Central administrators also moderated the pace of change based on faculty feedback about the implementation scheduling. Finally, because faculty did not want to have responsibility to be accountable for each other, also a familiar aspect of the collegial culture, they gravitated toward an outside, legitimate source, an accreditation team.

The archetypes were not a powerful enough explanatory lens to understand some of the unique ways that the robust design efforts were shaped on these campuses. For example, RSCC attempted to develop a robust design through a whole series of data collection efforts. Data collection seemed to be such a strong element of robust design because it reflected the campuses' drive to be responsible and to become more self-aware. Some of the types of data collection mechanisms are extremely self-analytic, including an organizational character index and a collective vision index. These different assessments focused on learning about the nature of the organization and working to develop a more functional culture and vision, if needed.

TABLE 19.3
Robust Design Strategies by Institution

Informal, Trusting University (Developmental)	Responsive, Self-Reflective Community College (Managerial)	Autonomous, Insecure University (Collegial)
Local planning; they know best[B]	Centralized communication, design at administrative level[B]	Goals and implementation plan designed at local level[B]
Accountability was connected to ideal of being a better teacher[B]	Setting expectations for accountability and gather baseline data and assess core processes over time[B]	Strong planning documents top-down design of project created tension[B]
Long-term orientation: visionary, future perspective part of leadership culture[B]	Long-term orientation: Data-driven planning[B]	Accreditation team provides support for initiative[B]
Celebrated accomplishments[B]	Outside perspective: Performance indicators in state heavily influenced planning[B]	Used externally generated legitimacy[B]
Informal communication facilitates momentum[T]	Reports written up and shared; esp. meeting-targeted goals[T]	Highly coordinated, intentional, structured communication[T]
Few planning documents[T]		Master document[T]
Uncoordinated, but loosely linked strategies[T]	Establishing plan by describing other campuses with similar plans[T]	Tapped campus insecurity for action[T]
Outside perspective did not play a role[T]	Type of data collection, organizational index[T]	Moderated pace of change through setting range of goals and obtaining feedback from faculty to change rate[T]
Did not put change in larger context[T]		Publicity of high achieving faculty[T]
		Putting change in broader context; trends among peer institutions[T]

Note: B refers to Bergquist Framework; T refers to Tierney Framework

Data collection that focused on students was also seen as important to better respond to their needs and to improve the learning environment. On most campuses with a developmental culture similar to ITU, a detailed and clear robust plan would be critical for moving forward with change. Yet, within ITU's family-type environment, it appears that there was little need for this type of documentation, which was unique to their distinctive culture. At AIU, the central administration built the plan around areas of insecurity and used faculty and staff insecurity as a lever to coalesce the campus around the robust design. They also used outreach to help gain momentum for the plan; for example, externally publicizing faculty's new ideas about general education. In the past, designs for change were thwarted at AIU; leaders knew it would be difficult to coalesce people without some strategy or crisis. Building on faculty insecurity was identified after months of searching for a motivational technique that would reach faculty, in particular. No generalized cultural archetypes would have been helpful in discovering these nuanced aspects of developing a robust design.

Visible actions. People need to see that their hard work is leading toward progress, thus visible actions are an important change process strategy. Table 19.4 reflects the following discussion. There were very distinct ways in which the three institutions used visible actions to facilitate change. The developmental culture at ITU, heavily tied to the growth of people on campus, appeared to necessitate a change in the people and their attitudes as a means to maintain momentum. This was achieved through the award of developmental grants for staff development and through a change in hiring policies aimed at bringing in new faculty. At managerial RSCC, goals needed to be met to maintain the momentum for change. A short-term action team was

TABLE 19.4
Visible Action Strategies by Institution

Informal, Trusting University (Developmental)	Responsive, Self-Reflective Community College (Managerial)	Autonomous, Insecure University (Collegial)
Needed people change; hiring criteria[B] Faculty development[B] Focused on personal growth[B] Local, informal multilevel action: guiding document written by faculty, institutional grants, faculty-led workshops[T] Make individual responsible[T]	Meet goals. Short term action—20% increase in graduation rates[B] Developed new policies and procedures[B] Incentives: small grants and monies provided for any initiative related to the change initiative[B] Gave national presentations and received national recognition[T] New leadership development program[T] Measure progress of student learning via data[T]	Secured new resources and prestigious grants[B] Allocated money to departments for related initiatives[B] Support structures: cross unit interest groups[T] Faculty ownership, immediate change in curriculum and department culture[T] Getting funding to support projects[T] Prestigious publicity and recognition[T]

Note: B refers to Bergquist Framework; T refers to Tierney Framework

established and initially documented a 20% increase in graduation rates. This strategy created a surge of energy, bringing many holdouts to the change initiative. The collegial culture at AIU focused on resources as a motivation. The acquisition of several grants provided the needed incentive to build the change initiative. Although each institution obtained grants for their initiatives, they seemed to be valued most at AIU. Allocating grant money to faculty within departments at AIU developed a sense of ownership and enthusiasm.

Two examples will help illustrate the ways that their unique cultures emerge within the visible-action-taking strategy. The informal culture at ITU appeared to result in numerous activities throughout the campus, falling under visible actions. This differed from most developmental campuses, where centralized staff development was the core feature. Activities ranged from a faculty group that wrote one of the guiding documents that created a new language on campus to centrally administered developmental grants to a regular newspaper column that described efforts to incorporate technology into classrooms. All these efforts helped to build momentum throughout this informal environment. However, at AIU, bringing in outside money seemed to provide the incentive that made the campus feel that they were becoming more prestigious, and therefore successful, in their change process. The insecure culture at this campus seemed to link outside recognition through money as a validation of its robust design and change initiative. Although the collegial culture would have predicted that money would be important to taking action, the consuming nature of this strategy would not have been predicted or understood purely through the cultural archetypes.

Staff development. Staff development, a set of programmatic efforts to build new capacities within faculty and staff, was extremely important to the change processes at all three institutions. Yet, it was enacted in very different ways, based on the culture of the institution. ITU utilized a local departmental model for technology staff development. Leaders within different schools or colleges led the efforts to develop the needed support for their colleagues. The training programs were focused on the individual and their needs. At RSCC, however, most of the staff development was produced by outside consultants or outside speakers. The decision to create the formal staff development program emerged from the president and vice president for transformation's office.

There was little if any input from individuals on campus about the content or approach for staff development. The focus of the learning was how to develop staff to better serve the college, an objective that is closely aligned with a managerial culture rather than personal development for the individual, as was stressed at ITU within a developmental culture. In AIU's collegial culture, several different models emerged. Many faculty were sent off campus to observe how their peers were working to transform general education. In addition, speakers were often brought to specific colleges and schools to describe new approaches to general education, particularly in disciplines such as engineering. Experts within each college were also called upon to describe innovative ideas and ways to facilitate the change process. The focus of the development was at the departmental level; the outcome was that the faculty member could serve his or her department more effectively.

What is the relationship between the individual cultures and the ways these strategies emerged? The developmental culture of ITU would have predicted staff development as the most important strategy for change. Yet, it was not emphasized heavily on this campus. The culture of this unique campus also seemed to affect the way staff development was enacted. The informal and trusting nature of ITU appeared to shape the staff development initiative, which was much more unstructured than that on any of the other campuses in this study or within the entire project. This institution drew exclusively on internal staff for development because of the deep trust they held, knowing they would be the best guides for assisting each other's growth. At RSCC, staff development was the dominant strategy in the change process, which appears to be related to their unique culture of self-reflection. This fact also counters the cultural archetypes, because robust design and senior administrative support would have been predicted to be the most important of the core strategies within a managerial culture. It appears that their great interest in self-reflection and personal transformation made this area a high priority and a successful strategy. The unique culture at AIU can also be seen in the way staff development emerged. The autonomy of AIU appeared to have resulted in multiple levels of staff development by various colleges/schools and throughout levels within the college—department, program, and other levels. Their insecure culture seemed to make them seek outside expertise, not trusting their own knowledge for various aspects of the staff development. Table 19.5 compares the variety of ways staff development played itself out across the three institutions.

TABLE 19.5
Staff Development Strategies by Institution

Informal, Trusting University (Developmental)	Responsive, Self-Reflective Community College (Managerial)	Autonomous, Insecure University (Collegial)
Focus on individual needs[B]	Outside expertise and administratively decided[B]	Faculty sent to off campus conferences by school, see what other faculty are doing[B]
Faculty development program[B]	Centrally coordinated leadership development program[B]	Department level, serve department[B]
Internal grants program[B]		
Decentralized by school or department[T]	Efforts were coordinated and purposeful[B]	Outside experts[T]
Technical support developed at local level[T]	Focused on serving college[B]	Different models across units[T]
Not well developed[T]	Central focus of the change process[T]	Cross-departmental teams[T]
Unstructured[T]	Transformation series[T]	
Tapped internal experts[T]		

Note: B refers to Bergquist Framework; T refers to Tierney Framework

DISCUSSION

The results of this study illuminate several new insights into higher education organizational change processes. In addressing the first research question, whether there appears to be a relationship between institutional culture and change, the results suggest that at all institutions and among every strategy there was a relationship. In examining the nature of this relationship (the second part of the first research question), several patterns were identifiable. First, exploring the strategies used by institutions to effect change through a cultural approach appears to provide a richer description of the often empty strategies, such as collaborative leadership or senior administrative support. Each campus enacted strategies in different ways. The distinctions are important, because the approach to senior administrative support taken at RSCC most likely would not have been acceptable on the two other campuses, and vice versa. The findings about how institutional culture and change are related also sheds light on the second research question, whether ignoring institutional culture can thwart change processes. Where strategies for change violate cultural norms, change most likely will not occur (Eckel et al., 1998; Schein, 1985). The three case studies illustrate the weakness of and the challenge to presenting change strategies as universal principles. Future research might be more insightful if it were more sensitive to the relationship of culture to strategies for change.

A second finding about how institutional culture and change are related is the recognition that Bergquist's four cultural archetypes are a helpful lens for understanding the ways in which culture is related to the change process. The findings note a relationship between institutional cultural archetypes and the way the change process was enacted. For example, AIU, a collegial campus, followed the predicted pattern of engaging in a change process where faculty and traditional academic governance structures and bodies were central to the change process, where motivation was derived from prestige, where collaborative leadership utilized the traditional academic leaders, and where key planning and decision making occurred at the college and departmental level.

A third result is the discovery that each campus' change process could not be explained by the archetypes alone. The distinct nature of the campus cultures cannot be overlooked in trying to understand how change processes unfold and which strategies institutional leaders should emphasize. The self-reflective tendency of RSCC would have been overlooked if that institution had only been examined through Bergquist's managerial lens. A structured change process, as predicted by the developmental culture, most likely would have derailed the change effort at ITU. Furthermore, the lack of structure to support change at ITU could not have been predicted by the developmental culture. Examining institutional culture in depth, beyond the four archetypes, provides a deeper and richer understanding of the change process and appears to facilitate change.

A fourth finding in this vein is the understanding that cultural archetypes and unique institutional cultures may help to determine which strategies might take prominence in the change process. For example, at RSCC staff development appeared to be the most important core strategy based on the self-reflective culture of the campus. At ITU, collaborative leadership seemed to play a prominent role based on the family atmosphere on the campus. Also, certain substrategies emerged as core strategies based on the culture of the institution in the same way as incentives did at AIU or communication at RSCC. Understanding the strengths and relative contributions of different strategies may help leaders determine where to focus their efforts.

These results clearly reaffirm what we assumed was the answer to our second research question—that change strategies seem to be successful if they are culturally coherent or aligned with the culture. In this study, institutions that violated their institutional culture during the change process experienced difficulty. Because of the culture's collegial nature, AIU's process was almost immediately halted when the president tried to initiate change. Not writing the word "draft" on documents hurt the process at RSCC, because it showed insensitivity to the feelings of faculty, who did not see themselves as the natural allies of administrators. These examples reinforce the idea that missteps in the change process are often cultural misunderstandings. Leaders might be more successful in facilitating change if they understood the cultures in which they were working.

These results have several implications for campus change agents. First, they need to attempt to become cultural outsiders, or as Heifetz (1994) suggests, they need to be able to "get on the balcony" to see the patterns on the dance floor below. Reading institutional culture in order to develop and match the strategies for change are fundamental to an effective change process. Change agents' strategies for achieving this outside perspective on campuses include working with a network of institutions, using outside consultants, presenting at and attending conferences where they publicly explore their assumptions, bringing in new leadership, and participating in exchange programs to broaden the horizons of personnel. Second, individuals or campuses interested in change need to be aware of the four cultures of the academy and how these are reflected within their campus. Bergquist's (1992) typology can be a useful tool for leaders undertaking comprehensive change.

Finally, future research is needed regarding culture and institutional change. Drawing on this analysis, there is evidence that working within the culture facilitates change. If change strategies violate the institution's cultural norms and standards, they might be viewed as inappropriate and stifle the change process. Yet, this study was not designed specifically to address this question. Are there certain instances (for example during a crisis) that cultural norms can be violated to affect change? Further research should examine, in what situations, it might be necessary or important to challenge institutional culture, rather than work within it. As noted in the literature review, some studies have identified how certain cultures facilitate and hinder change; these various lines of culture research need to be examined together (Curry, 1992). We want to emphasize that this study did not attempt to ascertain the efficacy of various change strategies, rather it sought to understand the relationship between institutional culture and strategies. Although working within the culture of the institutions appeared to assist institutions in moving forward, this relationship and its complexities need further study. Additionally, the archetypes were examined as exemplifying the institutional culture. Bergquist (1992) notes how campuses will have different subcultures that operate within a specific archetypal culture. These nuances and effects of subcultural archetypes need further investigation.

The intent of this study is to urge researchers and practitioners to reflect on change as a cultural process. As Bergquist notes, "one of the best ways to begin to prepare for (change) and to cope with challenges is to examine our own institutions in order to appreciate and engage diverse and often conflicting cultures that reside in them" (1992, p. 230). This chapter provides a framework for ways that institutions can begin to engage in this type of examination and reflection.

NOTES

1. Model and theory are not necessarily interchangeable, although many scholars use them this way. Instead, "theory" is a broader term suggestive of contemplation of reality or insight, whereas "model" delineates a set of plans or procedures. Certain disciplines tend to develop models of change, such as business or psychology, whereas other fields tend to discuss theories. We use the term "theory" generically within this chapter.
2. Although he did not focus specifically on the change process, instead focusing more on general issues

of administration and leadership and how these processes are influenced by the four cultures, a small component of his work did speculate on change and culture.

3. Birnbaum also examined different institutional types as representing different cultural archetypes (1988).

4. The researchers acknowledge that even more detailed data could reveal interesting subcultures within the institution that would also assist in our understanding of comprehensive change. These two frameworks are illustrative of the levels of culture but do not examine the department- or program-specific level of culture, for example. This is an area for future research.

REFERENCES

Bergquist, W. (1992). *The four cultures of the academy.* San Francisco: Jossey Bass.

Birnbaum, R. (1988). *How college works.* San Francisco: Jossey Bass.

Bolman, L., & Deal, T. (1991). *Reframing organizations.* San Francisco: Jossey Bass.

Burns, B. (1996). *Managing change: A strategic approach to organizational dynamics.* London: Pitman Publishing.

Chaffee, E., & Tierney. W. (1988). *Collegiate culture and leadership strategies.* New York: ACE/ORYX.

Clark, B. (1970). *The distinctive college*: *Antioch, Reed, Swarthmore.* Chicago: Aldine.

Collins, D. (1998). *Organizational change: Sociological perspectives.* London: Routledge.

Curry, B. (1992). *Instituting enduring innovations: Achieving continuity of change in higher education.* Washington, DC: ASHE-ERIC Higher Education Report No. 7.

Eccles, R. G., & Nohria, N. (1992). *Beyond the hype: Rediscovering the essence of management.* Cambridge, MA: Harvard Business School Press.

Eckel, P., Hill, B., & Green, M. (1998). *On change: En route to transformation.* Occasional Paper, No. 1. Washington DC: American Council on Education.

Guskin, A. E. (1996). Facing the future: The change process in restructuring universities. *Change, 28*(4), 27–37.

Hearn, J. C. (1996). Transforming U.S. higher education: An organizational perspective. *Innovative Higher Education, 21*, 141–151.

Hearn, J. C., Clugston, R., & Heydinger, R. (1993). Five years of strategic environmental assessment efforts at a research university: A case study of an organizational innovation. *Innovative Higher Education, 18*, 7–36.

Heifetz, R. (1994). *Leadership without easy answers.* Boston: Harvard University Press.

Kezar, A., & Eckel, P. (in press). Examining the institutional transformation process: The importance of sensemaking and inter-related strategies. *Research in Higher Education.*

Leslie, D., & Fretwell, L. (1996). *Wise move in hard times.* San Francisco: Jossey Bass.

Levy, A., & Merry, U. (1986). *Organizational transformation: Approaches, strategies, theories.* New York: Praeger.

Lindquist, J. (1978). *Strategies for change.* Washington, DC: Council for Independent Colleges.

Lunsford, I. (1963). *The study of campus cultures.* Boulder, CO: WICHE.

Martin, J. (1992). *Cultures in organizations: Three perspectives.* New York: Oxford University.

Miles, M. B., & Huberman, A. M. (1994). *Qualitative data analysis* (2nd ed.). Thousand Oaks, CA: Sage.

Morgan, G. (1986). *Images of organization.* Thousand Oaks, CA: Sage.

Peterson, M., & Spencer, M. (1991). Understanding academic culture and climate. In M. Peterson (Ed.), *ASHE reader on organization and governance* (pp. 140–155). Needham Heights, MA: Simon & Schuster.

Peterson, M., Cameron, K., Jones, P., Mets, L., & Ettington D. (1986). *The organizational context for teaching and learning: A review of the research literature.* Ann Arbor: National Center for Research to Improve Postsecondary Teaching and Learning, University of Michigan.

Reisman, D., Gusfield, J., & Gamson, Z. (1970). *Academic values and mass education: The early years of Oakland and Monteith.* New York: Doubleday.

Roberts, A. O., Wergin, J. F., & Adam, B. E. (1993). Institutional approaches to the issues of reward and scholarship. *New Directions for Higher Education*, No. 81, pp. 63–86.

Schein, E. (1985). *Organizational culture and leadership: A dynamic view.* San Francisco: Jossey Bass.

Smirich, L., & Calas, M. (1982). Organizational culture: A critical assessment. In M. Peterson (Ed.), *ASHE reader on organization and governance* (pp. 139–151), Needham Heights, MA: Ginn Press.

Sporn, B. (1999). *Adaptive university structures: An analysis of adaptation to socioeconomic environments of US and European universities.* Philadelphia: Francis and Taylor, Higher Education Policy Series 54.

Tichy, N. (1983). *Managing strategic change: Technical, political, and cultural dynamics.* New York: Wiley.

Tierney, W. (1988). Organizational culture in higher education. *Journal of Higher Education, 59,* 2–21.

Tierney, W. (1991). Organizational culture in higher education: Defining the essentials. In M. Peterson (Ed.), *ASHE reader on organization and governance* (pp. 126–139), Needham Heights, MA: Ginn Press.

Van de Ven, A. H., & Poole, M. S. (1995). Explaining development and change in organizations. *Academy of Management Review, 20,* 510–540.

20

Community College Organizational Climate for Minorities and Women

Barbara K. Townsend

Recent headlines from the January 5, 2004, issue of *Community College Week*—("Board calls for more minorities at Louisiana college" and "Utah minorities not getting enough college prep")—suggest that all is not well when we consider the organizational climate for minorities in community colleges. The headline about Louisiana alludes to the concern of Louisiana's Community and Technical College System governing board that not enough minorities are being hired in high-ranking positions in the system. In particular, the concern is that not enough Blacks are being hired, given the high percentage of Blacks in Louisiana (Dyer, 2004). In Utah, a report issued by the Utah Coalition for the Advancement of Minorities in Higher Education informed the state's Board of Regents about barriers to higher education for minorities, including the barrier of campus climate (Utah Minorities, 2004).

In addition to these recent headlines, there are studies that provide some sense of how women and minority community college faculty perceive their institution's receptivity to their presence. In a study Townsend and LaPaglia (2000) conducted within the Chicago system of community colleges, both female and male full-time community college faculty were asked their perceptions about certain issues. These included administrative attitudes toward female and male faculty and salary and rank differentials based on gender. There were statistically significant differences by gender as regards perceptions about salary and rank and perceived administrative attitudes toward female and male faculty. Women faculty were more likely than men faculty to perceive inequities in salary and rank. They were less likely than men to agree that their institution's administrators hold both women and men in the same regard.

Recently Hagedorn and Laden (2002) used a national data set on community college faculty to assess whether or not a "chilly climate" exists at community colleges for women faculty. Their major finding was that faculty of color and women are statistically less likely to agree that claims of discriminatory practices against minorities and women have been greatly exaggerated than are men or white faculty. In short, there are perceptual studies that indicate women and minority faculty view the community college's organizational atmosphere or climate differently and less positively than do white male faculty regarding receptivity to women and minorities (Peterson & Spencer, 1990).

What would be a positive organizational climate for women and minorities and how could it be achieved? To answer this question, I will first describe some traditional or standard measures of a positive organizational climate for women and minorities and then evaluate how well the community college is doing when examined against these measures. Next I will describe some structural manifestations of a negative climate for minorities and women. Some of these manifestations include negative discourse about minorities and women. In doing so, I will trace the development of some discourse patterns about these groups and provide some illustrative cultural assumptions that reflect these discourse patterns. I will conclude with implications for the community college, including some steps to be taken to improve the organizational climate for minorities and women.

EVALUATING COMMUNITY COLLEGES ON ORGANIZATIONAL CLIMATE

At a very pragmatic and easy-to-measure level, a positive climate for women and minorities would be reflected in the traditional or standard measures of (a) representation of women and minorities proportionate to their percentage in the population served by the institution, (b) equal pay for equal work, and (c) equal opportunity for promotion, regardless of race/ethnicity and gender.

How do community colleges nationally—and Texas community colleges in particular—look on these dimensions when they are specified as (a) proportionate representation of female and minority students and faculty, (b) equal pay for equal work as demonstrated by faculty salaries, and (c) equal opportunity for promotion as demonstrated by the percentage of women and minorities in the presidential ranks?

WOMEN AND MINORITY STUDENTS AND FACULTY IN COMMUNITY COLLEGES

Students

In all types of higher education institutions, women students currently outnumber men students and have done so since the late 1970s. In 2000, women constituted 57% of undergraduate enrollment in degree-granting institutions (Snyder & Hoffman, 2003). Thus, women students outnumber men students in the community college. The picture is no different in Texas where 58% of the annual public community college enrollment by headcount in fall 2000 was female (Texas Higher Education Coordinating Board Community and Technical Colleges Division, n.d.).

Minority students have also increased their presence in higher education from 15% in 1976 to 28% in 2000 (Snyder & Hoffman, 2003). At the 2-year college level, minority enrollment was 30% in 1997, as compared to 24% at 4-year colleges (Shek, 2001). According to the Texas Higher Education Coordinating Board (2002), non-Whites constituted almost 48% of the student headcount at public community colleges in the fall semester of 2000. However, minority enrollment is heavily clustered in some Texas community colleges, while others have very limited enrollment.

Faculty

At the national level, women constitute around 36% of the faculty when full-and part-time faculty are combined. However, in the public 2-year college, the percentage of female faculty is much higher. In fall 1998 women held 49.9% of faculty appointments in 2-year colleges (Snyder & Hoffman, 2003). In Texas, for the 2001–2002 academic year, 48% of the community and technical college faculty (full and part-time) were female and 52% male (Texas Higher Education Coordinating Board Community and Technical Colleges Division, n.d.).

Regarding the presence of minority faculty, a study by Perna (2003) that utilized the 1993 National Study of Postsecondary Faculty database found that the percentage of Blacks, Hispanics, and American Indians was somewhat lower at public 4-year institutions than at 2-year colleges. In fall 1998, the great majority of full-and part-time 2-year college faculty were White, non-Hispanic (over 85%). Of the remaining faculty, 6% were Black, non-Hispanic; 4.6% were Hispanic; 3.4% were Asian/Pacific Islander; and 1.1% were American Indian/Alaska Native (Snyder & Hoffman, 2003). In Texas during 2001–2002, 22% of full- and part-time 2-year college faculty were minority, with 12% Hispanic and 7% Black (Texas Higher Education Coordinating Board Community and Technical Colleges Division, n.d.). In other words, Texas surpasses the national average of minority faculty in 2-year colleges.

Perna's (2003) examination of 1993 national data on faculty led her to conclude that there was generally an absence of observable ethnic or racial group differences regarding employment-related experiences for faculty at public 2-year colleges, including faculty rank and salary. She concluded that this suggests that there is an absence of racial/ethnic inequity, but believes more must be done in order to correct the underrepresentation of faculty of color that continues to exist at community colleges. Given their underrepresentation, minority community college faculty, unlike women community college faculty, are subject to the pressures of being the minority group in skewed groups or where the majority-to-minority ratio may be as high as 85:15. In skewed groups, those in the numerically smaller group have very high visibility, exaggerated awareness by others and themselves of their differences, and stereotyping on the basis of their dominant differing characteristic, e.g., sex, race/ethnicity, sexual orientation (Kanter, 1977).

Before we begin congratulating ourselves on the strong presence of women faculty in the community college, however, we need to reflect on whether or not their presence is a result of choice or of circumstances, including the circumstances of 4-year colleges and universities' discriminating against hiring them. Luba Chliwniak, who has taught at the community college level, has asked whether the characteristics of the community college make it more accepting to women or, alternatively, is it that women who hold advanced degrees go to community colleges as an alternate work location. Thus, the question really is whether or not the community college is leading by choice or by default (Chliwniak & Bernhardt, 1999)?

Some evidence to answer this question is found in Townsend and LaPaglia's (1995) study in which the authors conducted an open-ended survey of full-time women faculty in the City Colleges of Chicago. They also surveyed a few women faculty in rural and suburban Illinois community colleges. Respondents were asked why they thought there were so many female community college faculty as compared to 4-year college faculty. Several reasons were given. One was that employment at the community college better enabled them to balance the demands of work and life outside work. Some also indicated that gender discrimination in 4-year colleges worked against women being full-time faculty there. When asked if they thought community college leaders had "consciously striven to hire women," those who responded gave a resounding "No."

EQUAL PAY FOR EQUAL WORK/FACULTY SALARIES

Regardless of institutional sector, male full-time faculty typically earn more than female full-time faculty. In 1999, male faculty earned an average of $61,700 compared with an average of $48,400 for female faculty. As depressing as this news is, the salary differential between female and male faculty is less than in positions outside academe. Nationally, in 2001, for every dollar a man earned, a woman earned 76 cents. In contrast, women assistant professors at doctoral institutions made only 9 cents per dollar less than men in 2002–2003 (Fogg, 2003).

The pay differential between female and male faculty is the lowest in the 2-year sector. In 2001–2002, the average salary for full-time female faculty in public 2-year schools was $49,276, as compared to $52,340 for male faculty. In all ranks, men earned more than women (The NEA 2003 Almanac, 2003).

EQUAL OPPORTUNITIES FOR ADVANCEMENT IN PRESIDENTIAL LEADERSHIP

Over the past two decades, there has been significant growth in the percentage of female presidents in both the 4-year and 2-year college sector. In the 4-year sector, 18% of college presidents are female, while in the 2-year sector 27% are female (ACE News, 2002: "Rate of increase for women and minorities as college presidents slows according to a new report on the college presidency from the American Council of Education." (Press release)). However, as Amey and VanDerLinden (2002) have noted, the representation of women in the administrative ranks still is not proportionate to their presence as students in the classroom or in the community college faculty ranks.

More minorities are now in college presidencies than a couple decades ago. In 2001, almost 13% of college presidents were non-Whites (*Chronicle of Higher Education*, 2003). In the 2-year college sector, 14% of college presidents in 1996 were minorities, as compared to 11% in 1991 (Phillippe, 2000). No easily accessible data are available specifically addressing the presence of minority or female community college presidents in Texas, so a comparison cannot be made at this time.

This picture of the increasing presence of minority and women community college presidents, relative equity in faculty salaries, and major presence of women community college faculty and students provides some evidence of a positive climate for these groups. There is also evidence of problems; and many of those problems are reflected in the limited presence of minority faculty and students. Using various indicators in examining national data sets, researchers such as Perna (2003) and Hagedorn and Laden (2002) have concluded that the environment or climate for women and minority faculty is better at 2-year colleges than at 4-year colleges. However, the 2-year college is by no means a place where women and minority faculty never encounter the barriers of discrimination, glass ceilings, or academic funnels.

STRUCTURAL MANIFESTATIONS OF POOR ORGANIZATIONAL CULTURE FOR WOMEN AND MINORITIES

What might be occurring in the community college organizational climate that prevents a more positive organizational climate for women and minorities? As one way of answering this question, it may be helpful to examine a description by Chesler and Crowfoot (1989/2000) of how racism can be manifested in organizational cultures. Their description can also be applied to manifestations of sexism in organizational cultures.

Chesler and Crowfoot (1989/2000) have explored racism in higher education from the perspective of five universal organizational elements that affect universities' policies and practices. Organizational or institutional culture is one of these elements. Although organizational culture is different from institutional climate in that culture is more deeply embedded and more difficult to change, Chesler and Crowfoot's description of how institutional culture is manifested should be helpful in our understanding of how climate affects perceptions. *Culture* is manifested in various ways in an organization including the presence of dominant belief systems reflected in values, rituals, technology, styles, and customs; norms for "proper" behavior and criteria for success; a degree of monoculturalism or pluralism of the approved culture; standards for the allocation of rewards and sanctions; and "rules of the game." Further, institutional racism is manifested in these aspects of culture through rituals and technology (graduation ceremonies, athletic mascots, pedagogy, etc.) that reflect White and Eurocentric dominance/exclusivity; monocultural norms for success being promulgated; a reluctance to explicitly recognize or promote alternative cultures; the view that diversity and excellence are seen as competitive/ contradictory/played off; a lack of explicit rewards for antiracist behavior by the faculty and staff; and a stance toward "racial incidents" that is reactive.

I believe these examples of institutional racism also can be adapted to reflect examples of sexism. Specifically, in sexist institutions, rituals and technology reflect male dominance/ exclusivity, and male norms for success are promulgated. Likewise, there are no explicit rewards for antisexist behavior of faculty and staff, and the institutional stance toward sexist behavior is reactive.

Feminists share the Chesler and Crowfoot's (1989/2000) belief that one group is advantaged over another through consequences of organizational structure, policy, or practice. To improve the organizational culture and, thus, the climate for women, specific actions that liberal feminists have sought and still seek include "equal pay for equal work, equal access to high-level positions, affirmative action in hiring, establishment and enforcement of sexual harassment policies, provision of child care facilities, establishment and use of a gender-inclusive language policy, and establishment of paid maternity and other family leave policies" (Townsend & Twombly, 1998, p. 79). Those interested in overcoming racism would clearly endorse some of these actions such as equal pay for equal work, equal access to high-level positions, and affirmative action in hiring. Both women and minorities would also likely view a positive organizational climate as one where the organizational structure, policies, and practices are overtly antiracist and antisexist. In such a climate there would be no denials that racism and sexism, including sexual harassment, exist; no backlash against affirmative action; no marginalization of multicultural and women's studies; and no research that blames women and minorities for not succeeding because they haven't adapted to the norms (White and patriarchal) of the academy.

CHANGES IN DISCOURSES ABOUT MINORITIES AND WOMEN

This last point about not blaming women and minorities for their failure to succeed is related to patterns of discourse about minorities and women. Sarah Theule Lubienski (2003) has recently conducted a study of changes in the discourse about cultural diversity. According to Lubienski, in the 1960s and into the 1970s, as well as fairly recently in Herrnstein and Murray's (1994) *The Bell Curve*, authors have emphasized the struggles of marginalized groups and typically framed these struggles as being the results of deficiencies in the group's culture. This is known as the "cultural deficit" model. For example, Daniel Moynihan's (1965) report about African-American families stressed such things as the prevalence of narcotics use, school dropout, crime, out-of-wedlock birth, and other negative aspects stereotypically attributed to this demographic group.

Beginning in the 1970s and 1980s, researchers began to focus on institutions rather than individuals. They began to examine schools' responsibilities in perpetuating the inequities present in capitalist societies (Lubienski, 2003). Thus, we have Bowles and Gintis' (1976) classic work, *Schooling in Capitalist America*, which examined how schools are predicated on a capitalistic culture and work to reproduce social class inequities through their curriculum and other practices. Likewise, Bourdieu's (1973) work on cultural reproduction led the way in demonstrating how schools, through their emphasis on upper-class and middle-class language, reproduce and legitimate class structure. In other words, this approach to diversity no longer views students from particular cultures as culturally deficient. Rather, it considers that their cultures are misaligned with the culture of schools. The cultures are simply different. Hence, this approach is the "cultural difference model."

What might be a solution to the differences in school culture and the cultures of non-Anglos? Educators need to bridge the gap between students' cultures and schools' cultures through reframing students' deficiencies as strengths (Lubienski, 2003). More specifically, faculty should utilize pedagogies and curricula that better match the preferred learning styles and cultural backgrounds of traditionally underserved students (Lubienski, 2003; Aragon, 2000). A limitation of this approach is that it "essentializes" groups, generalizing that all members of the group share the same essential characteristics and practices (Lubienski, 2003). Additionally, case studies of successful teachers and students are popular. A related approach is the celebration of diversity to emphasize the positive aspects of having a diverse student body. Approaches that concentrate on the positive aspects of diversity, as well as inspirational case studies, are heartwarming and motivating. However, Lubienski cautions that they may serve to divert attention from the larger structural problems that underlie inequitable school outcomes and processes. Problems that include the growing divide between the poor and the rich in our country and unequal power relations between groups based on race, class, and gender.

In reflecting upon how cultural diversity has been—and is currently—represented, one can see some parallels in the discourse about women, as represented by phases in the incorporation of feminist thought into disciplinary curricula. Mary Kay Tetreault (1985) has developed a theory about this incorporation and calls it "feminist phase theory." According to her, there are five stages or phases in the representation of women in curricula. The initial stage or phase is the *male* one, in which women are not even represented in the curriculum. Perhaps an equivalent phase for people from non-White backgrounds was their exclusion from any curricular representation.

The next phase in feminist phase theory is the "compensatory" one, in which exceptional women are presented and their achievements described. The phase seems similar to the current emphasis on case studies of academically successful students who come from non-White, economically disadvantaged backgrounds and of the teachers who help them succeed. Their exceptional achievements are celebrated but with the potential risk of raising the bar far too high for the average student or teacher or, in feminist phase theory, the average woman (Tetreault, 1985).

The third phase is the "bifocal" phase in which both women and men appear in the curriculum, but women are often presented as people with problems. They do not receive equal pay for equal work, they do not have equal opportunities for positions, they are sexually harassed, etc. By being presented as people with problems, they may become viewed as problematic and, therefore, to be avoided. This phase is perhaps equivalent to the cultural deficit model in viewing groups other than the White, middle-and upper-classes as culturally deficit (Tetreault, 1985). For example, Olsen, Maple, and Stage (1995) believe that a tendency persists in ascribing traits, behaviors, and attitudes to minorities and women that make them deficient or inappropriate as managers—whether it is an irrational fear of success or an enervating conflict between work and family/community life.

Part of the bifocal phase is an indictment of socioeconomic and political structures that have contributed to, or are the reasons for, women's problems. Concentration on these structural issues for women is similar to the emphasis on social and cultural reproduction of inequalities for diverse populations. Beyond the bifocal approach is the "feminist" approach in which women are valued in and of themselves and are not viewed as deviations from the male norm. In other words, they are no longer viewed as deficient because they are not men. Women are simply viewed as different and celebrated in their own right. This phase has similarities to the cultural difference model reviewed earlier (Tetreault, 1985).

The last phase in feminist phase theory is the "multifocal" phase in which human experience is treated holistically with femaleness and maleness viewed as "humanness." Men and women are studied on their own terms without differences being judged as deficiencies. This phase has rarely been achieved (Tetreault, 1985). For this phase, I am not sure there is an equivalent in the perspectives about cultural diversity.

EXAMINING CULTURAL ASSUMPTIONS ABOUT WOMEN AND MINORITIES

These views show how conversations about women and minorities have changed—and are changing—to emphasize differences rather than deficiencies. They can provide us with a useful lens through which to examine our own and others' assumptions about women and minorities. Assumptions are a key part of an organization's culture. According to Schoen (2000), any change to climate is possible only to the degree that a desired new climate is congruent with the underlying assumptions of the dominant culture. For example, in a culture based on competitiveness and individualism that has a control and reward system that values and encourages individual competitiveness, a new climate of cooperation and teamwork would be difficult, if not impossible, to create. Thus, it would be hard to have a receptive or positive organizational climate for minorities and women if this climate would violate tacit assumptions about these groups. In other words, we must be very aware of how tacit cultural assumptions affect our ability and willingness to change organizational climate.

What are some possible tacit assumptions about minorities and women? To what extent do these assumptions draw from the deficit model of viewing them (they are deficient because they are not white men)? To what extent do they draw from the cultural difference model (they are different from white men)? When we think about community college students, do we assume that when students of color do poorly in classes it is because they are inferior academically/intellectually to white students? Do we assume that minority students will perform less well than majority students? Likewise, do we assume that women aren't good in math and science and, therefore, should be advised into female-linked careers such as nursing, education, and social work? Lastly, do we assume that certain areas/disciplines will be weakened when more female students are enrolled in them?

Further, when we think about community college faculty and staff, do we assume that women faculty will be more nurturing of students than will men faculty? Do we also assume that minority faculty will be more effective than White faculty with minority students because minority faculty can relate better to minority students? Finally, do we assume that women faculty and staff need less pay because they are married and their salary is the extra one in the family?

Additionally, when we think about those who lead the community college administratively, do we assume that women can't be as effective leaders as men because women won't have the time to devote to the job because of their family commitments? Do we assume that when a woman president makes a bad decision that she did so because she is a woman and didn't know any better; i.e., she wasn't smart enough to make the right or good decision, or is incompetent because of her gender? Do we assume that when an African-American (or Hispanic or Native American) president makes a bad decision that it happened because he or she didn't know any better, or is incompetent because of her/his race/ethnicity?

Although speaking just about faculty, the thoughts of Olsen et al. (1995) concerning assumptions would seem to hold true for assumptions about students and leaders as well. They believe that cultural assumptions concerning how minority and women faculty function—and wish to function—may be just as damaging to their development and professional growth within the workplace as is the presence of institutional insensitivity and outright discrimination. Holding tacit negative assumptions about women and minorities, as administrative leaders, as faculty, and as students, is not conducive to a positive organizational climate for them.

CONCLUSION

My overall point is that the organizational climate for women and minorities will not improve until we embody in our own discourse, including its tacit assumptions, the perspective that women and minorities are not deficit because they do not fit the norms of White middle- and upper-class males. When we overtly move to discourse that claims minorities and women are different then White males, we must be careful that these differences are still not viewed as deficiencies.

With any new discourse and new assumptions, some of the standard structural characteristics that epitomize a positive climate (e.g., equal pay for equal work, equal opportunity for advancement) are more likely to occur. Some of the less traditional characteristics such as no or limited backlash against affirmative action and support of multicultural studies and feminist studies will take longer to occur. However, they can be achieved if institutional leaders will commit to several practices. First of all, institutional leaders must actively and overtly move to ensure that nondiscriminatory hiring practices and nondiscriminatory determination of salaries occur. Next, leaders must examine their own cultural assumptions about minorities and women in order to ensure that their speech and their writings do not reflect assumptions that minorities and women are deficient because they are not White males. Also, leaders should reflect upon organizational practices such as the unstated "rules of the game" for success within the institution to determine whether or not they are gender and/or racially biased. If the institution has a strong organizational culture of trust and openness of members toward one another, leaders should consider having study groups and workshops among faculty and staff to provide an opportunity for reflection about their discourse and institutional practices. Such conversations can be difficult and require careful planning and expert facilitation; but they can be an important means for improving the organizational climate for minorities and women. The community college, with the most diverse student body, faculty, and presidential leadership, has the opportunity to lead the rest of higher education in providing a positive organizational climate for minorities and women.

REFERENCES

Amey, M. J. & VanDerLinden, K. E. (2002). *Career paths for community college leaders. AACC Research Brief Leadership Series No. 2.* Washington, DC: AACC.

Aragon, S. R. (Ed.). (2000). *New Directions for Community Colleges: Beyond access: Methods and models for increasing retention and learning among minority students*, vol. 112.

Bourdieu, P. (1973). Cultural reproduction and social reproduction. In R. Brown (Ed.), *Knowledge, education, and cultural change* (pp. 71–112). London: Tavistock.

Bowles, S. & Gintis, H. (1976). *Schooling in capitalist America.* New York: Basic Books.

Chesler, M. A. & Crowfoot, J. (1989/2000). Racism in higher education: An organizational analysis. Reprinted in C. Brown (Ed.), *ASHE Reader on Organization and Governance in Higher Education* (pp. 436–469). Boston, MA: Pearson Custom Publishing.

Chliwniak, L. & Bernhardt, G. R. (1999). The gender gap in higher education: How it affects women and men students. *Michigan Community College Journal, 5*(1), 9–36.

Chronicle of Higher Education Almanac. (2003, August 29). Characteristics of college presidents—2001, p. 22.

Dyer, S. (2004, January 5). Board calls for more minorities at La. college. *Community College Week*, p. 3.

Fogg, P. (2003, April 18). The gap that won't go away. *Chronicle of Higher Education*, A12–14.

Hagedorn, L. S. & Laden, B. V. (2002). Exploring the climate for women as community college faculty. In C. Outcalt (Ed.), *New Directions for Community Colleges: Community college faculty: Characteristics, practices, and challenges*, 118, 69–78.

Herrnstein, R. J. & Murray, C. (1994). *The bell curve: Intelligence and class structure in American life*. New York: The Free Press.

Kanter, R. M. (1977). *Men and women of the corporation*. New York, NY: Basic Books.

Lubienski, S. T. (2003, November). Celebrating diversity and denying disparities: A critical assessment. *Educational Researcher*, *32*(8), 30–38.

Moynihan, D. (1965). *The Negro family: The case for national action*. Washington, DC: Office of Policy Planning and Research, U.S. Department of Labor.

Olsen, D., Maple, S. A., & Stage, F. K. (1995). Women and minority faculty job satisfaction: Professional role interests, professional satisfactions, and institutional fit. *Journal of Higher Education*, *66*(3), 267–293.

Perna, L. W. (2003). The status of women and minorities among community college faculty. *Research in Higher Education*, *44*(2), 205–240.

Peterson, M. W. & Spencer, M. G. (1990). Understanding academic culture and climate. In W. G. Tierney (Ed.), *New directions for institutional research: Assessing academic climates and cultures*, vol. 68. San Francisco: Jossey-Bass.

Phillippe, K. (2000). *National profile of community colleges: Trends & statistics*. 3rd ed., Washington, DC: American Association of Community Colleges.

Schoen, E. H. (2000). Commentary: Sense and nonsense about culture and climate. In N. M. Ashkanasy, C. P. M. Wilderom, & M. F. Peterson (Eds.), *Handbook of organizational culture and climate*. Thousand Oaks, CA: Sage Publications.

Shek, K. (2001, April 3). Transfer to 4-year colleges gets easier for minority students. *Community College Times*, XII(7), p. 1, 13.

Snyder, T. D. & Hoffman, C. M. (2003, June). Digest of education statistics 2002. Washington, DC: U.S. Department of Education National Center for Education Statistics.

Tetreault, M. K. (1985). Feminist phase theory: An experience-based evaluation model. *Journal of Higher Education*, *56*(4), 363–384.

Texas Higher Education Coordinating Board. (2002, June 17). *Strategic plan for Texas public community colleges 2003–2007*. Austin, TX: Author.

Texas Higher Education Coordinating Board. (n.d.). Position description and ideal candidate specification, Coordinator of Higher Education, Texas Higher Education Coordinating Board. Retrieved December 20, 2003, from http:// www.thecb.state.tx.us/cfbin/COMMISSIONER.pdf

Texas Higher Education Coordinating Board Community and Technical Colleges Division. (n.d.). *Texas public community and technical colleges 2002 statewide fact-book*. Austin, TX: Author. Retrieved January 10, 2004, from http://www.thecb. state.tx.us/reports/pdf/0505.pdf

The NEA 2003 Almanac of Higher Education. (2003). Washington, DC: NEA.

Townsend, B. K. & LaPaglia, N. (1995, April). Women community college faculty: How they perceive their status in academe and in the community college. Paper presented at annual meeting of AERA (American Educational Research Association), San Francisco, CA.

Townsend, B. K. & LaPaglia, N. (2000). The community college as a workplace for women faculty members. *Initiatives*, *59*(4). Note: This article was published in an on-line issue of the journal and the on-line address (http://www.nawe.org/ journal/59.4.htm) is no longer available.

Townsend, B. K. & Twombly, S. (1998). A feminist critique of organizational change in the community college. In J. Levin (Ed.), *New Directions for Community Colleges: Organizational change in the community college*, *102*, 77–86.

Utah Minorities Not Getting Enough College Prep. (2004, January 5). *Community College Week*, p. 15.

V

POLICY

Edward P. St. John, Section Editor

Higher education policy is an important subfield of study. Researchers seek to draw policy implications from their work; most students, faculty, and administrators feel the effects of policies that influence higher education; and most policymakers do not understand the complexities of higher education. Policy researchers can find themselves in the middle of many complicated discourses that intersect with law, economics, finance, science, and other fields of study. The five chapters in this section address different topics and take different stances. Yet, in combination, they provide a good overview. Given the range of topics, it may be hard at first glance to figure out what holds the topic of higher education policy together. I suggest you keep four issues in mind as you read, reflect on, and discuss these chapters: (1) The levels of government policymaking that influence higher education; (2) the role of the courts; (3) the rationales used in policy research and policy formulation; and (4) the unintended consequences of policy decisions.

LEVELS OF GOVERNMENT

In the United States there are three levels of government with interrelated policies: federal, state, and local. Education was left out of the U.S. Constitution and, as a consequence, primary authority for education was left to states in which schools and colleges had formed before independence. In both K-12 and higher education, there is a history of local school districts with corporate-style boards (this is especially true for community and technical colleges). Many states mandated education through eighth grade in the late 1800s and gave states direct authority.

There have been many debates about the roles and authority of state agencies and public institutions, especially research universities. In Chapter 21, Frank A. Schmidtlein and Robert O. Berdahl revisit this debate. Two authors with extensive experience in policymaking and research on policy explore the dilemmas of institutional autonomy in a decentralized system of higher education that faces increased calls for public accountability. While their stance is clearly pro-autonomy for universities, they recognize the state's roles in accountability. More recently, the federal government has taken a more assertive role in promoting accountability in higher education, as outlined in the report *A Test of Leadership: Changing the Future of U. S. Higher Education* by the Spellings Commission (U.S. Department of Education, 2006). Issues related to accountability and autonomy remain very current and unresolved, in spite of their long history.

Even though the federal government does not have primary authority over education, it has established a major role over time. The federal government sponsored some education programs before the 1960s, but federal laws passed as part of the *Great Society Period*—specifically, the Elementary and Secondary Education Act (ESEA) and the Higher Education Act (HEA)—created programs that continue to influence education policy in the states. In particular, the HEA, as amended over time, has had a substantial influence on developing student aid programs. The newest wave of federal policies have shifted the emphasis from grants to loans as the primary form of federal student aid; at the same time, states have reduced funding, causing tuition to rise (St. John, 2006).

Other chapters in this section address the formation and consequence of federal policies. In Chapter 22, Michael D. Parsons raises questions about whether there is any underlying rationale or agreement in the policy process, especially at the federal level. In Chapter 23, Ruth Zimmer Hendrick, William H. Hightower, and Dennis E. Gregory examine how the combination of state and federal policies influence tuition charges, the decline of student aid, and the difficulty of maintaining the commitment to open access in community colleges. In contrast, Clifton F. Conrad and David J. Weerts focus in Chapter 24 on the way federal implementation of desegregation policies influence states and institutions.

These chapters illustrate that the multi-tiered government system with shared responsibility for funding and regulation creates complexity for the governance of colleges and universities. While it might be preferable to some administrators in colleges and universities to plan for enrollment, curriculum, and other topics in relation to internal strategy factors, these chapters reveal a reality: planning, management, and other governing practices within colleges and universities must consider state and federal policy. With the overlapping responsibilities of state and federal governments, it is important to understand how the levels of public policy actually work, how they are divided, and how they influence practice within community colleges and four-year institutions.

THE ROLE OF THE COURTS

As readers may know from observing presidential elections, appointments to the U.S. Supreme Court are major, and the Court's role in education has been a politically contested topic. The Supreme Court's decision in *Brown v. Board of Education* (1954) set the stage for decades of litigation over desegregation, and the decision itself has remained a target of criticism for right-wingers who favor the state's rights. The *Great Society Programs* of the 1960s in both K-12 and higher education emphasized promoting equal opportunity, a national goal that emerged out of debates about equal education after *Brown*. The *Brown* decision did not directly apply to higher education. Only one state, West Virginia, responded to the decision by ceasing to maintain segregated colleges. Separated from Virginia because of its loyalty to the Union during the Civil War, West Virginia was the only border state to respond to *Brown*. Other border states with Historically Black Colleges and Universities (HBCUs)—such as Missouri, Ohio, Pennsylvania, and Maryland—did not respond, nor did the southern states. It was only after the Supreme Court's *Adams v. Richardson* decision (1973) that the federal government began requiring states to develop plans for desegregation and the strengthening of HBCUs.

In Chapter 24, Conrad and Weerts examine the evolution of the federal role in desegregation. This chapter addresses the legal remedies to segregation of higher education, a process that involves the federal government in monitoring plans accepted by the courts to remedy vestiges of de jure segregation in the dual systems of predominantly White institutions and HBCUs in the South. They explain how the federal government shifted after the Supreme Court's *United States v. Fordice* decision (1992), which shifted the federal role from encouraging states to equally fund HBCUs to rationalizing funding for new programs based on their ability to desegregate these colleges. The states of Mississippi and Alabama had cases decided by federal courts requiring them to develop programs and funding models for HBCUs that would attract Whites. Conrad was a witness for the federal government in most of the desegregation cases, so he tells the history from an insider's viewpoint.

In Chapter 25, Michele S. Moses also addresses higher education issues involving the courts. This chapter addresses the past, present, and future of affirmative action, a process of adjusting admissions practices to overcome historical inequalities. The Supreme Court has weighed in on affirmative action in *Bakke* (1978), *Gratz* (2003), and *Grutter* (2003). These decisions all confirmed the use of affirmative action, but held that colleges and universities could not set quotas or assign points for race. The latter two decisions set a time limit on the use of affirmative action. Moses has been an eloquent analyst examining the policy consequences of court decisions and state bans on affirmative action. While at first glance policy debates about desegregation and affirmative action might seem distant from the daily operation of colleges and universities, these and other court decisions have substantial influence on rules and regulations governing campus practices.

USES OF RATIONALES IN POLICY

There is a long history of research focusing on the rationales used in policy sciences. After World War II, systems approaches worked their way into public policy. For example, it has often been argued that program planning and budgeting provided the framework for the introduction of the HEA and ESEA, which firmly established the federal role in education. In recent decades there has been a shift in research (St. John, 2003; St. John & Parsons, 2004). In the 1960s, research by economists had a substantial influence on the formation of need-based aid programs, especially the 1978 reauthorization of HEA which created the Pell Grant program (as Basic Educational Opportunity Grants). However, these decisions were political even though research was used in policy arguments, a process of rationale building. Rationale building now plays a major role in policy. For example, Conrad had a program rationale in his arguments about funding HBCUs, a logic he adapted when the federal role shifted from building the capacity of these vital institutions to using programs to attract White students. Moses also demonstrates the artistry of rationale building in Chapter 25 on affirmative action. In litigation, researchers align with interest groups on both sides of issues, testifying for and analyzing positions using political arguments or ideologies.

In addition to the art of using logic to rationalize policies, researchers, policymakers, and lobbyists are part of a larger process as major ideologies shape policy. In the 1960s, the old liberal ideology dominated. Even in the 1970s, Richard Nixon, a conservative, created the Federal Pell Grant program, the largest federal grant program to date. After the introduction of Pell, there was a brief period of near equitable college enrollment rates for Hispanics, African Americans, and Whites (St. John, 2003), but substantial gaps emerged after the Middle Income Student Assistance Act (1978), which reauthorized the HEA's student aid programs to remove income caps. With the shift of need-based aid dollars to middle-income students, there were relatively fewer dollars for low-income students as costs increased; inequalities reemerged.

UNINTENDED CONSEQUENCES OF POLICY DECISIONS

In the current context of higher education policy there are serious challenges facing policymakers and administrators due to the unintended consequences of policies. One challenge is the economy, which increases the difficulty of adhering to historic practices in college finance. For example, Zimmer Hendrick and colleagues illustrate in their chapter how contradictory policies can be for institutions like community colleges that seek to maintain their historic missions. This chapter raises crucial questions about the unintended effects of declining state support for public colleges, the implementation of performance funding, and other neoliberal education policies. Specifically, the authors document the challenges facing community colleges that attempt to maintain a commitment to open admissions. In particular, they discuss how performance funding can undermine efforts to keep courses open to students who want to take one or two classes to attain a skill for the workforce because of the pressure on colleges and universities to graduate high percentages of students.

CONCLUSION

Higher education is an interesting and complex field, and public policy plays a critical role in the discourse. How you frame policy issues—your views on race, gender, inequality, privatization, and taxation—will influence how you interpret the chapters in this section, just as the political views of the authors shaped their analyses. People who make new discoveries have points of view. If they did not, they would not have much to say, especially about public policy. Thus, the art of reading and interpreting policy research involves discerning the interpretive positions. Does an author hold on to old functionalist reasoning, which is closely aligned with liberalism and the old liberal stance on education policy? Do authors make new arguments for resistance to policies because they think they are unfair? In the 1960s, conservative intellectuals (e.g., Daniel Bell, 1966) began to critique the inherent liberal positions. By the 1990s, a new conservative logic had come to dominate the policy literature with arguments about accountability and the new science of education. When you begin to read policy through a critical lens, it will be easier to discern the embedded logic, the rationalizing of research through political views.

When conducting research on higher education policy, it is important to have a perspective on the role research plays in supporting rationales for public funding and the difficulty of bringing high-quality research into certain discourses. Even the National Center for Education Statistics has made serious statistical errors in reports crafted to promote their agendas (Becker, 2004; Heller, 2004; St. John, 2003). Therefore, those who seek careers involving policy research or policy advocacy need to be well versed in theory and methods pertaining to their policy interests. The five chapters in this section are examples of exemplary policy-focused scholarship.

REFERENCES

Adams v. Richardson Civ. A. No. 3095–70, U.S. Dist., 356 F. Su92 (February 16, 1973).

Bakke vs. Board of Regents. 438 US 265 (1978).

Becker, W. E. (2004). Omitted variables and sample selection in studies of college-going decisions. In E. P. St. John (Ed.), *Public Policy and College Access: Investigating the Federal and State Roles in Equalizing Postsecondary Opportunity, Readings on Equal Education Vol. 19* (pp. 65–86). New York: AMS Press.

Bell, D. (1966). *The Reforming of General Education: The Columbia College Experience in its National Setting.* New York: Columbia University Press.

Brown v. Board of Education, 347 U.S. 483 (1954).

Gratz v. Bollinger, 539 U.S. 244 (2003).

Grutter v. Bollinger, 539 U.S. 306 (2003).

Heller, D. E. (2004). NCES research on college participation: A critical analysis. In E. P. St. John (Ed.), *Public Policy and College Access: Investigating the Federal and State Roles in Equalizing Postsecondary Opportunity, Readings on Equal Education Vol. 19* (pp. 29–64). New York: AMS Press.

St. John, E. P. (2003). *Refinancing the College Dream: Access, Equal Opportunity, and Justice for Taxpayers.* Baltimore, Maryland: Johns Hopkins University Press.

St. John, E. P. (2006). *Education and the Public Interest: School Reform, Public Finance, and Access to Higher Education.* Dordrecht, The Netherlands: Springer.

St. John, E. P., & Parsons, M. D. (2004). Introduction. In E. P. St. John & M D. Parsons (Eds.), *Public Funding for Higher Education: Changing Contexts and New Rationales* (pp. 1–16). Baltimore, Maryland: Johns Hopkins University Press.

United States v. Fordice, 505 U.S. 717 (1992).

U.S. Department of Education. (2006). *A Test of Leadership: Charting the Future of U.S. Higher Education*: A report of the commission appointed by Secretary of Education Margaret Spellings. Washington, DC: U.S. Department of Education.

21

Autonomy and Accountability

Who Controls Academe?

Frank A. Schmidtlein and Robert O. Berdahl

If a college or university is effectively to define its purposes and select or invent the means of attaining them, it must have a high degree of autonomy. Howard Bowen observed that the "production process" in higher education is far more intricate and complicated than that in any industrial enterprise.[1] Turning resources into human values defies standardization. Students vary enormously in academic aptitude, in interests, in intellectual dispositions, in social and cultural characteristics, in educational and vocational objectives, and in many other ways. Furthermore, the disciplines and professions with which institutions of higher learning are concerned require diverse methods of investigation, intellectual structures, means of relating methods of inquiry and ideas to personal and social values, and processes of relating knowledge to human experience. Learning, consequently, is a subtle process, the nature of which may vary from student to student, from institution to institution, from discipline to discipline, from one scholar or teacher to another, and from one level of student development to another. The intricacy and unpredictability of both learning and investigation require a high degree of freedom from intellectually limiting external intervention and control if an institution of higher education is to perform effectively.

These characteristics of colleges and universities have led Etzioni[2] to make a distinction between "administrative" and "professional" authority. This distinction has important implications for the tensions between the concepts of autonomy and accountability in higher education. Unfortunately, this distinction commonly is not understood nor, perhaps, appreciated by public officials who are more familiar with the "administrative" concept of organizational coordination and control and who believe that direct bureaucratic intervention can, or should be able to, effectively alter academic practices in institutions. Etzioni contrasts decision-making authority in organizations whose workforce is primarily composed of professionals with those where the primary workforces possess less complex skills: "Administration assumes a power hierarchy. Without a clear ordering of higher and lower in rank, in which the higher in rank have more power than the lower ones and hence can control and coordinate the latter's activities, the basic principle of administration is violated; the organization ceases to be a coordinated tool. However, knowledge is largely an individual property; unlike other organization means, it cannot be transferred from one person to another by decree. Creativity is basically individual and can only to a very limited degree be ordered and coordinated by the superior in rank." He then concludes that, in organizations made up of professionals, "the surgeon has to decide whether or not to operate. Students of the professions have pointed out that the autonomy granted to professionals who are basically responsible to their consciences (though they may be censured by their peers and in extreme cases by the courts) is necessary for effective professional work. . . . It is this highly individualized principle which is diametrically opposed to the very essence of the organizational principle of control and coordination by superiors—i.e., the principle of administrative authority."

AUTONOMY AND ACADEMIC FREEDOM

On first thought, one might identify academic freedom with autonomy. Certainly, a high degree of intellectual independence is necessary for faculty and students in choosing the subjects of study and investigation, in searching for the truth without unreasonable or arbitrary restrictions, and in expressing scholarly conclusions without censorship. Some forms of external control or even subtle efforts to influence teaching, learning, or research may endanger intellectual freedom. However, academic freedom and university autonomy, though related, are not synonymous. Academic freedom as a concept is universal and absolute, whereas autonomy is of necessity parochial and relative.

Presumably, state boards of higher education designating the missions of sectors or particular institutions after appropriate studies and consultation would not be an unwarranted invasion of autonomy. But specifying the content of academic programs, academic organization, curriculum, and methods of teaching for the attainment of designated missions is likely to be considered unjustified intervention. A coordinating or governing board might phase out a doctoral program at a particular campus (after appropriate study and consultation) without unwarranted invasion of institutional autonomy or violation of academic freedom. The federal government might impose antidiscrimination procedures in admitting students or in appointing and promoting faculty members without interfering unjustifiably in academic affairs, provided the means do not make unreasonable demands on the institutions or violate necessary confidentiality of records. If appropriate safeguards are followed, no invasion of academic freedom need be suffered.

Requirements for accountability may impose onerous procedures on an institution, but even these restraints may not endanger academic freedom. Whether restrictions on DNA research put an undesirable limit on choice of problems for investigation remains a controversial issue. In this case, public protection may justify some interventions that seem to infringe on academic freedom. One may agree that the absence of external controls does not guarantee academic freedom and that certain elements of external control do not endanger intellectual independence, but an institution's right to mobilize its intellectual resources—and within reasonable limits, even its financial resources—toward the attainment of its agreed-upon purposes is at least strongly fortified by a relatively high degree of autonomy.[3]

THE NATURE OF ACCOUNTABILITY

Zumeta,[4] in an excellent review of accountability in higher education, notes that institutions historically were viewed "as necessarily freewheeling and unconstrained." He quotes Trow, saying they "were treated with unusual deference by their state sponsors, who were often content to 'leave the money on the stump' with few questions asked." Today, however, Zumeta observes that colleges and universities face unprecedented external demands and "this shift in states' expectations and relations with colleges and universities is significant not only for academe's own interests but . . . for important societal values."

Growing external demands on institutions have produced conflicting concepts of how to maintain institutional accountability. Some states have reduced some substantive and procedural controls on institutions, usually to encourage market forces that are expected to promote consumer interests and innovation, while some have strengthened administrative controls. In some cases, states have reduced financial, personnel, procurement, and other procedural controls while imposing less direct substantive and procedural controls by mandating accountability, quality assessment, and performance budgeting processes. There is a vigorous debate over what mix of market incentives and administrative controls are appropriate and effective to assure that institutions meet their public responsibilities. Both administrative controls and marketplace pressures can restrict institutions' autonomy, but they generally prefer accommodating the more diverse pressures of the marketplace over the centralized imposition of administrative controls. A delicate balance is required between an unregulated marketplace and expensive and stultifying government-imposed administrative controls.

Shulock[5] observes that "the meaning of accountability has evolved as new models of public management have emerged in the last 15 years. The older view emphasizes accountability for sound fiscal management and following rules. The newer view emphasizes outcomes and argues that public managers should be given flexibility to produce the desired outcomes with minimal oversight of how funds were allocated or what methods were used—a kind of oversight viewed as micromanagement." She also points out that accountability and assessment of student learning are not the same: "State-level accountability is about the effectiveness of our institutions and public policies, *collectively*, in meeting the educational needs of the citizens of the state; it is not about assessing the effectiveness of each institution or providing consumer information to support the private choices of citizens" (emphasis in original).

Financial austerity causes legislatures, state coordinating boards, and even consolidated governing boards to look more critically at institutional roles, at the availability and distribution of functions and programs, at effectiveness, and at educational and operational costs. As the federal government extends support for higher education, it prohibits discrimination in the admission of students and in the appointment and promotion of faculty members. The public at large has become more conscious of its institutions of higher education. States and localities are more demanding of education and service, more critical of what they perceive institutions to be doing, and more vocal in expressing their criticisms and desires. Public institutions, always answerable to the general interest, can no longer avoid defending what they do or do not do. They increasingly have to explain themselves, defend their essential character, and demonstrate that their service is worth the cost. They will become increasingly answerable (i.e., accountable) to numerous constituencies for the range of their services and the effectiveness of their performance.

Accountability is not confined to an institution's external relationships. Internally, a college or university is a complex of mutual responsibilities and reciprocal pressures for accountability with a wide variety of ongoing and periodic performance assessments. As Etzioni[6] pointed out, professionals have a primary accountability to their peers for the quality and integrity of their efforts. These include not only the peers at their institutions but also those in their disciplines and professional fields nationally and, increasingly, internationally. External accountability to peers is accomplished largely through processes such as accreditation, peer review of manuscripts for publication, and peer review of research proposals. Important as these bases of accountability are, this chapter is devoted to a discussion of accountability to external agencies.

In this environment of increasing demands for accountability, intellectual freedom in colleges and universities generally has maintained widespread public and governmental support, although occasionally governmental officials attempt to sanction academics who express unpopular views or criticize government policies. Also some institutions have abolished tenure, thus potentially inhibiting faculty expression of unpopular views.

ACCOUNTABILITY TO THE PUBLIC

Ultimately, public institutions of higher education are broadly answerable to the people who support them. After California voters earlier failed to approve a state bond issue providing large sums for the construction of medical school facilities and gave other evidences of disaffection, the then president of the University of California recognized the ultimate public accountability of the university: "Make no mistake," he said to the Assembly of the Academic Senate, "the university is a public institution, supported by the people through the actions of their elected representatives and executives. They will not allow it to be operated in ways which are excessively at variance with the general public will. By various pressures and devices, the university will be forced to yield and to conform if it gets too far away from what the public expects and wants."[7]

At one time, the people were relatively remote from their public institutions, but citizens now find their future economic, social, and cultural lives increasingly influenced, in some cases virtually determined, by their colleges and universities. Consequently, public institutions have had to become responsive to a wider range of economic interests and to a more diverse pattern of ethnic and cultural backgrounds and aspirations. Minority groups are pressing for financial assistance, for remedial programs when necessary for admission or attainment of academic standards, and for academic programs that will meet their interests and perceived needs. As special interest groups have pressed the university to provide the services they believe they need, students have organized to promote their interests. With the prospect of declining enrollments in the 1980s, many colleges and universities responded to that student market by establishing new vocational and professional programs of study, and most institutions are struggling to redistribute faculty, equipment, and resources as students shift from liberal arts courses to vocational and professional curricula.

Serving the public interest is a complicated process; not all institutions will undertake the same missions or serve common purposes. Accountability is further complicated by a question of what special interests should be served and what should be put aside.

The interests to be served by an institution are determined through both external and internal political processes resulting in complex compromises and the accommodation of many, often conflicting, objectives. As a consequence, accountability, which implies agreed upon purposes and objectives, has significant political as well as technical dimensions. Many attempts to institute accountability processes have failed because they were based on an inaccurate assumption that substantial agreement was possible on a stable set of measurable institutional goals and objectives. The directions institutions take result from a constantly evolving complex set of compromises among a variety of contending internal and external interests and from the accommodation of resource and time constraints.

Conflicts over the appropriate locations for making various kinds of decisions have occurred since tribal times. They typically involve balancing collective and private interests. Schmidtlein describes a number of factors that influence where decisions are located. He observes that persons at various locations in governance structures have ready access to differing kinds of information. Those in state government are in a better position to observe the relationships among colleges and universities and typically have a more holistic sense of public sentiment. Consequently, they are likely to be more sensitive than institutions to the appropriateness of the entire pattern of institutions and their missions, the relationships among institutions, and priorities across the entire state system of higher education.

In contrast, those located in institutions possess more information about local circumstances and the trade-offs involved in making decisions affecting local issues. When decisions involve internal institutional issues, central officials are likely to have oversimplified views of the factors involved and make inappropriate decisions. Many highly relevant kinds of information are hard to quantify and communicate effectively to those in government and difficult for them to evaluate. Consequently, they are likely to delay decisions by requesting increasing numbers of costly reports and data to assure themselves that their decisions are correct because often they are aware of their relative ignorance of local complexities. Lacking intimate knowledge of local complexities, they also are more susceptible to simplistic solutions to issues, more likely to embrace management fads, and tend to focus more on information collection and decision-making processes than on the substance of the decisions.

In practice, higher education's systems need to achieve a balance between the benefits and costs of central and local decision making. Government oversight and steering are needed to assure, for example, that a set of institutions exist whose missions serve the diverse needs of the public and to counter occasional attempts of two-year colleges to become four-year institutions and four-year teaching institutions to become graduate/research universities.[8] Changes in institutional missions should serve the public interest; not be based primarily on institutional ambitions to move up the prestige ladder. Government oversight also is needed to assure that a diverse set of academic programs exists that meets the legitimate needs of the public while avoiding unnecessary duplication. Institutions, however, should have the freedom to design the content of their academic programs and courses and their research initiatives. They also should have the procedural freedom needed to pursue their programs in an efficient manner. As Berdahl notes[9] governments need to retain authority over substantive issues related to the character of higher education systems while institutions should be given a very large measure of freedom over procedural aspects of their programs. Unstructured competition reduces diversity and increases costs through program duplication, while excessive regulation restricts the ability of competent institutional leaders to take expeditious advantage of new opportunities and adjust to new circumstances. Government controls seldom remedy the errors of those lacking competence. Thus, accountability is both general (responding to definitions of the broad public interest) and particular (responding to more limited constituencies).

Later chapters in this book will elaborate on the tensions between autonomy and accountability in higher education for state governments, the federal government, and the courts. Here, we merely provide brief overviews.

GOVERNMENTAL INTERVENTION

The State Government

Accountability to the public is mediated by the operation of several governance layers between it and the institutions in question. Colleges and universities are answerable most immediately to their governing boards. Most public boards have statutory status: they were created by legislatures and are in nearly all respects under legislative control. Seven or eight states have given constitutional status to their public universities: "The idea was to remove questions of management, control, and the supervision of the universities from the reach of politicians in state legislatures and governors' offices. The universities were to be a fourth branch of government, functioning co-authoritatively with the legislature, the judiciary, and the executive."[10]

The purpose for creating universities' constitutional status was to give them a much greater degree of autonomy and self-direction than statutory status would provide. Their autonomy, however, has been materially eroded over the years. A study of statutory and constitutional boards in 1973 showed that the supposedly constitutionally autonomous university "is losing a good deal of its ability to exercise final judgment on the use not only of its state funds but also of those derived from other sources. It now undergoes intensive reviews of budgets and programs by several different state agencies, by special commissions, and by legislative committees, all of which look for ways to control."[11] Whether an institution has statutory or constitutional status, or even whether it is public or private, it is moving into the governmental orbit.

Most students of university governance believe that government officials should not serve on governing boards, since this identifies the institution too closely with political and governmental agencies. In California the governor, the lieutenant governor, the superintendent of public instruction, the president of the state board of agriculture, and the speaker of the legislative assembly are among the ex officio voting members of the board of regents of the University of California. Governors may also use their appointive power to attempt to influence governing boards, although most boards have staggered terms that prevent governors from appointing a majority of members until they have served several years in office.

However, sometimes governors can accomplish through other means what they lack the power to do through direct appointment of trustees or regents. For example, when Ronald Reagan was governor of California, he heartily disapproved of the way President Clark Kerr was handling the mid-1960s student uprisings. A minority of university regents agreed with Governor Reagan; to them he added a few appointments to seats that had fallen vacant. He still lacked a majority who agreed with him, however, until he emphatically noted that the university's budget did not have constitutional autonomy and that he would not look kindly at continued resistance to his point of view. Consequently, Clark Kerr, as he later commented, left the university as he had come to it, "fired with enthusiasm!" Enough additional regents had been intimidated by the governor's statements to swing opinions over to his side.

Although governors may thus influence institutions via their governing boards, they make their greatest impact "through the executive budget process."[12] The state finance or budget officer, who is ordinarily responsible to the governor, may also exercise an important element of authority by controlling shifts or changes in line-item budgets. Some state finance departments conduct preaudits of expenditures that not only pass on the legality of the use of itemized funds but also give the state officer the opportunity to rule on the substance or purpose of the expenditures.

But important as the executive officers of state government may be to public colleges and universities, state legislatures are more so. The institutions are dependent on the legislature's understanding of their broad missions and programs, its financial support, and its judgment of the institutions' educational effectiveness. Even a constitutionally autonomous public university is ultimately accountable to the legislature for the ways in which it uses its state-appropriated funds and for the effectiveness of its educational services. Legislators have become increasingly restless in the face of what some regard as the continuing neglect of undergraduate teaching and the overemphasis on research at graduate/research universities. Studies of faculty workload are common, with some legislatures considering mandated faculty teaching loads. At times the long arms of state finance officers have reached into academic affairs by conducting program audits or even program evaluations.[13]

> Issues raised in program evaluation include the consistency of the program with the assigned institutional role and function; the adequacy of planning in regard to the objectives, program structure, processes, implementation, and evaluation of outcomes; the adherence of program operation to the objectives, structural features, processes, sequence, and outcome appraisal originally specified or

the presentation of a sound rationale for any deviations from the original prescription; an evaluation of planning and operation and use of feedback for alteration and improvement; and provision for cost benefit analyses.[14]

State governments determine eligibility for state aid to both public and private postsecondary institutions. Most states charter and license degree-granting institutions, but some observers believe that in most instances the standards specified are insufficient to ensure quality. The Education Commission of the States has urged that the states establish minimum quality standards for all postsecondary institutions.

Student Assessment

States are seeking to hold institutions answerable for the attainment of their professed goals in the form of demonstrable changes in students. Historically, there appeared to be an implicit assumption that responsibility for learning outcomes should be placed primarily on students. However, over the past three or four decades, institutions increasingly have been viewed as having a major portion of this responsibility. Today, institutional demonstration of student learning outcomes is commonly viewed as part of their responsibility for public accountability and states are seeking evidence they are meeting this challenge. However, as noted earlier, Shulock asserts that demonstration of learning outcomes is *assessment* and is an internal institutional responsibility. Complex learning outcomes are extremely difficult to identify, to agree on and assign priorities, and to communicate to government officials and the public. This view may be simple in conception, but it is extremely difficult in implementation. First, it is essential to translate goals into relevant and agreed upon outcomes. An even more complicated task is to devise means of determining the extent to which students have attained these outcomes. The first question to be asked is, How has the student changed at a given point in relation to this characteristic at entrance? This requires information on how students vary at the starting point not only in previous academic achievement but also in general and special academic aptitude; information on students' intellectual dispositions, such as a theoretical or pragmatic orientation; and information on students' interests, attitudes, values, and motivations, to mention only some of the dimensions relevant to the educational process. These attributes establish baselines for estimating the amount of change over stated periods, and some are indicative of students' educability.

Studies of the influence of institutions on student development also require means of measuring or describing college characteristics, "the prevailing atmosphere, the social and intellectual climate, the style of a campus," as well as "educational treatments."[15] One of the complications involved in describing college environments is that student characteristics and institutional qualities are by no means unrelated. Furthermore, most institutions are not all of a piece and the total environment may have less influence on particular students than the suborganizations or subcultures of which they are members.

It is even more difficult to determine the impact of the environment on students. First, environmental variables probably do not act singly but in combination. Second, changes that occur in students may not be attributable to the effect of the college environment itself. Developmental processes established early in the individual's experience may continue through the college years; some of these processes take place normally within a wide range of environmental conditions, and in order to alter the course and extent of development, it would be necessary to introduce fairly great changes in environmental stimulation. Third, changes that occur during the college years may be less the effect of college experience as such than of the general social environment in which the college exists and the students live.[16]

For these and many other reasons it is extremely difficult to relate changes in behavior to specific characteristics of the college or to particular patterns of educational activity. Studies of change in students' characteristics reveal wide differences from person to person and detectable differences from institution to institution. Bowen summarizes the evidence on change in students in both cognitive and non-cognitive outcomes and also differences in the effects of different institutions: "On the whole, the evidence supports the hypothesis that the differences in impact are relatively small—when impact is defined as value added in the form of change in students during the college years."[17]

Given these complexities, the assessment of student learning outcomes and their implications for academic programs appear best accomplished within institutions by faculty who are the ones with detailed knowledge of the students and their academic progress and accomplishments. The appropriate role of state government and accrediting agencies should be to assure that institutions have appropriate policies and procedures for assessing student learning outcomes and to review the effectiveness of their academic programs.

Notwithstanding the complexity of the processes described above, a number of states have established policies seeking to assess student learning. But in most states, policy makers were persuaded to place the responsibility for developing the assessment program on each public institution, allowing each one to develop a program appropriate to its particular role and mission. Only by allowing for such diversity is it likely that any institution will gain a sense of ownership of the process and be encouraged to use the results for self-improvement.

The Federal Government

Autonomy/accountability issues of American higher education vis-à-vis the federal government primarily involve three major relevant federal policies areas: federal support for research, federal support for student aid, and federal interventions to support social justice. While later chapters in this volume will discuss both the federal policies and the role of the courts in much greater detail, here we present a brief overview of our perspectives on those key issues relating to autonomy and accountability. Issues in the research domain include the following:

- Are internal research priorities among major research universities unnaturally distorted by federal priorities?
- Does the peer review process for awarding federal research grants allow enough recognition to women and minority scientists at so-called second-level research institutions?
- Has the right balance been struck between the need for federal accounting requirements and the setting of indirect research costs and the need for research institutions to have both flexibility and sufficient research funds to cover their internal related costs?
- Are the costs and limitations of federal requirements for human subjects' protection and avoidance of fraud excessive?

Our response to the first research issue is not only to acknowledge that federal policies have obviously tilted research universities' priorities in ways that they might not have chosen, absent the federal funds, but also to point out that the bottom line has been to aid a small, but substantial, number of public and private research institutions to become world class, as noted by their international achievements. Thus, on balance, we regard this federal role as somewhat mixed but, overall, a very positive influence.

Similarly, on the criticisms of peer review as too elite oriented, while we welcome the broadening of most panels of peer review to reflect a greater diversity of institutions, we defend the basic principle of concentrating most of the federal research funds at a limited number of institutions and with a limited number of scientists widely recognized as constituting "the best." Obviously, the persons judging "the best" must be drawn from a fair cross section of qualified scientists.

The federal government's accounting requirements for institutions to justify their "overhead" costs are expensive, but they are designed to ensure that cost calculations are accurate and comparable across institutions. The federal government needs to work closely with institutions to minimize this burden, to avoid the impression of being driven by overzealous attempts primarily aimed at reducing federal costs, and to recognize and support the infrastructure costs associated with the research projects or programs.

The federal government has instituted extensive requirements to help ensure that researchers at colleges and universities do not engage in practices that harm research subjects and to reduce incidences of academic fraud. The principal issue is whether these requirements have become overly restrictive and so rigidly applied that they hamper legitimate research and add to its costs. There appears to be a tendency for the federal government to react strongly to individual cases of misconduct by imposing burdensome requirements on all receiving federal support. Reaching an appropriate balance between reducing misconduct through regulation, on the one hand, and the hampering of legitimate research practices and increasing the costs of research, on the other, is a difficult task that merits further attention.

Issues in the area of student aid policies relate to federal efforts to tighten up on student loan defaults, and more recent proposals from a few in Congress and in the U.S. Department of Education consider linking eligibility for federal funds to student attrition/graduation rates and even, possibly, to student grades and quality dimensions. Here we recognize that loan default rates have declined markedly in the face of reform efforts and then warn that proposed federal moves to link student aid to assessments of student quality outcomes may be no more successful than our earlier analysis of the shortcomings of state efforts along the same dimensions.

Issues concerning the federal role in promoting social justice pertain to the effects of executive orders and court rulings on such institutional policies as student admissions, faculty hiring and promotion, and composition of governing boards. We recognize that federal activities in these areas have obviously lessened the former autonomy of most public and private institutions but are justified to many observers, including us, in the name of broader social values. We realize that some aspects of this set of issues are still controversial and that people of good will can disagree.

JUDICIAL INTERVENTION

The increasingly intimate relationship between government and higher education means that colleges and universities are in and of the world, not removed and protected from it. Toward the end of the earlier period of student disruption on college campuses it was observed that "judicial decisions and the presence on campus of the community police, the highway patrol, and the National Guard symbolize the fact that colleges and universities have increasingly lost the privilege of self-regulation to the external authority of the police and the courts. . . . It is apparent that colleges and universities have become increasingly accountable to the judicial system of the community, the state, and the national government."[18]

William Kaplin's book on higher education and the law summarizes legal conditions bearing on higher education institutions and gives numerous examples of court decisions involving trustees, administrators, faculty members, and students, as well as cases involving relationships between institutions and both state and federal governments.[19] Recourse to the courts to settle disputes has increased greatly during the past four decades. Faculty members may sue over dismissal, appointment, tenure, and accessibility to personnel records. Students may sue to secure access to their records, over discrimination in admissions and over failure by an institution to deliver what it promised from the classroom and other academic resources. Institutions may take governments to court for the purpose of protecting their constitutional status and, as we illustrate above, in contention over the enforcement of federal regulations.

The traditional aloofness of the campus has been shattered. Kaplin pointed out that "higher education was often viewed as a unique enterprise, which could regulate itself through reliance on tradition and consensual agreement. It operated best by operating autonomously, and it thrived on the privacy which autonomy afforded."[20] The idea of the college or university as a sanctuary was once considered necessary to protect the institution and its constituencies from repressive external control and invasions upon intellectual freedom. Now, other means must be devised to protect an institution's essential spirit while it bows to the world of law and tribunal.

ACCREDITING AGENCIES

Accreditation is a process for holding postsecondary institutions accountable to voluntary non-governmental agencies for meeting certain minimum educational standards. Institutional reviews are conducted by representatives from institutions according to standards derived by member institutions.

Institutional and program accreditation are the two types usually noted. Six regional agencies are responsible for accrediting entire institutions' schools, departments, academic programs, and related activities. Program accreditation, extended by professional societies or other groups of specialists or vocational associations, is extended to a specific school, department, or academic program in such fields as medicine, law, social work, chemistry, engineering, and business administration. A variation is an agency for accrediting single-purpose institutions, such as trade and technical schools.

If the institutions or program being accredited fails to meet minimum standards, the obvious sanction is withdrawal of approval (or rejection for a first-time candidate). Since accreditation is, in theory, voluntary and nongovernmental, an institution or program judged inadequate will suffer loss of prestige but could presumably survive without it. However, in practice, since the federal government requires accreditation by some federally recognized accrediting association for the institution to be eligible for federal research and student aid funds, the process has in effect become much less "voluntary."

The issue then shifts to the federal government's decision to approve a given accrediting association for inclusion on the Department of Education's list. For these decisions the department is presumably influenced by the recognition status accorded the association in question by the recently formed (1996) Council for Higher Education Accreditation (CHEA). CHEA functions as an umbrella national group for accreditation activities and works actively with the federal government on matters of quality assurance, student outcomes, and internationalizing higher education.

EDUCATIONAL COSTS

Although "a tidy dollar comparison of costs and benefits is conspicuously absent," Bowen goes on to list the financial value of higher education.[21] First, the monetary returns from higher education alone are probably sufficient to offset all the costs. Second, the nonmonetary returns are several times as valuable as the monetary returns. And third, the total returns from higher education in all its aspects exceed the cost by several times.

It is usually said that institutions should be accountable for both effectiveness and efficiency, the latter having to do with the cost of the outcomes attained. But costs are extremely difficult to compute in analyzing differences in student change, both within and among institutions. And, as pointed out above, it is extremely difficult to relate changes to significant features of educational environments. Bowen and others have made a significant contribution to the analysis of institutional costs, including expenditures per student, cost differences among institutions, and the implications of cost data for administrative policies and decisions.[22] But we have a long way to go before sound means of determining cost effectiveness are developed.

CONCLUSION

Although autonomy cannot be absolute, only a high degree of independence will permit colleges and universities to devise and choose effective academic means of realizing their professed goals. First of all, institutions must ensure academic freedom to faculty and students. Autonomy does not guarantee intellectual independence, but some forms of external intervention, overt or covert, may undermine such freedom.

While intellectual fetters must be opposed, institutions may legitimately be expected to be held accountable to their constituencies for the integrity of their operations and, as far as possible, for the efficiency of their operations. Colleges and universities are answerable to the general public, which supports them and needs their services. Responding to the public interest, federal and state governments intervene in institutional affairs. At times, government pressure may induce an institution to offer appropriate services; at other times, government agencies may attempt to turn an institution, or even a system, in inappropriate directions. Only constructive consultation and requirements for accountability that recognize the fundamental characteristics of academe will effectively serve the public interest and give vitality to the educational enterprise.

Most institutions, including those supported by legislatures, are not immediately controlled by the general public. Public accountability is mediated by several layers of representation. Institutions are directly answerable to their governing boards. They may be responsible to a consolidated governing board. They may be first responsible to institutional or systemwide governing boards, and these in turn may be under the surveillance of statewide coordinating boards. They also must respond to the requirements of accrediting agencies. Institutions thus may be controlled by a hierarchy of agencies, an arrangement that may complicate their procedures for accountability but that may provide a measure of protection from unwise or unnecessary external intervention.

Colleges and universities are in a period when they are being asked to provide not only data on the attainment of defined outcomes, including changes in students during undergraduate, graduate, and professional education, but also evidence that results have been gained at "reasonable" cost. They are confronted with the difficult challenge of resisting inappropriate government accountability processes, with their added costs and damages to the academic enterprise, while recognizing legitimate state interests and avoiding the appearance of self-interest and resisting sincere efforts to improve their performance. Institutions need to communicate clearly the accountability and assessment practices they currently employ and take the lead in designing processes that are compatible with the character of colleges and universities and with the complex political and professional judgments faculty and institutional administrators must make to maintain and achieve a quality academic program.

NOTES

This chapter is a revision of a previously published chapter by T. R. McConnell, now deceased. It is dedicated to his memory.

1. Howard R. Bowen, *Investment in Learning* (San Francisco: Jossey-Bass, 1977), 12.
2. Amitai Etzioni, *Modern Organizations* (Englewood Cliffs, NJ: Prentice-Hall, 1964), 75–84.
3. Eric Ashby discusses the relationship between academic freedom and autonomy in *Universities: British, Indian, African* (Cambridge, Mass.: Harvard University Press, 1976), chap. 10.
4. William Zumeta, "Public Policy and Accountability in Higher Education: Lessons for the Past and Present for the New Millennium," in *States and Public Higher Education Policy: Affordability, Access, and Accountability*, ed. Donald E. Heller (Baltimore: Johns Hopkins University Press, 2001), 155–97.
5. Nancy Shulock, "An Accountability Framework for California Higher Education: Informing Public Policy and Improving Outcomes" (Sacramento: Institute for Higher Education Leadership & Policy, California State University, November 2002).
6. Etzioni, *Modern Organizations*.
7. C. J. Hitch, "Remarks of the President," address delivered to the Assembly of the California Academic Senate, June 15, 1970.
8. Frank Schmidtlein, "Assumptions Commonly Underlying Governmental Quality Assessment Practices" (paper presented at the 25th EAIR Forum, Limerick, Ireland, August 25, 2003).
9. Robert O. Berdahl, "Universities and Governments in the 21st Century: Possible Relevance of U.S. Experience to Other Parts of the World," in *Toward a New Model of Governance for Universities*? eds. Dietmar Braun and Francois-Xavier Merrien (London: Jessica Kingsley, 1999).
10. Lyman A. Glenny and Thomas K. Dalglish, *Public Universities, State Agencies, and the Law: Constitutional Autonomy in Decline* (Berkeley: University of California, Center for Research and Development in Higher Education, 1973), 42.
11. Ibid., 43.
12. John W. Lederle, "Governors and Higher Education," in *State Politics and Higher Education*, ed. Leonard E. Goodall (Dearborn: University of Michigan Press, 1976), 43–50.
13. Robert O. Berdahl, "Legislative Program Evaluation," in *Increasing the Public Accountability of Higher Education*, ed. John K. Folger (San Francisco: Jossey-Bass, 1977), 35–65.
14. Paul L. Dressel, ed., *The Autonomy of Public Colleges* (San Francisco: Jossey-Bass, 1980), 43.
15. C. R. Pace, "When Students Judge Their College," *College Board Review* 58 (Spring 1960): 26–28.
16. T. R. McConnell, "Accountability and Autonomy," *Journal of Higher Education* 42 (1971): 446–63.
17. Bowen, *Investment in Learning*, 257. Other evidence on changes in students over the college years is presented in Alexander W. Astin, *Four Critical Years* (San Francisco: Jossey-Bass, 1977); Patrick Terenzini and Ernest Pascarella, *How College Affects Students* (San Francisco: Jossey-Bass, 1991).
18. McConnell, "Accountability and Autonomy."
19. William A. Kaplin, *The Law of Higher Education* (San Francisco: Jossey-Bass, 1983).
20. Ibid., 4.
21. Bowen, *Investment in Learning*, 447–48.
22. Howard R. Bowen, *The Cost of Higher Education* (San Francisco: Jossey-Bass, 1980).

22

Lobbying in Higher Education

Theory and Practice

Michael D. Parsons

In the 1990s, I argued that the federal higher education policy arena could be defined as a communication community in which power rested on the ability of actors to define and solve problems (Parsons 1997, 1999a, 1999b, 2000). Policy actors could use this theoretical and conceptual construct of a policy community as they sought to understand and influence policymaking. This framework for explanation and understanding also provided a foundation for examining the development of rationales used to advocate for public support of higher education. In addition, the definition of a communication community of policy actors bonded by emotional, historical, intellectual, and social bonds could be used to inform policy development.

By the late 1990s, the community that had developed slowly over some thirty years came to a swift end (Parsons 2000). The federal higher education policy arena was hit by highly partisan politics, ideological divides, retirements by major policy actors, shifting public opinion, demands for accountability, a declining trust in government, and a movement in emphasis away from equity in favor of privatization. The problem solving and seeking of common ground that had defined the arena was replaced by a more primitive form of power as neoconservatives and neoliberals sought to enforce power over the policymaking process (Cook 1998; Gray 1995; Parsons 2000; Waldman 1995b).

In the Introduction to this text we lamented the decline of consensus that had guided policy researchers and actors and suggested that it might be possible to identify the basis for a new common ground. In addition, we hoped that the beginning of a new theoretical framework might be established that could be used to advocate for better-informed policy choices. These are rather lofty goals for a single edited volume, but policy scholars have an obligation to critique, to identify problems and solutions, and to dream.

The paragraphs above represent a summary of my position before reading the contributions of the invited scholars. After reading their chapters, I have reinterpreted past events and reconsidered how higher education advocates might best position themselves as they seek to influence public policy. The first section of this chapter briefly reexamines the old common ground and suggests that it was an illusion based on a small area of consensus and a large supply of federal funds. The next section questions the ability to find a new common ground. The policy arena of the last century has fragmented into multiple arenas that make a new common ground difficult, if not impossible, to achieve. The last section considers the use of postmodernism as a heuristic device for understanding and influencing public policy. Policy researchers and policy actors need not consider themselves postmodernists, but they will need to approach the policy arena with a strong sense of "irony and contingency" (Rorty 1989).

THE OLD COMMON GROUND

The formation of a common ground for the higher education policy started in the spring of 1964 when President Lyndon Johnson began planning for his next term of office. Sensing what would soon become reality, Johnson anticipated an overwhelming victory over Republican candidate Barry Goldwater and large Democratic majorities in the 89th Congress. Not wanting to miss a historic opportunity, Johnson instructed his staff to organize a number of task forces to work on legislative proposals for immediate presentation to the new Congress. The president wanted to present Congress with a massive social reform program and enabling legislation when it met in January 1965 (Graham 1984).

With the Higher Education Act of 1965, Johnson not only created a legislative program but laid the foundation for the development of a higher education policy arena. Over the next twenty-seven years, HEA would be reauthorized six times. From these common experiences, a communication community developed. One of the prerequisites of such a community is a common language that can be used and understood by all of the members. In the beginning, it did not have a common language; but today terms such as equity and access, Congressional methodology, direct lending, GSL, loan-grant imbalance, needs analysis, Pell Grant, Sallie Mae, TRIO, and dozens of others need no explanation or definition for community members.

Language by itself is not enough to foster fully understood communications. The community also needed widely understood signs and symbols to convey shared meanings. The hearings associated with each reauthorization were an opportunity to display these signs and symbols of the community. In addition, community members need to interact in cooperative activities because "the pulls and responses of different groups reinforce one another and their values accord" (Dewey [1927] 1988, p. 148). The various reauthorizations and associated activities provided scores of opportunities for cooperative activities between 1965 and 1992. The shared activities also produced emotional, intellectual, and moral bonds that helped bind the community. These prerequisites for a communication community produced a community that transformed the power of domination into the power of problem solving.

In addition to its focus on problem solving, the policy arena was characterized by low internal complexity, high functional autonomy, strong unity within types of participants, and cooperation among different participants. A small group of policy actors worked together on virtually every reauthorization. The White House was primarily a non-actor after 1965, leaving the field to the congressional committees and the higher education associations. In the House, Representative Gerald Ford had been an active participant starting with the Great Society programs. He was joined by long-term Republican members such as Representatives E. Thomas Coleman and William F. Goodling, who valued educational opportunity for students above party politics.

In the Senate, Edward Kennedy and Claiborne Pell had been there from the first days of HEA. Pell guided the 1972 reauthorization that created the framework for the major student aid programs. He was so highly regarded by his colleagues that they gave his name to the largest student grant program—the Pell Grant. As in the House, Republican senators such as Nancy Kassebaum and James Jeffords worked more closely with committee members than with their own party to fashion higher education legislation. Vermont Republican Senator Robert Theodore Stafford was so respected by his fellow senators that they gave his name to a student loan program.

Congressional staff members also played an important role in the community. Thomas R. Wolanin, who worked for Ford, was known in Congress for his detailed knowledge of HEA and in academe for his writing on higher education policy issues. David V. Evans started working for Pell in 1978. Given the broad jurisdiction of Senate committees, Evans shared the higher education workload with Sarah A. Flanagan, who joined the subcommittee in 1987. Terry W. Hartle was a key aide to Senator Kennedy on higher education issues. Hartle, a former policy analyst with the American Enterprise Institute, had also written on federal student aid programs.

While there are a large number of higher education associations, only a few were recognized as active policy actors. The major higher education associations are housed in the National Center for Higher Education at One Dupont Circle in Washington, D.C., and the address became a shorthand way to refer to higher education associations. Of the twenty plus associations that reside at One Dupont, only the American Association of Community and Junior Colleges (AACJC), the American Association of State Colleges and Universities (AASCU), the American Council on Education (ACE), the Association of American Universities (AAU), and the National Association of State Universities and Land-Grant Colleges (NASULGC) have been consistently active policy actors in the higher education policy arena. ACE, an umbrella organization, has often attempted to forge consensus positions on policy issues, getting as many associations as possible to speak with one voice on the issue before attempting to influence Congress or the Executive. The other five associations, all of which are institutional associations, provide the expertise on the issues that most affect their member institutions.

The higher education associations that work with the committees to shape higher education legislation benefit from an extensive circulation and flow of personnel within the policy arena. For example, Beth B. Buehlmann, William A. Blakey, John Dean, Rose DiNapoli, Jean S. Frohlicker, Richard T. Jerue, Patty Sullivan, Lawrence S. Zaglaniczny, and other professional staff have remained in the community for many years but have moved between positions within the community. While the leaders of the associations and congressional committees changed, the staff remained, providing an institutional memory. This movement contributed to the maturation of the communication community as policy actors gained shared experiences and multiple perspectives.

Over a nearly thirty-year period, the higher education policy arena evolved into a communication community devoted to problem solving. Higher education associations were powerful policy actors because of their ability to work with other policy actors to solve student aid and other higher education policy problems. Problem solving rested on an axiomatic system of beliefs, institutional relationships, and personal relationships that guided the higher education policy arena in the construction and design of student aid programs. Problems were frequently addressed on the basis of a recommendation from a policy actor with whom other policy actors shared personal relationships. The reason for following the recommendation was explained by policy actors in terms of knowledge, longevity, respect, trust, and other characteristics that define personal relationships. Institutions were defended because they were the institutions that policy actors knew. Programs were created and defended on the basis of what a member believed to be right.

FOUNDATIONS OF POWER

The foundations of power concept calls on earlier concepts of power developed in communicative action theories. It goes beyond the work of Arendt (1968, 1969, 1986), Dewey ([1927] 1988), Habermas (1979, 1984, 1986, 1987), and others to search for the foundations of power. Power rests on three broad foundations. These foundations, suggested by the historical and social context of the higher education policy arena, interact to give form, shape, and meaning to power.

One foundation of power is formed by *society's defining institutions and structures.* Visible structures of power are the products of decisions made in earlier policy arenas. Institutions are the "structures [that] define interactions among individuals and groups" (Rorty 1987, p. 10). They also house the persons and social relationships of the community. The institutional foundation answers the "where" of addressing problems, while persons and social relationships represent the "who," and beliefs and values the "why" of policymaking. As such, these structures represent the exercise of power in the past but are not generative sources of power in the present. Instead, these structures represent "the greatest achievement of power . . . its reification" (Clegg 1989, p. 207). These monuments to past power form the relatively fixed, obligatory passage points of power in the present. While they do not generate power in the present, problems must be addressed within these structures. Institutions become important when occupied and manipulated by humans who are addressing problems.

While institutional structures form the channels and boundaries within which the higher education communication community functions, alone, they are not generative of power. Without human occupants, the institutional structures are mere monuments to the past. Power in a communication community is generated through interactions between the foundations of power. The social foundation of power consists of the *rules governing the relationships between policy actors and programs* in a policy arena and includes, in addition, the personal relationships that develop between policy actors apart from any formal relationships created by the rules of the game. Over time, these relationships, formal and informal, become relatively fixed, but this stability should not be interpreted as permanence. Instead, what is being observed is adherence to customs, loyalties, and norms that have developed over the years and that guide the policy arena in the conduct of its affairs.

The third foundation of power is formed by *the beliefs, principles, and values of the community.* Many of these are well-defined, but the community often works with a tacit understanding of its beliefs and values. At times the values and beliefs that underlie student aid policies are unconnected, compartmentalized, and even conflictual. The policy arena does not seek philosophical coherence, nor does it have a mechanism for value clarification. Over the years, new programs and policies have been created to match policy actors' assumptions about problems without any concern over whether or not the guiding assumptions and beliefs mesh to form a coherent philosophy. This explains why supporters of seemingly contradictory policy proposals can each claim that his/her problem solution is grounded in the values of the arena and vital to its future. While the values and beliefs that guide policy are not always well defined and articulated and are at times conflictual and contradictory, successful problem solving is dependent on solutions that are grounded in the beliefs and values of the higher education policy community.

In addition to beliefs, principles, and values, traditions and emotional experiences serve as a basis for problem solving without first being developed into abstract principles or clearly articulated beliefs. These emotional reactions and responses to events are proto-beliefs that sometimes evolve into fully articulated beliefs, principles, or values. In considering the beliefs' foundation, it is important to recognize that beliefs may follow from the actions of policy actors as much as their actions follow from beliefs. Interaction between the three foundations generates power, regulates power, and provides the channels and boundaries of power in the higher education policy arena.

Communication communities, as defined by Arendt, Dewey, and Habermas, exist to solve problems. Problem solving in the higher education policy arena did not match the Habermasian ideal of communicative competence, nor is it an irrational activity that produces problem solutions through some random or accidental confluence of events that results in a policy decision. Instead, problem solving depended on, and was framed by, an axiomatic system of beliefs, institutional relationships, personal relationships, and values that guide the community in the construction and design of student aid programs. Successful problem solvers were those who built their solutions on these foundations and showed how the community's past and future were linked to acceptance of those solutions.

COLLAPSE OF THE COMMUNITY

The most remarkable thing about the communication community and the old consensus is that it was built on such a narrow base and that it lasted for so long. When President Johnson's task force fashioned what would become HEA, they put together a diverse group of interests. The intent of the legislation and the composition of its constituency are reflected in HEA's eight titles. Title I attempted to expand the land-grant extension concept to urban universities. This was included as a concession to ACE and to the U.S. Office of Education (USOE). Title II provided money to expand college and university libraries and to train librarians. This was supported by the USOE, the American Library Association, and the Association of Research Libraries as a necessary program to meet the demands of a rapidly expanding college population. Title III was designed to aid historically black colleges and universities but was drafted in terms that veiled the basic intent. Title IV, with its four-part package of financial aid, is the heart of HEA. The Democrats were finally able to gain student scholarships in the form of Educational Opportunity Grants to institutions. To forestall support for tuition tax credits and to undermine Republican opposition, a guaranteed student loan program for the middle class was included. College work-study and an extension of the NDEA loan program completed the aid programs. Title V established the National Teachers Corps. The Corps was to provide teachers to poverty-stricken areas of the United States. Title VI created a program of financial assistance for improving undergraduate instruction. Finally, Title VII amended the Higher Education Facilities Act, while Title VIII contained the law's general provisions.

Over the years each title has developed its own constituency, advocacy groups, and budgets. Still, the focus of most policy analysts and researchers has been Title IV. The narrow focus on Title IV caused most researchers to miss the fact that Title IV and other programs rested on a common ground no larger than a metaphorical dime. The narrow overlap of social and economic rationales shared by liberals and conservatives was enough to nurture, develop, and support a massive higher education policy arena. Obscured by the focus on student aid was the development of multiple interests within the policy arena, multiple centers of power, and multiple levels of decision making. It is not surprising that once the common ground vanished, there were no metanarratives to support new rationales for public funding of higher education. The possibility of creating a new common ground from which to lobby for higher education is addressed in the next section.

SEEKING A NEW CONSENSUS

In the Introduction we suggested that it might be possible to develop a new common ground by focusing on the public interest and considering how lobbyists might develop rationales to help us reach the common goals represented by the public interest. Reading the chapters submitted by the contributors makes the possibility of finding a new common ground seem remote. This is not pessimism. It is simply recognition of the new context of policymaking. What once was is gone and may never be again.

The generation of policymakers and education leaders that crafted federal policy between 1965 and the mid-1990s has now left the arena. A new generation will make higher education policy in the 2000s. Unlike the earlier period, higher education is today seen as a private consumer good rather than a social good whose benefits are publicly shared. Without higher education's status as a social good, universities and colleges become just one more special interest group seeking a public handout for its own private benefit. As such, they find themselves in competition with other interest groups seeking a portion of the federal budget. The federal higher education policy arena of the early 2000s is characterized by fragmented, specialized associations, with each one seeking to protect and expand its share of the budget.

Historically, the fault lines of the community can be seen even before it started to form into what we call the higher education policy arena in the mid-1960s. Thelin notes that the federal government has long supported the divergent goals of research and undergraduate student assistance. This helped produce different power centers with divergent beliefs, values, goals, social relationships, and institutional structures. The contemporary practice of earmarking further divided postsecondary institutions. On one level, those with the research infrastructure to receive earmarks were separated from those who did not. Within this group, those with powerful congressional sponsors were separated from those without powerful sponsors. Another level of institutions with no known ability or merit emerged simply because they enjoyed the support of congressional leaders who wanted funds to flow to their home states. With the expansion of earmarks, a new language emerged to justify earmarks and to distinguish the privileged from the disadvantaged. Merit, peer review, research performance, and similar long-used academic terms were replaced by fair share, equal distribution, need to develop research ability, and other terms more closely associated with entitlement politics.

Federal support of undergraduate student assistance highlights the development of different types of postsecondary institutions. Land-grant colleges and universities, historically black colleges and universities, research universities, and community colleges can trace their development to federal funding and/or federal policy decisions and recommendations. The growth of this array of institutional types was followed by the development of a full range of student aid programs. Today any student, from the truly needy to the truly comfortable, qualifies for some form of federal student aid. Given the diversity of goals and missions, it is not surprising that institutions, the various aid programs, and representative organizations developed different constituents, interests, and needs. What is surprising is that the flow of federal student aid funds was so successful in papering over these differences for so long.

Hearn and Holdsworth may be correct when they suggest that what we see today is "a *return to dissensus.*" The brief period of consensus that we saw in the 1970s was an aberration from the norm that existed before the passage of HEA. Even during this period of relative consensus, policy actors could not agree on program "goals, participants, and delivery systems." As programs multiplied, constituent groups grew around each program, offering different rationales for the support of their program at the expense of other programs.

While much of the focus of policy analysts has been on federal policy, actions at the state level and in the courts have also contributed to the fragmentation of the policy arena. One can read Zumeta, Hossler, and Trammel together to get a good sense of what is happening in the states and how it changes the way postsecondary institutions position themselves. As state support declines, public institutions increasingly position themselves as private institutions. Trammel notes that an even more dangerous turn could occur as institutions are tempted to craft appeals for state support that lack merit and do not "represent the values of the academic community."

Judicial policymaking is a political process that represents the intersection of federal, state, institutional, and individual interests. It is reviewed here to reinforce the claim that higher education policymaking has fragmented into multiple arenas and occurs on multiple levels. The shifting of issues such as affirmative action to the states clearly illustrates and supports this claim. As Brown, Butler, and Donahoo, as well as Conrad and Weerts note, higher education affirmative action cases are still decided in the federal courts, but the states are now the focus of power. States and institutions are the originators of policies and practices that produce decisions such as *Adams, Fordice,* and *Hopwood.* In addition, some states have moved to opt out of affirmative action, leaving unresolved the national commitment to higher education desegregation. Those states that have abandoned affirmative action justify their retreat by declaring that it is no longer needed to insure access and equity. States are also using the current budget crisis as an excuse to reduce their commitment to access and equity.

It is not necessary to review each of the contributions to this text to demonstrate the fragmentation of the higher education communication community. The fragmentation has made it impossible to find a new common ground from which to lobby for public support of higher education. One need not accept Thelin's metaphor of the public trough to accept that institutions are seeking the largest possible share of the $18 billion in federal grants and contracts and are not seeking to define an overarching rationale of the public interest. Hearn and Holdsworth have established that institutions use multiple rationales to lobby for federal student aid. The chapters that address affirmative action establish that any consensus that might have existed around access and equity has long since exploded. Each of the growing number of fragments that once were part of the old common ground now has formed, or seeks to form, its own set of rationales, arenas of action, centers of power, and institutions of control. It is within this context that advocates of public support of higher education must navigate in the early 2000s.

CONCLUSION: THEORY AND PRACTICE

Understanding the fragmented, decentralized higher education policy arena of the early 2000s calls for a postmodernist perspective. The use of the term *postmodern* will immediately produce as many definitions as there are readers of this text. The purpose here is not to define postmodernism. Instead, I want to use a postmodern perspective as a heuristic device for understanding and influencing public policy. What that means in this setting is defined below. In addition, I will combine a postmodern perspective with the foundations of power concept to show how it can be used to organize and use insights gained from use of the perspective.

Taking a Postmodern Perspective

Postmodernism has so often been used to undermine what are viewed as modernist perspectives that we forget that it also can be used to gain insight into possible solutions to modernist problems (Cahoone 1996). The intent here is not to attack but to discover. The use of a postmodern perspective as a heuristic device requires that the user accept certain positions. One is that there are no metanarratives that provide a single foundation for a uniform higher education policy arena. A second is that discourses over public funding of higher education are struggles over the production of meaning. A third is that rationales, or language used to define and support policy, do not carry meaning outside the context in which they are developed and used. Fourth is that rationales exist primarily within the social network in which they are created, thus the power of rationales can be expanded by increasing the scope of the social network. Finally, to borrow from the very modernist historian Richard Hofstadter (1970), one must be both "playful and pious" in using these positions. Playful in the sense of being open to new ideas and insights that might result from their application, and pious in the sense of treating seriously the obligation of scholars to act as social critics and social constructors.

A good beginning point in the application of a postmodern perspective is to accept that the metanarrative of access and equity that drove public support for higher education in the last half of the twentieth century is gone. Accepting this, advocates can then begin to explore and "play" with the narratives that explain student aid, state higher education financing, desegregation, institutional positioning, technology, and the many other higher education policy arenas. Each arena will have its own set of rationales, meanings, and social networks that characterize successful advocacy. Policy advocates must learn and apply the rules of success for each arena in order to effectively lobby for public support of higher education.

Advocates must also be "pious" and understand that postmodernism tends to be anti-communitarian, whereas higher education is dependent on communities. In seeking to understand the various narratives that define the multiple higher education policy arenas of the 2000s, advocates must apply post-modernism loosely. A strict application would focus on the differences that differentiate and divide the fragments of the old common ground. A loose application provides a way to understand the fragments while listening for elements that might be woven into a larger narrative capable of uniting some of the diverse fragments.

In the 1990s, advocates lost control of the evolving language of public support for higher education and remained mired in the old language of the policy arena even as the arena itself fractured. Liberals and neoliberals lost ground as neoconservatives and the right appropriated what had been the language of liberalism. In an effort to be more inclusive, liberals and neoliberals celebrated difference and rejected any discussion of commonality as essentialism (Martin 2000). Neoconservatives and the right were able to capture rationales for equal opportunity, equal educational opportunity, merit, and other arguments that had once belonged to liberals, and to use those arguments in ways that damaged affirmative action, equity and access, and public funding of higher education.

A strict application of a postmodern perspective is also dangerous in that it removes the foundational basis for rationales. If rationales have no ethical or moral foundation, then there is no claim of privilege for access, equity, desegregation, public funding, or other rationales designed to make higher education fair, open, and available. Without the ability to claim a special role or privileged position in society, higher education is nothing more than another special interest group feeding at the public trough.

Advocates need to be "playful" with rationales—listening to what is said in different arenas and then playing with those rationales outside the context in which they were first used. This may seem like a violation of the positions listed as a condition for taking a postmodern perspective, but it is not. The purpose of taking a postmodern perspective is to gain insight and understanding of policy advocacy. Recognizing that different fragments of the old common ground now speak in different tongues is one way to gain insight into those fragments. Carrying rationales from one fragment to another may be a way to increase lobbying effectiveness as different rationales are tested and used. Developing rationales that work across multiple arenas might build small islands of common ground from which to advocate for broader support of higher education.

Higher education advocates might also use this playfulness to sharpen their understanding of arenas of discourse as struggles for power. Discourse is not about conversation, debate, messages, or knowledge. Discourse is about the relationship between power and knowledge and should be seen as a contest to impose hegemony (Clegg 1989). The winner gains the right to impose meaning on the discourse. Lobbyists for higher education seem to have forgotten this in the 1990s. As a result, they often fell into the trap of using their critics' language in an effort to defend themselves and to develop rationales of support for higher education (Cook 1998; Parsons 1997; Slaughter and Leslie 1997). When one side controls meaning in the discourse, then it also controls the range of possible outcomes (Schattschneider 1970). If advocates are unable or unwilling to be "pious" about discourse arenas as arenas of contest, then they will continue to have the higher education policy agenda defined in ways that are not supportive of public funding for higher education.

The last position required for a postmodern perspective is that rationales exist primarily within the social network within which they are created and used. If lobbyists want to increase the power of their arguments for public support of higher education, then they need to increase the scope of their social networks. Advocates would seem to have ample opportunity to expand the scope of their networks, given that higher education has moved from access for the elite to access to the masses in a relatively short time. As we have seen in this text, higher education is now more important to more individuals, groups, and organizations than it ever has been. The multiple higher education policy arenas are teeming with potential friends and allies who could join the traditional advocates of higher education to form a powerful lobby.

Ironically, the traditional Washington, D.C.–based advocates of higher education seem to have moved in the opposite direction, becoming more exclusionary and aligning themselves with a corporate vision of education (e.g., Slaughter and Leslie 1997). This behavior might be attributable to several factors: the original HEA was created in secrecy; the Washington, D.C.–based associations have long worked inside the policy process; and the associations and other higher education advocates have seen themselves as being cleaner and more pure than common lobbyists (Cook 1998; Gladieux and Wolanin 1976; Parsons 1997). If advocates for higher education are going to be effective in the 2000s, they will have to become more like common lobbyists looking to form coalitions that will expand their social networks as well as expand the reach and power of their rationales.

Foundations of Power: Revisited

A postmodern perspective helps provide insight and understanding for policy actors who are willing to play with the positions. It helps us see that any "truth" about public support for higher education is not "the product of free spirits" but "is produced by virtue of multiple forms of constraints" (Foucault 1980, p. 131). Foucault and other postmodernists contribute to our understanding of constraints but not to our understanding of power. Nancy Fraser (1989) summarizes the problem of using Foucault and other similar postmodernists to understand power by noting that "the problem is that Foucault calls too many sorts of things power and simply leaves it at that. . . . Phenomena which are capable of being distinguished . . . are simply lumped together . . . a broad range of normative nuances is surrendered, and the result is a certain normative one-dimensionality" (p. 32).

How then can higher education policy actors and advocates play with a postmodern perspective and use the results to influence public policy? The foundations of power concept can be used as an approach to organizing knowledge about the multiple higher education policy arenas gained from the application of a postmodern perspective. In some ways this approach is similar to Foucault's effort to apply an archaeological approach to discourse. Here our concern is not with the rules of discourse but with the meaning of power in each of the policy arenas. More specifically, it is about using power, however it might be defined in an arena, to successfully lobby for higher education in each of the arenas that affect public policymaking.

Each arena, regardless of its nature, will have an institutional foundation, a social foundation, and a beliefs/values foundation. Understanding this, policy actors and advocates can use the foundations of power concept to organize knowledge gained from the application of a postmodern perspective. Each arena can be mapped, models of operation can be developed, and a classification system of power can be established. None of these can bring back the old common ground or create a new consensus for public support of higher education. At the very least, the proposal to combine a postmodern perspective with the foundations of power concept will increase lobby-ists' level of understanding and possibly their level of effectiveness as they advocate for public support of higher education. At the very best, this approach may create some small islands of consensus in a sea of dissensus.

Finally, while this approach promises an opportunity for success in the new context of higher education policymaking, the ability of higher education advocates to take advantage of the opportunity remains questionable. The post-1992 success of higher education advocates is attrib-utable more to institutional conflict than to any actions taken by the higher education associations and advocates. Important policy issues such as national service and direct lending were neither developed nor embraced by the higher education associations. The defense and protection of student aid in the 1995–96 budget battle between the Clinton administration and the Republican Congress was not, as Cook (1998) claims, due to the power and influence of the associations, but it was due to Clinton's willingness to close the federal government rather than accept Republican cuts in AmeriCorps, direct lending, and other student aid programs. With a different president controlling that obligatory passage point in the institutional foundation, the results could have been very different.

Federal and state higher education policymaking in the 2000s will be marked by fragmenta-tion, conflict, and coercion. The new context will not be friendly to an expansion of public sup-port for higher education. Indeed, any change, including program elimination, will be difficult to achieve because there is no common ground that spans the entire policy arena and because groups are more willing to engage in conflict. It remains to be seen if the higher education advocates will be able to meet the challenges of the new millennium. To understand higher education poli-cymaking, one must understand the meaning of power in the policy arena. To understand power, one must understand the institutional, social, and beliefs foundations on which it rests. If the past is a prelude to the future, then higher education advocates and associations have shown neither the ability to respond to the challenge nor an understanding of the changes in the new context of higher education policymaking.

REFERENCES

Arendt, H. 1968. *Between past and future: Eight exercises in political thought.* New York: Viking Press.

Arendt, H. 1969. *On violence.* New York: Harcourt, Brace, and World.

Arendt, H. 1986. Communicative power. In *Power,* ed. S. Lukes, 59–74. New York: New York University Press.

Cahoone, L. 1996. Introduction. In *From modernism to postmodernism: An anthology,* ed. L. Cahoone. Oxford, UK: Blackwell Publishers.

Clegg, S. R. 1989. *Frameworks of power.* London: Sage Publications.

Cook, C. E. 1998. *Lobbying for higher education: How colleges and universities influence federal policy.* Nashville, TN: Vanderbilt University Press.

Dewey, J. [1927] 1988. *The public and its problems.* Athens, OH: Swallow Press.

Foucault, M. 1980. *Power/knowledge.* Brighton, UK: Harvester Press.

Fraser, N. 1989. Foucault on modern power: Empirical insights and normative confusions. In *Unruly prac-tices,* ed. N. Fraser, 17–32. Minneapolis: University of Minnesota Press.

Gladieux, L. E., and T. R. Wolanin. 1976. *Congress and the colleges: The national politics of higher educa-tion.* Lexington, MA: D. C. Heath.

Graham, H. D. 1984. *The uncertain triumph: Federal education policy in the Kennedy and Johnson years.* Chapel Hill: University of North Carolina Press.

Gray, J. 1995. Senators refuse to save national service program. *New York Times,* 27 September, D22.

Habermas, J. 1979. *Communication and the evolution of society.* Boston: Beacon Press.

Habermas, J. 1984. *Theory of communicative action,* vol. 1, *Reason and the rationalization of society.* Boston: Beacon Press.

Habermas, J. 1986. Hannah Arendt's communications concept of power. In *Power,* ed. S. Lukes, 75–93. New York: New York University Press.

Habermas, J. 1987. *The theory of communicative action,* vol. 2, *Lifeworld and system: A critique of functionalist reason.* Boston: Beacon Press.

Hofstadter, R. 1970. *Anti-intellectualism in American life.* New York: Knopf.

Martin, J. R. 2000. *Coming of age in academe.* New York: Routledge.

Parsons, M. D. 1997. *Power and politics: Federal higher education policymaking in the 1990s.* Albany: State University of New York Press.

Parsons, M. D. 1999a. The higher education policy arena. In *Foundations of American higher education,* ed. J. L. Bess and D. S. Webster, 615–33. Needham Heights, MA: Simon and Schuster Custom Publishing.

Parsons, M. D. 1999b. The problem of power: Seeking a methodological solution. *Policy Studies Review* 16 (3/4): 278–310.

Parsons, M. D. 2000. The higher education policy arena: The rise and fall of a community. In *Higher education in transition: The challenges of the new millennium,* ed. B. Fife and J. Losco, 83–107. Westport, CT: Greenwood Publications.

Rorty, R. 1987. Method, social science and social hope. In *Interpreting politics,* ed. M. T. Gibbons, 241–59. New York: New York University Press.

Rorty, R. 1989. *Contingency, irony and solidarity.* New York: Cambridge University Press.

Schattschneider, E. E. 1970. *The semisovereign people.* New York: Holt, Rinehart and Winston.

Slaughter, S. E., and L. L. Leslie. 1997. *Academic capitalism: Politics, policies, and the entrepreneurial university.* Baltimore: Johns Hopkins University Press.

Waldman, S. 1995a. *The bill: How the adventures of Clinton's National Service bill reveal what is corrupt, comic, cynical—and noble—about Washington.* New York: Viking.

Waldman, S. 1995b. Sallie Mae fights back: The brutal politics of student-loan reform. *Linguafranca: The review of academic life* (March/April): 34–42.

23

State Funding Limitations and Community College Open Door Policy

Conflicting Priorities?

Ruth Zimmer Hendrick, William H. Hightower, and Dennis E. Gregory

Historically, according to *The Economist* (2001) and the National Governor's Association and National Association of State Budget Officers' (2002) *The Fiscal Survey of States report* education has accounted for roughly 1/3 of state spending. However, when only general fund spending is considered, states allocate roughly 48% of their budgets to education—35% for elementary and secondary education plus 13% for higher education (Prah, 2003).

Recent national budget shortfalls have caused many states to evaluate various ways to cut their budgets—including cutting education expenditures. "Education is no longer the sacred cow it used to be," according to Dane Linn, director of the National Governor's Association's education policy studies division (Prah, 2003, p. 1).

Budget shortfalls have come about in recent years primarily because tax collections have been less than the projected revenues (National Governor's Association and National Association of State Budget Officers, 2003). "State and local taxes as a percent of gross domestic product are at their lowest levels since the late 1980s" (McNichol, 2004, p. 2). Thirty states are now projecting deficits for 2005 (Johnson & Zahradnik, 2004).

In response to these shortfalls, states are slashing budgets. According to the Center on Budget and Policy Priorities, adjusted state spending is estimated to be 5.4% lower in 2004 than in 2001 (McNichol, 2004). Many states have suffered serious reductions in their budgets and have reduced their spending on higher education. For example, in 2003 Tennessee reduced state spending on education by 9% (Associated Press, 2003). In FY 2004, Massachusetts faced an 18.5% cut in its higher education budget (American Federation of Teachers, 2004).

While state spending is falling, college tuition and fees are rising. For 2003–04, the American Association of Community Colleges (AACC) estimated average annual tuition and fees for a full-time community college student would increase about 11.5% per semester over the previous year (National Association of Student Financial Aid Administrators, 2003). Minnesota "heralds the third and fourth year of double-digit tuition increases" in their community colleges for 2003 and 2004 (American Federation of Teachers, 2004) and a 2003 AACC tuition survey found that many states had planned to increase tuition for the 2003–04 year, from 3% in Georgia and Louisiana to as much as 63.6% in California (Larose, 2003).

In the last 40 years, 2-year college enrollments have exploded in the United States. Sheer numbers of students demanding higher education at the community college level—combined with issues of decreased funding and increased accountability—have put increasingly severe stress on the traditional open door policy of community colleges.

HISTORY OF THE OPEN DOOR POLICY

Community colleges began with an open door policy for a number of reasons, starting with the American ideal of an open society where every person is given a chance to move between class strata regardless of their condition of birth. Additional factors fueling the open enrollment policy included the democratic ideal of a learned populace taking an active role in civic affairs, the lengthening of adolescence in western society, industrialization's need for increasingly well trained employees, and businesses' desire to have their employees trained at public expense (Cohen & Brawer, 1996). Also, traditional postsecondary institutions were slow or resistant to adjust to an increasing variety of students that included commuters, part-time students, and employed students. The baby boom of the 1940s–50s and the civil rights movement of the 1960s provided additional reasons why community colleges were created with their doors open to all students.

There has been debate throughout the history of community colleges about the pros and cons of an open door policy (Kearney, 1981). While this debate continued, the originally intended positive results have occurred. Students are provided a stepping stone to the traditional baccalaureate degree, and advanced learning environments are offered to individuals who were previously blocked from higher education due to social or economic factors. The colleges also provide an adequately trained workforce to meet the needs of business and industry. They also offer a variety of accessible life-long learning experiences to the citizenry.

Critics of community colleges and their open door policy have often noted their concerns regarding curricular issues and the quality of the education provided at 2-year colleges. This concern has increased as community colleges provide more and more remedial education to many students at a level below what has typically been considered as "collegiate." Negative outcomes enumerated by Oliver (1995) include the idea that enrichment courses offered for credit are being used in place of academic courses, resulting in increased retention and student satisfaction, but not in the mastery of academic skills. Additionally, schools are attracting students with financial problems and/or a lack of direction, and these students never complete their academic programs (Oliver, 1995). Oliver also noted that an academically underdeveloped student base might result in a watering down of instruction. This can later result in transfer shock. Oliver also noted that secondary schools expect community colleges to assume the teaching of academic fundamentals (1995).

Additionally, the increasingly high costs of higher education are often at the center of the argument against an open door policy. This is particularly so because community colleges must be prepared to quickly respond to the fluctuation in student population size and to changing technology and employment needs.

HISTORIC THREATS

At numerous times in the history of the community college system, enrollment trends have threatened the colleges' ability to continue the open door policy. Threats to the open door policy have traditionally arisen during periods of economic downturn. This is when funding, in general, becomes more limited, and funding to nonessential programs (i.e., higher education) is most hard hit. These eras, combined with the continuous leaps in college enrollments, have led to time periods when community colleges have more seriously considered policies that might affect the open door.

During these periods of enrollment growth and funding decline, however, the open door did not slam shut. As Nigliazzo (1986) suggested, "the open door is not easily closed for community colleges because it has so long been part of the community and junior college mission; it has in fact shaped that mission" (p. 36).

Collins, Leitzel, Morgan, and Stalcup (1994) summarized the cost-saving policies traditionally enacted by community colleges. Seeking additional funds from local sources, and increasing tuition and fees were shown to be the primary defenses to counteract increasing enrollments and declining state support. As these authors note, other areas of community college operations traditionally impacted during these periods include adjustments in personnel (i.e., decreasing or eliminating faculty and/or support personnel raises, increasing the number of part-time faculty appointments or deferring hiring decisions), raising the student/faculty ratio, and decreasing or eliminating marginally successful programs and new program development. Budget cuts outside of instruction are traditionally enacted first. Even though these measures only indirectly affect access, increases in tuition and fees, increasing class sizes, and eliminating academic programs may limit access—particularly to marginal students.

While some cost-saving initiatives that have been historically enacted by community colleges have resulted in limiting access, the trend has been to select short-term coping strategies that favor preserving access. Few suggested policies for modifying the open door through prioritizing services (Kaster, 1979) or developing selective admissions policies (Rippey & Roueche, 1977) were taken seriously enough to reach implementation or analysis. For example, California's 1993 attempt to utilize differential fee structures (Chen, 1993) was subsequently dropped in January 1996, "marking a return to the broader notion of educational access that the community college represents" (Burstein, 1996, concluding remarks, p. 4).

THE CURRENT THREAT TO THE OPEN DOOR POLICY

The current threat to the open door policy of community colleges has come about for some of the same reasons that institutions have faced this crisis in the past: continued student population growth, increased accountability, and less discretionary funding. Additionally, the broad "all things to all people" traditional mission of the community college is expanding further than ever before. It now includes workforce development, distance learning, and increased remediation needs. It appears that community colleges have come to this point primarily because, as pointed out by Collins et al. (1994), long-term, permanent solutions to the issues related to open enrollment have not traditionally been sought by legislators or college administrators, and because the mission of the community college remains so broad.

Schmidt, in 1999, indicated increases in spending on community colleges of up to 14% in some states. However, paraphrasing David Pierce of the American Association of Community Colleges, Schmidt also noted, "this is restoration money, not new money" (1999, p. 22). Schmidt quoted Terri Standish-Kuon, spokeswoman for the Commission on Independent Colleges and Universities, who stated, "the recent surge . . . was serving mainly to make up for past neglect" (p. 18) as colleges continued to make up for the losses suffered in the economic slowdown of the early 1990s.

Referring to the late 1990s, Evelyn (2001, October) noted, "after a period of relatively flat national enrollment for community colleges—the institutions may be experiencing a boom" (p. 4). Factors causing this growth include population changes, increases in the college-age population, attraction of students who cannot find spaces at 4-year institutions, displaced workers seeking retraining, and a looming recession causing students to seek the lower tuition rates of community colleges. The ability of community colleges to quickly expand or change programming may also account for a large portion of this increase in enrollment. Growth in many states is similar to that expected in California. There, Smith (2004) reports that between 2001 and 2010 the Public Policy Institute of California estimates that "the demand for community colleges will increase by over 400,000 students" (p. 3).

At the same time community colleges are seeing a burst in enrollments, they are faced with softening support of higher education as the country enters its first recessionary period of the new millennium. As reported by Schmidt (2002), a survey conducted by the Center for the Study of Education Policy at Illinois State University reflects "the vulnerability of higher education to downturns in the economy (p. A20)." Many states are not receiving appropriations that include enough new money to stay ahead of inflation, and some state budgets are calling for reductions in higher education spending. With many states facing deficits in the coming fiscal year, public-college officials throughout the nation have said they hold little hope of winning substantially more state support anytime soon (Schmidt, 2002).

RESPONSES TO CURRENT THREATS

Higher education may be seen as entering the downward spiral of a cyclical pattern where there are too many students and not enough money. This leads many community colleges to consider and institute new policies that will allow them to continue operating. Such policies, some at the expense of complete open door access, may be divided into two categories including (a) access inhibiting and (b) funding-producing.

POLICIES THAT MAY INHIBIT ACCESS

Practices affecting the community college open door policy tend to limit or restrict enrollment either purposefully or as a result of their implementation.

Emphasizing Performance Based Funding

Although ultimately meant to require community colleges to gain efficiency, performance based funding (PBF) may also serve to limit enrollment when colleges place upon students an expectation that they will graduate, increase their incomes or transfer to 4-year institutions. With over 30 states utilizing PBF by either tying specific dollars to institutional benchmarks, or utilizing performance measures in consideration of funds allocated, colleges may implement practices that have the effect of scaring off some individuals (Honeyman, Wattenbarger, & Westbrook, 1996). Students with remediation needs, part-time students, and those students who enroll purely for personal development are less inclined to attend college when grade point averages, timely graduation rates, and elimination of less productive programs become primary benchmarks of institutional success (Roueche & Baker, 1987).

Limiting Program Admission

Admission to a community college is virtually guaranteed by the open-door policy. However, admission to specific programs of study within the college is often based on selective practices that, in effect, close the most lucrative doors to many students. Kearney (1981) identified the factors used in selective admissions practices, including: (a) over-subscription, (b) higher costs in health related programs, (c) limited classroom and clinical space, (d) state legislation permitting selective admission, and (e) regulations of program accrediting agencies. Thus, while seen as legal and often necessary for some degree programs, these restrictions limit access to the services of the community college and are being used at an increasing rate as a tool to limit the student population.

Instituting Waiting Lists

Another recent trend that limits access to the community college is to place students on waiting lists when funds are not available to hire new instructors or to meet other needs of the college. When their enrollment increased at a much faster rate than their state allocations, Oregon's community colleges placed thousands of prospective students on hold in 2000 while awaiting an infusion of state funds (Yachnin, 2001). With this tactic colleges hope to persuade legislators to pay closer attention to enrollments in deciding how much money to provide in their budgets. The most immediate effects are felt by part-time students needing one course to transfer or graduate and on students with specific or immediate workplace training needs (Yachnin). However, all students hoping to attend college may be affected.

Emphasizing Noncredit Training

Another enrollment-limiting trend in community colleges is exemplified in Virginia. There, the chancellor's annual report indicated that community colleges in that state had provided 10,510 noncredit courses to 3,218 companies, a 21% increase in noncredit training over 2002 (Virginia Community College System n.d.). By transferring courses and programs from the credit to the noncredit arena, schools may be able to sidestep funding formulas or increase their funds through profit making. However, this tactic also leads many students away from traditional academic training with a transfer or terminal degree option. While still meeting the community college mission of providing community service, this trend does limit students' ready access to some of the original purposes of the system.

Prioritizing Enrollment

California and other states are reviewing proposals to prioritize student enrollments, even though this concept was tried and then rescinded less than 10 years ago in that state. Reducing state subsidies to individuals who already possess a degree would provide expanded space for first-time college students. As Phelan (2000) noted, this plan would also ensure that the students who enroll have access to career programs and enhanced employability as a result. However, these prioritization plans limit access for some. The result, then, means open access is not available to all individuals.

Redefining Mission

Since a major cause of the current enrollment and funding dilemma facing community colleges is their broad mission, some would suggest that it is unlikely that the colleges can survive in their current form. Gordon (1995) noted that "to that end, they must abandon weak areas, focus on what they do well, and develop specialized niches" (p. 10).

Analyzing the Virginia Community College system as early as 1992, Levin, Perkins, and Clowes (1995) came to this conclusion.

> We suspect that the substance for the written mission statement of most community colleges has not changed since they were founded. The typical community college mission remains sufficiently broad to authorize every conceivable kind and scope of training, education and service. This "business as usual" approach to mission can no longer be tolerated in a time of declining finances. In the current economic setting, "business as usual" is likely to destroy college quality, college culture and college physical plant.
>
> (p. 114)

One traditional aspect of the community college mission, remediation, is sometimes considered "at the very heart of an open-door college" (Roueche and Baker, 1987, p. 72). Blair notes, however, that "higher education systems . . . are cracking down on students in need of remedial help" (Blair, 1999, p. 1). Although Blair was specifically discussing California and New York plans to remove students from senior level colleges, this trend is evident at the community college level as well. Community colleges are referring students who are unprepared for college level work back to high schools, adult education programs, and private, profit making agencies to complete costly remediation (Breneman & Haarlow, 1999). This practice may also limit access to the community college system.

Toughening Academic Standards

Tougher academic standards place one more block at the open door of a system that has, over time, come to accept all levels of preparedness in students. Similarly, a trend toward college requirements that students earn a higher grade point average in their core courses in order to receive a degree leads some to postulate that "struggling students will become discouraged by the new standards and drop out" (Haworth, 1999, p. 6). In defense of this increasingly common practice, Neal A. Raisman, president of Onondaga Community College in New York argues, "giving people an education with inflated grades is just going to insure that they fail in the future" (Haworth, p. 14). This practice indirectly restricts access, and if it does not close the "open entrance door," it at least shuts the "open exit." Miami Dade Community College's educational reforms of the early 1980's suspended or dismissed over 8,000 students not performing to required expectation levels (Nigliazzio, 1986). While measures like this do increase the overall level of student performance, they also scare off a large group of students with varying educational, social, and economic needs.

POLICIES THAT MAY INCREASE FUNDS

Perhaps for the first time in the history of community colleges, the institutions are beginning to look toward adding to their resources rather than taking away from their services in order to balance budgets. Numerous tactics that were previously only seen in the realms of business, private colleges, and some public senior institutions are being utilized by community colleges.

Private Fundraising

Forced into creativity, many community colleges are following the lead of 4-year colleges and universities by becoming fundraisers. According to van der Werf (1999), the money not only supplements operating expenses but also builds endowments. He states, "while amounts raised are much smaller than those given to 4-year colleges and universities, community colleges are surprising even themselves with their success" (van der Werf, p. 6). Community colleges have large groups of untapped sources in local organizations and alumni. Their student populations also tend to be older than those in traditional senior colleges and, thus, are more able to make donations while attending the college. In exchange for the expectation of increased private funding, community colleges are working harder to develop programs and partnerships with local businesses and industries. Nielsen (1994) notes trends focusing on economic development activities, sharing of facilities with other agencies, housing business facilities on college campuses, and providing off-campus training and degree programs at local businesses.

Beyond direct fund raising, community colleges are also actively seeking larger grants from foundations. This trend is illustrated by Bellevue Community College's receipt of a large grant from the William H. Gates foundation. There is also St. Petersburg Junior College's receipt of a $19 million art collection from benefactors (van der Werf, 1999, p. 14). Increasingly, community colleges are employing development and grant writing personnel.

Increasing Government Allocations

Additionally, there is a trend toward more active lobbying by community colleges. Increased lobbying, hiring professional lobbyists, and collaboration among lobbyists on proposed community college state legislation have led to significant effects on state allocations. Community colleges are even finding their way into federal arenas when national decisions have direct effect on their funding. As noted by Evelyn (2001), California's community college system recently employed a high-cost Washington lobbying firm in an attempt to maximize the size of the Pell Grants their students could receive.

Development of new monies, used for a wide variety of training and workforce development initiatives, is allowing community colleges to continue their broad mission of service to the entire community without restricting enrollments. Monies from lottery funds are being utilized in Georgia to provide HOPE scholarships to the state's students with good high school academic records. Tobacco settlement funds are serving to expand workforce retraining of displaced workers in numerous southwest and southside Virginia counties. Caution must be raised, however, that the beneficiaries of these funds often lose revenue from other government sources, typically through erosion of the general revenue share.

Redefining Finance

Budgetary pressures are forcing some community colleges to become fiscally creative. More colleges are utilizing practices traditionally used by private businesses including outsourcing and developing for-profit ventures. Examples include outsourcing bookstores, food service, facilities maintenance, and counseling services. Other examples include such ventures as the Saddleback Community College golf course and driving range that are located on campus (Nicklin, 1996). All of these endeavors may allow community colleges to maintain their open door policies and expansive mission. Cohen and Brawer (1987) also offer one solution that can be considered as redefining finance. They suggest that the major missions of the community college be divided into separate units within the college. These different educational functions would receive separate funding based on the tasks being performed and the ends being pursued by students. Thus, the unit managing academic degrees might be funded at a higher rate, with separate benchmarks and goals, from the unit coordinating service programming. Lack of need for faculty credentials in this latter unit would allow for lowering programming costs.

IMPLICATIONS FOR PRACTICE

From history and recent innovative practices, community colleges have a number of options to help deal with the conflicting trends of increased enrollment, higher accountability levels, and decreased funding. Some of these directions are contradictory to the traditional open door admissions policy. The path historically followed has been one of short-term, indecisive maneuvers. It is hoped that such maneuvers will be sufficient to hold off the problem until the economy again allows money to freely flow into higher education's coffers. A technologically savvy society demands increased accountability and questions how long our economy can continue to provide expanded services. These concerns suggest that holding a collective community college breath and waiting for the problem to go away would not be in the best interest of a system in search of permanent, long-term solutions to a problem it has faced on and off for over 30 years.

A second path open to legislators and system administrators is to allow trends to continue that would effectively limit access to the community college. This path ultimately would lead to a paradigm shift redefining the mission of the community college. If it is accepted that the community college cannot be all things to all people, especially when the definition of "all things" continues to expand, it could be determined that the community college system has reached its limits and must divest itself of some traditional areas of its mission.

Conversely, community colleges could move toward developing a long-term vision that focuses on resources. Improving performance, responding to external priorities, and improving or altering resource flows from traditional sources may allow community colleges to reinvent themselves with a new entrepreneurial spirit. This path could offer community colleges the opportunity to maintain the traditional open door while meeting increasing operational and capital demands. However, the question must be considered as to when the colleges would reach their next threshold of inability to provide services at a higher funding level. For the foreseeable future, though, this path may provide community colleges with their best chance to continue expanding to meet enrollment needs without closing the open door.

As is the case when similar situations occur within other organizational structures, community colleges are likely to select a mix from the paths mentioned above. We have yet to learn if the current period of consolidation and fiscal caution will lead to decisions driven by thoughtful debate about institutional purpose, or if those decisions will be made primarily to counter immediate fiscal problems.

REFERENCES

American Federation of Teachers. (2004). *State budget roundup*. Retrieved April 10, 2004, from http://www.aft.org/higher_ed/State_Budget.html

Associated Press. (2003). *State budget cuts may be pricing some Tennesseeans out of higher education*. Retrieved April 20, 2004, from http://www.wmctv.com/global/ story.asp?s=1346419&ClientType=Printable

Blair, J. (1999). N.Y., Calif. Cracking down on college remediation. *Education Week, 19*(15), 6.

Breneman, D. W. & Haarlow, W. N. (1999, April 9). Establishing the real value of remedial education. *The Chronicle of Higher Education*, p. B6.

Burstein, M. (1996). *The thin green line: Community colleges' struggle to do more with less* (Report No. EDO-JC-96–11). Washington, DC: Office of Educational Research and Improvement. (ERIC Document Reproduction Service No. ED400024)

Chen, M. K. (1993). *Into the downward spiral: The impact of fee increases and course reductions on LACCD enrollment and resources* (Report No. JD930313). Los Angeles, CA: Los Angeles Community College District Educational Services Division. (ERIC Document Reproduction Service N. ED358882)

Cohen, A. M. & Brawer, F. B. (1987). *The collegiate function of community colleges.* San Francisco: Jossey-Bass.

Cohen, A. M. & Brawer, F. B. (1996). *The American community college.* 3rd ed., San Francisco: Jossey-Bass.

Collins, S. E., Leitzel, T. C., Morgan, S. D., & Stalcup, R. J. (1994). Declining revenues and increasing enrollments: Strategies for coping. *Community College Journal of Research and Practice, 18*(1), 33–42.

Economist, The. (2001, August). Red ink rising. *Economist.com.* Retrieved March 30, 2004, from http://www.economist.com/displaystory.cfm?story_id=731539

Evelyn, J. (2001, August 3). Two-year colleges step up lobbying. *The Chronicle of Higher Education,* p. A23.

Evelyn, J. (2001, October 19). Many community colleges report a boom in their enrollments. *The Chronicle of Higher Education,* p. A36.

Gordon, R. A. (1995). Can community colleges do the job [Abstract]. *Leadership Abstracts, 8*(8), 2.

Haworth, K. (1999, January 22). Many 2-year colleges impose tougher academic standards. *The Chronicle of Higher Education,* p. A33.

Honeyman, D. S., Wattenbarger, J. L., & Westbrook, K. C. (Eds.) (1996). *A struggle to survive funding higher education in the next century.* Thousand Oaks, CA: Corwin Press.

Johnson, N. & Zahradnik, B. (2004, February 6). *State budget deficits projected for fiscal year 2005.* Retrieved April 13, 2004, from The Center on Budget and Policy Priorities at www.cbpp.org/10-22-03sfp2.pdf

Kaster, H. H. (1979). Modifying the open-door policy. *Community College Review, 6*(4), 23–33.

Kearney, J. C. (1981). *Selective admissions at the open door: A case study of a dilemma for an American community college.* Unpublished doctoral dissertation, University of Pittsburgh.

Larose, M. (2003, August 19). Budget cuts forcing tuition hikes across the country. *Community College Times* [Electronic version]. Retrieved April 10, 2004, from http://www.aacc.nche.edu/Template.cfm?Section=NewsandEvents&template=/ContentManagement/ContentDisplay.cfm&ContentID=10973&InterestCatego ryID=272

Levin, B. J., Perkins, J. R., & Clowes, D. A. (1995) Changing times: Changing mission. *Journal of Applied Research in the Community College, 2*(2), 109–121.

McNichol, E. (2004 February 25) *Fiscal crisis is shrinking state budgets.* Retrieved April 13, 2004, from The Center on Budget and Policy Priorities at http://www. cbpp.org/10-22-03sfp3.html

National Association of Student Financial Aid Administrators. (September 24, 2003). "AACC: State and local budget cuts account for most community college tuition increases." Retrieved March 30, 2004, from http://www.nasfaa.org/ publications/2003/rnaacctuitionsurvey092403.html

National Center for Policy Analysis (February 11, 2003). *College tuitions rise by double digits in some states.* Retrieved March 30, 2004, from http://www.ncpa. org/iss/sta/2003/pd021103c.html

National Center for Public Policy and Education. (2003 Winter). *College affordability in jeopardy: A special supplement to National Crosstalk.* Retrieved March 30, 2004, from http://www.highereducation.org/reports/affordability_supplement/affordability_1.shtml

National Governor's Association and National Association of State Budget Officers. (2002, November). *The fiscal survey of states.* Retrieved March 30, 2004, from http://www.nga.org/cda/files/NOV2002FISCALSURVEY.pdf

National Governor's Association and National Association of State Budget Officers. (2003, June). *The fiscal survey of states.* Retrieved March 30, 2004, from http:// www.nasbo.org/publications/fiscalsurvey/fs-spring2003.pdf

Nicklin, J. L. (1996). Finding the green on the fairway. *The Chronicle of Higher Education, 42*(43), 36.

Nielsen, N. R. (1994). Partnerships: Doors to the future for community colleges [Abstract]. *Leadership Abstracts, 7*(5), 1–4.

Nigliazzo, M. A. (1986). The fading vision of the open door. *New Directions for Community Colleges, 14*(1), 33–40.

Oliver, C. (1995). *The community college open-door philosophy: What negative outcomes have developed* (Report No. JC950529). (ERIC Document Reproduction Service No. ED388345.)

Phelan, D. J. (2000). *Enrollment policies and student access at community colleges* [Electronic version]. Education Commission of the United States. Retrieved March 30, 2004, from The Center for Community College Policy at http://www. communitycollegepolicy.org/pdf/3306_Phelan_policy.pdf

Prah, P. (2003). Education budgets, no child left behind dominate '02. In E. Fouhy (Ed.), *State of the States 2002, A Stateline.org Report*. Retrieved March 30, 2004, from http://www.pewtrusts.com/pdf/vf_stateline_states2002.pdf

Rippey, D. T. & Roueche, J. E. (1977). Implications of reduced funding upon the open-door commitment. *Community College Review*, *5*(2), 55–58.

Roueche, J. E. & Baker, G. A. (1987). *Access & excellence: The open-door college*. Washington, DC: The Community College Press.

Schmidt, P. (1999, December 17). As economy chugs along, states pour money into higher education. *The Chronicle of Higher Education*, p. A28.

Schmidt, P. (2002, January 18). State spending on higher education grows by smallest rate in 5 years. *The Chronicle of Higher Education*, p. A20.

Smith, M. S. (2004, March 20). Getting an education in California: Class (and hope) dismissed: Community colleges in peril. *The Sacramento Bee*. Retrieved March 30, 2004, from http://www.sacbee.com/content/opinion/story/8672823p-9600664c.html

van der Werf, M. (1999, April 9). For community colleges, fund raising has become serious and successful. *The Chronicle of Higher Education*, p. A42.

Virginia Community College System. (n.d.). *Virginia community college system workforce development services annual report*. Retrieved March 30, 2004, from http:// www.vccs.edu/workforce/reports/report03sum.htm

Yachnin, J. (2001, January 12). Two-year colleges in Oregon get emergency cash. *The Chronicle of Higher Education*, p. A23.

24

Federal Involvement in Higher Education Desegregation

An Unfinished Agenda

Clifton F. Conrad and David J. Weerts

Spanning several generations of debates, court cases, and compliance initiatives, the federal agenda to desegregate higher education remains unfinished. While a considerable distance has yet to be traveled, meaningful progress toward dismantling segregated statewide systems of higher education has been made—especially in the last decade. In particular, the leadership of the executive and judicial branches of the federal government has been instrumental in accelerating desegregation efforts. Guided by the U.S. Supreme Court's landmark ruling in *United States v. Fordice* (1992), many states and institutions—notably in the South—have implemented and continue to explore policies and practices aimed at eliminating dualism and reducing disparities between historically white and historically black institutions. Still, formidable barriers at the state and institutional level continue to stand in the way of completing the federal agenda to desegregate higher education.

The purpose of this chapter is to examine the federal government's involvement in seeking to eliminate the vestiges of segregation in higher education and to illuminate the challenges that stand in the way of desegregation. To that end, we begin by tracing the history of federal involvement—including both the judicial and executive branches—in promoting statewide desegregation. We then critique the federal legacy by examining both the strengths and limitations of federal leadership and involvement. In so doing, we argue that the federal government has been very influential in addressing issues surrounding liability both in the executive and judicial branches, but at the same time, it has not always been able to be a powerful vehicle by itself for bringing about change and reform at the state and institutional level—not least because meaningful change ultimately rests at those levels. Early in the new millennium some states are still grappling with designing desegregation policies and practices consonant with the aims of *Fordice*.

We conclude the chapter by identifying several major barriers through examining key desegregation challenges remaining at the state and institutional levels. We argue that—in light of the limitations of federal involvement and legal constraints surrounding practices such as affirmative action—the central remaining challenge is to encourage states and institutions to embrace desegregation. In particular, the political landscape at the state and institutional level and financial issues surrounding desegregation initiatives often stand in the way of finishing the agenda.

THE LEGACY OF SEGREGATION AND THE FEDERAL IMPETUS TOWARD DESEGREGATION

The end of the Civil War marked the beginning of opportunities for blacks to experience the full rights of U.S. citizenship. But these opportunities emerged only gradually and unevenly as a number of states—particularly in the South—were slow to grant blacks full privileges, including the right to an education. It would not be until the second Morrill Act of 1890 that the benefits of higher education would begin to be extended to blacks, allowing for the establishment of dual systems—composed of both white and black institutions—so long as the funds were equitably divided. Subsequently, statewide dual systems of higher education were established and remained undisturbed until 1954, when the U.S. Supreme Court ruled in *Brown* v. *the Board of Education of Topeka* that "separate but equal" educational facilities were unconstitutional (Conrad and Shrode 1990).

Although dismantling segregated higher education systems was implied in the *Brown* decision, meaningful steps toward desegregating higher education would have to wait until the 1960s when President Lyndon B. Johnson signed the Civil Rights Act of 1964. Title VI of the act restricted federal funding to schools and colleges that discriminated on the grounds of race, color, or national origin. Using his executive powers, Johnson charged the Office of Civil Rights (OCR) within the Department of Health, Education, and Welfare (HEW) with the responsibility of enforcing state compliance with Title VI standards for admission. Following its mandate, HEW eventually found ten states to be in violation of Title VI and requested plans from each of these states to address desegregation.

Despite federal orders, the mandate was largely ignored by most states. Frustrated by states' lack of compliance with desegregation orders, the NAACP Legal Defense Fund filed suit in 1970, alleging that federal funds had continued to be granted to institutions in violation of the law. In *Adams* v. *Richardson* (1972), Judge John Pratt from the U.S. District Court for the District of Columbia found in favor of the NAACP Legal Defense Fund. Subsequently, HEW obtained state plans for desegregation, but in 1977 Judge Pratt ruled that the plans were ineffective. Throughout the late 1970s and 1980s, HEW guided states in their desegregation efforts. By 1985 the federal government determined that fourteen states were officially desegregated.

At the same time, other states continued to struggle to comply with Pratt's orders, often falling short of making significant progress—especially in terms of black students matriculating at white institutions and black faculty being employed in white institutions. Perhaps most significant, program duplication and inequality between traditionally white and historically black institutions was conspicuous in many of these noncompliant states. While the *Adams* litigation was dismissed in 1990, the desegregation agenda gained new strength in 1992 with a landmark case that continues to shape contemporary efforts toward desegregating higher education: *United States* v. *Fordice*.

The Fordice Case (1992)

Although a number of states complied with Judge Pratt's orders in the 1970s and 80s, others, including Mississippi, argued that nondiscriminatory practices, as identified in *Brown*, were sufficient to meet federal standards for desegregation. Not convinced that this standard was just and adequate, Jake Ayers and other black citizens from the State of Mississippi filed a suit in

1975 demanding a more equitable state system of higher education. Emphasizing disparities in educational opportunities between historically white institutions and historically black colleges and universities (HBCUs), the plaintiffs called for increased funding for the state's three HBCUs. Over a twelve-year span Mississippi responded by adopting institutional mission statements that they considered race-neutral and by developing differentiated missions for the eight public institutions in the system. Although admissions policies no longer explicitly discriminated by race, the institutions remained largely segregated: historically black institutions remained predominantly black and historically white institutions remained predominantly white (Weerts and Conrad 2002). The district court in Mississippi finally heard the Ayers case in 1987, and while the court raised issues of discriminatory admissions policies, funding inequities, and program duplication within the state system, it ruled that the state's legal duty of desegregation did not extend to these areas. Instead, the court declared that states were only responsible for creating policies that were racially neutral, were developed in good faith, and did not contribute to making the institutions racially "identifiable." This interpretation of the law was subsequently upheld by the U.S. Court of Appeals for the 5th Circuit.

Not satisfied with the outcome, the federal government, through the U.S. Department of Justice, joined the plaintiffs and brought the case to the U.S. Supreme Court in what became known as *United States* v. *Fordice*. Relying on the findings introduced in the district court, the Supreme Court pointed to multiple practices in Mississippi that perpetuated segregation among the eight public institutions. While not limiting themselves to these areas, the Court focused on four areas that needed to be addressed to eliminate the vestiges of de jure segregation: admissions standards, program duplication, institutional mission assignments, and the continued operation of separate universities. Informed by guidance from the Court, these policy areas became the touchstones for designing desegregation strategies in Mississippi, Maryland, and nine other states. A number of states continue to explore desegregation policies and practices consonant with the four policy areas advanced in *Fordice*.

STRENGTHS OF FEDERAL INVOLVEMENT TO DESEGREGATE HIGHER EDUCATION

In reflecting on federal involvement in desegregation over the last forty years, it is clear that the federal government has experienced considerable success as well as some failure in advancing its agenda. Still, while the journey to desegregate higher education has been long and challenging, meaningful progress has been made due in large part to the leadership of the executive and judicial branches of the federal government. The strengths of the federal involvement to desegregate higher education are amply illustrated by examining the role of both of these branches.

Executive Leadership

At the executive level, President Lyndon B. Johnson played a critical role in advancing serious desegregation efforts in the 1960s. Foremost, he signed the Civil Rights Act of 1964—which achieved two critical aims. First, it enabled the federal government to bring lawsuits on behalf of black plaintiffs. Second, it restricted the spending of federal funds in segregated schools and colleges. The Civil Rights Act of 1964 created a clear and unmistakable desegregation mandate for America's colleges and universities (Brown 1999).

No less important, President Johnson's leadership paved the way for enforcement of desegregation in the higher education arena as he directed HEW to take the lead with the enforcement of Title VI standards for admission. A major strength of HEW involvement was that it was very thorough in defining parameters with which the administrative procedures for the Civil Rights Act of 1964 could be developed (Brown 1999). Still, HEW struggled to bring about meaningful reform, not least because most states—including Mississippi, Florida, and North Carolina—argued that they were already in compliance with the law (Williams 1988).

Even after the dismissal of *Adams*, HEW continued in its attempts to enforce state compliance with the desegregation mandate. By the end of the *Adams* litigation, HEW had already referred several state systems of higher education—including Tennessee, Alabama, Louisiana, and Mississippi—to the U.S. Department of Justice for litigation (Brown 1999). In a nutshell, HEW played a key role in keeping the desegregation mandate alive during a time of inadequate compliance initiatives and significantly diminished support from the judicial branch of government.

Following the lead of HEW, the Department of Justice was instrumental in pursuing the unresolved issues remaining from the dismissal of *Adams*. In particular, the department relentlessly pursued the desegregation agenda through the *Fordice* litigation. Joining the plaintiffs in the *Ayers* case, the Justice Department took a strong position in combating the argument that states were only responsible for creating higher education policies that were racially neutral, were developed in good faith, and did not contribute to making the institutions racially "identifiable." In *Fordice*, the Justice Department effectively and successfully demonstrated how vestiges of segregation continued to propel dual systems of higher education. Arguably, the leadership of the Justice Department in *Fordice* was responsible in large measure for bringing about a "sea change" in advancing desegregation effort by providing the legal and evidentiary foundation that persuaded the U.S. Supreme Court to develop a new standard for assessing liability in regard to segregation and desegregation in higher education.

Judicial Leadership

Noting the success of the executive branch's leadership—again, most recently through the U.S. Department of Justice—the judicial branch of the federal government has also played a pivotal role in advancing higher education desegregation. As evidenced by the effects of *Fordice* in terms of inviting and eventually bringing about statewide desegregation resolutions and remedies, the U.S. Supreme Court has had a very substantial impact by clarifying statewide responsibility for eliminating the vestiges of segregation.

The Supreme Court's leadership in *Fordice* was paramount because it set a legal standard for evaluating whether a state has addressed its duty to dismantle de jure segregation in its higher education systems. In so doing, the *Fordice* opinion made clear that the lower courts misinterpreted the law and failed to apply the correct legal standard for Mississippi's system of higher education. The Court noted that present policies perpetuated segregation even though racial neutrality was expressed in institutional missions. Simply put, the Court declared that a number of factors more or less predetermined an individual's choice of institution—and that this predetermination was based on race.

In *Fordice* the Court concluded that "if policies traceable to the *de jure* system are still in force and have discriminatory effects, those policies too must be reformed to the extent practicable and consistent with sound educational practices." Stated another way, the Supreme Court through *Fordice* made clear its intent to eliminate policies and practices that made institutions racially identifiable and thus wittingly or unwittingly steered students to attend a particular college based on their race (Weerts and Conrad 2002). *United States* v. *Fordice* continues to stand as the judicial guidepost for desegregation efforts across the country (Brown 1999).

In summary, the progress of the higher education desegregation effort since the 1960s can be attributed in no small measure to the concerted efforts of the executive and judicial branches of the federal government. Beginning with the signing of the Civil Rights Act of 1964 and the efforts of the Department of Health, Education, and Welfare (HEW), the executive branch has been instrumental in marshalling efforts to eliminate the vestiges of segregation in higher education. Most significantly, the U.S. Department of Justice and the U.S. Supreme Court have more recently fueled a powerful effort to finish the federal agenda to desegregate higher education. The Office of Civil Rights—now housed in the Department of Education—has successfully worked with several states in the last several years, including Maryland, to meet the standards set down in *Fordice* and continues to work with the remaining states in completing the desegregation agenda.

LIMITATIONS OF FEDERAL DESEGREGATION EFFORTS

This chapter has thus far highlighted the successes of the federal government's involvement in advancing desegregation. As the history of desegregation shows, however, there clearly are limits to the federal government's leadership. The limitations of federal involvement in the desegregation of statewide systems of higher education are threefold. First, the *Fordice* case provided a template for states and institutions to explore policies and practices to desegregate, but this template has nonetheless left states with many questions about the appropriateness of specific courses of remedy. Second, the relationship between the federal courts and the U.S. Justice Department has, at times, been more adversarial than collaborative. Finally, the Office of Civil Rights has arguably had to negotiate trade-offs with some states that may eventually compromise desegregation touchstones as envisioned by the Supreme Court in *Fordice*. While the combination of these limitations has contributed to the sluggish pace of some states and institutions as they have gone about responding to the federal directive to desegregate, we discuss only the first limitation in depth here.

Conceptually, the Supreme Court template for desegregation following *Fordice* is anchored in two policy directives aimed at increasing the other-race presence in traditionally black and traditionally white institutions. One addresses dualism—namely, the unnecessary (nonessential) program duplication between historically white and historically black institutions. The second addresses unequalness—that is, states are expected to address historic disparities in mission, funding, programs, and facilities between historically white and historically black institutions.

Many scholars and policymakers acknowledge that the general template advanced in *Fordice* has been useful in informing desegregation initiatives but also argue that its interpretation and subsequent implications for implementation remain murky. To illustrate, the Court made it clear that more than racial neutrality and good faith efforts are needed to eliminate the effects of prior discriminatory systems but left it up to the states to achieve these ends using "sound educational policy." Some scholars have interpreted "sound educational policy" with an emphasis on intangible elements—such as the quality of education for blacks—not necessarily the racial balance between whites and blacks (Brown 1999). Interpreted slightly differently, the basis for evaluating policy may be focused on the *intention* to discriminate. Thus, "sound educational policy" arguably may allow for the preservation of HBCUs while requiring white institutions to integrate (Brown-Scott 1994).

Adding to the uncertainty following *Fordice* is confusion over federal guidelines for Title VI compliance. Brown (1999) argues that "a lack of consensus exists regarding the remedy necessary to overcome the continuing discriminatory effects on higher education institutions plagued with vestiges of *de jure* segregation. The confusion surrounding the construction of universal standards for Title VI compliance leaves higher education grappling to articulate what it means to be desegregated or to have dismantled dual educational structures. This ambiguity allows states to continue circumventing and misinterpreting the legal guidelines issued in *Fordice*." Following this line of criticism, some scholars are critical that *Fordice* makes no official statements about whether additional funding is needed to achieve full dismantlement under the new judicial standards. They also point out that *Fordice* lacks an aggressive mandate for traditionally white colleges and universities' increasing their numbers of blacks and fails to create a long-term plan for continuous monitoring of the desegregation effort (Brown 1999). Anchored in these issues, some scholars claim that "*Fordice* raises more concerns than it resolves" (Stefkovich and Leas 1994). At the least, a major limitation of federal desegregation involvement is that important questions regarding remedy remain unanswered.

In light of these limitations—more precisely, constraints—concerning federal involvement in the desegregation of higher education, the next major phase toward collegiate desegregation will ultimately be left in the hands of states and institutions. Three major barriers to desegregation stand out. For one, both at the state and institutional levels, the politics of desegregation has not infrequently interfered with advancing meaningful reform in state systems of higher education. For another, the policy of affirmative action has not been a significant tool in advancing desegregation because it stands at the crossroads of political and legal disagreement. For still another, states continue to struggle to secure state funding to meet the aims articulated in *Fordice*—a critical factor that is central to the success of desegregation.

The Politics of Desegregation

Because the act of policymaking is deeply embedded in the political process, it is difficult to arrive at noncompromising solutions for many government initiatives and policies. Efforts to desegregate higher education are no different. As seen in the cases of *Adams* and *Fordice*, it is the breakdown of the political process that has led to litigation in states. As the Supreme Court declared in the desegregation case *Knight* v. *Alabama* (1994): "Many of the issues involved in this case essentially require political solutions. . . . The failure of politics has left this matter with the court" (Brown 1999). Still, the formation of policies and practices to advance desegregation are ultimately filtered through political means to more or less create "sound educational policy." As Brown (1999) put it, "the political dimensions of the policy making process are often played out between forces that advocate rational, systemic change and those that desire more incremental steps that maintain power and the status quo." These opposing forces are at work in many states and have resulted in desegregation plans that remain variously stalled in the political arena.

One striking example of a political standoff between factions can be seen in the debate over closing or merging black colleges with neighboring white institutions as a way to accomplish desegregation. Proponents of this policy argue that such a measure would be consonant with the *Fordice* mandate to address dualism and have the added benefit of promoting cost savings within the system. However, members of the black community often cite this option as an inappropriate remedy, pointing out the irony of closing the very institutions that sustained blacks during segregation as a way to combat its vestiges. Many black scholars and activists argue for the importance of black institutions as environments that preserve black culture and provide shelter, networks, and comfort for blacks (Brown and Hendrickson 1997). The debate over the future of black institutions is at the heart of the *Fordice* mandate to address dualism, which not least aims to increase the other-race presence in historically black colleges and traditionally white institutions. But whether closing or merging black colleges for the purposes of desegregation is "sound educational policy" has been subject to lively political debate—not the least in Mississippi, where one state plan proposed the closing of historically black Mississippi Valley State University.

Embedded in some of these political struggles are racial disputes related to desegregation. For example, claims of racial discrimination in Louisiana have plagued efforts to assemble a leadership team at a new community college in Baton Rouge aimed at advancing desegregation. In Mississippi, a proposal to expand the Gulf Coast campus of the University of Southern Mississippi has fueled great controversy as black critics argue that funds to be used for expansion are better spent enhancing the state's three HBCUs (Lords 2000).

Political obstacles at the board and system level have also existed. In attempts to increase the "other-race presence" at some institutions, there has sometimes been a lack of cooperation between four-year and two-year systems, thereby creating an obstacle to smooth student transfer between institutions (Conrad and Shrode 1990). Since governing and consolidated boards play an important role in promoting statewide desegregation efforts, states would be well advised to give fuller support to boards as they navigate the politics associated with desegregation.

Affirmative Action and Desegregation

Much of the activity surrounding increased access for blacks in traditionally white institutions lies in the politically charged—and legally challenged—policy of affirmative action. Affirmative action initiatives have taken a variety of forms both inside and outside the walls of the academy. On the inside, such policies seek to promote access based on characteristics associated with the economically or academically disadvantaged—factors that would disproportionately benefit blacks as a whole. Outside of the institution, efforts continue to be made to diversify boards of trustees, state coordinating boards, and planning commissions (Weerts and Conrad 2002).

During the last six years affirmative action policy has struggled to gain a consistent ruling in the courts concerning race-based scholarships and admissions. Guided by the Supreme Court's 1978 *Bakke* decision, for nearly two decades many institutions have taken race into consideration for the purposes of advancing educational diversity in higher education. However, in the *Hopwood* decision (1996), the 5th U.S. Court of Appeals suspended the University of Texas Law School's affirmative action admissions program, ruling that the *Bakke* decision was invalid. The court rejected the legitimacy of diversity as a goal, asserting that "educational diversity is not recognized as a compelling state interest." In deciding not to hear the case, the Supreme Court allowed the ruling to stand (Greve 2001).

Since *Hopwood*, other institutions have come under legal attack for giving minority applicants a specific point "boost" or putting them on a separate track in the admissions process. In September 2001, the 11th Circuit Court ruled that that University of Georgia's admissions system of awarding a half point to black applicants in the admissions process was in violation of the Constitution (Gose and Schmidt 2001). In 2003, the Supreme Court ruled that the University of Michigan's undergraduate admissions policy's automatic distribution of 20 points (out of 150 possible) to every member of an underprivileged minority was unconstitutional because it was not narrowly tailored to achieve the compelling state interest of educational diversity that the university claimed justified the program (*Gratz* v. *Bollinger*, 2003).

Eradicating affirmative action policy has already gone into effect in some states like Florida, where Governor Jeb Bush barred the use of race-conscious admissions by public colleges in an executive order. Bush's decision was upheld in July 2000 by Judge Charles Adams, who held that "affirmative action is no longer needed to ensure equal access to higher education" (Selingo 2000).

The juxtaposition of *Fordice* and the recent court cases challenging affirmative action policies has left some states and institutions puzzled as to how to fully realize their legal responsibilities to desegregate as well as their strategies for increasing diversity. In particular, the ambiguity surrounding affirmative action policy has been a barrier to desegregation as outlined in Fordice. The desegregation mandate is focused on eliminating policies and practices that make institutions racially identifiable; and affirmative action policy, by promoting a diverse student body, can be highly compatible with advancing desegregation. The present legal disputes about affirmative action as a means to advance diversity undermine institutional efforts to move forward with their legal duty to eliminate the vestiges of segregation. Simply put, progress toward desegregation has been undercut because states and institutions are unclear about the legal implications of improving black access to historically white institutions through affirmative action.

The Challenge of State Funding

Adding to the political and legal challenges faced by institutions attempting to desegregate is their constant struggle to obtain the necessary state resources to implement desegregation plans. A core expense of the effort lies in strengthening the institutional identities and uniqueness of HBCUs as a way to reduce program duplication and thereby eliminate unequalness and promote white matriculation. To achieve these goals, states are aiming to enhance missions, programs, and facilities of HBCUs. A central priority is to create high-demand, high-quality programs at the master's and doctoral level (Weerts and Conrad 2002).

But the current economy may interfere with the desegregation plans as public colleges face new reductions in state support. During the last budget cycle, governors of nine states instructed public universities to prepare for midyear cuts in state appropriations in the range of 1 to 7 percent. Many other states received the same warning signs of forthcoming reductions in support (Schmidt 2001).

To illustrate, the sluggish economy may significantly affect Mississippi's ability to deliver on its $503 million settlement plan to enhance Mississippi's HBCUs. The proposal calls for $246 million to support new academic programs, $75 million for construction projects, and $70 million for a publicly financed endowment over a 17-year period. The plan also calls for a $35 million privately financed endowment (Hebel 2002). State Senator Ronald D. Farris, a Republican, spoke out against the plan, saying that it would drain too many resources from the state's higher education system during tough budget times. Farris declared that lawmakers had to cut $60 million from college budgets in 2001, and the financial picture looks as bad, or worse, for next year, he added. "The money is not there," said Farris (Hebel 2002).

On the other side of the spectrum, opponents of the proposal argue that the settlement is not enough to adequately expand the roles of the state's three public historically black universities. In particular, critics argue that the proposal does not sufficiently improve college access for Mississippi's black students (Hebel 2002). Despite these criticisms, Mississippi senators have passed a resolution supporting the $503 million plan, which has since been approved by U.S. District Judge Neal B. Biggers Jr. (Gose 2002).

Like the plans themselves, financing higher education desegregation is mired in politics. Policymakers, scholars, and administrators have varying views on what should inform the dollar amounts to meet the aims of *Fordice*. As Senator Farris declared about the Mississippi settlement, "This settlement appears to be more about money than about desegregation. These expenditures, in my view, amount to mere reparations" (Hebel 2002). But others point to larger goals, such as enhancing the educational attainment for blacks, as the definitive measure for resources allocated to the desegregation effort (Brown 1999). Clearly, the issue of funding will continue to be debated as the remaining segregated states attempt to comply with *Fordice*.

CONCLUSION

The path to desegregation can be portrayed as a winding road that leads to a faraway and uncertain destination. On a path littered with more than century-old remnants of discrimination, obstacles still remain on the way to completing the journey. Nonetheless, the very considerable movement down this path, especially in the last decade and a half, has been fueled in no small measure by the strong involvement of the federal government. Executive branch leadership, initially through the Department of Health, Education, and Welfare (HEW) and the U.S. Department of Justice, and most recently the Office of Civil Rights in the U.S. Department of Education as well, has been crucial in moving the desegregation agenda forward. The U.S. Supreme Court—in *Fordice*—has set a standard by which states are held liable for perpetuating dual and unequal systems of higher education.

Still, the federal government's success in desegregating higher education is mixed. Notwithstanding strong leadership in the executive and judicial branches, questions still remain about the appropriate course of remedy to achieve desegregation. In light of constraints on the federal government, it will ultimately be up to states and institutions to finish the agenda. Challenged by the political process, continuing ambiguity surrounding affirmative action, and financial struggles, state policymakers and college and university representatives have their own barriers to overcome as they seek to follow the desegregation template advanced by the federal government. In the end, the extent to which federal efforts to desegregate higher education throughout the nation are fully realized will be left in the hands of states and institutions—and the public officials and institutional leaders who are responsible for, and committed to, maintaining fidelity to advancing desegregation.

REFERENCES

Brown, M. C. 1999. *The quest to define collegiate desegregation.* Westport, CT: Bergin and Garvey.

Brown, M. C., and R. M. Hendrickson. 1997. Public historically black colleges at the crossroads. *Journal for a Just and Caring Education* 3 (1): 95–113.

Brown-Scott, W. 1994. Race consciousness in higher education: Does "sound educational policy" support the continued existence of historically black colleges? *Emory Law Journal 43* (1): 1–81.

Conrad, C. F., and P. E. Shrode. 1990. The long road: Desegregating higher education. *NEA Higher Education Journal* 6 (1): 35–45.

Gose, B. 2002. Federal judge approves settlement of desegregation lawsuit in Mississippi. *Chronicle of Higher Education* 48 (March 1): A22.

Gose B., and P. Schmidt. 2001. Ruling against affirmative action could alter legal debate and admissions practices. *Chronicle of Higher Education* 48 (September 7): A36.

Gratz v. *Bollinger*, 123 S.C+. 2411, 2003.

Greve, M. 2001. Affirmative action is on the rocks, thanks to college leaders. *Chronicle of Higher Education* 47 (April 20): B11.

Hebel, S. 2002. Judge says he will sign Miss. desegregation settlement if lawmakers finance it. *Chronicle of Higher Education* 48 (January 18): A24.

Lords, E. 2000. Racial disputes stymie efforts to remedy desegregation in Louisiana and Mississippi. *Chronicle of Higher Education* 46 (April 28): A38.

Schmidt, P. 2001. Downturn in economy threatens state spending on colleges. *Chronicle of Higher Education* 48 (October 19): A22.

Selingo, J. 2000. Judge upholds Florida plan to end affirmative action. *Chronicle of Higher Education* 46 (July 21): A23.

Stefkovich, J., and T. Leas. 1994. A legal history of desegregation in higher education. *Journal of Negro Education* 63 (3): 406–20.

Weerts, D. J., and C. F. Conrad. 2002. Desegregating higher education. In *Higher education in the United States: An encyclopedia.* Santa Barbara, CA: ABC-CLIO Publishers.

Williams, J. B., III. 1988. Title VI regulation of higher education. In *Desegregating America's colleges and universities: Title VI regulation of higher education*, ed. J. B. Williams III, 3–53. New York: Teachers College, Columbia University.

25

Affirmative Action and the Creation of More Favorable Contexts of Choice

Michele S. Moses

Affirmative action has emerged as the most contentious of all race-conscious[1] education policies in the United States. The affirmative action debate attracts opinions from nearly everyone because many people believe that the policy personally affects them. Whether one supports or opposes the concept, it seems that affirmative action and its implications for equality, justice, and democracy strike a tender chord in the lives of Americans, who are "arguably the most 'race-conscious' people on earth" (Marable, 1995, p. 185). Christopher Edley, one of Bill Clinton's advisors on affirmative action, observed that the controversy surrounding affirmative action is primarily concerned with people's competing ethical values and moral vision (Edley, 1996). People have competing intuitions about the issue of nondiscrimination and the role that race and gender should play in the awarding of educational and employment opportunities.

College and university campuses across the nation are embroiled in the controversy over affirmative action. Students who support the policy have protested the scaling back or abolishment of affirmative action programs. For example, students at Florida International University staged a protest at Governor Jeb Bush's office in response to his plan to end affirmative action in admissions to Florida's public universities (Selingo, 2000). Students of University of California at Los Angeles were arrested because they refused to vacate an academic building as they demanded their university's noncompliance with California's ban on affirmative action (Basinger, 1998). These protests exemplify a continued passion for affirmative action policies and the democratic ideals that they represent. Students are likely driven to protest because they believe that abolishing affirmative action in college admissions will result in deep losses not only for campus communities but for individual students as well.

A CONTEMPORARY LIBERAL FRAMEWORK

Missing from the discussion of affirmative action policy is an analysis of affirmative action that takes into account students' vastly different "social contexts of choice" (Kymlicka, 1991, p. 166). The notion of a context of choice comes out of contemporary liberal political theory, the perspective I adopt in this chapter. For a long time the political theory of liberalism has been charged with being too atomistic, too oriented toward the individual, too blind to social and cultural embeddedness, and too noncommittal (neutral) about the good. Contemporary liberal theory transcends traditional liberal theory precisely because of its central concern with placing the responsibility for oppression and disadvantage within dominant societal structures, rather than with individuals. As a strand of liberalism that recognizes the critical importance of not only the individual, but of the individual's culture and community, it acknowledges as essential people's cultural and social contexts, within which a context of choice is framed by a society's history and structures in interaction with a person's cultural background (Kymlicka, 1991). It is thus important to distinguish contemporary liberalism from the traditional strands of liberalism (namely, libertarianism and utilitarianism) that view social problems as the responsibility of the individual, in such a way that social policy must somehow compensate for individuals' cultural deficiencies. Contemporary liberalism, rooted in the philosophy of John Dewey and supported by scholars like Kenneth Howe (1997), Joseph Raz (1986), and Charles Taylor (1991), attempts to move liberal political theory beyond the idea that education policy needs to remedy individual cultural deficits, toward the idea that oppressive social structures and systems need to be changed so that oppressed persons in general, and students of color in particular, may flourish. It also embraces a perfectionist stance on the good, rather than a neutral stance. This is significant because perfectionist liberal tradition allows for a focus on an ideal such as self-determination as a specific constituent of the good life.

Self-determination is a capacity that can be constrained or expanded by one's place within a dominant structural context and resulting life circumstances. In striving for self-determination, while the focus is on the individual, contemporary liberal theory also explicitly includes the individual's family and cultural community as crucial parts of the individual.[2] Because a just and democratic liberal society requires that its citizens be autonomous, or self-determining, the development of self-determination among young people becomes most important. The education system plays a significant role in whether or not students will be able to become self-determining in a meaningful way, that is, become the primary authors of their life stories. According to Raz (1986):

> The ruling idea behind the ideal of personal autonomy is that people should make their own lives. The autonomous person is a (part) author of his own life. The ideal of personal autonomy is the vision of people controlling, to some degree, their own destiny, fashioning it through successive decisions throughout their lives.
>
> (p. 369)

Richards (1989) in turn described this robust notion of personal autonomy as the reflective freedom to plan one's own life. A person with this reflective freedom is one whose life is characterized by self-determination, and who is able freely to choose one's own goals and relationships. Self-determination thus is more robust than the barest notion of autonomy defined only by the absence of coercion. Self-determining people make not only judgements, but significant judgments about substantial activities. Most importantly, they know the difference between the two. Self-determination is characterized, then, by a significant capacity for autonomy within which person's life choices are made in relation to their historical, cultural, and social contexts, and represent who they are and who they want to become, rather than who they cannot be due to unjust societal limits.

Because the ideal of self-determination is defined by the capacity to write one's own life story, self-determining persons do not have to capitulate to societal factors that are outside of their control. One major condition associated with the development of self-determination is that persons have a favorable context within which to make significant choices about their lives. This affects the character of people's choices; even if a choice is not directly coerced, it cannot properly be thought of as a meaningful choice if it is made within an impoverished context. Because of the dominant societal systems that privilege white skin, the social contexts of choice of people of color may be seriously constrained (Young, 1990). Constrained contexts of choice may limit individuals' real choices in such a way that their nominal choices do not reflect their potential talents, abilities, and aspirations. An unfavorable context of choice hinders students' development of self-determination, which is a crucial underpinning of an education for justice and democracy.

With this framework in mind, the purpose of this chapter is to take the ideal of self-determination, traditionally considered to be an individualistic, atomistic ideal that is not hospitable to people of color, and refocus the priorities associated with it. By relying on contemporary liberal political theory as described above, the ideal of self-determination is characterized as an inclusive and democratic aim of education that strongly supports race-conscious policies like affirmative action. A reconceptualization of self-determination may help race-conscious policies garner greater favor.

This chapter addresses two central questions: (1) How does affirmative action foster self-determination among students? (2) In light of the many critiques of affirmative action, can a defense of affirmative action hinging on the educational aim of developing students' self-determination take us beyond the standard arguments toward a place where critics and supporters might actually agree? In answering these questions, I undertake a detailed examination of the most common criticisms of affirmative action policy. It is with an understanding of these dominant themes of the debate that I then offer a new defense of affirmative action in relation to a contemporary liberal framework. I use the concept of self-determination to augment the qualifications argument for affirmative action described by Dworkin (1978, 1998), Gutmann (1987), and Gutmann and Thompson (1996). I argue that affirmative action is necessary because it fosters students' self-determination by playing a crucial role in expanding their social contexts of choice, both while they are students and afterwards.[3] I end with a discussion of the status of affirmative action policy in the United States.

The range of affirmative action programs is broad, from federal contracts to employment and promotion to college and university admissions. I specifically examine affirmative action policy for students of color in higher education admissions because colleges and universities are gatekeepers to most valued social positions (Gutmann, 1987). Higher education's gatekeeping role puts the selection of students for college and university places at the heart of the struggle for equal opportunity and social justice in education.

BACKGROUND FOR THE AFFIRMATIVE ACTION DEBATES

In 1961, President John F. Kennedy signed into law Executive Order No. 10925 (1961), which demanded more of employers than merely passive nondiscrimination in all employment practices. It required that employers act affirmatively to hire and treat employees fairly regardless of their race, creed, color, or national origin (Sovern, 1966). During Lyndon Johnson's presidential term, the 1964 Civil Rights Act became part of a substantial group of 1964–1965 legislation known as Johnson's Great Society and War on Poverty programs, which had the following goals: helping low-income people through education and health programs, stimulating the economy for new jobs, and removing race and sex barriers to educational and employment opportunity.

Most significant for affirmative action policy was the Civil Rights Act, specifically Titles VI and VII. Title VI "bars discrimination under any federally assisted activity" and Title VII bars employment discrimination according to "race, color, religion, sex, or national origin" (Sobel, 1980, pp. 1–2). Although the focus seemed to be on employment discrimination, Title VI also applied to college admissions. Any educational institutions that received active financial assistance risked losing their aid if they did not comply with the federal requirements. After the passage of the Civil Rights Act, Johnson added Executive Order No. 11246 to the civil rights legislation in 1965. Executive Order No. 11246 (1965) formally encompassed and overrode Executive Order No. 10925 (1961), so it is widely seen as the source of federal affirmative action policy.

Although one specific program may be a little bit different from another, affirmative action in higher education admissions is a policy that aims to take an applicant's race, ethnicity, and sex into account in making selection decisions. Generally, this means that if an applicant is African American, Latino, Asian American, Native American, and/or female, this fact is taken as one qualifying factor among many considered in the admissions process. Of course, just who is considered under affirmative action varies regionally according to specific populations. Massachusetts, for example, often includes Portuguese immigrants (Tierney, 1997).

In recent years, Bill Clinton supported race-conscious policies in general, and affirmative action in particular, yet he did not aggressively champion this portion of the civil rights agenda. In June 1995, he spoke on affirmative action and solidified his support for the policy even though he said that it needed reform. "When affirmative action is done right," he said, "it is flexible, it is fair, and it works" (Purdum, 1995, p. B10). Still, it was during Clinton's tenure in office that affirmative action policy faced the strongest attacks yet.

California has led the way in the backlash against affirmative action. Spurred on by Regent Ward Connerly, in 1995 the Regents of the University of California voted to bar the consideration of race and ethnicity in admissions decisions. In the November 1996 elections, California's Proposition 209, a ballot initiative entitled the California Civil Rights Initiative (CCRI), was passed with 54% of the vote. This constitutional amendment, written by two conservative academics, abolished all preferences based on race, ethnicity, and sex, but never specifically mentioned affirmative action. During the campaign, Clinton tried his best to stay out of the affirmative action debate, fearing that it would negatively affect his ability to get the White vote (Chávez, 1998). Opponents of the amendment challenged its constitutionality in court, but in 1997, the Supreme Court affirmed the 9th Circuit Court of Appeals ruling that had upheld Proposition 209. The impact on California's college student population was felt almost immediately. In Fall 1998, the most prestigious University of California campus, Berkeley, reported a 52% decrease in the number of African American and Latino first-year students for the first class admitted without affirmative action. Because of this, African American and Latino students made up only 9.9% of the first-year class compared with 20.7% the previous year (Healy, 1998). At Berkeley's law school, there was only one African American student in the first-year class of 1997–1998. The sentiments in California have spread to other states as well. The most significant developments have been in Texas, Washington, and Michigan.

In deciding the *Hopwood v. Texas*[4] case on March 18, 1996, the Court of Appeals for the 5th Circuit ruled against race-conscious affirmative action policies in higher education admissions, thus nullifying the Supreme Court's *Bakke* ruling in all 5th Circuit states: Texas, Louisiana, and Mississippi. The three-judge panel, who, not coincidentally were all Reagan-Bush appointees, prohibited the use of race-based admissions criteria to achieve diversity at the University of Texas Law School. They found for Hopwood based on the notion that a state's interest in acquiring a diverse student body was not compelling enough to justify a program like that of the University of Texas Law School. Texas appealed the case to the U.S. Supreme Court. In declining to review the case, the Supreme Court both upheld the ruling and limited its applicability to only the 5th Circuit states.

In Washington state, 59% of the voters approved Initiative 200 in 1998, a CCRI-like referendum banning race and sex preferences in public employment, contracts, and university admissions. It was in this political context that White applicants to the University of Washington Law School contested their rejection in the *Smith v. University of Washington* case. In two other cases, both the University of Michigan and the University of Michigan Law School also have been sued by White applicants who were rejected for admission.

As the legislative challenges to affirmative action continue, the theoretical and ideological debate about whether the policy is right or wrong continues to rage.

THE MAJOR ARGUMENTS AGAINST AFFIRMATIVE ACTION

To propose an innovative defense of affirmative action policy in higher education admissions based on the key educational aim of developing self-determination among students, it is important first to grapple with the major arguments both against and for affirmative action policy in higher education.

Discrimination in Reverse?

One of the most common criticisms of affirmative action is that it violates our idea of equal rights for all. Critics argue that when colleges and universities take an applicant's race or ethnicity into consideration in the admissions process it is tantamount to discrimination against White students. Steele (1990) maintained that affirmative action policies "have reburdened society with the very marriage of color and preference (in reverse) that we set out to eradicate. The old sin is reaffirmed in a new guise" (p. 115). According to critics such as Steele, this is an odious practice that results in the rejection of some applicants simply because they are White, which is just as objectionable as the rejection of applicants of color. However, supporters of affirmative action agree with attorneys Katzenbach and Marshall (1998):

> To speak of. . . [affirmative action] efforts as though they were racially biased against whites and to equate them with the discriminatory practices of the past against African Americans is to steal the rhetoric of civil rights and turn it upside down. For racial bias to be a problem, it must be accompanied by power.
>
> (p. 45)

Nonetheless, charges of reverse discrimination abound in the public debate over affirmative action. Although the 14th amendment to the Constitution guarantees equal protection to all under the law, nowhere does it preclude the consideration of race, ethnicity, or sex. In fact, sometimes to treat people fairly, it is necessary to be conscious of race, ethnicity, and sex in education policies (Appiah & Gutmann, 1996). Yet, when it comes to challenges that affirmative action has faced in court, the chief complaint against affirmative action is that it amounts to reverse discrimination.

The civil rights legislation of the 1960s championed nondiscrimination. At the time, it went unquestioned that nondiscrimination banned discrimination against people of color or women, because White men were not in danger of being discriminated against for educational or employment opportunities because of their color or gender. In fact, both sides of the affirmative action debate usually agree that race, ethnicity, and sex should not be used to discriminate against people of color or women.[5] The concept of nondiscrimination has evolved in such a way that policies that view a person's race, ethnicity, or gender as a qualification for selection are still considered legal. An applicant's race is a relevant qualification because the social purposes of (selective) colleges and universities include educating professionals and community leaders that can serve all communities (Gutmann, 1987). The notion of affirmative action was conceived as an active expansion of opportunities for people of color and women, not just as freedom from discriminatory practices. Given the past and present racism that is entrenched in American society, mere nondiscrimination can actually perpetuate the oppressive status quo. Young (1990) argued that it is precisely affirmative action's challenge to passive nondiscrimination that makes its case stronger, because it aims to combat the oppression and domination of marginalized groups. Oppression is the major wrong endured by people of color and women in United States society. Young pointed out that "if discrimination serves the purpose of undermining the oppression of a group, it may be not only permitted, but morally required" (p. 197).

Young's assertion underscores another important point: affirmative action policies take nothing away from White men that they actually earned or deserve to keep. Because of societal inequality, they enjoy many unearned privileges (McIntosh, 1989). Affirmative action, in part, attempts to remedy that situation. Studies have shown that increases in the numbers of students of color in higher education, although positive, have been small and "have been made without causing undue personal or financial hardship to white males" (Ethridge, 1997. p. 70). Of the approximately 1,800 four-year institutions of higher education in the United States, about 120 of the most selective schools practice "serious affirmative action" because the other schools have much less competitive admissions processes (Chenoweth, 1997, p. 10). A recent study by The College Fund/United Negro College Fund (UNCF) found that between 1984 and 1995, the majority of the top 120 institutions accommodated the increase in African American and Latino students by expanding their first-year cohorts in toto. For example, at the University of Virginia, the entire 1995 first-year class included a total of 292 more students, while the number of African American and Latino students increased by 237 (Chenoweth, 1997). Regardless of education, White males still had higher wages than women and people of color. White students attend their first choice of college, whereas African American and Asian American students are more likely than Whites to attend a second or third choice college (Hurtado & Navia, 1997). Interestingly, following the 5th Circuit's decision in favor of Hopwood and two other White students, a lower court charged with awarding damages to the plaintiffs considered it so unlikely that any of them would have actually been admitted to the law school, even under a race-blind policy, that they were each only awarded one dollar (Dworkin, 1998). In 1995, the Department of Labor found that out of 3,000 discrimination cases filed, fewer than 100 involved reverse discrimination; of these, only six were actually validated (American Council on Education, 1996). Still, the widespread impression is that White people unjustly lose out because of affirmative action. In a 1995 *USA Today*/CNN/Gallup Poll, 15% of the White males believed that "they've lost a job because of affirmative action policies" (Marable, 1995, p. 85). Whether or not this perception is based in reality does not change the fact that a portion of White people feel cheated by the civil rights gains in the United States. These feelings may cause one to question the fairness of affirmative action. This leads to another argument often raised by affirmative action's critics, that some students of color are less deserving of college admission than some White students with higher standardized test scores or grade point averages (GPAs).

Who Merits Admission?

The idea that affirmative action is discriminatory is a misconception that stems from the myth of meritocracy. Those who make this argument never consider how much privilege, often afforded by skin color and the arbitrary circumstances of birth, influences one's ability to meet traditional standards of merit. Without this deep understanding of the meritocratic myth, White students become resentful. All they see is that the rules of the game that privileged their fathers have changed; they cannot now always count on having the favored position.

Affirmative action caused people to question whether or not the students admitted under such policies were qualified enough, or worthy of admission.[6] Many White students believed that affirmative action policies came at the expense of their fair educational opportunities, at the expense of merit-based selection. Representative S.I. Hayakawa (Republican, California) protested affirmative action policies in 1979, even though he had supported initial affirmative action efforts to draw attention to the problems of discrimination. Hayakawa wanted "to keep those opportunities from becoming color-coded handouts" (Sobel, 1980). He was wary of opportunities that may have gone to people who did not merit them. This is the crux of the merit objection to affirmative action, perhaps the most prominent of all the opposing arguments. A main part of the contention that affirmative action desecrates merit-based admissions processes is that it reinforces the idea of White superiority by tacitly confirming that applicants of color cannot meet the traditional admissions standards, which is exactly the idea that the Civil Rights Act tries to overcome (Belz, 1991). A recent study by two researchers at the University of California at Davis Medical School examined the career paths of 356 medical school students who were admitted to Davis under affirmative action policies. They compared the affirmative action beneficiaries with a matched sample of students who were not admitted under affirmative action. Their findings directly challenge the idea that students admitted under affirmative action policies are necessarily less qualified and less able to compete and succeed in higher education. The graduation rates of both groups were quite similar; 94% of the affirmative action beneficiaries graduated compared with 97% of the matched sample. In addition, after graduation, both groups performed equally well in their residencies, as evidenced by their evaluations and rates of completion. Medicine is arguably one of the most challenging career paths one could undertake. This study makes it clear that although affirmative action helped some students of color gain entry, their qualifications and abilities enabled them to graduate and succeed as physicians.

An affirmative action policy such as the one at Davis Medical School is justifiable mainly because it compensates for biased and oppressive structural and institutional factors, rather than for the supposed deficiencies of students of color.[7] It was (and is) not uncommon for students of color to receive little to no encouragement from school officials to attend college. Consider the experience of a well-respected Chicano scientist: "I was in an accelerated class, I was in the top 10% of my high school graduating class. I wasn't dumb; I was pretty good, I thought. She [the counselor] told me, 'Well, you should go into vocational school'" (Gándara, 1995, p. 62). Structural factors such as the attitudes of K-12 educators have an impact on students' perceived future options. Affirmative action tries to offset some of the structural inequities suffered by students of color within their K-12 educations. As Sturm and Guinier (1996) contended, the "tests and informal criteria making up our 'meritocracy' tell us more about past opportunity than about future accomplishments on the job or in the classroom" (p. 957). Of course, the argument is made that students need better schools, college preparation, and encouragement from educators, not admittance to a college for which they are not qualified. Although this is certainly true, students should not suffer due to the inferior quality of their schools. It is also not right to assume that students of color do not have superior academic achievement. In 1998, Berkeley rejected 800 African American and Latino students who had perfect 4.0 GPAs (Takaki, 1998).

Still, critics will wonder why White students should suffer due to arbitrary circumstances of race. This raises an emotion-laden point. To be sure, White students should not suffer because of their race. However, the issue is far more complex than the answer intimates. Affirmative action policy does not entail that students be rejected because they are White. It also does not entail that students be accepted because they are Latino or Native American. It does entail that admissions officers select students who have the most to offer in accordance with the institution's mission and goals. When one of those goals is to educate students who will serve as leaders for all portions of United States society, then an applicant's race or ethnicity is a relevant qualification for admission (Dworkin, 1998; Gutmann, 1987).

Using race and ethnicity as a factor in admissions is somehow seen as being in opposition to regular or objective admissions criteria. What is perhaps more accurate is that it is the most thorny criterion. Race is one qualifying factor, not a sufficient qualification to guarantee admission. Other factors taken into consideration go relatively unquestioned. College and university admissions procedures have always taken special circumstances into account when selecting students. It is rather ironic that the practice of taking race into consideration raises such ire; the reliance on quantifiable scores to determine merit became standard practice only when more women and people of color began gaining access to college (Rodriguez, 1996). There is little (conservative) public outcry against other factors such as children of alumni (legacies), friends and children of large donors, athletic ability, veteran status, or geographic area. University of California admissions records from 1991 to 1996 show that influential people such as regents, politicians, and businesspeople often try to use their community standing to affect particular admissions decisions at the most selective institutions (Rodriguez, 1996). At Harvard, student legacies admitted in 1989 outnumbered all the African American, Mexican American, Native American, and Puerto Rican students, combined (Karen, 1998). Opponents of affirmative action nevertheless balk at the idea that selection criteria other than academic ability (as measured primarily by tests and GPAs) should matter in the admissions process. Although academic ability is very important, it is hardly the only, or even the most, important factor in deciding who should attend competitive institutions of higher education. As Gutmann (1987) wrote: "Academic ability is, by the best accounts, a very poor predictor of social contribution, however it is measured" (p. 197). This is especially so because an important institutional aim of selective colleges is that their graduates will benefit society in some way. Qualifications are not separable from the "social function" of the institution (Gutmann & Thompson, 1996, p. 324).

Interestingly, a study of affirmative action showed that within the selective schools' admissions records about 90% of African American applicants had higher standardized test scores than the national African American average and about 75% had higher scores than the national White average (Bowen & Bok, 1998). According to this measure, their level of qualification was quite high. Even so, the African American students at these schools had lower mean scores than the White students. Facts such as these cause affirmative action critics to argue that college-minded students of color should simply attend less selective institutions. This way, the argument goes, they have a better chance of succeeding academically and graduating from college. Here again, the evidence from the Bowen and Bok (1998) study is relevant. African American students were more likely to obtain graduate degrees when their undergraduate college was more selective, even if their GPA was lower than it might have been at a less selective institution.

A Faustian Bargain?

Do students of color lose more than they gain from affirmative action policies? Some scholars of color would answer yes to this question (Chavez, 1991; D'Souza, 1991; Rodriguez, 1982; Sowell, 1993; Steele, 1990). They argue that affirmative action victimizes students of color who end up feeling inferior, first because they doubt that their own qualifications earned their admission, and second because they cannot compete with other students at selective institutions. According to Steele (1990), disclosing one's race or ethnicity on a college application amounts to a Faustian bargain. If students of color disclose their race or ethnicity, they risk presenting themselves as victims in need of special help, which may be damaging to their self-worth and confidence. Along these lines, Belz (1991) contended: "As long as legal rights and social benefits are conditioned on racial victimization, . . . it appears to be impossible for the beneficiaries of preferential treatment to achieve full equality" (p. 263). Indeed, these critics believe that affirmative action forces students of color to sell their souls to gain opportunities.

Although this line of argument is undoubtedly heartfelt, and despite the possibility that some students of color may have feelings of self-doubt, it is not affirmative action policies that cause those feelings. It is racism that causes people to doubt the abilities of students of color and it is oppression that causes these students to doubt themselves. Unfortunately, people of color who achieve in the educational realm are often questioned, whether or not affirmative action is at issue. Their qualifications and abilities are called into question despite the evidence of educational achievement and success. Consider what this Chicano student has to say:

> I took my eighth grade diploma which was straight As, and I was valedictorian of my eighth grade
> . . . And I told him [the counselor] I would like to go to college and could he fit me into college-
> prep classes? And he . . . said, well, he wasn't sure I could handle it.
>
> (Gándara, 1995, p. 61)

This type of incident is all-too common and has nothing to do with affirmative action. The fact is that college students at selective institutions whose race or ethnicity was considered in the admissions process are largely successful. From 1960 to 1995, when affirmative action policies were implemented, the percentage of African American college graduates (ages 25–29) and law school graduates increased, according to Bowen & Bok (1998). Between 1970 and 1995, the percentages of Latino college graduates (ages 25 and over) and law school graduates also increased. Bowen and Bok (1998) also found that the 6-year graduation rate for students of color at selective institutions was similar to that of White students. White students had a 94% graduation rate, whereas the graduation rate was 96% for Asian American students, 90% for Latino students, and 79% for African American students. The more selective the college, the higher the graduation rates for all groups. Bowen and Bok observed that these statistics refute the notion that affirmative action should be abolished so that students of color would attend less selective schools where they would have a better chance of success. They also rejected the idea that affirmative action harms its beneficiaries. Their study found that students of color at selective institutions that considered race and ethnicity in admitting students had high levels of success and satisfaction, as measured by their graduate and professional school success, satisfaction with their college experience, and perceived intellectual benefit of attending a selective school. Far from damaging its beneficiaries, affirmative action does what it is supposed to do—it views a student's race and ethnicity as a relevant qualification for admission and provides students with the real opportunity to attend a selective institution of higher education. From most accounts, affirmative action programs do not cause students of color to suffer as Faust. Instead, they gain knowledge and success through their own abilities.

Are the Neediest Overlooked?

Many believe that affirmative action in higher education admissions primarily benefits students of color who need it least (D'Souza, 1991; Steele, 1990). It may be true that affirmative action disproportionately benefits students of color from middle or higher-income families rather than students from lower income families, because those from higher-income families are likely to have better college preparation and more family assets. That said, it is important to realize that in admitting students of color from any wealth background, colleges and universities are fulfilling their social purposes of, for instance educating officeholders and enabling graduates to choose from among good lives (Gutmann, 1987). It would be difficult to argue that only students of color from working class and poor backgrounds will offer something new to the diversity on campus or to postgraduate positions of leadership. Middle-class students of color bring relevant experiences to the campus related to their race and ethnicity. Through his research on the black middle class, Cose (1993) found "America is filled with attitudes, assumptions, stereotypes, and behaviors that make it virtually impossible for blacks to believe that the nation is serious about its promise of equality—even (perhaps especially) for those who have been blessed with material success" (p. 5). These are compelling reasons for the continued emphasis on race consciousness in affirmative action programs, even if students from middle-class families benefit the most. So, if the question is whether affirmative action should benefit a middle-class Latino child of an attorney or a poor child of a rural white farmer,[8] I would say the answer is both. We are, in essence, comparing apples to oranges. However, if we compare a Latino child of an attorney with a similarly situated White child, it is fair to say that the Latino student will have a different experience in that in her or his life, she or he will always have to deal with the issue of ethnicity (Edley, 1996).

There are those on both sides of the affirmative action issue who would solve the controversy by simply replacing race and ethnicity with socioeconomic class (D'Souza, 1991; West, 1993). They argue that the neediest Native Americans, Asian Americans, African Americans, and Latinos would benefit most from increased access to college. Middle-class students of color would then compete in the same way that White students do now. We must remember, however, that when affirmative action is done right, students of color do compete in the same way as White students. The only difference is that being White is not seen as a relevant qualification for admission, whereas being, say, Native American is. One major concern is that viewing class as a proxy for race would dilute the unique importance of a focus on race and ethnicity. In her study of law school admissions, Wightman (1997) found that using an admissions model focused on class rather than race does not help to identify a racially and ethnically diverse group of applicants. Similarly, Kane (1998) has found that substituting class for race as an admissions factor in California would favor low-income White and Asian students instead of African American and Latino students. Even though West (1993) favored class-conscious affirmative action, he acknowledged that race-based policy has been necessary given United States history. Another concern is that it seems dishonest to substitute class for race in the admissions process when the policy is still intended to benefit students of color. It is as if we are somehow pretending that race is no longer the central issue.

While using class as a proxy for race is neither an honest nor an effective solution, I think it is important to take class into consideration within the college admissions process because poor and working-class students would benefit from affirmative action in similar ways as students of color do. Feinberg (1998) maintained that there is a significant difference between racial injustice and injustices based on socioeconomic class, and I agree. However, he went on to argue that as a result poor people may sometimes be more to blame for their economic misfortunes than people of color are ever to blame for the misfortunes they face due to racial and ethnic considerations. This seems to be a wrong-headed way to resolve the contention that class should be substituted for race in affirmative action policy. On the contrary, class considerations fit appropriately into the socially conscious mission of selective colleges and universities. Students from poor families, depressed inner city neighborhoods, or those who are the first in their family to attend college have a background characteristic that is relevant in the admissions process. In addition, there are regional cases when it would be especially appropriate to take class issues into account (e.g., Appalachia). Nonetheless, I want to underscore the idea that a solely class-based system of affirmative action is not an effective solution to the lack of racial and ethnic diversity on college and university campuses. A class-conscious policy would likely benefit many poor White students, which is certainly good. However, because poor White people outnumber poor people of color, there would be fewer students of color at selective institutions.

Shouldn't We See Past Color Already?

As yet another argument against affirmative action, opponents such as D'Souza (1991) point to campus tensions surrounding issues of race as evidence that affirmative action policy augments racial divisions. Without a policy that admits students using race and ethnicity as a factor, students would not feel such separation due to race. Opponents argue that it is time to return to the ideal of color-blindness, that the divisiveness of affirmative action has been endured long enough. The separation that affirmative action policies create leads to racial conflicts between White students and students of color, often because of the resentment that White students feel. True, incidents of racism and hate on campus underscore this point. Nevertheless, proponents of this view appear to be overlooking the fact that conflicts related to racism and stereotyping are far more attributable to our past and present history of racial tension than they are to affirmative action policy. In addition, present racial oppression makes the ideal of genuine race neutrality in education policy little more than a pipe dream. Hurtado and Navia (1997) made the excellent point:

> Since social construction of inferiority and beliefs about cultural differences predate the implementation of affirmative action policies, the dismantling of these policies is not likely to eradicate the deeper problem of longstanding stereotypes or institutionalized racial, ethnic, gender, and class discrimination.
>
> (p. 114)

A study of college students shows that when a college or university has a strong emphasis on diversity, students gain more cultural awareness and a deeper commitment to promoting racial and ethnic understanding than they would have otherwise (Astin, 1993). Indeed, in reviewing the literature on the educational benefits of diversity, Milem and Hakuta (2000) found empirical evidence documenting that a diverse campus is beneficial for individual students, the campus as a whole, and society overall. More specifically, both the African American and White graduates in Bowen and Bok's (1998) study said they value the diversity to which they were exposed as undergraduates. One of the goals of affirmative action culled from the mission of selective institutions is to create a healthy climate, one in which students have a diversity of backgrounds, experiences, and opinions so that they can learn from one another and bring their knowledge into the community as graduates.

"Diversity" is an oft-cited justification for affirmative action (Chang, Witt, Jones, & Hakuta, 1999; Liu, 1998; Mann, 2000; Milem, 1999; Milem & Hakuta, 2000). This is due in part to the legal precedent of Justice Powell's *Bakke* opinion, in which he affirmed diversity as a worthy goal for which colleges and universities should strive. Recent research shows that campus diversity is beneficial for all students, as well as for institutions of higher education and society (Marin, 2000; Milem, 1999). Legal analysis by Liu (1998) posited diversity as a constitutionally compelling interest, intimating that the diversity rationale for affirmative action could withstand court challenges. The judges who heard the University of Washington Law School and University of Michigan undergraduate cases agreed with this rationale (Schmidt, 2000). With the understanding that the diversity rationale is crucial to the defense of affirmative action policy in court, it should not stand alone. Admitting a few students of color in the hopes of increasing campus diversity does not necessarily ensure intellectual diversity or diversity of viewpoint. Similarly, because a student body is diverse does not mean that different perspectives will be heard. A study of law school participation discovered that White men participate the most in selective law school classroom discussions, regardless of the racial, ethnic, or gender composition of the class (The Chronicle of Higher Education, 1998). However, this study also supports the notion that faculty and student diversity that is not token in nature does make a difference in the quality of classroom interactions. If the professor was a person of color, more students of color participated in classroom discussions.

What these findings show is despite the fact that affirmative action cannot guarantee that a campus will have a real and noticeable diversity of viewpoints, it can ensure that students of color will be represented in higher numbers. This, in turn, moves us toward the noble goal of a diverse and rich campus environment; when diversity is strongly lacking, White males tend to dominate the classroom discourse. Because the ideal of color-blindness sits well with many of us does not mean that it is a good, or even decent, course of action for education policy. Genuine race neutrality would be preferred if there were more doctors, lawyers, scientists, and teachers of color, but there have been small increases in these fields even with race-conscious policies. Reverting to so-called color-blindness and dismissing affirmative action will not solve this problem.

Color-blind policies cannot be championed in a society that is not color-blind. Consider these facts: 50% of African American and 44% of Latino children under the age of 6 years live below poverty level, as compared with 14.4% of White children (Edley, 1996); African Americans make up just 4.2% of all doctors, 5% of university teachers, and 3.3% of attorneys, even as they make up some 12% of the U.S. population (Feinberg, 1998); among accomplished graduates of selective colleges, Whites still earn much more than their African American counterparts (Bowen & Bok, 1998). In an experiment that placed a White man in a similar set of life situations as a Black man and as a Latino man of the same age and qualifications, the Black participant fared worse than the White participant 24% of the time, and the Latino participant fared worse than the White participant 22% of the time. The situations included a search for entry-level employment and a trip to an employment agency for a job referral. When it came to searching for housing, the Black and Latino men fared worse 50% of the time (Edley, 1996). Because race continues to matter in the United States, education policies ought to take it into account. Although in some aspects it would be nice if race neutrality could do the trick, the United States has not yet reached that point. Color-blindness will not reduce oppression just because we wish it could.

Having now considered the most common arguments against affirmative action put forth in the debate, I would like to move on to a defense of affirmative action that is not considered within the current discourse. Because the development of a sense of self-determination is a crucial educational aim if all students are to receive a good and just education, a race-conscious education policy such as affirmative action is necessary because of its role in fostering more favorable societal contexts of choice for students of color.

AFFIRMATIVE ACTION AND THE ARGUMENT FROM SELF-DETERMINATION

Good affirmative action policies implemented by institutions of higher education do much more than merely help students of color to gain admittance. When race is used as a factor in the college and university admissions process, the context from which students make their choices in life is greatly expanded. When an expanded context of choice is fostered by education policy, students are better able to become self-determining persons. The systemic oppression of people of color in the United States warrants an education policy that combats limiting societal structures. Because affirmative action policy places value on nondominant races and ethnicities and expands access to the opportunity structure, it counteracts oppression. Affirmative action policy, therefore, greatly contributes to the development of students' self-determination, especially students of color by contributing to the expansion of their contexts of choice.

In advancing this argument for affirmative action, I will first outline just how affirmative action helps students develop self-determination. Then I will show why this justification is both more defensible and more attentive to concerns of justice than the others presently available.

Expanding the Social Context of Choice

A well-respected Chicano political scientist recounts how significant it was for him to have a sibling who attended a top university. He explained: "My sister was a tremendous influence on me . . . I can remember, how many times I used to tell people my sister was at Berkeley. That was sort of a success image, a very important success image" (Gándara, 1995, p. 35). This political scientist is one of 50 Chicanos with doctorate, medical, or law degrees from selective institutions that Gándara (1995) studied in an effort to understand the factors that influenced their educational success and social mobility. One common theme was that examples of family success like a sister at Berkeley helped to expand the context within which these students made their educational and career choices. Gándara found that having role models of intelligence, achievement, and success made a big difference for these successful Chicanos. In addition, over one half of the study's participants attributed their enrollment in college and/or graduate school to out reach and recruitment programs such as affirmative action for students of color.

A higher education is widely viewed as key to the pursuit of equity and upward mobility. When higher education in America began, there was great concern about the role it would play for equality and democracy (The Institute for Higher Education Policy, 1998; Tierney, 1997). On measures such as teacher quality, money spent per student, and curriculum offerings, public schools with a large number of students of color enjoyed fewer resources than predominantly White schools (Darling-Hammond, 1998; Kozol, 1991). Inasmuch as affirmative action contributes to greater educational opportunities and possibilities of highly valued positions in society for students of color, it significantly enhances their ability to become self-determining in a meaningful way. In addition, it combats oppression and contributes toward a healthy democracy. Without people of color and women in positions of professional and community leadership, it is fair to say that there is a substantially reduced chance of eradicating institutionalized racism, sexism, and oppression. A corollary benefit is that when Whites embrace the need to share power with all members of society, their humanity becomes more meaningful, a notion championed by Freire (1970). Diminishing racial injustice can be seen as a special obligation held by White people (Gutmann, 1987). Until the policies and programs that fight oppression are protected, those who have traditionally benefited from the oppressive and racist societal structures remain morally stunted and less than fully human (Freire, 1970). According to Edley (1996): "The diversity we experience enriches our lives in immeasurable material and immaterial ways, changes who we are and how we develop. This has little to do with instrumentalism and everything to do with wanting completeness in our humanity" (p. 130). To be sure, there are those who will disagree with this idea, arguing that their humanity feels complete enough as is. In spite of that, it seems right and good to strive for a moral ideal where all people feel worthy of respect, can conceive of themselves in positions of power, and have an overall sense of possibility about their lives. Surely this a humanity worth wanting by all.[9]

When the dominant social structure places one at a disadvantage in competitive higher education admissions, thereby constraining one's context of choice, affirmative action policy adds to one's capacity for self-determination by taking that oppressive structure into account. By helping to expand the social context of choice of students of color, affirmative action takes a step closer to humanity worth wanting. The argument can be made that affirmative action programs restrict White students' contexts of choice. Prima facie this seems to be the case because as access is increased for students of color, White students may be displaced. However, that is not what has happened. Traditionally, top institutions of higher education have chosen instead to make more room for increased numbers of students of color (Chenoweth, 1997). Admissions examples from court cases like *Bakke* and *Hopwood* dramatize this issue by making it seem like a zero-sum calculus. However, in both cases, the White plaintiffs would not have been admitted even if the university's affirmative action policy had not been in place. What is most important is that affirmative action policy serves the interests of justice for students of color. Through affirmative action, students of color enter selective institutions of higher education in greater numbers than they would have otherwise been able to do. Graduation rates for White students and students of color are similar at such institutions (Bowen & Bok, 1998). Once students are accepted to college or graduate school, the context within which they make decisions grows much wider. Recent research measuring the value of a higher education proves this to be true. College-educated individuals enjoy higher rates of employment, improved health, better working conditions, higher salaries and benefits, greater personal status, and better overall quality of life (The Institute for Higher Education Policy, 1998). They are not forced to rely on only a high school education for the skills and training needed for good employment opportunities. These outcomes contribute to an expanded context of choice for college graduates, who enjoy greater life options. This has broader implications because that expansion leads not only to the development of self-determination and more worthwhile opportunities for individual students, but also to a more favorable social context of choice for other members of society who interact with college-educated role models of color.

Widening access to higher education through affirmative action contributes to justice (Dworkin, 1998; Lawrence & Matsuda, 1996). Dworkin noted: "We expect educational institutions to contribute to our physical and economic health, and we should expect them to do what they can for our social and moral health as well" (p. 100). Without college-educated role models of color in the positions of power to which affirmative action policies facilitate access, children receive unhealthy hidden messages. If they are White or male students, they learn that people in power usually look like they do; if they are students of color or female students, they learn that those in power do not look like them. Whether or not affirmative action is in place, Whites and males benefit from unearned race and sex privileges (McIntosh, 1989). With the implementation of affirmative action policies, we publicly recognize that people of color and women add something vital to college campuses and to society. It is this recognition that puts us on the road to fuller humanity. It is in everyone's best interest that all persons do as well as possible. The evidence shows that affirmative action expands people's social contexts of choice and their possibilities in life. According to at least one researcher, there is not much evidence of White backlash against affirmative action; White persons with personal experience with affirmative action programs are more likely to support race-conscious policies (Winkler, 1995). Because of firsthand experience with the way affirmative action programs work, White people recognize the overall benefits of affirmative action.

Nevertheless, we cannot necessarily assume that if White people understood why affirmative action is ultimately good, then they would support it in large numbers. It is predictable and even understandable that White people might not like affirmative action because they have benefited, both directly and indirectly, from long-standing preferences. Affirmative action does not feel like it is beneficial for most White people, who see it as an unfair policy. Some scholars of color charge that this is indicative of a tendency to deny real racial and ethnic oppression, despite evidence to the contrary. Patricia Williams, an African American law professor, recounted an incident in which she attempted to enter a Benetton store. Even though it was obvious to her that the store was open for business, the employee refused to let her enter. Williams spoke publicly about the incident and encountered a strong unwillingness to believe that things like this happen all too often to people of color (Williams, 1991). The catch is that not only do they happen, but they have a profound impact on the people to whom they happen. Incidents like this as well as more serious incidents cause people like Williams to question their inherent worth and place them in an impoverished context of choice. Those who refuse to believe that such incidents occur are also unlikely to support race-conscious policies like affirmative action. Accordingly, Edley (1996) noted that Americans have moral confusion over race-conscious policy.

One step toward clearing up this confusion is to use the principle of self-determination in conjunction with Gutmann's (1987) qualifications argument as the best philosophical justification for race-conscious policies like affirmative action. Because it advances the self-determination of students of color, critics and supporters can begin to view affirmative action as a fair and ethical policy. Affirmative action carries a moral cost (Edley, 1996). Whether Americans ultimately embrace or reject affirmative action, certain of us will likely feel worse off. Nonetheless, if we can all step back, even briefly, from the emotions surrounding the issue of race consciousness, we can begin to understand that social justice requires affirmative action and other such policies. The current oppression of people of color due to dominant institutional structures, systems, and ways of being is both undemocratic and unjust.

This portion of the argument is not likely to convert the most diehard of naysayers. It still will not feel good to certain White critics to embrace affirmative action as a morally just policy when it continues to use what they see as arbitrary characteristics—race, ethnicity, and sex—as factors in awarding opportunities. What they seem to choose not to see is that race and sex have always been factors. This time, however, it is not their own race or sex that is viewed as an important qualification, and that is somehow not palatable. In the final analysis, affirmative action is justifiable because race and ethnicity ought to be seen as relevant qualifications for admission (Gutmann, 1987). An important addition to this is that affirmative action improves the self-determination of people of color, while it does not significantly diminish the self-determination of White students. In the cases where a White student's context of choice became more limited due to affirmative action, we must realize that it was a context of choice based on intolerable injustice in the first place. As a result, the bottom line is regardless of its costs, affirmative action is morally justifiable because it plays a significant role in fostering marginalized student's development of self-determination, educating leaders and professionals, and reducing societal oppression. What is more, all told, it is the right and good thing to do.

Relevant qualifications. When a college practices affirmative action, both students of color and White students learn that the experiences, perspectives, and ideas that students of color bring to the campus environment are worth extra attention by admissions committees. It is important to a selective institution's mission to enroll students from a variety of cultural backgrounds that they consider minority, racial and ethnic background a plus factor. Being a person of color is seen as a qualification that is relevant to the mission and social function of a selective institution of higher education[10] (Gutmann, 1987).

The idea that one's race or ethnicity is a relevant qualification for admission to a selective college or university stems from the work of Amy Gutmann[11] (Gutmann, 1987; Gutmann & Thompson, 1996). She presents a presentist defense of affirmative action policies designed to diminish structural and institutional repression and discrimination. Her argument relies on the main principle of nondiscrimination, which stipulates that qualifications for selection be relevant to the social function of the institution (or job, as the case may be). Nondiscrimination prevents repression and allows educational opportunities to be distributed on grounds that are relevant to legitimate social purposes. Nondiscrimination entails taking all relevant qualifications into account in admissions decisions and hiring practices. For example, within public schools, it is essential to view sex as a relevant qualification when hiring elementary school principals. If schools are to be nonrepressive and fulfill their social purpose of educating all students so that they can rationally deliberate about different conceptions of the good life, then being a woman is a relevant qualification for the position of elementary school principal. Because most elementary school principals are men and most elementary school teachers are women, both boys and girls receive, implicitly through the hidden curriculum, an education in gender role stereotypes and power positions. According to Gutmann (1987):

> Girls learn that it is normal for them to rule children, but abnormal for them to rule men. Boys learn the opposite lesson. The democratic problem lies not in the content of either lesson per se, but in its repressive nature: the lessons reinforce uncritical acceptance of an established set of sex stereotypes and unreflective rejection of reasonable (and otherwise available) alternatives.
>
> (p. 114)

In order to provide the children with a nonrepressive and nonoppressive[12] education, more women need to be hired as elementary school principals. A similar, albeit more controversial, argument can be made regarding elementary school teachers, but this time male teachers would have an extra qualification for the job. Gutmann argued that affirmative action provides students with the experiences necessary in order for them to be able to deliberate in a rational way about differing conceptions of the good life. It helps to diversify the people in positions of authority and status as role models to whom students can look for a sense of what is possible in life.

A parallel example can be constructed regarding college and university admissions. There is a clear need for more physicians of color, both as role models for students and because they are more likely than White doctors to practice in underserved minority communities (Schroeder, 1996). As a result, race and ethnicity are relevant qualifications for admission into medical school. One of the functions of medical schools is to provide doctors for medical services in all types of communities. Fewer than 5% of all doctors are African American and Latino (American Council on Education, 1996). Due to affirmative action rollbacks in the 1990s, the number of students of color enrolling in medical school declined by 11% (Srinivasan, 1997). Because selective higher education is a privilege that one must earn, rather than a right that everyone has, qualifications matter (Gutmann, 1987). As part of their social function in a democracy, institutions of higher education serve as the gatekeepers to and educators for the highest status and highest power positions in our society. It is the exception rather than the rule that someone without at least a college degree could reach the highest levels of professional success and prestige in the United States.

Race is obviously not the only qualification considered by admissions committees. Academic ability, generally measured by standardized test scores and grades, is perhaps the most well-known and supported qualification for higher education. Opponents of affirmative action see it as the only relevant qualification. In actuality, academic ability has always been one of many factors that admissions officers take into account in selecting students who they believe have the best chance to succeed in higher education. Test scores predict a student's first-year grades, not overall college success. Therefore, admissions committees must also consider nonacademic qualifications. These qualifications need to be publicly defensible and related to the university's legitimate social functions (Gutmann, 1987). Nonacademic qualifications include intangibles such as creativity, motivation, maturity, and perseverance. It is within these categories that admissions committees can consider factors such as special talents, athletic ability, and hardships in life. It is often not the most academically gifted (at least as measured by standardized tests and grades) students who have the most to gain from and to contribute to higher education (Gutmann, 1987). Another relevant nonacademic qualification that is related to the university's social purposes is the ability to serve society and to help others. Insofar as a varied student body contributes to the robust exchange of ideas and to intellectual stimulation on campus, it is relevant to consider factors such as race, ethnicity, sex, ability, and religion. Of course, race and sex are also relevant because of how they serve the university's social functions of gatekeeping and educating office-holders. It is often students of color who have much to contribute in moving the university toward positive change.

In justifying affirmative action because it contributes to students' development of self-determination, I have been relying not only on Gutmann's qualifications argument, but on Howe's (1997) principle of nonoppression as well. Race and ethnicity are relevant qualifications for college and university admission; in admitting more students of color, selective institutions of higher education are taking an important step toward the reduction of societal oppression. Affirmative action combats the primary wrong of oppression. By having a policy of affirmative action, institutions of higher education begin to address institutional oppression and domination. For example, one study found that if law schools abandon their affirmative action policies, there will be a striking decrease in the numbers of law students of color (Wightman, 1997) and consequently, fewer lawyers who would be most likely to serve communities of color (Bowen & Bok, 1998). The increase in self-determination gained by college and professional school graduates and the concomitant contributions that they can make to society seem to be in the best interests of those on both sides of the affirmative action debate.

This is admittedly a forward-looking argument. Other arguments look more toward the past for a primary justification for affirmative action policy. Of these, the argument from historical debt is the most prominent. The argument from historical debt is based on the ethical need to redress the racist and sexist history of the United States. Generally, this defense only applies to groups that were either brought to the United States against their will or were already living here and were treated extremely poorly by White people. As such, affirmative action would only apply to women, African Americans, Native Americans, and Latinos. The argument, put forth recently by Feinberg (1998), goes something like this: We owe a special debt to women, African Americans, Native Americans, and some Latinos due to the outrageous violations of rights they suffered through our history of the subjugation of women, slavery, genocide, and cultural imperialism. Feinberg (1998) explained:

> The assault on a culture has real consequences for many people in terms of truncated expectations and opportunities both denied and overlooked and in terms of a general social attitude on the part of others that accepts as part of the natural state of affairs lower levels of material well-being. Affirmative action—that is, race-based, backward-looking affirmative action—can be part of a strategy for repairing the rupture. It attempts to reconstruct the opportunities to which intentions and expectations must be attached.
>
> (pp. 69–70)

Thus, according to the argument from historical debt, policies of affirmative action play one part in redressing the United States' shameful history by providing the affected groups with increased educational opportunity to make up for the legacy of the opportunities missed in the past.

The idea that the sole, or most important, aim of affirmative action policy is to correct past wrongs against people of color is faulty for two reasons. First, it emphasizes the past to the detriment of the present. There is no small amount of current discrimination in need of remedy. Second, and more compelling, to think of affirmative action as justifiable only or mainly because of the need to compensate for past wrongs is a significant roadblock to wider acceptance because individual persons today do not feel responsible for these historical wrongs. They refuse to accept the blame and the guilt that inevitably accompany this argument. Feinberg (1998) acknowledged this problem, but argued that even though White people should not feel responsible for historical racism, they should still feel obligated to personally right past wrongs. Although the very real debt that is owed to people of color in our society should not be overlooked, a better way of defining the aim of affirmative action policy is to correct present oppression. As some contemporary liberals have pointed out, the principle of nonoppression rather than nondiscrimination would satisfy the spirit of civil rights policy and contribute to the cause of justice for people of color (Howe, 1997). It would also place affirmative action firmly within the project of fostering social justice now rather than addressing wrongs committed by people in the past with whom many White Americans feel no kinship. Appeals to a reduction of oppression and injustice will likely carry more weight with most Americans. The argument from historical debt is just not the most compelling, especially for White people who believe that they had no part in that racist and discriminatory history. A more compelling justification relies on the idea that affirmative action furthers social justice goals both by helping students develop self-determination and by fighting oppression.

A mutually agreeable ideal.   One of the attributes that makes this justification of affirmative action especially appealing is that self-determination is a principle on which both proponents and critics of affirmative action can agree. Basing the argument for affirmative action on the ideal of self-determination gives it a favorable starting point that other points of arguments do not enjoy. If we ask people whether or not all Americans ought to have an education that fosters their self-determination, we are likely to garner mostly positive responses. This makes the argument for affirmative action from self-determination more viable than other defenses. One significant criticism of affirmative action offered by conservatives is that it constrains the freedom and autonomy of individual Americans. Belz's (1991) libertarian view exemplified this opinion. He wrote: "The chief historical significance of affirmative action . . . has been to promote statist intervention into the free market and weaken political and social institutions based on individual rights" (p. 265). Affirmative action is viewed disparagingly as a big-government policy concerned with the rights of groups to the exclusion of individuals, which is seen as undemocratic. What could be more democratic than the attempt to combat oppressive societal structures, broaden people's social context of choice, and, consequently, help them to develop meaningful self-determination? Self-determining citizens make the biggest contributions to a democracy because of their capacity to engage thoughtfully in democratic deliberation and participation. Our democracy was conceived with self-determining citizens in mind. Affirmative action policies deeply affect the lives and imaginations and consequently, the self-determination, of the individual students who benefit from them.

However, this argument could possibly be turned on its head. If one believes that affirmative action policies restrict the personal autonomy of White students, the ideal of self-determination would actually preclude the support of affirmative action. Using the example of Cheryl Hopwood, one could argue that because she could not attend the University of Texas Law School, her social context of choice was impoverished and, consequently, her self-determination restricted. Attending a less prestigious school would not afford her the same social capital as the highly selective flagship campus of the University of Texas. Although her individual context of choice was indeed limited by her Texas rejection, the contexts of choice of the students of color who benefited from the affirmative action program were expanded. The university's social purposes were fulfilled by educating a larger number of lawyers of color. Recall that I am not saying that there are no moral costs of affirmative action. I am saying that, on balance, affirmative action programs for students of color best serve the dual purposes of enhancing their individual development of self-determination and supporting the goals and functions of institutions of higher education. Unfortunately, there will be students like Hopwood who will not be selected because they lack some relevant qualification(s) for admission. Of course, Hopwood would most likely not have been accepted to Yale Law School[13] either. The nature of highly selective universities is that there are many fewer places than students who would like to attend.

The argument from self-determination does not solve all of the possible problems with affirmative action perfectly. It cannot; no argument could. The substantive components of specific affirmative action policies need to be carefully considered and constructed. One aspect that makes this argument for affirmative action policy defensible is that it is based on an ideal—self-determination—that has a good chance of mutual acceptance. Another is that it is centrally focused on resisting systemic oppression and promoting social justice. The lives of the individual students are profoundly affected by a policy that is often formulated, changed, scaled back, or even abolished without their input.

THE CURRENT STATUS OF AFFIRMATIVE ACTION IN AMERICAN HIGHER EDUCATION

As of this writing, affirmative action in higher education admissions is still alive and well in most of the United States. However, the U.S. Supreme Court has not ruled on it since the *Bakke* case. In the 1990s, state initiatives abolished affirmative action in two states and there were at least five court cases important to affirmative action's well-being. The legacy left by the *Bakke* case provides the legal guidelines for affirmative action policy.

Bakke as Law

It was widely believed that no other court case, not even *Brown v. Board of Education,* had attracted such immense media attention as the *Regents of the University of California v. Bakke*[14] case. After the University of California at Davis School of Medicine rejected the plaintiff, Allan Bakke for the second time, he decided to sue on the grounds of reverse discrimination that put the University of California at Davis School of Medicine in violation of the 14th Amendment and Title VI of the Civil Rights Act. *Allan Bakke v. Regents of the University of California* was adjudicated in California Superior Court, which ruled in favor of Bakke on both counts. On appeal by the university, the California Supreme Court also ruled 6–1 in favor of Bakke, but this time only on one count—the 14th amendment, not Title VI (Bennett & Eastland, 1979; Sobel, 1980). In the majority opinion, the justices cited the Davis School of Medicine admissions program as unconstitutional because the special program was "a form of an education quota system, benevolent in concept perhaps, but a revival of quotas nevertheless," which was in violation of the 14th Amendment (Ravitch, 1983, p. 286). Davis decided to appeal the decision to the U.S. Supreme Court.

On June 28, 1978, the Supreme Court announced its decision. They held 4–1–4 that "(a) the minority-admissions program of the University of California Medical School in Davis had discriminated illegally against a White male applicant, but (b) that universities could legally consider race as a factor in admissions" (Sobel, 1980, p. 145). In the swing vote, Justice Lewis Powell decided against the quota part of the Davis policy, but in favor of using race as a factor in admissions. Justice Powell became the court's majority opinion, because he was the deciding vote for both sides. This type of split decision showed that the justices were as divided as the nation.

Justice Powell's deciding opinion in the *Bakke* split decision stated that universities should be allowed to admit any students who they believe will add most to the robust exchange of ideas on campus; the search for a diverse student body, Justice Powell explained, is a constitutionally acceptable goal (O'Neill, 1985). Thus, race could be a legitimate factor to consider in admissions decisions. The opinion of the justices who sided with Bakke, written by Justice Stevens, cited that Title VI could be interpreted as forbidding quotas, saying that "race cannot be the basis of excluding anyone from participation in a federally funded program." This invalidated the University of California at Davis Medical School's admissions procedures because a specific number of spaces were set aside for students of color, which excluded Bakke presumably because of race (Sindler, 1978, p. 294). By contrast, the justices who sided with the Regents and University of California at Davis Medical School argued that Title VI and the 14th Amendment justified the use of racial preferences in university admissions (Sindler, 1978).

In Justice Powell's *Bakke* opinion, he appended Harvard College's affirmative action program as a guide to the constitutionality of such admissions programs. Within the plan, diversity was held as the most important rationale for affirmative action. Harvard officials believed that a diversity of students enhanced their student body (Sindler, 1978). With this in mind, the admissions committee looked at myriad activities, heritages, talents, and career objectives in selecting students for admission. One might conclude that because the Supreme Court rated Harvard's program as constitutionally permissible and fair, much of the debate over affirmative action in higher education admissions would have been squelched. However, that has certainly not been the case, despite the fact that prominent legal scholars have also endorsed the *Bakke* idea that well-crafted race-conscious admissions policies are indeed constitutional. According to Dworkin (1998), "we have no reason to forbid university affirmative action as a weapon against our deplorable racial stratification, except our indifference to that problem, or our petulant anger that it has not gone away on its own" (p. 102). Nevertheless, there have been various legislative attempts to bar affirmative action policies and to establish their unconstitutionality despite the *Bakke* precedent.

The Politics of Intimidation

Conservatives have led political campaigns against affirmative action in many states. As a result, voters in California and Washington State approved initiatives banning affirmative action in higher education admissions, contracting, and hiring.

The onslaught against affirmative action in the courts is led by the conservative Center for Individual Rights (CIR) in Washington, D.C. They are, by far, the leaders in the politics of intimidation that characterize the campaign against affirmative action. Attorneys for the nonprofit legal center represented the plaintiffs in *Hopwood v. Texas* and they represent the plaintiffs in *Smith v. University of Washington* and the two University of Michigan cases. However, their role goes beyond just helping disgruntled students sue universities. They are engaged in a crusade to intimidate administrators and officials of selective institutions of higher education. Their primary method is to spark fear of lawsuits and to recruit White students as plaintiffs against colleges and universities that have affirmative action programs. According to one CIR attorney, the group's ultimate goal is to see affirmative action policies declared unconstitutional by the Supreme Court (Greve, 1999). The CIR released two guidebooks, one for college and university trustees that focuses on how to avoid lawsuits over affirmative action in admissions and one for students that explains how to review institutional policies and sue to change them. The book for trustees warns college officials that nearly every selective institution of higher education is violating the law with their affirmative action programs, and that, if challenged in court, individual trustees can be held personally liable for those violations (Bronner, 1999; Healy, 1999a). Of course, those contentions are a matter of considerable public debate. The *Bakke* decision has not been overturned by the Supreme Court even though they have had the chance to do so, and there is no clear legal precedent for holding trustees personally liable for institutional policies (Hebel, 1999). In fact, in 1999 and 2000, the *Bakke* standards were upheld in Federal court during the *Smith v. University of Washington* and *Gratz* cases.

The Consequences of the Conservative Campaign

Those engaged in the politics of intimidation are making headway. After seeing a CIR advertisement in their campus newspaper and receiving the trustee handbook, officials at the University of Virginia began to review their admissions policies (Healy, 1999c). As a result, the policies were changed so that African American applicants no longer received qualifying points due to their race. Perhaps related to this change, the number of African American applicants seeking Fall 2000 admission to the University of Virginia decreased by 25% (Hebel, 2000). Similarly, in the aftermath of California's Proposition 209, the *Hopwood* case, and Washington State's Initiative 200, there have been decreases in the numbers of students applying for admission to and enrolling in the selective institutions in these states. There had previously been steady (albeit slow) increases in the numbers of students of color in the ranks of undergraduate and graduate students. Between 1985 and 1993, 36% more African Americans, 34% more Native Americans, 75% more Latinos, and 103% more Asian Americans graduated from college (American Council on Education, 1996). In 1994, these increases resulted in 7% of all college graduates being African American, 4% Latino, 0.5% Native American, and 4.4% Asian American. Although these are not high percentages, they are more substantial than they were before affirmative action policies were initiated. Between 1996 and 1998, while affirmative action was attracting negative publicity due to Proposition 209 and the *Hopwood* case, the percentage of students of color in the first-year classes at all colleges decreased by 1.8% (Geraghty, 1997; Reisberg, 1999). For the most prestigious University of California campuses, Berkeley and Los Angeles, the percentage of students of color accepted for admission to first-year classes declined dramatically the first year that affirmative action was not used. At Berkeley, for example, 66% fewer African Americans, 60.9% fewer Native Americans, and 52.6% fewer Latinos were admitted (Ramage, 1998). In 1999, the number of applicants of color to the University of Washington Law School declined significantly from the previous year. For Latinos, the decline was 21%, for Filipinos 26%, and for African Americans a whopping 41% (Selingo, 1999). As for University of Washington's undergraduate admissions, the number of Latino students in the 1999 first-year class decreased by 30%, African American students by 40%, and Native American students by 20% (Ma, 1999). No African American students were admitted to the University of California at San Diego's School of Medicine in 1997, even though 196 applied; only 4 of 143 Latino students were accepted (Selingo, 1997). In the 1998–1999 first-year class at the University of California at Berkeley Law School, only 1 of 268 students was African American. At the University of Texas School of Law, only 4 of 468 are African Americans. These admissions and enrollment statistics only begin to demonstrate the impact of the legislation and court rulings against affirmative action policies.

Court challenges within higher education. Court cases challenging affirmative action have been brought against the University of Washington Law School, the University of Michigan, and the University of Michigan Law School. It is likely that these cases will be the deciding factors regarding the status of affirmative action in higher education admissions. In *Smith v. University of Washington*, three White applicants who were not accepted to the University of Washington Law School sued the university with legal representation from the CIR. Even though Initiative 200 caused the university to abandon the admissions program under question, the case moved forward. A victory for affirmative action supporters came in December 2000 when the 9th Circuit Court of Appeals ruled that the University of Washington Law School's affirmative action program was constitutional.

In both cases against the University of Michigan, the university's defense relies on the *Bakke* precedent of using the argument from diversity to justify affirmative action in its undergraduate and law school admissions (Elgass, 2000). Like the lawyers for Bakke in 1978, the plaintiffs' lawyers from the CIR maintain that the University of Michigan's use of race as a factor in admissions violates the equal protection clause of the 14th Amendment and Title VI of the Civil Rights Act. The *Gratz v. Bollinger et al.* case, in which two White students are challenging the University of Michigan undergraduate admissions policy, is the first case that is not centered on law or medical school admissions. The first court battle was won by the University of Michigan. In December 2000, a U.S. District Court judge ruled against the students and the CIR. This case, as well as *Grutter v. Bollinger et al.*, the Michigan Law School case, are also unique in that they name the current and former presidents of the University of Michigan as personally liable. Officials at the University of Michigan are strong in their stance that the university will not back down on its commitment to affirmative action.[15]

Institutions that are not facing court challenges to their affirmative action programs have begun to change their policies. Like the University of Virginia, the University of Massachusetts at Amherst announced a preemptive strike on its affirmative action policy. Following the 1st Circuit's ruling against Boston Latin School's affirmative action program, the University of Massachusetts made race and ethnicity less significant qualifying factors for admissions even though the university is not facing any legal challenges. University officials estimate that the percentage of students of color enrolled could decrease as much as 6% (Healy, 1999b).

Recent court cases and state initiatives demonstrate that the politics of intimidation threatens affirmative action policies, highlighting the need for even more compelling justifications for affirmative action such as the argument from self-determination.

CONCLUSION

> Imagine, if you will, a world built over a long time by and for men, by and for whites. In that world there would be a thousand and one impediments to women and blacks working effectively and successfully. That world and its institutions would be suffused through and through with inhospitality to blacks and women . . . That's the world we still live in, isn't it?
>
> (Fullinwider, 1991, p. 13)

Indeed, that is the world we still live in. Affirmative action policies were implemented within higher education as part of an educational agenda for social justice that also includes other race-related policies such as bilingual education and multicultural curriculum policies.[16] Affirmative action is a crucial policy effort because it adds to students' meaningful self-determination by challenging dominant societal structures and expanding their social contexts of choice. A defense of affirmative action that rests on the ideal of self-determination goes beyond the established defenses of affirmative action and has a good chance of widespread acceptance because it leads to social justice.

I did not argue that colleges and universities generally have affirmative action policies in place that are good and sound. As evidenced by the court victories against the University of

Texas Law School and Boston Latin School, it is crucial for these policies to be well drafted and in keeping with current law in order for them to withstand inevitable court challenges. Of course, even a good affirmative action policy cannot eliminate all injustices in American education; dominant institutional systems and structures that are oppressive to people of color and women must be challenged on other fronts as well.

Federal affirmative action policy is at a crossroads. The ongoing dissatisfaction with affirmative action programs shows that many Americans want a more palatable alternative. Supporters stress the importance of affirmative action to ensure that oppressive practices against people of color are abated. Otherwise, as history has shown, the United States would surely retreat to a more discriminatory and oppressive time (West, 1993). As early as 1972, scholars said that in order to have sound affirmative action programs, "universities will have to develop and continually monitor and revise their affirmative action programs" (Shulman, 1972, p. 37). To that end, affirmative action must be reconceptualized in the public consciousness as a policy that creates more favorable social contexts of choice and, thus, a greater sense of possibility for people of color and women. Sound affirmative action policies successfully combat oppression against people of color, with the aim of promoting students' self-determination, and, ultimately, social justice.

NOTES

I express my sincere gratitude to Ken Howe for his thoughtful feedback, Linda McNeil for her insightful comments, and the Spencer Foundation for the funding that made this research possible.

1 I use the term *race-conscious* not because I see race as a signifier for some kind of immutable biological difference between humans, but because of the socially constructed place that "race" has in our society. Manning Marable (1995) made a relevant point: "Race only becomes 'real' as a social force when individuals or groups behave toward each other in ways which either reflect or perpetuate the hegemonic ideology of subordination and the patterns of inequality in daily life. These are, in turn, justified and explained by assumed differences in physical and biological characteristics, or in theories of cultural deprivation or intellectual inferiority" (p. 186).
2 See Kymlicka (1991) for a comprehensive treatment of the criticism that liberalism is only centrally concerned with individual autonomy and self-determination, to the detriment of culture and community. Kymlicka refuted the idea that contemporary liberal theory is too individualistic and insensitive to minority cultures.
3 In arguing for affirmative action, I primarily have the interests of students of color and female students in mind, although there are important instances where White students and male students would also benefit from an expanded context of choice. This issue will be addressed in a later section.
4 *Hopwood v. Texas,* 78 F. 3d 932 (5th Cir. 1996), certiorari denied, 116 S. Ct. 2582 (1996).
5 There are some exceptions to this, such as when being male may be seen as a qualification for posts as elementary school teachers. This will be discussed in the next section.
6 These questions were posed mainly regarding students admitted to elite and selective institutions.
7 Related to this, the idea that standardized tests should be a major criterion of selection has been vigorously challenged. See Sturm and Guinier (1996) for a critique of higher education selection practices.
8 This example is owed to Edley (1996).
9 The concept of something worth wanting was described by both Dennett (1984) and Howe (1997).
10 I have been focusing on selective institutions of higher education for that reason. Selective institutions aim to educate future community leaders. In addition, affirmative action is unnecessary in less selective or nonselective institutions because they admit almost all who apply.
11 These ideas were also provided by Dworkin (1978, 1998). However, I rely specifically on Gutmann's interpretations.
12 Howe (1997) conceptualized the principle of nonoppression as stronger than Gutmann's (1987) principle of nonrepression.
13 Yale Law School was ranked as the number one law school in the nation by U.S. News and World Report in 1999.

14 *Regents of the University of California v. Bakke*, 98 S. Ct. 2733 (1978).
15 See the University of Michigan website regarding these two cases: www.umich.edu/~urel/admissions/index.html for further information from the University of Michigan.
16 Perhaps it should not go without saying that decent health care, public schools, and academic preparation are needed for all students.

REFERENCES

American Council on Education. (1996). *Making the case for affirmative action in higher education.* Washington, DC: Author.

Appiah, K. A., & Gutmann, A. (1996). *Color conscious: The political morality of race.* Princeton, NJ: Princeton University Press.

Astin, A. W. (1993). Diversity and multiculturalism on campus: How are students affected? *Change, 25,* 44–49.

Basinger, J. (1998, May 29). 88 students arrested in protest at UCLA. *The Chronicle of Higher Education,* p. A32.

Belz, H. (1991). *Equality transformed: A quarter-century of affirmative action.* New Brunswick, NJ: Transaction.

Bennett, W., & Eastland, T. (1979). *Counting by race: Equality from the founding fathers to Bakke and Weber.* New York: Basic Books.

Bowen, W. G., & Bok, D. (1998). *The shape of the river: Long-term consequences of considering race in college and university admissions.* Princeton, NJ: Princeton University Press.

Bronner, E. (1999, January 26). Conservatives open drive against affirmative action. *The New York Times,* p. A10.

Chang, M., Witt, D., Jones, J., & Hakuta, K. (1999). *Compelling interest: Examining the evidence on racial dynamics in higher education.* Washington, DC: American Educational Research Association.

Chávez, L. (1991). *Out of the barrio: Toward a new politics of Hispanic assimilation.* New York: Basic Books.

Chávez, L. (1998). *The color bind: California's battle to end affirmative action.* Berkeley: University of California Press.

Chenoweth, K. (1997, October 30). Not guilty! *Black Issues in Higher Education,* pp. 10–13.

Cose, E. (1993). *The rage of a privileged class.* New York: HarperCollins.

Darling-Hammond, L. (1998). Unequal opportunity: Race and education. *The Brookings Review, 16* (2), 28–32.

Davidson, R. C., & Lewis, E. L. (1997). Affirmative action and other special consideration admissions at the University of California, Davis School of Medicine. *Journal of the American Medical Association, 278* (14), 1153–1158.

Dennett, D. (1984). *Elbow room: The varieties of free will worth wanting.* Cambridge: Massachusetts Institute of Technology Press.

D'Souza, D. (1991). *Illiberal education: The politics of race and sex on campus.* New York: The Free Press.

Dworkin, R. (1978). *Taking rights seriously.* Cambridge, MA: Harvard University Press.

Dworkin, R. (1998, October 22). Affirming affirmative action. *The New York Review of Books, XLV,* 91–102.

Edley, C. J. (1996). *Not all black and white: Affirmative action, race, and American values.* New York: Hill and Wang.

Elgass, J. R. (2000). University lawsuit gets court hearing. *The University Record.* Ann Arbor: University of Michigan.

Ethbridge, R. W. (1997). There is much more to do. In M. Garcia (Ed.), *Affirmative action's testament of hope: Strategies for a new era in higher education* (pp. 47–74). Albany: State University of New York Press.

Feinberg, W. (1998). *On higher ground: Education and the case for affirmative action.* New York: Teachers College Press.

Freire, P. (1970). *The pedagogy of the oppressed.* New York: Continuum.

Fullinwider, R. K. (1991). Affirmative action and fairness. *Report from the Institute for Philosophy and Public Policy, 11* (1), 10–13.

Gándara, P. (1995). *Over the ivy walls: The educational mobility of low-income Chicanos.* Albany: State University of New York Press.

Geraghty, M. (1997, January 17). Finances are becoming more crucial in students' college choice, survey finds. *The Chronicle of Higher Education,* pp. A41–A43.

Greve, M. S. (1999, March 19). The demise of race-based admissions policies. *The Chronicle of Higher Education,* pp. B6–B7.

Gutmann, A. (1987). *Democratic education.* Princeton, NJ: Princeton University Press.

Gutmann, A., & Thompson, D. (1996). *Democracy and disagreement: Why moral conflict cannot be avoided in politics, and what should be done about it.* Cambridge, MA: The Belknap Press.

Healy, P. (1998. May 29). Berkeley struggles to stay diverse in post-affirmative action era. *The Chronicle of Higher Education,* pp. A31–A33.

Healy, P. (1999a, February 5). A group attacking affirmative action seeks help from trustees and students. *The Chronicle of Higher Education,* pp. A36–A37.

Healy, P. (1999b, March 5). U. of Mass. limits racial preferences, despite vow to increase minority enrollment. *The Chronicle of Higher Education,* pp. A30–A31.

Healy, P. (1999c, February 12). U. of Virginia reviews race in admission. *The Chronicle of Higher Education,* p. A37.

Hebel, S. (1999, February 19). How liable are trustees in affirmative-action suits? *The Chronicle of Higher Education,* pp. A35–A36.

Hebel, S. (2000, February 18). U. Va. sees drop in black applicants. *The Chronicle of Higher Education,* p. A44.

Howe, K. R. (1997). *Understanding equal educational opportunity: Social justice, democracy, and schooling.* New York: Teachers College Press.

Hurtado, S., & Navia, C. (1997). Reconciling college access and the affirmative action debate. In M. García (Ed.), *Affirmative action's testament of hope: Strategies for a new era in higher education* (pp. 105–130). Albany: State University of New York Press.

Kane, T. J. (1998). Misconceptions in the debate over affirmative action in college admissions. In G. Orfield & E. Miller (Eds.), *Chilling admissions: The affirmative action crisis and the search for alternatives* (pp. 17–31). Cambridge, MA: Harvard Education Publishing Group.

Karen, D. (1998, November 16). Go to the head of the class. *The Nation,* 46–50.

Katzenbach, N. D., & Marshall, B. (1998, February 22). Not color blind, just blind. *The New York Times Magazine,* pp. 42–45.

Kozol, J. (1991). *Savage inequalities: Children in America's schools.* New York: Harper.

Kymlicka, W. (1991). *Liberalism, community, and culture.* Oxford: Clarendon Press.

Lawrence, C. R., & Matsuda, M. J. (1996). *We won't go back: Making the case for affirmative action.* New York: Houghton Mifflin.

Liu, G. (1998). Affirmative action in higher education: The diversity rationale and the compelling interest test. *Harvard Civil Rights-Civil Liberties Law Review, 33,* 381–442.

Ma, K. (1999, May 28). U. of Wash. expects fewer black freshmen. *The Chronicle of Higher Education,* p. A33.

Marable, M. (1995). *Beyond black and white: Transforming African-American politics.* London: Verso.

Marin, P. (2000). The educational possibility of multi-racial/multi-ethnic college classrooms. In American Journal on Education (Ed.), *Does diversity make a difference: Three research studies on diversity in college classrooms* (pp. 61–83). Washington, DC: American Council on Education and American Association of University Professors.

McIntosh, P. (1989, July/August). White privilege: Unpacking the invisible knapsack. *Peace and Freedom,* pp. 10–12.

Milem, J. F. (1999). The educational benefits of diversity: Evidence from multiple sectors. In M. Chang, D. Witt, J. Jones, & K. Hakuta (Eds.), *Compelling interest: Examining the evidence on racial dynamics in higher education* (pp. 1–41). Washington, DC: American Educational Research Association.

Milem, J. F., & Hakuta, K. (2000). *The benefits of racial and ethnic diversity in higher education.* Washington, DC: American Council on Education.

O'Neill, T. J. (1985). *Bakke and the politics of equality: Friends and foes in the classroom of litigation.* Middletown, CT: Wesleyan University Press.

Purdum, T. S. (1995, July 20). President shows fervent support for goals of affirmative action. *The New York Times,* p. Al.

Ramage, J. (1998, April 10). Berkeley and UCLA see sharp drops in admission of black and Hispanic applicants. *The Chronicle of Higher Education,* p. A43.

Ravitch, D. (1983). *The troubled crusade: American education 1945–1980.* New York: Basic Books.

Raz, J. (1986). *The morality of freedom.* Oxford: Clarendon Press.

Reisberg, L. (1999, January 29). Survey of freshmen finds a decline in support for abortion and casual sex. *The Chronicle of Higher Education,* pp. A47–A50.

Richards, D. A. J. (1989). Rights and autonomy. In J. Christman (Ed.), *The inner citadel: Essays on individual autonomy* (pp. 203–220). New York: Oxford University Press.

Rodriguez, R. (1982). *Hunger of memory: The education of Richard Rodriguez.* New York: Bantam.

Rodriguez, R. (1996). The dirty little secret of college admissions. *Black Issues in Higher Education, 12* (13), 12–14.

Schmidt, P. (2000, December 14). Federal judge approves Michigan's use of race in admissions decisions. *The Chronicle of Higher Education* [On-line]. Available: http://chronicle.com/daily/2000/12/2000121402n.htm.

Schroeder, S. A. (1996, November 1). Doctors and diversity: Improving the health of poor and minority people. *The Chronicle of Higher Education,* p. B5.

Selingo, J. (1997, August 8). No blacks are admitted by Cal. medical school. *The Chronicle of Higher Education,* p. A32.

Selingo, J. (1998, February 27). U. of Michigan changes the way it considers race and ethnicity in admissions. *The Chronicle of Higher Education,* p. A38.

Selingo, J. (1999, March 26). Washington law school loses black applicants. *The Chronicle of Higher Education,* p. A45.

Selingo, J. (2000, January 20). Sit-in forces delay in vote on Florida plan to end use of race in admissions. *The Chronicle of Higher Education, Today's News* [Online]. Available: www.chronicle.com.

Shulman, C. H. (1972). *Affirmative action: Women's rights on campus.* Washington, DC: American Association for Higher Education.

Sindler, A. P. (1978). *Bakke, DeFunis, and minority admissions: The quest for equal opportunity.* New York: Longman.

Sobel, L. (Ed.). (1980). *Quotas and affirmative action.* New York: Facts on File.

Sovern, M. I. (1966). *Legal restraints on racial discrimination in employment.* New York: The Twentieth Century Fund.

Sowell, T. (1993). *Inside American education: The decline, the deception, the dogmas.* New York: The Free Press.

Srinivasan, K. (1997, November 2). Medical school minorities decline. *The Denver Post,* p. 18A.

Steele, S. (1990). *The content of our character: A new vision of race in America.* New York: St. Martin's Press.

Sturm, S., & Guinier, L. (1996). The future of affirmative action: Reclaiming the innovative ideal. *California Law Review, 84* (4), 953–1036.

Takaki, R. (1998, October 5). California's big squeeze. *The Nation,* pp. 21–23.

Taylor, C. (1991). *The ethics of authenticity.* Cambridge, MA: Harvard University Press.

The Chronicle of Higher Education. (1998, July 17). Which students talk the most in law school? White men. *The Chronicle of Higher Education,* p. A53.

The Institute for Higher Education Policy. (1998). *Reaping the benefits: Defining the public and private value of going to college.* Washington, DC: The New Millennium Project on Higher Education Costs, Pricing, and Productivity.

Tierney, T. G. (1997). The parameters of affirmative action: Equity and excellence in the academy. *Review of Educational Research, 67* (2), 165–196.

West, C. (1993). *Race matters.* Boston: Beacon Press.

Wightman, L. F. (1997). The threat to diversity in legal education: An empirical analysis of the consequences of abandoning race as a factor in law school admission decisions. *New York University Law Review, 72* (1), 1–53.

Williams, P. J. (1991). *The alchemy of race and rights.* Cambridge, MA: Harvard University Press.

Winkler, K. J. (1995, November 17). A sociologist's research finds little evidence of white backlash. *The Chronicle of Higher Education,* p. A15.

Young, I. M. (1990). *Justice and the politics of difference.* Princeton, NJ: Princeton University Press.

Epilogue on the Future of American Higher Education

Paul D. Umbach, Lisa R. Lattuca,
Samuel D. Museus, Matthew Hartley, and Tatiana Melguizo

Below are predictive statements on emerging priorities, future trends, and new directions in American higher education. They are written by early and mid-career thought leaders in each of the five areas of study in the field. Also offered here are several possibilities for future research. These statements might be of interest to readers who wonder where higher education is likely to go within the next five years, and what challenges and opportunities are on the horizon for those who work at colleges and universities in the United States.

FACULTY

Charged with the task of educating students, and in many cases, with the production of new knowledge, college and university faculty function in a rapidly changing professional context. In this section, I explore three foremost environmental factors that will affect college faculty and their work in future years. I also examine ways in which researchers, administrators, and policymakers will likely contend with these issues. Specifically, I predict the following: Years of funding reductions culminating with deep cuts resulting from the most recent economic recession will markedly change the academic workforce and faculty activities; rapid changes in technology will continue to shape the way faculty do their work; and diversity of the professoriate will continue to lag behind that of the U.S. and college student demographics unless postsecondary administrators, faculty, and policymakers make a concerted effort for change. Each of these areas presents new avenues for well-designed research concerning faculty appointments, development, and support.

Financing Higher Education and Academic Workforce Changes

Researchers and faculty groups have become increasingly concerned with the changing mix of tenure-track and non-tenure-track faculty appointments. Years of cuts in state funding have resulted in some marked shifts in the academic workforce. Today, part-time and non-tenure-track faculty (e.g., full-time clinical and practice professors) make up the majority of college faculty members. States, facing massive shortfalls from the recent recession, have made even deeper cuts in higher education appropriations. These cuts, along with losses in endowment income and decreases in giving will likely cause continued reliance on part-time and non-tenure-track faculty. Colleges and universities, in the short term, will pare back their non-tenure-track workforce to trim their budgets. With continued lack of state support, it is not unreasonable to expect that the reliance on part-time and full-time non-tenure-track faculty will increase in upcoming years.

While the continued reliance on less-permanent appointments affords college leaders flexible and inexpensive labor, it likewise presents them with challenges. Recent research suggests that part-time faculty negatively affect the undergraduate experience. Although this evidence is far from conclusive and much work needs to be done to disentangle the complex relationship between faculty appointment type and the undergraduate experience, it does suggest that colleges need to examine their hiring practices and ways to better support part-time faculty. Higher education scholars would be wise to continue exploring the effects of contingent appointments on the undergraduate experience. Few, if any, researchers have examined disciplinary differences among contingent faculty. We also know relatively little about the trajectories, experiences, and labor market opportunities of faculty in these appointments.

Many also argue that the shift toward a temporary workforce is slowly eroding academic freedom, a core value of college faculty. This shift, along with recent court cases, has led many to question the future of academic freedom. Some would argue that long-term appointments would act in the same way as tenure in ensuring faculty members' rights. Still others maintain that academic freedom should be extended to all faculty members, regardless of their appointment type. Can academic freedom exist without the job security afforded by tenure? Administrators, policymakers, and college faculty would be wise to explore this issue in upcoming years, and researchers could provide assistance by examining the current state of academic freedom and the implications that various options pose.

One response to the continued growth of less-permanent academic appointments is the extension of collective bargaining to part-time and full-time non-tenure-track faculty. Given the relatively poor working conditions and low pay among part-timers, this should come as no surprise to postsecondary leaders and policymakers. The three major faculty collective bargaining units—the American Federation of Teachers (AFT), the National Education Association (NEA), and the American Association of University Professors (AAUP)—are already having some success serving part-time faculty, and I expect they will represent them at more colleges and universities in the future. Research on how collective bargaining affects working conditions for part-time faculty as well as the relationships between them and their full-time colleagues and administrators would be helpful in determining the effectiveness of such arrangements.

The steady decrease in state funding to higher education, rapid declines in public giving, and drops in endowment income, have also forced both public and private college faculty to become entrepreneurial in ways that they had not in the past. Nearly all faculty at four-year institutions have or will likely work in a world of public-private partnerships, grant writing, sales and services, paid advisory boards, and patents. Institutional pressure to generate revenue will only increase in the upcoming years and will continue to change the work that faculty do. Faculty members will increasingly become managers of small to very large enterprises, forcing them to spend their time dealing with complex budgetary and human resource issues. With their reported time already stretched to the limit, the emphasis on making money will likely stretch them even more. Furthermore, the type of research faculty do will become more market driven.

Technology and Changes in Faculty Work

In addition to changes ignited by financial pressures, rapid advances in technology and increased demand for online instruction will likely continue to change the way college faculty teach and do research. More and more faculty will be asked to teach courses online, regardless of the type of institution at which they are employed. Administrators will continue to be faced with the challenge of providing support for and training to faculty, many of whom have resisted teaching at a distance in the past. Faculty will need to keep up with current technologies to effectively deliver instruction. The traditional concepts of contact hours and student-faculty interactions in an online environment will need to be examined systematically and researchers will need to explore the outcomes of online learning environments.

As in the corporate sector, technology creates a global academic workforce. College and university faculty will increasingly teach students from other countries via distance education. Technology also has created the capacity for multiplying international research collaborations. Removing traditional boundaries presents both opportunities and challenges for college faculty. We know very little about how this affects faculty and their work. Colleges and their students could benefit greatly by supporting and capitalizing on these international faculty collaborations. Research on how international instruction and research collaborations affect the work and productivity of college faculty would be helpful to both institutions and policymakers.

Advances in instructional technology also will intensify competition from for-profit institutions. Already major players in the postsecondary market, for-profit institutions employ thousands of college faculty. This segment of the faculty workforce is relatively unexplored in the higher education literature. Given their growing numbers, issues related to for-profit college faculty are ripe for empirical investigation.

Diversity of the College Faculty

Faculty diversity, particularly in certain disciplines and in senior ranks, continues to lag substantially behind societal diversity. While college students and the U.S. citizenry continue to become increasingly diverse, we have seen relatively small gains in the racial/ethnic diversity of college faculty. Likewise, women still represent a small number of the science, technology, engineering, and math (STEM) faculty and senior professorships. Scholars and administrators offer several reasons for these inequities. Many point to an unwelcoming climate for women and minority scholars, while others speak to inequitable reward structures. Still others point to policies that do not support family responsibilities for which women most often bear disproportionate responsibility. The continued success of American higher education depends upon a concerted effort to diversify the faculty.

Paul D. Umbach
Associate Professor of Higher Education
North Carolina State University

CURRICULUM, TEACHING AND LEARNING

The abundance of national reports calling for greater accountability from U.S. colleges and universities and expressing doubts about the quality of undergraduate education should concern those who maintain responsibility for curriculum, teaching, and learning activities. Some campuses have responded positively to these concerns by offering information on graduation rates and students' post-undergraduate experiences. But in general, postsecondary institutions have not done as much as they could to reassure the public or themselves that their academic programs consistently provide well-designed learning experiences that simultaneously help students meet their goals while also contributing to the civic, cultural, and economic health of our nation.

Underlying public criticisms of higher education are some fundamental issues of concern related to curriculum, teaching, and learning. The first is the design of courses and program curricula that deeply engage students in the learning process, and thus result in desired educational outcomes. There is a significant empirical knowledge base to guide curriculum development, hence the issue is not so much the absence of knowledge, but more often that of effective dissemination, consistent application, and translating theory and research to practice. These issues are exacerbated by several factors, including the insufficient preparation of graduate students for their future roles as faculty; the tension between teaching and research obligations in four-year institutions; and steep increases in the numbers of part-time and non-tenure-track faculty who are not well integrated into academic programs. Some critical questions stem from these current realities: How can we ensure that all those who instruct our students have the commitment, knowledge, and skills to develop courses and programs that maximize opportunities to learn? How can we expand our understanding of teaching, which is often narrowly conceived as classroom performance, to include responsibilities for sound curriculum design so that these two essential activities are well-aligned and effective? How can colleges and universities support the professional activities and development of part-time and non-tenure-track faculty, as well as those who are tenured or tenure-track, so the integrity of academic programs is maintained and improved on an ongoing basis?

To respond to higher education critics, but more importantly to enable curricular and instructional improvements, practitioners and researchers must focus attention on student learning assessment. Effective assessment is essential at the course level because all students need specific and constructive feedback to learn. Program-level assessments yield useful data for decision making among those responsible for academic programs. The curriculum, teaching, and learning literature provides much guidance on assessment. More challenging, though, is finding ways to demonstrate via assessment data the quality of curriculum, teaching, and learning to external stakeholders (e.g., employers, the public, and policymakers). This is an area of tremendous research possibility for interested scholars. With its diversity of institutional types, missions, and curricula, there are no simple answers in the complex domain of U.S. higher education. Accordingly, practitioners and researchers must find answers that work in particular contexts and then disseminate effective models for adoption or adaptation. As will soon become clear, the concerns I have identified are highly interrelated.

Expanding Understandings of Faculty Careers to Improve Practice

One of the most fundamental, yet complex problems in higher education is ensuring that all faculty and instructors are ready and able to help students learn. Until recently, most Ph.D. programs focused exclusively on building students' research expertise. Still at many research universities, little to no attention is devoted to preparing graduate students to design courses, identify appropriate learning objectives, select instructional methods that have the potential to achieve those objectives, develop assessment tasks that truly measure what students have learned, and evaluate what they have done so it can improved the next time around. Although initiatives such as the *Preparing Future Faculty* program have transformed doctoral education at some institutions by addressing the multiple roles of research, teaching, and service that graduate students will someday assume as faculty, such programs are not universally available or required. Nor is it clear that all provide graduate students with an understanding of or skills in curriculum design and evaluation, which are part of effective teaching. Moving ahead, comprehensive preparation programs should be an institutional priority for doctoral and research universities. In addition to helping graduate students understand the faculty role and how it varies in different kinds of institutions, all programs should include information on how students learn, the principles of course design, and the array of teaching methods that might be used to meet different learning objectives.

College and university leaders must also assist current faculty and instructors in becoming more effective teachers. Many institutions have instructional development centers, but relatively few people take advantage of the services. The question for practitioners and researchers thus becomes how to motivate those who have not been adequately prepared to teach to engage in this learning process. Too often instructional support facilities are viewed as venues for remediation rather than resource sites for an ongoing process in which the development of knowledge and skills in curriculum design, teaching, and assessment skills are woven into the professional lives of faculty.

We must also examine institutional motivations and their impact on teaching. Research shows that faculty in all types of four-year colleges and universities, even those more oriented toward teaching than research, believe research productivity is the key to earning tenure. Whether perceived or actual, this contradiction between institutional values regarding research and teaching affects the choices that faculty make about how to spend their time and which aspects of their work to prioritize. A more holistic understanding of faculty interests, goals, work lives, and careers will help institutions create the conditions that support the development and delivery of excellent educational programs.

Addressing Costs without Compromising Pedagogy

As I write, the economic picture in the United States is improving, but the after-effects of the economic recession will be a continuing concern as higher education institutions contend with reduced endowments, cuts in state appropriations, and downward trends in annual giving for years to come. Concerns about instructional costs, however, predate current economic realities. College and university administrators have not met the challenge of working with faculty and instructional experts to develop pedagogically sound and cost-effective instructional methods. New technologies can be used in large lecture courses, for example, to creatively engage students in their learning. The literature on teaching in the disciplines includes descriptions of methods for scaling up instructional activities that have proven effective in classes of varying size. Ongoing professional development, as described above, would introduce faculty to innovations as they become available, help them modify these innovations for use in their courses and programs, and build their comfort and skill levels so they are willing and able to implement the innovations.

While imperfect, online learning can also provide educationally sound approaches to containing instructional costs. In the years ahead, practitioners and researchers will be required to work together to determine effective methods for teaching different types of content and skills, as well as ways to combine residential instruction, online modules and courses, and experiential learning. As e-learning grows in popularity, its impact on student learning, achievement, retention, and degree completion should be systematically studied. This topic could be explored in community colleges, four-year universities, and for-profit institutions or online learning contexts.

Assessing Learning to Meet Institutional Goals and Assure Quality

Many in the higher education community find it hard to conceive of an accountability system that would provide defensible comparisons of student learning outcomes across institutions with varying missions, educational goals, student populations, and academic programs. These concerns are sensible, as the diversity that is the strength of the U.S. higher education enterprise is also one of its greatest challenges. Nevertheless, educators will be expected in future years to demonstrate effectiveness in teaching diverse populations. In addition, identifying strategies for assessing learning among all students will also become a higher priority. Sophisticated assessment systems that yield trustworthy data can be used to improve academic programs as institutional leaders attempt to respond to external pressures for accountability.

Lisa R. Lattuca
Associate Professor of Higher Education
The Pennsylvania State University

STUDENTS

The changing characteristics of entering college students create a fascinating, yet complex context for the study of higher education. To effectively meet the needs of college students in the coming years, educators and institutional leaders must effectively adapt to an array of internal and external forces that ultimately determine who gets access to college, what they experience and how successful they will be post-admission, and what resources and strategies appear most effective for maximizing their learning and engagement. I outline below three of the most salient student-related issues with which institutional agents (faculty, staff, and administrators) are likely to contend over the next 5–10 years.

Increasing Access and Success in Financially Turbulent Times

First and foremost, access to U.S. higher education will continue to be a critical issue, one exacerbated by current economic realities. Access, as I have conceptualized it here, is not just about admitting more students to colleges and universities. It also includes affording students access to resources that enable success once they are enrolled and ultimately to the benefits associated with college degree attainment. Increasingly, access without attainment is being viewed as pointless (although many argue that *some college* is better than never having attended at all). Indeed, some populations are still disproportionately denied access to college. While a plethora of factors contribute to this reality (e.g., historical racism, unequal schooling, and socioeconomic disparities), the current economic climate may serve to intensify the denial of access to large numbers of prospective college students and success for many potential college graduates. Indeed, the growing costs of a college education, coupled with economic uncertainties and instabilities resulting from the recent recession, are already making it more difficult for many students to enter and persist through college. In fact, as I write this statement, professors and students are planning over 120 protests to challenge budget cuts at public universities in over 30 states across the nation.

Given the magnitude of this issue, higher education scholars will be charged with the task of expanding current understandings of the complexities around how financial factors shape students' choices and experiences. Specifically, researchers should seek to advance knowledge regarding the indirect impact of specific types of employment and financial aid on students' behaviors, choices, and dispositions. They should also generate new knowledge about the ways in which socioeconomic realities intersect with other factors to shape students' experiences. While higher education has made great strides in understanding the role of finances on student engagement and persistence, many questions remain about how those influences vary across gender, race, ethnicity, and citizenship. Thus, institutions will be continually pressed to find ways to ameliorate the negative effects of students' financial challenges. This could involve fostering a more seamless experience and addressing students' academic, cultural, financial, and social problems in more integrated ways during the admissions process and throughout the college years.

Responding Effectively to an Increasingly Diverse Student Population

The diversity of entering college student cohorts continues to grow. Of course, this is not a new trend, but more colleges and universities are witnessing unprecedented numbers of historically marginalized groups on campus, including undergraduates from lower socioeconomic backgrounds; lesbian, gay, bisexual, and transgender (LGBT) students; and racial, ethnic, and religious minorities. Higher education researchers and practitioners will continue to grapple with questions regarding how educators can engage, support, and graduate an increasing number of minority students. They must also figure out how they will most effectively take advantage of the diversity that such students bring to their campuses and utilize it to advance institutional missions.

Scholars are presently calling for the inclusion of voices from historically silenced groups in research, including Asian Americans, Pacific Islanders, multiracial students, and LGBT persons. A handful of universities are engaging those voices in campus-wide discussions that revolve around issues of diversity, identity, social justice, community engagement, and educational opportunity. And many institutions have established ethnic studies programs that engage racial minority students' cultural backgrounds as tools to increase success among students of color, facilitate white students' learning about cultures that differ from their own, and generate new ways of thinking about social problems. In these ways, some educators are proving that diversity is one of higher education's most underutilized resources. Nevertheless, these examples are exceptions rather than pervasive practices, and much more progress needs to be made in viewing minority students as educational assets that can enrich learning in courses beyond those offered in ethnic studies.

Moving ahead, educators and institutional leaders also must better understand and strengthen the connections between campuses and the communities from which diverse student populations come. It can be argued that postsecondary institutions serve their communities in myriad ways. But if educators are to effectively meet the needs of increasingly diverse populations, they will need to make the educational experience more inclusive of and relevant to the lives of those students and their communities of origin.

The Influence of Digital Technology on College Student Life

Entering college, student populations are growing up in increasingly sophisticated digital environments. Ten years ago, many students did not have cellular phones; rates of dependency on e-mail for communication and the Internet for academic work were lower; and even fewer undergraduates belonged to online social networking communities when they entered college. Today, a majority of college students are meaningfully connected in more than one of these ways—in fact, a sizeable fraction of the millennial generation is connected to all these technologies through a single mobile device. In addition, current students have instant access to endless amounts of information and get a substantial portion of their news from blogs and websites. These realities have important implications for higher education researchers and practitioners. Because technology is such an integral part of today's (and predictably tomorrow's) culture, educators must understand the role of digital media in students' lives in order to most effectively teach them, communicate with them, and meet their developmental needs.

Today, many researchers are asking questions about how educators can most effectively incorporate technology into academic experiences. As a result, many faculty members communicate with students via courseware (e.g., Blackboard), Facebook, and Twitter. To maintain relevance in future years, they must figure out innovative ways to incorporate digital media into lectures and discussions, and assign projects through which students can create their own digital deliverables. Social networking software that allows students to map community organizations and the relationships among them are being infused into classrooms. And, faculty members are creating their own blogs in recognition that this is the way to reach the masses of contemporary college students. More and more, professors will have to figure out ways to incorporate a range of technologies into their work if they hope to engage students.

Samuel D. Museus
Assistant Professor of Higher Education
University of Massachusetts Boston

ORGANIZATIONS, LEADERSHIP AND GOVERNANCE

In 1419 the wool merchants guild, one of the most powerful in all of Florence, Italy, held a competition to select an architect to erect the dome above the city's massive cathedral, Santa Maria del Fiore. What made the commission remarkable was that no one had any idea how such a feat of engineering and artistry could possibly be accomplished. The span to be bridged exceeded that of the Pantheon, the architectural glory of ancient Rome. Buttresses, an engineering solution employed elsewhere in Europe, were forbidden by the city fathers. It was not possible to construct wooden rafters long and strong enough to support the weight of an unfinished dome. According to one account the wool merchants set up a test for the prospective architects, asking them to balance an egg on a piece of marble. All failed. Then up stepped Filippo Brunelleschi. He took the egg and gently smashed the end of it, causing it to stand. When the competitors cried foul saying that any of them could have done as much, Brunelleschi quipped that they also could have built the dome had they seen his design. He got the job. He also spent much of his remaining life erecting the majestic octagonal dome and the lantern that sits on top of it.

Brunelleschi oversaw every aspect of the construction. He supervised a veritable army of skilled artisans whose autonomy and interests were advanced by guilds. The transporting and placement of more than four million bricks proved to be a staggering logistical feat. Necessity dictated that he invent a machine to haul building materials to the lofty heights of the cathedral. He made creative use of iron and stone chains to hold the rising dome in place. Six hundred years later, the Duomo remains not only the tallest building in Florence, but it is undeniably a crown jewel in the rich artistic legacy of the Renaissance. Brunelleschi's immortality as an artist was the result of his brilliantly marshalling expertise and resources (human and material) and using his own ingenuity to create something of lasting value to society. He did this by focusing his rapt attention on a lofty (literally and figuratively) goal and by moving towards it with single-minded intent, elbowing past the impossible when necessary. This is precisely the set of qualities that college and university leaders will most need in the decade ahead. The central governance issue of the twenty-first century is the definition of the higher purposes to which we are called and structuring the work of the academy (including its norms) to achieve them.

Other scholars in this book have written eloquently about the imperative for change—the maturation of higher education as an industry, the drive of competition from peer institutions and a proliferation of new entrants into the market, the pressing need to fashion a P-20 system of education that ensures the economic prospects of all people, the relentless ratchet of accountability—the litany could go on and it is a familiar one to presidents, senior administrators, and boards. Efforts have been made on many campuses to produce greater efficiency and cost savings. Strategic planning (or one of its many progeny) is being used to advance "best practices."

Development and admissions offices employ the most sophisticated marketing techniques to secure precious resources (money and students). New programs and centers have been established to foster access and to encourage student learning, engagement, and success. All of these activities are worthwhile. But we are facing challenges as a society on a scale that makes the discourse on "efficiency," or "competitiveness," or "accountability" in higher education seem like the parochial haggling of a group of wool merchants.

Like those merchants, decision makers in the academy (administrators, board members, and faculty) are, within their domains, influential. But we have spent long enough scrutinizing the rough foundation of a society that aspires to honor each person's humanity and potential. What we need now are academic communities committed to bridging the expansive gaps in our understanding: How do we address the historic legacy of legalized racism and ethnocentrism here and abroad—the kind that produces genocide, generational war, catastrophes like 9/11, and that allows us to turn a blind eye to the inexcusable poverty in our own inner cities? How do we create a planet that sustains life (and a life worth living) with a developed economic system addicted to oil and mass consumption and many developing nations deep in debt? How do we respond to the wholesale collapse of entire species unparalleled in the history of the world? How do we ameliorate the fear voiced by founding father John Adams that "there never was a democracy yet that did not commit suicide" in a time when a minority of citizens vote, understand, or care about the substantive policy debates of our time and most view government with deep distrust?

To remain relevant, our institutions of higher learning need to start thinking in a scale that is presently unimaginable. Try to imagine a series of Manhattan Projects that draw together and materially support faculty from a range of disciplines (and universities) whose collective aim is to eradicate poverty or to erase the achievement gap or to seek sustainable energy sources. It is not impossible. It has never been tried. But it will require fundamental shifts in the work of the academy and a radical alteration of expectations about what work is valued. It will require shifts in expectations around the production of new knowledge moving from a system that measures scholarly worth by the quantity of peer-reviewed academic journal articles that fill a hole in a specialized disciplinary literature to the application of multiple disciplinary lenses to pressing real-world problems by scholars from many universities where the measure of success is both advancing disciplinary knowledge and actually solving problems.

This sort of reorientation of the work of the academy will take a particularly bold and creative (and even stubborn) form of leadership; one that seeks to spark the imagination rather than secure buy-in. It will entail relying on expertise—cultivating leadership as an organizational rather than personal quality—while also challenging the efficacy of conventional wisdom about what is reasonable and possible. It will require leaders who, despite having navigated existing organizational structures and norms, are able to see through them and to envision new possibilities. This sort of leadership is not possible if the goal is greater efficiency or fear of competition—those conditions have existed for decades and produced precious little change. What is required now is the unconditional commitment of time and resources to goals that are far loftier, seemingly impossible. Increasingly in American society we think in news cycles or perhaps quarters. Tasks of this kind will take a far longer commitment—one that transcends any individual leader. But the heights of understanding and progress that are possible make it vital that we try.

Matthew Hartley
Associate Professor of Higher Education
University of Pennsylvania

POLICY

The current economic crisis can be an opportunity for the United States to redesign its higher education system and regain world leadership. The nation no longer holds the top position in terms of the number of first-time college students earning bachelor's degrees. It ranks beneath three European countries, and its completion rate is below the average of the Organization for Economic Cooperation and Development (OECD) countries. There are a number of explanations for this loss. First, unlike some European countries, U.S. graduation rates have remained stagnant in the last ten years, even though it spends twice the average amount of European countries on higher education. Second, the United States has focused on increasing access instead of making institutions accountable for educational outcomes. Third, the lack of K-16 articulation and the disconnect between high school preparation and college requirements have led to substantial remediation needs that necessarily translate into higher dropout rates or longer time to degree for students. Fourth, the increasing costs of American higher education, coupled with decreasing state and federal support for institutions, has resulted in higher tuition and fee costs for families and students. Fifth, changes in admission policies alongside shifts from grants to loans and need-based to merit aid have resulted in a socioeconomically stratified system of higher education.

The Obama Administration is currently implementing a number of programs and legislative efforts to tackle these problems. However, major systemic reform and regulation is necessary to reverse the current decline. In this statement, I describe three major issues that higher education researchers, policymakers, and college administrators need to address in the coming years. First among them are federal mandates that promote systemic changes at the state level. As a result of the financial crisis, federal and state resources to higher education institutions are going to continue to decline. At the same time, the federal government is going to play a major role in regulating the higher education system, and providing incentives to states to improve post-secondary educational outcomes. Second, the financial model of public flagship institutions is going to change. Public institutions can no longer subsidize the cost of education. Their financial model must change and the federal government needs to create incentives for them to be financially stable, outcomes-oriented, mission-centered, and firmly committed to serving the public good. The third and final issue I discuss is the move towards an articulated K-16 system. High schools need to work with community colleges and four-year institutions to define the skills and academic preparation necessary for students to succeed in higher education. States should take advantage of technological changes that makes it easier to follow students throughout the system to make each type of institution accountable for specific outcomes. In the following paragraphs, I describe in more detail each of these issues.

Federal Mandates that Promote Systemic State-Level Changes

There are serious problems with the current structure and financing of higher education institutions. The result is that costs continue to escalate, yet institutions remain unaccountable for ensuring that more students persist through degree attainment. The current economic crisis has required the federal government to intervene in unprecedented ways in the financial, health, and education sectors of the country. The increasing role of the federal government coupled with the willingness of the states to work towards a common goal (i.e., currently 48 of the 50 states are participating in the *Race to the Top* initiative to standardize math and English high school requirements) presents new opportunities that the Obama Administration cannot afford to lose. One challenge is that even though the federal government is providing financial support and incentives for states to work towards common standards in high school, there are currently no programs or laws geared towards articulating the whole education system from kindergarten to college. Therefore, it could be expected that the federal government might eventually provide incentives to states to also work toward better connecting all sectors of education. There is a need to create some sort of regulation that ideally includes federal financial incentives; otherwise, states can just use the money to solve current liquidity problems without really generating the systemic changes necessary to make a difference in postsecondary outcomes and attainment.

Changing Financial Models at Public Flagship Institutions

Currently, the states are subsidizing education, and despite skyrocketing costs, individuals who attend public institutions are paying substantially less than the true cost of the education received. Public institutions, specially the flagships, would need to change their current model to remain sustainable. One possible alternative is a hybrid between the high-tuition/high-aid model of the elite private institutions, combined with the best business practices employed by some high-quality for-profit institutions. Tuition increases are necessary, but they need to come together with high aid so that students and their families can afford the costs. There should also be some federal-level incentives for providing need-based instead of merit aid to students, which is essential to maintaining and increasing socioeconomic diversity.

Most elite private institutions are following a prestige maximization model, which has contributed to the cost escalation and what is known as *mission creep* (meaning, that other comprehensive and liberal arts colleges are following the same model). This is where the model implemented by some successful for-profit institutions might be applicable. There is evidence that some for-profit institutions are very effective in reaching out and supporting low-income students and students of color. They are appealing because they adapt to students' schedules, they offer degrees that are in high demand in the labor force, they use all the sources available to cover the costs of the tuition (unfortunately most of them rely on private loans), and they invest much into creating curricula that many faculty can deliver. A change in the financial model, coupled with the appropriate federal and state level support in the form of financial incentives, can guarantee that public institutions remain mission-centered.

Movement towards an Articulated K-16 System

The lack of articulation and insufficient accountability in the higher education system has led to a situation where open access institutions blame high schools for not providing the academic preparation necessary for success in college. More than two-thirds of recent high school graduates arrive at college with remediation needs. In most states, community colleges are now responsible for providing remedial education, and taxpayer dollars are being used to fund the cost of providing basic skills. This situation is not sustainable, as the costs for students, their families, the state, and the country are immense. States need to create the channels for high schools, community colleges, and four-year institutions to work together in creating a clear pathway towards the baccalaureate degree. The problem with the current system is that students are told that they need remediation, but there is not a clear support system for them to tackle these issues. States should continue to work towards an articulated system where each level is held accountable. Furthermore, states should continue to invest in longitudinal datasets with student identifiers so that students and institutions can be tracked.

Tatiana Melguizo
Assistant Professor of Higher Education
University of Southern California

Permissions

Altbach, Philip G., Robert O. Berdahl, & Patricia J. Gumport, eds. *American Higher Education in the Twenty-First Century: Social, Political, and Economic Challenges*, pp. 71–90. Copyright © 2005 The Johns Hopkins University Press. Reprinted with permission of The Johns Hopkins University Press.

Banks, J. A. (1993). The canon debate, knowledge construction, and multicultural education. *Educational Researcher*, *22*(5), 4–14. Reproduced with permission.

Birnbaum, R. (1988). *How Colleges Work: The Cybernetics of Academic Organization and Leadership*, pp. 3–29. San Francisco: Jossey-Bass. Reproduced with permission.

Brint, Steven. From *The Future of the City of Intellect: The Changing American University*. Copyright © 2002 by the Board of Trustees of the Leland Stanford Jr. University.

Clark, B. R. (Fall, 1997). Small worlds, different worlds: The uniquenesses and troubles of American academic professions. Daedalus: *Journal of the American Academy of Arts and Sciences*, *126*: 4, 21–43. Copyright © 1997 by MIT Press – Journals. Reproduced with permission.

Conrad, C. F., Johnson, J., & Gupta, D. (2007). Teaching-for-Learning (TFL): A model for faculty to advance student learning. *Innovative Higher Education*, *32*(3), 153–165. Reproduced with permission.

Gappa, J. M., Austin, A. E., & Trice, A. G. (2007). *Rethinking Faculty Work: Higher Education's Strategic Imperative*, pp. 3–23. San Francisco: Jossey-Bass. Reproduced with permission.

Gurin, P., Dey, E.L., Hurtado, S., & Gurin, G. (2002). Diversity and higher education: theory and impact on educational outcomes. *Harvard Educational Review*, *72*(3), 330–366. Copyright © 2002 by Harvard Educational Review. Reproduced with permission.

Hagedorn, Linda Serra (2008). Looking in the review mirror: factors affecting transfer for urban community college students. *Community College Journal of Research and Practice*, *32*: 643–664, 2008. Copyright © Taylor & Francis Group, LLC.

Harper, S. R. & Patton, L. D. (Eds.), Responding to the realities of race on campus. *New Directions for Student Services* (No. 120, pp. 7–24). San Francisco: Jossey-Bass. Reproduced with permission.

Hendrick, R. Z., Hightower, W. H., & Gregory, D. E. (2006). State funding limitations and community college open door policy: Conflicting priorities? *Community College Journal of Research and Practice*, *30*(8), 627–640. Copyright © Taylor & Francis Group, LLC.

Kezar, A. J. & Eckel, P. (2002). The effect of institutional culture on change strategies in higher education: Universal principles or culturally responsive concepts? *The Journal of Higher Education*, *73*(4), 435–460. Copyright © 2002 by Ohio State University Press (Journals). Reproduced with permission.

Kuh, G. D. (2009). What student affairs professionals need to know about student engagement. *Journal of College Student Development*, *50*(6), 683–706. Copyright © 2009 by The Johns Hopkins University Press (Journals). Reproduced with permission.

Lattuca, Lisa R. & Stark, Joan S. "External influences: sociocultural context", pp. 23–64 in *Shaping the College Curriculum: Academic Plans in Context*, 2nd edition. Copyright © 2009. Reproduced with permission of John Wiley & Sons, Inc.

Moses, M. S. (2001). Affirmative action and the creation of more favorable contexts of choice. *American

Educational Research Journal, 38(1), 3–36. Copyright © 2001 by Sage Publications Inc. Reproduced with permission.

O'Banion, T. (2007). Creating a new architecture for the learning college. *Community College Journal of Research and Practice, 31*(9), 713–724. Copyright © Taylor & Francis Group, LLC.

Orton, J. & Weick, K. (1990). Loosely coupled systems: a reconceptualization. *Academy of Management Review, 15*(2), 203–223. Copyright © 1990 by Academy of Management (NY). Reproduced with permission.

Rendón, L., Jalomo, R. & Nora, A. (2001). Theoretical considerations in the study of minority student retention in higher education. In J. Braxton (Ed.), *Rethinking the Student Departure Puzzle: New Theory and Research on College Student Retention.* Nashville, TN: Vanderbilt University Press. Reproduced with permission.

Schuster, Jack H. & Martin J. Finkelstein. *The American Faculty: The Restructuring of Academic Work and Careers*, pp. 19–26. Copyright © 2006 The Johns Hopkins University Press. Reprinted with permission of The Johns Hopkins University Press.

St. John, Edward P. & Michael D. Parsons, eds. *Public Funding of Higher Education: Changing Contexts and New Rationales*, pp. 60–73, 215–230. Copyright © 2004 The Johns Hopkins University Press. Reprinted with permission of The Johns Hopkins University Press.

Tierney, W. G. (1988). Organizational culture in higher education: defining the essentials. *The Journal of Higher Education, 59*(1), 2–21. Copyright © 1988 by Ohio State University Press (Journals). Reproduced with permission of Ohio State University Press (Journals).

Townsend, B. K. (2009). Community college organizational climate for minorities and women. *Community College Journal of Research & Practice, 33*(9), 731–744. Copyright © Taylor & Francis Group, LLC.

Townsend, B. K. & Rosser, V. J. (2009). The extent and nature of scholarly activities among community college faculty. *Community College Journal of Research & Practice, 33*(9), 669–681. Copyright © Taylor & Francis Group, LLC.

Turner, C. S. V., Gonzalez, J. C., & Wood, J. L. (2008). Faculty of color in academe: what 20 years of literature tells us. *Journal of Diversity in Higher Education, 1*: 3, 139–168. Copyright © 2008 by the National Association of Diversity Officers in Higher Education. Reproduced with permission.

Index